Forgotten Patriot

The Life and Times of
Major-General Nathanael Greene

Lee Patrick Anderson

"Forgotten Patriot"

"The Life & Times of Major-General Nathanael Greene"

by

Lee Patrick Anderson

Edited by

Lisa Skowronski

Universal Publishers
USA • 2002

Forgotten Patriot:
The Life & Times of Major-General Nathanael Greene

Portrait of Nathanael Greene on the cover was painted by Charles Wilson Peale in 1783
and is being used by permission from the Independence National Historical
Park of Philadelphia Library.

Universal Publishers / uPUBLISH.com
USA • 2002

ISBN: 1-58112-635-2

www.upublish.com/books/anderson4.htm

Dedication

To all of America's unsung heroes.

Acknowledgments

A special thanks to the folks at the Mulberry Mansion Society in Savannah, Georgia for their wonderful help. To Karen Ann Beaver for her outstanding work in putting the finishing touches on the project and a special thank you to Lisa Skowronski for the hard work in editing this manuscript from start to finish. Well done my friends.

Table of Contents

Nath Green

Major General, United States Army

"*Forgotten Patriot*"

"*The Life & Times of Major-General Nathanael Greene*"

By

Lee Patrick Anderson

Edited by

Lisa Skowronski

Chapter I

"From Cradle to Brigadier-General"

Quaker beliefs are as diverse as the New England fall colors. The lifestyles of the New England Quakers varied from those of their brothers and sisters in the Delaware Valley in and around Philadelphia, the largest city in the colonies at that time. Where one sect was fanatical in the writings and beliefs of their founder George Fox, another would look at those same writings and interpret them in a completely different way. How you should dress, how to conduct the weekly meetings, and how one should adhere to those beliefs were looked upon as a general guide by the Delaware Valley Quakers, but followed to the letter by Quakers in New England. However, almost all Quakers, no matter where their geographical home, would agree on some things. Diligent, rigorous work and the care and upbringing of their family was paramount in how a body should conduct itself on a daily basis. One such man who believed was named John Greene, a Quaker, merchant and surgeon who came from Salisbury, England in the late 17th century. He found himself in the coastal land called Providence, Rhode Island with his wife and three children. He would move his family inland because abundant land and prosperity called to him. However, he soon chose a far less inhabited area closer to the sea which was called Shawomet (Sho' wo' mot) near the town of Warwick. He purchased a tract of land on the left bank of the stream at the mouth of Greenwich Bay (now known as Narraganset), nestled between two hills where the stream formed a small pond. The homestead would be named after the land the Native Americans used for it, Potowomut (Poto' wamot), "place of all the fires."

It would be here, around the early 18th century, at the land called Potowomut, that Jabez would be the first settler of the land his grandfather, John Greene, had originally stacked out as the family homestead. Jabez Greene joined with Thomas Hill, as partners in the mills of the new settlement and together watched as this small part of the colony of Rhode Island began to grow in importance due to development of the new land and its expanding industries. At about 1740 though, the property was passed into the hands of the Greene family where the second Nathanael was one of six brothers of father Jabez. It was close to this time that this branch of the family had begun to follow the teachings of George Fox and become Quakers. Jabez had died without making out a proper will, but had declared early on that his oldest son, James, would inherit the estate and have it divided among all of his children. By the laws of the time in Rhode Island, James became sole heir of the property and the first thing he did was carry out his father's wish and divide it with his five brothers, the second Nathanael, being the fourth, and a Quaker preacher.

Nathanael was highly regarded in the community as an eminent, vigorous enforcer of evangelical truth in the Quaker meetings. But he also was an owner of large tracts of land as well as a good businessman who helped his brothers with the running of the family grist mill, flour mill, saw mill, merchandise store, and a large forge and all became very profitable. As early as 1743 the forge, store (along with all of its merchandise) was valued at L8,055, with L2,408 in uncollected debts. By that time, the chief care of the forge and mills seems to have been given to Nathanael. When his sons grew to young adulthood, they were admitted to the family business as partners.

The senior Nathanael had married Phoebe, a second cousin who he had known since they were children. They would have two sons and one daughter who was named for his wife, but would not live

1

to see her second year. Soon after their young child's death, Phoebe also died of Yellow Fever in 1730. Soon after the Senior Nathanael married his second wife, Mary Mott, they had 6 more children, all of them sons. The fifth of this second brood would take on his father's name, Nathanael. Born the twenty-seventh of the fifth month, 1742. Now in our modern calendar that month would be May, but in 1742 England was still under the old style calendar and had yet to adopt the Gregorian calendar we go by today. For all civil and legal matters in the old calendar March was the first month, so Nathanael would have actually been born in July. In 1752 England adopted the Gregorian Calendar, and so did all of its subjects, including those in the new colonies would now consider the fifth month May. So, in any book or correspondence speaking of Nathanael Greene you will see May 27, 1742 as his birth date.

Having 8 sons could only enhance the Senior Nathanael's business holdings, and business was growing by leaps and bounds. Sailing vessels owned or chartered by the Greene family firm brought wheat from the Virginia colonies. The flour from the Greene's mill was then sent to Providence and Newport, the principal markets in the early days of the American colonies. Coal, also came from Virginia, and the best iron to be found on this side of the Atlantic came from Pennsylvania. Even then the state of Pennsylvania was known for its iron and ore production. Being one of the chief suppliers of dry goods in the area, a steady supply of merchandise for the store was required to sell to new settlers entering the expanding area of New England.

Another of the Greene's family businesses was the production of anchors, which were made in the Greene's family owned forge. The further management of shipping the anchors to market for sale to various seagoing firms was also necessary. Last, but certainly not least, the collection, posting and accounting of proceeds to all these various industries and then put to appropriate use was probably the most important of all. Add the duties of preacher as well as being a farmer and it was easy to see that the senior Nathanael was a very busy man and in the need of as much help as possible

The family's farm was abundant with good soil and the family wanted for nothing on their large table, but had little in their bank account. However, the elder Greene had made many investments in land throughout different parts of the State. Many of the tracts were farms operated by local inhabitants who paid a small amount to the senior Nathanael from a portion of the crops they grew and harvested on his land. The Greene's were extremely interested in agriculture and the manufacture of the crops it yielded. But, "agriculture" in the early to mid 18th century was mostly unchanged from a century before when grandfathers taught their sons from generation to generation. This can be seen in many of the books consulted at the time of the junior Nathanael's boyhood, such as, "Book of Husbandrie" published in 1523 and Tusser's "Five Hundred Points" written in the mid 16th century. It was years and miles away from the modern use of agriculture. The use of chemistry for analyzing soils, plants, and manure would reveal the laws of natural matter and materials as a force in harmony with nature. A more prolific answer to crop growth and harvesting is now common at the beginning of the 21st century.

Nathanael Greene's eight sons were set to learn all of the family holdings and workings at a young age. The youngest would begin in the fields, and young Nathanael was no exception. They were taught seed sowing, the proper days for harvesting the crops at their optimum time, collecting the cut fields' bounty and chafing the grains afterwards. We learn from many of Nathanael's letters throughout his life that the fields were not of his liking. It was evident early on that Nathanael was a precocious child who had more energy than most his age. The fields failed to keep his interest, but he worked them for the time expected and until he was old enough to move to the next test of his responsibilities. When the children became older, say 10 or 11 years old, they would work in either the grist mill where the harvested grain was sent or they would work at the location of the grains final destination, the flour mill. The gristmill was a frame building on the west bank of the Potowomut River, just a few yards below the dam on the Greene's property. The constant noise from the millstone and crushing of the mill hopper, along with the constant gurgling of the water flowing over its gate on its way to the paddlewheel made it nearly impossible to talk in or around the mill structure. It would become one of young Nathanael's favorite places to study. Maybe because no one else would bother to venture there, or because he knew no one would bother to seek him out and attempt a conversation with him. It seemed perfect for uninterrupted reading, which would become Nathanael's life long passion.

Close to the mill, just on the lower area of their land, was the forge. A larger building than the mill, with a broad shingle roof coming so near to the ground that the Greene children and the local youngsters of the town played on it daily. Two large doors afforded a good breeze for back breaking, exhausting and overheated working conditions inside where three separate forges operated at least 12 hours a day. The forge had a huge bellows and two anvils with a separate one used for the anchors the family was famous for manufacturing. Off to the side was a modest forge, which was primarily used for blacksmith work. Working the forge was part of the Greene sons' training, but only the young Nathanael who excelled at the use of fire to iron, would carry it on as his young adulthood vocation. Each Quaker child was also expected to be trained in a handicraft. Young Nathanael would demonstrate his prowess at wielding a blacksmith hammer with more than adequate ability. At the end of a hot, tiring workday the Greene sons would meet on the bridge just below the milldam. From spring to fall, they enjoyed fishing for eels in the dark Potowomut waters and occasionally taking a swim in the warmer months.

The family house was a plain wooden, saltbox type with low ceilings, common for houses of early Colonial life. But it was substantial in size compared to most homes of the day and well adapted for a large Quaker family. The house was within ear shot of the forge and stood on the edge of a small hill which the boys would run down on their way to work in the morning. But it probably seemed like a steep mountain when they had to trudge up its face at the end of a long, hard workday.

In 1754 the Greene family would suffer a tragedy. Young Nathanael would lose his mother, but the senior Nathanael Greene would remarry after the usual time of mourning. His third wife, Mary Rodman, would bare no other children, but would always be known for quickly learning to treat her husband's children as her own. Years later, while in the Army of the Rhode Island militia, young Nathanael would echo those sentiments time and time again in his letters to his family and adopted mother.

The children were expected to not only absorb Quaker ideals and teachings, but also master a craft or vocation. Nathanael the father and preacher hoped that the two things would become one for at least one of his sons futures. Of course, this meant having one of his sons follow in his footsteps as a preacher, and also as a good businessman or farmer. The one who held the best chance of this was young Nathanael. But, he could not have picked a less willing pupil.

The family would travel two miles to the town meetinghouse. In most cases, father and mother would ride in a simple carriage, when used at all with the youngest behind on a bed of straw. The rest of the family, along with servants, followed obligingly by foot. Only Quakers with more than usual means rode in carriages, and the senior Greene was one such man. The children were expected to work long and hard in the fields, mills or forge and then study the teachings of George Fox the Quaker founder, and other writers like Townsend or Barclay. Required reading included literary masters such as, Fox & Townsend's "Apology", and Barclay's "Holy Scriptures." Reading was taught from Fox's, "Instructions for right Spelling and plain Directions for Reading and Writing true English."

Education in the late 18th century was simple and plain at best in most communities in the country. In the Quaker community, children were taught only the bare necessities of reading and ciphering (math). This would be all a Quaker child would need to get by in life and business. Most, but especially the senior Greene, did not believe learning to be important. Attempting to learn more than was needed was looked on as a form of vanity. What was the need to learn more than your neighbor, if

3

only to try and act as if you were smarter or better than he. What service did it hold for the community? Reading books took precious time away from doing more important services like work. The Quakers held idleness in contempt as one of the most horrible acts against the Lord that a Quaker could commit. Most did not work hard for material benefits. They worked diligently because George Fox taught that it was a form of thanks to the Lord for giving you life on Earth. If you were lucky enough to be given life, you should repay the favor by working as tirelessly as you can. It just so happened that by working so industriously, the reward was often prosperity as well.

As a result of their grueling 6-day workweek, they wanted for little. They had crops and animals for food, orchards for drink, funds for practical amounts of clothing, and a comfortable home to shelter them from the harsh New England elements. Family would gather around the father or head of the household and listen intently. He read religious passages and holy scripture to help each Quaker child understand the meaning of life and their obligation to God.

That is not to say that Quaker children and young adults had no time for a little fun. The Quaker calendar was made up of yearly, quarterly and monthly "great gatherings", when the doors of meeting-houses and homes were opened to all and their tables overflowed with meats, grains, "butters" and fruits. The senior Nathanael Greene's house was no exception. The occasions were used for teaching, but also for good cheer with friends and family. It was said that even the strictest Quaker would crack a smile at such occasions and find hope and joy with the young as well as old counsel. Talking of traditions, tales, stories, and even jokes that would cause the most stoic Quaker to break into laughter.

The "great gatherings" were not only a time for play, but also a time for teaching the young. By listening to these stories, the children would be taught Quaker history without reading about it. Life lessons were taught by bringing girls and boys together for a better understanding of the opposite sex. They danced, talked, and maybe even stole a kiss behind the barn or house. It also was a forum for young men to learn recreational competition. The Quakers did not want competition for the largest house or most luxurious carriage. But they did feel that competition for biggest crop; fattest calf or most productive sawmill could only help the Quaker community. So, tests of prowess were conducted between the young men within the community and between other meetinghouses. Games included who could stack hay the highest and firmest, who could furrow deepest in a field without straining the oxen, and who could lift the heaviest weight, usually a barrel of water or logs. Strong, young Nathanael was especially accomplished in this competition. He was exceptionally strong and could out lift most men in the area. After the competition or work for the day was finished, the young Greene boys were not immune to a swim in the summer or a slide on the ice in the colder months at the sheltered pond by their house. But the most prized merriment known to the boys by far was the husking parties on cool October evenings which were usually followed by dancing, much to the chagrin of the elder Quaker members. This was young Nathanael's favorite vice, but not his only one.

There are several stories told or written by his descendants of young Nathanael's feats of strength, sharpness of wit, and ability to sneak out of the house without his father's knowledge. One such tale, told in a biography on Nathanael Greene and written by his grandson tells how the senior Greene kept regular hours and would check all of the children before retiring at 9 o'clock. When young Nathanael was sure his father was in his own chambers, he would fix the covers to make it look as if he was under them, put on his clothes and slip out of the window and jump down from the second story. He would then go off to a husking party so he could dance. But one night it was close to midnight before young Nathanael got back home and as he turned the corner, he could see his father in the moonlight with the distinctive shadow of a riding crop in his father's hand. Young Nathanael managed to get close to the house without being seen, but could not get into the house because his father was barring the usual way. He happened to be on the side of the house where he had stacked a fresh bundle

4

of cedar shingles for repairing the roof. So he formulated a plan. He took two shingles and dropped them into the back of his breeches (short pants). Then when his father would undoubtedly inflict the rod, as to not spoil the child, he would be somewhat protected from a morning and a day of standing rather than sitting. Though it has all of the markings of a legend, rather than the truth, the story gives us a wonderful idea of how people considered Nathanael Greene to be a shrewd strategist.

The senior Greene could forgive young Nathanael for the occasional truancy and lack of decorum. But one thing that the senior Greene vehemently disapproved of was Nathanael's love of books. "The only aspect of my life that I lament is the want of a liberal education," Nathanael Greene would write about his early life as the son of a Quaker preacher in 1772. He would go on to say, "My father was very superstitious and also had great piety. He believed in governing in his conduct to humanity with kind benevolence, but his mind was overshadowed with prejudice against literary accomplishments." As we noticed before, Quakers considered math and reading to be necessary studies, if not only to study the Bible. Conducting business accurately and legally required knowing basic addition and subtraction so that you knew how to exchange lambs for grain for instance. If a James Olsen gave you 4 lambs in payment for 4 pounds of grain, you would need to know basic mathematics.

Reading beyond the standard knowledge needed in everyday life was not looked upon as necessary in the Quaker hierarchy and the senior Nathanael was a staunch believer that books outside of the Quaker tradition were useless. But the young Nathanael strongly disagreed. And at the age of fifteen, while walking from the town of East Greenwich, he happened upon a young man named Giles who was coming home from college for vacation. As the two young men walked, the subject of books came up and Giles proceeded to discuss what he had learned at college. It aroused young Nathanael's curiosity about what there was to learn besides basic Quaker teachings. From that day forward young Nathanael Greene was a new boy. He could no longer stand by the forge and conduct his daily life without thinking about the knowledge that lay just beyond his tiny world. He had always looked up at the night sky and wondered about the motion of the stars and heavenly bodies, and watched the waves on the nearby beach and asked himself why the tides came in and out. He looked at the fire in his forge and now wondered aloud, what makes the heat soften the iron? In the future, into what distant seas will my anchors splash? He no longer could find the answers to such questions in the books his father provided for nightly reading. The day of unquestioning faith was gone. He required answers and from that day on would seek them relentlessly until he completely understood them.

Days later, Nathanael would cautiously approach his father and ask if he could pursue a better means of studying. His father was less than sympathetic and it would take multiple appeals from the young son to the Quaker preacher to soften him and ultimately allow his son to go against his wishes. But, with time the senior Nathanael did soften. His son was an efficient and tireless worker in the forge as well as a completely dutiful son, so it was hard to deny the young Nathanael this one wish.

The young Nathanael Greene's journey for expanded knowledge would take him to the quiet hamlet of East Greenwich near where the mouth of the Masquachugh river flows into Narraganset Bay. Here was a small, unassuming wooden house inhabited by a man by the name of Maxwell. No record lists the circumstances of how young Nathanael found this place, but it would possibly be the most important discovery of his life.
Mr. Maxwell was a learned man. He had studied extensively at several schools and universities in his native Scotland and was an expert in Geometry and the ancient languages, especially Latin. He would pass along that knowledge to his new and apt pupil.

As his studies intensified, Nathanael felt the longing he had known but did not understand, begin to melt away. In its place had formed a distinct awakening of the desire to know the world beyond his limited experience. He started to understand what Giles had told him in the numerous conversations since they had met months before. This was knowledge beyond his basic Quaker upbringing that he had thirst for all his life. From numerous letters, we can see that the young Nathanael was finally experiencing the joy of learning and was enjoying it very much.

Latin did not seem to be Nathanael's forte. He struggled with it constantly with Maxwell. He was given several books that were required reading by the scholars of the 18th century. One of which was Seneca's "epistles", which were a collection of letters (scholars called them personal essays) written in Latin around 10 BC, to the people of Rome focusing on ethics and morality. Nathanael was said to have enjoyed the message Seneca was teaching, but had a hard time understanding it at first. Consider for instance, a 10 year-old child today trying to read Stephen Hawking's "A Brief History of Time."

But by far one of his favorite books was an immense, dog-eared, dark sheepskin volume of Horace's "Euclid." It was the very first book young Nathanael purchased with his own money and it was said that it "was hard to determine where his fingers ended and the book began." He was devoted to the study of this manuscript and did not go far without it. He would read it every chance he was allowed. When his boyhood friends would be playing, Nathanael would plop himself down under a tree and absorb every detail of every page. The "Euclid" was a collection of Horace's lyrical poetry that was written around 65 to 8 BC and had been reprinted about 1500 in Renaissance Italy. Nathanael especially enjoyed the poems about beauty and love even though he had yet to fully enjoy or understand them.

Another of the books Mr. Maxwell had lent Nathanael was Euclid's "Elements." Written over 2400 years ago, today it is still considered by scientist and mathematicians around the world to be the foremost manuscript on mathematics and the exact sciences. Euclid's "Elements" explains mathematics and scientific principles in layman terms. It would become the single most used formula Nathanael Greene would go by in his later years as a military strategist. With the mathematical equations taught to him by Euclid, Greene would be the foremost authority in mapping and surveying geographical areas that had no maps, no survey lines or posts and in some areas may have been the first white men to step foot on.

Nathanael was in love with books. His brother would kid him about the intoxication he had found in the books he would read. He never denied it, and in fact may have embraced the idea of knowledge taking such a hold on his being. He was no more than 13 years old and had discovered a part of himself that he truly enjoyed. Books. He wanted more, but could not expect his Quaker father to either give him the funds to buy books or have his father buy them for him. His father detested books outside the readings of Quaker beliefs. Young Nathanael would have to formulate some sort of plan to gain some meager earnings so he could purchase more books.

He finally discovered one, quite by accident. Nathanael was proficient with the hammer at his father's forge and was known to produce some of the best anchors in the seaside of Rhode Island. Once, while waiting at the forge for a piece of iron to heat up, young Nathanael had taken a scrap piece of iron shaving and absentmindedly twisted the metal in his hands. A friend who had happened by commented, "The iron shaving resembles one of your anchors, but much smaller." Nathanael did not think much of it at the time, but when it came time to produce earnings the idea reappeared and he set out to produce miniature anchors to sell as toys.

At that time, Newport was the major city in the colony of Rhode Island. With a larger population than his hometown and with a seaport as its main source of income, Newport seemed the perfect place to launch his small anchors venture. It did not hurt that Nathanael liked to go to the wharf at Newport and watch the collection of ships that had just days before been at distant places such as London and Bristol. He could also stop in at the Redwood Library near the Trinity Church and look upon more books than he could read in his lifetime.

6

But on one of these trips Nathanael would have a turning point in the progress of his pursuit of knowledge. While in a bookstore by the wharf, Nathanael asked the proprietor of the shop if there was a particular book he might recommend. At that moment, a gentleman wearing the garb of a clergyman turned to eavesdrop on the conversation between the young customer and the bookseller. "What do you like to read?" asked the shopkeeper. After some deep thought and short conversation about the few books Nathanael had at his disposal, the clergyman decided it was his time to step in and help the young man with the earnest face. It is unknown what book Nathanael decided to purchase at the bookstore. What is certain is that he came away with an important friend from the happenstance encounter. The man in the cleric clothing was none other than Ezra Stiles, future president of Yale University. Stiles would see thousands of young men prosper by the lessons and knowledge he would bestow on them over the years, but none would appreciate his lessons more than the young Quaker boy. Stiles never realized what an enormous impact his talks and lessons had on this young man who went on years later to fight for his country's freedom. Nathanael Greene on the other hand would never forget.

One of the first books Stiles would lend Nathanael was Locke's "Essay on the Human Understanding," this was a group of essays that spanned four volumes on numerous subjects, in which John Locke, philosopher, politician and writer described his own ideas on everything from God to air. As a student, Nathanael Greene would have been given this book by his teacher, Stiles, to help him to learn the study and laws of mental action. Basically, to think outside the box. Greene had been taught the Quaker way all of his life. He was a sponge to new things and was eager to improve his mind at every opportunity. Lessons from Euclid and Locke gave Nathanael rigorous training to demonstrate connected reasoning and further the power of his brain beyond anything he ever imagined. The young man had no idea there was so much he could learn, nor that he was so capable of learning. Stiles considered him an excellent student and would later use young Nathanael as a measuring stick for how well he would teach other young men. Years later, Stiles would write, "Few if any could live up to the scruttening that I would apply to them." Nathanael Greene would certainly be a hard act to follow.

In Greene's early lessons, Stiles knew that Nathanael wanted to learn more than the basics offered by the Quaker lifestyle. He was constantly questioning everything he assimilated in his first 15 years. Stiles planned on showing young Nathanael that there were always two sides to every problem and therefore, usually two answers. Having him read books by Locke, Horace, and other philosophers, Stiles could teach the young man different ways to approach a conclusion and at the same time expand his conceptions of how things could be processed with one's mind. It opened a new and wider field of inquiry into what could be accomplished and a better understanding of moral political truths. Another work that would further Nathanael's concept on such matters would be Watt's "Logic" and Rollin's series of essays on the frality of human logic. Far and away Nathanael Greene's favorite author was Jonathan Swift. The Angelo-Irish satirist and political pamphleteer who was known for his book, "Travels into Several Remote Nations of the World," more popularly known today as "Gulliver's Travel's." Although originally meant to be an acidic attack on the vanity and hypocrisy of statesmen, political parties and the royal court, the book was also intended to reflect on the bitterness of human nature. It would become and it remains today a classic favorite, read from grammar school to high schools around the world.

Years before, while Swift was dean to St. Patrick's Cathedral in Dublin and a foremost political activist, he issued the "Dapier's Letters" which was Nathanael Greene's favorite book. It was a series of letters to the people of Ireland attempting to bring an end to the royal patent granted to an Englishman coining copper halfpence in Ireland. Swift also was a champion of ancient literary works, which young Nathanael was also a great fan of at the time. Nathanael saw Swift as a hero to the under-privileged and illiterate and felt a strong tie to his writings. Another Revolutionary forefather also looked upon Jonathan Swift for guidance. Benjamin Franklin was known to be a follower of Swift's and injected many of Swift's beliefs into his own graceful and simple writing style.

Young Nathanael Greene's mind expanded by leaps and bounds. But even with this newfound knowledge that he now possessed, Nathanael never imagined a different occupation than the daily task of plowing and working the hammer on the anvil in his father's forge. He certainly wanted to learn more and experience as much life as possible now, but he also felt that the forge was his calling. This would remain his lot in life and the continued pursuit of knowledge was merely a hobby that he loved. But he also would write "I feel the mists of ignorance to surround me," and he would use his books to block out that ignorance and help him to ignore it. But being involved with Dr. Stiles only made it more unbearable. He came in contact with men of high learning and those men gave him glimpses of things beyond his small world that young Nathanael wanted and dreamed of experiencing. He felt the overwhelming attraction to experience all of the situations he had heard about.

Dr. Stiles often scheduled events for the benefit of Nathanael. It was at one of these meetings that Nathanael would meet the second most influential person in his life. A young man close to his own age and also born into a Quaker family, he was Lindley Murray, a young lawyer working for John Jay's firm in New York. Lindley had also yearned for more than a traditional Quaker education. Jay was the future president of the 1778-79 Continental Congress and later would be in the negotiation party of Paris with Benjamin Franklin and John Adams for peace between Britain and the United States. In the near future, Murray would become our country's foremost grammarian. Nathanael would learn the same things he also learned from Dr. Stiles, but by being closer to his own age Murray and Nathanael could discuss books that they had both read by looking at them with the blending of youth and faith that only young adults could experience. A humorous note about his strong relationship with a skilled grammarian like Murray you would imagine Greene would grow into a excellent user of the English language and a wonderful letter writer. Unfortunately this could not be farther from the truth. As we will see in the numerous letters Nathanael Greene would write throughout his life, he never became a skilled letter writer. Perhaps Greene could not escape the early aspect of his Quaker upbringing and the things he was taught. Years later he would comment on more than one occasion, "I lament the want of a liberal education." What all of this new education could do was take his training farther in later years when Greene would become more than just a reactionary Army officer. Nathanael Greene would be the foremost battlefield statistician of the entire Revolutionary War.

By now it was 1760, and Nathanael was beginning to take several trips a year to New York to see his close friend Murray. Also, at this time smallpox was rampant in the city and young Nathanael was less than secure entering the town without getting inoculated. The inoculation for smallpox had been available for years by this time, but most people were hesitant to accept it. The reason being that many times it was either useless, or condemned as a rebellion against the will of God. Most states out and out rejected the use of inoculation, including Massachusetts and Rhode Island, but Greene found a doctor in New York that would administer the shot. Many times the inoculation would cause a light case of smallpox and thus cause several pox marks to form on the face, body and extremities. Greene weathered through the inoculation and had only a blemish in the right eye that did not impair his vision. What he did have was confidence from that time forward to move within and about New York to visit. Greene's experience with the inoculation for smallpox would again be a teaching form that would follow him to his days with the Army.

One of his visits to see his friend Murray was a business call. The senior Greene had given young Nathanael the management of a family lawsuit that involved the death of two half-brothers. The principles of the case were so confusing and intricate that several appeals were sent over to England for rulings. When Nathanael was given management of the lawsuit by his father he bought another book he thought would come in handy, "Jacob's Law Dictionary," which he read from cover to cover until he felt that he had mastered the contents. During the exchange of consequences involved with the case,

Nathanael also formed lasting acquaintances with several associate members of the bench in New York, which would, again, come in handy in later years. And so, Nathanael Greene was well on his way to adulthood with the experiences he learned from and the knowledge he had gained from several noted scholars. He gained experience as a subtle scrutinizer of men and their actions. As well as a thoughtful observer of nature, a great listener, a fond cultivator of the genteel influences of society, an entertainer of the fairer sex, a great lover of books, a curious observer and inquirer into the cause and reason of things. He was a man without the ambition and hunger of fortune that many men of his day possessed. Nathanael Greene went into his adult life with no more want than to own a comfortable home, enough fortune to allow him the purchase of his beloved books, and just enough leisure time so that he may read all of them.

His father would gaze at him in puzzlement at times. An astrologer his father had known, Dr. Spencer, had announced at Nathanael's birth that he would "be a great man of Israel." The senior Greene had grave doubts of the prophecy's fulfillment. The outside knowledge young Nathanael had gained made it very unlikely that he would take one of the high seats in the meeting house his father had always hoped for his son.

Also, around the time of 1762 young Nathanael Greene began experiencing health problems. Most notably asthma, which kept him awake most nights, especially in the spring and summer. Although said to be around 5 foot 10 inches tall with strong build especially in the chest and shoulders, his right knee began to swell often and stiffen without cause or reason. He mentioned later that "was not enough to prevent me from running, jumping or wrestling with the strongest of active companions; but enough to be seen a limp in my gait." We gain a good insight into Nathanael Greene's appearance from a detailed description written by his grandson George Washington Greene from the biography he wrote in 1867, "a well-filled oval face, with a forehead that declare prominent attention. His eyes of clear, liquid blue and a nose that was rather Grecian than Roman. A deep-set mouth with full lips and a full, rounded chin." The ladies seemed to think he was handsome and he had no lack of suitors, it was said. He was also thought to be quite the comedian for his day. Always ready with a joke or an impersonation, although no mention of who he impersonated is given, other than an old family friend by the name of Dr. Slop.

His demeanor was considered of a nervous temperament at first, but he brought it under control and bore the reputation of being firm, but fair. There is no mention of a fiery or tenacious temper. He despised arrogance and so never allowed himself to show any. Looking back on his youth there is nothing that distinguishes Nathanael Greene as the great man of refined mind and character he would become. Nothing that indicates the intellectual fortitude, the systematic decision making or distinctive character many other famous public figures showed in their youth. Greene's private life bore no such criteria to show that this was a man who would display the personality and emotion that would lead him to be one of the greatest Generals this country has ever seen. Perhaps all of the qualities Greene possessed made him a great individual. Something you needed to become a leader of men in wartime.

By now, it was 1770 and the Greene family was prospering and looking to expand. The Quaker way of life was to never let the grass grow under one's feet, lest one would accuse you of slacking in time or effort. The senior Greene would never allow his family or himself to let that happen. So he decided to put to work a plan to expand the operations between the forge in Potowomut and the one that was built just before the younger Nathanael's birth in Coventry, some ten miles away. The iron used at the works from Pennsylvania was mostly shipped through the little seaport town of Apponaug in the northwest portion of Greenwich Bay. It was tough going to get the ore from there to the small town of Cranston. It was then carted by farmers on ox carts to be smelted and then taken to Coventry to be forged (mostly into anchors) carted again to Apponaug in ox carts, and then shipped by waterway to Newport. With the manufacturing business flourishing, the senior Greene who was in the latter part of his life, had to travel several times a year to manage the affairs of both forges. Ten miles does not sound like a large distance today, but in the summer of 1770 in the wilds of Rhode Island it was as if you were traveling a distance of 100 miles today. It was decided that the senior Greene need not make the bi-monthly trip with a group of young and strong sons at his disposal and it was decided that one son would become the manager of the Coventry forge and go to live there. When it came to pick which son would make the move it was not a hard choice. It would be the son with the most energy, the son with the broadest education and the son with wanderlust in his veins. The son that kept him up at night with worry, but who was destine to accomplish the most as his namesake; Nathanael.

This was quite an event for the younger Nathanael, who was used to living under the same roof with his parents and siblings his whole life. Although he was now twenty-nine, it was customary for Quaker families to live under the same roof well into adulthood. If they were to move, it was usually on the same property as their parents. To move to another town was therefore considered a life-altering event. With a heavy heart Nathanael said his good-byes with the added excitement of starting his life on his own. For a home he chose a site on the side of a hill overlooking the river that was shaded by woods on the western exposure. Beneath him was a broad strip of woodlands that stretched to the Coweset Bay and above was seen the summit of Warwick Neck. The house was a neat, two-story building with four rooms on each floor and divided by a wide entryway and on the outside showed a great resemblance to his old homestead of Potowomut which he missed very much.

When Nathanael was settled, he often would saddle his horse and take long journeys into his new surroundings. He loved horseback and unconsciously prepared himself for his next vocation, soldiering. An unknown, family friend later wrote about Nathanael, "His first visit, after a absence from home was always to the stable." When going on the new route he had laid out to Newport from Greenwich he would often meet a party of friends on the small, rocky island halfway down the bay known as Hope Island. There the friends would meet, have supper and finish the night in one of Nathanael's favorite pastimes, dancing. He was becoming, quite the distinguished party guest and would be very proud when he learned he was invited to a particular party given by an important person of the area. Several of his friends were left off the list. This was Nathanael's first, real experience with formal social activity and being put on the "A" list. It was hard for him to understand why he was picked over guests that were just as accomplished and willing to be invited as he was. When Nathanael was the one giving the party, it was just as hard for him to leave anyone off the guest list. So he usually did not. But on the other hand, with each party given with Nathanael being one of the privileged few, it was also hard for him not to think he was becoming someone of some sort of importance, and indeed he was becoming just that.

Greene was known for his hospitality and we get some insight into it from a letter written by David Howell to his sister at one such meeting. Howell was then a tutor at Rhode Island College and later a famous attorney, judge, and congressman for the state. He wrote, "Mr. Greene is a very remarkable man. I had rode down to borrow a book from him and found myself in conversation which naturally ran till late in the evening. Mr. Greene invited me to stay the night, but I arose very early the next morning before daylight in order to make sure of reaching home in time for my recitation. But I was surprised to find Mr. Greene up before me and pouring over a book by the light of the fire. I had apologized for the necessity to leave early in the morning and bid him goodbye that night and expecting no offer for breakfast. But when morning came the table was found set and breakfast was ready and waiting for my arrival."

Soon after Nathanael moved to Coventry, his father died. He would write soon after that it was, "an event, which turned all our affairs into different channels, that made it requisite for me to give the closest application and attention to the settlement of matters." But, in fact no serious changes were made in the family's business relations and transactions and everything continued as if nothing had upset the brother's concentration. The senior Nathanael had trained his sons well at the art of work with the feeling that while working for their father, they were actually working for themselves. When the estate was passed onto the Greene's sons, they were more than prepared to share the burden and the profits equally amongst them.

In Rhode Island state law stated that only the eldest son of a freeholder who held real estate valued at more than forty pounds sterling could vote. Back in 1760, Nathanael was the executor in the holdings of his half-brother Thomas who had died. One of the holdings that had been passed onto Nathanael was an estate in West Greenwich and according to the law made him a freeman in Warwick in April of 1765. A freeman, but especially a Quaker was expected to make a "solemn affirmation to the protest of bribery and corruption" as taught by their Quaker founder George Fox and the state law prescribed. At about this time, the passage of the Stamp Act was instigated and was headed into Parliament by a gentlemen that would become a future opponent in another matter to Nathanael, Lord Charles Cornwallis - Lord of the Bedchamber. Briefly, the Stamp Act of 1765 was a tax that was imposed on the American colonists on any printed paper product used by them. Legal documents, ship logs, newspapers, and even playing cards were taxed. The tax was minuscule by comparison to any other tax that had been levied to them in the past. But this tax enraged the colonists because it was used to raise money to defend the frontier (along the Appalachian Mountains) where taxes in the past had only been levied to regulate commerce. This was further viewed as another attempt to by-pass American colony legislatures and if allowed to pass without resistance would pave the way for England levying future taxes on the colonist whenever they deemed appropriate.

Needless to say, the colonist did not take kindly to this intrusion of power into their relatively quiet lifestyle. This was the beginning of the American colonist's rebellion to the motherland of England. So in 1768,when legislation for the non-importation resolution which would counteract the Stamp Act was introduced, Greene was chosen to head the committee for canvassing the county for necessary signatures to pass that resolution. When Nathanael moved to Coventry he was chosen to represent his new home in the General Assembly. His first official public act in the assembly was to start a movement to establish a school in his new hometown. His next important step was to draft a political letter which was addressed to Moses Brown, who later would become a famous Quaker educator and philanthropist in Providence. The letter addressed the opposition to the reelection of a Judge Potter in the upcoming election. Greene wrote, "I should be remiss not to give you timely information of all matters that were likely to concern civil polity or the well-being of the government and in an especially manner when I thought you would be likely to adopt any plan to obviate their schemes. I know not for what reason, but there is the greatest opposition forming against Judge Potter's ensuing election that I have ever seen in my life against any representative. His conduct and mine hath been almost uniformly the same in public measures. Was I not conscious that the Judge would do his town and the government better service than any other person in it, I would not be so strongly attached to his interest as to oppose any man better sort of the people thought worthy, by their suffrage, to represent them in the General Assembly." Why is this letter important? It clearly shows how Greene played on the power of reading character and controlling men as one of the founders of the soon-to-be nation. It is just a sampling of the strong virtue and unwavering leadership that Nathanael Greene would bring as a General in the Army of American Revolution in the Southern States campaign.

Although most of Greene's legislative accomplishments have fallen into obscurity, others have survived the test of time. Local details of legislation, like discussions on fundamental principals were foremost in Nathanael's mind. This was a subject he had long studied about and would not allow a moment to go by without a word or two about his convictions on the subject. When the resolution of 1774 against the "Importation of Negroes" was passed, he was no longer a member of the Rhode Island

Assembly. But his declaration a few years later is an example of his beliefs and how he would have voted had he still been a member of that body, "As for slavery, nothing can be said in its defense." Outside of the Legislature he was now a public man and took an active interest if not an active part in public measures. His training for dealing with men, all men, and taking responsibility for them had begun.

An example of Greene's heartfelt and growing patriotism are the incidents surrounding the grounding and subsequent destruction of "His Majesty's Ship Gaspee" on a shoal in Newport harbor. Legend has always placed Nathanael Greene at the insurrection and even had him leading the crowd involved. But in fact Abraham Whipple, a Rhode Island sea captain agreed to lead the band of 8 long-boats that silently rowed out to the Gaspee before the morning flood tide could free her. Whipple and his band crept onto the sleeping ship and found her captain, Horace Dudingston walking the deck. One of the colonists struck the captain and technically drew the first English blood of the Revolution. The captain and his crew were taken prisoner and removed to the village of Pawtuxet. Before Whipple and his men castoff, they set fire to the Gaspee, which burned to her waterline before the fire reached its powder magazine and blew-up. A letter written by Greene's close friend E. Brown to Artemas Ward, Jr., who would later distinguish himself as a General for the Continental Army, placed Greene with him that warm July evening. Greene did travel to Providence the next day and took the route along the bay where he would notice the smoldering hull floating in the harbor. However, his name was still attached with the band lead by Whipple.

Although American records show Greene to be elsewhere at the time of the Gaspee incident, the British government believed Greene was involved as official documents of the time indicate. The British government however offered a reward for information leading to the capture of the men and ringleaders of the Gaspee plot and announced that when the perpetrators were caught, they would be tried in England and not in the colonies. But the colonists kept the names of the men involved secret and no one ever claimed the reward. None of the men involved were ever discovered or apprehended by the British. Legend has it that Abraham Whipple was the first to utter the famous line about King George III and repeated several times during the Revolution, "If he's to hang me, he first must catch me!" Abraham Whipple would go on to distinguish himself further during the fight for Independence. In 1775, the newly named commander-in-chief of the Continental Navy, Esek Hopkins, sailed on one of the first ships commissioned by Congress, the Katy. Abraham Whipple was the captain and joined the other vessels in the Delaware River for operations defending Philadelphia against the British. In 1778, Whipple sailed to France in command of the frigate Providence, carrying munitions and the following year was responsible for taking a fleet of heavily laden East Indiamen, one of the richest prizes of the Revolutionary War. He was later taken prisoner in the siege of Charleston and was held prisoner the remainder of the war.

Greene and Whipple would be linked indirectly again during the ill-fated battle of Charleston where Nathanael commanded the infantry. But for now, Greene was busy defending himself against the burning of the Gaspee, while becoming offensive with the Rhode Island governing body which was assisting the British in their investigation of the matter. "When the new-fangled court," as Greene described it, assembled at Newport to receive information against the suspected persons taking a part in the destruction of the royal cutter, he condemned the General Assembly as "alarming to every virtuous mind and lover of liberty in America. The Assembly seems to have lost all that spirit of independence and public virtue that has ever distinguished them since they have first been incorporated, and sunk down into a tame submission and entire acquiescence to ministerial mandates." Already his views were embraced throughout the whole country and further letters were written by him to express his political sentiments toward union: "If this court and mode of trial is established as a precedent towards its people, it will naturally affect all of the other colonies."

Nathanael Greene's words echo many of the correspondence and documents of the day: James Otis's "Rights of the British Colonies," Josiah Quincey's "Observations on the Boston Port Bill," and John Adams "Dissertation of the Canon and Feudal Law." They were all required reading for the revolutionist and patriot of the day. They prepared the public mind for the open resistance that was to follow. Greene himself was expecting and preparing for the worst when he wrote, "the civil ministry seem to be determined to imbue their cursed hands in American blood." These sentiments brought him to the forefront with the popular leaders. In a letter to Samuel Ward, an associate judge at the time, dated January 25, 1773, he wrote, "I spent last evening with your father (Governor Ward), Mr. Marchant, and a sundry of other gentlemen at your uncle Greene's." The uncle being William Greene of the Warwick branch of the large family and who years later became chief justice and then governor of Rhode Island. Mr. Marchant was attorney general and only two years before had been sent to England to collect French & Indian War debt for the Rhode Island colonist. He would later fill the congressional seat that Samuel Ward had held earlier. Throughout the years leading up to the struggle that would become the American Revolution, men such as these always seemed to be brought together in one eventful goal. Liberty.

The idea of a General Congress was beginning to take shape. The Congress of 1765 was used as a means of obtaining redress at the time, and now the private talk in taverns and street corners of resurrecting that body was gaining influence once more. The first official action taken would be a town-meeting in Providence on the evening of May 17, 1774, instructing their "deputies to the General Assembly to use their influence for promoting such a Congress." The first election sent the leaders of Rhode Island's two great parties (Hopkins & Ward) to sit side by side in the newly formed Congress and work together in a single goal of a common defense. Greene obviously felt the solemn note of this act when he wrote, "Heaven bless their congressional consultations with her seasoning grace, and crown their resolution with success and triumph!" The choice of then governor Ward was particularly pleasing to him. "The mean motives of interest, of partial distinction of ministers of state, will have no influence upon his virtuous soul: like Cato of old, he'll stand or fall with the liberties of his country."

In the December session, although no longer a member of the state Assembly, he was put on the "committee to revise the militia laws of the colony and report as soon as may be." The events surrounding this time made this duty more important with each passing day. Cannon had already been removed from Fort George and a resolution was made for the immediate formation of a public powder magazine. Outfitted with lead, flints, and the recommendation "to all the inhabitants of this colony, that they expend no gunpowder for mere sport and diversion, and only in pursuit of game." The act of issuance for the report of the committee of militia laws to provide a monthly exercise in "martial discipline and for the manner in which the forces within the colony shall march to the assistance of any of our sister colonies when invaded or attacked." It was posted as if by prophecy less than 4 months before the standoff at a small bridge in Lexington and Concord, Massachusetts. Of all these preparations, none hit home to Greene's personal feelings than the organization of the Kentish Guards. They were an independent company from East Greenwich, Warwick, and Coventry, similar to other bodies of men and militias being planned and organized all over the country. Greene was bound to this particular organization because of its ties to three particular locations. Born in Warwick Township, he grew up meditating at the Quaker meeting-house in East Greenwich and currently resided in Coventry.

All of the members of this elite company were his neighbors, acquaintances and friends, and Nathanael entered the group at its inception as a private. The Kentish Guard was formed on September 24, 1774. Nathanael Greene was among the first petitioners of a charter for the group. The Kent County Courthouse, which still stands in East Greenwich, served as the group's first Armory. At the formation of the Continental Army during the siege of Boston in 1775, George Washington particularly noted how well equipped, trained, and disciplined the members of the Guard were. The Guard built

Fort Daniel at the entrance to Greenwich Cove, equipped with nine 18-pounders, and garrisoned it throughout the Revolutionary War. Among its first officers were James Mitchel Varnum, a man of "exalted talents" whom Greene "loved with the greatest esteem," and who would take an honored place in the civil and military history of the American Revolution. Another was Christopher Greene, who was to follow Arnold on the ill-fated attack on Quebec, and defend Fort Mercer against the Hessians at Red Bank, New Jersey. Later in the war he would fall and die, a victim of the negligence of militiamen, so often seen during many of the battles in the war. More than 35 men would move onto the regular army and the Continental line during the war.

The Kentish Guard would serve as sentries at Prudence Island in Narragansett Bay, Warwick Neck, Warren, Bristol, Portsmouth, Middleton, Newport and Tiverton. From 1776 to 1781 the Guards had duties and activities including: countering several attacks on Greene's hometown of Potowomut, East Greenwich, Warwick Neck and Wickford. They single-handedly launched an attack on and successfully destroyed a British artillery battery in Jamestown, Rhode Island. Is 1781 the Kentish Guard escorted the travel weary French troops under Rochembeau from Connecticut Island to their rendezvous with Washington in Yorktown, Virginia, as well as guard duty on Sachuest Beach in Newport up until the end of the British occupation of the city in 1782. The Kentish Guard operates to this day under their original charter, opting to stay as a separate organization in the early 1900's when the trend was to incorporate smaller groups into what is now the modern National Guard.

Soon after joining the Kentish Guard, many of Greene's friends tried to persuade Nathanael to petition for a lieutenant's commission. But they forgot something that would block their good-natured efforts. Nathanael's stiff knee, which gave him "a limp in his gait" would soon cause the foundation for an unwelcome turn of events from what originally was to be a noteworthy act. In the eyes of the village elders and leaders of the township, Nathanael's limp, although slight, was looked upon as a serious blemish, rendering him unfit not merely as an officer, but even as a private. A limping soldier in their elite ranks would be seen as a weakness of the entire company. Greene was beside himself with the ridicule he was receiving and took it solely to heart. His friends were indignant and Varnum threatened to withdraw his name as First Officer. The loss of Varnum to the newly organized company would be a serious blow to their credibility.

The resentment Greene felt to the village could not be explained by word-of-mouth to his friends and so he took pen to hand to write of his passion and duty as a soldier and a citizen. Dated Monday, two o'clock, P.M., Coventry. "Dear Sir, --- I was informed the gentlemen of East Greenwich said that I was a blemish to the company. I confess it is the first stroke of mortification I ever felt from being considered, either in private or public life, a blemish to those with whom I associated. Hitherto, I have always had the happiness to find myself respected in society in general, and my friendship courted by as respectable characters as any in the government. Pleased with these thoughts, and anxious to promote the good of my country, and ambitious of increasing the consequence of East Greenwich, I have exerted myself to form a military company there; but little did I think that the gentlemen considered me in the light of an obtruder. My heart is too susceptible of pride, and my sentiments too delicate, to wish a connection where I am considered in an inferior point of light. I have always made it my study to promote the interest of Greenwich, and to cultivate the good opinion of its inhabitants, the severity of the speech, and the union of sentiment coming from persons so unexpected, might wound the pride of my heart deeper than the force of the observation merited."

Greene goes on to describe the circumstances surrounding the commission his friends tried to obtain for him and then attempts to explain that it was they and not he who wished the promotion. But he continues with the following; "but if I conceive right of the force of the objection of the gentlemen of the town, it was not as an officer but as a soldier, for that halting was a blemish to the rest of my comrades. I confess it is my misfortune to limp a little, but I did not conceive it to be so great; but we are not apt to discover our own defects as others do. I feel the less mortified as it is natural, and not a stain or defection that resulted from my action. I have pleased myself with the thought of serving under you, but as it is the general opinion that I am unfit for such an undertaking, I shall desist. I feel not the less inclination to promote the good of the company, because I am not to be one of its members. I will do anything that's in my power to continue to procure the charter." Nathanael continues by asking his commander to halt any further protest by the men or his superiors. He felt that continuing any such actions would only bring disgrace upon the company and in closing writes. "I feel more mortification than resentment, but I think it would manifest a more generous temper to have given me their opinion in private rather than make proclamation of it in public; for no one loves to be the subject of ridicule, however true the case. I am, with great truth, your sincere friend."

The honest hurt Nathanael Greene felt is evident in his letter and it is hard not to feel sympathy for what he must have endured. Like most problems in one's life, this one had a happy ending. The circumstances of how the situation was resolved is lost to time and history, but safe to say that Greene remained in the company, but as a private. His next difficult problem, although less personal, would be no less important.

To be in the military, either regular army, militia or local guard, a soldier had to have five major articles. A coat or hunting frock, a canteen, a hat of some kind, shoes and of course, a firelock. Where would he find a flintlock (musket)? The military was already having difficulty getting gunpowder, muskets and assorted accouterments. He decided the best place to start was in Boston, where his business relations would probably be able to assist him in some way. The only problem was that it was the first year of the "Boston Port Bill" and that meant the British Crown effectively shut down the port of Boston to any incoming traffic or trade. Presumably until the town of Boston paid for the tea that the East Indian Tea Company had lost when several of their crates were unceremoniously thrown into Boston Harbor some years before. So, finding things like hats, shoes, English tea and muskets was difficult indeed to find in the later days of 1774.

When Greene journeyed to Boston he usually lodged at the "Bunch of Grapes Inn," on the small square just in front of Faneuil Hall. It is here some say the first whispers of revolution were uttered at protest meetings over the taxation policies of the British Empire. Several times many of the people involved in those meetings became agitated and the discussion spilled out into the street and became violent. Some of the instigators were men like Sam and John Adams, James Otis, Dr. Joseph Warren, and Josiah Quincy. Quincy had written several articles in the Boston Gazette titled, "Observations on the Act of Parliament Commonly called the Boston Port Bill." What is not well known is that after a group of British soldiers opened fire on a riotous group of protesters, killing 5 civilians in 1773, Quincy and John Adams were the defending attorneys for the British soldiers and had them acquitted. The 1773 event that many used as propaganda for the swelling of resentment toward the British occupation did not remain unknown to history. It has been called the "Boston Massacre." Due to Greene's past positions on several issues, it is easy to believe that he would have made time while visiting Boston to sit down with some of the men who would become the "Sons of Liberty" and discuss a bit of treason.

There are a few mentions in some of Greene's letters of the time, that alluded to a meeting he may have had with Samuel Adams and Dr. Warren, where they discussed the chance of recruiting 20,000 men to start a organized army. Massachusetts had just asked Rhode Island to join with New Hampshire and Connecticut to help raise such a force. They would have used Josiah Quincey's sixteen page pamphlet, describing how the General or First Continental Congress of Philadelphia had drafted a proclamation from Pennsylvania's Joseph Galloway with a plan to reconcile the colonies differences with Great Britain. It was a measure that was popular with the representatives present when it was drafted and it nearly passed, but with the arrival of the Suffolk County contingent (Boston) the debate brought defeat for the measure with a six to five vote. It was a cause for celebration in the streets of Boston and at the "Bunch of Grapes Inn" where we are told, that Nathanael Greene was a participant. Greene would have also used his time to procure a few items for his passion, books, at Henry Knox's bookstore. Greene writes of Knox and himself attending several of the morning and evening parades of the British troops through the streets by Knox's shop. Looking sternly from under the broad brim of his dark Quaker hat with his keen eyes fixed on the soldiers and mumbling unkind words between Knox and himself. Two short years later, the two men would be doing the same under the cocked tricorns of Brigadier-general in two short years. Greene finally procured a flintlock musket a few days later and on the trip back haphazardly met a British deserter and persuaded the man to go back with him as a drill-master to the Kentish Guards. But first he would have to hire a farmer to hide the musket in his cart, and only by following behind the cart at a safe distance as to not be suspected of being the owner of the flintlock could he begin his journey back home. Several villages were Tory held and staunchly loyal to the British crown. A gentleman by the name of Ditson had traveled through one such place called "Roxbury" and having his musket discovered by the Tories was tarred and feathered and ridden out of town on a rail. Greene had no such problem and soon was marching in formation with his newly obtained weapon and learning the manual of arms from the Guard's fresh drillmaster.

Nathanael Greene loved the out-of-doors. From the large amount of time spent working the family fields and spent outdoors when he had a moment of free time, he naturally enjoyed being unencumbered by walls. Even the mills and forge that Nathanael worked had an air of nature and openness about it. Much more so than the mercantile store the family owned, which we have learned Nathanael did not inhabit. So the time spent in camp, mustering and drilling did not bother Greene at all. He instead relished the moments, although he did complain every so often that drilling took most of the time he usually would have spent reading his books. His mode of reading was very deliberate and since he had only a small collection of books, he took to reading them one after another several times until he almost wore them out. His knowledge of his books was unparalleled and he mastered every word from cover to cover. After years of reading to this extreme, he was prone on occasion to exclaim, amongst his friends at least, that no one could get the substance out of books like he could. This, of course, was in part to the prejudice his father had shown toward what the senior Nathanael had called, "unnecessary amounts of education." So, Nathanael only had a smattering of books to speak of, including works of Fox, Barclay and Locke in subjects ranging from poetry to thought itself. But, once Nathanael could indulge in a wider range of study, and had his own home he furnished the house with books and built a library. A little room on the northeast corner of his house in Coventry was chosen as his study. The walls were covered with miscellaneous contents like a country store. A few of the shelves were set apart for his books. At the time of his acceptance into the Kentish Guard the number of books in his collection totaled two hundred and fifty. Many of his friends thought about the money he had spent on them and just shook their heads at him and said, "You never can read them all!" One of his first and favorite series of books, were the volumes of Euclid, about the theory of absolute truth. The volumes had helped bring him to the first consciousness that the world proceeded past his own front door. Another of his favorites was the four thick volumes of the "Dictionary of Arts and Sciences," which had hundred of answers to his constant probing questions and with numerous elaborate engravings as well. His collection even included a book called, "Book-keeping Methodized," which he would find very useful when pressed into service as the Quartermaster-general's department accountant. In the inside leaf of each and every volume, in a steady, bold hand is the signature of *Nathanael Greene* methodically and lovingly displayed to show each book's significance.

Very soon, the pen would be just as important an instrument as Greene's books. The earliest specimens of his writings were first preserved by his dear friend Samuel Ward, Jr., and most recently, "The papers of General Nathanael Greene." His writings, second only to those of George Washington's in volume, are currently being examined and cataloged for the Rhode Island Historical Society by the University of North Carolina at Chapel Hill, using only his letters from 1763 to 1783. Some are merely studies in composition, showing the progress Greene showed from his earliest attempts at letter writing dissertations on subjects in which he was well versed. His writings turn to the thoughts and opinions he felt near and dear to his heart. In one, he traces our action to "self-love" as the "primary mover and first principle of the all," and attributing the "hazardous actions of great and exalted spirits for the good of others" to the "passion of glory and the generous benevolence of worthy minds in the domestic way of life" to the "greater happiness with gratification that benevolence affords them." In another letter, Greene draws the comparison between town and country life. He unconsciously gives us a personal glimpse into his own enjoyment of country living. Town life reminds him of "a cloudy sky, country life of a clear one, each acting upon the other by a law of necessary succession which nature seems to move gently on, undisturbed by noise and tumult actions and affording us an opportunity of contemplating her order and beauty until we arrive at that pitch of knowledge and understanding that the God of nature has qualified us to soar to." In another of his writings, he goes on to define "virtuous manners as such acquired habits of thought and correspondent actions as lead to the steady prosecution of the general welfare of society. "Virtuous principles are such as to tend and confirm those habits by superinducing the idea of duty." The "Virtuous" manners of which he speaks are "a permanent foundation of civil liberty, because they lead the passions and desires themselves to coincide with the appointments of civil law." Strong convictions shown by a future Brigadier General in the Continental army of the Unites States and a simple outline of just some of Nathanael Greene's beliefs and thought processes. A process we will see used again and again in the hard fought campaigns of the American Revolution. It would also be a gauge or template so as to understand why Greene would do the things he did and the thought processes of how he made those decisions at the time.

Sometimes Nathanael's thoughts were close to malice when he described his Quaker upbringing, particularly how he was educated. On one occasion he wrote to a young friend, "I hope one day to see you shine like a star of the first magnitude, all glorious both evening and day...I lament the want of a liberal education. I feel the mist of ignorance surround me...I was educated a Quaker, and amongst the most superstitious sort; and that of itself is enough to cramp the best of geniuses, much more mine. The constrained manner of educating their youth has proved a fine nursery of ignorance and superstition instead of piety, and has laid a foundation for farce instead of worship." He goes on to say, "it was not the original intention of the Friends to prevent the propagation of useful literature in the Church, but only to prohibit their youth from reading such books as may make them fools by industry; that they considered youth to be the great opportunity of life, which settles or fixes most men in a good or bad course; that, falling upon an age of priestcraft, they were disgusted with a system of education the only aim of which was to cultivate the youthful mind to be subservient to the afterviews, and failing to distinguish where the evil lay, and arguing from the abuse to the disuse of the thing, they confounded literature with a vain philosophy and while they aimed only to lop off the dead branches, superstition and ignorance, creeped into the decay of learning....This, my dear friend, was the foundation of my education." Although Nathanael Greene was outspoken on numerous subjects other than his Quaker education, this was a subject that drove and haunted him till his dying day. No matter how much knowledge Greene amassed, he would always feel that he could have learned even more if given the chance from an earlier age. And for this, and only this, he chastised his early Quaker teachings.

At about this time, Nathanael was beginning to fall in love with the sister of his dear friend, Samuel Ward. Nathanael had watched her grow from a young girl he had known during his youth into what he described as; "a fair maiden in whom all the noble instincts of the father and brother looked out through soft eyes of bluish gray, strengthening the harmony of well-matched features, deepening at times the tints of her rosy cheeks, and imparting dignity to a form which is full of grace." As Greene saw and talked with her more and more, he came to the realization that she could only return the feeling of friendship. He constantly attempted to change her feelings and look upon him as a suitor rather than just a friend, but his efforts were in vain and, as he wrote, "the discomfort and overwhelming distress and pleasant pain brought variance with myself and thoughts and meditative habits of my natural disposition of life, greatly contributed to prolonged agitation." Although heart broken about his first attempt at love, it was fortunate for him that another, more demanding pursuit would soon command a large share of his attention.

The Colonies dispute with England was rapidly deteriorating, and making it necessary for men of all classes to choose their side in the contest that was most assuredly approaching. For Greene this decision involved another decision, which he could not make easily. He realized long before that nothing but an appeal to arms could save the Colonies from British subservience. He felt that his country wanted and needed his services, which he was more than willing to give. But he knew that he could not take a sword in his hand without exposing himself to dismissal from the religious society he had lived in since he was a child. In the grounds surrounding the small meeting-house where he worshipped was the grave of his mother whom he helped lay to rest at the age of ten. Years later, he would return to the spot more times than he would like to recall. There he would bury two brothers and his father along side of his mother. How could he ever cut himself off from a building where he had so often listened to his father's voice preaching, and give up his rightful place in consecrated ground by the graves of his family members?

The Greene family had strong attachments to the people and government in the surrounding area, and the local inhabitants felt a personal kinship to the Greenes. But the Society of Friends had firm and deliberate resolutions condemning members from military service. The meeting-house elders made no decision on Nathanael until he made his profession public at a military parade at Plainfield, Connecticut near the Rhode Island
border. It was not until then that the Friends gave public notice concerning the Greene's. As the record showed: "At our monthly meeting, held at Cranston on the 5th of seventh month, 1773....Whereas, this meeting is informed that Nathanael and Griffin Greene have at a place in Connecticut of public resort where they had no proper business, therefore this meeting appoints Ephraim Congdon, Jared Greene, and Cary Spencer to make inquiry into the matter, and to make report at our next monthly meeting." When that next meeting came together, it was further resolved to: " Monthly meeting at East Greenwich ye 2nd of the eighth month, 1773. The committee appointed to inquire into the conduct of Nathanael and Griffin Greene report that they have had no opportunity with them as yet. Therefore it is continued to our next meeting." Actually, the committee did uncover evidence against the pair, but was reluctant to say so or to proceed against the son and nephew of an eminent and posthumous preacher. The next meeting was held, but with little progress in the matter. "Cranston on ye 6th day of ye ninth month, 1773 - In the matter referred to this meeting concerning Nathanael and Griffin Greene, the committee reports that they have treated with them, but they have given no satisfaction as yet. Whereupon this meeting continues it once more, and desires the clerk to inform them of the same." The pair were reprieved again and another month passed. This time it is held in East Greenwich in the very building they had seen Nathanael's familiar face as a member for almost thirty years. But on this date the clerk enters: "ye 30th day of ye ninth month - The matter referred to this meeting concerning Nathanael and Griffin Greene, as they have not given this meeting any satisfaction for their outgoing misconduct, therefore this meeting doth put them from under the care of this meeting until they make satisfaction for their misconduct, and appoint John Greene to inform them of the same." Already the year 1773 had seen Greene skirt the accusations surrounding the Gaspee incident, as he wrote to Samuel Ward, "One of the Gaspee people has sworn against me as being concerned in the destruction of her....I should be tempted to let the sun shine through him if I could come to him." He had entered the Kentish Guard

only to be asked to leave due to his weak knee, and now he was unceremoniously driven out of his childhood meetinghouse. His separation from the Quakers was complete and irrevocable, so he began to stock his home library shelves with military books he had purchased from the bookstore Henry Knox owned. Up until now, Knox was merely the bookseller Greene bought from in Boston. Soon, they would meet in camp as Kentish Guards and strike up a friendship that was cherished by both men until the day they died.

It was now time for Nathanael to find true love. Not that he had been looking, but the three ladies that bore his affection did not return the same feelings. It was early 1774 and Greene had occasion to make several trips to East Greenwich. At first Nathanael's trips were designed to do advanced scouting for the Rhode Island College Board of Trustee's. Since the College's establishment in February of 1764 it had been searching for a permanent location for the growing institution. They had not found one as late as December of 1770. Nathanael was one of many men taking part in the long and argument filled debates, discussing the location of the colleges. Almost every principal or large town in the state thought its location was best and East Greenwich was no different, claiming their town as the best location for the college. But, that was not the only reason Nathanael started making frequent trips to the town. It also happened to be the home of a particular young lady who had stolen Nathanael's heart. Her name was Catherine Littlefield, but everyone called her Caty, and she was the niece of Catherine Ray, wife to William Greene, Jr., future governor of Rhode Island and uncle of Samuel Ward, Nathanael's young friend. The courtship between Nathanael and Miss Littlefield moved very smoothly and swiftly, an arrangement Nathanael was not accustomed to with his past lady acquaintances. His friends thought Nathanael would never marry. Even a close friend was once motivated to write, "Nat and Miss Nancy Ward had gotten in such a way of leaning backward that I have given them over entirely." The same friend suggested that Nathanael's brother William "go right off and see Polly Greene, Caty Littlefield, or some agreeable girl." Instead it was Nathanael, who had known Caty since she was a young girl at his Aunt Catherine Greene's home, that had won her affection.

Caty was born in 1751 on Block Island, which is just off Point Judith, Rhode Island in the southwest entrance of Narragansett Bay and almost the same distance from Montauk, Long Island, New York. The daughter of John and Phoebe Littlefield, Caty was sent to her Aunt Catherine's when she was ten years old. Caty had lost her mother a few years earlier and it was becoming clear to her father that a young girl coming of age could not be properly educated in the finer and delicate forms of womanhood on a small, desolate island in the Atlantic Ocean. Her aunt was an attractive, vivacious woman who was known far and wide as a charming hostess. She was to be a character in many letters of Benjamin Franklin. He would stay at their home whenever he was visiting Boston. Caty's book learning may not have been as extensive as Nathanael's, but she was an apt pupil of her Aunt's charming ways, which, when combined with her natural good looks and animation, made her a favorite of the local and visiting dignitaries. Nathanael was thirty-two years old, nine years Caty's senior at the time. Nathanael accompanied her on several occasions when Caty made trips to Block Island to visit her father and sisters. Her sibling would arrange parties where the guests ate, drank, and danced all night.

And so, on the 12th of July 1774 the bands of marriage were entered for Nathanael Greene to Catherine Littlefield. Certified in Coventry by David Sprague, Clerk, who wrote, "to all whom it may concern, That the intention of marriage was Published in the congregation assembled For Divine Worship in Newshoreham meeting-house Three days of Publik Worship between Mr. Nathanael Greene of Coventry in the County of Kint and Catherine Littlefield a daughter of John Littlefield Esq. at Newshoreham in the county of Newport and being no objection made to forbid their marriage." On the very same day, the worshippers at the "Episcopal Church at Providence received notice and testified by book-copy to the rector, J. Greaves." By the 18th of July a third certificate was given to and entered into court records by Stephen Arnold, Court of Common Pleas Clerk of the requisitions of law and custom. Nathanael, the happy bride-groom-to-be wrote to his dear friend Samuel, "Please deliver the enclosed cards to your sisters. On the 20th this instant, I expect to be married to Miss Kitty Littlefield, at your uncle Greene's. As a relation of hers, and friend of mine, your company will be required on that occasion. The company will be small consisting only of a few Choice spirits. As she is not married at her father's house she declined giving invitation but a few of her nearest relations and most intimate friends. There will be my brothers and their wives, Mr. Varnum and his wife, Polly Greene, Phoebe Shuffield, Betsy Greene, Christopher Greene and Griffin Greene and their wives, Mr. Thomas Arnold and who from Block island I know not. These are all expecting your family." But suddenly the note that started by evoking thoughts of glad tidings about Samuel's family turns decidedly towards stronger and sterner subjects. "The Ministry seems to be determined to embrace their hands in American Blood, and that once Wise and Virtuous Parliament, but now Wicked and Weak Assembly, lends an assisting hand to accomplish their hellish schemes. The Soldiers of Boston are insolent above measure. Soon very soon expect to hear the thirsty Earth drinking in the warm Blood of American sons. O how my eyes flash with indignation and my bosom burns with holy resentment. Should any of that Pest of men, those Scourges of Society, fall a sacrifice, how would the Earth heave in her very bowels to disgorge such Poisonous matter as runs from their veins. O Boston Boston, would to heaven that the good Angel that destroys the Army of Sennacherib might now interpose and rid you of your oppressors. How is the design of government subverted!" This was a plain view of Greene's thoughts and feelings of the events that were sure to come and influence their lives forever.

The 20th of July finally came, and in the small southwest parlor which overlooks the valley to the west, Nathanael Greene received the hand of his bride Catherine Littlefield, and then took her to his house in Coventry where they would share their lives together. But, news and events would disturb their tranquil country life sooner than anticipated. Already the state legislature was meeting often, and in each session more questions than answers were raised. A man by the name of Solomon Southwick of Newport had just published Lord Somer's "Judgement of whole Kingdoms and Nations concerning the Rights, Powers, and Prerogatives of the People." It was a collection of dissertations aimed at "resisting evil and destructive princes." The legislators of Rhode Island, as well as many Colonists in New England, were finally realizing that such resolutions made their path plain and began to feel that "the time was near approaching when we must gird on swords, and ride forth to meet our enemies." Greene felt obligated to let his feelings known once more, and in a letter to his wife writes, "Remember me to the Doctor, and tell him if he does not make a perfect cure, or lay a good foundation for it, I'll put him on board of a man-of-war and send him to England to be tryed for the heinous offense of disaffection to Arbitrary Government and Ministerial tyranny." It is from these letters that we know how Nathanael must have been in conversations. His single-mindedness aside, his patriotism and call of duty would become legendary, and a matter no one could ever question.

The drills of the militia and independent companies pressed on. The calls to arm became constant, and manufacturers suddenly sprang up in different parts of the state to supply them. The action of Congress was approved in an extra session of the State Assembly. Committees of inspection, called "Department of Safety for the defense of the local area" were put on the alert. All eyes were turned anxiously towards Boston, where money and provisions were sent to the inhabitants to counteract the Port Bill. In December, the dismantling of Fort George was already described. The cannons from the fort (six twenty-four pounders, eighteen eighteen pounders, and six four pounders) were secured for use by the colony. The use of tea was halted. "We will have nothing to do with the East India Company's irksome tea, nor any other subject to like duty." At Providence, about twelve o'clock noon, the town-crier passed through town giving notice, "At five o'clock this afternoon, a quantity of India tea will be burnt in the market-place. All true friends of their country, lovers of freedom, and haters of shackles and handcuffs, are hereby invited to testify their good disposition, by bringing in and casting into the fire a needless herb which for a long time hath been highly detrimental to our liberty, interest, and health." About three hundred pounds of tea were burnt that day "by the firm contenders, for the true interest of America. On this occasion the bells tolled and whilst the tea was burning a spirited son of liberty went along the streets with his brush of lampblack and obliterated or unpainted the word tea on the shop signs," a newspaper wrote the next day, 17th of March 1775.

The anxiety and preparations for battle were gaining strength through those weeks leading up to the first days of April. Then, on the afternoon of the 19th, a messenger fresh from the field reached Providence, with news that the Regulars and the Colonists were fighting at Lexington. The news passed quickly from mouth to mouth, each man giving it more color and exaggeration than the last to speak the words, "War, war, boys!" One young man, by the name of John Howland, wrote that he heard another exclaim, "there is war; the regulars have marched out of Boston; a great many men are killed; war, war!" Men gathered into groups on the parade, inquiring about the news, the officers of the four independent companies among them. The drums began to beat out call to formation and it was sundown before the last man fell into ranks. Lieutenant-governor Sessions, would not bend to their appeal to give them marching orders and Governor Wanton, who lived in Newport, was over thirty miles away and could not be contacted. The officers were reluctant to march without permission because their legal authority would have ceased the moment they crossed the state line. At first glance a band of armed rebels hesitant to march because they lacked the proper authority may be a little odd. But on the other hand, you had to admire their hindsight. A group such as the Kentish Guard would have surely lost their hard-earned charter and been disbanded if they had marched on their own. They did however, dispatch a communiqué to Boston, stating that if they were needed as reinforcements, they would march on a moment's notice, and damned the governor or any other legislative body.

Meanwhile, time passed without word from Boston and it was already early evening when they finally got word to Nathanael Greene in Coventry. When he got the word he said good-bye to his young wife and immediately mounted his horse for the ride to East Greenwich to form up with the Guard. He had to make a stop, however, at the house of a friend whose name is lost in the annals of time. He had left home so quickly that he had scarcely had time to put on a coat. Unfortunately, his money was in his other coat and he stopped by the friend's house to borrow a few dollars of hard money, in case they marched out tonight. The Guard did set out at dawn the next morning with James Varnum as their leader. Later that morning they arrived in Providence. "I viewed the company as they marched up the street," wrote John Howland, "and observed Nathanael Greene, with his musket and as a private. I distinguished Mr. Greene, whom I have frequently seen, as one of his legs was shorter than the other." It was the ever present stiffness in his knee that gave him, as they use to say, "the halt in his gait" and gave the allusion that he had one leg shorter than the other. At Pawtucket, just as they were crossing the line, a messenger from the Governor, at the time suspected to be a Tory, ordered them to halt at once and turn back immediately. The company, with little other political backing, obeyed and struck for home. But Greene procured a horse from an acquaintance in town and pushed on with three companions, two of them his brothers. On the way, messengers met them with information that the British troops had driven into Boston.

On the 22nd of April, the Assembly met in Providence and voted "be resolved that fifteen hundred men be enlisted, raised, embodied as aforesaid, with all the expedition and dispatch that the thing will admit of." This little army was to serve at home as an observation unit, "and also, if it be found necessary for the safety and preservation of any of the colonies, to march out of this colony and join and cooperate with the forces of the neighboring colonies." In the same session a committee was appointed to wait upon the General Assembly of Connecticut to consult with them upon measures for the common defense of the four New England Colonies. Besides Connecticut, they were Massachusetts, Rhode Island, and New Hampshire. Samuel Ward and William Bradford made up the committee, but Bradford was unable to serve due to his duties as delegate to Congress. Ward contacted the Assembly and nominated Greene to be appointed in Bradford's place. The Assembly voted on it and Greene was appointed the following day. In the following weeks the Assembly met again, not in Newport, as prescribed by the rotation of towns ordered in their charter, but in Providence. It was felt Providence would offer a greater sense of security due to the nature of the meeting and the organization of the army of observation. The fifteen hundred men that they had originally fixed as a number would be formed into one brigade and be under the command of a brigadier-general. The brigade would then be divided into three regiments, one of which would be commanded by one colonel, one lieutenant colonel, and one major. Each regiment was to consist of eight companies, one of the companies to be trained in the art of artillery drill and to have the use of all of the Colony's available field pieces. The list that was passed for the choice of officers had the name of Nathanael Greene placed as the brigadier-general. At first glance it seems like an obvious choice given the name of this book! But in light of the historic and military importance of the events that would follow, it would be at least prudent to look at such a choice logically.

Why Nathanael Greene as your brigadier-general? The man had never been a member of an army unit until his short training in the Kentish Guard as a private, let alone holding any military commission. The Colony's militia had been formed for years and its major general was a well-trained, organized, veteran soldier of the French & Indian War whose name was Simeon Potter. Why not have a man with a military association background? Then there was Varnum, Colonel of the Kentish Guard, a popular man who was also brilliant. Why go to his ranks and pick one of his privates? Greene had an extensive background in militia laws, and on a mission to Connecticut where military organization would be more or less the paramount discussion topic, his knowledge would certainly come in handy. Also, it is probable that his late military reading had given precision and distinctive answers in the language of military questions and knowledge. Still, it can't be helped but to think that the primary reason was that he had a personal relationship with Samuel Ward, whose political clout at the time was unmatched, even by governor Wanton. Rumor has it that Nathanael was not their first choice, but in fact another man was offered the position, but declined on the grounds of his religious beliefs. A second man, this one from another congregation, also declined for the same reason, religious beliefs. The third choice was Greene, and when it was explained who the other two men were, smiled and rose from his seat after the vote that made him brigadier-general of the brigade and commented, "Since the Episcopalian and Congregationalist won't, I suppose the Quaker must. I accept the commission gentlemen." Of course it is only hearsay from stories passed down through generations of the Greene family, but it would not surprise me knowing Greene's personality and quick wit.

Wanton, was re-elected governor despite his Tory tendencies, but Henry Ward was secretary of the Colony and was, "authorized and fully empowered to sign the commissions of all officers civil and military,....receiving therefore, out of the general treasury, two shillings and eight pence for each commission." And so, on the 8th of May 1775, on a copy of the State's legal parchment, with the bold Rhode Island anchor symbol in the left-hand corner which is still among the official papers of Nathanael Greene, it reads;

"By the Honorable General Assembly of the English Colony of Rhode Island and Providence Plantations in New England America.

To Nathanael Greene, Esquire,

Greetings:
Whereas, for the Preservation of the rights and liberties of His Majesty's loyal and faithful Subjects in this Colony and America, the aforesaid General Assembly have ordered Fifteen Hundred Men to be inlisted and embodied in an Army of Observation, and be formed into one Brigade under the command of a Brigadier-General, and have appointed you the said Nathanael Greene that Brigadier-General of the said Army of Observation: You are, therefore, hereby in his Majesty's Name George the Third, by the Grace of God King of Great Britain, &c., authorized, empowered, and commissioned to take, and exercise the office of Brigadier-General of the said Army of Observation, and to command, guide, and conduct the same, or any Part thereof. And in Case of Invasion or Assault of Common Enemy, to disturb this or any other of his Majesty's colonies in America, you are to alarm and gather together the Army under your Command, or any Part thereof, as you shall deem sufficient, and therewith to the utmost of your Skill and Ablility you are to resist, expel, kill, or destroy them in Order to preserve the Interest of His Majesty and His Good Subjects in these Parts. You are also to follow such instructions, Directions, and Orders as shall from Time to Time be given forth, either by the General Assembly or your superior Officers. And for your doing so this Commission shall be sufficient Warrant.
"By Virtue of an Act of the said General Assembly, I, Henry Ward, Esq. Secretary of the said Colony, have hereunto set my Hand and Seal of the said Colony this Eighth Day of May, A.D. 1775, and in the Fifteenth Year of His said Majesty's Reign.
Henry Ward

Details of the organization and preparations, followed with questions to arrange final details with the government, and at the last moment, with the Committee of Safety left Greene's time to organize his own private affairs short. They certainly would have needed some of his attention as well, but he threw them on his brothers and from that moment on barely gave them as much as a careless look again. A final detail he did attend to was to contact his tailor. A Mr. James Gould of Newport, who had made many suits for the public, now was commissioned with the task of designing and tailoring a uniform, and when completed was directed to, "send it along to Cambridge by Wednesday." By the 2nd of June Greene wrote to his wife from Providence: "My dear Wife,--I am at this moment going to set off for camp, having been detained by the Committee of Safety till now. I have recommended you to the care of my brethren; direct your conduct by their device, unless they should so far forget their affection for me as to request anything unworthy of you to comply with. In that case, maintain your own independence until my return, which, if Providence allows, I will see justice done you; but I have no reason to think but that you'll be very kindly and affectionately treated in my absence. I have not so much in my mind that wounds my peace, as the separation from you. My bosom is knitted to yours by conjugal love. It had been happy for me if I could have lived a private life in peace and plenty, enjoying all the happiness that results from a well-tempered society, founded on mutual esteem. The social feelings that accompanies such an intercourse is a faint emblem of the devine saints inhabiting eternity. But the injury done my country, and the chains of slavery forging for posterity, calls me forth to defend our common rights, and repel the bold invaders of the sons of freedom. This cause is the cause of God and man. Slavery shuts up every avenue that leads to knowledge, and leaves the soul ignorant of its own importance; it is rendered incapable of promoting human happiness or piety or virtue; and he that betrays that trust, being once acquainted with the pleasure and advantages of knowledge and freedom, is guilty of a spiritual suicide. I am determined to defend my rights, and maintain freedom, or sell my life in the attempt; and I hope the righteous God that rules the world will bless the armies of America, and receive the spirits of those whose lot it is to fall in action into the paradise of God, into whose protection I commend you and myself; and am, with truest regard, your loving husband, N. Greene."

And so, at the age of thirty-two, and with all of the knowledge he could gain from the mountains of books he read countless times, Nathanael Greene went on his way. To use all of the experience he gained through his years; the accuracy of business life, the physical strength he gained from working the forge, fields and mill, with principles drawn from his time reading and meditating by the stream where he lived as a boy, his self-training of listening and observing the world around him both of nature and man; the cautious formation of opinions, but quick and determined to act; experienced in dealing with men and the responsibility of commanding them, he left the safe, tranquil pleasures of domestic life for the uncertain, dangerous and tragic life of a soldier to fight battles for his beloved country. This would only scratch the surface of what Brigadier-general Nathanael Greene would be party to in the coming years of arguably the most historically significant time in the infancy of the United States of America.

Chapter II

"From Rhode Island to Boston"

Greene would now enter upon a new phase of his development. Because he would have a new profession to learn, but learning was a passion for Nathanael and he brought the study of his life-long habits of work ethic and experiences from his public life with him and used them to their fullest. One of the traits that bore him so well through life was all that he had learned and gathered through his experiences in dealing with the different personalities of men. Those experiences would come in handy on a certain Saturday, on the 3rd of June 1775, when he reached the Rhode Island camp at Jamaica Plains and found what he described later as "a great commotion, and the men in a rebellious mood, and the officers unable to control them, and several companies with clubbed muskets and set upon the point of starting for home; a few days more, would have proved fatal to the campaign." His arrival was perfectly timed. "Never," Greene writes, "was a man so little deserving such a welcome. He immediately, "made several arrangements for order and change, applied myself strenuously to the task, and brought the confusion under check, and with it, gained the men and officers respect, as well as their confidence. It was hard work to limit people accustomed to so much latitude." Apparently his efforts met with good success, because on the 5th of June he writes to his wife, "I am well, but very much fatigued,...not having slept above six hours in two nights. Things here are well at last though." Colonel Varnum had not yet arrived with his regiment and writes to his brother Jacob, "I wish you could forward Colonel Varnum's regiment, he will be a welcome guest in camp; I expect much from him and his troops' example."

On the very same day he was summoned to a meeting with all of the generals at Cambridge in a house Ward had established his headquarters. With Spencer, Putnam, Heath, and Thomas, he was trying to assemble the inexperienced soldiers into some shape or resemblance of an army. Early on in the war each colonial general commanded its colony's troops independently. Since each colony had assembled them, fed and paid them and was supplying them, each colony obviously expected to run each under their own guise. So, until Congress mandated otherwise and selected a supreme or commander in chief to watch over the entire army, Ward had been selected to the job. In the beginning, Greene had more than enough to keep him busy within his own brigade, he saw and knew that discipline was first and paramount if the army would continue or survive. The commanders of the early enlistees would soon find out that it would become impossible at times to keep their men together, let alone prepare them for service by teaching them how to fight against the most powerful armies in the world at that time. Fortunately, many of Greene's fellow commanders and officers had been taught how to drill in the manual of arms by the British deserter who became drill-master and who had been employed by the Kentish Guard to teach them. Greene was thus able to at least give his three regiments a working knowledge and uniformity in their drilling. Many of the other commanders did not have that luxury. They were teaching their men their own self-taught system, or the Norfolk exercise, or the 1764 manual of arms the King's troops were using. Most, therefore, had not universally accepted any one drilling exercise and it would not be until the winter of 1777 and spring of 1778 that it would take the help from a obscure Prussian officer to make this rag-tag collection of farmers, merchants, and tradesman into soldiers.

Daily exercises were ordered for commissioned as well as non-commissioned officers and at four in the evening the whole battalion was called to muster and paraded. No one was excused but the sick and those men on picket and fatigue duty. Regimental orders posted on the 8th of June give us some idea of what daily and weekly orders consisted of, "That Colonel Hitchcock's regiment parade on Wednesday every week, precisely at half after three o'clock, and march from camp, around the Square and back again. The Colonel expects, in that parade, that every officer appear in his uniform, and that care is taken by the officers that every soldier be clean, and as neatly dressed as possible; and that no one who has breeches be permitted to wear overalls, nor to parade without having on his stockings and shoes; and that, during the march, no soldier be permitted to talk. As the regiment has gained honor from this regular performance of exercise, 'tis fully expected by the Colonel, that the officers spare no pains to instruct themselves in the exercise." This order would have been typical throughout all of the other regiments as well.

Another order, issued on the 10th provides for the proper cleaning of the firelocks: "That the officers of several companies in Colonel Hitchcock's regiment call their companies together this afternoon, and see that every soldier's firelock be washed clean, and that some non-commissioned officer strictly attend while the guns are washed, and take special care that no one washed his gun without taking off the lock. 'Tis expected that every company washes their firelocks with hot water." It can not be stressed enough how important the care of a soldier's musket in the 18th century was to the entire regiment. The standard British flintlock musket used during the war was the Short-Land Musket better known as the "Brown Bess". Early in the war the Continentals favored this gun over the one most militiaman were using, which was not much more than a semi-military gun frequently made from a mixture of parts from other guns that no longer worked. But, most of the guns the men had brought with them from home would not pass muster if used over a long period of time, also most would not allow the bearer to affix a bayonet on the militia fowlers and it was a necessity that a soldier of the 18th century have a musket that a bayonet fitted onto. The name "Flintlock" comes from the firing action that is affixed to the stock or furniture of the musket. The original design is from the early 1600's, with a mechanism that had a spring-loaded, rotating cock with small steel clamp and held the hand hewn flint stone in tiny teeth. When the trigger was pulled the flint in the lock would turn, coming down and striking an L-shaped piece of thin steel called the frizzon creating a spark The frizzen would rotate forward and expose a small priming pan filled with a tiny amount of gunpowder that the frizzon was covering. The ignited powder would result in a small flash of fire that was forced through a small hole in the barrel called a "touch hole" in turn igniting a charge of gunpowder inside the barrel and projecting the lead ball out of the barrel. The flintlock was a muzzle, single loaded, and was a smooth bore barrel weapon. Meaning that it had no grooves cut on the inside of the barrel like modern rifles, permitting the bullet to travel in a tighter, straighter trajectory. The musket ball was in fact, .10 inches smaller than the barrel of the musket. Brown Bess were.75 caliber guns and with a ball smaller than the barrel the ball would literally bounce around until it came out the end and making it less than accurate. It was also a heavy weapon, about 12 pounds, making it hard to handle and maneuver, especially in combat. It had no rear sight and although the ball could travel up to 300 yards, it was completely ineffective beyond 75 to 100 yards. Black powder was greatly affected by temperature, high humidity, and even wind. The gun could not be fired if it rained or snowed. If any adverse condition existed on the battlefield the musket simply would not fire. As a result, if you look back on the history of the Revolutionary War, less than a handful of battles occurred during those conditions and except for Washington's first attack on the Hessians at Princeton, New Jersey on December 26, 1776, no battles occurred in the winter months.

Because of the gun's deadly inaccuracy and difficulty in loading, troops had to fight shoulder to shoulder and fire in ranks of 20 or 30 per company or unit and fire shots in volleys. Firing volleys meant that the musket balls would be fired all at once and thus had a better chance of finding some semblance of a target. An effective soldier was taught to load and fire about 3 to 4 times a minute, it was not just orders and regulations but in most cases in the course of a battle could mean your life. So, the weapons must be kept very clean if expected to fire on a regular basis, and in some cases even that did not help. Having a clean firelock and in good working condition was not enough. Each man had to learn drill so they could work as one, as a team, as a cohesive unit. The better the unit, the better the soldier and the better chance of staying alive. The early militia men and independent unit soldiers were no match in this area against the best-trained troops in the world at that time. It was found that each daily drill was an exercise in frustration for the officers. Each regiment was using their own manual of arms to drill their men. It was going to be necessary to establish a drill that all units could master together. On July 6th the order was posted, "That a drill be established for the instruction of those who are deficient in exercise, from ten to eleven o'clock in the forenoon every day; that the drill be commanded either by a commissioned or non-commissioned officer of the several companies by rotation, and 'tis expected that every officer will strictly see that all those who are deficient in exercise in their company constantly attend the same at the time fixed for holding drill."

Greene soon discovered that his greatest obstacle would not only be to establish good discipline with his men, but with his officers as well. He found that most would perform their duty, whatever was asked of them. But Greene saw a growing concern with several key officers. The problem was that the officers just could not make the transition from home life to military life. Many of the officers came from families of distinction or considerable wealth and were use to having some of their simple tasks, for instance dressing in the morning, done with the assistance of a valet or servant. Needless to say then, camp life was exceedingly difficult to these men and the circumstances it produced led Greene to write, "Some captains, and many subordinate officers neglect their duty, some through fear of offending their soldiers, some through sheer laziness, and some through obstinacy. This makes the task of the field officers very laborious. I have warned them of their negligence many times, and am determined to break every one for the future who shall lay himself open to it." One corporal in Hitchcock's regiment had already been reduced in rank for repeated neglect of duty, and disobedience to his captain.

Another obstacle to good order in Greene's troops, as well as every regiment in the army at that time was drunkenness. One such case was reported in Hitchcock's regimental orderly-book in a court-martial case against one, Peter Young for the offense of intoxication while on duty. Jeremiah and Stephen Olney were the presiding president and member of the court. The orderly-book reads, "Young was sent for and examined, plead not guilty of the charge." Captain John Angell, captain of the guard and future participant of the battle of Fort Mercer two years later, wrote his deposition and said, "Peter Young was confined in the guard-house by Colonel Miller, at ten o'clock at night, being found in liquor; who, when confined, behaved himself in a very indecent and contemptuous manner; damning the man that confined him, and also the man that kept him in confinement, throwing his hat about the guard-house. The prisoner being present heard Captain Angell's evidence, and said he had no evidence to confute the same. The court, upon mature deliberation, are of opinion that the prisoner, Peter Young, be sentenced to ride the wooden horse fifteen minutes, with two guns tied at his feet, and ten minutes without guns, as an adequate punishment for his crime." Riding the wooden horse was a punishment that was consistent with drunkards, slackers or soldiers that were particularly argumentative. The act had been used as a punishment since ancient times and was primarily the same as being ridden out on a rail. The soldier would sit with his feet dangling as to not touch the ground on a rail post. But the difference with riding the rail, this rail was placed between two foundations that served as legs. With the soldier sitting on the rail it would punish his crotch and tailbone. In the case of adding the guns to his feet, multiplying the discomfort. If the offending soldier were particularly troublesome four men would pick up the rail and jostle him for a short time frame prescribed. However, drunkenness in individual cases was not the real problem. The problem was so wide spread that Greene wrote to the Provincial Congress of Massachusetts, requesting that they impose their authority and prevent the sale of intoxicating liquors within the limits of the camp.

Another problem Greene had run up against was adapting civil punishment to military offenses. Legislators shrank at first from the severity of punishments. But as the war continued and the cases mounted to the point of being habitual, the Legislators did impose stronger guidelines for punishment. For instance, the Rhode Island "Rules and Orders for the Army of Observation," only had three articles out of fifty-three detailing how to impose capital punishment; and in two out of the three the member of the court-martial imposing those punishments was left to order, "such other punishment as they may think best." Even whipping, though familiar to the public mind, as limited to what was termed the "Mosaic" rule of "thirty-nine stripes, and in practice not to exceed fifteen, ten, or five." George Washington was not an advocate of soldiers receiving severe lashings and later in the war even sent a communiqué to General Howe who was the commanding general of the British troops at the time that the severity of lashes for both armies should not exceed thirty-nine. It was not unusual for a prisoner in the army to receive up to one hundred and fifty lashes for what was deemed a capital offense.

Greene's men and officers were not alone in attempting to adapt to camp and soldier life. Greene himself admitted that it was a great change from his quiet life in Coventry and wrote of it. "My tasks is hard, and fatigue great. I go to bed late, and rise early. The number of applications you cannot conceive of, without being present to observe the round of business." Back in Rhode Island, when he was singled out by his acquaintances of the Kentish Guard for special consideration he felt somewhat surprised by the attention. Now he was feeling the same kind of treatment by the general officers of the neighboring camps. "Were I to estimate my value by the attention paid to my opinion, I should have reason to think myself some considerable personage. Fatal experience teaches me every day, that mankind are apt to pay deference to station, and not to merit. Therefore, when I find myself surrounded by their flattering attentions, I consider them as due to my office, and not to me." Greene was full of self-reliance, which is a prerequisite for command, but did not seem presumptuous, or conceited, considering he was a remarkable self-made man. "I shall study to deserve well," he continues, "but cannot but lament the great defects I find myself to discharge, with honor and justice, the important trust commited to my care." With only a minimum of training in law and with more experience as an anchor-smith than a lawyer, Greene was marked by his friend Judge Howell of Coventry as a "very extraordinary man." At hearing the questions and remarks by Greene at a recent court-martial he presided over, Timothy Pickering of Cambridge pronounced him, "a man of true military genius, and decidedly the first man in the court." No one was more ready to acknowledge his superiority than the officers and men under his immediate command. "I must assume," Greene writes, "my own officers and men are generally well satisfied,--nay, I have not heard one complaint."

In the coming weeks, the preliminary planning for the occupation of Bunker Hill was beginning, but on the day of the battle Greene was in Rhode Island. By the time news arrived, it was well into the evening, but he immediately mounted his horse and began to ride toward Boston. He rode all-night and arrived at camp the next morning to discover Charleston smoldering and the troops engaged on the other side of Cambridge Bay. A thousand men were sent over to Roxbury to help secure the entrenchments that were being constructed on Prospect Hill. Although the battle had actually taken place on Breed's Hill, the American troops who fought, under the command of Colonel Prescott, led the retreat after the battle to Bunker Hill, but the British commander, General Gage soon overran that position as well and forced the American troops to the new position on Prospect Hill. Several hundred of the men sent to the new position were from Varnum's regiment under the direct command of Major Christopher Greene, who would go on to a number of glorious campaigns in the coming years.

Greene and part of his force were eventually stationed at a position in Roxbury. It was the first time Nathanael had come under live shelling and wrote of that day, "The excitement of battle was not yet passed away. The British are constantly firing canon-shot both on Prospect Hill and on the new position at Winter Hill. But the troops are in high spirits and we wished that we could sell them another hill at the same price." Although the colonists lost over 400 men in the horrendous clash of armies, the British fared much worse losing almost 1000 men killed or wounded. The toll for the position was so costly that it prompted General Henry Clinton to utter the now famous phrase, "It was such a dear victory, another such would have ruined us."

The entire workings of both sides bore every aspect of an active siege, and something the British were quite experienced at, but the Americans would be learning as they went. The British made several half-hearted attempts to deceive the Americans into thinking they had stronger defenses and a larger force of men than they actually had. But by this time the entrenchment's, particularly on Prospect Hill, were high enough for the Americans to see everything the British were doing and were aware of their movement at all times. The British troops were hard at work converting the crude ditches on Breed and Bunker Hills into two formidable redoubts, which they had now furnished with several 24 and 18 pound canons. Soon, shells were being lobbed over to Roxbury on a regular basis and it was beginning to unnerve the less experienced American army. The colonists were now faced with another weapon that was hard to defend against and that was demoralization. The constant bombardment made it almost impossible for the men to get any sleep. Fatigue parties would finish supporting a wall and suddenly a bomb would destroy the hard work that may have taken days to complete, only to be started all over again. Supplies were running dangerously low due to the fact that few men would brave the shelling to cross the bay and retrieve the supplies needed. But also, it was hard to know who was a friend and who was foe. War brings out the best in some, but the worse in many. Faithless agents, heartless speculators, cowards, traitors, selfish partisans and lukewarm patriots, just to name a few. For every person in America that fought for Independence, another fought against it, and another cared little for the war at all, but only what it would bring to them in fame or fortune. Such a nest of men appeared in Boston and added to the unrest the Americans at the hill defenses were feeling about this time. By the 4th of July Greene had had enough and wrote in a complaint to the Deputy-governor of Rhode Island James Cooke, "There is continual complaints made to me about provisions falling short, some barrels not having much more than one half and two thirds the quantity they ought to contain. I wish your Honor would desire the committee throughout the colony to examine all the provisions sent to camp, for I am very positive they must have been greatly imposed upon. The field-officers are continually complaining to me of the imposition, and requesting me to have a stop put to it as soon as possible. Many people in camp suspects the fidelity of the committee, to suffer such repeated impositions, and still no check put on them. Such unfavorable sentiments propagated abroad must do great injury to their characters, and perhaps render it very difficult for them to settle their accounts with the colony, and do justice to themselves and those they are concerned with." In most cases the food sent to the camp was unfit to eat. Many times, meat that was expected to be beef, was in fact horse and dog mixed in with a portion of beef. Other times, the beef had to be condemned because it was rancid or crawling with maggots. Bread was either dirty or moldy and the same was said for the potatoes and vegetables sent to the troops on a weekly basis. The people contracted by the government were paid for the supplies an inspector had checked and then the supplies were replaced with the less desirable contents. It would be a recurring complaint throughout the war. Not enough food for the troops or dishonest merchants and agents whose only interest in the fight for Independence was indifference and the amount of gain they could procure from the people involved.

On a far decisive note, on the day before the battle of Bunker Hill Congress had finally made a decision on a commander-in-chief of the army, George Washington. On the 2nd of July Washington reached Cambridge with an escort of mounted citizens and a troop of light horsemen. It was a Sunday, but the British were not taking the Sabbath as a reason for rest against the weary Americans on the lines near Boston Neck. Washington may have even heard the cannonade on his usual morning ride, but on the next day he took formal command of the Continental Army under a broad elm tree that still stands on Cambridge Common. Only the few troops bivouacked at Cambridge were able to see the ceremony, but the next day Greene writes, "I sent a small detachment of men to Cambridge and with the colonel commanding them a letter of address, to welcome his Excellency to camp. The detachment met with a very gracious reception, and his Excellency returned me a very polite answer, and invitation to visit him at his quarters." At the time Washington's aide-to-camp was Charles Lee, who many said was the most accomplished soldier in the entire army. Many speculated that Lee resented the appointment of Washington as commander-in-chief over himself, but the next fifteen months would show how far his opinion would go. Lee questioned whether Washington was on the side of duty, toward the fight for freedom, or merely just another disinterested private individual out for nothing but personal gain, like so many other men in the military and government that were involved in the inner workings of the war.

Greene approved of the appointment of Washington almost immediately, as he writes several days later, "I received a letter directed to his Excellency from the General Assembly appointing Gen. Washington to command all of our troops; all of which is perfectly agreeable to me and I shall conduct myself accordingly, and hope by his wise directions accompanied with my best endeavors, and that all of my officers, to promote the service of the colony agreeable to their wishes. I expect him the next day after tomorrow to visit our camp." The day after Greene wrote to the senior Samuel Ward, who knew Washington personally, "His Excellency, General Washington, has arrived amongst us, universally admired. Joy was visible in every countenance, and it seemed as if the spirit of conquest breathed through the whole army. I hope we shall be taught to copy his example, and to prefer the love of liberty, in this time of public danger, to all the soft pleasures of domestic life, and support ourselves with manly fortitude amidst all the dangers and hardships that attend a state of war. And I doubt not, under the General's wise direction, we shall establish such excellent order and strictness of discipline as to invite victory to attend him wherever he goes."

With Washington's arrival in camp, a new period began and a system of organization was about to take hold. Considering the imperfect trials and tribulations of the army up until this point, any organization would be a welcome sight contrary to the conditions the troops had suffered under previously. Washington's own experience with regular troops had been confined up until this point to the short service on General Braddock's British army staff during the French and Indian War and like most of his officers, had not had a great deal of command experience and had much to learn. Most of Washington's knowledge was from textbooks; a mixture of so-so facts to be used at best as a guide, but somewhat incomplete in its layout. General Washington's experience up to this point with the new fledgling army had been with irregular troops and a feeble government. But, he had just arrived in camp and already had provided better supplies to his men, learned to deal with prejudice, ignorance, obstinacy, and sloth. His staff had yet to become what it would aspire to be further into the war, but men whose names we would come to know and respect; Mifflin, brave and eloquent, and once, like Greene, a former Quaker who now stood alongside Washington and held his confidence, although in the not so distant future Mifflin would become bitter enemies with Washington and Greene. Jonathan Trumbull, young and ambitious, but with a keen mind of an artist. Horatio Gates, adjutant general, who brought experience from the French and Indian War, but would become Washington's most bitter rival of all. And Reed, whose fine culture and polished address made him a welcome and close companion to the general, but his command of the English language and his ability to seize upon important points of subjects others had long forgotten, made his services as Washington's secretary invaluable.

The first step in the organization of the army was to convert the independent colonial bands and militias into a regular army, the army of the United Colonies. "I am informed by his Excellency," writes Greene, "that the idea of colony troops is to be abolished, and that the whole army is to be formed into brigades, and the generals to be appointed by the Congress." The upheaval this announcement caused within the camp was unimaginable to say the least and men began to anxiously ask each other who the new generals might be. Greene was also viewing the prospect of not serving as general with a bit of jealousy and regret when he wrote, "I should be extremely sorry for any schisms that might creep in through the ports of honor, from real or imaginary degradation." But in his defense he follows with, "if continued I am prepared to serve cheerfully, if not to submit patiently. I wish only that good and able men may be the objects of the Continental choice, rather than subjects of particular interests." When the appointments were made and finally announced, he was found at the bottom of the list as brigadier-general, last to be precise.

The army was divided into three grand divisions, Greene being placed with seven regiments in the left wing, under General Charles Lee and with John Sullivan at the head of six regiments as senior brigadier-general. In all, 5,670 men, stationed at Prospect Hill, just across from the enemy lines on Bunker Hill and cut off by the desolation of Charlestown behind them. Just at the bottom of Prospect Hill was an old farmhouse called "Hobgoblin Hall," where Lee had taken up his headquarters. It was a comfortable two-story building with convenient rooms for living and an area for the constant officer meetings that were called all hours of the day or night. One room had an excellent view of the parapets along the British lines. Two miles down the road at a stately mansion, Washington had made his headquarters. Years later, Longfellow wrote some of his best poems and works in that same mansion.

Three of the regiments in Greene's brigade were his own Rhode Island troops, 1085 men in all, led by Varnum, Hitchcock, and Church who were men of strong will, along with Colonel Christopher Greene, the two Olneys, the two Angells and Simeon Thayer and rich collection of majors, captains and lieutenants, one of which was his young friend Samuel Ward. No troops in the army of 1775 were better equipped or appointed with tents, officers' marquees, muskets, and canons. Greene wrote, "we spare no pains, night or day, to teach them their duty. And with Varnum and Hitchcock as excellent disciplinarians we can do no worse than succeed. I flatter myself that they comparatively derserve it." The rest of his brigade was made up of four Massachusetts regiments consisting of 713 men under the command of Whitcomb, Gardner, Brewer, and Little.

The siege began to grow in earnest as one by one Prospect, Winter, Ploughead, and Cobble Hills were occupied and secured, as well as areas like Lechmere Point and Sewall's Farm became part of the chain of fortifications which became a stronghold of a eight to nine mile semicircle over the entire area of water and with the enemy in the center. Every day the American lines added to their strength, but almost everyday an artillery skirmish of cannonade shells and balls fell within the American works, sometimes killing, sometimes maiming, but never producing more effect than the Continental troops could endure. Of the over two thousand shots fired at the American lines, twelve persons were killed and only minor damage to a few buildings and ramparts. "I have no doubt," Greene writes to his wife, "that I shall be safely conducted through the shower of Tory hail. But whatever be my fate, let my reputation stand fair for the inspection of all my inquiring friends." Yet the first sight of the real effects of cannon shots to the human body shocked and sickened him. Adjutant Mumford, of East Greenewich and a member of Varnum's regiment was beheaded by a direct hit by a canon ball as he leisurely walked across the parade ground to Greene's quarters one day. That day Greene wrote to his wife, "My sweet angel, the anxiety that you must feel at the unhappy fate of Mr. Mumford, the tender sympathy and distress of his poor lady, the fears and apprehensions for my safety, under your debilitated state, must weigh too great for you to support. We are all in the hands of the great Jehovah; To Him let us look for his protection. I trust that our controversy is a righteous one; and although many of our friends and relatives may suffer the same untimely fate, yet we must consider the evil sanctified

31

by the righteousness of this dispute. Stifle your own grief, my sweet creature, and offer a small tribute of consolation to the afflicted widow. I could wish, from my soul, that you never witness the scene of this horror, altogether inconsistent with the finer feelings of a delicate mind. My heart melts with pity for the loss to his poor lady, but dumb silence must speak my grief until I am in a situation to give scope to the natural sentiment of the human heart." But before the year was done, Greene would become all to familiar with violent death and would send one of his officers to announce such an event to the family of the deceased. Before long though, he would become callous and unmoved by the almost daily event and cease the custom all too soon.

The army soon fell into the daily routine of a siege and before long merely went about the monotonous duties involved with camp life; drilling, cleaning, digging, marching, and drilling again. Civilians from the local area began to find their way to the outskirts of the camp and even sit with a picnic lunch in hopes of seeing some military action like they were watching a theater show. Some came by horseback and others by carriage, many of them family members of both enlisted men and officers. Many only came in hopes of catching just a glimpse of the, "tall and majestic figure of His Excellency General Washington." a newspaper once wrote. They also were beginning to get restless of the continuing siege. People started to ask, "If, without this preparation they had held Bunker Hill so long against the best troops in the British army, why can they not, with the increased strength which discipline gives them, drive the enemy from Boston?" The same subject was brought up more than once in the council of war. The first council had determined not to occupy Dorchester, or defend it if the British should attempt to occupy it. But should they do the same with Boston? Greene felt that, "an attack upon a town garrisoned with eight thousand regular troops was serious object." He knew, as Washington knew, that no matter how much the troops appeared to be veteran-like to the civilians, to any soldier's keen eye they were still raw, untested and undisciplined enough to go head to head with a complement of regular British troops. But Greene did think that an army of twenty thousand men, might attack and succeed. "It would be hard if we could not find twenty thousand who will fight manfully. There must be as many cowards among them as well as among us." Greene wrote.

Time passed slowly and the summer months dragged while the early days of autumn quickly approached, when on the 3rd of August 1775, a council was held at Washington's headquarters and during a simple accounting of supplies it was discovered on a report to the Massachusetts committee that instead of the 485 quarter casks of gunpowder in the magazine, they only had 35 half barrels accounted for that day. That adds up to about 1/2 a pound of powder a man. When Washington heard the report Greene witnessed, "he was struck so much by the danger of it that he did not utter a word for half an hour." The entire command was equally surprised indeed and messengers were dispatched to all of the Southern colonies to call in their stores of powder. This was a dangerous turn of events and every attempt was being made to keep this information from everyone in the army, but the most senior staff personnel and Greene was one of the unfortunate few to have access to the information. He must have felt a bit unnerved standing by one of his silent canons while listening to the constant roar of the British artillery pieces at night, and he wrote, "the track of their shells, a long train of light on the darken sky. How can I hold this hill, if they come out now?" But soon the crisis was alleviated with the shipment of powder from the Southern states.

But no sooner than one problem would be solved then another would take its place. It was evident early on that the line officers had a problem with many of the junior officers in their ranks. Discipline amongst them was paramount to Washington and his officers and a lack of it would only fuel a deficiency of it within the non-commissioned officers and men as well. The army had just solved the problem of the low supply of gunpowder when it came to the attention of Greene that many of his men were wantonly wasting it on firing at geese. There was a standing order prohibiting this action but it was being completely ignored. The sound of musket fire could be heard throughout the camp every time a flock flew over. It prompted the new standing order written by Greene and dated November 7th, 1775 that read, "There being an open and daring violation of a general order, in firing at geese, as they pass over the camp, General Greene gives positive orders now, that any person that fires for the future be immediately put under guard. Every officer that stands an idle spectator, and sees such a wanton waste of good powder, and don't do his utmost to suppress the evil, may expect to be reported." But the same subject recurs and is updated to read, "That all cartridges delivered out this day, if the bunches are not broke, the captains collect them out when occasion calls. Every person that fires his gun without positive orders, is to be punished immediately by a regimental court-martial; and if these orders are not obeyed, the General will order the first transgressor to be tied up and whipped, for an example." The problem of the geese hunting is finally curtailed then another rears up to take its place. It comes to Greene's attention that, "the soldiers have got into the practice of stealing cartridges from one another, and those that go on furlough, or are discharged, carry them home. As this conduct is both dishonorable and villainous, the General hopes there are but few, if any, that are so lost to honor and honesty as to commit so dirty a crime. If any are detected in the fact, they may expect to be punished without mercy." The punishment would most assuredly be 50 to 100 slashes from a cat-o-nine-tails.

But the waste of powder continued, but always in a different text. Every alarm sounded brings the immediate firing of sporadic musket fire, which prompts another standing order from Greene saying, "The officers of this brigade are once more desired to pay particular attention to the preservation of cartridges. There continues to be such a wanton waste, for some time past, and still continues, upon every alarm, that it is really disgraceful. It is impossible to conceive upon what principle this strange itch for firing originates, as rather a mark of cowardice than bravery to fire away ammunition without any intention. If the soldiers are desirous of defending their rights and liberties, the General desires they would deprive themselves of the means to execute so laudable a purpose." Appeals to the patriotism of the troops are not always successful and a large number of what we may term, bad elements, would seem to filter into the army with even the best intentions and screening process. Early on in the war the process was somewhat selective of recruits. Age, stature or height, and experience played a part in being admitted to the army. From the frequent court-martials recorded by Greene's orderlies, it would appear that the process was in need of revamping. Stealing and drunkenness were the principal crimes, but disobedience, desertion, and even mutiny were not immune of rearing their ugly heads and were punished by fines, imprisonment, whipping, and in the case of corporals and sergeants by a drop in rank. The reports of court-martials fill page after page of orderly books, showing clearly that love of country was not always the only motive which brought recruits and volunteers to the camps after Boston.

Nathanael Greene's responsibilities by this time were wide and diverse. He went to bed late, got up early, did a lot of horse riding to reach all of his regiments, wrote a great deal of orders, letters, communiqué, and pages of journal entries, frequent meetings with the council at headquarters, presided over daily details involving breakdowns in discipline, and to top it all off, the daily stress with the progress of the siege. Greene exacted several orders for the daily inspection of the soldier's arms. He demanded that an in-depth inspection be made of the arms, ammunition, locks, flints, and right down to making a daily count of every man's cartridges. It was so serious that Greene issued an order to his captains that read, "for every cartridge that is lost, the soldier will be charged one shilling lawful money; and for every flint missing, three pence; a report to be made daily to the regimental colonel of what condition they find the guns and ammunition. Any officer neglecting to report their findings may be put on report to the general of brigade and forward the report to headquarters." Since it was well into November by this time the days were beginning to shorten considerably and Greene expected his officers to rise at least a half hour earlier than his men so they could get a jump on all of the duties Greene expected them to perform each day. From inspecting arms to sentries, Greene demanded his officers and non-commission officers take the brunt of responsibility for their men's actions. The proper details of sentry duty were especially important with the close proximity they had to the enemy. It was not unusual for sentries to just walk back to their tents if their relief was not there at the appropriate time to relieve them and thus leaving no sentry at all at that post. Greene drafted exact instructions of every minute detail on how the officer, sergeants, and privates were to relieve and be relieved on sentry duty. Today we would call Greene Anal Retentive, but checking every minute detail was Nathananel Greene's way of accomplishing goals and it would do him well in the war years to come.

Greene felt his paramount responsibility was the constant provision of the defenses for his brigade. He especially wanted the artillery to be at a high degree of readiness at the first hint of an alarm. For this to be accomplished he expected the artillery officers for each gun to be at or near his post at all times. If they could not be at the post, he wanted an individual the officer could trust to be there in his stead. They also were asked to be quiet and attentive since they were the first lines of defense for the entire army. November was an exceptionally anxious month with new arrangements being made for the long nights and short days. The field officer of the day needed to inspect each and every sallyport in the fortifications, check that the chevaux-de-frise were all in good repair and in order, make sure the pickets were in place and if not, fix them and have the guns and ammunition well supplied and in good working order. To save ammunition the daily routine of firing a gun for morning reveille and evening call was discontinued. This was also a sound defensive strategy. By not firing the canon from the exact same location every day the British could not pinpoint and zero in on that gun's location when hostilities did break out. They were also careful to post sentries in closer intervals on the parapet and keep a higher air of awareness about so they could hail every person in the vicinity of the walls and ask for the daily cosign/password. All soldiers who were not on duty were ordered to be in their quarters by 9 o'clock at night. By restricting the foot traffic within the fortifications sentries could concentrate on the outside walls and anyone on the inside walking around would be quickly inspected, figuring them to either be thieves, drunkards or the enemy.

If an assault did take place, one of the weapons of choice to repel an invader was the spontoon or spear. Officers primarily carried spontoons since they could not carry muskets and few officers carried pistols. But Greene decided to try a new approach to an old form of defense that dated back thousands of years. His order read, "Every colonel or commanding officer of a regiment are to appoint thirty men that are active, bold, and resolute, to use the spears in defense of the lines, instead of guns; to form in the centre of the rear of each column and to stand ready to push the enemy off the breastwork, if they should attempt to get over the parapet and beyond the lines. Let those be appointed that are the worse equipped of arms, and those that have none at all, provided the size, strength, and activity are agreeable for the purpose of their appointment, to be commanded by a subaltern and sergeant." Greene was obviously becoming nervous with the long, drawn out siege process and was only outlining steps for the best defense of his men. It also shows us in detail how Nathanael Greene evolved from the private man to the General and the steps of how he attained his military knowledge, comprehension, and leadership characteristics.

With the onset of autumn and winter quickly approaching, yet another problem was looming on the horizon. The army was enlisted for only a few months since the council had no idea at the beginning of hostilities how long the action would take. Those few months were almost over and if not rectified soon New England would be left undefended. What was England planning? Congress finally took charge of the situation and appointed a committee of three, lead by Benjamin Franklin to go to camp to consult with General Washington about how the new army was progressing. While the committee was en-route, Washington called his own council of general officers to examine the subject for themselves and to arrive at a course of action. The consensus of Washington and the officers was that 20,000 men would be required to continue the siege. On the 15th of November the committee reached headquarters and Greene was present. "I had the honor," Greene writes the next day, "to be introduced to that very great man, Dr. Franklin, whom I viewed with silent admiration the whole evening. Attention watched his lips, and conviction closed his periods." Franklin knew the Greene family name and was very familiar with Greene's wife Caty, who after all, was the niece of one of Franklin's dearest friends, Catherine Ray. It was the first time Greene had been in contact with members of Congress from the South colonies. He took full advantage of the situation to speak to them about what he had labeled, "the groundless jealousy of the New England Colonies," which he felt was a stumbling block in Congress's willingness to help the army. "When I mentioned this subject," he wrote to the senior Ward, "the gentlemen of Congress assured me that no such sentiment prevailed in Congress nor among the Southern inhabitants of any respectability. I am sorry to find they were mistaken and it grieves me that such jealousies should prevail. If they are nourished, they will sooner or later sap the foundations of the union and dissolve the connection. God in mercy avert so dreadful an evil."

Greene felt that discontentment of colonies against each other and among the regiments was the prime factor for an army to self-destruct. If men who were banded together to fight a foreign foe could not put aside their petty differences, how could they act together as one to fight the British? Greene writes, "As troops are considered Continental and not colonial, there must be some systematic plan for the payment without any reference to particular colonies; otherwise they will be partly Continental and partly colonial. His Excellency has a great desire to banish every idea of local attachments. It is next to impossible to unhinge the prejudices that people have for places and things they have a long connection with. For my own part, I feel the cause and not the place. I would as soon go to Virginia as stay here. I can assure the gentlemen to the southward that there could not be anything more abhorrent proposed than a union of those colonies for the purpose of conquering the Southern colonies." "The interest of one colony are no ways compatible with the interest of another," Greene wrote in a letter dated 31st December, 1775. While , an English statesman in parliament stated, "It will not be an easy matter to bring the American States to act as a nation; they are not to be feared as such by us. Their climate, their staples, their manners, are different; their interest opposite, and that which is beneficial to one is destructive to the other." The British went into the war believing that America was nothing more than a group of territories and land joined by nothing but the borders drawn on a map. The little colony that was desperately trying to become independent, would sooner than later have to become the United States if they had any hope of winning a war they were not prepared to fight.

There were other subjects to be anxious about in the early days of the revolution. Just before the arrival of the committee led by Franklin, Nathanael Greene had a surprise visit from his first mentor, Master Maxwell. Greene had not seen his old friend in years, but Maxwell had not come merely for a visit. He had brought with him a letter from Henry Ward, Secretary for the Colony of Rhode Island. The mysterious envelope contained a letter written in cipher or code, which some woman from Boston had attempted to send on-board the H.M.S. Wallace, which had been anchored in Narraganset Bay since before the beginning of the war. Greene immediately brought the letter to Washington. They had no idea who the author of the letter could be or what her intentions were, but they had to discover the answers to those questions. The first obvious step was to question the messenger who had been captured long with the letter. The messenger soon furnished the name of the woman in question and she was brought to Washington's headquarters the next day. A man by the nickname, "Old Put" was the agent given credit for finding the woman. He forced her into a carriage and drove all night to reach General Washington. When they reached Washington's headquarters it was said the woman was dragged kicking and screaming in terror. As the front doors of the house were flung open, there in full regalia and with the sternest look the general could muster, stood the Commander-in-Chief of the

Continental army, George Washington. He assured the spy that nothing but a full confession could save her from a hanging halter. In a low, mousy voice the name, Dr. Church, was all that was heard.

Dr. Church was a man who had been well known as one of the foremost patriots of the cause. He was well respected, beloved, trusted, and an author and spokesman against the British. A traitor? He was immediately arrested and all of his papers seized. The letter was deciphered and the scope of the treachery was revealed the following day at a General Court of Province which Greene attended and wrote about the proceedings to his wife, "Dr. Church's examination relative to his treason. With art and ingenuity surpassing whatever you saw he veiled the villainy of his conduct, and by implication transformed virtue into vice. But, notwithstanding all his art and address, and his faculty of making the worse appear the better reason, he could not establish his innocence either satisfactory to the public in general or the General Court in particular." He was condemned to close solitary confinement for several months and when his health began to fail, then was given permission to sail to the West Indies in exile and was never heard from again. The scope of Dr. Church's spying was never truly revealed, but the British had gained important information of troop strength, movement, and artillery placement, most of which was rectified before any real harm could be done.

It was now January 1776. A new year called for a new beginning and the strong whispers of independence were starting to turn into shouts. Congress had drafted the "Olive Branch Petition" which was sent to parliament and King George III just four months before. In it, Congress issued a petition declaring its loyalty to the king and stating its hope that he would help arrange reconciliation and prevent further hostilities against the colonies. Several of our founding fathers signed the document, including Benjamin Franklin, Thomas Jefferson, Patrick Henry, Samuel Adams, John Adams, and John Hancock. Richard Penn and Arthur Lee were each commissioned to bring a copy by separate ship to the king and on the 21st of August they were received by Lord Dartmouth, Secretary to the king for the State of the Colonies and Penn and Lee asked his lordship to present the petition to the king on their behalf. But King George III would not even read the petition saying, "Since I did not receive the petition on the throne, no answer will be given." In actuality, the king had no intention of doing anything but reject it and declared the colonies in rebellion and war was the only means of punishing their rebellious and disloyal ways. Congress had no other choice by 1776 but to pursue independence and to raise a large army as quickly as possible to establish strong forces against the superior force of the British army.

Greene was a strong supporter of independence and the sooner the better. His reasoning was present when he wrote, "We have already took steps in the present establishment of the army. Under one commander, raised and appointed by the same authority, subjected to the same regulations, and ready to be detached wherever the occasion may require. A larger force is needed. It will be infinitely safer, and more expensive in the end, for the continent to give a large bounty to any number of troops in addition to what be ordered on the present establishment that will engage during the war, than enlist them from year to year without a bounty. The tyrant, in his last speech, has convinced us that to be free or not depends upon ourselves. Nothing, therefore, but the most vigorous exertion on our part can shelter us from the evils intended us. It is no time for deliberations; the hour is swiftly rolling on when the plains of America will be deluged with the blood of its inhabitants. Resolves, deliberations, and all the parade of heroism in words, will not obtain a victory. Arms and ammunition are as necessary as men, and must be had at the expense of everything short of Britain's claim."

The question of America's domestic enemies, the Tories, was also becoming an issue. The most pressing problem was whether or not the Tories would harbor or supply the British with food, arms or ammunition. Commodities the Continental army was sorely lacking and needed more desperately than the British. The want for arms compelled Washington to retain the weapons of anyone leaving the army, whether they were private property of the men or of the army. This was not a popular law with the men or the people, but it was a necessity if they were to gain supplies needed in the long campaign ahead. Washington was very disappointed in the stance the common people took in his actions and Greene, although infinitely loyal to Washington, sided with the people on this subject. He writes, "His Excellency is a great and good man. I feel the highest degree of respect for him and welcome the opportunity to serve under so good a general. But his Excellency, has not had time to make himself acquainted with the genius of this people. They are naturally as brave and spirited as the peasantry of any other country; but you cannot expect veterans of a raw militia of only a few months' service. The sentiment of honor, the true characteristic of a soldier, has yet got the better of interest. His Excellency has been taught to believe the people here a superior race of mortals. The country round here set no bounds to their demands for hay, wood, and teaming. It has given his Excellency a great deal of uneasiness, that they should take this opportunity to extort from the necessities of the army such enormous prices." But his relationship with Washington was becoming closer and one who was so reserved and cautious as Washington was beginning to "lean his great arm upon him for support." Washington often expressed to Greene his uneasiness with the expenses the army was incurring and that they far exceeded the expectations the Congress had budgeted. Washington had commented, "I am afraid they will sink under the weight of such charges."

Greene felt that the economy of the war should not be the essential subject for Congress. The facts were, no one knew where the money for such an endeavor as waging war against Britain and their allies the Hessians was ultimately going to cost in gold as well as lives. To Greene's mind, "The duty of Congress is plain. If they wish to put the finishing stroke to this war, they must exert their whole force at once, and give every measure an air of decision. Our preparations in all parts of the United Colonies ought to be so great as to leave no room to doubt our intentions to support the cause and obtain our conditions." Greene called for an additional 7,000 men at once to be stationed in each of the coastal towns to protect against piracy and invasion. These men would be separate from the grand army and at the disposal of Washington's discretion. To hold down expenses in such an endeavor and to hold down the constant deluge of request to go home on furlough, Greene suggested the Southern and Northern troops rotate or exchange every six months. Congress had other ideas and came up with a plan to defer the expense by paying part of the troops their wages and put the other part on furlough with their families until necessity proved otherwise. Greene was against such a plan and wrote, "The colonels are the best judges of the prudence and good economy of their soldiers. Those who behave well and make a prudent use of their money want no agent; for they will receive monthly payments, and such part as they can spare for the support of their families can easily be conveyed home."

Greene pushed his suggestion to form a great army that would be, well organized, thoroughly disciplined, properly supplied with food and clothing, enlisted for the whole war and be paid regularly. He felt this was the only way to surely bring the war to a prompt and decisive end and enlisted his good friend Henry Ward as the agent to convey this idea to Congress. In the meantime, Greene looked on in disgust at the people of the towns surrounding the various camps as, "the lower class, but of the merchants and wealthy farmers who have raised the prices of many articles, four times the first cost, and many of them cent per cent. These are the people that wound the cause. When people are distressed, it is natural for them to try everything and everywhere to get relief; and to find oppression instead of relief from these two orders of men, will go near to driving the poorer sort to depression and creatures of a day, and present gain and gratification, though small, has more weight with them than much greater advantages at a distance." Greene, always thinking, always devising, always watching the progress of events revolving towards the great contest that was surely to be engaged soon. Suddenly, his horizon became enlarged and his thoughts flowed into broader channels then he had ever thought possible. Ideas twelve months ago that Nathanael would have deemed outrageous or down right bordering on insane, now filled his thoughts every minute of every day. But his recent habits had changed little in the previous months. He still awoke with the dawn, went to bed later and later, spent hours in the saddle, and spent longer hours with pen in hand writing letters, transcribing notes, and dictating orders for the following day. He was still an attentive listener, a patient thinker, and always remained faithful to his books and reading. Finding time became a struggle within itself, but he felt it was necessary at times to calm his mind and regenerate his spirit which was beginning to show the wear of command and the monotony of the days upon days dealing with the never-ending siege.

Once in awhile Greene found the time for a pastime he considered one of the blessings in life; relaxation in socializing with fellow officers and distinguished guests in camp by entering into spirited exchanges of ideas, and opinions, neither of which Nathanael Greene had a lack of indeed. Within the brigade there were his early friends Varnum, Christopher Greene, and Ward. But too soon, arrived a friend of his aide who was a Universalistic chaplain by the name of John Murray. Greene also began to strengthen an earlier acquaintance he had had with Knox and began to bring him into his confidence which in the course of their lives remained rock solid. With Lee, Nathanael began to get very close and had found on occasion to show Lee his letters from Henry Ward. Dinners at headquarters had become friendly meetings, "I am now going," he writes to his wife, "to dine with his Excellency General Washington and Mr. Murray. I wish you could fly to Cambridge so you could partake of a friendly repast." Only one habit that used to be second nature to Nathanael in his youth, which seems to have been broken was reading the sermon on Sunday's. "Mr. Murray gave us a sermon to-day. This is the first sermon I have heard since your first arrival at Jamaica Plains." Greene wrote to his wife a few weeks after her first visit to camp. As the evenings grew longer, he wrote to his wife several times requesting more of his books and new books and, almost as an after-thought, he asked his wife to send more shirts as well. It was easy to see where Nathanael's personal priorities lay. Being in the military sometimes means long periods away from home. If the assignment is one that has long periods of boredom attached with it like Greene was experiencing, the mind automatically turns to thoughts of home, for this I write from my own experience. On one such evening Nathanael Greene wrote, "It is past nine o'clock; the room is still, and my company is gone. My attention is turned towards you. Permit me to address you, my dear, with some sentiments of warm affection. My soul breathes a secret prayer for your happiness, amidst these times of general calamity. How fondly should I press you to my bosom, were you with me. Cruel separation! But I console myself that you are happily provided for, and I in the way of my duty, offering my small services, united with others who are endeavoring to preserve an oppressed people from the worst of miseries, slavery. May God speed our efforts, crown us with success, and wing our way home before we lose the alter of Innocence."

To make Greene feel even more restless, in September he had lost the company of two of his closest friends, Samuel Ward and Christopher Greene, both of whom volunteered for the ill fated Canada expedition led by Benedict Arnold which was a coordinated attack on the British garrison in Quebec City. Greene had done everything in his power to dissuade both men from undertaking such a expedition that late in the year, but he merely marked it to the, "zeal of youth and the ambitious power of distinguishing himself with a reasonable offer." What Ward saw it as was underlying feelings of jealousy due to the fact that Nathanael was not able to join his friend in an adventure he called, "a very pretty tour through the Northern wilderness." Needless to say that news from the expedition was a regular topic of Greene's from that time forth. In late September, Greene received news from Ward that they were leaving Fort Weston and setting off the next day to meet up with General Montgomery and his troops. By late November there was no more news from the party and it was a very bitter winter in camp, it was imagined that it could only have been worse farther North in Canada. By early December it was discovered that the attack was a failure. Only a few hundred of the 650 that started out had made it. The others had either turned back or died due to lack of food because most of it had rotted, not enough cold weather clothing, or exposure. Arnold, Christopher Greene, Montgomery and Ward were captured and would be imprisoned until a prisoner exchange could be organized to free them.

Another event that was occurring was the news that the town of Falmouth, Massachusetts had been burned by the British and that orders from England had been intercepted stating that, "all seaport towns on the continent that would not lay down and deliver up their arms, and give hostage for their future good behavior," were to be burned as well. The city of New York had suffered a similar fate. All of this was startling news for a Rhode Islander, considering the entire state was basically one large seaport town. Greene immediately sent off an express message to the new Governor, Cook, who had succeeded in ousting the decidedly Tory sympathizing governor Wanton. "By these accounts we may learn what we have to expect. I think Newport should be fortified in the best manner it can be. Doubtless the enemy will make an attempt to get the stock of the island. Provision should be made to defeat them. Death and desolation seem to mark their footsteps. Fight or be slaves, is the American motto. The first is by far the most eligible."

But now the newest subject was the forming of the new army. When would it happen? How would it be raised? The last thing the general officers wanted was for the soldiers they had been training for over 8 months to be packed up and sent home just as they were beginning to be real soldiers at last. By December Greene writes, "the troops enlist very slowly in general. I was in hopes that ours would not have deserted the cause of their country. But they seem to be sick of this way of life, and so homesick, that I fear the greater part and the best of the troops from our colony will go home soon. The Connecticut troops are going home in shoals this day. Five thousand of the militia, three from this province and two from New Hampshire, are called in to take their place. There is a great defection among their troops, but from the spirit and resolution of the people of that Province, I make no doubt they will furnish their proportion without delay. New Hampshire behaves nobly; their troops engage cheerfully. The regiment raised in the Colony of Rhode Island has hurt our recruiting amazingly. They are fond of serving in the army at home, and each feels a desire to protect his own family."

By New Years day of 1776, the Continental Army was being reorganized in accordance with the Congressional resolution which placed American forces under the command of General George Washington. The General Court of the Colonies began to supply the armies more regularly with clothing, food and provisions. Although Congress had made December 31st the last day of the old enlisted soldier's service, recruitment of new troops became less of a struggle when the men began to see conditions improving. The army starts to fill its ranks again and the recruit prospects brighten for the spring. A time, generally, when many of the soldiers who turned the earth for a living prior to the war would drop their muskets to return home for spring planting. But many of the new recruits were actually coming in from the country, which seemed to help the morale of the troops a bit and make them more cheerful. But Greene still feels that recruitment could be strengthen even further with the initiation of a bounty system for the men and approaches his friend Henry Ward with the idea in hopes he may recommend it to Congress, "a bounty is necessary. But his Excellency General Washington has often assured us that the congress would not give a bounty, and before they would give a bounty they would give up the dispute. The cement between the Northern and Southern Colonies is not very strong if forty thousand lawful will induce the Congress to give it up. Do you think we should hesitate a moment to recommend a bounty if we felt ourselves at liberty to do so? We should then have an opportunity of picking the best men, filling the army sooner, keeping up a proper discipline, and preserving good order and government in camp. There is nothing that will encourage our enemies, both external and internal, like the difficulties we meet in raising an army."

The "Bounty" Greene was speaking of were government land grants that States would award to the veterans at the conclusion of the war. Of course, there were a few catches to the bounty. First of all, the soldiers would have to serve until the end of the war, plus the States would not award the land until the war had concluded and the British had been defeated. Also, several northern States, such as

Delaware, New Jersey, New Hampshire, Rhode Island, lacked the appropriate vacant land to support such a policy. But States like Connecticut, Massachusetts, New York, Pennsylvania, Maryland, Virginia, Georgia, and North and South Carolina, had more than enough land in their western frontiers to enact such a policy. In fact, these nine States welcomed such a move with open arms. By awarding the bounty land in the western frontiers to the veterans, the States were virtually placing a full-time military force to protect the settlements from Indian incursions, and in turn encouraged other settlers to populate the lands as well. To further encourage the veterans to accept the bounty, most States granted tax exemptions on the lands from years to the life of the time they remained on the property. On the other hand, many of the soldiers that chose not to continue in the army and went home were met with such a negative reception that many thought it easier to return to camp. Many of the men were looked upon as quitters and unpatriotic for not continuing with the army. Others were even looked on with contempt and not given food or shelter on their long journeys home.

On the afternoon of New Years Day 1776, a communication from the British, with the king's speech denouncing war, confiscation and death arrives in Boston. Washington, not knowing of the speech as yet, orders the Grand Union flag hoisted above the camp at Prospect Hill in compliment of the United Colonies. The Grand Union flag is the British national flag, and at about this time Loyalist in Boston are busy circulating the recent speech by the king. In it, the King was offering the Continental forces favorable terms if they laid down their arms. Now they look over to Prospect Hill and see the Grand Union flying in full regalia and the Loyalists assume this is a sign from Washington that the king's speech has impressed the Continental forces to such a great degree that it has convinced them into surrendering and have flown the flag of England to show respect to King George III. Again, the Continentals had not even heard about the speech until January 4th at about the same time that Washington was getting reports asking if he had surrendered? Nothing could be further from the truth as Washington wrote that day, "By this time, I presume, they begin to think it strange we have not made a formal surrender of our lines." Obviously, a new flag was needed and it is here that the great debate as to who and when the first American flag to be formally introduced is waged. On the 5th of January, General Washington orders a flag hastily sewn that shows the Grand Union where our field of blue with fifty stars now lay and thirteen, six pointed stars blaze across a field of red where the thirteen red and white stripes would be today. A short display of patriotism is shown when the artillery companies are permitted to fire thirteen rounds as the troops cheer their new flag. In actuality, several versions of flags are flown over camps, regiments, forts, and ships for several years before a single flag is commissioned and adopted as the new national flag.

But the British look out from their cozy confines in Boston city and are confident that the submission of the Continental forces lie in the not so distant future. Indeed, the Americans begin to grow anxious and draw a long breath many a winter evening wondering, "When will the British attack?" Greene writes, "The enemy must know our weaknesses and be prepared to profit by it; I myself manned the lines upon the hill this day, and felt a degree of pleasure that I have not felt for several days. Our situation has been critical. We have no part of a militia here, and the night after the old troops went away I could not have mustered seven hundred men, notwithstanding the returns of the newly enlisted troops amounted to nineteen hundred and upward. I am now strong enough to defend myself against all the forces in Boston." Added to the alarm the Continental forces were already showing was the talk of a small-pox epidemic already known to be in Boston, but rumors that the enemy was trying to introduce it by emissaries into camp heighten their already frayed nerves. A strict system of fumigation was established, and everyone coming from Boston was compelled to submit to it before he or she was allowed to enter the lines. Greene remembered his first visit to New York, and how he had himself inoculated at a time when most people still hesitated from inoculation because it was considered ineffective and an act against God. But now, he urged the adoption of immediate measures to have the army inoculated, and gave up his house in Coventry as a hospital for officers.

It was always a happy day for Nathanael when his wife joined him in camp, and by late January Martha Washington joined the commander-in-chief at about the same time as Caty came to see Nathanael. It was not unusual for wives of both sides to join their husbands and travel with the army. Anyone from some privates all the way up to Generals had their families with them throughout the war. They would be given jobs as water carriers, seamstresses, charwomen, cooks, etc. and make a few extra shillings for the family and help pay their way as well. Officer's wives would not do such mundane jobs, but would usually play hostess for their husband or his superior officer and maybe even do some light shopping for the officers. Greene's relationship with Washington in the meantime was becoming a bit closer. Washington was known to have a good sense of humor, and at that time a man by the name of Moses Brown was doing some correspondence work for Washington. On one occasion Brown was being sent to Cambridge for some business which would involve dealing with the Quakers. When Brown approached Washington for some background on how he should deal with the Quakers, Washington smiled and told him, "We have an authority on Quakers in our very midst. Go to General Greene, he is a Quaker and must know more than I. His social relations in that regard will put you on a better footing with them than I could ever hope too." Greene's wife was well trained by her aunt in society and social standing and was seen to be so well fitted to the task that Martha Washington incorporated her knowledge more than once for parties and dinners she and General Washington put on for VIP's and his general officers. A close friendship therefore sprang up between Katy Greene and Mrs. Washington which, in turn, strengthened the bond between the women's husbands so much so that the Greene's first baby boy was named George Washington Greene and their second child, which was a daughter, was named Martha Washington Greene.

By this time the long siege was drawing to an end. General Knox had reached camp with the train of fine artillery he had procured from the enemy at Fort Ticonderoga with great difficulty earlier that month. All winter long the Americans had been counting on the ice in the harbor to arrange passage into Boston for them. In early February the weather turned colder than it had been and preparations were being made to finally attack the British. Greene had contracted jaundice and proclaimed, "I am a yellow as a saffron and my appetite all gone and my flesh hangs upon my bones. I am so weak I can scarcely walk across the room. But I am in hopes that I am getting better and would be grievously mortified if my confinement holds me from making an appearance at such an important period of the American war. The bay at Cambridge is now frozen over; if the weather continues a few days longer as cold as it has been, it will open the passage to Boston with need. Sick or well I intend to be there, if I am able to sit on horseback." Like Washington, he believed that an attack might succeed. But the weather did not hold and turned warmer before final arrangements could be made for an attack. The British had occupied all the heights around Dorchester. By seizing Dorchester Heights it would force the enemy to fight, since whoever held it commanded the bay and its shipping, and Washington was about to do just that.

Battle preparations were made rapidly and as secretly as possible. By the first day of March, the troops were ready and the army was in place. In an attempt to draw the attention of the enemy away from where they intended to attack, they began an artillery barrage from Cobble Hill, Lechmere Point, and Lamb's Dam. The British immediately returned fire and there was an almost incessant roar of cannon and mortars firing through the evening, all night, and into the next day. On the 2nd of March, a 13-inch exploding shell from a mortar reached Prospect Hill and burst just above the ground with little effect, while a ball from one of the Americans 18-pounders struck the Brattle Street Church outer wall where it remains embedded to this day. There was a short respite from the bombarding, but by the night of the 4th, it started anew and with even more intensity. Witnesses wrote that the cannonade was so fierce that it seemed to form an unbroken line of fire. For miles around, houses shook and windows rattled with each cannons roar. Hundreds of anxious civilians surely thought it was the end of the world as it continued unabated throughout that long night. When morning came, people left their houses and gathered on Penn's Hill to hear the amazing roar of guns and watch the steady flight of shells cross paths against each foe. "O, how many of our dear countrymen must fall with each shot." wrote Abigail Adams, wife of John Adams, who was one of the many participants witnessing the bombardment. But the British took a far different view of the proceedings. In a word, perplexed. What were the Americans trying to achieve? Did their plans include burning down the town and storming the forts on Bunker, Fox, and Breed Hills and thus cut off the approach to Roxbury? A Captain John Montresor constructed the works built on the aforementioned area. A man quite educated to the engineering of forts and redoubts and well versed in American defenses as well. Montresor was the chief engineer in the construction of another fort that would play an intricate part in the American Revolution. But instead of using it as a defensive position, he would be employed to take an offensive stance in its destruction. That fort was built on a small, water logged island appropriately called Mud island and was one of many such islands on the Delaware River and just outside the city it was built to defend, Philadelphia. The fort was unceremoniously named Mud Fort, but would be better known years later as Fort Mifflin. The batteries and redoubts Montresor had built in Boston harbor were almost impregnable and suffered little damage from the American barrage of cannon fire. But on the 5th of March, the one year anniversary of the battle of Lexington and Concord, the first rays of morning sunlight pierced through the gray haze of gun smoke to reveal the Dorchester heights covered with American built redoubts. This prompted the British commander General Howe to comment, "The rebels have done more in a night than my whole army could have done in a month." Howe well knew that if the Americans were allowed to hold that ground, his fleet would be driven from the harbor and they would be hard pressed to return anytime soon. He made immediate preparations to attack the American strongholds.

Washington, of course, was anticipating Howe's plans and prepared to meet them as best he could. He sent General Putnam out with over 4,000 men in two divisions to assault the city on the waterside. Greene, with the second division, was to land just south of Barton's Point and secure Copp's Hill. Then, joining the first division under Sullivan, help force the enemy at The Neck, and let in the troops from Roxbury. Both divisions were drawn up by Fort #2, just a half mile in front of the Cambridge lines, and about three quarters of a mile from Putnam's quarters, a large house near the main street of Cambridgeport. Just before them lay the Charles River, covered with various boats and craft of all kind. Anything that would float was put into use to carry men and supplies. Three huge floating batteries, which carried five 24-pound cannons, were among them, along with flatboats that could hold 40 men each. Beyond the broad tract of lowland, with the bay on their left, they could barely see Boston, bristling with cannon, redoubts, strong picket lines and Mount Horam, where the grenadiers were laying in wait in the shadows of Beacon Hill. The Americans knew that thousands of pairs of eyes were anxiously peering out from every housetop and steeple in the city and surrounding ground, and every point that could get a glimpse of the bay. It was under this gaze that the American troops would have to row, right up to the heart of the British strongholds. The hours passed slowly and must have weighed heavily on the nervous soldier's minds. When noon came, and the signal they were expecting from Roxbury steeple still did not come, it must have only intensified the waiting more and worked further to play on the young troops minds. Messengers came and went. Some of them must have brought word from Dorchester that the British were preparing to load their troops into the boats. They could see the British ships of the line in position to cover the landing and then take part in the assault. Washington himself was nervous, and to try and alleviate his tension he mounted his horse and rode among the men to remind them that this was the anniversary when the struggle began. The British had drawn first blood on that day, but this was the day they would acquire some vengeance for that deed.

But by afternoon the clocks that should have pealed the hours were unearthly quiet. They may not have rung out loud, but every man heard them in their heads as the hours passed and soon turned into night. The expectation of battle, became the uneasiness of waiting. Waiting for a battle that did not come.

As the night wore slowly the winds grew fast. The Charles River foamed between its narrow banks. Down in the bay, the waters lashed into waves and curled into foam. Nature would have a hand in what would take place now, and men stood in silent awe as the howl of wind and water took the place of cannon and bursting shells. It was hard to decide which was louder or which was more intimidating. The wind finally brought the rains, which fell in sheets and lashed out at anything that stood in its path. The tempest, as they were called then, raged all night and all of the next day, and by the following evening, a Captain Erving succeeded in making his escape out of Boston to bring word that the British were preparing to leave the city. Relief soon replaced disappointment with the embittered troops. Washington and his general knew that this was not the end and that their work was only beginning. On the 13th of March, a council was held at General Ward's quarters in Roxbury. Washington, Ward, Putnam, Thomas, Sullivan, Heath, Greene, and Gates were all present. They decided that, if the town were not evacuated the next day, they would fortify Nook's Hill. The British did not leave, and weary with their loitering, Washington brought things to an immediate start by fortifying without delay. Howe had no choice but to flee, or drive the Americans from their stronghold, which he did not have very much faith in doing. It was worried the battle would not turn in their favor and the last thing he wanted was to watch his ships and his only means of escape destroyed and sunk at their moorings. On the morning of the 19th, just after sunrise, boats filled with soldiers and Tory citizens were seen putting off from the wharves, and when the sun set that day the city was once again in the hands of its own people.

But Washington did not rest with ease. He still did not know or trust the enemy's intentions, as he watched their fleet linger for days in the lower bay. The British had begun the war making a huge error in strategy. By allowing themselves to be cooped up in a place that had more political strategy involved in the decision than military, they allowed the Americans to force them into wasting mountains of time and energy on a location that could not further their occupation strategy. But, by occupying New York and seizing the passes of the Hudson River, they could, without even firing a shot, cut off communication between the Eastern and Middle States, and secure their own communication with their troops in Canada. Washington had little doubt that this was Howe's new objective and General Heath had already been sent on with his brigade the day after the evacuation. The only concern for Washington was, "might the British, before he struck this blow, attempt with his concentrated forces a parting blow on us in our new positions?" Washington had written in his journal. Washington, therefore, continued to watch Howe's every movement, holding his troops well in hand and preparing himself for any contingency. The command of the city was given to Greene. "General Greene," say the orders of the day for the 24th, "will dispose of the regiments in Boston to the best advantage. The wagon-master and a company of carpenters in the city are to receive and obey all such orders and directions as Brigadier-General Nathanael Greene shall think proper to give." Things remained quiet and an uneasy calm fell over the daily duties of the troops and people in the city. Then, on the 27th of March 1776, the British fleet finally made sail and made its way out to sea. Just a day after, Nathanael had received heart-breaking news from home. His very dear friend, Governor Samuel Ward, had died of smallpox which was still committing its dreadful ravages throughout much of the New England states. Nathanael's other friend, Ward's son Samuel, was still up in Canada where the disease was decimating the army there as well. But young Samuel had taken Nathanael's advice and had been inoculated against the disease, unlike his father who felt he was too busy to be inoculated. And so, a wise, earnest man, was lost in Congress. Ward would not live to see what he had helped advocate for so long, independence. And the state of Rhode Island would greatly miss his wise counsel in the coming years, when they would be ill prepared for the path history would shape for the colonies. Greene felt the loss even more so; who would he now tell his thoughts and feelings to concerning all the great questions he had about his ability to command men's lives? The form would be in the shape of John Adams, who he had met years before in his time at Cambridge. Although the character of Nathanael's letters would change somewhat from here on out, his close, careful study of situations and search for remedies to his questions would still shine through.

Chapter III

"Boston to New York"

Two years before, the British troops had given Nathanael Greene important lessons in minor tactics with their daily exercises on the Common, and now they left a still more important lesson behind them in their redoubts and works in the city and on Bunker Hill. Greene took the task of studying the British engineering to heart. Fortification after all, was the only chapter in his art of war, which he had studied extensively to this point, and here were classic illustrations that far exceeded anything he had ever seen or read about. But Nathanael did not have time to study, he was soon issued marching orders, and at sunrise on Monday, the 1st of April, Brigadier-general Greene took command of his brigade. It was made up of Varnum, Hitchcock, Little, Reed, and Bailey's regiments, along with a detachment from Knox's artillery which was added at the last moment to complete the brigade. The quartermaster supplied them with "necessary teams of horses and sufficient provisions for the march and receive a warrant for five hundred pounds, lawful money, upon application at head-quarters." The route taken lay from Providence to New London, where transports were to meet the troops and convey them directly to New York. But, before they were on their way came an express message from Governor Cooke, saying that, "A ship of war had arrived in the harbor of Newport, along with twenty-seven other ships, undoubtedly having the ministerial troops onboard, were within Seconnet Point." Greene was ordered to hasten his march, and a messenger dispatched to Sullivan, who with six regiments, was on the road to Norwich to direct Greene where to file off toward Providence. "The enemy has the best knack of puzzling people I have ever met with in my life." Washington had written to Reed, who was watching the fleet in Boston Bay when they departed. "This may be a stroke of their same game." But a sharp blow dealt to Rhode Island by the British would be felt throughout the colonies Washington surmised, and could force an evacuation of Boston. So, Greene pushed on, becoming very nervous that the tide of war was about to turn in the direction of his own home, and that he might soon have to fight under the eye of his own friends and townsfolk.

The truth known, the entire country was in a state of alarm, dreading an attack at almost every vulnerable point of its long line of coast. While every person in the colonies was worried about the outcome of this new threat, three particular soldiers stood on a hill just below Newport at their lookout station. They had made a calculated error. They had mistaken the undulations in the fog that morning for the sails of hostile ships. A messenger was immediately dispatched to the governor at Providence before they scarcely had time to think, and a quick decision making aide to the governor failed to wait for confirmation before whisking off an urgent message to Washington in Boston. But unlike the immediate response of electronic systems like e-mail or cell phones, in 1776 things were much different. Messages were written, riders had to take the messages miles on horseback on rough roads, usually with frequent stops and they may get there in a day. In this case, another night and day to verify that indeed it was not an invasion force and more messages. This time to contradict the earlier warnings and to call off the alarm. Greene received the message outside of Providence and was able to make his way to New London, scarcely able to turn his glance toward his family in Coventry when he marched by on familiar roads only a few miles from his home. The trip proved bothersome to say the least, with the spring thaw the roads were muddy and in spots impassable, and the local people were less than helpful to the soldiers when the baggage horses gave out and new ones were needed to replace them.

As mentioned in the past, for every citizen soldier fighting on the side of the Americans, another fought on the British side and another cared little for the struggle at all, unless it involved him in some outside source. Such as having to give up good horses for little or no pay for them.

This was the first march with troops for Greene. It would become an everyday occurrence in only a couple of years, but for now it was tedious at best. Here he met up with the transports that would convey him and his brigade to New York. Just before he was about to sail, Washington passed through on his way by the shore road and plans were finalized. The night Greene and his men sailed a vicious snowstorm arrived and dispersed his small fleet, the very ship Greene rode on almost capsized just miles from shore, and slowly but surely the ships all met in New York on the 17th of April. Greene found Washington engaged in the preparations for the defense of the city, completing the works and redoubts that had already been laid out months before and the building of new ones. The British ships of the line, "instead of lying within pistol shot of the wharves, and their sentries conversing with ours, while they received every necessary that the country afforded, were driven down to the Hook, and their intercourse with the inhabitants cut off." Greene would write to his brother. "It was hard times for quiet people. New York is no more the gay, polite place it used to be esteemed, but is become almost a desert, unless for the troops." Dissatisfied citizens, in great numbers, thought it a unwelcome restraint to their freedom to be required to be within doors by a stated hour and have a pass with them at all times. On the 24th, the regiments were brigaded again, and Greene was put in command of his old Rhode Islanders, under Varnum and Hitchcock, along with the regiments under Wayne, Little, and Irvine. This was the first time Greene had met Anthony Wayne, who would later become a close friend and would serve with him in the Carolinas. But before they could proceed with any other plans, news out of Canada was received. The department that Washington deemed, "more trouble and concern than my own," requested additional troops to reinforce the Northern army. Sullivan was appointed to command it, Wayne and Irvine's regiments were placed under his orders as well. Greene's brigade now counted as the Third, with Hand's regiment, which took the place of Wayne's and Irvine's, numbered in all 1,307 men fit for duty out a total muster of 1,761, most of whom had influenza. Washington ordered Greene's brigade to, "encamp, tomorrow morning at ten o'clock, on the ground marked out upon Long Island."

The field was much broader before him now, with a wider range of duties and a greater weight of responsibility laid on his shoulders. Although the enemy had not yet made an appearance, there could be little doubt that the line of the Hudson River was his objective, and that part of the first blow, if not the whole weight of it, would fall onto Long Island. To prepare for this was Greene's first assignment, an assignment so familiar to that of the campaign in Boston, that he made his daily rounds among the works, and daily revolved his mind in the means of their defense, and the possibility of strengthening them. He must have felt like this was all the same and merely applying lessons of the old campaign to a new location. In the science of engineering, the British army was far superior to the Americans. Gridley, whom Washington was told to be "one of the first engineers of the new age," did not lack for brilliant ideas, but surely lacked the energy to carry the plans out. Gridley was given the task of rebuilding and strengthening the defenses of Boston and progress was creeping along at a snail pace. In war, speed is the utmost of tools and time is a luxury seldom afforded. On the other hand, Rufus Putnam had shown proof of his talent and energy, but deficient in the scientific training of engineering. The forts and works at Cambridge had been "planned by a few of the principal officers of the army, assisted by Mr. Knox, a gentlemen from Worcester. I have but one, " writes Washington, "on whose judgement I should wish to rely in laying out works of the least consequence?" Greene's taste for mathematics was clearly similar to the studies of engineering and Washington leaned toward Nathanael as a candidate for the engineering position. Lee was the first to suggest works be constructed in Brooklyn, and it is impossible to determine with certainty how far his plans were changed by Greene, or how fully they were carried out by his successor. Still, very little had been accomplished when Greene took command of construction of the works General Charles Lee had already begun, but had to abandon due to his departure for the South in spring of 1776. All that was done after the 1st of May was engineered and built by Greene and with the help of Brigadier-general William Alexander Stirling, better known as Lord or Earl of Stirling, who was never officially given that title but was addressed by it to his dying day. Stirling was given the job of finishing the series of abatis, entrenchment's, fraise work, and redoubts Lee had started, and was well involved with their construction when Greene was put in charge of their completion.

Brooklyn, or Brookland as Greene preferred to call the location, at the time was regarded as a narrow peninsula, separated from the main land of Long Island by Wallabout Bay, and Gowanus or Gowan's Cove and creek, which ran deep inland from the south. There the landline was reduced to no more than a mile and a third wide, and presented a natural front to an enemy with both flanks protected by water. Within this line and on the heights near the water, Lee had built a redoubt, in conjunction with a battery on the Manhattan side, which he had hoped to use to secure the entrance of the East River. Lee also chose the site for two other redoubts, in that forming an entrenched encampment large enough for 3,000 men. With these works already in place, Greene began his work. Near the Wallabout, where Washington Square now stands, stood a wooded hill commanding a water range of a little over a mile from Wallabout Bay to Corlear's Hook, and a land range which covered the two principal roads from the interior of the island. On this Greene built Fort Putnam, a redoubt with five 18-pound guns. By cutting down the trees between the guns and the road, the line of fire for the canons was unimpeded. An entrenchment running a northwesterly course down the hillside to the edge of the Wallabout secured the approaches on the north. Another zigzag entrenchment connected it with Freek's Millpond, a body of water at the head of Gowanus Creek. But to make this entrenchment, which was already naturally protected by the slope of the ground, still easier to defend, he strengthened it by building another redoubt of five guns, halfway between the millpond and Fort Putnam. This new fort was named, by him or someone else, Fort Greene, which was the custom of the day to do and not at all unusual. Near the head of the creek, and still within the peninsula, was another high hill, called Cobble Hill by the old English settlers, but Ponkiesberg by the Dutch. On this, a third redoubt was erected, armed with only three 12-pound guns, but strengthened by an entrenchment which ran in a spiral down the cone-shaped hill, which gave birth to its name, the Corkscrew Fort. Between this fort and Gowanus Cove was Box-hill Fort, a fourth redoubt; and two more small redoubts, one on the slope of Bergen Hill and one near the Jamaica road, and a little south of Fort Putnam, which completed the lines of defense on the landward side. On the waterside, a strong guard was stationed at Red Hook, where works had already been thrown up in haste and another at Governor's Island, halfway between Red Hook and the Battery. Here two substantial redoubts were named Fort Stirling and Fort Defiance, with two smaller redoubts that were of little importance to have names, but carried a few 18-pound cannons, most of which were old iron guns that were honeycombed with rust. More than a few volleys from them and they would most likely explode on the men who were firing them.

Hand's regiment was stationed at the Narrows, to keep a sharp lookout from that important point, and the shore carefully patrolled by pickets. To prepare himself for defending the ground between his lines and the landing places on the coast, Greene went about making a painstaking study of that area in every direction. The first thing Greene needed to do was push the building of the works as quickly as his men were able. While this small force of men worked as fatigue parties, another, larger force was required as pickets to guard the workers. This became a sort of catch-22 scenario, since Greene needed as many men as possible to build the works quickly, but needed even more to guard the large area that the men were working, but with more men he could complete the work faster, yet he dared not because, "I cannot safely enlarge the fatigue party," he writes in July, "without injuring the health of the people, for they are one day on and one day off duty now." Also, to secure the earliest intelligence of the enemy's approach, a system of signals was planned by a committee composed of Sullivan, Greene, and Stirling. With the appearance of any number of ships by day, from one to six, a large flag was to be hoisted on the highland of Neversink on the heights of Staten Island; upon the appearence of any number, from six to twenty, two flags, and for any number greater, three flags. The flags would be hoisted on flag staffs arranged from east to west about twenty yards apart from each other. In the event the sighting occurred at night, an equal number of bonfires, arranged in the same sequence would be used in the flags place. The orders from the Commander-in-chief specified, "we recommend the day signal be given using large ensigns, with broad red and white stripes, the country is take the alarm, and communicate it as soon as possible, for the purpose of calling in the militia." The militia the commander was speaking of was the "Flying camp" that was to be established in Perth Amboy, New Jersey. Congress sought to build a force of 13,800 militiamen from Massachusetts, Connecticut, New York, and New Jersey for defense of "the middle colonies." Needless to say, this attempt was a total failure. There was an insufficient response to their appeal, and the militia, mostly made up of two regiments, one from Maryland, the other from Delaware numbered 1,200 by most accounts and were sent almost immediately to New York a few days after their arrival and the Flying camp soon passed out of existence by the end of the summer.

A good series of lookouts was manned day and night in addition to the flag alarm guard, as well as a group of riders on constant stand by so as to spread the alarm on a moment's notice. At the moment the alarm was sounded the Committee of Safety had arranged a "rendezvous spot" for each regiment where the militia would meet up with them. While all of this was being planned, Greene, ever vigilant of the enemy about to start the open attack at any moment, had other problems to combat, which sprang from within the city itself. Like all towns throughout the colonies, New York had its share of Tories; but on Long Island the number was so great that Greene had to worry about their effect constantly. When the king's troops succeeded in landing on the island, it was assured that the British would put themselves in communication with the partisans of the crown almost immediately. The Tories had much more familiarity with the terrain and Greene could be sure they had agents mapping the American defenses and every move the Americans made could be passed along as information to help the British. This would make the Tories invaluable assistants in every operation the enemy would venture and Greene could do little but watch and wait. Serving as spies upon the patriot army, the Tories made almost no secret of their intention of covertly assisting the British the minute they landed, and skillfully set to work causing suspicion and spreading rumors in the American troops' camps. They exaggerated enemy statements, put out false reports, made up malignant slander about the Continental officers, thus making their men suspect their effectiveness during battle, and anything else they could use in the dangerous art of propaganda and sabotage.

Washington, apparently feeling he was the direct agent of the Committee of Safety, decided it was his duty to root out any and all of the suspected Tories in the area, but especially in and around Queen's County. This area, near Flatbush, was witness to increasingly brazen acts of activity for the enemy and collusion with the British. Washington had his troops on the alert for any such sightings deemed threatening to the army's safety. On the 16th of July Greene wrote, "a Mr. John Livingston and his barber were taken into custody near the Jamaica Road by a captain in Lieutenant-colonel Cornwell's division. Papers found on him indicate notorious or unfriendly participation with the help of the enemy. I shall deliver them into the hands of the Committee; accordingly I have sent a number of officers with them in their care." Some days later another incident prompted Greene to write in a letter to Washington, "The officers tell me that not less than four or five hundred stands of arms have gone by the camp with the past few days. I have given orders that in the future, no such trips shall pass until I know your pleasure." Greene grew increasingly tense with this type of blatant disregard for the

48

garrisoned troops and let it be known in a letter to Washington on the 4th of August, "I received information last evening that thirty or forty Tories were on a little island at the entrance to Jamaica Bay. Three boats full of men were seen off there day before yesterday, but they did not land nor speak with any boats that the guards could discover. I sent a party of sixty men to scour the island this morning, and to take all they found there as prisoners." Sometimes the brigadier just got plain old riled up. A few days later Greene wrote, "In obedience to the within order and warrant of spying against the United States, I sent a detachment of my brigade, under the command of Colonel Vernon, to the house of the within named David Mathews, Esq., at Flatbush. The detachment surrounded the house and seized his person at precisely at the hour of one this morning. After having made him a prisoner, a diligent search was made after any of his papers; but none could be located, notwithstanding great care was taken that none of his family should have at least opportunity to remove or destroy them." Measures that seemed stern at the time, had to be made. As Washington wrote to Greene, "These matters, far advanced from tenderness are necessary, and I have reason to repent the indulgence of lenity I have shown our enemies in the past. It has been attributed to fear, with men like Mathews, and restraint with duty to itself and to the people who trust us, proves we are compelled to impose them. The same men talked loudly of violated rights and injured innocence. They must speak of the foe they claim are their rightful domain."

One of Greene's favorite people was indeed Henry Knox. Knox, known for his warm heart and sound mind loved to pal around with Nathanael also. Many times they endeavored to reconnoiter the grounds and works, supervising their completion and on one particular day they found themselves on Manhattan Island near the King's Bridge where the home of congressional member, Gouverneur Morris stood. Putnam, who was with the two men at the time, would write later, "the commanding height near the Morris's house was pointed out as a position which, if properly fortified, would be nearly impregnable." But some insisted, with Greene and Heath, "that even if it were made as strong as Gibraltar; it would be a mere trap from which it would be impossible to extricate the army itself from, unless the high grounds above the bridge were occupied at the same time." Both opinions were ultimately accepted, and Fort Washington was built on the first height and Fort Independence on the second. Nothing else could be done, but wait for the British.

At camp before Boston, Nathanael Greene's regiments had been said to be the best disciplined in the entire army. But since then many changes had taken place in the organization of his brigade. Some of his men had left the army and the new troops had not been properly trained in musket and battle drills as well as his old charges. Still, as time passed, mixing together, and working and living closely together, an attachment sprang up between the old and new guard eventually which Greene carefully fostered as a means for success. Greene knew that without it, many of his men would perish in battle, and he could not hold to that fact the more he thought about it. He also began to fully appreciate the importance of exact and regular reports, both preserving discipline by keeping officer and soldier alike, constantly under the eye of their commander, and for enabling himself to then ascertain in almost an instant, at any moment or situation, the number, morale and condition of his men. Knowledge such as that would be invaluable in the heat of battle, and in the long run, keep himself and his men at the ready at all times. The state of each company was the subject of a morning report, from the corporal to every officer in the company; the state of each regiment, of a daily report from the adjutant to the commanding officer; there were daily reports of the sick and absent; provision reports every other day to the quartermaster; returns from the adjutant three times a week, and the same number of returns from the surgeon; daily reports of guards posted, and twice a week reports of the arms and ammunition. Add with these courts-martial, orders, correspondence, and miscellaneous regimental papers and the task of yeoman and clerk must have been daunting under reams of paper month after month. But Greene was well organized and extremely analytical and expected every i dotted and no t went uncrossed. Greene's brigade lightened a great deal of the material burden, much to the delight of

Washington who greatly appreciated it.

The problem of recruiting a sufficient number of men for a war that Greene was sure would last for several years, was still in question during preparations for the British attack on New York. It was now late July, Congress had finally made the country's path known to King George and his army. There was no turning back and all out war was now a forgone conclusion by this time. Congress had spent considerable time on the debate of Independence. Greene now felt it was the appropriate time for Congress to realize that wars were not won because of vast differences sitting and staring at each other in committee after committee. The discussion of how to work on entrenchments and redoubts was now merely a question of affirmation. What Congress had to decide now was, where would the men needed to fight come from and how would the army keep them until the entire business with England was decided one way or the other? "If I am to form a judgement of the success of recruiting," Greene writes in a letter to Congress, "from what is past, the time is too short to raise the troops and be in readiness to meet the enemy; and as every argument has been made use of upon the present plan of recruiting to engage people in the service, there must be some new motive added to quicken the motions of the recruiting parties. With the approach of danger, recruiting will grow more and more difficult. If Congress was to fix a certain means of support upon every officer and soldier that was maimed in the service, or to the families of those that were killed in defense of their country, it would have as happy an influence towards engaging people in the service and inspire those engaged with as much courage, as any measure that could be fixed upon it. I believe it is nothing more than common justice, and puts those in and out of the army upon more of an equal footing than at present, and that the desperate game you have to play, and the uncertainty of war, may render every measure that will increase the force and strength of the American army worthy consideration."

For one in Congress, his friend John Adams agreed with Greene about the justice of such a measure, but doubted its acceptance by Congress. Greene wrote back, "the activity and zeal of the troops also falls entirely upon the animation given them by their officers. The field officers in general, and the colonels of regiments in particular, think themselves grievously burdened upon the present establishment; few, if any, of that rank that are worth retaining in service will continue, if any dependence is to be made upon the discontent that appears. One of their grievances was the necessity of acting as factors of the regiment and drawing from the Continental stores for wholesale, and delivering out to the troops in retail, thus paying a great loss of bad accountants. To much of this duty is the responsibility of the colonel in the regiment and too much of his time has been engaged in that employment of this business mode for the good of the service. His time would be better served on military business and a remedy would be to have an agent for each regiment to provide the troops with clothing on the easiest of terms."

Another cause for complaint, and one that would be seen throughout much of the war was insufficient pay and distribution of it. Greene writes, "They say, and I believe with too much truth, that their pay will not defray their expenses. Many of these men were engaged in the service in the early part of the dispute without any consideration of paid reward when they started; few, if any, thought of its continuance until the present; but its duration will reduce all that have not independent fortunes to attend to their families concerns. Novelty may attract new men to the service, but if the present officers quit it, it will not make up for the injury the army will sustain by the loss of every good and well-trained officer. A young officer, without experience in the military art and knowledge, unless he is a very uncommon genius, must be totally unfit to command an entire regiment." If it has not been made clear until this point, I should explain what makes up a regiment of the Continental army in 1776. It would consist of eight companies of 76 privates each, with the usual officers, non-commissioned officers, along with fifes and drums. By standards of the time the pay and provisions were more than sufficient and generous. The pay for officers ranged from $50 a month for a colonel to $13 1/3 for an ensign.

Privates were to receive $6 2/3; but out of this sum there were deductions for clothing furnished them at the rate of $1 2/3 per month. But, as we also have learned, the expedience and frequency the men were paid came into question constantly. It did little good to be the highest paid army in the world, if you did not get the pay. Also, because of widespread inflation and depreciation of the Continental money, which Congress had printed too much of to have any real value, troops had to pay exaggerated fees for clothing sold by merchants outside the army and high prices for food to feed their families, and on occasion themselves.

Exaggerated ideas of the strength and condition of the army had been spread through the country. Ideas that made it very desirable to give to the enemy, but very dangerous for our own people to believe. It fostered expectations that the army just could not stand up too, and the civilian population relaxed, thinking the British could not possibly harm them. This laid the groundwork for dangerous suspicions and unjust complaints against Washington and his army. "You would think," Greene writes to Adams, "that the present army, assisted by the militia, would be sufficient to oppose the force of Great Britain. Formidable as it appears on paper, I can assure you it's necessary to make great allowances, in the calculation of our strength, from the establishment, or else you'll be greatly deceived. I am confident the force of America, if properly exerted, will prove superior to al her enemies, but I would risk nothing to chance; it is easy to disband when it is impossible to raise troops. If the force of Great Britain should prove near equal to what it has been represented, a larger augmentation shall be necessary for the completion of our duty." Up until now the total amount of troops had added up to about 28,000. Putnam, Spencer, and Sullivan's divisions, with the Connecticut militiamen accounted for about 19,800 in all, and were posted in and about the city. Heath's division was separated into several parts; Mifflin's brigade of 2,400 men was on Manhattan Island at Fort Washington, and George Clinton's 1,800 were at Kings Bridge. Two regiments of Greene's division were on Governor's Island. Greene himself, and the rest of fewer than 4,000 men were on Long Island. The American troops on the eve of the battle roughly totaled 28,000 men.

When Howe had to evacuate Boston, it was already apparent to the British crown that their early plans for crushing the American colonies rebellion had been conceived on a scale that proved to be too small; Howe's 7,000 men just were not going to be enough to finish the job. By October, 1775, the plans to enlarge the occupying force had already been put into effect and a call for an additional 55,000 men, plus 12,000 sailors with the Royal Navy would bring the British troop total to 74,000 men. Recruiting had already begun in all parts of the British Isles; but, as an English historian wrote, "hardly any enthusiasm for the war among the classes from which soldiers were drawn." The British Isles were enjoying a terrific year of crop prosperity the years prior to the war and so the chief incentive for men enlisting, hunger, was unknown. This was one reason why England turned to Germany for help. But unlike most Revolutionary War historians, I disagree with the label of "mercenary" that is always associated with the Hesse-Kassel troops, better known as Hessians. The primary reason the German troops were enlisted to fight in the American rebellion was so the crown princes of Germany could pay off the enormous hospital debt that Germany had incurred in the Seven Years War. At that time, the losing participant of a war would have to pay the winner the cost of hospitalizing the enemy's casualties. The German leaders saw a way out of most of their debt with England by hiring out the Hessian troops and at the same time, maintaining a well trained and supplied army without incurring the cost. In the kindest of terms, the Hessians should be classified as "Hired Allies."

On June 25th, three British ships of the line with General William Howe aboard sailed into lower New York Bay. General Howe had just come from Halifax, Nova Scotia and was in New York to prepare for the next level of the American conflict. He had decided that New York would be used as the base for the entire British army and navy and would be a better location for his plan to conquer the American colonies. The force Howe had with him was small, but only a forerunner of what was soon to come. On the 29th, the full magnitude of Howe's plans began to show itself when forty-five British ships of the line sailed into the lower bay and on the 30th, another eighty-two appeared on the horizon. One hundred and thirty ships of war and their transports unloaded 9,300 soldiers onto Staten Island. This was only the beginning of what would be a major build-up of men, equipment and arms that England had decided was necessary to ultimately win the war. Admiral Lord Howe, brother of the general, followed with a fleet of one hundred and fifty sailing vessels, full to the gunwales with material and fighting men fresh from England. By July 12th, the fleet, along with the other ships and troops, joined forces on Staten Island, along with the 2,500 troops and ships of Admiral Sir Peter Parker, that were just arriving from their recent defeat at Charleston, South Carolina. Commodore Hotham brought his six men-of-war and twenty-eight transports by August 12th, and carried aboard 2,600 British Guard under the commands of General Henry Clinton and General Lord Cornwallis and 8,000 Hessian allies. In the already formed British camp of Staten Island, directly across the Narrows from Long Island, there were no less than twenty-seven British regiments-of-foot, four battalions of light infantry, four grenadiers, two of the Guards, three brigades of artillery, one light dragoons under the command of Howe, Clinton, Lord Percy, Lord Cornwallis, and another 8,000 Hessians with Von Heister. These troops alone could easily overwhelm the Continental forces, all of them were highly skilled in the science of war and the art of command. A total of 32,000 trained, disciplined, professional soldiers, completely armed, fully equipped with the up to date weaponry, unlimited supplies-the greatest expeditionary force that Great Britain had ever unleashed from its shores. They were supported by a fleet of ten ships of the line, twenty frigates armed with 1,200 guns, and hundreds of transports, manned by more than 10,000 seamen. Britain had drawn from her war chest the tidy sum of more than L850,000. A staggering amount of money at that time in history. Britain had decided that defeat was not an option they were willing to live with.

On the other side of the Narrows, the Americans had roughly 19,000 untrained, undisciplined, untried amateur soldiers, poorly armed, meagerly equipped and supplied at best, led by either very young amateur officers or very old ones that had not fought in years and at this scope of war, and they were all led by an untested commander-in-chief who had gained his experience as an amateur officer with the British army during the French & Indian War twenty years before. They did not have a single warship nor transport, only a few row galleys, equipped with a single 18-pound cannon on its bow, and their war chest was in large part a printing press in the city of Philadelphia issuing paper money at will and worth whatever the holder could induce another person into giving them for its value which seemed to diminish with each passing day. But these men had something specific to fight for that the British could not see nor fully understand, because independence was something very sacred and dear in their hearts since its declaration in early July of 1776. If things did not look grim enough for the Americans, they had another obstacle to hurdle in their fight with the British and that was that their inadequate force was divided in two between New York and Long Island with the East River separating them from each other. If British warships were to engage either of them, they had no line of communication with the troops on the other side of the river, and communication is the lifeblood of army troops even today. The Americans could not see the British camp; but their ships were only too visible. Greene kept a very watchful eye on them, and on the 10th of August he transmitted a communication to Washington that read, "four prisoners of Staten Island tell us that they went on board the fleet as they lay at the Hook, several boat-loads of them and that if a sharp watch is not kept, the people of Long Island will do the same at the earliest opportunity. Our people are firing with nine-ponders at the Narrows, but have not heard whether they have done any execution. There was a smart fire heard at the west end of Staten Island about four this morning. It is supposed to be an attack upon Fort Smith, in the south part of that island." It was about this time that Greene received some happy information from Congress. The new appointments were made, and when four new major generals were chosen, Nathanael's name was one of the chosen. His name, again, came up last on the list. On the parchment, in scripted letters, the general orders of his promotion still ran the same name as when he was commissioned a brigadier-general, a commission with the United *Colonies* of America. One of the first benefits that Greene experienced in this higher grade was the lightening of his mountainous clerical burden at last, for he was entitled to not one, but two aides. "I have made a choice," he writes to the brigade yeoman, "of Mr. William Blodget and Major William Livingston for the position of my aides-de-camp."

Also at this time, Nathanael gained another new and dear friend. While attending a meeting at Washington's headquarters in New York, he walked by way of The Park, which was nothing but open ground and frequently used for drilling and parades. On this particular day a company of young artillerists were drilling. Greene was impressed by the groups soldierly appearance and was drawn to the company's commander, who seemed to be the size of a boy, but went through his duty with uncanny military precision that is usually attributed to veterans. When the parade was over, Greene sent a note to the young officers commander complimenting on the proficiency the young officer had shown with his company, and invited this young officer to join him and a group of other officers that were going to dine in town that night. The young man who accepted the invitation would shortly become one of Washington's aide-de-camp in the coming months, and his name was Alexander Hamilton. That night, the two men found they had a lot in common. Both appreciated each others talents, gained confidence in each others motives, had equal devotion to the cause in which they were fighting, and seemed to have the same open opinions to the great questions involved with the struggle that other officers had a tendency not to discuss openly. It showed as a source of deep strength in character, and maybe a bit of ego in the case of both men, but also showed that they were both more than a little ambitious. They both agreed that the war would soon escalate, without question, as they looked over the river at the five hundred dark hulls and forest of masts openly displaying the colors of His Majesty King George III. The sights exhilarated men like Alexander and Nathanael, and caused panic in the hearts of half the inhabitants of New York who supported independence, while gleams of joy could be found in the eyes of the other half that were opposed to it and supported the British.

The first sign of aggression from the British was when two warships, the *Phoenix* with forty-four guns and the *Rose* with twenty-one, and their two tenders moved in towards town one morning. In the American camp the alarm was sounded; troops took their posts as the ships swept by the town on their way up the North River. The artillery batteries there and the ones on Pauls Hook (now Jersey City) opened fire on them. The two British ships replied with broadsides, which threw the town into a mad panic. "We have our coach standing before our door every night, and the horses harnessed, ready to make our escape if we have the time," writes one civilian, a daughter of John Morin Scott, "We have hardly any clothes to wear; only a second change." One night the family mistakenly identifies a thunderstorm with one of the alarms and they hurry off, making their way towards the interior of New Jersey as best they can, but are "obliged to stop on the road and stay all night due to the poor conditions of the road. And all our lodgings they say can get are a dirty bed on the floor. How hard it is for us to live this way, us who have always been used to living comfortably." They would be inconvenienced many times in the coming years and even led Washington to write of the inhabitants and especially the women of the town, "When the men-of-war passed up the river, the shrieks and cries of the poor creatures, running every way with their children, were truly distressing, and I fear they will have an unhappy effect on the ears and minds of our young and inexperienced soldiers." Day after day, past the numerous batteries that were constructed for the very purpose of preventing their passage, the ships held their course to Tappen Bay, forty miles above the town. Fireships were time and again sent against them, but with little or no success. Six days later, they came back, running the gauntlet of American artillery, only to anchor in the Narrows once again, completely unharmed.

A black servant brought in by the rifle-guard from Staten Island reports to Greene that 800 blacks are being formed into a regiment by the British that very day. The next day, more ships come to anchor in the Narrows, armies of soldiers are seen standing on their decks "in the Highland habit" and Greene knows all to well that their comrades, perhaps the Highlanders themselves can not be far behind. Also by now, the wheat crop in the area was ripening in the fields along the Utecht and Gravesend shores. These crops could not fall into the hands of the enemy. "For everything they destroy or carry off will be a matter of triumph," Greene writes to Washington on the 25th of July, "I apprehend that an order from Congress will be necessary for its removal." He also adds, "if your Excellency would like to visit this post, when at liberty, to see if there are any opinions or any alterations or further regulations necessary upon the preparations of defense."

Some of Greene's troubles do not come from the enemy or the Loyalist, but from his own officers, who make him look foolish and waste his time on situations better spent on the battle at hand. A Lieutenant Dunworth, discharged just a few days before from Little's regiment, had challenged Captain Talbot, of Varnum's regiment to a duel. A hint of this quarrel had already reached Greene beforehand, and, in fact, he had already spoken to Washington of the possibility of its coming to a fever pitch between these young men, and ultimately resulting in one or both challenging the other "on the field of honor." Washington, also had his hands full at the time, and responded, "I wish to know nothing about it General Greene. They are your men and your responsibility; use your own good judgement, and dispatch the problem in haste." But when the challenge was actually sent and accepted, and Greene was known to have been informed of it, he was, "not just a little perplexed, knowing dueling to be against all laws, both civil and military," yet, he had the feeling, apparently, that the question of personal courage was so involved in it that it would be extremely difficult to step in and prevent the event from taking place. But, somehow he did prevent it, though by means that are not fully explained, and Talbot's life was preserved for better things to come. Meanwhile, Greene's eyes still turned anxiously seaward, scanning the relentless paths of the British ships moving up and down below the Narrows. And yet another cause of alarm is raised in the following days, "The troops are in general exceedingly sick, great numbers taken down every day. If the state of the army will admit of a reinforcement at this post, perhaps it may be prudent if it does not. I will do the best with what I have." That evening, Greene himself, goes down to the Narrows, and counts the ships he sees. From the uniforms, the troops seem to be the Guard and artillery. "If your Excellency has leisure, perhaps it may be worth while to pay a visit to the Narrows, only if to reconnoiter, and count the ships."

Chapter IV

"The Retreat from Long Island and the Aftermath"

By Wednesday, the 7th of August, the day passes without much change. But by nine that evening a report from Colonel Varnum arrives from Red Hook, "as many as a hundred boats coming from Staten Island, full of men. Three other ships were observed going towards your location after taking on thirty boatloads of soldiers. Everything seems to indicate a general disembarkation. The clouds, at last, are about to burst." Not quite yet, but those clouds are gathering with the other clouds and growing darker by the day indeed, and hangs over the Americans as a deepening menace on the horizon. The ships Varnum mentions, along with the soldiers that were loaded, are still in the Narrows by the 10th of August. "I was at Red Hook this morning about three o'clock," writes Greene, "It is a dangerous place, with its dank, mist-laden atmosphere, for a man born and bred in the pure air of Rhode Island, but it affords a sight that almost repays the risk; for there, in the gray morning twilight, lies the entire English fleet, just within the Narrows,-two hundred vessels in all, seven of the largest drawn up in a line nearly two miles advanced of the rest." In all fairness to Nathanael, presenting a conclusion in the fog and the sheer confusion of spars, masts and hulls, closely packed, one upon another was not a simple task. By the time he made his observation and count, the British ships more accurately numbered close to three hundred. As another night passes, the booming of a cannon breaks the silence. This would be the arrival of the Hessian fleet surely, and the hearts of the Americans sank, while the bile in their throats rose. The Hessians were a hated lot, but also feared and dreaded more than any other troops in the world. The stories of the Hessian grenadiers, in their tall mitre caps, reportedly as much as 7 and a half feet tall, with row, upon row of great spiked teeth, who devoured babies, raped women, pillaged towns, and drank the blood of their enemy, the rumors had run amuck through the American camp for weeks. But, Greene had a different perspective of the Hessians, "here they were, just off shore, and ready to devour the lovely fields, and reveling already in fancy their work of desolation. Call them victims if you must, rather, poor, deluded victims of greedy masters, driven, many of them, at the point of the bayonet; lured by some of the crown princes of Germany, by lies and misrepresentations; some drawn away by the errors of youth."

By the 14th of August, the 8,000 Hessians are seen landing on Staten Island, they parade on the beach, happy to be rid of the swaying deck of the past fourteen weeks, and glad to have solid ground under their feet once more. They then March up the hill toward the flagstaff, and are not seen again, due to the weather, which grows thick and stormy that evening. Nothing will be heard from them for days, but on the 15th Greene receives unwelcome news. Hitchcock's regiment, which has been with him since the beginning, have received orders to move to another defensive position where they are badly needed. Greene was relying on his well-trained men to be with him when the battle began. These were carefully disciplined, well drilled, well-equipped men of good order. It was because of those particular reasons that Washington was relocating them to an area he felt they would be better utilized. But Greene disagreed with his commander this time, "not only do we have as particular an attachment to the old regiments, but to be taken from me and replaced with strangers to the ground we have trained on is unbearable. I suspect the troops in their replacement are undisciplined, and badly furnished with arms to take their place. I have long been acquainted with these men who were not only attached to each other, but to this place, would support each other in time of action, as strangers are mere acquaintances of a day, and could not be expected to do the same business. You Excellency, if it can possibly be dispensed with, and absolute necessity does not require their removal, I wish them to stay." But they did go, and the militia, and the "promise of the lieutenant-colonel, has yet not come. Should they delay coming in any longer than this day, I am determined not to be trifled with, and shall let them feel my resentment by vigorous spirited exertions of military discipline, and those powers with which I am invested." Part of the militia, under the command of a Colonel Smith, do join him by the 16th, and immediately given marching orders to, "send out scouts and parties to gain intelligence. If the enemy should make their landing good on any part of the island, and hear of your coming, they may send out a party to interrupt your march. Keep a good front, flank, and rear guard at all times, to prevent being surprised and captured."

Among all of the stress of the impending battle, the "troops appear to be in exceedingly good spirits, and I have no doubt but that, if the enemy should make their attack there, he would be able to render a very good account of them." Greene reported. Meanwhile, other duties had to be performed in preparation for battle. He gives orders to, "carry out the execution the late resolve of Congress, respecting the removal of the cattle, dismantling of the mills, removing the grain already threshed, and having that which is still in sheaf so stacked and disposed of that in case of attack, it may easily be destroyed." The next day, the 17th of August, Greene is, "confined to his bed with a raging fever, but hope, through the assistance of Providence, to be able to ride, before the presence of the enemy may make it absolutely necessary," one of his aides-de-camp, W.S. Livingston writes for him. The British showed no appearance of any immediate preparation for an attack, but still the fever increased. "I am sorry to inform your Excellency," writes Livingston on the 17th, "that General Greene had a very bad night of it again last night, and cannot be said to be any better this morning than he was yesterday." His other aide-to-camp, William Blodget, writes for him the next day with better news, "The general desires me to acquaint your Excellency that he finds himself considerably better this morning; and hopes, in a few days, to be able to go abroad, though he is still weak." In the 18th century, whenever someone was describing "go abroad," they were merely speaking in terms of traveling from where they were living to another location. Unlike today, when we use the same term to describe someone who is traveling across a vast ocean.

The only action seen, is when "five small vessels, with troops on board, had made their appearance at Hog Island Inlet, and two pettyaugers off Oyster Bay, a marauding party expedition in search of livestock." Greene immediately detaches a party of five officers on horses, and 220 men. And so, the days pass on, the fever still holding Nathanael down to his bed most of the time, but his strong will making himself rise to the job at hand, and the danger of attack so imminent. But on the 20th of August, Washington fears Greene is not getting better due to the work load he puts on himself, and sends, first Sullivan, and then Putnam, to take his place, and Greene is carried over to the city to see a physician. He is then sent to the home of John Inglis in Sailors Snug Harbor, no more than four miles from his command post to that quiet suburban street, and on what is now the northwest corner of Ninth Street and Broadway. But Greene struggled with the feeling he was letting down his men and wrote to his brother Christopher, "it seems that the whole fleet, or any part of it, might land their troops at any time on the north end of Manhattan Island and cut off the whole army from any possible retreat, to bag it at leisure. I have been sick for near three weeks; for several days there was a hard struggle between nature and the disorder. Gracious God! to be confined at such a time! The misfortune is doubly great, as there was no general officer who had made himself acquainted with the ground as perfectly as I have." But the days passed and the British did not allow their movements or intentions known. However, from the time of the first arrival of the British, what form the attack would take, whether against New York or against Long Island, remained an open question, puzzling and harassing to Washington and the American command. The question would not remain open long for the nervous

Americans.

The question was at last answered on the 22nd of August. At dawn on the 22nd of August three British frigates, *Phoenix, Rose* and *Greyhound*, and two bomb ketches, *Carcass* and *Thunder*, took station in Gravesend Bay, Long Island, about a mile east of the Narrows and no more than three miles from where Major-general Nathanael Greene lay in his sick bed. Another frigate, *Rainbow,* anchored in the Narrows off Denyse Point, the part of Long Island nearest to Staten Island. Seventy-five flatboats, eleven bateaux, and two row galleys, built for the occasion and manned by sailors from the fleet, were assembled at Staten Island, and 15,000 soldiers, fully equipped for active service, along with forty field pieces which were drawn up before the British camp. At eight o'clock in the morning a British advance corps, consisting of four battalions of light infantry and Preston's 17th Light Dragoons, and a reserve of four grenadiers, the 33rd and the 42nd, or Black Watch Regiment, and Colonel Carl Von Donop's corps of Hessian grenadiers and jagers, 4,000 men in all under the command of Clinton and Cornwallis, embarked. By noon 15,000 men had been landed without opposition or delay. On the 25th of August, they were joined by two brigades of Hessian grenadiers under the command of General Philip von Heister, a seasoned veteran of the Seven-Year War. The column of Hessian and British troops was not marching under the usual pomp and rigid discipline to which these soldiers were accustomed. It was said that, "the muskets were sloped in the columns, and the soldiers and sailors seemed merry as in Holiday, and regaled themselves with the fine apples, which hung everywhere upon the trees in great abundance." It would appear that the troops of King George III felt the Americans would not be much of a challenge in the battle of Long Island.

With no American opposition up until this point, Cornwallis, with his reserve of ten battalions of light infantry and Von Donop's Hessians, captured the village of Flatbush and made camp there. The main body of army traveled on and encamped near the shore, along the road running from near the bay in the vicinity of Gravesend to New Utrecht on the west, and the camp extended from there to the Flatlands village onwards to the east. The British now occupied a broad, low plain extending from the shore northward from six miles and eastward to a distance of at least seven miles. Looking to the north from camp, the enemy now faced the most prominent feature of the terrain, and that would be their battleground. Stretching northeast from near the waterside at Gowanus Cove nearly all the way across the island and forming a barrier between the British army and the Brooklyn defenses was a ridge or range hills, varying in height from one hundred to one hundred and fifty feet high. This was called the heights of Guan, or Guian. On the southerly side, fronting the British, the rugged face of the heights rose abruptly forty to eighty feet from the plain, and continued to gradually rise to the full height of the ridge. On the northerly side, the ground sloped more gradually to the lower land below and the entire surface of this ridge was covered by dense woods and thickets that were impenetrable, except to single men on foot, and even then with great difficulty. It was completely impassable by horse-drawn artillery or by troops in formation. Only one of the roads went westerly to the end of the main ridge; the others went through at different points toward the east and away from the battle zone.

With the arrival of the British to Staten Island and their route now known, changes had to be made in the command of the American troops on Long Island. With Greene still ill in bed in New York with fever, Washington turned the command of the troops around Brooklyn over to Major General John Sullivan. This change would prove unfortunate, because Nathanael had already proven to Washington that he was more than an able commander, and that he was much more qualified to lead the troops he had been with and trained for this very endeavor. "The misfortune of my confinement is doubly great, as there was no general officer who had made himself acquainted with the ground as perfectly as I had. I have not the vanity to think the event would have been otherwise had I been there, yet I think I could have given the commanding general a good deal of necessary information." Greene would write to his brother after the battle on the 30th. Hindsight is 20/20 and we will never know, but logic dictates that the turn of battle may have changed somewhat if Greene had been in charge at the time. We know that Nathanael had a thorough knowledge of the Long Island terrain, while Sullivan knew little of the lay of the land and this would prove costly during the battle and the ensuing retreat. To make matters even worse, by the 24th, Major General Israel Putnam superseded Sullivan in general command on Long Island, with Sullivan retained as Putnam's subordinate. Putnam knew practically nothing of the topography of the island, and further, was totally unfit for the control of this vital position which he was now put in charge. Along with these changes, others cropped up at the same time. Washington immediately sent Mile's Pennsylvania riflemen to help defend Brooklyn on receiving orders of the British landing. With the Connecticut regiments, New York Independent companies, Drake's minutemen, and several musketry battalions, this meant that of the 5,800 men on the Brooklyn lines more than two-thirds were made up of militia. These men were historically undependable, and would run at the first cracks of musketry, even behind entrenchment's, and were totally unreliable when made to stand-up fight in an open field situation.

Although Washington knew of the enemy's landing on Long Island, he was led to believe by his intelligence reports that the enemies' troops amounted to no more than eight or nine thousand, a minor part of the entire force. He then deduced by this that the British were only planning an attack on "our works on the Island and this city at the same time," and thus retained three-quarters of his whole army on the New York side, including many of the better skilled regiments. In reality, the major portion of the British and Hessian troops and most of its general officers were on Long Island, and that without a doubt the grand attack and in fact, the only immediate attack, was to take place in Brooklyn. Because of poor intelligence reports, Washington sent no reinforcements and left the majority of his reserves, about 2,000 dependable regimental soldiers from Smallwood's Maryland and Haslet's Delaware regulars. Washington was also expecting an immediate attack, and by the 24th, when no attack had come, Washington began to get nervous. Howe was settled in and in no hurry at all. Von Donop on the other hand made a move against Bedford Pass, evidently just to try it out, but they met a sharp fire from Hand's corps. Von Donop's troops returned to their former position, but not before they burned some houses they had held, and the Americans retired to their post on the ridge. But by the afternoon of the 26th, Cornwallis, leaving the Black Watch and the Hessians in the Flatbush camp, moved the rest of his troops to the Flatlands village, where the British headquarters had been established. This movement to Flatlands should have indicated to an American intelligence observer that neither Flatbush nor Bedford Pass was to be the scene of the main attack, but obviously none of the American troops stationed on the ridge seemed to notice the movement or just did not understand its meaning.

Later that evening Washington had come over from visiting Greene in New York and checking his condition. Finding him, "with no strength or appetite and scarcely able to sit up for more than an hour at a time," he knew he would have to proceed into battle with the British without one of his most able and trusted general officers. By this time Washington had come to the realization that the major strength of the British was on Long Island, and that "the grand push" was going to be against Brooklyn. He then ordered more men over and with this, put Putnam's command on Long Island to about 7,000 men fit for duty. But on their left, more than a mile and a half distant at the Flatbush Pass, in what would be the center of the battle lines, was a detachment of Rhode Island and Massachusetts Continental troops under the command of lieutenant colonels Elias Cornell and William Henshaw, along with a detachment of Connecticut Continentals, with fewer than 1,000 men in all. There, they held a very crude fortification of fallen trees, and mounting all of three 18-pound cannons and one howitzer. At the Bedford Pass, about a mile to the east were stationed Colonel Samuel Wyllys and his Connecticut Continentals and Colonel John Chester's State Regiment, about 800 men, with three guns and a fortification like that at Flatbush Pass. Another 400 Pennsylvania riflemen rounded out the troops, thus bringing the total to a paltry 2,800 along more than three miles of the densely wooded ridge in separate detachments, no visible communication between them except sentinels that had been stationed at regular intervals. It was a long, thin line; pierced at any point, it would surely give way, and facing them on the plain below were seven times their number; crack, efficient, dependable, man for man, one could speculate that that would make the number twice that of the Americans with the enemy's experience behind them.

At dawn of the 27th of August, 5,000 British veterans of General Grant's troops marched up the Jamaica Road and swung left at the Red Lion Inn. It was noted by one of the American observers afterward that the sun that morning "rose with a red and angry glare, as if portending the coming of evils." At about eight-thirty in the morning, the first sounds of artillery fire could be heard by the detachment that was guarding the Gowanus Road, and by the time it was all over by noon of August 27th, all the Americans that had escaped death or capture were within the fortified lines on Long Island, expecting with anxiety a concentrated attack, for which none came. Perhaps about 9,500 men were within those works, with nearly 14,000 British troops no more than 150 rods from Fort Putnam. Greene would write from his sick bed, "Great events, sometimes depend upon very little causes...I think, from this manoeuvre, the General purposes to retreat to King's Bridge, and there make the grand stand....If this is the determination, two to one New York lay in ashes." Nathanael's brother Christopher was with him during the days of the battle, and brought news from the field as fast as they could gather it. When Nathanael had heard how hard Smallwood's regiment had taken casualties, he wept uncontrollably for hours. During those anxious, forty-eight hours of battle, there was no more anxious, heavier heart than that of Nathanael Greene's. By the morning of the 28th, the British had dug trenches and built a breastwork that was a menace of disaster to the Americans. For two days following the Battle of Long Island, the Americans held their position. That afternoon a northeasterly storm blew in and a downpour ensued. The rain continued all day and all of the next day after that. The camp became a quagmire, with ankle deep water with the fort and in some parts of the entrenchment's the men stood waist-deep in muddy water. They had brought none of their tents during the retreat and so their clothing was drenched, and their ammunition soaked through. Even those men who had some how managed to keep a few of the paper gunpowder cartridges dry could never hope to use them. The muskets were practically worthless, as all of the flints, priming pans, barrels, and touchholes were also too wet.

Howe was reluctant to storm the works immediately, the memory of Bunker Hill was still fresh in his mind. He had learned a hard lesson about the steadfastness and the deadly fire the Americans could rain down on their advisory. It is believed, and can be debated for some time to come, that the minutemen at the redoubt on Breed's Hill saved hundreds of lives on the American side at Long Island the day after the retreat. That hard lesson can be the only reason Howe was waited for two, three, and even a fourth day after the battle. If he had stormed the American works immediately, and followed it with a charge of bayonets on the American lines the British could have easily finished the war right then and there. The Americans were in no shape to fight, and had few bayonets to go up against the British and even fewer men who knew how to use one. The only other answer that it could have been was that Howe assumed that his brother's fleet could prevent an all out American retreat, and that the expense of a full frontal assault was not worth the cost. Howe was known as a veritable Caesar on the battlefield throughout his tenure as Commanding General of his Majesty's troops, Howe was commonly sluggish before and after the fighting. Some historians even theorize that Howe may have been more than a little sympathetic with the Americans cause, and down right bristled at the King and his ministers continued diplomatic policies. It is said that Howe may have secretly wished to join the side of the Americans, rather than fight them but was unwilling to give up all of his money, homes and land holding in the name of the cause. It can only be speculated at the reason and thoughts behind his generalship.

On the morning of the 29th Washington decided that time was on their side. The longer the British waited to attack their impoverished army, the more Washington realized that he was getting a second lease on tomorrow. He ordered General William Heath at Kingsbridge and Hugh Hughes, assistant Quartermaster General in New York, to gather every boat of every sort fit for transporting troops and to assemble them on the New York side by that evening. Was he planning to retreat? He would not say, but contradicted his orders to Heath and ordered the lines reinforced. But Washington and his generals agreed that it was "eligible to remove the Army to New York." Retreat. If the truth had leaked out to the shelterless, famished, penned up militia and volunteers a panic to be the first in the boats would have issued. But Washington quickly issued the following order: "As the sick are an encumbrance to the Army & Troops are expected from the flying camp in New Jersey, under General Mercer, cover is wanted for the new troops, the Regt's are immediately to have such sick and wounded men removed...As the above Forces under Gen'l Mercer are expected this afternoon and proposes to relieve a proportionate & make change in the situation. Therefore, men with their Arms, Accouterments and Knapsacks, at 7 o'clock are to parade at the Head of the encampment and there wait for Orders." Washington could lie with the best of them when needed. He told a least half a dozen of them in that one order.

At dusk the boats began to arrive. Two amphibious regiments, Glover's from Marblehead and Hutchinson's from Salem, Massachusetts, all fishermen or sailors, took charge of the crossing. Between nine and ten o'clock the regiments on parade were drawn off one by one, the volunteers and militia first. With everything they owned on their shoulders or on their backs they marched to the ferry landing for embarking. One regiment would be marched into their place or extended while another marched into their place and so on and so on. The embarkation had to be performed in the utmost silence and orderliness, and in fact was begun in almost complete darkness. The work continued until men, as well as stores of ammunition, supplies, provisions and pieces of artillery were brought to the landing. At two o'clock in the morning, with everything seeming to go without a problem, an error occurred that might have been fatal to the entire American army. Major Alexander Scammell, acting as aide-de-camp to Washington, went to General Mifflin and told him that the boats for the covering party were waiting and he was to march his men to the landing at once. In spite of Mifflin's protest that there must be some mistake, Scammell insisted that there was no mistake. Mifflin called the sentinels and advanced posts in, and the entire detachment abandoned the front lines and marched toward the landing. They were well on their way when they met Washington, who was inspecting the retreat progress. He was horrified when he saw the Mifflin detachment and thought they were deserting their post and duty. "Good God!" Washington exclaimed, "General Mifflin, I am afraid you have ruined us by unseasonably withdrawing the troops from the lines." 'I did it by your order, sir.' Mifflin answered angrily, and Washington said that it could not be so. 'By God sir, I did.' said Mifflin. Washington replied that it was a dreadful mistake, that there was confusion at the ferry, and unless the covering party could resume their posts before the enemy discovered their abandonment, "the most disagreeable consequences would follow." Washington was always known for the masterpiece of understatement. The troops were about-faced and returned to their post, which had been unguarded for over an hour. Major-general Heath characterizes the immediate return of these men to their posts as "an instance of absolute discipline and true fortitude. Whoever has seen troops in a similar situation, or duly contemplated the human heart in such trials, will know how to appreciate the conduct of these brave men on this occasion."

To those troops holding the line within the sound of the British working with pickaxes and shovels scraping the earth no more than one hundred yards away, the night must have been the longest of their lives. If they were not called to leave soon, these few hundred would be forced to face an attack from thousands. Near the break of dawn, at last the order was received to embark, and the steadfast battalions marched away at quick step. At about this same time, a small British reconnoitering party was investigating the American lines. They had grown suspicious of the unnatural silence with the American lines, and were already creeping up to spy on the camp just as Mifflin's detachment was departing. Within thirty minutes the British pickets were inside the American works and sounding the alarm of the Americans' retreat. If they hurried, there was still time to at least catch the rear guard at the landing and score a morale victory, but Nature again played a part in this outcome. As the sun slowly rose that hot August morning, a dense fog settled in as well. Within minutes the British could barely see ten rods in front of them, and after a short march could not see at any distance. Under the same cover the last boats with the last regiment and Washington himself pushed off from the debacle that was the Battle of Long Island. Although Washington was disappointed in the outcome, he knew his army could have fared much worse indeed. By seven o'clock in the morning the hardy Marblehead fishermen of Glover's regiment and Hutchinson's skilled Salem boatmen had rowed and sailed 9,500 men, all of their baggage, filed guns, horses, equipment, stores, and provisions, "even the biscuits which had not been and raw pork which had not been eaten" were safe in New York. Major General Nathanael Greene still lay in his sick bed in New York, but was able to write to his brother of the event, "the works, indeed, with which we had toiled so hard to make impregnable, are lost, but men, equipage, baggage, and his Excellency are saved. It was the best effected retreat I have ever read of or heard of, considering the difficulties." Charles Stedham, an officer with the British army wrote at the time, "particularly glorious. No military operation was ever conducted by a great captain with more ability and prudence." Other great men of the day called the retreat, "one of the most single achievements of the war," and, "a master stroke of energy, dexterity and caution, by which Washington saved not only his army, but his country as well." Also, "a feat that seemed impossible." And finally, from General Francis Vinton Greene, a military critic of distinction of the day, said, "A more skillful operation of this kind was never conducted." But, it also exposed Washington, and Howe as having a lack of respective abilities as military leaders. Howe for failing to follow up his first success with an assault on the Americans lines that easily could have finished the war. And Washington, although brilliant in retreating, was less than masterful in allowing the British to encircle his army at the Jamaica Pass and exposing his inadequate force.

The results of the battle created a great sensation on both sides of the Atlantic. The surrender of Boston was devastating to the English, and news of the retreat in America was looked on as a terrible defeat. Silas Deane, an American agent in Paris trying to drum up support from the French wrote, "The last check on Long Island has sunk or credit to nothing. I must start all over again." Throughout America disappointment and gloom were widespread. Greene, still at the home of John Inglis, but finally able to get out of his sick bed wrote to Washington, "The city is in a panic. It seems as if the entire country is struck with it." Washington himself was said to be in a great depression, and wrote to Congress that the defeat had, "dispirited too great a proportion of our troops and filled their minds with apprehension and despair. The militia...are dismayed, intractable and impatient to return to their homes. Great numbers of them have gone off; in some instances, almost by whole regiments...their example had infected the whole part of the army. I am obliged to confess my want of confidence in the generality of the troops." Washington urged Congress to put no dependence on "the militia or other troops than those enlisted and embodied. Our liberties might be lost if their defence is left to any but a permanent army; one must exist during war." Washington and Greene had been screaming for a "standing army" since the war began. Congress finally overcame its dread and resolved on September 16th, 1776 that eighty-eight battalions be enlisted "as soon as possible to serve during the present war."

If the morale of the American army was not already at its lowest, the fever that had brought Nathanael to his knees was now rampant throughout one fourth of the army. Within nine days after the retreat, sickness and depression made it difficult to comfort these sick men, and with inadequate general and regimental hospitals, and the incompetence of the regimental surgeons, many men who had fought fearlessly against the British army and survived the bloody Battle of Long Island, was now being carried by a comrade to the hospital, or even the grave. A more pressing matter at hand also had to be addressed also. Where was the army to go now? Should they run and gamble the lives of New York as well as have the city set to the torch or stay and guard the city against the superior enemy and not only lose the city, but the entire army as well? Greene, almost completely cured of his sickness, sat with pen in hand and explained his thoughts to his Commander-in-chief. "Your Excellency; The object under considerations, whether a general and speedy retreat from this island is necessary or to stay. It would appear to me the only eligible plan to oppose the enemy successfully, and secure ourselves from disgrace. I think we have no object on this side of King's Bridge. Our troops are now scattered that one part may be cut off before the others can come to their support. Should the enemy make a run up the North River with several ships force, and a number of transports at the same time, and effect a landing between the town and the middle division of the army; another party from Long Island should land right opposite; these two parties form a line across the island, and intrench themselves. The two flanks of this line could easily be supported by the enemies shipping; the centre, fortified with redoubts, would render it very difficult if not impossible to cut our way through. It has been agreed that the city of New York would not be tenable if the enemy got possession of Long Island and Governor's Island. They are now in possession of both places. To hold this unfit place, notwithstanding, would be to hold it to a great disadvantage. The city and island of New York are no objects for us. Part of the army already has met with a defeat, any capital loss at this time may completely ruin the cause. Tis our business to study and avoid any considerable misfortune, and to take post where the enemy will be obliged to fight us on our terms. The sacrifice of this vast property has no influence upon his Excellency's measures. Remember the King of France. When Charles the Fifth, Emperor of Germany, invaded his kingdom, he laid whole providences to waste, and by that policy starved and ruined Charles's army; and defeated him without even fighting a battle. Two thirds of the city of New York and its suburbs belongs to the Tories. We have no great reason to run considerable risk for its defence. I give it as my opinion, that a general and speedy retreat is absolutely necessary, and that the honor and interest of America require it. If the enemy gets possession of the city, we never can recover it without a superior naval force to theirs; which we do not have at this time. If the city once gets into the enemy's hands, it will be at their mercy either to destroy it or save it. The temptation of the general market, and the supply of the sake of gain to the city's people will make it nearly impossible to keep possession of it for a long period of time. Allow the enemy to use it as they will until after they have made use of it as they think proper. At a retreat I would order the army to take the King's Bridge, post along Westchester shore, where barracks can be procured for a part of the army and tents used for the rest. If my zeal has led me to say more than I ought, I hope my good intentions may atone for the offense. I shall only add that these sentiments are not dictated from fear, nor from my apprehension of personal danger; but are the result of a cool and deliberate survey of our situation, which I had much time to contemplate during my long illness. Should your Excellency agree with me with respect to the first two points, that is, that a speedy and general retreat is necessary, and also that the city should be burned, I would advise to call a general council upon that question, and take every general officer's opinion upon the question."

The same questions were agitating Washington's own mind. He writes to Congress on the 2nd of September, "Till of late I had no doubt in my own mind of defending this place; nor should I have yet, if the men would do their duty; but this I dispair of....If I should be obliged to abandon the town, ought it to stand as winter-quarters for the enemy?" This, and on the heels of Greene's letter, did not improve Washington's mood, and on the 7th, laid the situation of the army before the council of general officers which he calls at Greene's suggestion. But, an exaggerated importance is attached to the preservation of New York, and Congress decides for them that the army is compelled to leave it with "no damage" and abandoning the "poor city." The council, by a large majority, decides to try and hold the city with 5,000 men, and post the rest of the army at King's Bridge and other intermediate points. Greene left the council-room with a heavy heart, but by no means ready to accept the decision as final. It was a delicate thing to do, the lowest major-general of the army to request a reconsideration of the council's decision before a full board of general officers, and it was a still more delicate matter, and would still be looked on even today as rebellious, to collect the opinions of subordinates on a matter that had already been discussed and determined by superior officers. But this was just another excellent example of Nathanael Greene's ideas of how men in an important situation such as this, should not make a rash or halfhearted determination without fully weighing all of the options. After consulting almost all of the subordinate field officers and most of the general-officers once again, Greene presented Washington a petition for a second council on the 11th of September. It was signed by Nixon, Mifflin, Beall, Parsons, Wadsworth, and Scott; his name standing at the head of the others, and the only major-general on the list. It would seem that Washington, feeling the same way in this matter, was waiting for just such a turn of events, because the very next day at General McDougall's headquarters, the decision of the first council was reversed with only three dissenting voices, Spencer, Clinton, and Heath. 8,000 men were to be left "for the defence of Fort Washington and its dependencies" and the remaining army would march out within the next few days.

Every nerve in Greene's body was now strained as the removal of stores, baggage, and the sick seemed to drag on forever. A general lack of transport was the problem, although every horse and wagon that could be procured in the town was pressed into service. Even boats were used to ship the cargo up the Hudson, but both methods were too little, too late. Twelve precious days had already been wasted, and by the 15th of September, Howe landed at Kip's and Turtle Bay, at the end of what is now Thirty-fourth Street. Howe knew that the American army would be stretched over a large area of the city and the surrounding area in a defensive position, with its weakest element midway between the two ends, and so decided to cut it in two and defeat the ends separately. And on the 13th, four frigates, the *Phoenix* and *Roebuck* with 44 guns each, and the *Orpheus* with 32, and the *Carysfort* with 28, passed up, and "in supreme Contempt of the Rebels and their Works, did not fire a Gun." By the 14th, another warship and six transports joined them, and the *Renown* with 50 guns, the *Repulse* and *Pearl* with 32 each, and an armed schooner, also went up the Hudson, daring the American batteries, which fired on them "as furiously as they could," but with little effect. The British anchored above the American works, and thus prevented the further removal of stores from the city by water. The stage was set for the next act. Howe was ready to attack Manhattan.

From the first appearance of the enemy on the waters of New York, great pains were made to secure New Jersey and open communications with Philadelphia. The flying camp was still, barely in operation, and the militia was called out to build works at important points on the Jersey side of the river. Special importance had been attached to the building of Fort Constitution, on what would become the old Palisades Amusement Park. It was hoped, with Fort Washington on the opposite bank of the Hudson, that it could effectively command the passage of the river, and thus secure both the country above and the crossings at the ferries. General Mercer and General Livingston were stationed at Fort Washington, and had been active in every measure of the construction and the intelligence reports given to Washington from their vantage point. Greene was ordered to take command of the Jerseys, with his headquarters in Fort Constitution. The detachment in the fort was composed of three brigades, Nixon's Clinton's, and Irvine's, with two regiments commanded by Bradley and Dey, and finally the militia, forming a total of 5,707 present, with 3,521 rank and file, fit for duty. The position Greene commanded was one of the most important he had ever been given, and was highly flattered by the great responsibility and confidence Washington was showing in him. That trust would not be misplaced or wasted. During the days surrounding the action in and around New York, Committee of

Correspondence member, William Duer, was at a dinner, when the question of Washington's safety was posed. The conversation ensued with several high ranking officers about the possibility of Washington being killed, and who, in case of such a misfortune, was best qualified to take his place. Duer would write later, "Within a heartbeat, the name was spoken by each and every man in unison, Greene, it was acknowledged by all, was the proper man to become commander." Everything now depended upon whether the American army was able to make a stand before the enemy, and keep them at bay, or at least retard their advance and draw out the campaign without giving them an opportunity to strike another blow like the one they suffered on Long Island.

On the morning of Sunday, September 15th, five warships took station in the East River, in a line from Kip's Bay towards the south at about two hundred yards from the shore. At ten o'clock eighty-four flatboats laden with British soldiers put out in four divisions from the Long Island shore. By eleven, the ships opened fire on the entrenchment's along the New York side of the river, "such a fire as nothing could withstand. About 70 large pieces of Cannon were in lay, together with Swivels & small arms, making so terrible and so incessant a Roar of Guns few even in the Army & Navy had ever heard before." All of this fire was poured upon the American entrenchment's at Kip's Bay held by Captain William Douglas with a brigade of Connecticut militia. An entrenchment may have been too strong a word to call them. In fact, they were nothing more than a ditch dug along the bank of the river, with the dirt thrown out towards the water in a pile. The boats came up with the line of ships, and the fire ceased, but the boats came on, crowded with redcoats and looking for a good place to land. They reached the shore at Kip's Bay and the light infantry leaped out, and clambered up the steep and barely accessible rocks of the hill, finding no one opposing them. Douglas's troops, their scrawny defensive position already beaten down by the cannonade, had fled "with the utmost precipitation at the sight of the British." Wadsworth's brigade, next below them, followed suit, with Parson's and Scott's militia, farther south, taking note of these goings on, retreated up the Bowery Road at a run.

Washington, at Harlem when he heard the sound of the bombardment, took horse and rode full speed to the scene of the action. On the Post Road, now Lexington Avenue, about where Forty-second Street crosses it, he met Douglas' men, still retreating precipitately and in great confusion. "The demons of fear and disorder seemed to take full possession of all and everything that day," one of them said later. Parson's brigade, also in complete disarray hurrying north for safety's sake, was right behind them. Washington tried to halt them, to rally them, "Take the walls men." he cried. "Take the cornfield!" Some ran to the walls, others to the cornfields. With Putnam and several other officers he tried to form them behind the walls, but there was no controlling them. Washington's anger was spectacular as he, "dashed his hat upon the ground in a transport of rage." Crying out, "Are these the men with whom I am to defend America?" He even snapped a pistol at them, and with a riding cane, "he flogged not only private soldiers, but officers as well," a colonel, even a brigadier general, but nothing would do. At the sight of sixty or seventy Hessians coming at them they broke, flung away their muskets, knapsacks, even coats and hats and ran "as if the Devil himself was after them." It was said later that the ground was literally covered with such discarded encumbrances that you could not walk without stepping on one or the other. And there they left Washington, practically alone, and within eighty yards of the oncoming Hessians. Blinded by rage or with despair, he sat upon his horse, taking no heed of his imminent danger. He would have been shot or captured had an aide-de-camp not seized his bridle and "absolutely hurried him away to safety."

Putnam, seeing that that no stand could be made, galloped south right through what remained of Wadsworth's and Scott's brigades coming on in full retreat, to attempt the rescue of Sullivan's brigade, Knox's artillery, and the others still in the town before the British could stretch across the island and hem them in. He gathered what troops he could find in the city, abandoned the heavy guns and the remaining military stores, and started north. But he knew as little of the geography of

Manhattan as he had known of Long Island. The Post Road on the easterly side, the main artery leading north and the only one he knew, was held by the enemy. He would have easily found himself hopelessly trapped, had not a young Aaron Burr, his aide-de-camp, guided him to an unfrequented road along the west side, close to the Hudson. The day was becoming intensely hot, and dust hung in stifling clouds above the troops' heads. The water in their canteens had already been exhausted, and with the dust in their parched throats, sweat streaming from their faces, they slogged along dejectedly. It was hard to keep them moving at a reasonable speed, but Putnam now displayed his best native qualities, courage and energy. He rode up and down the two-mile long column, heartening his men, hurrying them along. They met a detachment of the enemy, beat it off, and at long last, well after dark, ended their twelve-mile exhausting march in the main camp at Harlem, where the rest of the army had now collected.

The first division of the British army was led by Howe, Clinton, Cornwallis, Vaughan, Matthews, Leslie, and Von Donop. It comprised three battalions of light infantry, four battalions of British grenadiers, three of Hessian grenadiers and jagers, and the brigade of British Guards, about 4,000 in all. Immediately upon landing, Leslie and the light infantry swung to the right. Von Donop's Hessian grenadiers turned left, and met Wadworth's retreating New York militia in the middle, and after a short engagement captured over three hundred and fifty of them. During that afternoon detachments of the British forces had ranged about, picking up prisoners here and there, sometimes single men and sometimes entire companies. The Americans lost 17 officers and 450 men that day, nearly all of them captives; very few were killed in the limited engagements. But the Americans also lost about sixty cannons and a considerable amount of ammunition, stores, and baggage that had been left behind in the city. That night, the British rested in comfort, in their billeted houses and barns, and had set up hundreds of tents in a camp that stretched across the island from Bloomingdale on the Hudson to Horn's Hook on the East river. The Americans were not so lucky, sleeping in their hastily dug entrenched lines on Harlem Heights. "our soldiers," wrote Colonel David Humphrey, "excessively fatigued by the sultry march of the day, their clothes wet by a severe shower of rain that succeeded towards the evening, their blood chilled by the cold wind...their hearts sunk within them at the loss of baggage, artillery, and the works in which they had been taught to put great confidence, lay upon their arms, covered only in the clouds of an uncomfortable sky." The wild flight that was Kip's Bay was a sad exhibition of the army's discipline. Washington called it "disgraceful and dastardly," but it isn't fair to give those men such harsh epithets. Douglas' men were ill trained, inexperienced, and not well disciplined soldiers; they were raw militia. When their puny defenses were battered by cannonade before their eyes, and a well-trained foe of overwhelming numbers attacked, it was purely human nature that they would merely turn and run in self-preservation. It would be repeated several times in the coming months. Only by training regular, experienced soldiers into disciplined, seasoned veterans who would turn the tide of battle in the positive for the Americans.

While Washington and his beaten army were camped in their retreated position of Harlem Heights, Howe encamped no more than a mile from their lines. Washington had much confidence in the strength of his position, but not in the steadfastness of his troops. In the early morning of the 16th, a small corps of rangers, about 120 volunteers chosen chiefly from the Connecticut regiments for detached duty, scouting, and such, were out on patrol under the command of Captain Thomas Knowlton, "a fine figure of not, over six feet high, erect and elegant in figure and formed more for activity than strength," wrote Greene, "cool and courageous in battle, courteous and affable in manners, one of my favorite subordinates, and a favorite to many of the superior officers and his soldiers in camp." While across the American positions, across the Hollow Way, and up through the woods, just a short distance from where the main body of the enemy lay, Knowlton and his company came upon a stone house. At about the same instant, they came upon pickets for two battalions of British light infantry under General Leslie, who was using the house as an advance scout post. At the alarm, about 400 light infantry advanced, and the Rangers took a position behind a stone wall and opened fire. The American had fired about eight rounds when they realized that the 42nd Highlanders, the Black watch, was coming up on their left and threaten to out flank them. Ten of Knowlton's men had fallen by this time, and he gave the order to retreat. The British light infantry pushed forward after them through the woods, but the Rangers got away in good order. As Knowlton's men came within sight of the American camp, the sound of the firing alerted the camp and they started to form up for an attack. When the light infantry saw the American army under arms, they were just within sight by the Americans, emerging from a clump of woods, hot on the trails of Knowlton's men, but halted at the edge of the plateau, out of musket shot of the Americans. Pleased by the Rangers in retreat, the British "in the most insulting manner sounded their bugle-horns as is usual after a Fox-chase. I have never felt such a sensation before--it seemed to crown our disgrace," a Colonel Joseph Reed wrote to his wife days later. Washington, the old fox hunter, certainly recognized the taunting notes of the horns as the customary signal of a fox gone to earth. On top of yesterday's affair at Kip's Bay it must have been too much for the commander-in-chief to bear. He immediately planned a frontal feint with a small force to draw the British light infantry down to the open ground of the Hollow Way, so that a stronger detachment could encircle their right flank and cut them off. For the feint, he ordered out 150 volunteers from Nixon's brigade, led by Lieutenant Colonel Archibald Crary of Rhode Island. Knowlton's rangers and three companies of riflemen from Weedon's 3rd Virginia Regiment, under the command of Major Andrew Leitch, were to be the flanking party, about 230 men in all.

Crary's detachment advanced boldly down the Hollow Way. Responding to this challenge the British light infantry "immediately ran down the Hill, took up possession of some fences and bushes and a smart fighting began, but at too great a distance to much execution on either side." Crary's men fell back to draw the enemy on, still maintaining their constant fire. Nixon's brigade, about 800 men, were sent down to support them and give more credence to the attack. By now, the flanking party, guided by Colonel Joseph Reed, was making its way through the woods to the east of the fighting. Within a few hundred yards, it was about to spring the trap on the light infantry and sweep around the rear of the enemy. For some reason a few of the "inferior officers" could not restrain their glee, or perhaps could not control their nerves, either or both, but they gave the order too fire too early. The British realized the danger they were in and promptly withdrew to a safe distance about two hundred yards behind from where there were. Crary's men followed them, and the flankers joined in the fight. The fire on both sides was described by one participant as "extremely hot and continued for some time." Meanwhile, on top of the height and within ten minutes of each other, the two flanking party commanders, Knowlton and Leitch, fell mortally wounded. Here was the chance for the Rangers and Virginia riflemen, both now leaderless, to breakup in confusion and repeat the disgrace of Kip's Bay. But this time, they were the pursuers and seeing the back of the red coats must have been a stimulating sight. The company commanders took charge and pressed the men "with splendid spirit and animation and continued the engagement with the greatest resolution. Washington sent in reinforcements and watched from the height as his little affair, involving a few hundred, now was growing into quite a battle. His men were redeeming themselves from yesterday's disgrace. The fighting grew hotter, the Americans firing steadily and the British stubbornly holding their ground. As more of the American reinforcements came on, Leslie called on the British reserve in that quarter for more troops. From their post three miles in the rear, on the run "without a halt to draw breath" came British grenadiers, the 33rd of Foot Regiment, a battalion of Hessian grenadiers, and a company of their jagers, along with two field pieces, brought the number of British engaged up to 5,000 men.

For two hours, from noon to two o'clock, the combat was spirited to say the least. The British guns fired over sixty rounds, while the Hessians and Scotsmen, their ammunition almost out, retreated.

The Americans followed in hot pursuit for some distance. The rest of the British reserve was near at hand and looking to get into the fight. Washington, seeing the little affair was developing into a full force general engagement, which had not been his contention, sent orders to disengage and withdraw to camp. "The pursuit of a flying enemy was so new a scene that it was difficult for our men to be brought to retire." The losses on both sides are sketchy. Both sides tended to minimize their losses and exaggerate the others casualties, but a conservative estimate had the British with 14 killed and about 78 wounded, the Hessians losing 70 dead and 200 wounded, and the Scots with 24 dead and 100 wounded. Washington said his losses were "about sixty," but were probably closer to 30 killed and 100 wounded or missing. With the deaths of Knowlton and Leitch, the Americans suffered their severest losses by far. Knowlton was in Greene's words, "a valuable and gallant officer. His loss will be felt by myself as well as this army for the remainder of the war." Though gallantly fought on both sides, still it was just a small engagement. Yet its effects in both camps were immediate and extremely important, especially for the Americans. Among the Americans, the depression by the recent succession of defeats and retreats was dispelled. Many of the soldiers who had fled from Kip's Bay without firing a shot had now helped drive the British and Hessian regulars back more than a mile, had fought them in the open at forty yards for more than an hour, and had withdrawn in good order to their own lines only when commanded to do so, without being pursued. Caesar Rodney wrote to his brother about the event, "That New England men placed to defend the landing place (Kips's Bay), behaved in a most dastardly, cowardly, scandalous manner, is most certain; but that courage is not always to be found the same, even in the same person, is equally true, and verified in the very same men; for some of them the day following were in the other engagement and behaved with great bravery." Even more so, the "Southern" and New England troops had fought side by side with equal courage; neither could criticize the other. Teamwork and camaraderie between the southern and northern colonies was something that had been sorely lacking since the beginning of the war. Another, less obvious benefit, was that for the first time in the war the British witnessed a rebel army that was capable of fighting. It was quite an eye-opening experience to the British and Hessian soldiers. Up until then, the Americans had not exactly distinguished themselves on any battlefield other than Bunker Hill, and the British command was more than a little concerned that this could turn into a trend and end the reign of the British army's superiority on the battlefields of America.

The next face-to-face confrontation around New York for the King's troops and the rebels would be at Throg's Neck and Pelham. Greene would write, "It seems very strange then, and seems very foolish now, that Sir William Howe, after taking possession of New York, should wait so long before he again puts his army in motion. Our army are now so strongly fortified, and so much out of the command of their shipping, we have little more to fear this campaign." With a more well organized army that would certainly be true. But even with the morale victory of Harlem Heights now under the Americans belt, the British and Hessian armies were still a far superior force than that of the Americans in every aspect. Howe was planning something, but Washington and his general officers could not agree in their series of councils what that move might be. Several of the officers believed that Howe would try and become master of the entire island, and thought the reduction in force of Fort Washington would be first attempted. The stronghold, on a height overlooking the Hudson, was a mile or so behind the rear of the American lines, and it was not all too clear what plan for its conquest by the British, also involved a frontal attack on Washington's entrenchment's first. Others of his general staff, including Greene, looked for a landing at some point on Long Island Sound to the rear of the Americans more northerly defenses, and in that way Washington would be flanked. Since Washington and his generals could not agree on a particular opinion, they decided in council to guard against either or both scenarios occurring. Ten thousand men were held on Manhattan Island near Fort Washington, and another 10,000 would be held at the King's Bridge sector of the upper end of the Harlem River. A floating bridge was quickly constructed across that body of water so that reliable communication lines with the other troops could be maintained. Greene would continue to command 5,000 men on the other side of the Hudson at and around Fort Constitution.

On the 22nd of September, Washington summoned Greene to his headquarters. He was selecting Nathanael for the command of communications master with Congress. Washington felt the necessity of having a man that he could call upon with confidence for other duties besides those of watching the enemy and leading men into battle. Greene writes to the president of Congress the next day, "I have been instructed by his Excellency to send and express to acquaint you that the army are in great want of a large supply of cartridges, which no person can be spared to make; therefore he requests that you will order all that are now made in Philadelphia to be sent forward in light wagons that can travel with great dispatch, as they are really very much wanted; and, as none can be made up here, that persons be employed at Philadelphia to continue at that business to furnish a full supply for the army. Commissary Lowry is also in great want of a supply of salt, which he begs may be sent to Trenton, to enable him to furnish provisions for the army at King's Bridge, as the supplies from Connecticut may shortly be cut off; I have great reason to believe the evil will soon take place, if not wholly, in part." From this day forward, Washington would rely heavily on Greene's communication with Congress and stack a great multitude of important and trivial request to Congress which Nathanael would carefully dispatch with a watchful eye. No request received a lesser amount of watchfulness, whether it is large or small.

These became days of intense anxiety for the American army, knowing the British were planning an attack, but not knowing when. Everytime the British were on the move, Greene could see from his lookout on the Palisades, "Whig families hurrying unprotected before them, with their clothing and a scanty supply of provisions, seeking shelter for the coming winter, not knowing where." This was a painful reality of war that Nathanael did not particularly care for, and thought it could easily be his own family in those same dire straits. Washington in the meantime, was in the midst of an accounting of troop totals. On paper Washington had 25,000 men, but only on paper. At present he really only had 16,000 on station and fit for duty, and a large portion of these men were militia, no more to be depended on than "a broken staff," Washington was known to put it. On the 22nd of September, Washington, fully realizing the difficult position he and his men were in, wrote to his brother, "to describe the task I have to perform. Fifty thousand pounds would not induce me again to undergo what I have done." Meanwhile, Greene had his hands full as well with the British Navy. Early in October three frigates went up the river apparently unharmed, "a gentleman on board one of them walking along the second deck, seemingly in command, as if nothing was happening, and seven forts keeping up a constant fire at the ships with little effect." Greene would write. But on several occasions, shots were seen striking the ships, and great care was taken to keep men below decks whenever possible to reduce the harm. The *Phoenix* and *Rose* continued to run up and down the river, keeping close to the western shore, trying to avoid what seemed to be a well-directed fire from Fort Washington's guns. It was assumed, that if the passage of the British ships could not be completely prevented, they would at least render the trip extremely hazardous.

"This being a critical hour," Greene writes to the president of Congress, "when the hopes and fears of the country and city are continually alarmed, and yesterday there was considerable heavy cannonade for most of the day. A ship moved up river early in the morning on the 22nd, and began a brisk cannonade upon our shore. Colonel Magaw, who commanded at Fort Washington, got down an eighteen-pounder and fired sixty rounds at her; twenty-six went through her. The gun was mostly loaded with chain-shot. The confusion and distress that appeared on board the ship exceeds all description, and without a doubt she lost a great number of her men. She was towed off by four other boats sent to her assistance; she slipped her cable and left her anchor. Had the tide run flood one half hour longer, we could have easily sunk her. A cannonade and fire with small arms continued at Throg's Neck almost all day with very little intermission. We lost only one man, but several of the enemy were killed; two or three our people got brought off the field, and several more had to be left there. The firing did not cease until late in the evening, and has not been renewed as of this morning." General Heath, who was involved in the battle praised it as "a pretty affair...conducted with good address." Like Glover's little fight the month before, this enterprise did little strategically in the scheme of the war, but was chiefly valuable to stimulate the fighting spirit of the American army instead.

White Plains would be the next position the British would use to attempt to dislodge the Americans from the area. Charles Lee would again return to the main army, and Sullivan and Stirling as well. Released in a prisoner exchange for General Richard Prescott, taken by Montgomery when he captured British ships in Montreal, Stirling was traded for Montfort Browne, a former royal governor of West Florida. With the additions of these veteran generals the American army would be reorganized once again. To celebrate the return of General Lee from his victory in Charleston, Fort Constitution was renamed Fort Lee in his honor. An occasion that was not wasted on Major General Nathanael Greene. Greene was completely against renaming the fort in Lee's honor. He felt that Constitution was a stronger name and acknowledged what the army was fighting for in New York. It did not help that Lee and Greene hated each other with a passion. Now, it was no secret throughout the American troops from the camp privy cleaner to Washington himself that this feud had been festering for some time. Up until now it had been an out and out war without blows being thrown or calls for satisfaction, but merely a battle of words and accusations. That was not to say that this event could not indeed escalate the situation. It had started some months back when Greene was picked over several, better qualified, more deserving gentlemen for the rank of brigadier-general. Lee spoke up to everyone who would listen and exclaimed that Greene was too young, inexperienced and a cripple to boot. It was well known that Greene himself did not believe himself brigadier material, but accepted the position and rank with honor to serve his country. Yet, Lee did not endear himself to Greene's circle of friends with the remarks, especially since Lee had little or no real knowledge of Greene or his background. That is what Nathanael was most hurt and angry about and caused the situation to escalate. When Lee returned from South Carolina he had bellowed to Washington that it was he who should have command of Fort Constitution and not the upstart Greene. Then when the fort title was renamed in his honor it only made things worse instead of better. It is my opinion that Lee was not half the man Nathanael Greene was, but throughout his life made it his job to tell whoever would listen that he was indeed a better man and general. Lee did not have the heart or the head that Greene possessed, but did have the self admiration that far exceeded Nathanael's self confidence. Lee conceived unfounded hope and unwarranted designs from Washington that the victory in Charleston only compounded. When the fort was renamed Fort Lee, Charles Lee felt it necessary to level several low blow remarks at Greene during its dedication. Facts of Lee's characteristic malevolence toward most people other than himself, but especially his contempt at Nathanael Greene.

The tide of war was slowly turning northward in the thick wooded hills between Fort Lee and the main army. The season was quickly changing from fall to winter, and the armies would be in search of quarters. The British had firm control of New York city, but the Americans were in the fields and forest and did not have strong hope of wrestling New York away from its enemy. So, the opposing armies clashed again on the 28th of October. Lee's division of about 1,500 men, were sent to meet the British advance by Colonel Rall's Hessian grenadiers. The Americans retreated throughout the day, holding a position until nearly being outflanked, and then retreating again. After the retreat, Washington ordered Colonel Haslet and his Delaware regiment to reinforce the men at a place called Chatterton's Hill, about a half mile from the right of the main American lines. Before long Putnam, McDougall, Smallwood, and Ritzema were also sent into the fray. Before the field pieces could arrive, the whole British Army seemed to be bearing down on the troops. As soon as the British line was formed a battalion of Hessians, supported by a British brigade, with Von Donop's grenadiers, started towards the river. The river was unusually high from the recent rains, and the crossing was obstructed by trees and branches, making the river extremely hard to cross. The British led the charge with bayonets, but the hill where the Americans were entrenched was steep, the trees too thick, and the fire from the rebels was merciless. The attackers were thrown back, but were soon supported by the rest of the British corps and the Hessians. The Hessians managed to turn the Americans and at the same time Birch's British light dragoons came galloping down with sabers flashing and trumpets and drums pounding. The militia, which was in front of them, had never seen cavalry in action and promptly tried to flee in a very disorderly fashion into a small group of trees. The expert horsemen cut off their path of retreat to the camp, falling upon them in scattered groups and literally, hacked dozens of the 300 fleeing Americans. The flight of the militiamen uncovered the Americans right flank, and left the Delaware regiment unsupported on that side. Rall's Hessians fell upon them in full force with bayonets and three of the Delaware companies tried to hold but were eventually driven from the field. The New York regiment and Smallwood's Maryland regiment fought desperately to support the Delaware regiment, but the Hessians turned their flank as well and with Smallwood himself wounded two times, the regiment was thrown into confusion by the weight of the onslaught. Fighting with gallant, yet futile effort, McDougall and the remaining Americans retreated to a road leading to the American camp and held them there to protect the withdrawal of the scattered troops standing alone in the field of battle. The loss of the Americans has various reports, with as few as a hundred killed and wounded to as many as three or four hundred casualties, including prisoners.

The British army was now dug in on Chatterton's Hill, establishing that position would extend the left wing of entrenchment's eastward in a curve and threaten both flanks of the American lines. Greene was now strengthening defenses at Fort Lee. He knew the British would soon move in his direction and he secretly longed to be a part of the struggle. Meanwhile, Congress had finally sent Greene a response to his long list of communications, "Inclosed you have a copy of the letter in answer to yours to this congress. Colonel Biddle, in Amboy, is in possession of ninety thousand cartridges at that post, as well as light wagons, powder, and provisions, which you have requested. Another fifty thousand is in route as I write. You may expect them with the week." This delivery of musket cartridges would prove less of a blessing and more of a distraction before the struggle was through. On the 30th of October, at three o'clock in the morning, a sentinel looked out from the rampart of Fort Lee to see a sudden glare of lighting up in the wooded heights of Tettard's and Valentine's hills, sending a lurid gleam on the still waters of Spuyten Devil. Greene was awaken and hurried to the ramparts himself. The barracks around Fort Independence must be ablaze, and Greene mounted a horse and quickly crossed the river to investigate and see if anything could be saved. "Colonel Lasher burnt the barracks yesterday," he writes Washington the next day, "he left the cannon in the fort. When I went to investigate I found between two and three hundred stands of small arms that were out of repair as well. The company must have put up a good fight with the enemy for several days, but the troops on the other side are so much fatigued that it must have been a work of time."

The enemy was within sight once again, but Greene was having difficulty deciding what their intentions might be and wrote to Washington on the 31st of October, "The enemy have possession of Fort Independence and the heights above King's Bridge. They made their appearance the night before last; just after we got everything of value away. I should be glad to know your Excellency's mind about holding all the ground from King's Bridge to the lower lines. We are not able to determine, with any certainty, whether the troops that have taken post there are the same troops or not that were in and about Harlem several days past. We suspect them to be the same troops you engaged in Sunday's skirmish. Six officers that were taken by the enemy, made their escape last night and came here. They tell me that six thousand foreign troops who were on board the ship they were held on are suffering from scurvy, many of whom have died. The ships seem to be making sail for Rhode Island in the next few days. They inform me after the Sunday action, an officer of distinction was brought into the city, badly wounded. They report that they believe it to be General Howe himself. I forwarded your Excellency a return of the troops at this post, and a copy of a plan for establishing magazines. I could wish to know your pleasure as to the magazines as soon as possible. The motion of the grand army will best determine the propriety of endeavoring to hold all the ground from this position to the lower lines. I shall be as much on the Island of New York as possible, so as not to neglect the duties of my own department. I can learn no satisfactory account of the action of the other day." The "duties" Greene speaks of is Fort Washington, which was under the command of General Putnam, but since Greene had a hand in the construction of the works there, he felt a connection with it, and some degree of responsibility with its defense since Fort Lee was directly across the river from them.

The proximity of the British army, literally resulted in the Americans being uncomfortable in more ways than just their thoughts. When they got back to camp after the Battle of White Plains they found that their baggage had been removed by the British. "For three or four nights the American soldiers slept in the woods without bedding or blankets, covered only by the snow that fell upon them." On the 31st, the American army slipped away to the North Castle heights, leaving Stirling's brigade to hold their old position. The garrison at Fort Washington was not moved or reinforced. Howe, on the other hand reinforced by two brigades from Percy's force on Manhattan, now had about 20,000 men. He immediately took possession of the old American lines but made no other hostile move for the next four days.

Washington busied himself with his entrenchment's. Three redoubts, with a line of earthworks in front, were erected with what must have appeared to Howe to be magical swiftness. There was a bit of magic involved with the works, which is to say that they were a sham, an illusion. The line of earthworks was, in fact, largely made up of cornstalks pulled from a near-by field, with large lumps of frozen soil clinging to the roots. They were piled, top inward, clods of dirt outward, and covered ever so loosely with more dirt. Howe looked at what appeared to be formidable defenses, and altered his plan for attack. During the night of November 4th, the pickets at the American outposts heard the rumbling sounds of heavy wagons in the British camp. By morning it was seen that their advanced sentinels had been withdrawn, and hostile movement of the British army was apprehended, the American army was ordered under arms. But it appeared, in time, that the enemy forces were on the march toward the southwest in the direction of Greene. They were, in fact on the way to a site called Dobbs Ferry.

Needless to say, the Americans were more than cheery at the sight of the British withdrawal. They were again feeling satisfied, in spite of Chatterton's Hill, since they had by now "good flour, beef and pork plenty, with grog to wash it down." It certainly was true that an army marched on its stomach; especially when rum or grog was involved. The Americans indeed had much to be safe and happy about. They had been retreating and retreating, but it appeared that it was Howe who had balked this time after repeated attempts to get behind the Americans and hem them in. Contentment with the results of their strategy, war worn and ragged though they were, soldiers and officers alike were "in high spirits, loath to give an inch to their enemies."

The northernmost part of Manhattan Island, extending from Washington's old lines on Harlem Heights to Spuyten Devil (Duyvil) Creek, a distance of about four miles, is nothing more than a narrow tongue of high land lying between the Harlem River and the Hudson, its width no more than about three-quarters of a mile. It is bordered on both sides of the river by rocky cliffs a hundred feet high. These flank a plateau, which rises close to the Hudson, to a narrow hill one mile long and two hundred and thirty feet high above the water. In 1776, this hill was known as Mount Washington, it is now known as Washington Heights. On the Harlem River side was Laurel Hill, nearly as high. Between these two hills was a narrow valley, a gorge through which a road led to Kings Bridge and beyond, Harlem. The sides of these two precipitous hills were steep, rocky, and rugged cliffs and the entire tongue of land was densely wooded.

On Mount Washington, Colonel Rufus Putnam, the American army's chief engineer, had laid out the lines of a fort named Fort Washington. The fort was a pentagonal earthwork with five bastions. It covered about four acres of ground, but it was simple, open earthwork with a surrounding abatis, but no ditch worth mentioning. It had no casemates or bombproofs, no barracks, no building of any sort, except "a wooden magazine and some offices," no fuel for their fires, and no water source. No well, no creek nearby, no interior water supply whatever. In case of a siege, water could be got only from the Hudson, two hundred and thirty feet below them. It had no outworks except "an incipient one at the north, nor any of those exterior, multiplied obstacles and defences, that could entitle it to the name of fortress, in any degree capable of withstanding a siege," wrote Captain Alexander Graydon, second in command of Fort Washington. The fort's function was to defend the eastern end of a line of sunken hulks and chevaux-de-frise stretching across the Hudson. The purpose of these was to prevent the passage of British ships up the river. The western end of the line was supported by Greene's garrison at Fort Lee on the Jersey shore. To think that they could hold such a fort against Howe's entire army of more than 20,000 better equipped, superior trained sailors and soldiers would be insane. British ships had sailed to and fro through the obstructions and past the forts for weeks now without any effective intervention by the Americans. But, as the always exuberantly optimistic Israel Putnam put it, "I have an overweening confidence in the impregnability of Fort Washington." Colonel Magaw, its commandant, said he could "hold it till the end of December. Should matters grow desperate, we would carry the garrison and the stores to the Jersey side." Strangest of all, even Greene, now considered by most as the most competent general officer in the army, held a similar delusion. "I could not conceive the garrison to be in any great danger. I am sure that they would, and could, be brought off at any time." Greene wrote just prior to the battle.

In another communication, Greene updates Washington on what he hopes to accomplish, "By an express message from Major Clarke, who I have stationed at Dobb's Ferry, I find the enemy encamped right opposite, to the number of between three and five thousand; the Major's disposition is that they are searching after boats, and design to cross the river soon. Colonel Tupper still thinks he can transport any provisions by flatboats. A second attempt shall be speedily made, after we lost one. General Mercer write me that the Virginia troops are coming on in haste. They are now in Trentown (Trenton, NJ). He proposes an attack on Staten Island that would halt the motions of the enemy. On York Island, the enemy have taken possession of the far hill nearest Spuyten Devil, and I think they will not be able to penetrate any farther. There appears to be fifteen hundred of them there. From the enemy's motions, I should be apt to suspect they were retreating from your army, and altering their operations. The officers of Colonel Hand's regiment have arrived, and the officers of the Pennsylvania regiments think it a grievance that the men be given privileges of enlisting their men before they get orders. I have stopped it until I learn your Excellency's pleasure. You'll please to favor me with a line on the subject."

Washington, held no such fantasy. He wrote to Greene, who was commanding the troops in both forts by this time: "The late passage of the 3 Vessels up the North River...is so plain a Proof of the Inefficacy of all the Obstructions we have thrown into it, that I cannot but think, it will Justify a Change in the disposition which has been made. If we cannot prevent Vessels passing up, and the Enemy are possessed of the surrounding Country as you say, what valuable purpose can it answer to attempt to hold a Post of which the expected Benefit cannot be had; I am therefore inclined to think it will not be prudent to hazard the men and Stores at Mount Washington, but as you are on the Spot, leave it to you to give such Orders as to evacuating Mount Washington as you Judge best."

Greene immediately answers Washington the next day, "Your Excellency's letter yesterday was received this morning to my hand. The stores at Dobb's Ferry, I had just given orders to the quartermaster to prepare wagons to remove them. I think the enemy will meet with some difficulty in crossing the river at Dobb's Ferry. However, it is not best to trust too much to the expected difficulties they may meet there. The passing of the ships up the river is, to be sure, a full proof of the insufficiency of the obstructions in the river to stop the ships from going up; but that garrison employs double the men to invest it that we have to occupy it. They must keep troops at King's Bridge to prevent a communication with the country; and they dare not leave a very small number, for fear our people should attack them. The enemy seem to be disposing matters to besiege the place. If the enemy do not find it an object of importance, they will not trouble themselves about it; if they do, it is an open proof they feel an injury from our possessing it. Our giving it up will open a free communication with the country by the way of King's Bridge; that must be a great advantage to them and injury to us."

But Washington was not convinced, and even though the man he thought of as his best advisor and field general, as well as most of the members of Congress agreed with Greene, Washington wrote this note the next day. "The best accounts obtained of the enemy assure us of a considerable movement among their boats last evening; and so far as can be collected from the various sources of intelligence, they must design a penetration into Jersey, and to fall down upon your post. You will therefore immediately have all of the stores removed which you do not deem necessary for your defense; and as the enemy have drawn great relief from the forage and provisions which they have found from us and in country, and which our tenderness spared, you will do well to prevent their receiving any fresh supplies there by destroying them; as well as any stock the inhabitants will not drive off, and remove their hay and grains in time. Greene answers, "I shall follow your Excellency's advice respecting the cattle and forge. I shall collect our whole strength and watch the motions of the enemy, and pursue such measures for the future as circumstances may render necessary. As I have your Excellency's permission, I shall order General Stephen on as far as Aquackanonck, at least. That is an important pass. I am fortifying it as fast as possible."

Part of the army was now crossing the Hudson at King's Ferry, and it was evident that the enemy's plans would soon manifest itself. Washington, too, would soon be at Fort Lee. Meanwhile a letter to Washington from Greene was sent, "Your Excellency, I am taking every measure in my power to oppose the enemy's landing, if they attempt crossing the river into the Jersey's. I have about five hundred men posted at the different passes in the mountains. Another five hundred more are marching from Amboy directly for Dobb's Ferry. General Mercer is with me now. I shall send him up to take command of these men immediately." On the 11th of November, important intelligence was brought in by Justice Mercerau, of Staten Island. Greene communicated it to Washington, and on the same day, directly to the President of Congress, "I am informed by the gentleman that fled from Staten Island that there are ten thousand troops embarked for South Carolina, to be commanded by Lord Dunmore. He is a man of credit and truth, and is a good friend of mine to cause and a sensible man, and his account can be believed and confirmed. Mercerau further informs me that a large fleet are at watering-place on Long Island or Staten Island, all ready to sail to England. It is reported the fleet consists of one hundred sails. By several accounts of different people within the city, it appears our prisoners are in very suffering situation. They are being held in mastless ships in the harbor. Humanity requires that something should be done for them.

On the 13th, Washington arrived at Fort Lee and was now convinced that one of the immediate objects of the enemy was "the investing of Fort Washington; and that it was evident that, if the garrison were to be withdrawn, they must be withdrawn without loss of time," Greene would later write of their conversation. The matter was discussed at length, "but nothing final concluded upon," wrote Greene after the meeting. Instead, Washington left the Fort, and would forever through history be second-guessed for failing to give Greene positive orders to evacuate the fort. It would be a mantel of indecision cast on Washington of an instance of his recurring indecision throughout the war which beset Washington's mind, and is proved by his own words in his letters. Various historians are of the opinion that Washington's faith in Greene's decision making, and of all things Congress's bullying of Washington on occasion, were some of the conflicting considerations which "caused that warfare in my mind, and hesitation which ended in the loss of the garrison," Washington would write in his memoirs years later.

Two days after his visit to Greene, Washington was summoned to Fort Lee again. The British had arrived and requested Colonel Magaw and his garrison surrender. It was returned with, "a spirited refusal to defend this post to the last extremity," Greene wrote to Washington in his request for Washington to return and follows with, "The contents of Colonel Magaw's letter is inclosed, and requires your Excellency's attention. I have directed Colonel Magaw to defend the place until he hears from me. I have ordered General Heard's brigade to hasten on and reinforce them. I shall go to the Island soon and ask that you join me." Washington immediately hurried back to Fort Lee, but was told that Putnam and Greene had gone over to Fort Washington to assess the situation. Washington instantly followed, and was halfway across the river, when he met Putnam and Greene on their way back. It was late, and the evening shadows made the riverbed seem black, and the flag wavering over Fort Washington was barely visible in the last rays of the cold, autumn twilight. It was decided to return to Fort Lee, but Putnam and Greene assured Washington that they were hopeful that they had left Magaw and his troops with the confidence that they could make a good defense of the fort. Encouraged, though certainly not fully sharing their confidence, Washington returned with them to the western shore. The three men climbed the steep hill of the Palisades, pausing from time to time at the sound of single shots from small arms fire. It must have been a long, anxious night for the Americans of both forts, fixing a watchful eye for the enemy attack that was sure to come.

As morning shone, Howe indeed attacked, with the booming cannonade from the north and south. Magaw's force in the force was made up of his own and Shee's regiment, numbering about 700 of all rank and file, including many of those on sick list and were unable to be evacuated. Greene, while waiting for Washington's reply had sent additional men to the fort over the course of two weeks which brought the entire body of troops in Fort Lee to about 2,800 men. "Too many," Greene had explained later, "merely to hold Fort Washington." Although the council on September 12th, 1776 had declared that 8,000 men would be necessary for the task. Magaw did all he could to honor the orders Greene had handed down to him. He disposed part of his force to the northern end of Mount Washington, half a mile from the fort, Rawlings and riflemen held a small redoubt and a battery of three guns. In a couple of fleches on Laurel Hill near the Harlem River, Colonel Baxter and his militiamen were posted, and two miles to the south, Lieutenant Colonel Lambert Cadwalader had Magaw's and Shee's Pennsylvanians, a part of Miles's Rangers, and some others, about 800 men. They occupied the front line of the old entrenchment's on Harlem Heights. A few other small detachments were posted at other points, scattered around the fort, leaving Magaw with only a small band of soldiers to defend the fort.

Howe devoted 8,000 of his men to simultaneously attack the three points mentioned. Lord Percy was to go with his brigade of Hessians and nine British battalions and fight against Cadwalader. General Matthews with two battalions of light infantry and two of the Guards, supported by two battalions of grenadiers and the 33rd of Foot under Cornwallis, perhaps 3,000 men were to cross the Harlem River and take out Baxter's militia. General Wilhelm von Knyphausen had claimed the honor of making the main attack with the German troops alone. Rawling's position was therefore assigned to him, his force to number 3,000 Hessians and Waldeckers. The 42nd Highlanders under Colonel

Sterling would make a feint attack from the Harlem side between Cadwalader's position and the fort, trying to confuse the Americans. Needless to say, although the Americans put up a valiant effort outside the fort, they were out flanked by the superior forces and were either overrun, killed or captured at their post or made a mad dash to the fort, only to be outmaneuvered by the enemy and captured as well. Some of Cadwalader's men managed to reach the fort just before Rall and his Hessians arrived within a hundred yards of the fort and took position behind the fort's large storehouse.

Rall immediately demanded a surrender. Magaw demurred, hoping to get some relief from Fort Washington, and asked for time to consider his offer. Rall venomously refused. By this time Washington, Putnam, Greene, Mercer, and Knox, with their aides, had crossed the river in the excitement, and were watching the enemy's approach from the old headquarters at Morris' house. Washington was unable to give any new orders or to intervene, only observe the troops and the enemy's positions as they got closer to Fort Washington. He reluctantly agreed to withdraw, just in time to escape capture, because fifteen minutes after departing an English patrol stood on the very spot he had been standing moments before. Rall sent a second and final summons to surrender. With more than 2,500 men in the fort, crowded one upon another in fear for their lives, completely in the open, if a bombardment came it would be a hideous slaughter pen. Magaw's "last extremity" had arrived long before his folly boast of "late December." Washington watched from Fort Lee's walls as the flag over Fort Washington was lowered, signally their surrender. Magaw presented his sword to Knyphausen, who came up with Schmidt's column a little after Rall. Two Hessian regiments, Rall's and Lossberg's, were drawn up in lines, as the Americans marched downtrodden between them, and laid down their arms in the fort, giving up their colors, "which were yellow, red and light blue." It was said that Knyphausen, a grim and silent man, looked on the American banners with disdain, and spat upon them. It is historic irony that some of these same Hessian regiments, thus especially honored, would surrender their flags to Washington within six weeks.

Although this was a huge victory for the British, their casualties were far more severe than the Americans, but what the Americans saved in dead and wounded, were more than made up for in prisoners taken. The fort's defenders had 59 killed and 96 wounded and the British had 78 killed and 374 wounded. Of these the Hessians share were 58 dead and 272 wounded. But the Americans loss of prisoners and material taken, especially in cartridges was stupendous. Officers numbered around 230 and 2,607 private soldiers fell into the hands of the British. The amount of precious material lost was absolutely staggering in numbers from Fort Washington and Fort Lee, which fell to the British just a few days later without opposition. One hundred and forty iron and brass guns, ranging from the smallest to 32-pounders, 12,000 shots and shells, 2,800 muskets in working order, and over 400,000 cartridges, many of which had just been sent up from Congress especially at Greene's request, along with tents, entrenching tools, and various other sorts of equipment. It was one of the greatest military disasters of the war for the Americans, and the blame for it must rest upon the shoulders of Nathanael Greene and Magaw for their inexplicable infatuation in attempting to hold a fort that could not be held with the troops allowed them. Washington is only partially to blame for his vacillation and indecision when prompt and decisive action might have prevented his inferior officers from persisting in such a military folly. Although Greene has, and should bear a significant portion of the blame, his commander-in-chief was present the entire time. It was necessary to formulate a difficult decision by using his subordinates as a sounding board and listening to their varied opinions. But the true test of a superior officer in the military has always been quick and decisive decision-making abilities. Washington was the deciding factor in this event and did not show a significant aptitude for making a tough call against the majority in this case. That would have been to take their lumps and retreat in an orderly fashion to New Jersey with 2,000 more men and military material that they desperately needed and were surely going to miss in the coming months.

Chapter V

"The Long Journey Through New Jersey"

"The loss of Fort Washington rendered Fort Lee useless;" So wrote Nathanael Greene the day after, arguably, the most embarrassing loss the Americans would suffer in their entire military history. After the Fort Washington disaster, the main American army was still divided into three parts. The three divisions in North Castle, commanded by General Lee, those men from Generals Sullivan and Spencer, each composed of two brigades and seen with a paper strength of 5,500 able bodied men. General Heath had four brigades around Peekskill, with about 3,200 effective men, and Washington and Greene had the rest, 5,400 on paper, closer to 3,000 effective soldiers. It would appear from all reports combined that there were about 12,000 able-bodied private soldiers that could be relied on for the rest of the campaign, a substantial force indeed. But their numbers were dwindling quickly and winter was coming on. The nights were already frosty and the November rains sometimes turned to snow. They lacked tents, blankets, good men's clothing, the meager things they have been wearing throughout this campaign were beginning to become ragged and could not keep them warm in the height of the winter months ahead. This seemed years away from the time just after the events of White Plains, where they sat idle at North Castle with an abundance to eat and drink, and the men were cheerful and hopeful. But the catastrophe of Fort Washington had been a cold dish to serve and eat. An English officer had noted in his diary just after the fall of Fort Washington that, "many of the Rebel who were killed in the late affair, were found to be without shoes or Stockings, & Several were observed to have only linen drawers on, with Rifle or Hunting shirt, and without a proper shirt or Waistcoat. The weather has been somewhat mild before now, but in just the past month it had turned cold and they must now be suffering extremely." The term of enlistment was soon to expire for most of the army, especially the troops under Greene as of December 1, and the entire army would be free to leave by the 1st of January 1777.

Washington had taken the troops he commanded to Hackensack, the remaining troops would meet him just outside that town, and Greene, with his contingent of men were still within sight of Fort Lee trying to ascertain what the British army was going to do next. Howe, with his freedom of movement, intended to take full advantage of it and attack Fort Lee on the 20th of November. At nine o'clock on a very rainy evening the night before the attack, the 1st and 2nd battalions of the British light infantry, two of the British and two Hessian grenadiers, two of the Guards, two companies of Hessian jagers, and the 33rd and 42nd British Regiments of Foot, about 4,000 in all, struck their tents and proceeded to the landing site. By the next morning, Cornwallis was put in command of the attack, and landed on the Jersey side of the Hudson at Closter, five or six miles above Fort Lee, and marched down the shore of the river, intending to cut off the forts garrison from retreat to Washington's army in Hackensack by penning it up between the Hackensack and Hudson Rivers. By a great stroke of luck, an American officer on patrol discovered their advance, rode down to the fort, got Greene out of bed, and told him of the oncoming British column. Greene relayed the news to Washington, who ordered his men under arms and out of the fort, and hurried them away to the head of a small stream in his rear, thus gaining the road to the bridge over the Hackensack River. Greene wrote a report some days later to Governor Cooke of Rhode Island, "His Excellency ordered an immediate evacuation accordingly. All of our valuable stores were sent off. The enemy must have got intelligence of it; since they were in possession of the Harlem River, they brought their boats through that pass without our notice. They crossed the river in a very rainy night, and landed, about five miles above the fort, about six thousand, but most accounts say eight thousand. We had then at Fort Lee only between two and three thousand effective men. The troops at Fort Lee were mostly from the flying camp, militia, and irregular and undisciplined; had they obeyed orders, not a man would have been taken yesterday. I returned to the camp two hours after His Excellency had marched the troops off. Colonel Cornwell and myself got off several hundred more; yet notwithstanding all our endeavors, still near a hundred remained hid about in the woods."

Lee, who was still near North Castle, had been given instructions by Washington that had said, if the enemy moved westward into New Jersey, "I have no doubt of your following with all possible dispatch." Cornwallis was going to attack with all of his forces in New Jersey, and it seemed that this time Lee was going to have to come to the aid of Washington. Colonel William Grayson, one of Washington's aides-de-camp, wrote to Lee the day after Fort Lee fell, "His Excellency thinks it would be advisable in you to remove the troops under your command on this side of the North River." Washington would add the next day, "I am of the opinion that the publick interest requires your coming over to this side." Like so many times in the past, Lee did not see these letters as stating the terms of these orders as "positive", and thus were interpreted by Lee to mean at his discretion, and so, did not move immediately, suggesting that part of Howe's army might still move against New England. Lee wrote a reply to Colonel Joseph Reed, Washington's adjutant general: "Dear Sir; His Excellency recommends me to move...to the other side of the river...but we could not be there in time to answer any purpose." Again we see another example as of how vain Lee was, and he never denied the fact, and his vanity had been fed to the bursting level by the admiration and adulation of everyone since he first joined the army. "Congress has made generals out of booksellers, farmers, lawyers, and blacksmiths, whose meager sort of military knowledge could not compare to my enthusiasm." Here is where Lee's contempt for Nathanael Greene bore fruit out of a single seed. Lee was one of the only professional soldiers who from the age of fifteen had worn the coat of a military man and had flashed his sword on many of the battlefields in Europe and America. Lee, always ambitious, tended from now and then, to seperate his own division from that of the commander-in-chief, and use his own judgement rather than follow Washington's recommendations. At this crucial time in his career, Colonel Reed encouraged him to act independently. "You have decision, a quality often wanted in the minds otherwise valuable." We can only suspect he is speaking of Washington and Greene. "You are likely to be necessary; an indecisive mind is one of the greatest misfortunes that befall an army; We are in a very awful and alarming situation-one that requires the utmost wisdom and firmness of mind." You may draw your own conclusion as to who Reed is referring too. Lee answered back, "That fatal indecision of mind which in war is a much greater disqualification than stupidity; in so pressing a manner as almost to amount to an order, I have various reasons for not coming at once; but will come soon, for to confess a truth, I really think our Chief will do better with me than without me."

Washington and Greene could not hold Hackensack, even if Lee had arrived with his troops. The force Washington had was not only to small, about 3,000 able bodied men, but also that the outlying country was described by Washington as, "almost a dead Flat land." And since the fall of Fort Washington almost meant the loss of some "500 intrenching tools," they were in danger of being caught in an area that held no natural place for protection and thus cooped up in a narrow space between the Hackensack and Passaic Rivers. Washington and Greene decided to leave three regiments to guard against a crossing of the river using the bridge, and marched westward to Aquackanock, crossed the Passaic there, and hurried on to Newark, arriving the very next day. The rear guard they had left in Hackensack destroyed the bridge at the approach of the British and hurried to join the main body of the troops. The great journey, known as the retreat across New Jersey had already begun in earnest.

Stirling's brigade of eight regiments, about 1,200 men, had already been sent ahead after its crossing of the Hudson and reached new Brunswick well ahead of Washington's main body and waited there for them to arrive. By that time, like the rest of the army, Stirling's brigade was also in deplorable condition. One of Haslet's Delaware regiment remarked, "We arrived at Brunswick broken down and fatigued--some without shoes, some had no shirts." By this time, Washington considered the entire American cause to be in the gravest danger of failing completely. A conversation he reportedly had with Greene went something like this; "Should we retreat to the back parts of Pennsylvania, will the Pennsylvanians support us and the cause after such dispirited defeats? Greene supposedly answered, "If the lower (eastern) counties are subdued and give up, the back counties will do the same." Washington remarked, "We must retire to Augusta County in Virginia. Numbers will be obliged to repair to us for safety and we must try what we can do in carrying on a predatory war, and if overpowered there, we would cross the Allegheny Mountains." Whether the conversation took place has been debated by historians for centuries. A contemporary historian by the name William Gordon related the story in a book he wrote some time after the war, in which he claimed to have been present during the entire meeting and conversation. Whether the validity of its authenticity can be determined is unsure. But it does represent a good example of just how desperate the American army's situation was at that particular time.

Dispirited by their succession of defeats, wearied with marching day after day, always retreating with no final destination in sight, lacking tents, blankets, clothing, and shoes, Washington's force was "the wretched remains of a broken army." The British were becoming increasingly optimistic that the end of the war was near. Many of them wrote home, "Peace must soon be the consequence of our success." Howe was so confident that the war would soon be over that he divided his army in half and sent over 6,000 of his men, under the command of General Clinton to take possession of Rhode Island and have the army winter there. An army that took Rhode Island without opposition and who would remain in and around Newport for three years.

Washington's fear that the army would be forced back to the Delaware River was nearly realized. By late November, from his camp in New Brunswick, Washington had called on Congress for the Philadelphia Associators, a volunteer organization to march to Trenton where he would meet them. They had already started out, but had not arrived as of yet. The New Jersey militia failed to respond to the call. By this time Cornwallis' troops were in sight of New Brunswick in hot pursuit of their quarry, Washington's rear guard of Stirling's brigade. By the 30th of November, the enlistment's of the Maryland and New Jersey militia brigades under General Reazin Beall and Nathanael Heard, with their 2,000 men had expired and had refused to continue longer in service. Things only got worse for the American army, as Washington wrote, "Altho' most of the Pennsylvanians are inlisted till the first of January, I am informed that they are deserting in great numbers everyday." The same conditions existed in Greene's camp in Princeton, "We have yet another convincing proof of the folly of short inlistments: A unit of five months enlisted men were engaged, and their time expired at the actual period of retreat from Hackensack. Two more left us in Brunswick, notwithstanding the enemy were within two hours march and coming on. The loss of these troops at this critical time reduced his Excellency to the necessity to order a retreat again here to Trentown. We retreated to Hackensack, from Hackensack to Equacanach, from Equacanach to Newark, from Newark to Brunswick, from Brunswick to Trentown (Trenton); here we are endevoring to collect a sufficient force to give the enemy battle, or at least to stop their progress."

With Washington's letter to Congress there is a postscript dated December 1, "The enemy are fast advancing, some of 'em in sight now. We have had a smart cannonade whilst we were parading our Men, but without any or but little loss on either side. It being impossible to oppose them with our present force with the least prospect of success we shall retreat to the West side of the Delaware River and have advanced about Eight miles." At Princeton he stopped and met up with Greene and his men. Pushing on in full retreat they then came to Trenton the next day. The safety of his army was paramount in his mind now, and the other side of the Delaware offered just such a haven. Greene writes to Governor Cooke on the 4th of December, "Here (Trenton) we are endeavoring to draw our forces together for a final push. When we are finally collected together, I am in hopes it will be a respectable body of troops. I am in hopes the General (Washington) will give orders to advance upon the enemy to-morrow: our numbers are still small, not to exceed 5,000, but daily increasing. We left Brunswick with 3,000 men, a very pitiful army to trust the liberties of America upon...I wish the inlisting may go on favorably, but I fear the contrary: 'Tis impossible to oppose the enemy successfully without a good, firm body of troops, subject to proper discipline and well officered. Our men are good; nothing is wanting but officers and discipline to make the American troops equal to any in the world."

By the 7th of December 1776, Washington and Greene, strengthen by arrival of the Pennsylvania Associators and part of Colonel Nicholas Hausegger's regiment of Pennsylvania and Maryland German volunteers, decided to cross the river. But they lacked information about the movement of the British at New Brunswick, Washington decided to "face about and such Troops as are here (Trenton) fit for Service and march back to Princeton and there govern myself by Circumstances and the movements of General Lee." Meanwhile, Lee had continued for many days to follow his own judgement rather than the recommendations of the commander-in-chief. Greene had received a report from Major Clarke about the enemies whereabouts and also of General Lee which he forwarded to Washington, "General Lee is at the heels of the enemy. I should think he had better keep upon the flanks than upon the rear of the enemy, unless it were possible to concert an attack at the same instant of time in front and rear. I think General Lee must be confined within the limits of some general plan, or else his operations will be independent of yours. His own troops, General St. Clair's, and the militia must form a respectable body." Within a few miles of Princeton, Washington and Greene met Stirling and the remnants of his troops in full retreat. Howe had arrived in New Brunswick the day before and had sent Cornwallis ahead to meet the Americans head-on. While the Americans were marching, Cornwallis was on his way to the same destination. They would have to turn back yet again and return from where they had just marched from the day before.

Cornwallis had marched slowly and cautiously, with flankers thrown out on both sides to scour the woodlands and guard against ambushes. The British troops had reached Trenton, just as the last of the Americans were putting off over the Delaware to the Pennsylvania shore. A short fight between the American rear guard and British light infantry and jagers flared up, but the enemy was greeted by the American batteries already on the other side and lost about thirteen men, prompting them to break-off the skirmish. An American soldier named Anderson would write, "we were in the woods and bushes and none were wounded that I heard of...That night we lay amongst the leaves without tents or blankets, lying down with our feet to the fire. We had nothing to cook with, but our ramrods, which we run through a piece of meat and roasted it over the fire, and to hungry soldiers such as we it tasted sweet." The British ranged up and down the river, looking for boats, but found none. Washington had already instructed Glover to get all that he could find by hook or crook and to have every boat that could float on the other side.

The crisis would deepen in the next few weeks. As an American officer put it, "Such is now the gloomy aspect of our affairs that...strong apprehensions are entertained that the British will soon have it in their power to vanquish the whole remains of the Continental army." It was by far the darkest hour in the war, with Newport and New York already in the enemies hands and Philadelphia, the largest and finest American city, as well as the seat of the young country's government, lay unfortified, virtually ungarrisoned, and open to attack from all sides. Just thirty miles away was the enemy army with 10,000 British and Hessian soldiers buoyed by the recent victories and confident with their overwhelming strength over the rebels, poised and eager to have Philadelphia as their next prize, along with pleasant winter quarters that the location would hold.

Washington had more than just the British to contend with during these dark and gloomy days. John Adams, a close friend of Nathanael, and an advocate to Washington, was in a long, well deserved, three month visit to his family in Massachusetts whom he had not seen in almost two years and had just survived the horror of a Yellow Fever epidemic. With his absence, the burden of power was scattered among many of the Congress delegates for a time, making it almost impossible for Washington to get any timely authorization on delicate situations that called for immediate action. In this delicate and embarrassing moments of the war, Washington seems to have placed a great deal of reliance on Greene's opinion for consul. Greene did not have the luxury of the late Samuel Ward to rely upon, who would have definitely brought the subjects to Congress much quicker than what Washington was experiencing. One of the major subjects, was Washington's repeated argument that the burden of the military decision power should be given to him. The army was suffering greatly at the expense of the civil power now in charge of it, and Washington often needed immediate answers to decisions in the field and not long, drawn out discussions for which Congress was famous.

By the 20th of December, the American army looked more like scarecrows, shod like mere tramps in their worn and ragged garments than the appearance of the effective fighting force it was attempting to be. Huddled at their unprotected posts or attempting to sleep without blankets or tents in the shivering cold air, these wretched men were trying to protect 30 miles of river shoreline against a far superior enemy that could strike at any time and at any point along those 30 miles. The river held no substantial barrier against the British reaching the American forces. The material for the British to construct their own boats was all about them and two lumberyards were close at hand. If all else failed, they could go into Trenton and dismantle houses and use the wood to build the boats they needed. If that weren't enough, the weather was turning decidedly colder. The Delaware was already freezing and would easily be thick enough in the next few days to take the weight of the pursuing British marching men, their wagons, artillery, and baggage. But ever the optimist, Greene was fond of saying, "Although I am far from thinking the American cause desperate, yet I conceive it to be in a critical situation; we the guidence of God and his providence to a noble cause, we have the ability to calculate and pave the way against the disagreeable evils that stand before us."

By the 20th of December, Howe and his brother were prepared to take full advantage of the Americans weaknesses. They came to America, not only as military leaders, but also as peace negotiators. They bore the King's commission "for restoring peace to his Majesty's Colonies and Plantations in North America." In New York, Admiral Lord Howe issued a proclamation, signed by Sir William and offering, "a free and general pardon to all who return to their just allegiance and take oath accordingly." The effect on the army and the inhabitants of new Jersey was instantaneous. Already the colony known to be the most disaffected to the American cause, New Jersey desired to remain neutral in hopes of keeping its property. It also wanted to remain on the winning side whoever that may be at the time, and at present, the Americans were definitely not the winning side. So they flocked in great numbers to the British and took the oath and received protection papers against their own countrymen. Washington was disgusted by the desertion of the cause, "The Conduct of the Jerseys has been most Infamous. Instead of turning out to defend the Country and affording aid to our Army, they are making their submission as fast as they can." Greene was known to give his opinion on such occasion whether it was asked for or not, "The disposition of the Jerseys is a dangerous manoeuvre. 'Tis an endless task to attempt to cover the country; but it is my opinion they will be peaceable if you will; for, from the best accounts we can get, they consist of the invalids of this country towards the army."

At such a grievous time for the army, Greene would also be preoccupied by the events in his home and Rhode Island, and the increasing reports that he had performed badly and without foresight at the fall of Fort Lee. In a letter to Governor Cooke he wrote, "By your letter to General Washington, I find the British troops have occupied Rhode island and hold it. The Eastern delegates made application to General Washington for me to come to Rhode Island, but the General would not consent. He thinks more to the force of this country then just one provence. They may attempt to plunder the shores, but nothing more than that, this winter; for I am confident they have no hopes of penetrating into the country. I am also told some malicious reports propagated industriously about me, respecting the loss of the baggage and stores at Fort Lee. They are as malicious as they are untrue. I can bring very good vouchers for my conduct in every instance, and have the satisfaction to have it approved by the General under whom I serve. Everything was got off from that place that could be, with the wagons we had to move the stores with. The evacuation of Fort Lee was determined upon several days before the enemy landed above us, and happily all the most valuable stores were away. The enemy's publication of the garrison and stores there taken is a grand falsehood. Not an article of military stores was left there, or nothing worth mentioning." We know this to be half-true. But at the time, Greene believed in what he was saying, and went to his grave thinking he had done the best job that he could at Fort Lee.

After the appalling conduct of the Jerseys, Philadelphia also took notice. Its inhabitants, thinking that their continued liberty from the British was contingent only on how well the American forces could protect them, did not like the odds. They began leave the city in droves for the safe haven of the outlying countryside. An observer of the exodus related what he witnessed, "Numbers of families loading wagons with their furniture &c., taking them out of town...Great numbers of people moving...All shops ordered to be shut...Our people in confusion, of all ranks, sending their goods out of town for protection." The once busy, overcrowded, and sprawling capital of the newly formed United States was reduced to a ghost town, almost overnight. Even Congress became unnerved and "has been removed to Baltimore."

At the same time, was a slight man of small stature by the name of Thomas Paine, who had been a volunteer aide-de-camp to Greene at Fort Lee, and had marched with musket on his shoulder, day after day, in the weary retreat with the army. But while in Newark, the Irish immigrant began to fight with the weapon he was more accustomed to, a pen. He wrote a letter to America and sent it to a publisher in Philadelphia who turned it into a pamphlet called, *The Crisis*. It began with some of the most powerful words known throughout the history of the United States: ***These are the times that try men's souls: The summer soldier and the sunshine patriot will, in the crisis, shrink from the service of his country; but he that stands it Now, deserves the love and thanks of man and woman. Tyranny, like hell, is not easily conquered; yet we have this consolation with us, that the harder the conflict, the more glorious the triumph.*** The little book was flying "like wildfire through all the towns and villages." Most of the soldiers in the army of 1776 were illiterate, so corporals and sergeants that could read gathered small groups together and read it out loud. It may have been meant to stir the patriotism of the civilians and boast their faltering confidence in the army, but it did even more. It strengthens the beliefs of the poor soldiers in the field. Suffering defeat after defeat, always retreating from their superior enemy, enduring the endless hardships day in and day out. The men of the American army found a new animated feeling of worth and helped them gain a strong determination to finish what they had begun. To prove to themselves and the world, that they would be all-season soldiers and all-weather patriots.

With the removal of all military stores to Christiana Bridge in Delaware and the complete abandonment of Philadelphia by Congress, the directive Washington had requested for months finally came. Washington was awarded complete control of army operations with "full power to order and direct all things relative to the military department and to the operations of war until otherwise directed. The next day, Howe disclosed that he was suspending military operations until spring and retired with the greater part of his forces to his winter quarters in New York, leaving only a line of military outposts to hold New Jersey. An immense pressure was lifted off the Americans' shoulders that were holding the river. There would be no boats coming across, no soldiers marching over the ice and attacking them. As happy as the patriots of Philadelphia became, the Tories were all the more downcast.

Meanwhile, General Charles Lee, still leisurely retreating southward with the remaining troops he still had, decided to stop in Vealtown, New Jersey and camp so his men and he could rest. While his soldiers foraged the countryside for provisions, Lee decided to ride three miles to a tavern in Basking Ridge to spend the night, and indulge in that "folly and imprudence...for the sake of a little better lodging." During this leisure time, Lee was having breakfast and found a moment to pen a short note to his good friend General Horatio Gates, in which he characterized Washington as "most damnably deficient." He did not get time to send the message when British cavalrymen surrounded the tavern. They had been scouting the area for weeks in search of Lee's army and received word that Lee himself was in the tavern. Within twenty-four hours, Lee was led off in chains and was imprisoned in New Brunswick. His captors were from the very same regiment that he had led during his European military career, which had made him so famous. Although the news of Lee's capture was seen as just another dreadful calamity that was to befall the American army, it may have actually turned out to be a service to Washington as well as the army.

General John Sullivan, Lee's second in command, promptly marched his troops into Washington's camp on the 20th of December. Although it was only 2,000 of the 5,000 Lee had left New York with, it was 2,000 more than Washington had had the night before. With the Philadelphia Associators, Gates' regiment, the rest of the German regiment included in the troops Greene was commanding, the American troops on Christmas eve numbered 6,000 men listed as "fit for duty". But more important was evidence of Washington now looking to Greene as the sole trusted counselor in his camp. Washington had always been gratified at the honor and unwavering support Greene had shown him. And now, at a time when Washington was formulating plans for an audacious counterattack upon the British detachments, he would require that trusted counsel more than ever before.

It was never Washington's intention to permit the enemy to keep the possession of the Jerseys undisturbed, but where and when to strike the first blow was a question of ultimate difficulty. After a meeting Greene had with Washington, he wrote to Governor Cooke, "I hope we shall give the enemy a stroke in a few days," he was alluding to a plan that he and Washington had obviously decided on already. But on the 22nd of December, Reed sent some necessary intelligence reports that may have made their decision easier, as Greene shows in a letter to Colonel Biddle, "If your business at Newtown will permit I should be glad to see you here. There is some business of importance to communicate to you, which I wish to do to-day. No butter, no cheese, no cider,--this is not for the honor of Pennsylvania. Colonel Griffin is at Mount Holly, collecting great numbers of the Jersey troops; they have drove the Hessians and Highlanders many miles. Yesterday a great firing was heard there; the consequence I have not learned." The business was evidently to tell Biddle that Trenton was their goal, but wanted to keep it as much a secret as possible.

The only public record of Greene's involvement in the battle was a letter he wrote to his wife on the 30th, "Before this reaches you doubtless you will hear of the attack upon Trenton. We crossed the river Delaware at McKonkee's ferry, eight miles above this place, on the 25th we attacked the town by storm in the morning. It rained, hailed, and snowed, and was a violent storm. The storm of nature and the storm of the town exhibited a scene that filled the mind during the action with passions easier conceived than described. The action lasted about three-quarters of an hour. We killed, wounded, and took prisoners of the enemy between eleven and twelve hundred. Our troops behaved with great spirit. General Sullivan commanded the right wing of the army, and I the left. This is an important period to America, big with great events. God only knows what will be the issue of this campaign, but everything wears a much better prospect than they have for some weeks past."

When the battle was over, Greene went with Washington to visit the dying Rall. Rall had called Washington to his deathbed to plead mercy for his wounded and captured men. Greene would write of the meeting, "I felt that his Excellency was harden by the circumstances surrounding the capture of Fort Washington. It was rumored that Rall had a hand in having his troops bayonet our capture comrades. The General said not a word, and we went out of Rall's room." Meanwhile, Greene was all for following up the surprise attack on Trenton with another rapid pursuit of the enemy and an immediate attack upon their other posts. But Knox was the only other field officer who agreed with him, and Washington, not yet feeling confident with overruling the opinion of a majority, reluctantly accepted its decision to secure Trenton and rest in the town for the moment.

The year 1776 had come to a close. Robert Morris would write, "I am heartily glad of its passing and hope you nor America will ever be plagued with such another." But the campaign was far from over. The surprise attack and victory at Trenton had buoyed the country, but it was necessary to prevent it from lapsing into the dread that November and December had brought. The enemy was startled and it was necessary to turn their alarm into fear, just as they had done to the Americans in New York. Washington had resolved to follow up the victory with another blow against the enemy, before his troops, most of whose terms of service were just expiring, would be gone and Washington would be in dire straits with troops once again. With another decisive strike, maybe the soldiers would re-enlist and they could deliver the Jerseys from the British.

With personal appeals from Washington and a promise of ten dollars in bounty, most of the eastern men were talked into staying for an additional six weeks. But there were reports that many of them only stayed long enough to secure their money and then left before the six weeks were up. Forces under the command of Cadwallader and Mifflin, about 3,600 men in all, were called in from Bordentown and Crosswicks. The men reached Trenton on the 2nd of January 1777 and had just settled in for what they had thought was going to be the first real meal cooked over fires and the prospect of sleeping in beds under a roof. But suddenly the fife and drums called the soldiers to formation under arms. The reason they had been recalled to Trenton was not for rest and rehabilitation, but to become the forward troops to meet the enemy, who was advancing on the old road from Princeton under the command of Cornwallis.

The battle had hardly begun when Greene was ordered up with a strong detachment to support the advance. A soldier in Greene's regiment on that day wrote years later, "dashing up to meet the company I was in, the Rhode Islanders under Hitchcock, I could hear in a clear, loud voice, calling out to us, "Push on, boys, push on! From General Greene while he rode on horseback." Five thousand weary Continental troops were about to meet 8,000 well-rested disciplined men from the British ranks. The only passage for retreat was by a bridge over the Assanpink. On the east side Washington sat watching the progress of the fight, and with a "firm, composed, and majestic countenance," which the men were said to look on as they passed and grow confidence from him. As the last of the troops were safe across, the cannon, which had been pushed aside to let the troops pass, were again brought into position and immediately open up a well directed fire upon the advancing British. The British were forced to check their steady advance and regrouped on the other side of the bridge. As evening drew, the cannonade on both sides ceased, and with both armies settled into camps with only the narrow Assanpink separating the troops, they waited for morning to resume the bloody fight that was sure to come.

That night, Washington summoned his officers to council at the headquarters of General St. Clair, his own now in the hands of the enemy. St. Clair would write of the meeting, "His Excellency would ask; What shall be done? Shall we retreat down the Delaware, on the Jersey side, and cross it over against Philadelphia; or shall we remain where we are, and try the chances of battle? Each course had its advocates, when a voice was heard, saying, 'Better than either of these; let us take the new road through the woods, and get in the enemy's rear by a march upon Princeton, and if possible, onto Brunswick even." Who had made the suggestion? St. Clair claimed it as his own, and we have no doubt in his assertion. Nowhere is it documented where the idea sprang, but whoever it was, it was the inspiration of true genius and was promptly agreed on by all the officers involved. When the meeting broke up a sudden change in weather had taken place. A mist, which had been hovering over the landscape all morning, had now disappeared. And although the night was dark, it was void of clouds and moonless. There was no hint of wind, but the air was bitterly cold and the ground was frozen and snow covered. The ill-equipped Americans huddled by their fires, unseen by the British, and ate their suppers, some thinking that come tomorrow it would have been their last meal.

First, the baggage guard was sent ahead towards Burlington. A strong fatigue party had been assembled and sent to work on an entrenchment near a mill, so close to the enemy's lines that the British could hear the heavy blows of the pickax and spades hitting the frozen ground. The forward observers or even Tory spies would have run back to Cornwallis to inform him to sleep in that morning. The Americans would not attack. They were digging in and determined to hold the ground where they were. Then the Americans were ordered to heap as much wood as the fires could hold and keep them burning till told otherwise. The fires were so numerous by midnight that the British sentinels must have thought the Americans were crazy. Fire upon fire down the lines of the Americans could be seen for miles flickering above the trees. That is exactly what Washington wanted the British to think. But in fact, the Americans had cautiously closed camp, except for the fires and were prepared to march as soon as the order was given.

The road the Americans were traveling was brand new to Sandtown, and littered with low tree stumps on the path. So the pace of the soldiers was dictated by the artillery, whose cannon wheels had quite a problem getting over the rugged and rutted new road throughout the night, and the troops frequently had to halt and wait for wheels to be repaired. Dozens of infantrymen were said to take the opportunity "to stand with their arms supported, fast asleep where they stood, until the order to move on came and the scene was repeated throughout the long night."

When they got to Sandtown they took the road to Quaker Bridge and when day dawned that clear and very cold January morning, the column swung toward the northwest on the road leading directly into Princeton. The sun was just rising over a hill as they approached Princeton, and just to the east was seen the "brandishing of steel glint in the morning suns rays, and someone called, 'it must be the enemy, because our muskets have no glint to them." One of Washington's aides-de-camp observed it also, and ran to tell Washington near the head of the column, but when they looked again they saw nothing. Greene sent two of his riders to investigate and bring back news of what they found. The men did not return and with that, received their answer. It was indeed the British and closer than the American army knew.

The British force in Princeton consisted of three regiments, the 17th, 40th, and 55th of Foot, with three troops of light dragoons, a Lieutenant Colonel Charles Mawhood commanded the entire force. Mawhood had been ordered to march the bulk of his force that day to meet up with General Leslie at Maidenhead, and then push on to Trenton. While the British were marching out of Princeton, a forward guard had noticed the ragtag Americans, a small contingent of Mercer's troops, just emerging from the woods and alerted Mawhood at once. Thinking that it only a small part of the American army fleeing from the defeat at the hands of Cornwallis in Trenton, he sent a small band to reconnoiter the approaching army and shadow their movements until Mawhood could get his army into position and attack the American column. Mawhood brought his troops around, ordered them at quick march, and dashed them into an orchard just ahead of the advancing Americans. But that was the exact moment that the Americans caught sight of the British and with equal speed, gained the position Mawhood was trying to get, because they were slightly closer to it.

From a ridge forty yards away the British set their lines. With eight guns keeping up a continuous fire of grape and canister shot, the Americans were pinned down and began to break in

84

confusion back towards the woods. Washington arrived a moment later and tried to rally the troops, waving his hat to the huddled groups as his passed on horseback. He immediately dashed to the front line, galloping ahead of the troops to within 30 paces of Mawhood's line, trying to encourage his men to follow his example. Suddenly a burst of grapeshot exploded near his position, and the smoke enveloped Washington and his horse. A member of his staff was thought to have seen him and the horse go down, and the aide turned his head and covered his eyes at the thought of the sight he would open them too. But as the smoke cleared, there was Washington, horseless, but still standing, unhurt and calling to his men to race to his side. They responded to the sight, turned the battle and defeated the British. Greene, who was racing to his troop's position, was riding with another officer and heard of the scene where Washington was said to have been wounded. The two men spurred their horses and after a short distance the other officer pulled up his reins to avoid stepping on a wounded soldier in his path. Greene was rumored to say sternly, "O sir, this is no time for stopping."

The British were said to have lost over 400 men, 100 of who lay dead in the field. The Americans had 40 killed or wounded, but among the dead was one promising and merited officer, Colonel Haslet and another close friend of Washington's, General Mercer, who died of his wounds the next day. The Americans also gained two brass field pieces, but because they were short on horses, could not carry it away. They did manage to gather much needed blankets and shoes though. Like Trenton, Princeton was a terrific morale victory if only a small strategic one. It again buoyed the American cause and proved to the people of the states that their struggle had hope of completing their ultimate goal of freedom from England.

Thus far, Washington's bold strategy had succeeded in the last month of the New Jersey campaign of 1776-77. The road to Brunswick was open, and prisoners, including Lee were there, abundant stores and supplies were available there; as well as a military chest, reported to hold seventy thousand pounds in hard money. To seize this bounty had been Washington's original plan, but was halted by the fact that his men were exhausted and sadly undermanned at that. With the approval of the President of Congress, Washington's hungry, and fatigued troops were ordered to Morristown to fix winter quarters there. Greene was already on his way there when the decision was finalized, thinking it was the most logical choice at the time. That night the troops bivouacked at Somerset Courthouse, many of them finally able to sleep on blankets, rather than the frozen ground. By the 6th of January the entire American army, or what was left of them, reached Morristown, wayworn and destitute, but victorious and able to say they had saved the Revolution for now.

Chapter VI

"The Calm Before the Storm"

With lightened hearts, though weary limbs, the patriot army set up camp in the little village of Morristown on the Raritan River. They must have enjoyed telling tales to the wide eyed inhabitants of the town who looked on them as heroes, the story of how they had crossed the Delaware three times, had fought the Hessians for one and the British regulars another, and defeated them both. Then stole away at night under the very nose of Cornwallis, to mark the occupation of the Jerseys by wintering over here in Morristown. The camp sight they chose could not have afforded them better protection. With the Passaic on one side, the rugged hills where they camped was set on a high table-land, with steep slopes on two sides and a large ridge called Thimble Mountain on their west. They could actually look down on the lowlands where their enemy lay, but the British had no intention of forcing an engagement with the Americans if it meant exposing themselves at every step on a deadly angle such as this.

Forage was abundant and within easy reach, provisions, though less available, were enough to carry them through the rest of the winter encampment. This was the second winter encampment for many of these men, and even more of a percentage of the officers who had already served two campaigns together. This meant that they were beginning to know each other's strengths and weaknesses. A necessity in the military, but especially needed in war.

The camp was not so hard that many of the officers and non-commissioned officers called for their wives and ladies to meet them in camp for the winter, including Martha Washington. Caty Greene was unable to join her husband until the winter camp was broken, and the new campaign was about to begin. So, Nathanael chose to reaffirm his friendships with Knox and Hamilton, and was often invited to join the Washington's whenever they had a party or event at the headquarters. He writes to his wife, "I lodge at Mr. Hoffman's, a very good natured, doubtful gentleman. He has a charming wife, a great lover of the clergy. Major Clarke, a member of my aide-de-camp, is eternally perplexing her with doubts and difficulties of a religious nature, by dark hints and oblique insinuations respecting the purity of manners and principles of the Church of England....The smile of Heaven has changed the face of affairs. Respect and courtesy flow in upon us from all quarters. This is the picture of human life. I see the difference betwixt moving on with the tide of success, or sinking under a load of misfortunes."

Washington seemed to be under the load of misfortune, for he still encountered the same problems at the winter camp outside of Boston a year before. He must raise a proper army, an old army to disband, recruit and drill raw, new troops, keep up the spirit of the people throughout the country, who were vital links for the army's success, and keep the enemy at bay by harassing them and cutting off their foraging parties. But most important of all, was the question and discussion he must have with Congress to correct the past mistakes made and prepare for a more decisive future if they were to survive. Most of those thoughts can be found in Washington's memoirs. We will only concern ourselves with the part Greene played in those thoughts, and how his counsel directed Washington when he was asked for an opinion.

The questions raised were foremost in Greene's mind as well, "I am exceedingly happy," he writes to his wife on the 20th of January, 1777, "in the full confidence of his Excellency General Washington; and I found that confidence to increase every hour, the more difficult and distressing our affairs grow." But this also became a painful time for Nathanael Greene as well. One of his earliest military friendships had been with Daniel Hitchcock, who had been with Greene since the Kentish Guard and accompanied him to Boston as a colonel in one of the three original regiments Greene commanded in the Rhode Island contingent. From that time until Morristown the two men had performed closely together in camp and in the field of battle. Apparently the fatigue and latent exposure from the rugged campaign of the past few weeks had taken a toll of Hitchcock's health. He had been sick off and on for several weeks and it had even kept him from the field at Trenton and Princeton. A few days after the army's arrival in Morristown, Hitchcock died. He was buried, in what became during the course of the war, a popular burying ground for many famous men of the Revolutionary War, including his other good friend, Christopher Greene, who would lose his life a year later. In a letter to no one in particular Greene would write, "He was buried with all the honors of war, as the last mark of respect we could show him. Poor General Mercer, also dead of his wounds he received in the Princeton action. A fine companion, a sincere friend, a true patriot, and a brave general. May Heaven bless his spirit, as others, with eternal peace! Several more brave officers and men fell that day; particularly one Captain Neale, of the artillery. The enemy refused him quarter after he was wounded. He has left a poor widow overwhelmed with grief. She is a fine a woman as ever I saw; her distress melts the hearts of all around her...Such instances paint all the horrors of war beyond description."

Greene's own health had not suffered since New York, trying his best to keep sickness at bay. His equipment had not fared as well though, "I am miserably off for want of a horse;" he writes to a friend, "you'll oblige me very much, if you can get me a good one." Daily riding over rough tracks and all types of weather during the last campaign had worn down his horse very quickly. The way Greene spoke so tenderly of horses indicates that they must have been his favorite animals, but for now his want for one was purely sound military thinking. Without one he would not be involved with the next campaign which would surely follow their winter camp.

Next on the agenda was recruiting. Congress had finally adopted the bounty system that Greene had advocated for two years, but some of the eastern states had raised their offer higher than that adopted by Congress. Many surmised that some eastern states were making allowances for their men who came from areas with rougher climate than some southern states, and so the expense of clothing was greater for those men and it was reflected accordingly in those bounties. But Rhode Island, feeling alarmed by the presence of the British, confined their exertions not on bounties, but raising recruits as quick and quietly as they could. Out of the wake of such a hasty plan emerged the filling of only "two Continental battalions set on foot two regiments of seven hundred and fifty men each, and one regiment of artillery of three hundred men to serve for fifteen months." Washington was overwhelmed and strongly condemned the measure of Governor Cooke in Rhode Island. But even more upset was Greene, who felt that the honor of his native state was at stake and wrote a strong letter to Cooke, "I am exceedingly unhappy to hear of your resolution of raising troops at the expense of the State, before your proportion of the Continental regiments is completed. The forming of new regiments only serves to burden the State, without giving it any additional strength. There is not a State on the Continent whose interest and happiness depends so much on a union with others as yours. You are the most exposed and the least capable of making a separate defense; consequently, it is your interest to cultivate every measure that may tend to form the union of strength; and must be considered bad policy to give such an example to others, from which you can derive little or no advantage, and that may prove so ruinous in its consequences." The letter went on like that for 7 pages, and ended with, "I shall close this long letter with a strong recommendation of the filling the Continental regiments immediately."

Greene had written in, as he put it, "the style and freedom of one friend to another;" but the Governor was quite put off by it and laid the letter before the Assembly, who were also quite perturbed by Nathanael's letter. It seems they felt their measure to be the most prudent at the time, and defended their policies by asserting that their troops were designed as much for the Continental service as for the service of the state. The difference in the time of service, fifteen months, instead of three years or till the end of the war, was the only differences from their plan and that of Congress. Greene was repentant, "I am now exceeding happy on the receipt of yours, to find my information erroneous, and my apprehensions and fears in a great degree groundless respecting your departure from the union and general plan. I hope the House will pardon the freedom with which I delivered my sentiments, when I assure them that it was from a full persuasion that the reports were true, and that the measure was calculated to fix a lasting disgrace upon the legislators. I have felt no small share of unhapiness in remaining so long ignorant of the true history of your proceedings;"

It becomes evident around this time that the relationship between Washington and Greene became stronger and even more intimate. And during the months in Morristown, Washington relied even more heavily on Greene than he had in the past. Discussing even the most minute details of future plans of action, correspondence with Congress, and the freedom Washington gave to Greene to air his own opinion without shame or recourse. It is evident from the mountains of letters between the two men that they shared discussions on a wide range of subjects; from every interest of the army to what Martha had served at tea that day. If the letters of Washington and Greene that were written at this time are examined, the reader would see for themselves that during the months in Morristown these two great men applied their experience and knowledge of the first two campaigns, and calmly weighed the obstacles that lay before them, and the means for overcoming them. These two men became so tightly drawn together by the full accord of opinions and their motives, that smaller minds throughout the army and even Congress, began to look upon their union with jealousy. Thus, the enemies of one man, became the enemy of both in time.

There was one essential difference between their present situation and their situation in the Boston camp, and that difference was widely in their favor. In Boston and New York, smallpox ran rampant and took more than a few good men needed for the army. The danger was clear. Gather a few thousand men together in a constricted area for common dwellings and the monster would surely raise its ugly head sooner or later. The best attention to the killer disease had always been inoculation, but during this winter, a regular system was instituted, and whenever a new recruit was enlisted, they were automatically inoculated. If a new recruit carried the disease before he entered active duty, he was sent to a designated district inoculation center, one of which was in Morristown. In order to induce the inhabitants of the town to open their doors to the sick men, the army surgeons were directed by Congress to first inoculate the entire families without charge. The beneficent measure was a complete success and no record of any smallpox epidemic was reported during the entire winter encampment at Morristown.

Now that the hospitals were organized, hundreds would be saved rather than to die waiting for beds. Provisions began to trickle into the camp quartermaster stores. As soon as coats, blankets, and shoes were delivered, they would almost immediately be issued since half the army was either almost naked or at the least had been without shoes for months. When the commissary finally brought in his supply of provisions, most of the men were on the brink of starvation. Last, but not least, the paymaster came round with money for the first time in three months. Unfortunately, with the rise in inflation at a record pace, both soldier and officer had already pledged most of the funds as credit to local merchants and were left with less than half of their pay for as long it took to get paid the next time.

A few bright spots also shone on the beleaguered army of the Continentals. The morale boost of the successes at Trenton and Princeton had not been wasted on just the soldiers who fought in those victories. The civilian population was also showing a new degree of patriotism as well. "The Tory's are melting away very fast in this country," Greene wrote to his wife in late January. "The different treatment they meet with from the enemy from what they expect works great reformations." The

British very rarely ventured out of their strongholds, but when they did they were met with a sufficient degree of volleys that it was not worth the aggravation they received. For instances, on February 24th, a letter from Baskingridge to the Adjutant-general reads, "A large foraging party by the enemy came out yesterday from Amboy, consisting of about four hundred men; our people attacked them with various degrees of success." The reports of encounters like this one were few and far between. Generally it was a winter of little movement from either side.

Greene used this time to correspond with his friend John Adams who had finally returned to Congress after his long absence. Greene now had a voice that could speak for the army directly to that body, and would hopefully elicit the help or protest that the army so desperately needed on the inside. A letter from Greene to Adams, dated March 3rd reads, "It has been a long time since I wrote to you or you to me; who stands in debt upon the score of letters I cannot tell; therefore I shall begin anew. If you have time and the inclination, you will give this matter an answer; if not, I shall consider it as the ladies do their visits after marriage: if there is no return, then the acquaintance is dropped. I believe you are aware of the observation I made last summer, which was that you were playing a desperate game. I fancy your ideas and mine differed very widely at that time respecting the state of things. I am sensible, from a review of the last campaign, there appears some considerable defects in the counsels and conduct of its operations; but give me leave to tell you, sir, that our difficulties were inconceivable to those that were not eye-witnessed to them." Another system that Congress had enacted that drew Greene's anger was the choosing of general officers from each state in proportion "to the number of men which they would initially furnish... I confess this is a strange mode of reasoning; even for that body of government."

By this time, General Benedict Arnold was in camp from the north, and was a constant companion to Greene. Arnold and Greene had served together for a short time in the waning days of the New York fiasco, but had not seen each other since. But other events would warrant Greene's attention besides the reacquainting of old friendships. The envy towards Washington by of some those in Congress would soon raise its ugly head once again. In spite of Washington's repeated earnest attempts at clear representation, Congress had never taken measures to fill up the army, and make the necessary appointments of officers. While the army encampment lay in the shadow of the enemy forces, Congress drafted a resolution that was clearly a slap in the face of the army's commander-in-chief. In one particular paragraph it read, "an earnest desire of Congress to make the army under the immediate command of general Washington sufficiently strong not only to curb and confine the enemy within their present quarters, and prevent them from deriving support of any kind from the country, but by the divine blessing, totally to subdue them before they are reinforced." Four states were against the paragraph, three abstained, and six States, four of them eastern and two southern, Virginia and Georgia, were in favor of it. Mr. Burke, delegate from North Carolina explained it best when he wrote, "There appeared, without much question, through the whole debate, a great desire, in some of the delegates of the Eastern States, and in one from New Jersey, to insult the General."

Washington had to counteract this letter, with its half-drawn dagger in it. But how? "Could I accomplish the important objects so eagerly wished by Congress. I should be happy indeed. But what prospect or hope can there be of my effecting so desirable a work at this time? The inclosed return, to which I solicit the most serious attention of Congress, comprehends the whole force I have in Jersey." That force amounted to 3,000 men fit for duty, 2,000 of them were militia. When Lord and Sir William Howe had issued the proclamation to any American who would take an oath of allegiance to the British Crown, Washington issued a counter-proclamation. Washington called upon all who had taken out protection with the English general to give those up, and take an oath of allegiance to the United States. The General's proclamation is a violation of our civil rights," wrote Mr. Clark, of Congress, "Each State requires an oath to that particular State. In many other things the proclamation is exceptionable, and very improper. I believe the General is honest, but I think him fallible." This, from a man who was once considered one of Washington's trusted advocates. Washington was not fully aware of the extent of hostile spirit within Congress toward him. But he was aware that it would take more than a letter to reply to these accusations. going to Philadelphia himself at this precarious time was out of the question. Publicly speaking to Congress, and even to each individual member hostile toward him, would most certainly fill the ever-widening breach to his personal character. He had to send someone, and the decision was not a hard one. He chose Nathanael Greene to speak in his stead, and in fact, on his very behalf.

To James Wilson he wrote, "Dear Sir,--Give me leave to introduce to your attention Major-General Greene, who obliges me by delivering this. He is a gentleman in whose abilities I place the most entire confidence. A long acquaintance with him justifies me in this....The danger of communicating by letter, our present situation, and the indispensable necessity of Congress knowing it, have compelled me, though I can ill spare so useful an officer at this time, to send him to Philadelphia....His perfect knowledge of our strength and of my opinion enables him to give Congress the most satisfactory accounts they can desire. I am, dear sir, Your most humble servant, Geo. Washington." Greene's instructions were clear; "Make Congress well aware of the many matters essential to the well-being of this army." With the documents from Washington in hand, and his mind set to the important matters ahead, Greene promptly left for Philadelphia. It was Nathanael's first time in the Quaker city, and his first in-person meeting with Congress. At eleven o'clock in the morning, Greene presented himself at the door of the Pennsylvania State House (Independence Hall), and while waiting to be announced and seated, struck up a conversation with several important city fathers on the welfare of the army. Then, with ceremony somewhat borrowed from England, he was ushered into the main hall. There, he was seated in a chair on a raised platform, just above the floor, almost directly in front of John Hancock, and just to the side of Secretary Charles Thompson. "A bit nervous," he would tell friends later, "being among such lofty men as these, in the room that bore the union, and the salvation of our country." He must have also been thinking of the right words at such a time. After all, he was not there for himself, but to speak in General George Washington's name; and his heart and mind told him that Washington's name and reputation would be at stake. He would have to depend on his keen mind to speak firmly, yet wisely for Washington's sake, as well as his own.

He stood in committee for two days, and the discussions did not end with the setting sun. Much of the discussions, sometimes turned into debates, and were removed to the local tavern for the subject of full and free discussion in the interest of the authority and councils of war. What Greene tried to impart to the men of Congress was that Washington only acted with cautious consideration which his peculiar position with the army, and in government circles required. He was bound to the opinion of Congress, even when it differed from his own. What was the intention of Congress to these thoughts was the question Greene brought before the committee. Their recommendation became; "Resolved, That General Washington be informed that it never was the intention of Congress that he should be bound by a majority of voice in a council of war, contrary to his own judgement." But Congress was far more skilled in framing resolutions than carrying them out. In May of 1778, the battle of Monmouth was fought against the opposition to the decision set down by a council of war. It would not be the only time that Congress itself would be shown to be the body of government known to falter in the resolve of speedy decisions by useless delays.

Greene felt he had done his best in Philadelphia, and in a letter he wrote to Washington the day before his return to Morristown he outlines some of his conclusions for Washington: "Your Excellency, The time spent with the committee of Congress for two hours in chambers, and two evenings with the latter, was for the business of the cartel and other matters under consideration. I believe the business of the cartel will be settled agreeable to your wishes, that is, General Howe

90

acknowledging General Lee as a prisoner of war, and holding him subject to exchange whenever we have an equivalent to offer,--the full execution of the old cartel to take place as your Excellency and General Howe can agree. I explained fully the state of the army to the Congress; but I fear they can not do but little more than has already been done. There has gone from the city about seven hundred men (recruited) within the past week past, a thousand more will be ready in eight or ten days. Inclosed is a return of the situation of the quartermaster-general's department, the wagons, spare carriages, etc., not mentioned in the return, are in great forwardness, General Mifflin informs. Also, I am told by Congress, the pay and establishment of the light-horse is completed and forwarded. I believe I have impressed upon Congress, in the strongest manner I was capable, the necessity of keeping the paymaster fully supplied with cash. The House requested estimates. The Secret Committee have given me to understand that a large quanity of arms, ammunition, and brass cannon are daily expected. I shall stay to-day and to-morrow in town, and then set off for camp, unless I am detained by the Congress."

The business side of Greene's trip was complete, but another reason for his visit now had to be accomplished. The state of the nation's inhabitants, but especially the people of Philadelphia had to be determined. The city had had quite a scare in December, but seemed to have recovered quickly with the sight of happy and prosperous people about. Greene also noticed a number of French officers, he was told that the number of these gentlemen had increased in the last month. There was a sprinkling of other country's military officers, a few German and occasional Pole, but mostly French. Greene thought this interesting and filed it in the back of his mind. He stayed in a private house, and marveled at the sumptuous dinners served up on fine bone china, and rich wines in rare varieties, such dinners as headquarters never saw were now his for the few days he was a visitor to the capital city. He wrote to his wife, "The faces of Philadelphia appear angelic." Greene said he loved the place, but finished with the task he was sent there to do, he turned his face back to the bleak hills of Morristown and left the pleasant scenes he had witnessed behind him.

Greene returned to camp life and immediately began longing for home. "The great distance there is between us," he writes to his wife on the 30th of March, "and the few opportunities I have to hear from you, leaves me in a very disagreeable suspense. Eight long months have passed amidst fatigue and toil since I have tasted the flowers of domestic felicity." A few days later he received word of his second child's birth, a daughter. "I read the letter with a trembling hand. Some superstitious fears had been hovering round me that something would happen to you. What gave rise to this troublesome train of visitants I cannot tell. Heaven be praised for this second pledge of conjugal affection! When I shall see the poor little one God only knows. I am exceedingly happy at your being at Potowomut, and rejoice to find the brothers so kind and attentive to your wants."

But Greene would have cause for anxiety once again. At the moment he is recalling his thoughts to his home state of Rhode Island, the presence of the enemy had caused the first general alarm which was followed by a resolution to attack them. The officers in immediate command of the state were Spencer and Arnold. Greene, under the proposal of Washington, drew up a plan of attack; but all general officers in camp and Rhode Island agreed, unless a good and trustworthy force could be raised, any attempt, no matter on which plan, would be highly suspect and doomed to failure. No such force could be raised, and Arnold writes to Greene from Providence: "The wise Assembly of this State have passed a vote, declaring it disgraceful to the States of New England, and to this State in Particular, and of course to the general officers of the army, that the enemy of Rhode Island have remained so long unmolested, and have requested and directed general Spencer to attack them immediately. Included is a copy of votes of the Assembly. I send it to you as a curiosity." Greene reply's, "I fear the Assembly's measures were hasty ones. I am very sure their hearts are right, and their zeal warm, but I fear they do not give themselves time to deliberate properly." Greene said to Washington of Arnold at that time, "Surely, a more active, a more spirited and sensible officer fills no department in your army." Greene and Arnold had seldom served together, but they had a close personal relationship and corresponded frequently. Arnold often wrote to Greene to update him on the movements of the enemy and the whether they were close to his home and family. Greene liked Arnold and believed in him, as many officers in the army did, right up until the day of his disastrous fall from grace.

Spring had finally arrived, and Washington was making plans for pulling up winter quarters and moving on to the next campaign at hand. Final plans and preparations weren't completed as of yet, and while they are watching the enemy, they held their collective breaths for the steps Congress would take for the safety of the entire country. Congress was too absorbed with the care of their own individual safety to concentrate on the States as a whole. Greene would write to John Adams, "I have neither seen nor heard any resolution of Congress for preparations for defense of all States. Different States make preparations for their own defense, in such a situation as we are in, surrounded by imaginary and real grievances,--claims by one State, and refused by another."

The new army should have also been in camp by now, armed, equipped, and well on their way to being drilled into shape. But the new levies not only came in slowly, but were, in part, composed of the worst material to draw on for a patriot army; "convict servants," which the recruiting officers had purchased from their masters due to the negligence of duty in properly seeking worthy soldier candidates instead. Meanwhile, the question on everyone's tongue was, "What will the enemy do?" Greene writes, "Since my return to camp, I am more at a loss to guess the enemy's intentions than ever. They are fortifying Brunswick. Two spies who left that place a few days since say the greater part of the troops are gone to Staten Island; drafts have been made from several corps. If the States furnish their men, and we have a good train of artillery provided seasonably, and General Howe don't shut himself up in some inaccessible post, ten to one but ruin awaits him before fall. But if every State is at liberty to furnish only a part of their men, and those at their pleasure, we shall have another crippled campaign, indecisive and perhaps disgraceful."

Greene's personal life would invade his daily routine of inspections, drills, and meetings at headquarters when he becomes somewhat agitated that he has not received word from home in some time, "I impatiently waited for the post to-day, in hopes of a letter, but, to my great mortification, not a line, he writes in one letter to his wife. In another, he sounds rather sarcastic, "I had the pleasure to hear from you to-day by letters from Brother Kitt and Sister Caty," and another begins, "They write you are cleverly, and in a way of getting well soon. God grant you may! The child, also, they say is in a fair way. Heaven be praised for its goodness! I most ardently wish to see you, but when or where I shall the Lord alone knows. I don't expect to visit Rhode Island till the close of this campaign, if fortune should preserve me through it." Day after day passes without word from home, although he writes to his wife "by every post and every private opportunity." In one he writes, "My Dear, it is now a month and upward since I received a line from one of the family. I think it exceeding unkind; if you are unwell, and incapable of writing, surely some of the brothers might do me that friendly office. However disagreeable consequences may be, it is some consolation to know them. Pray, my dear, let me know the worst, that I may accommodate my mind to the evil. The last accounts I had from you, you was exceeding unwell, taking four grains of mercury every day. Think how you would feel if I had been in my engagement, and left your mind under the torture of suspense for upwards of a month. O, how cruel!"

Greene's wife had been ill. Imagine the embarrassment when he discovered her condition? "I was almost thunderstruck at the receipt of your letter. How different its contents from my wishes! A lingering disorder of five weeks' continuance, and from the present symptoms a confinement of two months longer. Heaven preserve you, and bless you with patience and fortitude to support yourself under the cruel misfortune! O that I had but wings to fly to your relief!" When word that Caty was better, Nathanael wished to see her, but his responsibilities forbid it, "My dear angel, since I wrote you

92

this morning I received your letter of the 29th. The contents have wrung drops of blood from my heart. Gracious God, how much I wish to come to you!....But the General will not permit me to go. I have had exceedingly hard duty this spring. The General keeps me constantly upon the go. The love and friendship he has for me, and the respect and kindness he shows me, goes a great way to alleviate my pains." The love and respect between Washington and Greene went both ways. Martha Washington Greene was the name he chose for his eldest daughter, and George Washington Greene was the name of his eldest son. But the time for soft and warm personal affairs would have to be put aside once again, while the war invaded the life of Nathanael Greene and so many other patriots of the American Revolution the year of 1777.

Summer was quickly approaching, and it was time for both armies to show their hands. Washington would be the first to wager a bet on the cards he was holding. Fearing that Howe might make a swift march from New Brunswick directly down to Princeton and then on to Trenton, thus marching thirty miles south of Middlebrook and within striking distance of the encamped Americans, Washington chose to break camp and march an additional twenty miles south of Middlebrook, about eight miles from New Brunswick. Here, the Americans could watch the pass between Amboy and New Brunswick and road to Philadelphia which passed between the Watchung Mountains. Smallwood's Maryland and Delaware brigade and Hazen's 2nd Canadian Regiment under Sullivan were positioned at Princeton to protect that area.

Howe would make his counter move on June 12th, 1777. He assembled all of his forces that were operating in New Jersey at that time, about 18,000 rank and file, and marched them to New Brunswick to two columns: one, led by Cornwallis, marched to Somerset; the other, under von Heister, went to Middlebush just outside Somerset. There, they hoped to lure Washington down from his position, which would also cut off Sullivan from Washington's main force in the process. But Washington was wise to this maneuver and ordered Sullivan and his troops to Rocky Hill, a small hamlet to the southeast where he could cover the road to Pennington and a path from which to retreat if necessary. While Sullivan was there, Washington ordered him to "harrass the Enemy by incessant parties whenever they attempted to march thro the country," without risking a major engagement for which he was undermanned to accomplish. Sullivan eventually slid over to Flemington and was now on the British right flank. Making it impossible for Howe to accomplish his original purpose; to draw Washington down from his position and engage him.

By the 21st, Washington called a council of war in which it was determined to advance upon Brunswick. Greene was immediately pushed forward to Woodbridge with his own division strengthened for the occasion by Wayne's brigade and Morgan's riflemen, with orders to fall upon the enemy's rear. Orders were also sent to Sullivan and Maxwell to give their complete cooperation to Greene. This was the first time that Morgan, "the wagoner," had served with Greene. Three years later he would serve for him again in the decisive battle of the Cowpens. They marched along the banks of the Raritan once again. It was early morning when the advance guard unexpectedly came upon the enemy pickets. They were Hessians, perhaps recalling the thrashing they received at Trenton, turned and ran in wild disorder towards the town, hotly pursued by Morgan and his riflemen. Within minutes the American advance and the British rear guard stood face to face close to the bridge. Within a few moments more the remainder of the rifle corps, and Wayne with his entire brigade, briskly charged without hesitation through the town, "compelling the enemy to take refuge in their redoubts" on the east bank of the river. Morgan's blood must have been up that day and eager for a fight. Greene was not the type of man to hold such a commander back. He felt that they had the upper hand on surprise and strength; and without waiting for the enemy to find out just how much they outnumbered the Americans, Greene's men leapt into the fire.

As the day advanced, Washington drew out his entire army onto the high grounds in front of his camp, watching anxiously as Greene's troops continued to push the enemy from their works and pursued them to Piscataway. But Sullivan had received his orders too late to get up into position to press the fight, and Maxwell did not receive his orders at all. Greene had to break off the pursuit, and with Howe's rear guard sorely pressed, he took his main body of troops and continued on to Amboy. On their way the British set everything in their path to the torch, at the shock of the civilians farmers and merchants who little dreamed the war would ever set foot at their door. Howe had failed again to gain the upper hand he so sorely tried to accomplish. Stedman would write, "Sir William Howe being now sensible that every scheme of bringing the Americans to an engagement would be unattended by success, resolved to retire from the Jerseys." Howe withdrew all of his troops to Amboy and then onto Staten Island. By the end of June 1777, the entire State of New Jersey had been eradicated of the Kings Troops.

Howe had tried to conquer by numbers and discipline and had completely failed. He tried maneuvers and strategy and had accomplished nothing. 'What would he try next?' was the chief question in the American camp, and the subject of many long conferences between Washington and Greene. They compared notes, reports from their spies, and had even consulted ancient books on the calculations of war. What it had mostly accomplished could not be seen on the battlefield. What had happened, was by the many conferences, talks, meetings and correspondence between the two men had harbored an infusion of confidence, and buoyancy of hope that their goal could be accomplished over time and effort together. Of this hope, one of the chief resources would have to be popular enthusiasm of the people in America. No sooner had Howe left New Jersey than the militia began to rise on every point of the compass. The same Jersey militia which had sulked away to avoid taking up arms for either party when the British army first made an appearance, and even more cowardly had asked for the invader's protection when it looked as if the American army might lose the war early. Through the ravages of winter and with the break of spring, the Jersey militia had become convinced that there was no protection for them but in the sword.

General John Burgoyne had arrived in Quebec early in May and this had made Washington very anxious. It was no secret that Burgoyne was planning an expedition southward by way of Lake Champlain and the Hudson Valley to Albany. He set out with a force of 8,000 British, Brunswickers, Canadians, and Indians in plans of meeting Howe's troops in Albany. To accomplish that feat Howe would have to sail his fleet from New York harbor and north up the Hudson. These subtle movements seemed to indicate the armies would merge soon, and prompted Washington and Greene to plan their next move. With the British keeping their eventual plans completely secret for now, Washington looked suspiciously at the passes between the highlands of New Jersey and advanced his armies to Morristown once again. Next they would move on to Pompton Plains and eventually to Rampo Clove. In the midst of all this movement and posturing disastrous news arrived from the north, "General St. Clair," Greene writes on the 13th of July, "who commanded at Ticonderoga, has evacuated that important post. His garrison consisted of between four and five thousand men, in good health and high spirits. With such a garrison, strongly entrenched and well armed, fully supplied with provisions and ammunition, and the works defended by one hundred and seventy pieces of cannon, it was evacuated without firing a gun. General Schuyler had two thousand men with him at Fort Edward. General Nixon was on his march from Albany with upwards of one thousand Continental troops, the militia of the country coming in from all quarters to the aid of the garrison; and the commanding officer, fully acquainted with all these circumstances, has abandoned the post. What could induce him to take such a measure God only knows! Burgoyne's whole force is suppose to consist of five thousand five hundred men,--the whole is a mystery to all the army. Charity obliges me to suspend all ill-natured reflections, but I fear there has been some misconduct somewhere."

It was evident that someone would have to be sent to the north immediately. Washington knew the necessity, but hesitated in his choice. "It is not determined who goes to Ticonderoga," Greene writes to his wife of the decision, "I can plainly see that the General wants me to go, but is unwilling to part with me; he has set several persons to sound my inclinations. I will go if the general give the order and the good of the service requires it; but I feel a reluctance, and the more so as it is disagreeable to you. If I am left at liberty to consult my own inclination, I shall not go; but if my honor and reputation becomes an interest, I must consent, and I am sure your love and affection is such, if my character is at stake, to give your consent also." Washington indeed must have been reluctant to send Greene, because in his stead he ordered Lincoln to Ticonderoga, when Greene was the logical choice. It wasn't because Greene was afraid to go to Ticonderoga, but that he may not have had the confidence yet that was needed for the commander of a second front. By staying with Washington he gained more useful information on generaling and commanding troops without the help of others with only your wits and own merit to guide you. He would gain those initiatives quickly enough and use them to their fullest in a few short years.

Washington was nearly certain that Howe would take his great fleet and go to meet Burgoyne in Albany. But there were several other possible destinations that Washington felt could also be the site for Howe; Philadelphia, for instance, by way of the Delaware River or Chesapeake Bay, or even Charleston, South Carolina. "His conduct is puzzling and embarrassing beyond measure," Washington writes to Schuyler on the 23rd of July. "So are the informations which I get. At one time the ships are standing up toward the North River; in a little while they are going up the Sound; and in an hour after they are going out of the Hook." On that very day, Howe's fleet of more than 260 warships and transports, laden with between fifteen and eighteen thousand soldiers, innumerable horses, fieldpieces and small arms, quantities of ammunition to numerous too mention, provisions, and military equipment of every sort, set sail for Sandy Hook. It must have been a remarkable sight, an armada such that had never been seen on the North American continent. Just below the Hook the transports formed two divisions; the 64-gun *Eagle*, and the 32-gun frigate *Liverpool*, led the convoy. Just behind sailed the 64-gun *Augusta*, and her sister ship the *Isis* with 50-guns. They sailed, but no one on the American side had any idea where.

Washington received another report on the sailing and had felt he had guessed wrong, that Howe was now on his way to Philadelphia. He immediately ordered Sullivan, Stirling, and Stephen, with their divisions, Morgan's riflemen, and the squadrons of dragoons led by Shelton, Moylan, and Bland to proceed immediately to Philadelphia. He detached Wayne from Greene's brigade and sent him to Chester, just south of the city to command the militia there. With Greene and the rest of his army, Washington headed south to cross the Delaware yet again. But after six days Howe's fleet had not been sighted off the Delaware capes. Washington had marched his troops to the Jersey side of the Delaware, at Trenton, called Coryell's and Howell's Ferry to try and anticipate Howe's eventual destination. Washington was just beginning to question himself again, when suddenly he received word from Henry Fisher, a pilot at Lewes, Delaware, at the mouth of the Delaware Bay. The fleet had been sighted. Washington was 150 miles from Lewes, and had received the report in just less than 24 hours. Quite a performance by men and horses considering the roads in 1777.

Howe's fleet had sailed from Sandy Hook on the 23rd of July, 1777. With calm seas and following winds, the fleet had made it to the Delaware capes by the 29th. But it is here, that the decisions Howe made have puzzled historians for over two hundred and twenty years. After meeting the *Roebuck*, captained by Sir Andrew Snape Hamond, which had been stationed at the capes for weeks, Captain Hamond boarded Howe's flagship to report his findings on the conditions of the rivers and bays of the Delaware and Chesapeake. Was it Howe's intention to go directly up the Delaware to Philadelphia, which would make the most sense or had he intended to sail up the Chesapeake all the while? In a letter to Germain dated before he left New York he wrote, "I propose going up the

Delaware." After his arrival he wrote to Germain again stating, "Arrived off the Capes of the Delaware...when from information, I thought it most advisable to proceed to the Chesapeake Bay." That information was that the Americans had a fleet of "one frigate, two xebecs, one brig, two floating batteries, and a number of row galleys," that the river itself was too intricate and hazardous to navigate, and tides and currents at that time of the year were tricky at best. In addition there was the ongoing construction of two fortifications just south of Philadelphia, Fort Mifflin on the Pennsylvania side and Fort Mercer on the Jerseys. Along with a series of Chevaux-de-Frise erected from Chester, Pennsylvania to just above the river fortifications, it seemed to Howe that with the information that Washington would not go north to fortify New York, it would be more advisable to travel south and easily enter the Chesapeake without as much as a ripple of inconvenience.

The fact of the matter was that there were no fortifications or obstructions south of Chester which was only fourteen miles south of Philadelphia and afforded several good landing places for troops and supplies. New Castle, Delaware, only thirty-three miles, was a known port for overseas vessels, and the river from that point would have afforded more than enough room to anchor the number of ships Howe had in his complement. Instead, Howe decided on a landing at Head of Elk, Maryland which was fifty miles south of Philadelphia. The sailing took an additional week under the hot July sun, with conditions varying from adverse to dead calm winds and inclement weather with rough seas. A voyage that was suppose to take no more than a few days turned into two weeks. Supplies were running low, horses were dying from lack of feed and fresh water, and the filth building up onboard was beginning to draw an adverse effect on the soldiers and sailors within the fleet. As Trevelyan would later point out, "after all the delays and all those hardships, the same army, but in larger numbers at Head of Elk was ten miles farther from Philadelphia than it had been the previous December at Amboy." Howe had calculated that by choosing the Chesapeake route he could possibly cut off Washington's communication between the middle and southern colonies and maybe force Washington into a disadvantageous fight somewhere east of the Susquehanna River. He later could open up a safe and formidable supply route up the Delaware after he captured Philadelphia. Whatever the ultimate plans, Washington now had a clear vision of Howe's objective for the first time in months and ordered Sullivan to join the army "with all convenient speed," General Nash to "hasten with your brigade," and Proctor to "deliver your artillery to Chester," and for Greene to "march all of the troops to-morrow morning very early towards Philadelphia and onwards." News of the American victory at Bennington, New York on August 17th had arrived by the 23rd, and a great cheer erupted within the soldier's ranks. It would be the last time they would have reason to cheer for almost a year, for the bloody Philadelphia Campaign was about to begin in earnest.

Chapter VII

"The Battle of Brandywine"

With word of Howe's arrival in the Chesapeake Bay, Washington wasted no time in hastening preparations for the British army's obvious next objective, Head of Elk. Early on the 23rd, the army was put into motion and marched his troops through the streets of Philadelphia along Front Street and down Chestnut and out of the city and down the road to Wilmington in a quick, continuous march without halting. Both Tory and Whig had to be impressed as the Continentals streamed pass as they passed along blocks of people watching the procession of soldiers marching down the street. As a citizen of Philadelphia who witnessed the spectacle wrote, "The companies were impressive with the rank and file stacked from short to tall, some with uniforms, and some with hunting frocks, and some with common clothes. Many had cocked hats, some without, and those that did cock them, not all of them wearing them the same way, but each man with a green sprig in his hat, emblem of hope, each bearing his firelock with what air of skill his is trained to be."

They marched to Darby that evening, and moved on to Naaman's Creek the next day, and were given orders to "encamp in the first good ground beyond it." The cavalry was instructed to continue on to Wilmington before encamping, and Washington, Greene and their new charge, Lafayette, along with their aides continued along with the horsemen and made headquarters in Wilmington in a house on Quaker Hill. They learned from intelligence reports that the enemy was beginning to disembark and land that very morning "about Six Miles below the Head of Elk opposite to Cecil Court House." Washington gathered all the available troops, called on Armstrong to send on "every man of the Militia under your command" at Chester and Marcus Hook "that is properly armed, as quick as possible, to march them, indeed, that very night if need be." Greene instructed Stephen's and Sullivan to, "Bring such men as you have Ready." But not to "press hard in their march, for they must no doubt have been greatly harrassed in their expedition against Staten Island and undertaken at Hanover." The next morning Washington, Greene, Lafayette, their aides, and a strong troop of horse, rode southward on a scouting expedition. From the top of Iron and Gray's Hills they scanned the countryside for some glimpse of the British army. Gray's Hill was within only two miles of the enemy's camp and the only spot in the neighborhood of Elkton high where they could see the British tents, but could not arrive at a satisfactory estimate of their numbers. As night fell on the small reconnoiter party "a tempest of such sudden wind and rain" hit the men that they immediately took shelter in a neighboring farmhouse. Although the group was just a few men, they became increasingly aware that the house was not made for such a number. Drenched and cold from the sudden downpour, Washington had no inclination to wander out on such a night again. But his companions urged him that the danger of capture was real, and citing the fate of General Lee in almost the exact circumstances, tried to impress on the Commander-in-Chief the reason for a quick get-a-way. Washington would have none of it, and they nervously stayed where they were until daybreak. They would learn later that the owner of the home was a Tory, and that he did not send word to the British of his late night charge would have been a miracle. If Washington had been captured it could have easily signed the end of the struggle right there and then. Afterwards, Washington himself acknowledged that his "imprudence at the time was not in the best interest of their cause."

That next morning Greene, with one of his brigadiers, Weedon, was sent to select a position for a camp. After a careful examination, Greene fixed upon the "Cross-roads about six miles from

Elk." With open country behind to draw supplies and reinforcements from, and good skirmishing ground in front from which it would be easy to harass and annoy the enemy while he was engaged in collecting provisions. But before Greene could report his findings and selection, word reached him that he was needed at headquarters for a council of war. There, they decided upon another position and another policy. An encampment was chosen right in the enemy's path, Redclay Creek, nearly at the halfway point between Wilmington and Christiana. "You would not hold your ground if they advance," Greene would argue. And when the council urged that unless the way was blocked, Howe would push straight on for Philadelphia, Greene replied, "Howe will not think of such a thing until he has beaten this army." In the meantime, a great deal of work was made to remove all of the stores with which the countryside abounded, and to keep them out of reach of the enemy. With Greene stationed behind Whiteclay Creek, most of that duty would fall upon him. "Inclosed," he writes to Washington on the 2nd of September, "is a letter from Mr. Levi Hollingsworth, relative to the situation of the stores in that quarter. General Muhlenberg has marched with his detachment to cover the removal of the stores. If your Excellency thinks an additional force is necessary it shall be sent immediately. I wait further orders."

At the same moment a new figure appears on the scene, one that will often be repeated in the sequel of events and day to day operations during the most active portions of the Southern campaigns. "Captain Lee was reconnoitering yesterday near the Head of Elk," wrote Mr. Hollingsworth to Greene, "He says that they saw signs of a detachment of troops from the enemy having gone towards Notingham. Captain Lee supposed them, by their track, to be about five hundred horse and foot." Captain Horis Lee was a gallant young Virginian who would become a constant companion to Nathanael Greene in the coming months and beyond. A friendship that would span beyond the life of Greene and end forty-one years later in suffering and obscurity in Rhode Island, under the roof of Greene's youngest daughter.

The British had dropped anchor in the Elk River, just opposite the Cecil County Courthouse on the 25th of August, and disembarked by the next day. But they still had not begun their march by the 28th, due to several strong summer storms that roared through the area and made the roads impassable. Along with the fact that the troops were still recovering from their rough journey from Sandy Hook to the Chesapeake and needed the time to refresh themselves, as well as the "miserably emaciated" horses"-those that survived the trip-were in no shape to be used. But by the 29th, the weather finally cooperated and the roads being somewhat dried enough, the army marched out to Elkton, a small hamlet of "about 40 well built brick and stone houses," from which 1,000 men under the command of Colonel Patterson had been bivouacked since Washington's troops had arrived. Their job was to watch the movements of the British troops and report their whereabouts at all times to headquarters. The members of Patterson's "Philadelphia Light Horse" fled to Gray's Hill, and fled again when Howe's advance guard came up quickly and invaded Elkton, where they found "Storehouses full, consisting of molasses, Indian corn, Tobacco, Pitch, Tar and some Cordage and Flour." Necessary items that the both armies would need, but items the British got to first, because the American troops had failed to remove them when they had the opportunity. A huge mistake that would be amplified in the coming weeks ahead.

The British army would leave Elkton with the newfound gains and depart in two grand divisions. One was commanded by Cornwallis, and the other, under Hessian general, Wilhelm von Knyphausen, who had crossed the Elk River and encamped at Cecil County Courthouse. The maneuver would permit the army to advance up both sides of the Elk and join at a point seven or eight miles south of the Christina River. Both armies would stay encamped for five more days. There were several minor skirmishes with the American infantry over those days, but nothing that developed could be deemed a battle. What did occur was the massive buildup of foraging parties for both sides. For instance, one such party, a large detachment from von Knyphausen's troops, made a discovery of "261 head of long horned Cattle, 568 sheep, and 100 horses." Another party discovered 350 sheep, 55 horned cattle, and 204 horses and mules. Horses were always a much-needed commodity for any army, but the British were especially in need of the animals. Over 300 had died during their voyage, and another 100 were rendered unfit for duty. The rest of the livestock was well-intended fresh meat for the hungry army, which usually was sustained on porridge, hard tack, and if they were lucky, salt pork. The British were content to sit until the 2nd of September, until they were sufficiently rested and fed their fill.

Washington was encamped on the Neshaminy and was still in doubt of Howe's intentions. He was almost sure that the British would march that day, and sent Colonel Daniel Morgan from Greene's brigade, north to meet up with Putnam's riflemen in the north, to reinforce that army facing Burgoyne. Then Washington chose 100 men from each of the remaining six brigades which would form a light infantry corps under the command of Brigadier General William Maxwell of New Jersey. Maxwell and his men were posted in the vicinity of Cooch's Bridge on the upper waters of the Chirstiana. Washington had warned Maxwell that the enemy army had intended to march by the 2nd and begged him "to be prepared to give them as much trouble as you possibly can."

The two British army columns did march the 2nd of September, von Knyphausen's troops up the road along the Delaware and Chesapeake Canal to Buck Tavern, also known as Carson's, and Howe by way of the road to Rikin's (Aiken's) Tavern as to avoid the American troops encamped on Iron Hill. Howe had expected to meet von Knyphausen by the tavern (currently the town of Glasgow), but when he "did not perceive them," they pushed on through to "close country in the woods within shot of the road frequently in front and flank of points towards the Road." The regulars were unfamiliar with fighting on this type topography and preferred combat in the open in fields where they could draw their regular battlelines which they had been trained to fight in for years. A short running fight with some Hessian jagers and British light infantry against Maxwell's men, had them running back to cover and retreating to "several close" points to the British, which kept them from gaining a position to the Americans rear flank. But the "spirited skirmish" was enough to drive Maxwell's troops into complete disorganization and caused them to retreat in full flight back with the main army on the White Clay Creek.

The next four days, the British were busy reconnoitering the countryside, bringing up provisions from the fleet, some 25 miles away, and sending back the sick and wounded. "Nothing new in camp since I wrote you last," writes Greene to his wife on the 7th of September, from his camp near Wilmington, "only that the army are advanced in line with me. 'Tis said this morning the enemy are coming out. A note, this moment received from Captain Lee, of my light-horse, favors the opinion. I am just going out upon a reconnoitering party. You must excuse my short letter." The day before the British had indeed moved up. Grant, with two brigades left in Elkton, was now with Howe's army. All communication with the fleet was ceased, and the entire fleet withdrew down the Chesapeake Bay.

Greene, along with Stephen's divisions, mostly Virginia Continentals, under Brigadiers Muhlenberg, Weedon, Woodford, Scott, and Sheldon's light-horse, were advanced to White Clay Creek with the main body of the American army. But a council of war decided the position of the Americans, although carefully strengthened, which was found to be better equipped to concentrate itself in the northerly side of Red Clay Creek on the road to Philadelphia, Howe's obvious destination. Washington and Greene were informed that the British army had unburdened themselves of their baggage and tents, indicating a quick march in their general direction. The American army was ordered to do the same, except for men who had greatcoats to keep them, and their blankets. Everything else was transported to Chadd's Ford on the Brandywine. Now ready for action, the Americans sat on the banks of the Brandywine and waited for the enemy's next move.

"The enemy marched out the day before yesterday," Greene writes his wife on the 10th of September; "they took post in a position to turn our flank, the Christiana Creek being on our left. His Excellency thought our situation too dangerous to risk a battle, as the enemy refused to fight us in front. His Excellency ordered the army to file off to the right, and take post at this place. A general action must take place in a few days. The army are in high spirits, and wish for action....Here are some of the most distressing scenes imaginable,--the inhabitants generally desert their houses, furniture moving, cattle driving, and women and children traveling off on foot,--the country all resounds with the cries of the people,--the enemy plunders most amazingly. The militia of the country are not like the Jersey militia; fighting is a new thing with these men, and many seem to have but a poor stomach for the business." Greene has been riding back and forth, reconnoitering along the lines, and trying to find a stronghold that his troops may use when the British attack. He writes to his wife that same day, "I am exceedingly fatigued. I have been on horseback for upwards of thirty hours; and never closed my eyes for near forty. Last night I was in hopes of a good night's rest; but a dusty bed gave me asthma, and I had very little sleep the whole night; but little as it was, I feel finely refreshed this morning." This is the first mention of the asthma Nathanael Greene had suffered from since childhood. He must have struggled with the painful disease increasingly in those days to mention it at all.

The battle the Americans knew was coming was anxiously awaited. Early in the morning of the 11th, the enemy was sighted approaching by the Nottingham Road (now US Route 1 or the Baltimore Pike) running eastward through Kennett Square on its way through to Chadd's Ford and then to Chester, and Philadelphia. This was where Washington expected the principal effort to be made. Washington drew up his main body of troops, with Wayne's Pennsylvanians and Proctor's artillery in the front, behind an entrenchment on the bank of the river, and Greene with his two brigades on the heights in their rear. The foggy morning wore away into a blazing sunshine and sweltering heat, as small skirmishes and cannonade broke the silence every so often. Washington and Greene were passing the time in a small house about three quarters of a mile from the ford, using it as their headquarters, and waiting for the decided action to take place. About an hour before noon a messenger from Sullivan, who was two miles higher up the stream in command of the right flank, came saying that a very large body of the enemy was marching for the upper fords by the great valley road. Suddenly Washington and Greene realized that this force in the front was not the main body at all, and Howe was repeating the maneuver, which had given him the victory at Long Island. Washington instantly decided to cross and attack the enemy on the opposite side of the ford. Orders were sent to Sullivan to cross at the same time, and fall upon the left wing. Greene immediately put his brigades in motion, and was already over the ford with the advance when another messenger came. There was no large body on the great valley road after all, the whole British army was in front, and Greene and Sullivan were rushing upon certain destruction if they continued in that direction. Greene was recalled by Washington, and Sullivan was directed to wait for further orders until more accurate information was acquired. Accurate intelligence information would be the single reason for the outcome of the Battle of Brandywine.

Two more anxious hours passed. Another messenger came; no longer with hearsay and conjecture, but with an eyewitness account whom barely escaped with his life from the hands of the enemy. Howe's maneuver had again succeeded, and Cornwallis was already on the left bank, pressing down toward the rear of the Americans. Sullivan was hurried off to meet Howe, and Wayne was ordered to watch the ford, where the body that all the morning had been feigning an intention to pass would now, doubtless, try to pass in earnest. Greene was directed to hold himself in readiness to reinforce either Wayne or Sullivan, as circumstances might require. Washington remained with Greene at the headquarters, waiting for the first sounds of the approaching conflict.

More anxious waiting, when at last, between four and five in the afternoon, a sudden burst of cannonade and musketry was heard from the northwest. The noise of the full scale battle could be heard in the noisy streets of Philadelphia, and was said to bring the members of Congress Hall out into the street, where groups of citizens had already gathered, muttering nervously, raising their voices in high pitched questions of the battles outcome. "The groups," it was written by a citizen who was witness to it at the time, "were divided into Tories, by themselves, the Whigs, too, by themselves, looking at each other askance in silent expectation." The sound of battle came faster and faster and in heavier surges, swelling at last into a continuous roar. Washington quickly gave Greene his orders, "Meet with Weedon's brigade and press the march by the nearest road. Wait there in reserve and hold the road to Philadelphia."

Greene and Weedon had nearly four miles to go, and only forty minutes to get there. Quite a distance in that short of time would be amazing. To do it on a horribly hot September afternoon would be a miracle in itself. But, the American line had to be formed on the northern slope of a round hill a hundred rods southeast of Birmingham Meetinghouse. Northeasterly through the valley ran the Street Road from Painter's Ford. The American line curved around the face of the hill, which De Borre's brigade holding the right; Stephen's division next; and Stirling's after that, composing the center. Sullivan would hold the left with the help of four pieces of "judiciously placed" artillery out in front of the line. "This position," wrote Captain John Montresor, chief engineer of the British forces in America and former builder of Fort Mifflin, "was remarkably strong, having a large body advanced, small bodies still further advanced and their rear covered by wood wherein their main body was posted, with natural glacis for 3/4 mile." The flanks also rested in the woods. Even Cornwallis, observing from the top of Osborne's Hill noticed the arrangements of the Americans and remarked, "The damn rebels form well." Quite a compliment from a man who was known to give few.

Cornwallis decided to move his observation point to an area closer to the fighting. When he emerged from some woods, a Quaker youth by the name of Joseph Townsend observed this and commented in his journal later that day, "He was on horseback, appeared tall and sat very erect. His rich scarlet clothing loaded with gold lace, epaulets &c., occassioned him to make a brilliant and martial appearance." He continued about Cornwallis' men, "Most of his officers were rather short, portly men, well dressed and of genteel appearance, and did not look as if they had ever been exposed to any hardship, their skins being as white and delicate as is customary for females who were brought up in large cities and towns." He also commented on the Hessians he saw, "Many of the Germans wore their beards on their upper lips, which is a novelty in this part of the country." He obviously got around that day, because he also saw Howe and said of him, "he was mounted on a large English looking horse, much reduced in flesh....The general was a large, portly man, of coarse features, and appeared to have lost his teeth, as his mouth had fallen in."

Meanwhile, the Americans were preparing for the grand attack and Washington was getting impatient just waiting at headquarters. Washington called for one of his aides to get his horse, he was leaving to get closer to the scene of the action, but he did not know the way to it. Among several groups of country people who had become refugees from their homes from the advance of the British, an old man was standing near Washington by the name of Joseph Brown. Washington requested him to lead the way by the shortest road to the fighting. Brown, of course, refused, stating that the reason he was there was to stay away from the battle. Why should he go toward it when he didn't have too? One of Washington's aides dismounted, threatened the old man with his sword, which persuaded Brown to change his mind, and he was hoisted onto the aide's saddle. Across the country they bounded; three miles as the crow flies, Washington continually crying out, "Push along, old man! Push along!" Washington's staff trailing behind them, trying to keep up. They finally came out on the road leading to Philadelphia, half a mile west of the Dilworth Inn. Greene was already there, with Weedon's brigade in advance, Muhlenberg's following close behind. Greene and his troops had covered the four-mile distance in less than 45 minutes.

Cornwallis was now edging his troops toward the Americans' extreme right and directly toward where Washington and the men were standing. The Americans would have to wheel, over and over again in order to avoid being outflanked. For an hour and forty minutes, under the heavy fire of the British artillery, the Americans on the hill kept the enemy at bay. For almost an hour during that time the battle was fought "almost Muzzle to Muzzle, in such a manner that General Conway, who has Seen much Service, says he never Saw So Close & Severe a fire," Wrote a captain of the Delaware regiment. "Cannon balls flew thick and many a small arms roared like the sound of rolling drums." On five separate occasions the Americans were driven back, and five times they surged forward to their old position again.

Meanwhile, Greene, Weedon, and Muhlenberg joined in the fight. Both Weedon and Muhlenberg came from Virginia. Weedon was born there and was just an innkeeper in Fredericksburg when he joined the army, but Greene would write of his brigade leader, "he was zealous, as he fanned the flame of sedition when war broke out. So much so he was made a brigadier when the 1777 promotions were made." Of Muhlenberg, Greene would start his letters to him, "My dear old friend." Muhlenberg was a Pennsylvanian German by birth, and studied in Gottingen Germany, ordained a minister in London, and made the pastor of a parish in Virginia at the opening of the war. Another example of a religious man taking arms up against what they deemed a "rightous act against an invader of our shores" in the fight for American independence.

Although the right of the American line had retreated, the fierce left side was yet to see any heavy action. Until now; while the British Guard and Hessian jagers were pursuing Sullivan's retreating brigade, they followed them into a "very thick, entangled woods, and were unable to further engage the enemy." They had, in fact, gotten lost in those woods. When they stumbled out of the forest, they had "came blundering through the woods--accidentally, but most opportunely--upon the uncovered flank of the American centre," and the entire American line fell back. The British followed, and gained "one height after another as the enemy withdrew." Without wasting time, but in a vain effort to check the tide of the American army's flight, Greene ordered his men to open ranks as the British light infantry troops advanced. He then ordered them to promptly close again when they had passed. The artillery was also directed to keep up a constant fire to hold the enemy from reinforcing the advance guard. They marched, halting, fighting, and marching again, for nearly half a mile, when they came to a narrow defile flanked by woods on both sides. Commanding the road by which the army was to retreat, Greene ordered Weedon to hold the road with his own brigade, while he crossed the road and held it with Muhlenberg.

By this time, the hot sun was setting and causing a fog to form at the treetops. Greene knew the fight was probably lost, and had no idea at the time, but he had gained some important information on tactics used by Cornwallis which would come in very handy at the next campaign the two antagonists would meet. The Americans were held in check as the last rays of sun were setting over the Pennsylvanian hills, but Muhlenberg was not quite finished with the struggle. As the Hessians jagers, now under the personnel command of von Knyphausen advanced on the American troops, the order to fix bayonets was given. Muhlenberg swung his troops around, fixing their own bayonets and marched toward the seasoned Hessian troops. Greene wrote after the battle, "Muhlenberg had a wild, boyish, look upon his face while he advanced the ranks toward the enemy. And the hated Hessians could be heard to say, 'Hier kommt Teufel Piet!' Here comes Devil Pete." The Hessians seemed to be in shock as bayonet met bayonet, thrust for thrust, man against man in hand-to-hand combat. Weedon was forced to firm Muhlenberg's rear when the Hessian line seemed to engulf his troops. Then Greene, having accomplished what they had set out to do, ordered his troops to retreat through the woods. Muhlenberg broke off the attack just as a band of the Queen's Rangers and the 71st Highlanders were seen in the distance to reinforce von Knyphausen. The troops hurried to join the American main body, which was retreating toward Chester. And with that, the Battle of Brandywine was over.

It had been a fierce and many faceted fight. Although the losses for the British are probably underestimated at 90 killed, 480 wounded, and 6 missing, the American casualty report was not much better, with Howe estimating more than 300 killed, 600 wounded, and almost 400 made prisoner. Those are most likely inflated, but the Americans did lose a great number of seasoned veterans, although the American wounded accounted for most of the British prisoners, one wounded soldier was able to travel with the retreating army. The young, French officer who had just entered the war, Lafayette, had been wounded in the leg with a musket ball. Although his horse had been shot from beneath him, he was able to find another and escape capture.

They had battled the superior British troops better than in any previous occasion, but had lost once again. Although tired and hungry, they retreated in an orderly fashion to regroup outside of Chester. Washington and Greene had brought off their gallant brigades in good order. Although exhausted with the labor of a good fight, excited by the days events, and the roar of battle still echoing in his head, Washington would have to perform one more duty before he could rest. "Congress would have to be written to," Washington told Greene that night, "someone must do it Nathanael, for I am too sleepy." Pickering, the Adjutant general was given the duty. After composing the letter, Pickering gave it to Washington to study and came back to say, "I wrote it and gave it to the General to read. He, with perfect composure, directed me to add a consolatory hope that another day would give a more fortunate result. And that was the most important point of all." The Americans were merely at the beginning of a long and frustrating campaign road. It would be nearly 8 months before they could call a battle "a more fortunate result."

Chapter VIII

"Philadelphia"

Howe's army camped on the battlefield, then he sent the 71st Regiment, Fraser's Highlanders, to take possession of Wilmington, Delaware. At the same time, Howe's guard was taking possession of John McKinly also. McKinly was President and commander-in-chief of the state, and Howe imprisoned him on the frigate "Soleby", lying in anchor in the river just out from the town. In Philadelphia, John Hancock was arisen at four in the morning by a messenger delivering Washington's letter. Hancock would respond to the general, "I am sorry for the unfortunate issue of the day, but from the troops keeping up their spirits, I flatter myself it will still be in our power to retrieve the loss of yesterday. I have thought proper, in consequence of the intelligence received this morning, to call the Congress together at six o'clock."

At exactly six o'clock that morning Congress met, heard Washington's letter, and ordered it to be published. Then at ten, they passed a resolution to call out the state militia to "hasten forward to the Continental; and reinforce the army under General Washington." By five that afternoon, they ordered "a proper vessel or boat to be provided without delay to convey the wounded Lafayette to New Jersey." And finally by evening, they directed "that the Commissary-general purchase, on the most reasonable terms he can, thirty hogsheads of rum, and that the same be presented to the army, with Congress's compliments, and distributed among the soldiers in such manner as the General shall direct, for their gallant behavior in the late battle of Brandywine," Washington directed that each man was to receive "one gill (about 4 oz) per day, while it lasts." It is thrilling, even today, to think Congress could all agree, ratify, and order a resolution in as fast a time as it took them that day. There is a lot to be said for ones safety becoming a strong motivating force.

Meanwhile, the defeated army was rapidly returning through Darby to the banks of the Schuylkill, Greene covering the rear with the brigades he had commanded at Brandywine. By the 13th of September, the army was encamped on the edge of Germantown. Even with the defeat at Brandywine, Washington's army was still between Howe and Philadelphia, and those were his standing orders. He guessed that the British would attempt to turn his right flank, cut off a retreat path to his west, and force him to be caught between the Schuylkill and Delaware Rivers. To keep that from happening, Washington broke camp on the morning of the 14th and marched west to the area of Warren Tavern and the White Horse Tavern, and "with a firm intent of giving the Enemy Battle," maneuvering his army between the British and the Swedes Ford across the Schuylkill, where Washington thought they would attempt to cross at that point.

Back in Philadelphia, Congress was debating on who was to blame for the army's defeat at Brandywine, and unjustly laid the blame at Sullivan's doorstep. They were in the process of compounding the injustice further by recalling Sullivan from the army, while an official investigation was conducted. Washington decided to conduct his own investigation, and one that would allow a valuable officer continue in his service, rather that having a new, inexperienced general take his place at such a crucial time. Congress yielded to Washington's opinion, and within days, the official investigation was completed, showing that Sullivan was without blame in the defeat, and exonerating Sullivan completely. The official investigation had shown that, like the defeat of Long Island the year before, the fault lay not with the generals, but with the means of command that they had a their disposal. If there was much question about who was to blame, Weedon would write as to whom may have been responsible for perhaps saving the entire army. "In that hour and a quarter of hot action, General Greene had confessedly saved the park of artillery, and indeed the army, from the fatal effects of a disagreeable rout;" Although Congress attempted to find someone to chastise for the Brandywine defeat, they did not bother to look for anyone to decorate. Several days after the battle, Washington was in the company of several officers, and was known to have said, "You, sir, are considered my favorite general by many; Weedon here, and his brigade, like myself, are Virginians; should I applaud them for their achievement under your command, I shall be charged with partiality; jealousy will be excited, and the service injured." Weedon said that Greene responded, "Your Excellency has enough to distress himself; let us not add to your perplexity." How true the conversation was, will never be known. One thing that cannot be denied is the fact that Greene was Washington's favorite general.

Washington had no intention of allowing Sir William Howe to take possession of Philadelphia without a terrific fight. If he did somehow succeed in getting it, he would not allow Howe the tranquillity of holding it for long. It was a busy time for the encamped army where the men had time to refurbish their arms, resupply rations, and prepare for a battle they knew was coming. It was even busier in Ole' Philadelphia, where the Whigs were hurriedly packing their belongings for a sudden removal, Congress with pressing issues being discussed, moving public stores to a safe place, and sending off the principal Quakers—"six wagons of them with a guard,--to be taken to Virginia in the hope of checking the readiness which the brotherhood had so freely manifested to keep up a treasonable correspondence with the enemy;" An early form of detention for people suspected of enemy activity, because of their heritage or religious beliefs? And every village surrounding Philadelphia was abuzz with the talk of "the American army losses were much more serious than expected," and that "the British army is already just outside the city;" and every town and hamlet suspecting that their village would be the next bloody battlefield. Where could they go? Where would they hide? But the busiest site was the headquarters in Germantown, toward which every soldier's eyes were turned with anxious expectation. Where would we meet the enemy next indeed? But first Washington had to solve an ongoing problem when the weather began to turn cold. The troops would need more shoes, blankets, and provisions. There was wide spread disaffection to the army throughout the country, and supplies were becoming a difficult commodity to produce. To make matters worse, the British fleet would soon attempt to force its way up the Delaware, and the defenses, long before begun, had not yet been completed and strengthened. The British army would soon be trying to reach the Schuylkill, but from which of the several fords would they try? By the 14th, the Americans again turned their faces southward toward the enemy, and the path that Howe was surely about to travel forward toward Philadelphia. Washington broke camp and marched the army by way of the Lancaster Road, and got between the enemy and Swedes Ford. By the 15th, they reached the Warren Tavern.

The next morning, by about nine o'clock, the scouts brought back word that the enemy was advancing and sure to offer battle. Detachments were instantly sent forward to support the advance guard, and to help hold the British in check while the line was forming. But the ground they were on was not the ground on which Washington would readily choose to fight. It was open and level, baked hard by the past weeks of sweltering sun. Washington decided to send out troops to scour the area for a better-suited ground that would be to the Americans advantage. Finally, Pickering, Adjutant general, discovered an area, in the valley behind the center and left of their line. The ground was exceptionally wet, considering the recent weather, the ground soft, and impassable to artillery. The only area that was not of this condition was to the right of the line, in the rear of Greene's division, "where there was firm road," Greene observed. Washington, and a number of his field generals were gathered in a group consultation when Greene arrived with Pickering. He wrote of the meeting, "Pressing my horse forward to learn of their object, I found that they were still debating whether to receive the British where they were, or cross the valley and make a stand on the high ground on the other side of it." In the distance, small arms fire could be heard from the front. Wayne and Maxwell, with an advance guard, were detached forward to observe the enemy's movements on the Chester-Dilworth Road, and were already engaged with Knyphausen's column, and part of the Hessian jagers, commanded by Colonel von Donop, near the Boot Tavern. Wayne and Maxwell's troops took a position "on high ground covered with a cornfield and orchards." Unfortunately, the jagers were expert fighters on this type of terrain, and almost immediately gained the upper hand, as a "considerable amount of fire was exchanged," before the Americans fell back "through a dense forest," and came upon the main American body for support.

A real battle seemed to be on the horizon when Nature herself took hold. It was September 16th, and the weather, which had been nothing but a sweltering heat all summer, had turned considerably cooler the day after the battle at Brandywine. A decidedly "hard North West wind" had blown in and dispelled the hot, humid air with cold, dry air. The result can be found in any elementary science book; Thunderstorms, which were in most cases, violent. By the 15th, the winds shifted to the northeast and "increased in violence;" the sky drew dark and ominous, and the clouds became overcast, and heavy with moisture. It was one o'clock in the afternoon, and Washington ordered Greene to draw up the troops into a new position on the higher ground. Count Casimir Pulaski, the recently appointed "Commander of the Horse," was sent to the forward British position and try and delay their advance while the main body of the army moved into the new position. A light drizzle had already begun to fall, and Washington suddenly noticed that Knyphausen's troops to his left, had just been joined by Matthew's troops and had a clear path into the Americans' flank. Washington, seeing he was in trouble, ordered the complete withdrawal of all troops to the higher ground to the west. The armies were in position, and were within a quarter mile and facing each other, ready to reprise the engagement they had had just five short days before.

Suddenly, the skies could hold the rain no longer. It was said to come down in buckets. One Hessian observer, a Major Bauermeister commented afterwards, "It came down so hard that in a few moments we were completely drenched and sank in mud up to our calves." Low clouds dropped down through the valley and the driving, wind swept rain, completely obscured the opposing hilltops where the armies were facing each other. The two combatants were hidden from each other and unable to even assemble a bayonet charge, let alone fire muskets or cannon. "We could nearly see the hand in front of our faces, let alone a quarter mile away," wrote General Henry Knox. Powder was soaked, guns sodden and useless, and one hundred and fifty thousand, extremely valuable, paper cartridges were ruined. Knox continued, "this was a most terrible stroke to us." It would be deemed the Battle of the Clouds, where Nature had won out over the two battle equipped armies. In the words of historian Edward Gifford, Jr., "It was the peace of God that interfered."

The deluge had dampened more than just the battlefield. Washington was sorely disappointed, and with a heavy heart, again put his wet and weary battalions on the march across the Schuylkill and toward Warwick Furnace (Reading), where the strong ground would allow his troops to rest, repair and clean their arms before moving against the enemy once again. He sent Greene forward with Tilghman, one of Washington's aides, to choose a position. Greene chose one on the range of mountains which, extending from Valley Forge to the Yellow Springs,--"difficult access," easy descent, well suited for skirmishes and partial actions, but impossible to force a general engagement upon. Greene had his own thoughts on what the Americans should do next. With Wayne close to the enemy's rear, and the main army within striking distance of his flank, Greene thought that a crippling blow could be dealt to Howe if he should attempt to cross the Schuylkill, and a safe retreat secured in case of disaster." Washington approved of Greene's plans, but at Redclay Creek, while Greene was making his study of the surrounding ground, a council of war had decided to act by the front. Washington accepted their decision, and Greene's enemies took this opportunity to accuse Greene that, with his plan he was all too

106

willing to sacrifice Philadelphia. Most of the influence to adopt the frontal action was pushed by the southern influence. In the sentiments of Greene, "never a body to concur, or approve, neither my plans or submissions."

The main body of the American army remained in Warwick Furnace to await a new supply of ammunition from the main magazine. But they had to wait, it was still raining three days after the Battle of the Clouds. Washington decided, that if the ammunition could not come to the army, the army was going to go to the ammunition. Again the Americans were on the march, this time to Yellow Springs, a twelve mile march, across the Schuylkill at Parker's Ford, through chest deep water, camped there that night, marched another seven miles toward Swedes Ford and then ten miles to Richardson's Ford, twenty nine miles in two days. Certainly a great feat of endurance in the distressed condition most of the soldiers were in. Many had no shoes, some only blouses and tattered breeches, no greatcoats, and blankets were hard to come by still. But, Washington had managed to maneuver his beleaguered troops to east of the Schuylkill and between Howe and Philadelphia. They camped along the Perkiomen Creek.

By comparison, Howe's army movements were a walk in the garden. Although they "suffered much from the weather," by the 18th, von Knyphausen had marched three miles to the White Horse, where he joined Cornwallis and then eight more miles to camp at Tredyffrin. At Valley Forge, a foraging party found a "store of rebel supplies: 3800 Barrels of Flour, Soap and Candles, 25 Barrels of Horse Shoes, several thousand tomahawks and Kettles and Intrenching Tools and 20 Hogsheads of Resin." On the 19th, when the Americans were making that grueling march, the British found "halting very necessary for the men and particularly for our horses," they had marched a mere 12 miles and arrived at the Bull's Head and Mouth Tavern where another foraging party "relieved the inhabitants of 150 horses" at New Town Square. By the 20th, a post was established at Valley Forge.

In accordance with the council, Wayne's division, partly made up of the 2nd Pennsylvania Regiment, with four fieldpieces, was still detached in the American rear. Here he met with the bloody disaster at Paoli, known to many as a massacre, although a rout. It had no resemblance to a massacre. The detachment was in the neighborhood of Warren Tavern in a position to fall on the enemy's rear guard and baggage train at any given moment. Howe knew this and formulated a plan. He sent Major General Grey, with the 40th, 42nd, 44th, and 55th Regiments of Foot, along with the 2nd Battalion of light infantry, and a handful of light Dragoons on a little surprise party for Wayne and his troops. It was already dark when they got to within 200 rods of the American camp. Grey ordered his men to march with unloaded muskets, and those who could not draw their loads to remove their flints, and set out at ten o'clock in the evening. They advanced up the White Horse Road, picking up inhabitants as they went along to prevent them from sounding an alarm. Near the Warren Tavern, Grey came upon Wayne's pickets and bayoneted them to death. But, one of the sentries got off a single musket shot, alarming the main camp. Wayne ordered his men into ranks and drew up the artillery for action. The men kept their campfires lit and the British could clearly see their outlines in the fires glow, making them easy targets, while the British were invisible in the darkness. Grey fell on the unsuspecting men and bayoneted them, while the Americans barely got off a shot. In the confusion, one of the fieldpieces got lodged in an opening in a fence and caused the American soldiers to get bunched up in a large group, making them easy prey for the British bayonets. The quick strike attack was over in less than 20 minutes and caused the death of 33 Americans, and over 100 wounded, all by the bayonet. Another 200 were claimed to have been captured by Grey. Wayne was ordered to stand trial for dereliction of duty in a courts martial. He was found not guilty and exonerated of all blame, but forever claimed it was his fault and carried the incident to his grave.

Wayne's defeat relieved Howe of any fear that the Americans could attack his rear guard. On the 21st of September, he set off confidently from Tredyffrin in a northern course, marched to Valley

Forge and encamped along the Schuylkill from the Forge to French Creek. Washington, who had anticipated a southern route, was confused by this "perplexing manoeuvre." The movement of Howe's troops spelled danger to the stores at the Reading Furnace, and he marched his troops north to meet Howe. "One old Whig with a telescope," we are told by Muhlenberg, "shuddered when he looked out upon the tents of the British army from his peaceful home. 'Here I am old, worn out, with a sick wife subject to hysterical paroxysms, have with me two daughters, two sons wives with two infant children, and my son's parents-in-law, and expect every day and hour that a British division will cross the Schuylkill and treat us without distinction, as the providence of God had ordered and will allow. We cannot well fly, for there is no place safe. Where the two armies do not reach there are thieves, robbers, and murderers, who take advantage of people like myself and the time and conditions.' I felt badly for the old one. But I was told, 'to come out upon the great road at the house and prepare fro the British Advance.' I left the old pastor and resolve that he and his family go to New Hanover. He tried to persuade his wife to go and leave, but she said she would rather live, suffer, and die with him in Providence." The daughters, children and other adults moved on to New Hanover, but the old folks stayed behind. We have no record of what became of them after the 21st.

Meanwhile, Howe was maneuvering to get possession of the lower fords, and through them, the road to Philadelphia, by causing Washington to second guess whether he was also after the stores at Reading. Howe had no intention of moving on the stores, or try to outflank Washington, but instead countermarched swiftly southward during the night to Fatland Ford and Gordon's Ford, blasted away a slimly held American militia post at Fatland with only "a few cannon-shot to dispense the cowards," and sent the Guards, a battalion of light infantry and six guns, along with 25 dragoons, cross the river to hold the opposite end of the ford, and with von Donop, and 60 jagers, 20 horse, and 100 grenadiers cleared the way at Gordon's easily and crossed there. There, "at the rising of the moon" the entire British army crossed at the flatland, and by eight o'clock the next morning all except Grant's brigade of British infantry, covering the baggage, provision, and artillery train, were on the east side of the river without nearly a shot fired. The rest of the troops soon followed, and thus again Howe, with all the ease imaginable, had outwitted the American commander-in-chief once more.

When the unwelcome news reached headquarters, "everyone was astonished," says Gordon. Washington was over twenty miles from Flatland, and with "Our Troops harassed as ours had been with constant marching since the Battle of Brandywine, it was in vain to think of covering that distance in time to seize the opportunity," wrote Washington. Another reason Washington noted as a strong reason "against being able to make a forced March is the want of shoes," Washington wrote to Congress that day. A council of war agreed with him that the best course of action was no action at all. Stay where they were until rested and reinforced. Howe continued his march unopposed, "till three o'clock in the afternoon when we arrived at Norriton" and encamped there, just seventeen miles from Philadelphia, less than half the distance the American army was from it.

"On one of these dreary nights," writes Pickering, "as the army was encamped on the eastern side of the Schuylkill, I fell in with General Greene while riding horseback. We descended the bank of the Perkiomen Creek together, and while our horses were drinking, I said to him: 'General Greene, before I came to the army, I entertained an exalted opinion of general Washington's military talents, but I have since seen nothing to enhance it.' I did not venture to say it was sensibly lowered, though that was the fact; and so Greene understood me, for he instantly shook his head and answered in these words precisely: 'Why, the general does want decision; for my part, I decide in a moment." Greene had no right to question Washington's decision, and then comment on it to a subordinate. But that was Greene's way, and he would prove that his independent acts were successful. But Greene was one of Washington's closest friends and should have been supportive, especially at a time like this. As is the case today; it's quite easy to stand on the sidelines and call the plays, if you aren't the one whose butt is on the line if you call a few bad plays and cost your team the game.

Nothing but a battle could save the city now. Congress had already withdrawn with the intention of reassembling at Lancaster, although afterwards they decided to remove themselves again and relocate to Yorktown. But before they left, they decided to strengthen Washington's hands by an important resolve. By conferring upon him dictatorial powers for sixty days. A battle was still expected and needed, especially by the Pennsylvanians who had the most to lose by the British destructive marches and countermarches toward the city. However, Washington felt he must stay in reserve a few days longer, no matter what the public sentiments thought or said. Reinforcements were on the march and expected at any time. The troops needed rest, more blankets and especially shoes before they could have another long march. Washington was determined that, the next time he and Howe met, the American army would come into it strong-handed and prepared for the conflict.

Howe entered Philadelphia on the 26th of September amid the cheers of the Tories, and the deep dejection of the few Whigs who, by chance, were unable to leave the city. This was only Howe's first step, and it had cost him a battle and thirty days marching, though the distance from the landing site at Elkton was only sixty miles. Two miles a day with fighting at every turn and starvation at the end of the road, did not look like they were successfully putting down the rebellion this campaign. But the British and their partisans in America, as well as those back in England spoke boldly of the victories they had already won, and promised themselves still greater ones to come. Here they had captured the rebel capitol. Not only holding the largest city and port on the American continent, but the pride of what such an event was doing to the rebel morale. Howe still had another step to take. He held the port, but not its waterway. What good would it be to have 8,000 troops in the rebel capital, if they could not be resupplied. They had the city's harbor, but could not use it because the Americans, with their inferior navy, still commanded the Delaware River. Without control of the river, there would be no direct communication with the fleet, and consequently no sure base for supplies to the city and Howe's men.

Provisions had long been dear in Philadelphia, especially those from the West Indies and Europe. But, immediately after the British entered it, articles of daily use rose so high in price that few of the inhabitants could continue to pay long without exhausting their financial resources. Washington had a plan, even before Howe captured Philadelphia, "If Howe is to capture Philadelphia, so be it. But let him hold it." he would say. His plan was simple; shut out the British fleet from freely going up and down the river, and thus starve Howe into evacuating the city. To do this, Washington and the Pennsylvania Board of Safety had constructed *chevaux-de-frise* in the channel, supported by row galleys, floating batteries, and three forts;--Fort Mercer at Red Bank Plantation on the Jersey bank, Fort Billingsport, about three miles just to the south of Mercer, and Fort Mifflin on Mud Island, just off the Pennsylvania bank of the Delaware. Along with the defenses, reinforcements were on their way from the north and Virginia, and with their aid a severe blow could be struck against the Royal army before it could settle down in contentment to its winter quarters in Philadelphia.

Accordingly, on the 28th, two days after Howe occupied the city, a council of war was assembled to decide whether it would be better to wait for the reinforcements or to venture an immediate attack with the 8,000 Continentals and 3,000 militia already in camp, against the roughly 8,000British and German regulars who were now stationed in Philadelphia. Greene, and all of the major generals, along with five of the brigadiers, were agreed that attacking was the answer, but not right away. Their plan was to take a strong position nearer the city, and from there they could mount their advance, or use it as an avenue of retreat, as circumstances required. Wayne, with five other brigadiers, was for attacking at once. Washington accepted the decision of the majority, and on the 30th of September 1777, the army moved forward by the Skippack Road to within sixteen miles of Germantown, where a part of the British forces lay in reserve for Howe. The Americans kept a vigilant guard on their new camp, and constantly sent out light parties for intelligence. One of the early fruits of this watchfulness was the interception of two letters, from which it was ascertained that Sir William Howe "had detached a part of his force against first Billingsport, and then the other two forts on the Delaware." A second council of war was promptly called. All agreed in a vote to immediately attack, and the Battle of Germantown was a result of that vote.

The British position at the time seemed to invite an attack. Part of their forces, as we have noted, had been detached to act against the defenses of the Delaware, another part had been stationed in Philadelphia, and still a larger part lay at Germantown, now a part of the city, but then merely a village of a single street, two miles in length, and four miles from the outskirts of the city. Here the main body of the British were encamped, their center near the center of the village, and at right angles with it, and their wings stretching out into the country in the midst of gardens and orchards, and covered in front by the German chasseurs on their left, and Simcoe's Queen Rangers on their right. The British pickets were at Mount Airy, two miles farther up from the main street of Germantown.

Beside this main road, there were two other roads to the village,--the Lime-kiln Road, leading to the center of their camp, and nearly at a forty-five degree angle, and the old York Road, which led to the rear of the camp, by a similar angle. Both of these roads were on the British right. On the left, the village was bordered by the Wissahickon Creek, which runs for some distance almost parallel with the village, and then eastward until it empties into the Schuylkill. There was another road as well, known as Ridge Road, which crosses the creek not far from its mouth and led directly into the Hessian troop camp. The plan was to strike the British, front, flank, and rear, simultaneously, and therefore rendering it impossible for one body to come to the aid of another. Doing this would crush them all at once, by using four separate attacks. To accomplish this the American army had to separate into four columns, each to take a separate road, but act as one. Timing was going to be everything.

Sullivan led the right wing, which would attack the enemy's front by the main road. Greene would attack the left, which would come in to the enemy's right by the Limekiln Road. Meanwhile the attacks to their rear guard was entrusted to the Pennsylvania militia, under the command of Armstrong who was coming in by the Ridge Road, and the Maryland and Jersey militia, under Smallwood and Forman, would arrive by the York Road. Light parties were to scour the roads and fields in front, and keep up an open communication line between the different corps as the army advanced.

At about seven in the evening on the 3rd of October, the Americans broke up their encampment at Metuchen Hill on the Skippack Creek, and set out that night to march the sixteen miles to their destination. The country in which they passed through was of an irregular grade, dotted with woods, orchards, and enclosed fields, with a valley here and there, and in some places a marsh or small watercourse.

Sullivan's advance was the first on the grounds. As they descended into the valley near Mount Airy, the sun was just rising with the promise of a clear day, but the cool October evening gave way to an unseasonably warm, morning sun, and fog was beginning to develop. The vapors began to grow thick, only opening from time to time to give short glimpses of objects only forty yards away, and then suddenly closing again. It was hard for Sullivan to recover what he was seeing one moment, and then being blind, only to see something completely different the next time he got a glimpse. He was beginning to lose his perspective of the land, but he was doing his best. Not knowing how far he had traveled in the fog, he suddenly came upon the British outpost by surprise, and drove right into them, fighting, pushing forward, and then losing each other in the fog for a moment, only to find themselves in front of another foe. But the British rallied at every turn and new troops were coming on in support, making his advance by way of the main road almost impossible. By now, he must have thought, it should be time to hear from Greene's troops, but not hearing anything of him and fearing for his left flank, Sullivan orders Wayne to form on the east road, on ground assigned to Greene in the original plan of attack.

In that plan, the entire army was expected to be on the same ground by daylight, but the difficulties of the terrain, and the fog rolling in, retarded Sullivan's advance and caused him to be late. Greene had a guide that got them lost an had an additional two miles to travel due to the mistake, amounting to a longer march and getting to his position late. There also appears to have been a mistake in the calculations or estimating the distance each force was to march. With it, the course of what time each force would arrive did not correspond with the times they were given, and so each column arrived at a different moment. Thus, it was about half an hour after Sullivan's brigade attack before Greene and his column arrived. Then with the changes Sullivan enacted because of the time mistakes, Greene came in where he was suppose to, but Wayne was already on that ground. Stephen's brigade, coming in from the west, Scott, Muhlenberg, and McDougal from the east, all came in at the same time, but were displaced because of the problems with Greene and Sullivan and thought they were on the wrong ground and confusion reined with disastrous effect. When Stephen advanced, he found Wayne's corps in his front, where he had expected to find the enemy, and mistaking them for the enemy, fired upon them. Wayne's troops, equally surprised to find themselves attacked from the rear, were thrown into a momentary confusion, and before the error could be corrected and order restored, Stephen's division was inadvertently separated from Greene's division, and a dangerous gap was made in the American lines. Still Greene pushed on at the head of his column. Muhlenberg leading his own gallant brigade, which had made the great stand at Brandywine, while Scott and McDougal led theirs. A soldier, who described the fight later, said the incessant battle was so continuous that "it sound like the crackling of thorns crushed under a heavy pot, or non-stop peals of thunder." The first force Greene met was a body of light infantry, and driving it before them, and sweeping relentlessly on, in a few moments they found themselves in front of the British right, all drawn up and ready to receive the American troops.

Although the fog was so thick they could only see forty yards in front of them, and with the haze lifting and falling, the line of hostile fire must have been somewhat magnified. It may have also caused the British force to appear to be larger and stronger than it actually was. But they did have the flash from the enemy's muskets to guide them. And with every flash, Greene ordered his men to aim right at the flashes, and firing rapid volley upon volley, soon the British line wavered and shrunk. Greene ordered his troops to countermarch to the right, avoided the British left wing which had been bearing down on them. They attacked the wing with such ferocity, that the entire wing collapsed back toward the market house. Suddenly, Muhlenberg advanced forward, with bayonets fixed, they crashed like a wave on the shore, and the British soldiers, hard trained in the art of the bayonet, were unaccustomed to having bayonets used against them, broke ranks and fled. Muhlenberg and his troops chased them back through their camp and into the village. It seemed to Greene and Muhlenberg's men that the moment of victory was at hand.

However, when the British were forced into the village, the well-trained soldiers were prompted to turn the danger onto their enemy. Dashing through the main street, they threw themselves into a great, square stone house on the east main road. It was the house of Chief Justice Benjamin Chew. Colonel Musgrave and his 40th Regiment of Foot reached the home first and he closed the thick shutters, barricaded the doors, and posted 120 men at the second floor windows. From this spot they delivered a continuous and deadly fire upon Sullivan and Wayne's men passing on either side of the house.

What could they do now? Washington and Greene consulted with the other generals. Some of them were for falling back and leaving a regiment to immobilize the garrison in the house and going after the troops Muhlenberg's men had pursued. But Knox and Greene, deeply imbued with the lessons they had learned while studying the military classics in his bookshop, wanted to halt the proceedings. While penetrating an enemy's country, you must never leave an occupied castle in your rear. The Chew home was just such a castle. Washington, always respectful of Knox's larger store of military science, as well as Greene's military genius, agreed. The "castle" must be subdued in due form. An officer, sent with a flag to discuss a parlay, was fired upon and killed. "So much for the British firm belief in military honor and classical warfare." Knox had commented. The death of this officer made him boiling mad by the brutal act and single handily turned one of his 6-pounders upon the stronghold and lit the powder. It instantly blew in the front door and killed six British soldiers standing behind it. Knox's artillery crews responded by firing the other cannons at their disposal and smashed in every window, and blew apart a hastily constructed barrier where the front door use to be. But the 6-pound balls merely bounced off the thick, stone walls. The British inside, oblivious to the danger, built another barrier with Judge Chew's expensive oak furniture in the hallway, and backed by a group of bayonet armed soldiers, denied any attempt at storming the stronghold by any degree. "Burn it, then." cried Greene to his men. They tried, but they would have to toss the incendiary device through one of the windows, since there was nothing that would burn on the outside. Even the roof was made of pottery shingles. But when the would-be incendiary bomb was thrown, a British sharpshooter shot it out of the sky. In spite of all their failures to gain entry, the Americans did not give up. Two high spirited youths, a Colonel John Laurens of South Carolina and the Chevalier de Mauduit du Plessis from France, volunteered to try again. Laurens went behind the house to the stables and got several bundles of straw. Mauduit forced the shutters of a window, and mounted the sill. A single British officer, flintlock pistol in hand, demanded to know what the Frenchman was doing there. "I am merely taking a walk." The British officer, red with anger replied, "Surrender, sir!" But before Mauduit could answer, a British private came into the room, took a shot at the Frenchman, and promptly hit the British officer instead. Mauduit escaped unharmed, but Laurens received a musket ball in his shoulder for his trouble. The artillery resumed its futile attempt to extract the enemy from within the Chew House, with Maxwell's division joining in doing nothing but uselessly wasting ammunition.

Meanwhile, Sullivan and Wayne were driving at the British center, each on his own side of the main street. They had been fighting longer than expected, and though they had started with forty cartridges per man, rather than the usual thirty, the ammunition was beginning to run low. General Grey, now known as "No Flint Grey" due to the infamous Paoli incident, was not finding the pressure he was expecting at his position on the left. At the same time, General Grant was bringing up the 5th and 45th Regiments from the British right center and attacking Sullivan's left, which was left without support due to the earlier mix-up. Since they were engaged on their front and both flanks and quite alarmed by the scene at the Chew House in the rear of them, Sullivan's troops suddenly fell into a panic on the sudden arrival of a light horseman crying that they were surrounded, an old calvary trick. Part of Sullivan's line broke then more, and finally the rest. Their officers tried in vain to rally them screaming, "Form up! Form up men!" But to no avail and, "With as much precipitation as they had before advanced, they turned tail and ran."

Greene was in the same predicament; he had no support, right or left. The British and Hessians who been fighting Sullivan let his men run without pursuit and wheeled around to the center against Greene. He was now caught on both sides. Muhlenberg was far off, maybe more than a thousand yards in the rear of the enemy, far behind their camp. But when he saw Greene and his troops in trouble, he ordered his men to an about wheel and turned his bayonets back against the encircling British line. All at once charging from their backs forcing the British line to give way and Muhlenberg charged through it and joined Greene with all of his regiments now together but one. Colonel Matthews, with his 9th Virginia, had been conspicuously daring, but successful. He had led Greene's advance, crushed the resistance at Luken's Mills the division swung in from the Limekiln Road, and fought all the way to the market house, driving the enemy before him and taking a hundred prisoners. He tried to draw a company off of Luken's Mill, but a breastwork that had previously been abandoned, had been manned again with a superior force. While they detained him, the British right wing enveloped him. He first lost his captives, then his 400 men, and then he was also captured. That was the one regiment Muhlenberg and Greene were missing.

Now Greene, with Muhlenberg, Scott, and McDougall, faced the division of Grey, Grant, and Agnew drawn together to oppose him. Their long march and the strain of the battle wore out the Americans. There was little fight left in these men, but they did continue to fight, because they had too. They fought as they withdrew through the village. They fought from the fences and walls, using them, and houses as a delaying action against the British rear-guard. Greene, one of the few major generals that carried a gun, along with a sword, was shooting as fast as he could load it. During his early days with the Kentish Guards, Greene had learned to drill with a flintlock musket. It was a lot less time consuming loading a pistol then a musket, and he had become quite astute at it. He had bragged to his brothers that he could load and fire it as many as six times a minute when necessary. This was a time when it was necessary. His men knew what had to be done, so he did not have to waste his hoarse voice screaming commands every few minutes. He did order the field pieces off from the fight to clear the path for the infantry's retreat. When one of the carriage wheels for a 12-pound cannon shattered, Greene leapt from his horse, assisted three of the crew in picking it up and depositing the remains in a wagon close by and sent it off.

His friend Muhlenberg was having problems of his own. While riding in the rear of his retreating men, his tired horse refused to leap a fence. His men quickly came up and attempted to take the fence down, and while they toiled with the stubborn, high picket fence, the exhausted Muhlenberg fell fast asleep in his saddle. He did not wake up until a musket ball barely missed his ear and the oncoming enemy was so close he could hear their screams as they charged with their bayonets.

Washington, frustrated with what he saw as a lost opportunity slipping away, tried to "check the retreat, and rally the fugitives, exposing him to the hottest fire." But it was useless. The entire army was swept up in full retreat, the men running past Washington, held up their empty cartridge boxes to show him why they were running. The problem was that it was not an orderly withdrawal. It was, in fact, a mass of confusion, as Greene would later recount, "past the powers of description; sadness and consternation expressed in every countenance that swarmed the Skippack Road." Cornwallis has now entered the fray, joining the pursuers with fresh troops and ammunition, and they pressed the retreat with new vigor. Pulaski's small calvary, which formed a rear-guard, was attacked by British dragoons, fled, and in their flight, rode directly through Greene's men, who mistook them for the British dragoons and scattered in every direction. Greene thought he would have to abandon the guns all together, but managed to get just enough men to save them. By this time, musketballs were whistling all around Greene and his men and his officers anxiously attempted to get him farther from the rear pursuit. But he knew that his men would turn to him for encouragement in the face of such danger. Watching him stand tall in his saddle in the midst of a firestorm, gave his men the added strength they needed to retain as much semblance of order as they might muster.

The fire from the British was so fierce, that a musket-ball struck the wig of one of Greene's aides, Captain Burnet, as he rode next to him, knocking the wig to the ground. "Burnet," cried Greene, "you had better jump down, if you have time, and pick up your queue." "And your curl, too, General?" Here, a musketball had severed a curl from the side of Greene as well. Greene laughed out loud and said, "I feel curls and queue are the least of our worries at the moment captain." The celebrated Thomas Paine, who was on Greene's staff and recording the following conversation, also said afterwards, "The retreat was extraordinary. Nobody hurried themselves." And for good reason. These men could all but put one foot in front of the other to stay awake as they marched.

Despite the complete destruction of the plans before the battle, the Americans nearly won. While Greene, Sullivan, and Wayne were still in the fight, along with Muhlenberg who was piercing the enemy's line, victory was within their grasp. It was said that the British had actually arranged a rendezvous point in Chester for after their expected defeat. If Stirling and Maxwell, with the reserve, had not been held up at the Chew House, or if Stephen had not disobeyed orders and taken his division away from Greene. If Wayne had not turned around and shot on Sullivan, and if Smallwood and Armstrong had not been delayed. If any one of those mistakes had not occurred, the Americans most certainly would have won. Even after all of those follies, it still almost happened. But instead, it was a comedy of errors that resulted into another British victory. The Americans were said to have lost 152 killed, 53 of them alone lay on the front lawn of the Chew House during the siege, four on its doorstep, and a field general, General Nash. Five hundred and twenty one were wounded, and almost 400 captured. The British lost two important field officers as well. General Agnew, and Colonel Bird, 66 from the rank and file, 30 officers, and 420 wounded.

A tragedy in the wake of the defeat was the discovery of General Stephen, an extremely brave and competent officer, totally drunk, and lying in a fence corner. He was immediately cashiered from the service, and said to have never been sober again. Lafayette, who had been appointed a major general, but without a command, got Stephen's division. It was noted that several of the field generals had an incident or two of indiscretion according to the code of officer's conduct. General Conway, a magnificent and brave officer, was found asleep by an aide to Washington in a barn on the road during the retreat, and Pulaski, whose merit was undeniable, was found asleep by Washington himself in a farmhouse at the same time. The total exhaustion is undeniable in the case of these men. But they were mounted the entire battle, and some of the work was done by the horse. What it shows is the terrific stamina that a foot soldier must have to endure hours of endless battle commands, carrying several pounds of equipment, a musket, and then march for miles after the battle before he would be allowed to sleep. These men endured far greater hardships and fatigue than their officer, but never seem to get the respect or recognition they desperately deserve in the history and record books.

Chapter IX

"Defense of the Delaware"

And so another defeat of the American army follows close behind the defeat at Brandywine and the strategic loss of Philadelphia. Meanwhile, the Northern Army was boldly pressing the campaign with Burgoyne, another attempt at invading Canada, and fighting decisive battles that they were winning; Bennington, Saratoga, Ticonderoga, and even Arnold trying his hand at an admiralty on Lake Champlain. Although he did not win that battle, he was successful in delaying the British fleet enough to keep them where they were through another winter. The Congress was having a field day at the expense of Washington. Their tone was absolutely indignant that he and his advisers could blunder along so, and display so little enterprise for success in a campaign that was so important, keeping Philadelphia out of the hands of the enemy. Among Washington's and the army's critics was none other than Nathanael's friend, John Adams, who in September, professed himself "sick of Fabian systems in all quarters." But in October, rejoiced "that the glory of turning the tide of arms was not immediately due to the Commander-in-chief." James Lovell, who wrote in November, "our affairs are Fabiused into a very disagreeable posture, and you will be astonished when you come to know accurately what numbers have at one time or another have been collected near Philadelphia to wear out stockings, shoes, and breeches."

Some Generals, too, shook their heads in disgust, Pennsylvania generals in particular, who thought that Philadelphia ought to be protected at all cost. Foremost among these generals was Mifflin, who, neglecting his duties as Quartermaster-general, had retired to Reading in disgust at Washington's refusal the summer before to march directly to Philadelphia, instead of waiting to know where Howe was going. Some in Congress would write, "According to Mifflin, the ear of the Commander-in-chief was exclusively possessed by Greene"; "neither the most wise, the most brave, nor most patriotic of counselors." Even Wayne, though probably in a different spirit, complained to Gates of the loss of Fort Mifflin and of Washington's "listening too much to some counsel."

And so, from Congress and even some from within Washington's own camp, eyes were beginning to turn hopefully toward Gates. Some letters began to appear and were written, unsigned, northward to encourage that fortunate general in drawing flattering comparisons between Gates and the Commander-in-chief of the army, in hopes of luring him into stepping forward and taking over Washington's job. When Congress was looking for a Commander-in-chief two years before, Gates' name was one of the first to be mentioned, just behind Charles Lee. But Lee had actually served in Europe with the British army and been considered "just too English" by Benjamin Franklin. Gates was thought by many to be the next obvious candidate, but had been declined for being too old, and a bit too timid. It had been suggested by as late as the great victory at Saratoga, that the true hero and commander of the defeat over Burgoyne should have been given to Arnold rather than Gates. However, Gates was the commander of the Northern army at the time, and so received the full recognition of the victory over his subordinate. The dark clouds of resentment toward Washington and many of his senior generals, including Greene, was not just centered in Pennsylvania, but throughout the country. Washington and Greene had become almost hated during the time directly after the loss at Germantown.

Disappointed, though not entirely disheartened by the negative attention he was receiving, Washington now directed his attention toward the defenses of the Delaware. Howe was already having trouble feeding his huge army, bivouacked in Philadelphia. Washington had banked on this happening from the beginning. If the forts could just hold out a few weeks longer, at least until cold weather and ice made navigating the river impossible, Howe might be compelled to return the troops to his ships and sail back to New York. Washington would write to his brother, "if the river defenses can be maintained General Howe's situation will not be the most agreeable; for if his supplies can be stopped by water, it may easily be done by land and the acquisition of Philadelphia may, instead of his good fortune, prove to be his ruin."

Every effort was made to "divert the enemy's attention and force." On the 16th of October, Washington advanced again to the ground which he had held before his attack on Germantown. Light parties familiar with the roads were kept hovering around the enemy, ready at every opportunity to strike at his foragers and intercept his supplies being moved overland. On one occasion, Greene was ordered to cross the Schuylkill, and attack a supply train, which was said to be on the road to Chester with an escort of 1,500 men. But, remembering the disastrous effects of rain on the American cartridge boxes at Warren Tavern and the Battle of the Clouds a month before, Washington felt the need to amend his instructions to Greene, and added, "Come back if it rains." As is common for the area during that part of the season, it did indeed rain and rained for several days. So Greene obeyed his orders, retraced his steps as to not bring attention to his troops, and returned to camp. McDougal was the next to attempt to draw havoc upon the British, and was told to take a detachment, and advance on some very accurate information that the enemy was marching with supplies being guarded by 4,000 men. They advanced "in great spirits," marching most of the night, to attack a post which the enemy was known to be forming at Grey's Ferry, to protect the bridge there that was vital for the route of their supply trains. However, McDougal arrived, only to find the half-constructed post deserted, and the bridge destroyed.

The forts that would be used in the river defenses were Fort Mifflin on Mud Island, better known as Mud Fort at the time, and Fort Mercer on a Quaker plantation called Red Bank on the Jersey shore. Both were a little less than seven miles south from the center of Philadelphia, and near enough to the American camp southwest of the city to hear the Americans heavy guns, as well as the many of the Royal fleet.

Howe's first obstacle, Billingsport, defended the lower section of the double lines of chevaux-de-frise that extended from the Jersey shore across the channel to Billings Island in the middle of the river. The *Chevaux-de-frise* were crate-like structures made of heavy timber, floated out into the river where they were then sunk by loading large stones into the crate to sink them. Wooden beams, topped by large iron points atop them, were pushed into the stone filled crate slanting them upward to within three or four feet of the river surface. The tips would be pointed downstream, so they could be more effective during low tide, and were capable of ripping even the copper sheathed bottom of any ship attempting to pass over them. They were quite effective, if not only for their psychological purpose.

Billingsport redoubt was not so formidable and in fact was merely an inconvenience to Howe and his brother, the Admiral. On October 2nd, Howe sent the 42nd and parts of the 71st Regiment, under Colonel Stirling, and attacked it from the rear. The small garrison that was defending the unfinished redoubt spiked its guns, set fire to the stores and barracks, and fled to Fort Mercer. Captain Hammond on the *Eagle* cut through the lower chevaux-de-frise and opened a passage large enough so six of his frigates could pass through.

The next obstacle would not be so easy. Thirty chevaux-de-frise were strung in a triple line from Mud Island, a little below the mouth of the Schuylkill, and across the channel to Red Bank on the Jersey side. Fort Mercer and Fort Mifflin defended them from both sides of the Delaware. Above that lay the American fleet, if you could call it a fleet, comprising of the frigate *Montgomery*, a brig, a schooner, two xebecs, thirteen row-galleys, two floating batteries, fourteen fire ships, and several fire rafts. The best vessel, the frigate *Delaware* with thirty-two guns, had run aground during a storm on September 7th on the Jersey shore, then set on fire by hot shots from the British batteries and had ultimately surrendered.

The first attempt against the major forts was made on October 22nd by the Hessian Colonel von Donop with three Hessian grenadier battalions, a regiment of foot, four companies of jagers, and a small contingent of artillery, about 1,600 men. They would cross the Delaware river at Cooper's Ferry and attack Fort Mercer at Red Bank. The fort had been occupied by a small force of New Jersey militiamen, but Washington soon garrisoned it with Continental soldiers from two Rhode Island Regiments. A portion of the 1st Rhode Island Regiment was commanded by Colonel Christopher Greene, cousin to Nathanael, and one of Arnold's majors during the ill-fated attack on Quebec. The remainder of the Fort Mercer garrison was made up of over half of Colonel Israel Angell's 2nd Rhode Island Regiment, along with part of the New Jersey militia that stayed, bringing the total rank and file to 475 men. Nathanael Greene was quite concerned with the Delaware defenses. Washington and Greene's enemies would surely rejoice if they failed once again, and Greene felt an obligation to this grave responsibility after the Fort Washington debacle. He still believed that Fort Washington could have been successfully defended. He knew that Fort Mercer must be. Because of the British success at Fort Washington, Greene believed that Howe would be over confident, thinking the Americans were incapable of defending such a fort against his army. Greene would write to his cousin, "This will be handed to you from my Lieutenant-colonel (also a Greene, but no relation,) who commands this detachment from my division, and is being sent down to reinforce our posts on the Delaware. They are exceeding good troops in the army. I am in hopes, with this additional strength; you will be able to baffle all attempts of the enemy to dislodge you. The Baron Arendt, colonel of the German battalion, an officer of experience and ability, is coming down to take the command of Fort Mifflin, agreeable to the determination of the council in the first instance. He is thought to be an officer of great spirit. Remember me to all of our friends. "Yours affectionate, *N. Greene*"

Washington had also sent a young French engineer to assist Col. Greene to strengthen the all-important fort. The Chevalier de Mauduit du Plessis, the same man caught on the windowsill at the Chew House in Germantown, attempting to toss a bomb into it, was well regarded as a fort specialist. He found that the Americans were, "little practised in the art of fortification," and helped Col. Greene reduce the works from "beyond their strength" and "transformed them into a large redoubt nearly of a pentagonal form." The walls were made entirely of earth, guarded only by a ditch and a row of abatis. The garrison had fourteen guns.

The Hessians marched down from Haddonfield where they had camped the night before, and thought that they were mounting a surprise attack on the Americans. However, Greene had learned about the attack the evening before and had expected them before noon. The Hessians had been harassed by a number of New Jersey militia detachments throughout the morning and were delayed for several hours and arrived "within cannon-shot" to the fort just after noon. Col. Donop, the Hessian commander was so confident of the attack that he had his troops stop and eat their lunch. Finally, at a little after four in the afternoon, a drummer, and a British Lieutenant-colonel along as interpreter, marched up to the parapet of the fort. From a distance of about forty rods, the British officer demanded its surrender by saying, "The King of England orders his rebellious subjects to lay down their arms and they are warned that if they stand to battle, no quarter will be given." A brash, young Lieutenant-colonel by the name of Stephen Olney, Greene's third in command was sent forward to reply and said, "We shall neither ask for quarter, nor expect it, and shall defend the fort to the last extremity." The Hessian interpreter and drummer had scarcely returned when von Donop opened fire with the few mortars he had available to him. Point in study, the Hessians had only five field-pieces, and the three mortars with which to attack. If the Hessians had brought several more cannon, the battle could have easily tipped the other way.

After a short volley against the fort, the infantry slowly moved forward for the main attack. Coming from the northeast, von Donop and his officers saw the portion of the fort which Col. Greene and Mauduit du Plessis had abandoned to make the fort more defensible. The Americans allowed the Hessians to easily gain this ground, only to open up with their cannons, full of grape and canister shot at close range. The results were devastating, and almost a hundred casualties were recorded on the first wave of this attack. The results were not much better in other areas of the fort. The row of abatis had been constructed out of the plantation owner's apple tree orchard that once stood next to the battlefield. The tree branches and limbs had been so expertly intertwined that it resembled a wall, and the Hessians had failed to bring any instruments, like axes, hatchets, or saws, that could be used to hack through the jungle of trees lying on their sides and facing the attacking enemy. So they used the only things that were available to them, swords. This only resulted in more devastating loses when the troops were forced to bunch up along the close proximity of the fort walls, all of which is explained in detail in my book on this battle; "Forty Minutes by the Delaware." Due to the restructuring of the fort, along with its new defenses, the Hessians were often caught in a shower of deadly crossfire, rained down with muskets and cannons filled with grape and canister shot. Von Donop was struck by one of these blasts about halfway into the attack and was said to have no less than eleven bullet holes in him when he was discovered. The remaining men of his columns did not fare any better and went down in rows and were heaped dying or dead, one upon another. "It may be well doubted," writes Trevelyan, "whether so few men in so small a space of time had ever delivered a deadlier fire." The entire affair was over in forty minutes. The loss to the Hessians was almost 300 killed, and 71 caught or wounded, including 22 officers. Counted in the mortally wounded was their over-confident commander, Colonel von Donop, who had brashly commented that, "I will capture Fort Mercer and rename it Fort von Donop or die trying." He received his wish and died of his wounds three days later about a mile from the battlefield.

Samuel Ward had fought by Christopher Greene's side at Cambridge, Quebec, and now Fort Mercer. Now Colonel Greene asked him to compose a letter and send it to Washington about what they had done at Red Bank. The letter was long, simple, modest, calm, but almost severe in its tone. It spoke of how a small group of ordinary men, raised up, held their ground in the face of incredible odds, and conquered an army that was suppose to be superior to them. Men would have to stand and fight if they ever had dreams of going home to their families someday. They had to finish what they had begun to be successful against the most powerful force the world had ever seen. The little country that stood and proclaimed itself free would have to oust the country, most had once called home, if they had any hope of retaining the land they now called the United States of America.

When the letter was read in the main American camp, there was great rejoicing. Finally, someone had turned the tide and had stopped the string of heartbreaking losses to the enemy. "I heartily congratulate you upon this happy event," Washington wrote to the successful Colonel Greene and his men, "and beg you will accept my most particular thanks, and present the same to your whole garrison, both officers and men. Assure them that their gallantry and good behavior meet my warmest approbation." Even Congress got into the act. "Resolved, That Congress have a high sense of the merit of Colonel Greene and the officers and men under his command in their gallant defense of the fort at Red Bank on the Delaware River, and that an elegant sword be provided by the Board of War, and presented to Colonel Greene." "With the greatest pleasure I congratulate you on your late brave and successful defense," writes General Greene of his cousin. "The attempt was bold, and the defense noble. Honor and laurels will be the reward of the garrison."

So much for Howe's three pronged attack on the Delaware River defenses. To make matters worse, he had lost two of his largest frigates. The *Augusta*, with 44 guns, ran aground attempting to intervene in the Mercer attack, only to catch fire and blow up the next day. The explosion was so severe that the American troops heard it in their camp, and were concerned "that it was the forts that had met with dire straits." The *Merlin*, a 32-gun frigate, also ran aground, could not be released, and was abandoned and burned by the British. But even with setbacks such as these, Howe was not going to permit the Americans to retain their hold on the Delaware without an all-out fight to determine the final outcome. It was late October, and the weather was already beginning to turn quickly. Ice could already be seen creeping out from the riverbank. Howe was running out of time.

"Griffin informs me," General Greene continued in another communiqué to Lieutenant-colonel Samuel Smith, the commander on Mud Island, "you are in great fear of a siege, and it will be impossible to defend the place any length of time should the enemy lay siege to it. I am sorry to learn that the garrison is growing sickly. Their labor and fatigue while fighting their own battle, assisting Mud Island's garrison must be intolerable. A strong reinforcement will be sent you immediately. I believe three hundred have marched today, and more will march to-morrow. You may depend that my influence, so far as it extends, shall be exerted to relieve the anxiety of the garrison at Red Bank and Mud Island."

Efforts indeed, were made to reinforce the river defenses immediately with militia, but with little success. Few answered the call, and of those, few possessed the enthusiasm that Colonel Greene's men had shown in the past few months as he wrote, "that there was very little to expect from them." Washington went so far as to direct Varnum, "not to bring them into the forts, for I am of opinion they would rather dismay than assist the Continental garrison." Varnum then decided to march his own men to assist Colonel Greene. But what Washington really wanted to do was attack Howe when he seemed now to be at his weakest. Provisions were beginning to run out in Philadelphia, and with the addition of several thousand Loyalists in the city, it was starting to put a strain on Howe's nerves. To make matters worse, Howe had to contend with the Americans sending light parties into the outskirts of the city to harass the British outpost whenever they could. Washington even sent out his best officers, including Nathanael Greene, to reconnoiter and spy on the British. However, for the Americans to attack with any prospect of success required more strength than the Americans possessed at that time. The added strength they needed could only come from the victorious army of the north, and Washington dispatched his trusted aide-de-camp, Alexander Hamilton, to urge General Gage to march south as quickly as humanly possible.

Fort Mifflin, sister fort to Mercer, and better known as Mud Fort by its inhabitants, was situated just a short distance off the Pennsylvania shoreline on an island, that really wasn't an island at all. It was really nothing more than a large mud flat that had developed over time, and had grown just off the bank of the river. Since it was not much more than a muddy sand bar, at high tide the fort would be virtually under a foot of water, thus giving the garrisoned position its name, Mud Fort on Mud Island. Rumor has it that it was not called Fort Mifflin until a year later, named for the terrible, murky job Mifflin had done as Quartermaster-general of the army. I suppose they thought the name fit appropriately. The structure that was called a fort, itself had been "unskillfully constructed," with one observer calling it "a Burlesque upon the art of Fortifications." During the early days of its construction the engineer who was given the job of supervising the building of the fort was none other than, Captain John Montresor, Howe's chief engineer for the British army. Years before, when America was still a peaceful colony of the British Empire, the fort had been started by the Pennsylvania Board of Governors as a fortification to Philadelphia, the largest city in the Empire. Construction was halted when Monresor's superiors felt the warmth of the Colonies growing disfavor with its sovereign and ordered Montresor to abandon the project. Once the forts designer and creator, Montresor would now be given the unalienable task of destroying it.

The men on Mud Island, approximately 450 soldiers, were scattered among a number of regiments throughout the Colonies. Men from Connecticut, Virginia, militiamen from Pennsylvania and New Jersey, and several Rhode Island soldiers sent over from Fort Mercer, which was still under the Americans control. The fort was equipped with only about a dozen cannon, 18, 24, and 32-pounders but, with no trained artillerymen to fire them effectively, they were nearly useless. The British, on the other hand had built 5 batteries on Providence Island, just north of Mud Island, mounted with ten heavy guns, 24 to 32-pounders, two howitzers, and three mortars. Add to that the floating battery the British had positioned in the channel behind the fort, with twenty-two 24-pounders fixed on it, plus the hundreds of guns set on the British ships in the river, and it spelled disaster for the out-gunned garrison on the island.

On November 10th, all of the British guns opened fire on the fort and continued all day long. At night, they sent only an occasional blast of hot-shot from one of the ships cannon, setting fire to the four blockhouses and barracks, and leaving the men without shelter in the cold, wet mud. The bombardment continued for five days, the rain had turned into a tempest, allowing the channel behind the fort to rise and allow two small galleys filled with marines to get within 40 yards of the fort. The marines climbed into the ships rigging and were able to shoot any man that showed himself inside the fort. Of the approximately 200 soldiers in Fort Mifflin, over half were killed or wounded. Her commander, Lieutenant Colonel Samuel Smith, saw the hopelessness of the situation and ordered the remaining survivors to row over to Fort Mercer the evening of the 15th of November. But not before setting fire to everything that would burn and was not already destroyed. Colonel Smith had ordered that the flag remain flying, so as to trick the British into thinking the Americans were still within the crumbling fort while they made their escape across the river. If they had "Struck the flag," it would have signaled that the garrison in the fort had surrendered and the men would all have been captured.

The defense of Mud Island was one of the most brave and stubborn fights of the entire war. Only 200 men, many of them killed or wounded during the five day bombardment, no shelter from the elements, no food or supplies, and no relief sent, held off the powerful British flotilla long enough to cause them great distress. The American fleet, under the command of Commodore Hazlewood, was of no use, and ultimately, the fleet had to be destroyed with the advance of Howe's navy. With that advance, Mercer was doomed to fall into enemy hands at any moment. Colonel Greene, seeing the position his troops were in, evacuated Mercer and marched to Burlington to reinforce it. Cornwallis meanwhile, was marching north from Billingsport with over 2,000 men to attack Mercer. Washington, hoping to save Mercer from the fate of the fort on Mud Island, sent General Greene to Bristol where he would cross the Delaware into the Jerseys and meet up with Cornwallis and his troops. That evening Greene wrote his wife, "I am now on the march for Red Bank fort. Lord Cornwallis crossed over to Jersey day before yesterday, to invest that place with a large body of troops. I am in hopes to have the pleasure to meet his Lordship. This eccentric movement will lengthen out the campaign for some weeks at least, and it is possible may transfer the seat of war for the winter. The enemy are now getting up their stores and fortifying the city of Philadelphia as strong as possible. The weather begins to get severe, and campaigning of it disagreeable, but necessity obliges us to keep the field for some time. . . .I had a fall from my horse some time ago, but have got entirely over it except a sprain in my wrist. . . . I lodge in a fine country-house to-night. The Marquis of Fayette is in company with me; he has left a young wife, and a fine fortune of fourteen hundred pounds sterling per annum, to come and engage in the cause of liberty; this is a noble enthusiasm. He is one of the sweetest-tempered young gentlemen; he purposes to visit Boston this winter; if so, you'll have an opportunity to see him. . . . Your brother, I am told, behaved the hero the other day, in the attack on Red Bank."

However, by noon the next day, Greene learns of the fate of the American fleet and the evacuation of Mercer. Greene halted his march and learned that Varnum and his relief column, made up of General Glover's brigade and Morgan's corps of rangers, had retreated to Mount Holly. Greene would write to Washington, "General Varnum has retreated to Mount Holly. I purpose to see him and General Huntington early in the morning; if this is practicable to make an attack upon the enemy it shall be done; but I am afraid the enemy will put it of my power, as they can easily make us take such a circuitous march by taking the bridge over Timber Creek. I cannot promise anything until I learn more of the designs of the enemy, their strength, and the position they are in. If it is possible to make an attack upon them with prospect of success, it shall be done." Fort Mercer would anger and frustrate Cornwallis one last time when he arrived to find it destroyed and empty. Meanwhile, the chief purpose of Greene's expedition was lost. The British now had a stronghold throughout the Delaware Valley and Greene had no choice but to give up and remain in Mount Holly for further orders.

The river was already beginning to freeze. Howe's fleet just managed to sail up to Philadelphia before the start of the long, cold winter. This caused Howe to scrap his plans for a final push into the country to rout Washington's men and perhaps finish the war right there and then. But the British also had control of the Delaware from the Capes to Philadelphia, and no one on Earth was going to displace him now. Instead, Howe, comfortable in his winter quarters, felt it was more prudent to wait until spring to attack the Americans. After all, they would have no winter quarters to hold up in through the bleak months of a Pennsylvania winter.

The Americans still encamped in Perkiomen, engaged in no military action for another month. They were too busy resting the beleaguered troops, and searching the countryside for blankets, clothing, food, and shoes. Especially shoes a commodity that had been hard to come by for months. Greene was still in Mount Holly, and communicated his frustration to Washington in a letter dated 24th of November 1777; "I have nothing new to communicate to your Excellency with respects to the motions of the enemy here in the Jerseys. They remain, or did last night, at Woodbury, with a guard at Timber Creek, consisting of about six hundred men. The militia of this State is dwindling to nothing, General Varnum says there were upwards of fourteen hundred a few days since; they are reduced now to between seven and eight hundred. I will endeavor to inclose your Excellency a return of our strength in Continentals and militia this afternoon if possible." Washington sends back a letter, suggesting that Greene attack the British anyway. Greene sends back a flippant communiqué, "Your Excellency observes in your last, you must leave the propriety of attacking the enemy to me; would you advise me to fight them with very unequal numbers? Most people, indeed all, agree they are near or quite five thousand strong; our forces is upwards of three, exclusive of the militia, which may be from seven to eight hundred at most. The situation the enemy are in, the ease with which they can receive reinforcements, and the difficulty of our knowing it, will render it absolutely necessary, when we advance from this place, to make the attack as soon as possible. I had much rather engage with three thousand against five than attack the enemy's lines, and there is a much greater prospect of succeeding, but still cannot promise myself victory, nor even a prospect of it, with inferior numbers." The building frustration in both Washington and Greene would be strengthened, rather than relieved in the coming weeks. Greene received news from Glover and his brigade, along with Burnet and his troops. It was encouraging and gave Greene hope that he may yet have the opportunity to meet Cornwallis head-to-head in battle.

A brash, young Colonel in the New Jersey militia was beginning to catch the attention of senior members of the Continental army, including Nathanael Greene. Adam Comstock, who, unlike many of his comrades in the militia, longed for a brush with the enemy. "O, how I want to give them a flogging before they leave the Jerseys for good!" he writes to Greene in one of his many letters to the general. Under Comstock's command the militia as late, had made several bold attacks upon the enemy's pickets and taken several prisoners that furnished Greene with important information about the movements of Howe's army around and within Philadelphia. In another letter to Greene, Comstock writes from Haddonfield, "This moment I arrived from a reconnoitering tour near Little Timber Creek Bridge; sent a smart young woman, who had a sister in Gloucester who was a spy there. She has returned, and I believe has received no other damage than a kiss from a Hessian general,--this is as she says. She reports that a very large number of British and Hessian troops are in Gloucester; that they are embarking in boats and going to Philadelphia; and that her sister there informed her they had been embarking since early that morning. That Lord Cornwallis quartered at Colonel Ellis's house, and the Hessian general at a house opposite, who asked the young woman where the rebels were. She answered she could not tell, she had seen none of them. She said she passed many sentries before she came to Little Timber Creek Bridge, where she passed the last. I do not need this information General Greene. I fear they will be too quick for us. Colonel Hart's regiment is here."

Greene immediately wrote to Washington, "This moment (four o'clock) received intelligence the enemy are embarking from Gloucester and crossing to Philadelphia. I have ordered General Varnum's and General Huntington's brigades to advance immediately, to fall upon the enemy's rear, and prevent their getting off their stock. I wait your Excellency's orders to march where you may think advisable." Comstock passes more information to Greene a few hours later. "Seven prisoners just arrived here from the enemy, taken by the militia about three miles from this place on the road to Gloucester. The prisoners explained to me that the main body lies about four miles from here on the Gloucester road encamped; that their line forms a triangle; that they are to wait there till they have embarked all the stock for Philadelphia, which will take them all day; that the army expect to embark to-morrow, and go into winter quarters; that they have two six-pounders in front, ditto two in the rear, and some smaller in the centre; that they were not in the least apprehensive of any of the Americans army being within miles of them; otherwise, they should not have been taken prisoner in the manner they were."

Meanwhile, a new question had arisen at headquarters. Washington had reconnoitered the enemy's works; and Stirling, Wayne, Scott, and Woodford were eager for an attack upon Philadelphia. "The enemy's force is weakened," wrote Stirling, "by the absence of Cornwallis; and, if we bring three columns suddenly against their north line, and enfilade their works from the hills on the other side of the Schuylkill, while Greene, embarking two thousand men at Dunk's Ferry, enters the city at Spruce Street, secures the bridge over the Schuylkill, and takes the lines in the rear, we shall surely suceed." That evening the council met to discuss that very question. The discussion became heated, and for probably the first time, Washington went against the majority and stood alone on his own decision. "I have just this day returned from investigating the enemy's works." Washington said, "They are to strong, and the cooperation of Greene's troops depend upon so many contingencies, as to make it extremely doubtful whether it would be possible for him to reach the city in season, if he reached it at all." But Washington admitted that the opinion of the people called loudly for an attack, any attack to be made against the British. The council broke-up that night, but Washington directed his officers to give their opinion in writing of what they should do next, and expected them the next morning. Of the officers present, only four supported an immediate attack, while eleven against it. Of those eleven were counted, Greene, Sullivan, Knox, DeKalb, DuPortail, and Lafayette, the best and most experienced officers in the army.

Greene was now in Haddonfield. He had already started his march out to meet the enemy, and had not heard of the new orders. By the afternoon of the 26th of November, the new orders from Washington had arrived. Greene acknowledged their receipt with a letter; "Your Excellency's letter of the 25th reached me at this place. I have halted the troops, and await the remaining column in the town. General Varnum and Huntington's brigades got to this place before I received your letter. I am sorry our march will prove a fruitless one; there is but one road that leads down to the point where the enemy are embarking on their ships, on each side the ground is swampy and full of thick underbrush, that makes the approaches impracticable almost; these difficulties might have been surmounted, but we could reap no advantage from it, this country is so intersected with creeks, that approaches are rendered extremely difficult, and retreat very dangerous. We have a fine body of troops, in fine spirits, and every one appears to wish to come to action. The Marquis is charmed with the spirited behavior of the militia and rifle corps; they drove the enemy pickets above half a mile from their troops, and kept the ground until dark. The enemy's pickets consisted of about three hundred, and were reinforced during the skirmish. The Marquis is determined to be in the way of danger. I believe the enemy has removed most of the great chevaux-de-frise; there went up sixty sail vessels this morning. Our intelligence is uncertain whether any of the enemy has crossed the river; prisoners have told us they evacuated Carpenter's and Province Islands, as they are no longer necessary. I propose to leave General Varnum's brigade and the rifle corps at this place for a few days, then return to Mount Holly. My division, Huntington's and Glover's brigades, will proceed with all dispatch to join your Excellency. I could wish the enemy might leave the Jerseys before us."

Washington knew that Greene was frustrated and upset that his troops were unable to attack the British column in Gloucester. He also detected from Greene's letter that, discretion is the better part of valor, and that the attack could have easily turned wrong and would have then accomplished nothing and dealt a serious blow to the effort at this place and time. It was prudent to wait for a better opportunity when the time was more favorable to their side. He wrote to Greene, almost in sympathy, and signing as he almost never did, "With sincere regard and affection--Our situation, as you justly observe, is distressing from a variety of irremediable causes, but more especially from the impracticability of answering the expectations of the world without running hazards which no military principles can justify, and which, in case of failure, might prove the ruin of our cause; patience, and a steady perseverance in such measures as appear warranted by sound reason and policy, must support us under the censure of the one, and dictate a proper line of conduct for the attainment of the other; that is the great object in view. Think therefore, I beseech you, of all these things, and prepare yourself by reflection and observation to give me advice on these several matters. It has been proposed that some of the galley's should fall down to or near the mouth of Frankfort Creek, in order to prevent troops from coming up by water, and falling in the rear of our pickets near the enemy's lines; Will you discuss with Commodore Hazlewood on this subject? Will you also ask what is become of the hands that were on board the vessels which were burnt?

Greene received Washington's letter and corresponded a reply, "The greater part of the troops returned to this place last night, and marched early this morning to cross the Delaware. I shall set out immediately for Burlington. I have given Lieutenant-colonel Abeel orders to procure wagons and send off all the spare ammunition to Huntington, the heavy cannon to Bordentown. At my arrival I will inquire of the Commodore respecting the matters by you directed. I think there are as many troops gone forward as will be able to get over to-day. I shall push on the troops as fast as possible without injuring their health." The next morning he writes, "Three brigades are now on the march for head-quarters,-- my division and General Glover's brigade. General McDougal's division is not yet come to town. I am afraid the want of provisions has detained them this morning. It is with the utmost difficulty we can get bread to eat. The commissary of purchases of flour is very ill managed; there is no magazine of consequence, and the army served from hand to mouth. A prisoner from Gloucester says Lord Cornwallis' detachment consisted of about six thousand; he also adds that the reinforcement consisted of about twenty-five hundred. General Howe designs to make an immediate attack upon our army, unless he weather is bad. I am told the prisoner thinks the enemy design to burn and destroy wherever they go. Germantown is devoted to destruction. The enemy plundered everybody within their reach, and almost of everything they had. They design to divide our land as soon as the country is conquered. They say the obstinate resistance made at Mud Island has broke the campaign."

Washington returned his reply, "Every account from Philadelphia confirms the report that the enemy mean to make a speedy move. I shall not be disappointed if they come out this night or very early in the morning. You will therefore push forward the rear brigades with all possible expedition, and the moment the troops and baggage have all passed, let the boats be instantly sent up the river to Coryell's Ferry; for one part of my information is that the enemy are preparing to send boats up the Delaware, and it cannot be for any other purpose than to destroy the remainder of our water-craft. I shall be glad that you would come on immediately upon the receipt of this message, and send word back to the brigadiers to hasten their march."

And so ended Greene's week in the Jersey's. "If an attack can be made on Lord Cornwallis with a prospect of success, I am persuaded it will be done," wrote Washington to the President of Congress on the 23rd of November. "General Greene has not been in sufficient force to see Cornwallis in the field," wrote Reed to the President of Pennsylvania on the 30th. On the same day Cadwalader wrote to Reed from headquarters, "Greene and the detachment from New Jersey are all arrived in camp." Greene had intended to attack Cornwallis, and had made his plans known, but Washington prudently declined the effort. The attempt would have been suicide, as 2,000 or 3,000 men could not have been thrown in the rear that quickly, and reinforcements sent over to Gloucester, even during the night, would have been detected almost immediately. Even more, a council of war was comprised to see if any judgment on conduct could be submitted against Greene for his intended action. A member of Congress, with Washington's comments available to him wrote, "Washington still hoped to recover much of what had been lost. A victory would restore the Jersey shore, and this object was deemed so important that General Greene's instructions indicate the expectation that he would be in a condition to fight Lord Cornwallis. That judicious officer feared the reproach of avoiding an action less than the just censure of sacrificing the real interests of his country by engaging the enemy on disadvantageous terms."

The expectations of an attack by Greene were well founded. On the 4th of December, the British general came out with all his strength and headed up the Germantown Pike, and took post on Chestnut Hill, in front of the right wing of the Americans. Howe had marched with two days of provisions and baggage, and he had hoped to outflank the Americans at the encampment in Whitemarsh. On the 3rd, Major John Clark, Jr., operating for Washington in Philadelphia, had gotten word to the American commander that the British were "in readiness to march with an end to surprise attack the Americans encampment." Washington's army spent the next two days on high alert of the British activities. On the morning of the 5th, the Cornwallis's column was fired upon by Captain McLane's picket station at Beggar Town (now Mount Airy.) Before retreating, McLane sent word to Washington of the British troop strength and their path of attack to Whitemarsh. In retaliation for being fired upon, the British burned several houses in route, which had harbored American troops. The British reached the American camp by dawn, and headed up the Bethlehem Pike to reconnoiter their position. In the hills above them they saw countless fires and thought the number of American troops was larger than first reported. What they didn't know was that Washington had directed soldiers to make extra campfires on the hills surrounding their camp to deceive the British, and it worked.

The Battle of Whitemarsh was ready to proceed. To begin, Washington sent out 600 Pennsylvania militiamen to meet Cornwallis. The Americans drew extremely heavy fire and quickly turned and ran from the British advance. They skirmished off and on for the remainder of the day and dozens of Americans were killed or wounded, while the British loses were light. By evening, the British marched down the Bethlehem Pike to St. Thomas Episcopal church and encamped there. The night was extremely cold and dipped down below 20 degrees. General Howe awoke the next morning and commented, "this American weather is excessive cold," as he climbed the church bell tower to survey the American positions which were a little more than a half mile away. Howe saw that

Washington was reinforcing his defenses, but decided to probe the American lines with some artillery fire. Unfortunately, the shells couldn't reach the lines and he decided to try attacking the left. Howe formed his troops of solid, high ground, but the Americans defenses were set on higher ground still. For once, Washington had dictated the line of battle and controlled the flow of action.

By the 7th, when the British tried shifting their troops to attack the Americans center, the Americans were prepared again and sent a fluid design of troops to follow Howe's every move. Howe was partial to flanking maneuvers, but was unable to accomplish them this time since Washington, at higher ground, could see Howe's every move and counteract each one. Howe tried one more maneuver. He shifted his troops yet again toward Edge Hill where Daniel Morgan's riflemen were posted. This was left of center to the American lines, and Morgan, along with Colonel Gist's Maryland troops assaulted the British with guerrilla tactics. "Using every tree, wall, rock, and building," to set down cover fire until Howe was so frustrated, he ordered his 33rd of Foot Regiment into the fray to counteract the small American detachment. Morgan decided it was time to withdraw and moved back to the American center just in time for Howe to send in another detachment of his own.

This time he ordered in Major Baurmeister's Hessian grenadiers. But they found the defenses of "strong abatis, trenches, and nine covered pieces of artillery," too formidable and fell back. Shortly after this, the 2nd Continental Regiment under the command of General John Cadwalader and Colonel Joseph Reed came against British General "No Flint" Grey's Light Infantry and Queens Rangers and the battle was beginning to turn in the favor of the British. Just then, Reed's horse was shot out from under him, but the animal had fallen on his leg and he could not move it. At the same time, a detachment of Hessians noticed the prone American officer and charged at him with bayonets. General Cadwalader saw this and drew his sword as he "drove his horse at all speed," in order to attempt to intervene in his friend's behalf. At the exact moment Cadwalader and the Hessians were about to meet at Reed's location, over a rise Captain Allen McLane, at the head of a squad of horsemen, had also noticed Reed's predicament and had charged across the open field at great haste. The horsemen arrived in time to intervene in the two officer's behalf, but not before "cutting down several of the fleeing barbaric Hessians first."

As night fell, two more Hessian regiments were brought in to strengthen the British line. It seemed to Washington that everything was in place for another major engagement the following morning. That night was even colder than the night before, and come sunrise the next morning Howe had lost the stomach to fight. He had used up all of his two day provisions, and he thought, "Why sit on a cold, frozen hillside, when he and his troops could be warm, rested, and fed at their quarters in Philadelphia? Besides, the Americans defenses were too well fortified." So by the afternoon of the 8th, the British started marching back to the comfort of Philadelphia. The Americans half-heartedly chased after the British rear column, but a detachment of Hessian jagers formed up on an elevation above the Americans and fired a few volleys at them to shoo them away. The Americans were satisfied that they had made their point and returned to their encampment. Surgeon Albigence Waldo who was traveling with Washington and his aides commented afterwards, "We were all chargrin'd at the British retreat as we were more willing to chase them in as far as Philadelphia."

On the 11th, Washington, with a touch of humor, wrote to Governor Livingston of New Jersey:--"General Howe, after making great preparations and threatening to drive us beyond the mountains, came out with his whole force last Thursday evening, and after manoeuvring round us till Monday following, decamped very hastily, and marched back to Philadelphia." And to Congress he reported, "I Sincerely wish they had made an attack as the issue, in all probability, from the disposition of our troops, and the strong situation of our camp, would have been fortunate and happy. At the same time I must add, that treason, prudence, and every principle of policy forbade us quitting our post to attack them. Nothing but success would have justified the measure; and this could not be expected from their position. Howe's little expedition into Whitemarsh had gained him nothing. A local Tory wrote trying to understand Howe's mindset as, "if the sole purpose of the foray was to destroy and spread devastation and ruin, to dispose the inhabitants to rebellion be despoiling their property." The three-day battle had resulted in over 300 British casualties, and about 100 for the Americans.

At the same time, Washington could not remain at Whitemarsh indefinitely. It was too close for comfort to Philadelphia, and it wasn't a good location for a long encampment. Winter season was almost upon them, the weather was already growing colder by the day, and the troops were suffering for want of clothing and shelter. While the British sat comfortably in good winter quarters in Philadelphia, the Americans pondered the route they should take. Where should the American army take up winter quarters? The overall sentiment was in favor of a line from Lancaster to Reading. Greene, with Cadwalader and a few others, thought Wilmington a better position. At last, after much discussion, and principally upon the opinions of the officers and VIP's from Pennsylvania, Washington decided on Valley Forge. "According to the original plan," writes Reed to President Wharton, "A brigade of Continental troops was to be left with the militia on this side of the Schuylkill, and this plan, which when I wrote I thought was approved by his Excellency, has upon other advice been totally changed. General Greene, Cadwalader, and myself had fixed upon this plan as the most eligible to quiet the minds of the people and cover the country at the same time."

Chapter X

"Valley Forge"

Although the distance from Whitemarsh to Valley Forge is no more than thirteen miles, the American army under Washington had been on the road to its new winter campsite for more than a week. They first marched north for three miles to Gulph Mills and bivouacked there, celebrating the "Thanksgiving Congress had ordered for the brave officers and men." But there was no turkey, no corn, not even biscuits and gravy. For four days and nights winter struck with its full fury. The wretched, ill clad, tired soldiers huddled around campfires, were trying to cook their meager provisions or to sleep, unsheltered and in tattered, wet clothes, thousands of them without blankets, on the snow covered ground. Their tents and baggage, sent from Whitemarsh at the time of the British attack, were now at Trappe, eighteen miles to the northwest. The night the baggage train finally arrived, the snow had turned to rain; but before morning the temperature plunged below the freezing mark once again, causing the all ready rutted, slush-covered roads to be congealed into icy ridges. The army had to wait three additional days for the weather to break so it could permit its barefoot men to march.

On the 19th of December, in the closing days of 1777, their march resumed. That often repeated story of bloody footprints was unimpeachably confirmed by a letter Washington authored to William Gordon, a noted historian after the war, that "you might have tracked the army from Whitemarsh to Valley Forge by the blood of their feet setting the path." "It is impossible to exaggerate the misery of the troops at this time," wrote Greene, "One half of our troops are without breeches, shoes and stockings; and some thousand without blankets."

The Quartermaster-general had not been near the army since July. The commissaries, in spite of Washington efforts, were constantly behind with their supplies of food, the hospitals were full, the graveyards were filling daily. There were "eleven thousand and eighty-nine men in the entire army as of the 19th of December 1777, and of these two thousand and eighty were unfit for duty," according to a report submitted by the army surgeons. "A quarter of the whole number that are unfit, because they are barefoot and otherwise naked," the report continued. In fifteen days, from the 4th to the 19th of December, the ranks "decreased near two thousand." "The Quartermaster's department, as well as the commissariat, has completely broken down," wrote Washington to Congress, "While the army is suffering, for want of shoes &c., hogsheads of shoes, stockings and clothing are at different places upon the country and in the woods, lying and perishing, for want of teams and proper management. Where is Mifflin?"

Nevertheless, the army staggered on and came at last to Valley Forge, "a deep, short valley on the west bank of the Schuylkill, and about twenty miles from Philadelphia, forming the first step of the hills that reach to North Mountain, or the Blue Ridge," Greene wrote to his wife, "A small creek runs through the upper part of the valley, turning the wheels of a Mr. Potts' forge in ancient times, from which the valley took its name." The creek flow was east to west, Valley Forge being on its southern side. From the creek the land rose steeply, over 250 feet in two-fifths of a mile, to an undulating plateau about two miles long and a mile and a quarter wide. The slopes on the west and on the north to the Schuylkill are less steep, and the elevation is heavily forested with a variety of trees. The area within what is now Valley Forge National Park, has changed little in almost two hundred and twenty five years.

Washington allowed his troops to rest as best they could for a day or two, but work had to be started on shelter and defenses. Along the southern edge was drawn an irregular line of entrenchment's.

Similar entrenchments and an abatis, running roughly north south guarded its western end, also by certain redoubts and redans, forming a sort of inner stronghold. The western creek side was thought to be sufficiently defended by the abruptness of approach from that quarter, and the north side of the width of the Schuylkill.

Throughout this space the various brigades were posted, each having its own little village of huts drawn up in lines facing each other with streets between. Washington's first general order at Valley Forge prescribed the plans and specifications for constructing these huts. "They are to be fourteen feet by sixteen in size, with log walls six and a half feet high, the interstices between the logs stopped with clay, the fireplaces and chimneys (directly across from the door) made of clay-dubbed wood, the steep-pitched roofs of planks or slabs of wood." Twelve men were to occupy each hut. Washington offered "a twelve dollars reward to the party in each, which finished its hut in the quickest and most workmanlike time and manner." The winning hut was constructed in less than two days. The team was made up of mostly carpenters and woodcutters, who had the best chance among an army of store merchants, farmers, and vagabonds.

Washington and Greene refused to seek other shelter for themselves while the men could not be afforded the same luxury. They both stayed in Washington's marquee, made only of coarse homespun linen. They lived in it for a week, and then Washington established his headquarters at the western end of camp in a large stone house owned by a Quaker by the name of Issac Potts. But Greene and the other general officers, gave into convenience, and although the original plan had the officers "each to occupy their own hut," they soon discovered that there would be little drilling during the onset of winter, and distributed themselves into neighboring houses, mostly outside the camp. The general officers had serious issues with their winter quarters. "None but an interested speculator or ill-wisher of the General's," writes DeKalb, "can have suggested to him the idea of wintering in this wilderness." Instead of a camp to rest in while new recruits were brought forward, and preparations made for taking the field in the spring, he looked forward to a hard winter campaign. "Who knows but what we shall meet with a misfortune this winter?" "It is unparalleled in the history of man," writes Varnum, "to establish winter quarters in a country wasted, and without a single magazine." How far Greene shared in these gloomy anticipation's we will never know. His letters show none of the low morale and disenchantment of his comrades. He seems to have gone about his business of planning the spring campaign and carrying out the decisions of his commander-in-chief.

On the afternoon of the 22nd of December, intelligence came to him that a strong foraging party of the enemy was "advancing towards Darby." Orders were immediately issued for the "troops to hold themselves in readiness to march." When, "Behold," writes Washington, "to my great mortification, I was not only informed, but convinced, that the men were unable to stir on account of provision, and that a dangerous mutiny had begun the night before, and which with difficulty was suppressed by the spirited exertions of the officers, was still much to be apprehended for want of this article. This brought forth the only commissary in the purchasing line in this camp; and with him this melancholy and alarming truth, that he had not a single hoof of any kind to slaughter, and not more than twenty-five barrels of flour! From hence form an opinion of our situation when I add, that he could not tell when to expect any."

"Howe himself could have easily come out and taken the army completely without a fight," it was suggested by Washington. "The attempt will be exceeding hazardous and the success doubtful," said most of the officers whom Sullivan consulted by Washington directions. "I am so weary of the infernal clamour of the Pennsylvanians, that I am for satisfying them at all events, and risking every consequence in an action. Possibly we may be successful; if not, they may be satisfied; and even Congress itself may gain experience, and learn to censure with more caution." The alarm of the enemy foraging party passed without incident, but more serious problems, like the joint discontent by the officers and men because of the lack of food, was just as alarming.

On the 1st of January 1778, Greene writes of his concerns to Washington, "It gives me the greatest pain to hear the murmurs and complaints among the officers for the want of spirits. They say they are exposed to the severity of the weather, subject to hard duty, and nothing but bread and beef to eat morning, noon, and night, without vegetables, or anything to drink but cold water; this is hard fare for people that have been accustomed to live tolerably. The officers observe, however disagreeable their situation, they would patiently submit to their hard fortune, if the evil in its own nature was incurable; but they think by proper exertions spirits may be procured to alleviate their distress until they have an opportunity to provide for themselves. Lord Stirling was mentioning yesterday that he had made a discovery of a considerable quantity of spirits, sufficient to supply all the officers. Supposing his Lordship's information to be true, will it not be consistent with good policy to seize it and distribute it among the regiments for the use of the officers,--about thirty or forty gallons for each regiment? While the officers complained about the lack of "spirits" while suffering with only "bread and beef morning, noon, and night," the soldiers were suffering far greater agonies. Yes. They had shelter that passed for sorry dwellings, but they were far from weatherproof. When it snowed, it filtered through the crevices, when it melted or rained, it poured through. When the constant, cold winter winds blew it went through the walls like a sieve. The poorly designed fireplaces had no flues and filled the huts with throat-choking smoke almost 24-hours a day. The floors were made of dirt that was usually mud. Their bunks were made with crude wood planks, thinly covered with straw and many of the men had no blankets. True, there was warmth within the crudely constructed walls and more protection then being exposed to the outside elements, but the food supply situation was growing desperate. Shelter, somewhat. Food was almost non-existent, and clothing was another issue.

Lafayette wrote, "The unfortunate soldiers were in want of everything; they had neither coats, hats, shirts nor shoes; their feet and legs froze until they became black and it was often necessary to amputate them to save their lives." Doctor Albigence Waldo, a surgeon of a Connecticut regiment, pictured a typical incident in Valley Forge that winter. "There comes a Soldier, his bare feet are seen thro' his worn-out shoes, his legs nearly naked from the tattered remains of an only pair of stockings, his Breeches not sufficient to cover his nakedness, his Shirt hanging in Strings, his hair dishevell'd, his face meagre; his whole appearance pictures a person forsaken & discouraged. He comes and crys with an air of wretchedness & dispair, I am Sick he tells me, my feet lame, my legs are sore, my body covered with this tormenting Itch." (a disease common in the camp).

The common soldier had inadequate shelter, lack of clothing, and dangerously low amounts of food. The officers complained that they needed spirits to keep them going in these horrible conditions. A class structure system was just as alive and well in the new nation of the United States as it was in its old homeland of England.

The severe and torturous conditions were becoming too much for the men. General Varnum reported that his division had been without meat for two days and three days without bread. In the waning days of 1777, Washington informed Congress that, the lack of food had caused "a dangerous mutiny" which was suppressed with difficulty, and that there was in camp "not a single hoof of any kind to slaughter and not more than twenty-five barrels of flour remaining in camp. Unless some great and capital change suddenly takes place in that line, this army must inevitably be reduced to one or other of these three things,--starve, dissolve, or disperse, in order to obtain subsistence in the best manner they can." Salted pork and beef was almost as scarce as fresh meat. The shortness of these commodities was supplemented by barrels of salted herring, which, more times than not, were rancid or decayed when they were opened. A common staple became "Firecake." A small amount of flour mixed with water paste baked on hot stones and made into thin cakes. "Firecake and water for breakfast," cried Dr. Waldo, "Firecake and water for dinner! Firecake and water for supper! The Lord send that our Commissary for Purchase may have to live on fire-cake and water himself!"

To make conditions even more harrowing, disease was an unwelcome visitor throughout the camp. Smallpox was a frequent guest, but not as frequent as the "putrid fever," better known as typhus. Medical knowledge was still in its infancy and the proper treatment of the deadly illness went unchecked in most cases. It did not help that there was an inadequate supply of doctors or surgeons as well. Improper diets for the men only compounded the problem, leaving the men weak when the fever set in and usually making the ailment fatal. Several hospitals had been established just after the battles of Brandywine and Germantown and were already filled to capacity with wounded. The largest hospital was in Yellow Springs at which 1,300 cases of typhus were being treated by the unskilled surgeons there. When that hospital filled up, they were sent to the Adventist Sisters care in their community in Ephrata. The Moravian Brethren at Bethlehem, and two other smaller hospitals in nearby towns, were also established. All of them were filled to capacity by the end of winter.

Many of the sick were sent to the same hospitals as the wounded, 500 from the battle at Brandywine alone. Room was so scarce that they had to be put up in tents with nothing but straw for their beds. Problem was, the straw would be used over and over again without being changed. A Dr. William Smith said he had, "known from four or five patients die on the floors and used again and again before it was changed." The typhus patients were brought in from Valley Forge and put into the same wards with the wounded men who were still weak and healing. The Valley Forge men weren't only brought in with the highly contagious disease, but also "attired in rags swarming with vermin." The deadly combination became a cocktail for fever and epidemic throughout all of the hospitals. The doctors, nurses, and orderlies came down with the disease as well. At Bethlehem, "not an orderly man or nurse escaped, and but a few surgeons." At a hospital in Lititz there were 250 invalids cared for by two doctors. Both doctors fell ill of typhus and died. Of the more than 1,500 patients received in that hospital alone, over 500 died. Forty men from a single Virginia regiment caught the disease and only three survived. "Those hospitals were but way stations on the road to the grave," wrote one doctor. It would be spring before the ravages of the disease were subdued at Valley Forge and those who survived would return to duty.

Even Greene fell to the discomforts of Valley Forge, although to a much lesser degree. Nathanael had felt a great deal of pain in his left eye. The eye that had been affected by the small pox vaccine when he was in New York before the war. He wrote to his brother Jacob on the 3rd of January 1778: "Our army is tenting themselves; they are almost worn out with fatigue, and greatly distressed for want of food and clothing, particularly the article of shoes and stockings. The present mode of clothing the army will always leave us without a sufficient supply. The change in the Commissary department has been a very distressing circumstance; Mr. Trumbull left it. The Quartermaster-general's department also has been in a most wretched condition. General Mifflin, who ought to have been at the head of the business, has not been with the army since it came into his State."

Foraging parties were the main supply of food at Valley Forge. While "Mad" Anthony Wayne worked in New Jersey herding and securing cattle for the army, he earned himself a second nickname, "The Drover." Henry Lee secured himself a nickname as well, "Light Horse Harry" for his expeditions into Delaware and bringing up cattle that were getting fat on the marsh meadows along the river for the use of British army. But Allen McLane was known as "the most dashing of all the raiders." Like most foraging parties, he preyed off the helpless local farmers, but he got a lot more enjoyment out of cutting off British detachments sent out from Philadelphia to pick up their fatted calves, and taking the cattle from them. McLane was made a Captain of an independent corps of men, made up by a small troop of horsemen, a hundred militiamen, some mounted and the others on foot, and a band of Oneida Indians. Once known only as a forger, he now added scout, and raider to his resume. Working everywhere from Philadelphia to beyond, and even working in disguises in the city. Greene said of him, "He became known to everybody as the constant hero of surprise and daring." Greene would soon need him, and all of his talented attributes.

While the army remained living from hand to mouth, one day without bread, another without meat, and often going without either, Washington was formulating a new path of action to acquire supplies and to keep the supplies coming. Washington had originally planned to have each individual State that the army was operating in at that particular time, pitch in with contributions. But states that had been host to the army for long periods of time, such as New Jersey, were reluctant to invest any more time or money on that plan, and Pennsylvania was quickly following suit. Especially the inhabitants all around the camp. They felt they had given more than their fair share to the army and quite frankly, were deeply disaffected, and consequently unwilling to give up their cattle and grain for American certificates when they could always get British gold for them in Philadelphia. Besides, most of the people in the area of Valley Forge believed that the British would ultimately be successful in the end, making the American certificates worthless. One must remember, for every American fighting on the side of the colonists, another fought for the British, and the third wanted no part of the war whatsoever.

Never since the retreat through the Jerseys had the army been so close to dissolution. A day did not go by that a commissioned officer threaten to resign. The flood of desertion was at a fever pitch, and Washington could not seem to come up with an idea that could stop his woes. He finally resolved to send out a large foraging party, and seize by strong-arm, if necessary, whatever they could get that could not be purchased. He gave command of the party to Greene. Nathanael was less than enamored by the decision, but knew that part of the job of being a soldier was doing the dirty jobs just as well as commanding troops into battle. But how much his heart was into the job shows in a letter to Washington, dated February 14, 1778, "We are posted at this place. I have set-up headquarters at a house across from the Springfield Meeting house for the purpose of collecting all the cattle, carriages, etc., etc., in and about the neighborhood to-day; to-morrow we purpose to take post at one Edwards' Tavern about six miles in our rear."

Sickened by the ineptitude of Mifflin as Quartermaster-general, Washington finally assigned someone who he thought would organize the effort to secure food, forage for the troops, and attempt to supply the clothing, so desperately needed by his men at Valley Forge and to push that resolve to its every extremity. The only man Washington ever considered for the job, was Greene. He knew Nathanael was diligent, thrifty, and strong willed. Whatever duty was set before him was always accomplished with determination, intelligence and in a decisive matter. All were attributes needed for this pursuit.

As much as Greene despised the job, he began to throw himself into his newest command with as much fervor as he could muster. He wrote to one of his commanders, Colonel Biddle, "I must beg you to exert yourself in obtaining forage, otherwise the business will go on slow and we will be required to remain here. Tell all the wagoners, and the officers that have the superintendence of the wagons, that I will punish the least neglect with the greatest severity. You must forage the country naked, and, to prevent their complaint of the want for forage, we must take all their cattle, sheep, and horses fit for the use of the army. Let us hear from you and know how you go on."

Reports were beginning to come in, but they were not as favorable as he had hoped for. That afternoon, Greene writes to Colonel Biddle again; "I received two letters from you within an hour past. I am very sorry to find so small a collection of wagons. Search the country through and through. Mount your pressing parties on horses for expedition's sake. Harden your heart and dispatch business as fast as possible. I have got many parties out collecting wagons, horses, cattle, hogs, and sheep. The wagons I shall forward to you as fast as they come in. We have made considerable collection of horses, and I think it will be best to send them to camp to-night, that as many wagons may be rigged out as possible, to come on for forage. I think I shall move from this position to-night or to-morrow morning; we are in the midst of a damn nest of Tories, and we are in the neighborhood of the enemy, a change of position becomes necessary for security's sake."

Greene was unable to change position until the following day, and during the move sent a message to Washington: We are in want of some of the deputy quartermaster-generals to conduct the business of that department; plèase sir to send us one. I received two letters from Colonel Biddle; he has got but a few wagons; the inhabitants conceal them; the Colonel complains bitterly of the disaffection of the people we are trying to fight for. I sent out a great number of small parties to collect livestock yesterday, but the collection was inconsiderable; the country is very much drained; the inhabitants cry out and beset me from my quarters; but like the Pharaoh of ancient I harden my heart and do not hear their pleas. Two men were taken up carrying provisions to the enemy yesterday morning. I gave them a hundred each (lashes with the cat-o-nine-tails) by way of example. I have sent off all the livestock. I will send on the forage and all further collections that may be made as fast as possible. I determine to forage the country very bare. Nothing shall be left unattempted."

Another message was sent the same day, "As provision will be scarce, especially of the meat kind, if the commissaries could purchase a quantity of sugar, the troops, with wheat, might make a fermity; a diet that would contribute to their health, be palatable and nourishing to the troops. I think it would be very good substitute for meat, and not much more expensive if any." By the following messages it seems that Greene has sniffed out Washington's ploy to make him Quartermaster-general and began to negotiate the placement of men in important departments Greene desired. "Lieutenant-colonel Ballard was out on foraging business yesterday down by Darby, and got intelligence that the enemy's bridge was being removed, and that even with this difficulty, attempted to relieve their guards, but as you can see from the inclosed report, he was by no way successful. But he was successful in foraging some cattle, sheep, and hogs, and returning with all and his men without loss of any. I hope the committee of Congress will not lose sight of him and Colonel Cox; both these men will serve their purpose better than any. Your Excellency may remember I named Mr. Lott for that department; please to name him to the committee."

In the meantime, Greene and his foraging parities had moved to a new headquarters at Providence Meetinghouse, but had come up with the same results. "I am afraid there will be nothing considerable, as the country appears much drained. Hay is the plentifullest article that there is in the country; sixty or seventy tons may be had in this neighborhood. . . . .To-morrow we shall mount a press party on horses to press wagons the back of Brandywine. The inhabitants hereabouts if they have any wagons or harness they concel them well." His best man, Ballard, had a little run in with a small group of British light-horseman, but after some heavy exchange of small arms fire, no one was injured and they proceeded, empty handed, to the next foraging site that Greene describes on the 16th of February, "I received your Excellency's answer to my last yesterday morning. I propose the burning of the hay on the Jersey shore, also another forage in Buck's County. Upon revolving the matter over in my mind, I think the following would be the best plan to execute it upon. Wagons cannot be got in this country, and to attempt to collect them in Bucks County will explain our intentions too early for the safety of the party. I would, therefore, propose a press-warrant to be sent to Colonel Smith at Lancaster, and for him to apply to the executive council for a hundred wagons to be got ready in three days; and in case they don't furnish them by that time, that Colonel Smith collect the wagons with his press-warrant; but if your Excellency thinks our situation will justify dispensing with an application to the executive council, the press-warrant will be the most speedy and certain method of getting complement of wagons seasonably. I will do everything in my power here, but the face of the country is strongly marked with poverty and distress."

Finding foraging an increasingly hard fight over the past week, the kind hearted, easy-going

Greene began to take his own advice and "harden his heart" to the plight of the inhabitants. He issued a standing order to the foraging parties to take everything that was not nailed down. If the inhabitants did not cooperate, they were to be locked in their houses. If they were found to be hiding livestock the army was asking for; "Your Excellency's letter of this day is in hand. I had given orders to all the press parties to bring the inhabitants prisoners that concealed their cattle or carriages, and examples shall not be wanting to facilitate the business I am out upon. General Wayne will cross over into the Jerseys from Wilmington, to execute the design of destroying the hay and driving in all the stock from the shores, which he proposes to forward on to camp by the shortest and safest route. By this detachment my party will be much diminished. Great numbers have already been sent home that have fallen sick and got their feet sore in all the marching. I think it will be best, therefore, to send two of my field-officers to camp, they being altogether useless to me. I sent to camp yesterday near fifty head of cattle. I wish it had been in my power to have sent more. Captain Lee writes of the increasing distress of the army. God grant we may never brought to such a wretched condition again."

Conditions at Valley Forge grew worse by the day. The horses that Greene had foraged, over 500 of them, died of starvation anyway. They could hardly be buried in the frozen ground, so their carcasses rotted in piles throughout the camp and endangered the health of the men. The soldiers were not faring much better. Washington would write to Greene: "For some days past there has been little less than a famine in the camp. A part of the army has been a week without any kind of flesh and the rest three or four days. Naked and starving as they are, we cannot enough admire the incomparable patience and fidelity of the soldiery, that they have not been excited enough by their suffering to begin a general mutiny and dispersion."

Greene continued with added fervor to forage the country wherever he could. "Colonel Harmer is gone with a party on the back of the forks of the Brandywine, a little above the route of the enemy. Colonel Spencer is gone to the township of Goshen, to rendezvous at the meeting-house, collect cattle, etc. I shall continue here until the impressed wagons, and all those from camp are loaded. I am afraid there will be but few to what our wants demand, and what might be loaded here with hay. Grain there is but little to be got. The business I am upon is very disagreeable; but I should be happy in executing it, if our success was equal to our wants."

By the 20th of February, Greene had almost completed all he could on his forage party detail. He wrote from Providence Meetinghouse: "General Wayne has successfully crossed over the river from Delaware into the Jerseys. He intends to collect all the stock he incounters and burn all the hay along the river that will be within the reach of the enemy. If he executes the business effectually, the only chance the enemy will have for foraging will be between the Schuylkill and the Delaware, at a place called Point-no-point, which already may be burned. Colonel Biddle writes that he had loaded forty wagons yesterday. Captain Lee was at Wilmington before he left and sent word that he saw no cattle. Colonel Spencer wrote from Goshen that he got a few cattle. I have not heard from Colonel Harmer since he set off for the forks of the Brandywine, but have heard of cattle coming into camp from that quarter, and therefore must suppose they were sent by him. Many people in this country refuse certificates for their horses and cattle. The next move I make from here I shall order home all the troops except one division; they will be so remote from the enemy that there will be little or no danger from them, and the country will be pretty well gleaned. The troops had been quartered constantly in houses, so that they suffered very little, except for the heavy marches they have gone through." And so ended Greene's first forage expedition. It would not be his last.

Greene returned to Valley Forge and picked up pen to write to his old friend Knox, who was visiting family in Massachusetts and also busy campaigning for supplies and provisions from the New England states. "I must beg your pardon for not writing you before, but I have put it off from time to time to learn the determination of the committee of Congress respecting the establishment of the army.

A mystical darkness has spread over the councils of America and prevents her counselors from seeing her true interest. The army has been in great distress since you left it; the troops are getting naked, and they were seven days without bread. Such patience and moderation as they manifested under their sufferings does the highest honor to the magnanimity of the American soldiers. Happily, relief arrived from the little collection I had made and some others, and hopefuly prevented the army from disbanding. We are still in danger of starving. The commissary's department is in a most wretched condition, the quartermaster's in worse. The committee of Congress have seen all these things with their own eyes."

For the moment the army was relieved. One of the committee of Congress members was William Greene of Warwick, who would soon become governor of Rhode Island, witnessed the conditions at Valley Forge and wrote: "I have seen lately that they now are well fed, which was afforded me much satisfaction, as I am convinced, and that long since, that under God, our all depends upon making them more comfortable, so as to create in them a cheerful inclination to carry on our reasonable and very necessary defense." In other words, let's make sure that the soldiers don't starve so they can keep us safe. Par for the course from a member of Congress. Because the relief was only temporary, and as glad as Greene was to escape from the unwelcome duty of foraging, his feelings were still severely tried by the amount of suffering which he could not alleviate. Although Greene still did not consider himself the Quartermaster-general or wear the title, he was in all actuality the Quartermaster-general of the army, and along with his other daily routines, the added mantle he had been given by General Washington would point that fact out everyday. Working in the context of Quartermaster-general would bring him into contact with some of the worse offenders of human morals and decency imaginable, and in turn, cast shadows upon his credibility as an officer and a gentleman in the process that would be rumored two hundred and twenty-two years later.

Chapter XI

"Quartermaster-General of the Army"

In the original formation of the department of Quartermaster-general, the appointment of the officer had been left to Washington, who had appointed Thomas Mifflin, a member of his own military family at the time. During his first year, Mifflin fulfilled the duties of his office with efficiency and zeal, and resigning of his own accord, Stephen Moylan, another Washington aide, was appointed in his stead. He too soon resigned, and Mifflin, by a special resolution of Congress, which had now taken the matter into its own hands, was "authorized and requested to resume the office; his rank and pay as Brigadier-general" being given to him. But Mifflin did not bring back his original enthusiasm, and in the following year, entertained a cabal against his Commander-in-chief: withdraw from the army under the pretext of ill health, and without resigning, virtually abandoned the office as Quartermaster-general and went back to his home in Lancaster.

Greene had been working in the guise of interim Quartermaster-general for a few weeks, but knew it was only a matter of time before he was either asked or ordered to take over the duties and title of Quartermaster-general of the army. That time finally came on the 3rd of March 1778 when the committee of Congress for the reorganization of the army drafted a letter to the president of Congress, "We had flattered ourselves that before this time the pleasure of Congress would be made known to us respecting the Quartermaster's Department. We find ourselves embarrassed in entering on this subject, lest a bare recital of facts should carry an imputation on those gentlemen who have lately conducted it." Speaking of Mifflin and his cohorts. "We are a sensible lot and with it could show just allowances that need be made for the peculiarity of their situation, and we are perhaps not fully acquainted with their difficulties. But we find the property of the army dispersed over the whole country; We need not point out the effects this circumstance will have on the new draughted troops, if not carefully guarded; they are too obvious to need enumeration. A character has presented itself, which, in a great degree meets our approbation, judgement, and wishes. We have opened the subject to him and it is now under his consideration. When we are at liberty we shall introduce him to your notice; but delicacy forbids our doing it until he has made up his mind on the subject, and given his consent to the nomination." The character they speak of is, of course, Greene. How he felt about becoming a staff officer over after having his line command is clear. As he explains in a letter to Knox: "The committee of Congress have urged me for several days to accept the Quartermaster-general's appointment. His Excellency, also, presses it upon me exceedingly. I hate the place, but hardly know what to do; the General is afraid that the department will become ill-managed again unless some of his friends undertakes it that the operations of the next campaign will in a great measure be frustrated. They also are pleased with how the commissary-general's departments are being more economically managed with than they have been for some time past. I wish and hope for your advice in the affair, but am obliged to determine immediately."

The pressure on him from all sides must have been great. Washington, whom he revered, appealing to him in the name of their personal friendship and love of country, and the committee, urging him in the name of public and private duty. How could he say no? He first told Washington, "Your task is too great as Commander-in-chief to concern yourself with the Quartermasters duties. I will serve one year, unconnected with the accounts, without any additional pay to that I have major-general." It was a good thing Greene felt that way. The office and title of Quartermaster-general carried with it no additional pay, but a great deal of responsibility. With all of the parties involved content with the proposition Greene proposed, Nathanael Greene was resolved to become the new Quartermaster-general of the Continental Army for the period of one year.

Greene had made only two conditions in his acceptance; the appointment of John Cox and Charles Pettit as assistant quartermasters-general, and his reason for doing this was simply to aid himself by having men he knew and trusted where he could place them in his full confidence. Without these two, well chosen men, it would be impossible for Greene to conduct so extensive and complicated a business. Cox was a colonel in Greene's regiment. Before the war, he was a Philadelphia merchant, but held a commission in the first regiment raised by the city. Charles Pettit, who was also from Philadelphia, brought a thorough knowledge of affairs and strict methods for economical purchasing. Both men had been very successful in the private sector and obviously were extremely familiar with the details of business. It also did not hurt that both were connected by marriage and friendship to Greene's good friend Joseph Reed, a member in good standing with the Committee that nominated and appointed Greene as Quartermaster-general.

His next appointment would be one of his most important that of commissary-general of purchases. Colonel Jeremiah Wadsworth of Connecticut, who had recently been elected commissary general of purchases, was chosen by Greene from the recommendations of friends in New England. He was well known to be an energetic, cheerful, and consummate merchant who always showed a profit. That's because by modern standards he would be classified as a wheeler-dealer. A salesman who could sell blankets to the Native Americans. His vigorous, intelligent, and sound judgment was the perfect combination to be of great service to Greene in many a trying emergency that would arise in the next few months. Wadsworth stationed himself in New England where he knew the climate was better suited to patriot movements and gentlemen could be persuaded to either donate articles the army needed, or to sell it at a reasonable profit. Also, unlike Pennsylvania, Delaware, and the Jerseys, goods could be found there in large amounts. Wadsworth put his nose to the grindstone and procured a collection of foodstuffs and clothing. Greene in the meanwhile, "was to perform the military duty of the department, attend all the issues, and direct the purchases." His first duty was to work on transportation needs, and gathered wagons and horses, repaired bridges, built and mended roads, and organized a corps of wagoners. Now livestock and provisions that either died or rotted waiting to be fed or transported could be brought to camp in a timely manner. Colonel Cox was to "make all purchases, examine all stores and the like," and Mr. Pettit was to "attend to the keeping of all accounts and cash. Forge-masters, wagon-masters, etc., must of necessity be in the appointment of the quartermaster-general, who is, or ought at least to be responsible for their conduct, forming a part of the general system."

Greene had offered to perform the military duty of the office for a year without any addition to his pay as major general, but when he found out that there were no additional funds allowed to his position he requested a stipend for family expenses. The committee, who was anxious to put the department onto a permanent footing, denied the request. An addition to base salaries, they feared, would lead to a general demand through the entire army officer's corps for an increase of salaries. They speculated, "when once that mode had begun no one can tell where it will end except in public bankruptcy." The committee had grave objections to the payment of a commission on expenditures, and that there was "no possibility of obviating speculation but by drawing forth men of property, morals, and character." It was therefore decided, "that any compensation would be a commission of only one percent on the money issued to the department, and to be divided between Greene, Wadsworth, Cox, and Pettit. A separate pay scale would be afforded to the wagon-master-general and his deputy which is absolutely necessary." But Greene proposed an equal division of profits, saying, "the commission of two and a half per cent now paid on forage alone will, we believe, exceed the allowance of the new establishment."

By late March, Greene was well into the duties of his office. "We have been looking over your plan for the forage-master-general's department," he writes to Colonel Biddle. "We wish to have a plan of the relative state the forage-master's department stood in to the quartermaster-general's heretofore. . . . .You will give us an account of your former conditions of serving,--who were paid by the month, who received a commission, what it was, and on what it arose. Give us as full a history of the matter as may be necessary for our full information to compare the two plans."

By the end of March he was already on the warpath with Congress: "I received my appointment as Quartermaster-general through the hands of the committee of Congress here at camp, by whose special solicitations I engaged in the business of the department. I am very sensible of the importance of the trust, and the difficulty of putting the business upon a tolerable footing at this advanced season. My utmost exertions, however, shall not be wanting to answer the expectations of the Congress and to accommodate the army; and I am sensible the gentlemen who are appointed my assistants will give me all the aid in their power. The demands are so extensive, and the resources so few, that the shortness of the time in which we must provide the necessaries for the ensuing campaign will not leave us at liberty to make the most advantageous contracts. This is an inconvenience to which the public must be subject, in consequence of the business of the department being taken up at so late a period, and will necessarily call for a large and immediate supply of cash. Colonel Cox will wait upon Congress in a few days, and give then further information upon his head. I hope by this time they are impressed with proper ideas respecting the situation of the department, and they will know how essential it is to the operations of the ensuing campaign that the most speedy preparations should be made. If I am not properly supported, if I am not aided with all the influence of Congress in the several States, I am fully persuaded our utmost endeavors will fall vastly short of the desired effect; the army will be distressed, the public disappointed, and our reputations ruined. I hope, therefore, that every possible encouragement will be given to enable us to answer the demands of the army."

His close relationship would also help him in accomplishing his duties as quartermaster-general. "I received your Excellency's letter containing a list of the counties in Virginia where wagons might be got, and the properest persons to employ to make the purchases. I am also obligated to his Excellency for the letters of introduction to those gentlemen you recommend to accept and engage in the business at hand. I must apologize for not waiting upon your reply, being very busily engaged in the arrangement of matters abroad."

The next day Greene sent an express in New England with instructions, orders, and commissions, and among them contractor's commission for his brother Jacob, who had served with him in the State legislature, and was now living in the house at Coventry as superintendent of the iron works.

By the last day of March, Greene had studied the subject of magazines, and prepared himself to decide upon the proper places for them. "I agree with you there is not a moment's time to be lost in fixing upon proper places for magazines," he would write to Colonel Clement Biddle: "I have been thinking upon the subject, and am of opinion that the following must be the great outlines of the chain of magazines; the quantity to be laid in of particular stores upon the river and at intermediate posts to form a proper communication, must be regulated by circumstances.
200,000 bushels of grain upon the Delaware, and as much hay as can be got.
200,000 bushels of grain upon the Schuylkill, and as much hay as can be bought.

200,000 bushels of grain at the Head of Elk and the intermediate posts to camp, and as much hay as can be bought within forty miles to camp upon that route.

100,000 bushels of grain upon the line of communication from the Susquehanna to the Schuylkill, from Reading through Lancaster to Wright's Ferry, and as much hay as can be got.

100,000 bushels of grain from the Delaware to the North River, to be proportioned to the consequence of the several posts forming the communication, and a necessary quantity of hay.

40,000 bushels of grain round about Trenttown, within a circle of eight or ten miles, and as much hay as can be got."

"As there has been a post kept at Trentown it is more than probable the forage must be principally drawn from Burlington and Monmouth. The forage at the North River must be proportioned to the number of troops to be kept there. I am ignorant of that at present, but believe it will amount to five thousand, and as it is on the direct route of communication from the Eastern States, the quanity must be considerable; the river will enable you to form that magazine very easy." No detail was too big or too small to Greene when he was in the process of formulating a plan of action and then carrying it out. "When forming your magazines, give all sorts of grain the preference to wheat. Oats first, corn next, then rye, and so on. You must get a number of screws made to screw all the hay, and employ hands to do it either at the farmers barns or at the magazines. You cannot set about this too soon; there must be a number of forage carts provided to be employed in no other business. I shall call upon you this afternoon, if possible. I find my present situation to be very inconvenient for the Quartermaster-general's department, and propose to move to More Hall as soon as possible."

The next day he submits the plan for Washington's approval, which Washington does, posthaste and without fanfare: "I approve the above places for magazines, with this proviso, that the one in Trenton shall not in its full extent be immediately formed, and that the others upon the rivers shall be tolerably high up for security purposes." And so, Greene's first official plan of action as quartermaster-general is enacted.

Now, another great source of anxiety was the selection of deputies and agents. One such appointment would require a great deal of investigation. He writes to General Heath, "I have sent a considerable order for goods and stores in that way, to be purchased by Mr. Benjamin Andrews, a merchant in Boston, since which I have heard his character has been called into question, respecting some dealings with some of General Burgoyne's officers. I had conceived so good an opinion of him as to think him a suitable person to be employed, but at the same time I would not chose to continue him in the employ if his character is so far injured as to hurt his usefulness to us, or if even becomes doubtful. I shall, therefore, be obliged to you to furnish me with the history of this charge against him, together with your sentiments concerning his fitness to be employed as Deputy Quartermaster-general at Boston."

Then, last but not least, dealing with the procrastinating body Congress. "You have been informed as of March 26th," he writes to the president of Congress on the 3rd of April, "that a large sum of money is absolutely necessary for the completion of duties within the Quartermaster's department, to enable us to make due preparation for the ensuing campaign, and I expect before this reaches you, Colonel Cox will have stated that necessity to you in a still more pointed light. Hitherto, however, we have yet to receive as much as a single shilling, though we have daily demands for large sums not only for expenditure here, but to be distributed into different parts of the country to draw supplies; and until these distributions are made, out utmost efforts will not have the desired effect. I have, therefore, drawn on the Treasury Board for fifty thousand pounds in favor of Robert Lettis Hooper, Jr., Esq., an active and useful deputy quartermaster for the district of Easton, who, I expect, will lay it out to good advantage. I therefore hope the draught will be duly honored. I also hope Mr. Hooper will not be disappointed in his expectations of receiving the cash, as much a disappointment would be greatly injurious to the service as well."

The army is still encamped in Valley Forge, and a great deal depends on the temper and quick action of the State of Pennsylvania's government at this point. Greene decides it would be prudent to travel to Lancaster and meet with the State legislature face to face, but thought it would first be wise to master the parts of local laws that relate to the immediate subject for which he was there to demand help. "If you have, or can procure the Pennsylvania State law respecting the wagon department," he writes to Colonel Biddle, "please to send it down to me by the bearer. I wish to consult fully upon the subject before I write to the legislature."

The next job on the agenda for the newly appointed quartermaster-general of the army was the subject of transportation, which had prior to this time served as a reason for the numerous delays and failures of the commissary. "This will be handed you by Mr. John Hall," Greene writes to Colonel Henry Hollingsworth, "who offers himself from this department, and comes warmly recommended. I wish you to employ him under you as an assistant, for I am persuaded there is more business than you can execute yourself. The Commissary-general has made a demand upon me for a large number of teams to remove a great quanity of provisions from the Head of Elk. I wish you to procure all you possibly can either by hire, purchase, or impressment. I must beg your utmost exertions to forward the business. I hope you have received my letter requesting you to purchase a large number of horses, and have taken the necessary measures accordingly."

Soon after sending the letter, Greene was ready to start out for Lancaster to meet with the Pennsylvania legislature. "I received your urgent note," he writes to Colonel Biddle the day he was to leave. "I had intended you should have traveled with me to Lancaster, as I am almost a stranger to all the assembly. If there is no particular objection, I wish you to go still. I have sent your agreement signed. I note your observation respecting Colonel Hollingsworth. I purpose to set of this afternoon, and wish you to be in readiness to go with me. Mrs. Greene's compliments to Mrs. Biddle."

On his travels he takes careful note of the bad roads, and resolves at once to have them repaired. "The road from camp to this place is exceeding bad," he writes to his assistant Charles Pettit from the Red Lion, "and as it is the greatest communication between camp and Lancaster, and between camp and Yellow Springs, where our principal hospitals are, it is our interest to set about mending it as soon as possible. Apply to his Excellency for fifty men to work upon this road, and fifty more upon the Reading road. I also met and overtook several wagons that were stalled yesterday. The sick they were removing, in distress, and the cattle almost ruined by repeated strains in attempting to get through the most difficult parts of the roads. More attention must be paid to the roads than heretofore to save our men, cattle, and our wagon-hire. We must get some good man to survey the road, and direct the operations of the fatigue parties. We have the misfortune to have a rainy morning, which I am afraid will detain me here to-day, as it is now past twelve o'clock."

Finally arriving face to face with the legislature in Lancaster, the Pennsylvania records show that body in less than a gracious mood to receive Greene. The Pennsylvania legislature had been a front runner in the subject of displeasure in the way the army was being run and a lack of cooperation that followed. Greene arrived with an added piece of ammunition. A letter from Washington that read, "I beg leave to introduce Major-general Nathanael Greene to you, who is lately appointed Quartermaster-general. Upon looking over the late laws of the State for regulating the manner of providing wagons for the service, he has found out some parts, which he conceives might be amended so as more fully to answer the valuable purposes intended. He will lay the wished amendments before you and the Council for your consideration, and if you think with him, that the service will be benefited by them, I have no doubt but you will recommend them to the Assembly at the opening of the next session."

"There is a grievance complained of by many persons, inhabitants of this State, who attend the army of Continental employ as quartermasters, wagon-masters, teamsters, etc. They are called upon to do duty in the militia, and if they do not appear are fined to the amount of their substitute money. This they conceive to be very hard upon them as they are in the service of the States, and ought to be as much exempted as officers or soldiers. General Greene will represent this matter fully to you, and point out an equitable mode of redress. He is interested in the matter, as the persons who complain generally belong to his department."

The next day Greene appeared before the Council Washington had spoke of, and for three days pleaded his case and laid out his recommendations. On the 18th of April 1778, the Council entered into its records that, "Major-general Greene having represented to this Council that there may probably be cases of great and immediate necessity for wagons for the use of the army which cannot be supplied in the mode pointed out by the wagon law, so as to answer such emergencies; and he expressing an earnest desire of acting in the discharge of his duty as Quartermaster-general in perfect harmony with this State, and of conforming to the laws of it, proposed that some further authority be given by law to him and his deputies in extra cases. The subject being duly considered, this Council are of the opinion, that whenever a sudden and extraordinary emergency shall make the impressing of wagons by a military force absolutely necessary, that necessity must, from the nature of things, justify the impressing by force of arms, but that it would be improper to entrust such powers in the military by law. The Council is of the further opinion that wagon-masters and teamsters, in consequence of the demands made on them for their services in the militia, or for payment of substitution money in lieu of such service: on consideration, the Council are of the opinion that wagon-masters and wagon-drivers actually enlisted in the Continental service for a reasonable time are not liable to serve in the militia during the time of their continuing in such service, nor subject to the payment of substitution money; and that an enlistment in either of these services for six months or longer time ought to be considered by the lieutenants and subalterns of the respective counties of this State as good and sufficient cause to forbear levying the substitution money in such cases."

Somewhat pleased, but not thrilled by the lukewarm response of the Pennsylvania legislature, Greene returns to camp and follows up on the other issues, each of which he is attempting to keep airborne, like a performer who spins plates on the top of a thin stick. Spinning the plates as they balance at the end of the stick and attempting to keep them spinning for fear they will fall to the ground and shatter. If you spend all of your time on one plate, others will fall, and another will lose momentum while you spend time with another. Eventually causing a chain reaction that causes all of the plates to fall and shatter. Greene was going to do everything in his power to not let that happen in his department.

The next step he tackled was the wanton negligence he felt was occurring in the army. While inspecting a roadwork detail, he noticed countless accouterments scattered over the roadside from soldiers who had marched by during the winter. It was a common practice for the soldiers who were responsible for the companies cooking pots and tools, to get tired of carrying them and throw them off at the side of the road as they marched. He did not blame the tired and hungry soldiers, but their officers for the lack of instilling discipline in these soldiers. "Your apology on behalf of your men is sufficient," he writes to Varnum. "Please to retain the axes for the use of your brigade. I am very sorry to be obliged to call for the axes belonging to the regiments in this way. I hope the necessity won't remain long."

The Congress and the Treasury Board continued to drag their feet. Greene was determined to make them feel that if he was to do his work, and he means to do it at all cost, they must cooperate and do theirs. "Having received information from Joseph Borden, Esq., the loan officer for the State of New Jersey," he wrote to the president of Congress, Henry Laurens from South Carolina, "that he has on hand a considerable sum of money which he wishes to be called out of his hands, as he thinks his situation at Bordentown is not safe, and as Colonel Cox did not obtain a sufficient quanity of cash from your treasury to distribute through all the channels which immediately call for it, and a large sum is wanted in New Jersey to give vigor to the purchasing of horses and other necessary supplies, I shall hope to receive by the return of this express an order on the loan officer of New Jersey for one hundred and fifty thousand dollars. Near one half of that sum he has on hand; rest we will draw from him as it comes in, or take in certificates which we can negotiate in the country. I hope this business will meet with no delay, as the agent for purchasing in New Jersey will wait the return of this express." As is the custom of Congress at that time, instead of the $150,000 that Greene requests, the Treasury Board issues a report to Congress that they would only vote to allow $50,000.

A problem that does not directly involve Greene, but is just as much a problem and plagued the entire army since its inception, is the question of appointments, and the mixing up of civil and military ranks. This practice had been started by Greene's predecessor, Thomas Mifflin. "My blacksmith is a captain," DeKalb writes Greene. "The numerous assistant quartermasters are for the most part people with no military education, often the common tradesman, but collectively they are all colonels. . . .The army swarms with colonels." Greene decided to ask the question of what rights were available to him? He drafted a letter to Congress. "This will be handed to you by Lieut.-Col. Hay, who acted as deputy quartermaster-general to the Northern army the last year by an appointment from Congress. Upon my offering a new deputation, he informed me that as Congress had been pleased to give him his present rank in the army, he could not, without acknowledging that to be canceled, accept of a new one, he could not with propriety accept it at present; that he was ready, nevertheless, to act under his old appointment or a new one, provided his military rank were preserved, but wanted to know the mind of Congress on these points, previously to his entering on business, and therefore would wait upon you for an explanation. The business of deputy quartermaster-general is so distinct from any idea of military rank, that I apprehend they have no necessary connection nor relation. I believe Colonel Hay to be a very good officer, and it should be very proper that he remain in his appointment, but clearly, as well from he nature of the business, that herethrough, I make any resolutions towards appointments of any kind, and at the same time I shall always be ready to gratify Congresses wishes in favor of any particular person, just so as long as the person and occasion be necessarily to be preserved in the business of quartermaster-general."

A great amount of writing to simply say, Congress has no business hiring men for my positions and giving them big titles. I'm the quartermaster-general, and if there's any appointments to be handed out, I'll do the appointing. Two weeks after Greene's letter was received by Congress, a special referendum was drafted and duly acted upon. The committee Greene had referred to as "appointing subordinate officers" was now strictly the job of the quartermaster-general and no other person, but "Udney Hay, Esq., could no longer claim the office under his old appointment; and that no persons hereafter appointed upon the civil staff of the army, shall hold or be entitled to any rank in the army by virtue of such staff appointments."

Time passed swiftly among all these cares and worries, and Nathanael persevered through all of them. Conditions grew more favorable for the troops camped over the long winter at Valley Forge and gradually provisions began to arrive at a steady pace. Mostly due to the unwavering fortitude of Greene and his tireless companions, Wadsworth, Cox, and Pettit. When spring finally arrived in all its majesty, the troops had a regular daily allowance to each man of a pound and a half of bread, a pound of beef or fish or pork and beans, and a gill (4 ozs) of rum or whiskey. Fruits and vegetables from the surrounding countryside supplemented their diets. The Schuylkill had a annual run of shad that ran up river to spawn every spring that brought so many that men could literally walk into the river and pick up as many as they needed. Using a far more conventional method, like a net, teams of fisherman could harvest thousands of the tasty fish for the troops in Valley Forge. What the soldiers could not eat they salted them down in hundreds of barrels for future consumption. "Soldiers cheeks filled out again, their arms recovered muscle and their step regained its spring; while the invalids who had survived the winter came back to the ranks by the hundred."

One item that needs to be addressed is the common misconception being batted around by modern historians these days of how Jeremiah Wadsworth got so rich after his position as commissary general. Wadsworth made no distinction between patriotism and profit. He could not understand why you couldn't do one without the other, and as long as one did not interfere with one another. Because of Wadsworth's flagrant profiteering, Greene has come under fire in the recent years that perhaps he also was a profiteer, or may have operated with merchants in illegal activity. Not a single piece of evidence to this subject has surfaced, and chances are that two hundred and twenty-two years may have erased any facts of this if they do exist. The judgment of this author is "Who cares." Must we always dig up unwarranted dirt on celebrities and historic figures? We must investigate the facts and then weigh them to see the outcome. If Wadsworth, Cox, Pettit, and Greene participated in profiteering whom was hurt by it? Congress at most, and we had no income tax at the time so the common man was not affected. What did men like Wadsworth and Greene accomplish by their actions? Food and provisions were provided so the troops at Valley Forge did not starve to death and the struggle of these mighty men could continue. Better road service to bring the provisions and supplies to camp more effectively, better management of supplies, provisions, and how they were appropriated and ultimately held at stations so they could be readily transferred to the troops when needed. Due to their actions the American army was able to survive, gain strength, train, continue the war with England which they ultimately won and established the United States of America, the first democratic country, becoming the template for other countries around the world, and establishing democracy as the foremost body of government in the world at the dawn of the 21st century. If everyone's actions that were thought to be questionable resulted in that conclusion, then I would certainly feel at ease if we saw more actions just like those men. It isn't always how you accomplish your goal, but what it ultimately accomplishes. Sometimes, the end DOES justify the means.

There remained only one problem that the army faced in the spring of 1778. The number of soldiers fit for duty in the American camp. Death had decimated the troops at Valley Forge; even more telling was the total of desertions that reduced their numbers. Many of the weaker spirits who could not endure the hardships walked out of camp "in great numbers, whole companies, ten to fifty at a time." Many of the deserters, one estimate had the number at 2,300, were foreign born and ran to Philadelphia to join the British army. The provincial governor, Joseph Galloway, said, "Many of them came to my office seeking help. Of these, half were Irish, one-fourth English or Scottish, and the rest American." You could not blame the Irish, British, and Scottish for going to the English army. They had not been in the country long and just thought they were finally fighting for their home army now. Because of this, Washington's army was now reduced to only about 5,000 men of which almost half were not fit for duty. Efforts had to be made, with relative success, to quickly build up the enrollment by new enlistments'. However, it was going to be difficult to induce men to submit themselves to the hardships they were sure to hear about from the men who were either in camp or had left it. It was no secret that the American army had almost starved to death over the winter. Even after the enlistment's were raised, the men could not go into the new campaigns ahead with the limited training they had going into Valley Forge. They must be trained in the European style of warfare. Lines of disciplined troops, with dedicated officers and men, firing volley after volley of musketry, and then willing to march forward to chase the enemy from the field at the point of the bayonet. They had such a weapon, and this is where von Steuben would come in.

Even in the harshness of Valley Forge, "several of the general officers were beginning to send for their wives," writes Lafayette to his own wife in France, "and I envy them not their wives, but the happiness of being where they can see them." Caty Greene had joined her husband early in January for a short visit, and left the children with her father and sister. She did bring the effervescent personality she was famous for, along with her latest hobby, attempting to learn the French language. A study that quickly made her the darling of the foreign officers and the subject of gossip with the women of the village and other officers wives. One of Caty Greene's favorite friends became Lafayette, who was not yet twenty-one, but already a husband, fathers, and major general. Lafayette was a strikingly handsome gentleman and loved by all, especially Washington and Nathanael Greene. A rumor that Lafayette and Caty Greene had seen each other several times without anyone else in attendance ran rampant. It was never substantiated that they had a torrid love affair, only that they were seen alone together, which in 1778 was as bad as sleeping together, because it was assumed that you had if a man and a woman were alone. One of those that fostered the gossip was none other than Major-general Fredrick William Augustus Baron von Steuben. He was recently assigned to Washington by Congress to assist the army in drilling the soldiers in the proper battle drill needed to fight the British. Baron von Steuben could not speak English, but could speak a little French. But, von Steuben had brought along a young Frenchman by the name of Peter Duponceau, who knew some German and could interpret for him. It was a well-known fact that the German and French people did not care for each other all that much. So was it between von Steuben and Lafayette. People had noticed that the two men had taken an immediate dislike to one another, and it showed from the time they met, until they parted company at the end of the war. Von Steuben was from the court of Frederick and was skilled in the ceremonial arts of conversation and it did not hurt that he wore the uniform of their republican army, with a glittering star on the breast, and numerous medals and awards on his lapels. How much the two men despised each other is told to us by DeKalb, a good friend of Lafayette, who wrote, "Lafayette thinks Steuben is a methodic mediocrity, and Steuben thinks of my friend as a display of vanity and presumption." Lately, it has even been suggested that von Steuben did not like Lafayette because he had spurred von Steuben when the young man had been sexually propositioned by the elderly gentleman. All that aside, the man who called himself Frederick William Augustus Henry Ferdinand baron von Steuben, may not have been what he proposed to be, but he would become a savior in the cause of the American Revolution.

He arrived in camp with a letter of introduction from Congress and from Benjamin Franklin and Silas Deane who were busy in Paris drumming up support for the cause. There they met baron von Steuben who they believed was a lieutenant general in the army under Frederick the Great. He told Franklin he had property, lands, and titles galore. It was all a ruse. His given name was Frederick, but all the others were window dressing. Even his last name wasn't Steuben at all, it was Steube. He thought it would appear more regal with an "n" at the end. And he had no lands, and certainly wasn't a baron. He was an officer in Frederick the Great's republican army, but he had never achieved a rank higher than captain. Unlike the Hessian soldiers on the British side, von Steuben, or Steube, whatever his name was, was a simple soldier of fortune and he was looking for a position to fill. He was described as, "an old forty-seven years of age, German, a man of middle height (about 5'3"), solidly built, heavy-featured, with a high forehead, a long nose, a strong chin, a full-lipped mouth that was more often smiling than not." He was aware that Congress cast a weary eye at "foreign officers aspiring for office," and knew he could make his way up the merit ladder in the America if he could only get his foot in the door. He constantly surmounted, "I do not seek any rank or pay. I wish only to join the war as a volunteer," which endeared him first to Franklin, then Congress, and now his peers. He would ask only that his necessary expenses be defrayed while he served his new country. His request was granted.

Washington received him graciously, saw the military ability within him, and asked him to join his army with the title of volunteer acting inspector general in charge of training the troops. When von Steuben first set eyes on his new troops, he was heard to say, "These are not troops. They are skeletons." He was both shocked and horrified and would write after the war, "The men were literally naked, some of them of every color and make, saw officers. . . .mounting guard in sort of dressing gown made of an old blanket or woolen bed-cover. With regard to military discipline, it was safe to say that no such thing existed. . . .There were no regular formations, the formation of each regiment was varied as their mode of drill dictated and which consisted only of the manual exercise. Each colonel had a system of his own, one according to Prussian, one English, another French style . . .. The greater part of the captains had no roll of their companies and had no idea how many men they had . . .. When asked of a regiments strength, the usual reply was 'Something between two and three hundred men." With the coming of spring and the promise of new life, the army would prosper too, and have a new direction, better provisions, and a new way of fighting. It would closely resemble the English version, but less complicated. It would be the on Steuben manual drill exercise.

Von Steuben first had to recognize what he had to deal with, analyze it, and come up with a solution that worked. It would be based on the Prussian system of drill, but with modifications that took American conditions into consideration. One problem that arose with von Steuben's system was how he would pass out his orders. Von Steuben knew no English, but he did know German and French. He would write his orders down the night before in French, hand them to his aide Pierre Duponceau who would then attempt to translate it into English, hand it over to Washington's aides-de-camp John Laurens and Alexander Hamilton who would them smooth it out into readable English form. When the English version was done, it would be presented back to von Steuben who would then have to memorize the English orders by rehearsing each command in front of the three young aides for hours on end until von Steuben felt he had it perfect. The first copies of von Steuben's drill manual were done by longhand due to the absence of a printing press. Since the drillmaster for each company needed a copy, hundreds had to be produced by hand. Speed was also essential since the year's opening campaign was less than a couple of months away. Everyday, von Steuben's orders were composed, translated, and polished from the original into copies starting on Monday night to completion for Wednesday morning.

The importance of drilling the army to absolute proficiency cannot be stressed enough. The English and Hessian armies were some of the most well trained and disciplined troops in the world. The American army was far from that level and had to be at least close if they were to continue the struggle of the American Revolution and ultimately win it. To accomplish this far-reaching feat, von Steuben would have to do something that was quite unheard of in its time. He would drill the troops himself. It was the English, as well as the American practice to have the sergeants drill the soldiers. To have an officer drill common soldiers was very radical. However, for von Steuben to get his drill technique down quickly and effectively he would have drill the men himself. First, he would organize a model company from a hundred men selected from the various regiments. When this was accomplished he would break them into smaller squads and would walk through "the position of the soldier." Because of the language barrier, von Steuben would act out the drill in pantomime, assuming each step himself to every man and having him imitate him, changing his faults and cheering each little accomplishment.

While he was drilling his squad, the rest of the model company watched, as well as most of the army, thousands of men looking on in amazement. He drilled the groups for a week, teaching officers to then drill the squads, and then having the entire company perform as a whole with von Steuben standing close by to exact his wrath at the slightest imperfection in their movements. They were taught several, basic variations of the Prussian manual of arms, how to carry the musket properly, load it, fire it, and the most important of all fix and charge bayonets. Most of the Model Company were veterans who had served the entire war and fought in several battles with the experienced British troops. They had witnessed what well-trained troops with experience could accomplish and they wanted to be just like them. So the men were eager to learn the new movements, and picked them up in record time, while the thousands of onlookers, almost the entire army, were instructed chiefly by picking it up themselves by mere observation.

Von Steuben, even with his language handicap, was a strong-willed man, but gracious under fire. He was known for his explosive temper and when his lack of English would cause an entire brigade to split into a scene from a Three Stooges movie, and he would punctuate the air with curse words in French and German. When that did not work, an occasional broken English, "God damn." It is no wonder that his fiery disposition and flamboyant personality soon made him the darling of the men in camp, and by far, the most popular officer in camp as well.

The main point von Steuben focused on was the lack of discipline in how the American army had marched in columns up until this point. They had always marched Indian file, where each column would reach a distance four times what it should have been, sometimes marching in single file. Von Steuben went to work teaching the men how to march "in compact masses with steadiness and without losing distance." This type of marching would also infuse discipline, preventing groups of individual soldiers from straggling out from the line, but making it difficult to get into position at a moment's notice when attacked. A perfect example of this was at Brandywine and Germantown, where the heads of columns had arrived in time, but their rears came in too late. As the soldiers learned more and more and became more skillful, they also became more soldierly, and their pride increased, and with that, the morale of the men, "a new morale, never more to be extinguished, soon pervaded the ranks of the Continental Army." wrote Nathanael Greene from Valley Forge in April of 1778.

But all was not as well with the higher echelon of the Continental army. The Congress was still snipping at the heels of Washington's strength as a commander and even an effective soldier, and at the same time, Major General Nathanael Greene's ability came into question as well. Commenting on a particularly menacing letter from a member of Congress, Greene wrote: "Had our forces been equal to General Howe's, or at least as much superior as the northern army was to Burgoyne, he must have shared the same fate. But, alas, we have fought with vastly superior numbers, and although twice defeated have kept the field! History affords but few examples of the kind. The people may think there has not been enough done, but our utmost endevors have not been wanting; our army with inferior numbers, badly found, badly clothed, worse fed, and newly levied, must have required superior generalship to triumph over superior numbers, well found, well clothed, and veteran soldiers. We cannot conquer the British force at once, but they cannot conquer us at all. The limits of the British government in America is their out-sentinels."

One critic cast suspicion on the entire army. "The general contempt shown to the militia by the standing army is a dangerous omen; in every victory as yet obtained by the Americans, the militia have had the principal share; the liberties of America can only be safe in the hands of the militia; the honorable Congress, in many cases, have been too much led by the military men; such precedents may, in time, become dangerous; the increasing of the standing army is not right unless better methods are adopted for supplying the same; no action has yet been lost for want of men able, willing, and fit to fight the present army with the militia are sufficient to conquer the present force of the enemy, at least, they were not long ago, and finally, if the army is not better managed, numbers will avail nothing."

Censures such as these were making their way into private circles, and even through secret channels to Congress, enabling members of Congress that had straddled the opposition fence against the commanders of the army, to finally make a decision one way or the other. It usually was toward the negative, and enabled more members of Congress to fan the flames of discontent, and helped to formulate an outward hostility of correspondences against the commander-in-chief and some of his generals, and turned the tide of Washington's popularity with the public as well. The perception some members of Congress were trying to get across was that Washington and some of his senior generals, like Greene, were beginning to think of themselves as deities and perhaps getting too big for their

145

breeches. For example, John Adams wrote; "you would have thought that the turning of the tide at Red Bank was directly attributed to the Commander-in-chief, his general, and the southern troops. If it had been idolatry and adulation would have been unbounded: so excessive as to endanger our liberties, for what I do not know. Now we can allow a certain citizen to be wise, virtuous, and good, without thinking him a God, or a savior."

Ordinarily these complaints would not go very far. But with the brilliant achievements of the northern army under General Gates the complaints were not without merit. Howe leaves New York and sails unopposed into Head of Elk, right on the heels of the announcement of the great victory in Bennington. The Battle of Stillwell, another northern victory was accomplished a few days after the embarrassment of Brandywine. While Washington and his weary soldiers were marching and then countermarching over and over on the same ground surrounding the Schuylkill, the northern army meanwhile was holding Burgoyne and his superior force from Canada at bay near the headwaters of the Hudson. A river that Washington and Greene were not unfamiliar with themselves. Then there was the second battle at Stillwater, which finished in a draw, while at the same time the "grand army" of the south fought the indecisive battle of Germantown. On one hand the people of the Unites States saw Gates as the successful general who forced the surrender of Burgoyne and his troops. While on the other hand, we had Washington whose greatest triumph up until this point was a successful retreat from Howe. Gates had been Congress's first choice in the beginning to be the commander-in-chief of the army back in 1776, but had been discounted by his age. Gates' qualifications were now being outweighed against the question of his years on this earth.

General Horatio Gates was born in Essex, England about 1728. Trained as a British officer, but left the service in 1773 at the rank of major due to the fact that his humble, middle-class upbringing would preclude him the possibility of his attaining a higher rank in the British army. Upon his arrival in America from England, he purchased a plantation in Virginia not far from George Washington's Mount Vernon where he remained until 1775 when war broke out. Due to his friendship with the commander-in-chief of the army, Washington appointed Gates the first adjutant general of the Continental Army, and he was commissioned a Brigadier-general on 17 June 1775. He received a field command some months later by seizing control of the Northern Department from General Phillip Schuyler after the two disputed over the command for more than a year. Gates was extremely ambitious and was not going to let anyone hold him back from his thirst for power as they had in England. Gates was the commanding officer that presided over the victories at Saratoga, Bennington, and other Northern Campaign battles, but had little to do with any of the actual engagements. The main credit for those tremendous victories should have gone to Colonel Daniel Morgan and Major-general Benedict Arnold. In fact, Gates was known to hide in his tent whenever an important decision over strategy or tactics had to be made and taking days to decide in a decisive manner when hours were important. Although his role was extremely minor in those battles, a strong movement by many high level officers in the army, as well as several members of Congress was begun to replace Washington with Gates as commander-in-chief of the army.

By this time Gates and Washington had long been estranged, not that it mattered to Gates. Whether they were friend, family, or relation, Horatio Gates was not going to let anyone get in the way of his assumption and the adulation he felt he deserved. The timing was perfect for Gates. Command of the victories in the north, Congress still stinging from Washington's ineffectiveness in the south. As a result, Congress decided to diminish Washington's authority by establishing the Board of War, and naming General Gates as its president. And as if to inflict further embarrassment, two of Washington's other adversaries were given positions that directly affected his effectiveness. One, Brigadier-general Thomas Conway is to be named Inspector general of the army, the other, named as a member of the Board of War, Thomas Mifflin. Washington's enemies were sure their plan would work to perfection and force the commander-in-chief to resign in disgust. Thus allowing the way to be clear for the henchmen to name Gates as the new commander-in-chief of the Continental Army.

One of the first proceedings that Washington had gotten wind of from a friend he had on the Board of War, was that the board draft a motion to proceed to Washington's headquarters at Valley Forge and take the Commander-in-chief into custody. Congress would then bring him back to Philadelphia where he could be put up on charges for dereliction of duty in the numerous defeats of the army. Unfortunately for the Board of War, they underestimated just how many supporters Lewis had in Congress and with the people, who the congressman represented. The board's trick failed completely and, in fact, would work in the opposite direction. Washington would gain supporters and many of the conspirators of the board lost confidence in their plans and jumped shipped. Rejected in their coup and detested by the majority of Congress, the complete opposite of what Gates, Mifflin, and Conway were attempting to achieve would bring their downfall all too quickly.

The Marquis de Lafayette was a strong supporter of Washington and Greene, and had even been looked upon in the light of son-like to the two men. Conway had been a friend to the young Lafayette, but the Marquis wrote Conway off soon after he found out of his conspiracy against Washington. Congress decided that a late winter campaign against Canada might succeed with the downfall of Burgoyne, and their plans included the naming of Lafayette as the expedition commander, who they felt would easily influence the French Canadians. Although the young Frenchman had proved his worth in battle, Congress still felt that Lafayette would need an experienced officer to help him when necessary. They decided on an officer they felt had too much time on his hands for far less important issues and named Thomas Conway as Lafayette's lieutenant. Washington refused to allow it, and named DeKalb as the more suitable second in command which was another slap in the face to the conspirators. The expedition would ultimately fail, and it would soon become clear that it was less of an expedition against Canada, and more of an expedition against Washington as Commander-in-chief. "A Don Quixote expedition to the northward," Greene would write to Rhode Island governor William Greene. And to his good friend Henry Knox, he says, "I look upon the whole plan to be a creation of faction lick't into publick form to increase the difficulties of the General."

Since the braggarts involved could not touch Washington with their initial path, it was decided that they would choose another. Going from beneath and working they're way up. It was Greene's turn to be the focus of innuendoes and accusations. Greene's major detractor would be Mifflin. Feeling slighted at the fact of being succeeded, rather unceremoniously, by Greene as Quartermaster-general, Mifflin routinely told anyone who would listen, that Greene "had taken the office in order to be out of the way of bullets." A friend of Greene's, George Lux, who had been present at one of Mifflins oratories, wrote to Greene, "Now, I do not think it would be amiss for you to take an opportunity of telling him in public company, that it has been reported, but cannot be recollected by any author, that he has said so and so, and ask him if it is true; if he acknowledges it will be saved the trouble of producing the author; and if he denies it, it will be stamping the character of a liar effectually upon the man, for the whole army knows he said so."

Greene decided to take a more decisive course of action, and wrote to Mifflin and asked him directly if he had said the things he had been hearing. Mifflin vehemently denied the charges. Lux wrote back to Greene, "The man is a Christian liar, and I would have you however, communicate to the man that I have been at one of the places he spoke these lies, and then express to me what he has to say." But Greene let the matter dissolve. What was of note is the fact that many people were becoming aware that certain officers and a part of Congress were hostile to Washington and Greene, and many people began to ask the question, what had these men done to prove their superior devotion to their country? It was true that the army, under the present command, had lost several battles and were compelled to retreat almost as many times, but whose fault was it that the army had not been properly furnished with the means of defense? Yes, Washington and Greene's judgment had sometimes been less than perfect. Even some of Gates most trusted friends and supporters were convinced that Mifflin had done an awful job as Quartermaster-general. Of those that continued to support Gates and Mifflin, almost all of them were perplexed and annoyed at their alignment with the dimwitted Conway. By late April, it was evident that the attempt to displace Washington and discredit his senior advisors like Greene had failed miserably. "I am happy to inform you," wrote Nathanael to his brother Jacob, "that the faction raised against his Excellency has sunk into contempt. Ambition is a dangerous evil in a free state when it happens to rage in an unprincipled bosom."

Now the plotters were attempting to hold on to their own safety net. Gates wrote to Washington, trying to deny any wrongdoing and setting blame on his co-conspirators, especially Conway. But Washington was having none of it. "It is my wish," wrote Washington to Gates, "to give implicit credit to the assurances of every gentlemen; but in this subject of our present correspondence, I am sorry to confess, there happen to be some unlucky circumstances, which involuntarily compel me to consider the discovery you mention, not so satisfactory and conclusive I might add, as you seem to think it. I therefore find that I am unhappy to reconcile the spirit of your different letters and sometimes of the parts of the same letter with each other." Driven to the wall by the stern response by Washington, Gates denied "all personal connection with Conway," asserting that he was "of no faction and disliked controversy," and hoped that Washington would not "spend another moment upon the subject." "I am as adverse to controversy as any man," wrote Washington in reply, "and had I not been forced into it, you never would have had occasion to impute to me even the shadow of a disposition towards it." Washington's confidence in Gates was damaged beyond repair, but there was never another mention of the subject from that letter forward. Gates had lied to Washington and Gates knew that Washington knew it.

"I learned," wrote George Lux to Greene, "that General Mifflin has publicly declared that he looked upon his Excellency as the best friend he ever had in his life. I would enjoy seeing one of his other friends, for I believe there are no others." Lux would again write, "It is reported that General Mifflin has wrote his Excellency declaring he esteems him above all men, both as an officer and a gentleman, and his particular friend, and wondered how so many reports injurious to him could have propagated? I myself heard him condemn him for his partiality for you and General Knox."

"The scheme," Washington wrote to Landon Carter, "originated with three men who wanted to aggrandize themselves. Finding no support, but on the contrary that their conduct and views, when seen into, were likely to undergo severe reprehension, they shrunk back, disavowed the measure, and professed themselves my warmest admirers."

Mifflin's days as a military man would wane and he would eventually move into Pennsylvania politics. "He found," writes Joseph Reed to Greene, "his enmity to the General was a fatal objection; he has, therefore, been obliged to recur to his old ground though, that he did not oppose the Commander-in-chief but his favorites, yourself and Knox who had undue influence over the General; that is the language he is obliged to talk or he would be even more utterly rejected than he already is."

Forever after in history known as the "Conway Cabal," the man who gave the scheme its name, Conway's fall from grace within the colonies was even farther than his two friends. In another moment of spite, he wrote another of his rude letters to Congress, lamenting the treatment he and his associates had received in the Washington matter. He again threatened to resign his commission, which sounded so much like an actual resignation that Congress took him up on it and under the guidance of Gouverneur Morris, accepted it. Conway sent assurances that he had been misunderstood. "The gentleman, however," wrote Morris to Washington, "had been so unlucky as to use the most pointed terms, and therefore, his aide, was told that the observations he made came too late. I am persuaded that he will attempt to get reinstated, if the least probability of success appears, but I am equally persuaded that his attempts will fail." Conway did attempt it, in New York, in his attempt to raise a suit to force the issue he wrote to Gates for help. Gates did not even reply to his numerous letters. Gates was attempting to distance himself from his co-conspirators as much as possible. But Conway's mouth would get him into more trouble. He was called a liar by Cadwalader, and in a duel with him, was wounded badly in the neck and mouth. On what Conway feared was his deathbed he wrote to Washington, "I express my sincere grief for having done, written, or said anything disagreeable to your Excellency. My career on this earth will soon be over; therefore justice and truth prompt me to declare my last sentiments. You are in my eyes the great and good man. May you long enjoy love, veneration, and esteem of these States whose liberties you have asserted by your virtues." But Conway lived, recovered, stayed in New York a few months, deserted, and returned to France where he was never heard from again.

Greene had been in the service of his country for three years now. He had grown from a private in his states private militia to the man most people in the country considered the general in which Washington most confided, a counselor to his troops, deliberate in inquiry to important issues, and a prompt decision maker. But, as of yet Nathanael had not been afforded the opportunity to display all of his true military abilities, his far-reaching resource of mind, and the great force of his will. But the time would soon afford itself. "It is very true, what cousin Griffin told you," he writes to his brother Jacob in late March, "that I wanted to retire to private life again, provided it was consistent with the public good; but I never will forsake the cause of my country to indulge in domestic pleasures. Nevertheless, it would be agreeable to retire if no injury was to follow to the public, for the splendor of the camp is but a poor compensation for the sacrifices made to enjoy it." It would seem the pressure of his duties as quartermaster-general, and the long-suffering winter had given Greene a small case of cabin fever. With the showers of late April, it was not only flowers that the cool rains brought to the camp, but the coming of a new ally, and new found strength and morale as well. Washington would soon be making plans for this year's, well anticipated, new campaign against the enemy. Greene did not want to be left behind.

Chapter XII

"A New Army"

"There seem to be but three general plans of operation, which may be premeditated for the next campaign," wrote Washington on the 20th of April. "One, the attempting to recover Philadelphia, and destroy the enemy's army there; another, the endeavoring to transfer the war to the northward by enterprise against New York; and a third, the remaining quiet in a secure fortified camp, disciplining and arranging the army till the enemy begin their operations, and then to govern ourselves accordingly. Which of these three plans shall we adopt." Opinion differed widely among the general officers, as usual. Greene was for keeping the main body of the army in their present quarters, under the command of General Lee, while Washington with 4,000 regulars and the eastern militia made an attempt upon New York. But news from Europe was already on its way across the Atlantic, giving a whole new aspect to the campaign being planned.

Greene's duties were not going to stand in the way of taking a lively interest in the progress of the plans. Greene saw that the progress of von Steuben's training and intelligent supervision had already brought the troops to a higher level of discipline than they had ever reached previously. The men were strong, of a high morale, and ready for a good fight. But with his pride and anticipation of commanding his men again, his duties as quartermaster-general would slowly seep back into his daily routine. "The wife of Mr. Jacob Brick," he wrote to General John Lacy, "complains that some of your people have taken from her husband one of their horses, which they are in want of to enable them to move to Reading. I wish you to inquire into the matter, and if there is no capital objection, to order the beast to be delivered to the owner again. The war brings enough sufficient calamity under every possible restraint; but where people are influenced by private prejudice, it only increases the distresses of the inhabitants beyond conception. These evils can only be restrained by the generals, whose duty it is to protect the distressed inhabitants, as well as govern and regulate the affairs of the army. I hope you will pay particular attention to this affair, as the age and distress of the complainants appear to claim it."

In early May, the welcome news that the French had entered the war had reached the camp and caused unbridled joy and a brand of confidence the army had not seen in almost three years. With an alliance formed between with the United States and France, according to many, the struggle would soon be over and our independence was now assured. Greene was not among these happy optimists, instead he only thought that this news would bring important changes to the campaign plans. The enormous sums he was compelled to call for almost startled him, and he felt that they would startle the country and Congress even more, though all of them knew that the actual state of the currency was a imperfect representation of the real sum of money. This is where the attacks of wrongdoing would be centered, and Greene knew even then that he would have to prepare himself for what he foresaw as a potential problem. He wrote to Washington on the 3rd of May, "Your Excellency, it appears to be absolutely necessary to make very extensive and speedy preparations for the ensuing campaign, especially in horses, teams, tents, and other articles of high price. In consequence of this apparent necessity, I have given extensive orders, almost without limitation, for the purchase of these articles; apprehending from the prospects at that time, the utmost exertions we could make would not procure more than a sufficiency for the necessary accommodation of the army. From intelligence lately received, the aspect of our affairs is essentially changed; and it may be that in consequence of this change, the plan of military operations may undergo such material alterations as may, in a considerable degree, abate the demand for those expensive preparations which some weeks ago were thought indispensably necessary. And as I would not willingly enhance the expenses of the quartermaster-general's department further than prudence and good economy absolutely require, I take the liberty of addressing your Excellency on the occasion, to request the favor of your advice and direction whether the plan above mentioned for obtaining supplies ought to be retrenched, and in what degree the plan of preparations ought to be continued, and particularly, as the prospect of the local situation of the army may greatly altered by these changes, what alterations should be made in the plan, lately approved by your Excellency for establishing magazines of forage in the different parts of the country." It is almost as if Greene is anticipating questions in how he would proceed with the tremendous amount of cash that was about to come over his desk. He wanted Washington to know he could be tempted to procure some of the funds, but that he would do what's best for the army and try to control himself. A less than saintly conclusion, but one that would return again and again over the coming months of 1778.

Meanwhile, it had been resolved to celebrate the French alliance with overwhelming ceremony. Von Steuben had a somewhat checkered resume of orchestrating such occasions in Prussia, and so he was given the duties of planning and preparing the grand festivities. On the 5th of May, the outlines of the festival were announced in general orders of the day. By Wednesday the 6th, the happiest morning that the gloomy valley had seen in a year dawned early with the army happy, and more hopeful than they had been in years. At nine o'clock that morning, the brigades were drawn out, to hear the chaplain read the announcement of the alliance from the postscript to the Pennsylvania Gazette from the 2nd of May. Prayers and a thanksgiving sermon, the American Te Deum, followed at the head of each brigade. Next came von Steuben's well-earned hour of triumph, and as the first signal-gun boomed through the valley, the troops, steeping briskly into line, were soon all under arms and marching smartly. The formal inspection came next, exact, rigid, stern, von Steuben himself, hair fully powdered and dressed in his best Prussian army uniform, with the gold star of the order of Fidelity shining brightly on his chest. He strode with every eye of the army fixed upon him, as he passed slowly through the ranks, scanning them closely with his experienced scrutiny. Barber, Brooks, Davies, Ternant, and Fluery came closely behind, inspecting, first the dress, then arms, and then accouterments of each and every brigade, and then forming them into battalions, and when all were arranged, announcing, each to his brigadier, with military precision, that the men were ready for their officers. The brigadiers then assigned to each battalion its commanding officer for the day, and the men, loading their muskets, stood with grounded arms, waiting the second signal-gun. It was now half past eleven, and the sun was looking down upon them from a clear sky, an occasional bright flash from a gleam of light bouncing off the polished steel of a musket or sword. The signal-gun was fired, drum and fife began, and the troops took up their grounded muskets and prepared to march. The entire army, with Stirling commanding on the right, Lafayette on the left, and De Kalb the second line, advanced in five columns to the appointed position on the heights, where Washington and Greene and the other officers not on duty had taken their stand to witness the services. What a sight it must have been. This was years and miles away from the collection of half hearted patriots and disenchanted youths that formed the army on that green in Massachusetts three years before. Washington now had what he always inspired his army to be. An exact copy of the British army he admired so much. This was a new army, with a new ally, and a cause that was destined to survive and succeed in the end. How could they do any less?

The review finally ended, Washington and the general officers repaired to a kind of amphitheater in the center of the encampment, and when all were ready, the third signal-gun was fired, and instantly cannon after cannon followed, one for each State. When the cannon ceased, the muskets began a running fire from Woodford's right, straight along the first line. The second takes up on the left, and on it ran, rattling down to the right again. Finally, silence for a moment as the thick smoke slowly floated away, and at a given signal, one loud "huzza" and "Long live the King of France," was shouted from more than 10,000 voices. Then another thirteen cannons fired, and one more "huzza" for the American States.

The festivities on the parade ground concluded, it was now time to do something the army had not been able to do for more time than they cared to remember. Sit down and stuff their faces with every imaginable food item. While the officers were set on the outer circle of the amphitheater under tent-cloths stretched out on poles; in the center, tables for invited guests, officers of higher rank, and a smattering of ladies present for the parade, and with marquees to protect them from the sun, it almost seemed to form one vast enclosure. Under the main marquee sat Washington, with Greene, Stirling, and Lafayette, noticeable by his ever-present white scarf. Here too were the wives that were present in camp at the time. They were, Martha Washington, Caty Greene, and Lady Stirling with their daughter Lady Kitty, who had been in the encampment throughout the winter, helping with the sick.

Of course the guests of honors were the foreign officers in attendance, representing the Americans new ally, and their new best friends. The talk was cheerful, wine flowed freely and there were numerous toasts to the King of France, Congress, and any other friendly powers of the States that they did not want to leave out. A band was present and played patriotic and martial airs and the thoughts of the worst winter in memory was pushed aside for a few hours. As the evening moved on and after a few more huzzahs and toasts, the festivities were broken up by the seizure of a British spy who had been captured by the guard on duty. "What shall we do with him?" asked the officer on duty. "Let him go back and tell his employers exactly what he has seen. Twill pain them far more than to hear of his detection and death."

The night of merriment still in their heads, the business at hand was now the next item on their agenda, and a council of war to decide their plan of operations adapted to this change in the political situation was formed. For the first time since the Conway Cabal, Gates and Mifflin were sitting in on the proceedings, just steps away from the man who they had recently plotted to unseat as the commander-in-chief of the army. To say that there was as much tension in the air as excitement over starting this new campaign would be an understatement. The foreign officers in attendance for the first of many of these meetings commented afterwards, "The uneasiness in the room over subjects we were unaware or accustomed to was ever present at our first war meeting with General Washington." But with the underlining issues aside, the council got down to business and quickly decided "to remain on the defensive and wait developing events, not attempting any offensive operation against the enemy, till circumstances should afford a fairer opportunity of striking a successful blow."

However, the opportunity they had wished for would be delayed for a time. Changes in the British army hierarchy were taking place at that moment. Parliament, increasingly unhappy and weary with the progress of the "American Rebellion," as it was known in England, was making a drastic change in leadership from Sir William Howe to Sir Henry Clinton. This was the same Clinton who had come to the aid of Howe at the battle of Bunker Hill, and who Howe had never forgiven for what he deemed, "that terrible digression." The English were also working on damage control with the entry of the French into the conflict. The British were in the process of drafting new terms of reconciliation with the American citizenry, in the hope of producing a division in the country and strengthening to the hands of the Tories.

Before this intention was even discovered, Congress had taken similar steps themselves by drafting a new oath of allegiance. The resolution had passed back in February, but it was not until May that it was actually acted upon, and gaining additional importance from circumstances unforeseen before the alliance with France had been finalized. The general officers in camp were the first to take the oath together before Washington, the rest of them, including Greene, taking it some weeks later, due to the fact that their duties delayed the proceedings. Greene, in fact was one of the last to take the oath, because of his operations in New Jersey at the time.

On the 15th of May, we find Greene by the Hudson, writing from Fishkill to General Gates, "You were polite enough to offer to regulate and settle the quartermaster-general's department at Albany. I shall be much obliged to you for doing it. You'll be so kind enough to transmit me your regulations and orders thereon as soon as the business is completed." If Gates was to be kept in command, Greene was going to make certain that Gates would not have the opportunity to make any trouble within the department. The trip also afforded Greene the opportunity to look up an old friend he had not seen in some time, Mr. Lott. With him was a letter that would normally be unimportant in a subject like this biography, but is a bit of interesting insight to the daily trials and tribulations a gentleman of the 18th century had to endure. Greene would write to Colonel Wadsworth, who was in Morristown at the time, "Mr. Lott, a friend and gentleman of this place, purchased a small quantity of rum and salt in Boston, which he cannot get on, owning of the States laws. I should be obliged to you to give him a pass, that his property may come forward; he wants the salt for his family use; part of his spirits he proposes for sale, and his business has been poor as late. Mr. Lott's character for generosity and hospitality is too well known to say anything upon the subject. I am under particular obligations to him; and shall esteem myself so to you, if you will be so kind enough to enable him to get forward his property. The propriety and the best forms you are the best judge of, and I therefore submit this matter to your opinion and discretion."

By the 25th of May, Greene is back in camp again, writing a letter to his family relation, William Greene, who had just been chosen Governor of Rhode Island. "I am exceedingly happy to hear you are elected Governor of our fair State, and beg leave to congratulate you upon the occasion. I am told Dr. Bradford took some very disingenuous means to supplant you. The duplicity of his conduct met with deserved punishment. I am persuaded you have taken the reins of government from the best of motives, and that you will discharge your trust with the greatest integrity. Nevertheless don't flatter yourself that the most upright conduct will secure you from reproach. The pride and ambition of some, the spite and envy of others, will always find occasion through misrepresentation to wound the reputation for a time. But truth and virtue will triumph at last. I beg leave to congratulate you upon the agreeable news from France. Our political alliance is most excellent. It is strongly reported Spain has acceded to the treaty also. I don't doubt all Europe in a few months, not in alliance with Great Britain, will declare us free and independent States. The enemy are making the greatest preparations imaginable for the evacuation of Philadelphia. Their further intentions and destination is unknown. We have the best intelligence the whole of the British forces are to rendezvous at New York; but whether they are going to leave the continent or go up the North River, remains yet to be discovered. Upon the enemy's evacuating Philadelphia we shall move towards the North River, where General Gates is now commanding. Pray, how does General Sullivan agree with you? He is a good officer, but loves flattery. That is his weak side. General Lee has joined this army with his usual train of dogs. I feel singular happiness at the different situation of the American affairs between the time he left us and the time he joined us again. Major Ward left this army some time since to join his regiment in Rhode Island. Mrs. Greene is on her way home. Poor girl! She is constantly separated, either from her husband or children, and sometimes, from both."

Meanwhile, an updated, old problem arose for Greene by this time. Difficulties in relation to the defective organization by the former head of his department have popped up, which threatens a collision between he and the Board of War. "Considering the weighty affairs," Greene writes to the President of the Board, "which must constantly claim the attention of the Board of War, it gives me no

153

small concern to find myself in a situation which obliges me to ask their interposition. It has been my constant aim in the appointments I have made, to engage such men in different branches of my department as were in every point of view most suitable for the business, giving the preference where I conceived it could be done with propriety to those I found in office. In particular the position of purchaser of stores, which I had heard was held by Colonel Chase was Deputy Quartermaster-general in Boston; and as I knew of no cause of complaint against him, I did not choose to displace him; but at the same time, being wholly unacquainted with his character and mercantile abilities, I thought it most prudent to send an order of so much importance to a gentleman of whose character and fitness for the business I had a more thorough knowledge. Among the order, was one to Mr. Benjamin Andrews, of Boston, for a large order of duck and other materials for tents and knapsacks. Mr. Andrews lately has made considerable purchases, and some goods are on the way to Boston hither; but his partner, Mr. Otis, complain that they have been much obstructed by the interference of Colonel Chase, founded, and is alleged, on authority derived from the Board of War; and he claims an authority superior to mine, and determined to bid as high for purchases as any one; for a large quantity of duck, tent cloths, etc., lately arrived at Boston, and which the Navy Board intended to deliver to Messrs. Andrews & Otis as purchasers for this department, till Colonel Chase demanded sufficient himself to make 4,000 tents, and which he said he had orders directly from the Board of War of a later date than my order to Messrs. Otis & Andrews. From whatever motive Colonel Chase may have been actuated, this kind of competition is surely injurious to the public in a high degree. The business is not only retarded by it, but must finally be effected at a greater expense by raising the prices of the commodities purchased. I cannot, therefore, doubt the Board will make the necessary inquiry into the entire affair and give such directions as will be proper on the occasion and in the future."

If that were not enough, troubles with some of Greene's agents with negligent purchases, and the blame ultimately fell on him. "Your favor of the 29th is before me," he writes to Colonel R.L. Hooper, one of his deputies, "The horses you mention are arrived, but I am sorry to inform you there are a great many of them barely fit for service, and make but a very indifferent appearance. I must beg you to be very particular in the purchases, and orders given to those that purchase for you, that no more bad horses may be brought to camp. The public will find themselves saddled with a great expense in the purchase of horses, and if there is but little or nothing to show for it they will think themselves greatly injured."

By the 1st of June, another pressing issue weighed heavy upon Greene's mind. He wrote about it to Gouverneur Morris, "On the subject of the Quartermaster's department, I intend to follow your advice in order to my own justification, and to silence the faction. I have represented the substance of what I wrote you (only more fully) in a letter to the General, requesting his advice and direction as well, which he has given much in the same terms as you did. But I am frightened at the expense. I have drawn on the Treasury already for upwards of four million dollars, and it seems to be but a breakfast for the department, and hardly that. The land carriage is so extensive and costly; the wants of the army so numerous, and everything selling at such enormous prices that our disbursements will be very great. I dare say they will far exceed your expectations. I have written to Congress for their sense and direction upon several matters respecting the department. I beg you will endeavor to bring the matter to issue as soon as possible, as I am much at a loss to know how to proceed. Sir Henry Clinton sent out a letter to his Excellency a few days ago, respecting certain acts of Parliament lately passed in favor of America, as he terms it. This letter, I suppose, has been before Congress before this time. Pray how came General Mifflin to be ordered to join this army? This is a phenomenon in politics. General Conway was at last caught in his own trap and suffered for it, and I am most heartily glad of it. I wish every such intriguing spirit may meet with the like disappointment in his ambitious designs. He is a most worthless officer as ever served in our army. What progresses have you and Congress made in the establishment of the army? The half-pay you have fixed at seven years. Most of the officers are discontented with it, and I am sorry for it."

By early June, Caty Greene finally left for Rhode Island after staying with Nathanael at their winter residence of a Mr. More, known as More Hall. Mrs. Greene had not been home in almost three months, their children had been staying with family the entire period. These would be the first of many trips Caty Greene would make to visit her husband, while leaving her children in the care of family members. A few days after she has left him, Greene writes to her. "Captain Bowen is just going and I have only time to tell you now that I am here in the usual style; writing, scolding, eating, and drinking. But you are not here to spend an agreeable hour with. Colonel Hay writes me you passed Fishkill in great haste. I hope you got safe home. I received a letter from Billy; he says the children are well; I wish it may be so. Pray write me a full history of family matters; there is nothing will be so agreeable. Kiss our sweet little children over and over again from their absent papa. You must make yourself as happy as possible; write me if you are in want of anything to render you so. Mr. More and his family all inquire after you with great affection and respect, and I believe with a great degree of sincerity. Mrs. Knox returned to camp and is living with General Knox. The enemy remain in much the same situation in Philadelphia as I wrote you before. My kind love to all the family, Cousin Griffin and Sally, Mother Greene, and all other friends."

But by the 15th of June, Clinton was making plans to move the British army out of Philadelphia the next day. Washington had been told he would, but was patiently awaiting the move at any time. He surmised that Clinton would move his troops in the most direct route to New York from Gloucester, New Jersey, just opposite of Philadelphia, move on to Haddonfield, Mount Holly, Crosswicks, Allentown, Cranbury, New Brunswick, and then Staten Island. That route would offer no natural defensive positions for the enemy until they reached Cranbury, but just above that small hamlet lie a group of hills that could block further advancement by the enemy.

Washington did not need to do a great deal of planning for his course. Unfortunately, the path was all too familiar to Washington and his army. From Valley Forge they could cross the Schuylkill at Swede's Ford, go eastward to the Crooked Billet Tavern (now Hatboro), go north through Doylestown, then east again across the Delaware at Coryell's Ferry. Once in New Jersey, go by way of Hopewell and Kingston, and then into Cranbury. If the American army left immediately, they could almost certainly beat Clinton to that point and be sitting and waiting unexpectedly for their arrival, then pounce on them. Clinton's route would have a seven or eight mile shorter march than the Americans, but the British would be traveling with an enormous baggage train, while Washington's would be significantly smaller, and the roads the Americans would use were somewhat better. It seemed like a fair race that Washington could win.

On the morning of the 16th, Washington was just finishing final preparations for marching. Stripping the redoubts of the field artillery, while at the same time, several advance British and Hessian regiments were already crossing the Delaware River at Cooper's Ferry. But Clinton was dragging 10,000 more men, a mountain of provisions, 3,000 Loyalist, men, women, and children. By the 18th the rest of the British army had left Philadelphia, marched about four miles to Gloucester Point and crossed to Gloucester in flat-bottomed boats. At that same time the remainder of the British fleet, mostly transports with only a dozen or so war vessels, dropped down the river and into the Delaware Bay. "Not a shot was fired, nor did an Enemy appear until the whole were on the opposite shore," wrote Major André which was far from the truth.

A small skirmish broke out between the last of the British troops and a small band of militiamen commanded by an Allen McLane "by way of Bush Hill . . .. between the 9th and 10th British redoubts." At Second Street they came upon the rear guard and captured a captain, a provost marshal, a guide, and 30 privates, with no loss of life to either side. That night, a disguised McLane, slipped into the British camp in Haddonfield, and reported his findings to the officer appointed the commander of the evacuated city, General Benedict Arnold.

Arnold sent a rider by the name of George Roberts to Valley Forge, and arrived in camp just before noon on the 18th, telling Washington that the evacuation by the enemy was complete. A council of war was held to hammer out the final plans of the campaign, and the majority were against attacking the enemy on its passage through the Jerseys, a decision led by the newly arrived General Lee, but somewhat disagreed on by Washington, Greene, and Knox. "The country," said Greene at the meeting, "needs to be protected; and if in doing so an engagement should become unavoidable, it would be necessary to fight." So, Washington halfheartedly agreed with Lee and decided to hold off on attacking the British column. Washington based part of his decision on the fact that Nathanael Greene was known as an aggressive commander normally. Hence, Washington felt that the added burden of Greene's last few months at his Quartermaster-general duties had perhaps made him, "less than timid searching for a fight." Washington would write to Lord Stirling later, "These were the first active movements of General Greene since becoming Quartermaster-general, and although the promptness with which everything that depended upon that department was done, demonstrated the possibility of what had hitherto been deemed impossible, and proved my confidence had not been misplaced."

On the 19th, Greene wrote to Colonel Pettit: "Intelligence has been brought from Philadelphia, that enemy have evacuated it. Part of our army begins their march towards the Delaware this afternoon, and the whole will be in motion to-morrow morning. General Lee seems to think they are going towards Maryland. But his Excellency and I am fully of the opinion they are going to New York. The balance of evidence at present is much in favor of this conjecture. The sooner you can join us the better. Colonel Cox is going into the city immediately, and I, poor soul, shall be left all alone to do both the field and family duty." The race across the Jerseys was on.

Clinton moved as slowly as expected, but with the intention, as Washington, Knox and some of the other officers believed, to draw the Americans "into the lower country, in order, by a rapid movement, to gain their right, and take possession of the strong grounds above them." The Americans moved slower than expected though, because the weather had turned oppressively hot for June, and the roads became heavy with the frequent rains, making the deep sand impassable in most places. On the 21st, they crossed the Delaware in force at Coryell's Ferry, Greene marking out the route and order of march with appropriate places of encampment; a duty that kept him more than half the time in his saddle.

Even with Greene's Herculean, ongoing effort to obtain provisions for the troops, basic food like beef, lamb, or pork were still hard to come by. Because of it, Wayne's detachment left their camp without sufficient rations and suffered badly their entire expedition. Greene felt responsible and assured Wayne that food was on its way. Several of Wayne's detachment suffered from malnutrition before the provisions finally arrived. At Hopewell, on the 24th of June, another council of war assembled. Lee, supported by a majority of field generals, still opposed an attack on the British column. After a long discussion it was decided "that a detachment of fifteen hundred men be immediately sent to act, as occasion may serve, on the enemy's left flank and rear, in conjunction with the other Continental troops and militia, who are already hanging about them, and that the main body preserve a relative position, so as to be able to act as circumstances may require."

Although all of the officers signed the resolve, he, along with von Steuben, Duportail, Wayne, Paterson, and Lafayette, disagreed with the number of troops being used as inadequate and suggested that number be raised to at least 2,000, and preferably 2,500 or more. He was dissatisfied that he and the other officers who disapproved of the final plan, were being ignored, and addressed the issue in a letter to Washington. "Your Excellency, although the plan to attack is a sound venture, several officers and myself are displeased with the number of troops being incorporated into the attack. I urge you, with all respect to your title Excellency, to attack the enemy's rear by a larger detachment than that decided, and a general engagement, if the main body could be brought into a favorable position for it. I humbly ask that you reconsider the final plan, and look to inforce the number of troops of the detachment to be used." It was out of character for Greene to be so direct and informal in approaching Washington, but when Washington rebuffed Greene's suggestion, Greene was so empowered with what he felt was a folly of General Lee's insistence, that he went even further to try and change Washington's mind. With Washington's trusted aide-de-camp, Alexander Hamilton in tow, Greene requested, and was granted an impromptu, personal interview to discuss the matter. Granting the meeting, Greene was only more convinced that Washington agreed with him, but only needed further convincing to change the plans accordingly. Repairing to Washington's marquee, Greene and Washington met. "I know what you have come for," Hamilton related some days later, "you wish me to fight; as the General rose and approached Major-general Greene, the two gentlemen had a brief discussion, and the orders were issued for a full engagement, which led to the Battle of Monmouth."

Chapter XIII

"The Battle of Monmouth"

Plans for an attack on the British took a momentary backseat for Greene. He had not heard from his wife in some time and was beginning to be concerned. The last time Caty was unable to write due to a serious illness, and Greene was worried that this was the case again. His anxious mood is evident in a letter to her from the American encampment in " Camp Hopewell, near Princeton, New Jersey, June 25, 1778. I have not received a single line from you since you left camp. I am afraid your letters are stopped and opened by some imprudent scoundrel. I have wrote you five or six times. I had the pleasure to hear of you on the road, and that you were well. I hope you got home safe. The enemy have evacuated Philadelphia, and are now on their march through the Jerseys; they are at this time about fifteen or twenty miles distant from us at a place called Crossix; we arrived here last night, and shall march for Princeton this afternoon. Colonel Cox is at Philadelphia and Mr. Pettit at Congress, and I am left all alone, with business enough for ten men. Mrs. Knox has been in Philadelphia and is now gone to Morristown. She is fatter than ever, which is a great mortification to her. The General is equally fat, and therefore one cannot laugh at the other. They appear to be extravagantly fond of each other; and, I think are perfectly happy when in eachs company. Pray write me at the first opportunity of everything and particularly about the children: My love to all friends." Nathanael seemed to be a little envious of the Knox's marriage. They were an older couple with a grown daughter and the three were thus able to travel whenever General Knox marched to their next encampment. Absence does not always make the heart draw fonder, but sometimes only makes for one to feel they are in a relationship that is going nary and brings the question of the sincerity of the missing person.

Caty Greene was not one to allow the grass to grow under her feet. Nathanael knew her reputation as the consummate hostess, because it was one of the things that drew her to him in the first place. She had been well taught by her Aunt on the art of preparing parties, socializing, conversation, and just being charming and ultimately being the belle of any ball. Her dinner party exploits, during the short period she was with Nathanael at Valley Forge became famous among the other couples there. She was always quick with her wit, able to speak on any subject with enough knowledge to make herself charming, but especially with the officers in camp. Most women of the day were unfamiliar with politics and military actions, and almost all of them felt it was a mans domain where women need not tread. Instead, Catharine Littlefield Greene had been taught to always be noticed by all of the men in the room. Marriage was not a reason to stop being noticed. Rumors and innuendoes flew about any room she entered; most to this day can not be substantiated. But the fact remains that Caty Greene was a career hostess to a fault. It was even suspected that she favored socializing and parties over the care of her children. During General Greene's career during the war, she traveled to see him without the children several times, staying at least half a dozen times for more than a month. It was also theorized that all of this socializing could not hurt the rise of Nathanael's stock within the army, and that was all she was attempting to do. In the meantime, it is hard to judge a woman over two hundred years later without the proper evidence. All that was known at the time was that Nathanael Greene missed his wife and young children very much and ideas clouded his thoughts daily of what had happened to his wife? What would become of the children if she were gone? The idea of leaving the army was not foreign to Greene and on the eve of battle; it may have been crowded his mind more than military strategy.

On the 27th of June, Washington called General Charles Lee to his headquarters with Greene, Lafayette, Wayne, Maxwell, and Scott also in attendance. Washington knew of Lee's contempt for his leadership ability. On more than three occasions Lee either countermanded Washington's orders by saying he had interpreted the orders from Washington to only be requests and not direct orders. Sometimes he ignored the orders all together. Washington had grown tired of Lee thinking he should be the commander-in-chief instead of, what he described as, "this civilian upstart playing at General." So, Washington staged this meeting so as to have a number of witnesses to his orders to Lee and making sure there was no question as to what he was summoned and ordered to do. He directed Lee to engage Cornwallis' grand division as soon as it was in motion the next morning, promising to support him, if necessary, with the rest of the army. Bowing to Lee's military experience, Washington prescribed no particular plan, but requested Lee to call together that afternoon the general officers of his division and arrange the details of the attack. Further, Washington asked the other generals to waive the respective claims to precedence of rank, to submit themselves to Lee's orders and to fight wherever and whenever they were directed to do so.

Lee had his conference at about 5 o'clock that afternoon. He proceeded to tell the officers in attendance that since the numbers and exact situation of the enemy was not completely known and the terrain had not been carefully examined, he would make no plan. He would move cautiously and rely upon his officers and men to act according to the circumstances. Truth be told, as was his practice, Greene had indeed canvassed the area to check the terrain and scout what either army could possibly use to their advantage. Greene mentioned this to Lee who said he would follow-up on Greene's recommendations. But during the night, Lee made no effort to secure the information he had been given and later used that excuse as the reason for not adopting a set battle plan.

Late that evening, when Washington was told Lee was not following up on information afforded him, Washington sent an order directing Lee to detach a party of observers to lie close to the enemy's camp and give notice of when they may move. The order was given to Lee at one o'clock in the morning, but it was not until six o'clock before Lee sent out a detachment of 600 men, composed of Grayson's Virginia regiment, Scott's brigade, and part of Varnum's, along with four guns, all under the command of Colonel William Grayson. They started from Englishtown, about five miles from the known British camp. The road from Englishtown to Monmouth Court House first came from Freehold Meeting House. From there it continued in a southeasterly direction to Monmouth Court House, where it stopped at a right angle to the road which ran northeasterly to Middletown and Sandy Hook which could be used for a British retreat. Another road ran north to Amboy. Stretching out from the area are three ravines. The first one ran west, and through it ran the Wemrock Brook and was crossed by a bridge on the Freehold-Monmouth road about two and a half miles from the MeetingHouse. A mile to the southeast was the middle ravine; through it ran the main stream of the Wemrock Brook. A causeway crossed here. This is the road the Americans would use to advance to Monmouth. The third ravine was to the east, and ran parallel to the road from Monmouth to Middletown and some distance to the west of the Sandy Hook road. There was no bridge crossing here, but the area would become important early in the battle.

The observers finally got to the British camp, which was stretched in a line along the road from Allentown and continued past Monmouth through Middletown to Sandy Hook. It appeared they were formed on a right angle to the road from Englishtown to Monmouth. The American troops could easily advance up this road to meet them.

Clinton knew that Washington was not just there to capture his baggage train. He was aware that they planned on a major engagement as well. Clinton ordered Knyphausen's Hessians, with a part of the army's wagons, to move forward on the Middletown road at about four o'clock that morning, while he and Cornwallis, with a larger force prepared to follow right behind. Cornwallis' command consisted of the 3rd, 4th, and 5th British infantry brigades, the 1st and 2nd battalions of British grenadiers, all the Hessian grenadiers, the British Guards, the 1st and 2nd battalions of British light infantry, the 16th Light Dragoons, and the Simcoe's Tory Queen's Rangers. All were comprised of the elite portion of the British army.

General Dickinson with the New Jersey militia was stationed with the observers throughout the night. When he discovered Knyphausen's grand division on the move he sent word to Lee and Washington. He was perched on a hill just east of the west ravine when he came in contact with a detachment of the enemy and they began to exchange musket fire. Thinking it was the second division of the British army; he retreated across the ravine, just as an American forward detachment was coming up. This small detachment was only a flanking party thrown out by Cornwallis, and when the Americans advanced over the bridge, the British force quickly withdrew. This was to be the prelude to the Battle of Monmouth.

When Washington received Dickinson's message, he sent word to Lee that he "desired you would bring on an engagement, or attack the enemy as soon as possible, unless some very powerful circumstance forbid it, and that I would very soon be up to your aid." It was also reported that Washington ordered Lee to attack so he could make an impression on the enemy, but be careful not to be drawn into a major scrape.

Lee did move his troops from the Englishtown road about seven o'clock in the morning, Colonel Richard Butler with 200 men, followed by Colonel Henry Jackson with another 200 men, then part of general Woodford's brigade, 600 men with two guns. General Varnum's 600 men with two guns followed, along with General Wayne's command of 1,000 men and four guns, General Scott's 1,400 men with four guns, and General Maxwell's 100 men and two guns.

The column arrived at the Meeting House, where Lee halted them for half an hour because he had received word from von Steuben's aide that the British had not yet marched forward. They obviously were speaking about Cornwallis' division, because Knyphausen had marched hours earlier. When Dickinson arrived from the scuffle with the flanking party, Lee launched into a tirade about him giving false information. Dickinson, known to be less than a Lee supporter, screamed back at the general that he was a bloody egomaniac and should check information before flying off half-cocked to someone. The argument almost escalated into a brawl when a Captain Benjamin Walker, aide to von Steuben, had to literally restrain Dickinson. Lee, considered an unstable minded person at best, was more than a little thrown off by the altercation. They began to march, only to stop again. Lee seemed to be lost in thought, and when asked the reason for the halt, demanded that Wayne go forward and relieve Colonel Grayson of command of the advance detachment. When pressed for a reason, Lee gave none.

From this point on Lee's force half-heartily moved forward, moved to the left, then to the right without much reason. No serious engagement of the enemy had been met. This portion of the battle has been recorded by historians in the past 223 years as "the most confusing in its movements and the most difficult to present or follow in any detail of any battles of the entire Revolutionary War." Lee's troops were said to be centralized between the east ravine and the road to Middletown, but that would be a general deduction at best.

Lee's army was not drawn into any formal battle lines. Various brigades and detachments were disposed into an irregular pattern and shifted every which way imaginable over the course of two hours. There were periodic skirmishes here and there, occasional advances, subsequent withdrawals, arrangements and rearrangements of the troops, with shifts of one brigade with another regiment, but with virtually no rhyme or reason to the movements in relation to the engagements involved. Lee constantly gave orders, only to be countermanded almost immediately. It was becoming obvious to the officers involved, as well as with the rank and file soldiers that whoever was in command had no fixed plan of battle or even a grasp of what the bloody hell they were doing. Even Wayne, known to be very decisive, got caught up in the confusion of the day. He would direct orders to other officers on the field, only to have them ignored or carried out, it did not seem to matter to what degree. Complete pandemonium was about to take hold if someone did not step in and take command soon.

Clinton had followed von Knyphausen about eight o'clock, leaving the rear guard to cover Monmouth. Lee decided it would be a good idea to try and cutoff this covering party and had even sent word to Washington that "the rear of the enemy was composed of only, 1,500 to 2,000 men; and that we expect to fall in with the enemy with great certainty of cutting them off." One of his aides, empowered with Lee's over confidence, commented to Lafayette, "The rear guard is ours," whereas Lee made a similar statement and began to move his troops with that conclusion in mind. The problem was, Lee did not tell any of his field officers his idea and gave them no orders or directions on how they were to accomplish this harebrained plan. So, having no idea of what they were suppose to do, and in most cases, receiving only minimum, general orders, the officers made ineffective and uncoordinated reliance's on their men.

Some strong fighting had already begun between several individual regiments of the American and British rearguard, both giving and taking to a virtual standstill up until this time. Clinton noticed that this was only the preliminaries to a major engagement in the making and sent a brigade of British foot and the 17th Light Dragoons from von Knyphausen's division to cover the exposed right flank, then faced about and marched in to face the oncoming American attack. Within moments, Lee's glorious plans for cutting off the rear guard were dashed into impossibility.

In turn he ordered Lafayette, with three regiments of Wayne's detachment and some artillery, to march forward against the oncoming British and their left flank. Lafayette, having moved into position, believed he could not attack without exposing his troops to a British thrust. He began to move his men to a new position. Scott and Maxwell took this as a retreat that would leave them cut off from the main force and decided to fall back. Colonels Grayson and Jackson saw these troops fall back, and without proper orders from Lee, decided on their own that they should retire. Soon after, Lee did give the order for Lafayette to retire, and with it, the entire force began to retreat. Before long, disorganized regiments in no order at all, marched into regiments who were in good order and a wave of American soldiers were suddenly massed into an enormous mishmash of 5,000 soldiers looking for direction. The temperature was reported to be 96 degrees in the shade, the heat was sweltering, soldiers were dropping from heatstroke more than from battle wounds. Five thousand sweating, thirsty men tramped along the road back towards Englishtown, with Lee leisurely riding along upon his horse. Reports after the battle suggested that Lee was self-possessed, and even seemed to be smiling. He seemed to be enjoying the entire affair and harbored quiet satisfaction that an impending defeat of this half-witted attempt by a commander less qualified than himself would bode well for him. After all, Lee had disapproved and voted against such an attack and was overjoyed with a sort of I-told-you-so sort of satisfaction. Several officers later reported that Lee had carried out a masterful job of covering the rear-guard actions, and that the movements were necessary to avert a crushing blow from Clinton's force. That could not be further from the truth.

Washington and Greene were with the main army, a bit larger than Lee's advance force, and had been marching to his support since they received word about Clinton's movements from Monmouth. They stopped on the way at a house for a late breakfast, while their men continued. Here, they received Lee's message about the attempt at cutting off Clinton's rear guard. Knowing the number of troops involved on both sides, they had no reason to believe the battle was not progressing well. It was therefore understandable that Washington almost went through the roof when he received a subsequent message that Lee's army was on the retreat. The poor fifer that delivered the news was put under arrest by the fiery tempered general for spreading false alarms. Washington forgot about his breakfast and continued on toward the front lines when he met several men who gave him the same information. But he still would not believe the story.

161

Pushing on with Greene, he met a large number of retreating soldiers, then a whole regiment, then more men in complete disorder, the men completely exhausted from the heat. Washington sat in complete amazement as he watched regiment, after regiment, come pouring down the road. They then met with Ogden who angrily said, "we flew from shadows." Washington finally came upon Lee. Several accounts have made their way into history and lore, at least fourteen by my count. The one I tend to believe goes something like this; Washington asked Lee, "I desire to know, sir, what is the reason--whence arises this disorder and confusion." On the defensive by his commander-in-chief's angry tone, Lee stammered out, "Sir? Sir?" "Why all this confusion, sir?" Washington demanded. "And what is the cause for the retreat?" From here I am reluctant to copy down the remaining dialogue that was said to have occurred. Suffice it to say that it was more than a little colorful, and very explicit language was used. A few officers present, and known not to be present, said that Washington called Lee a "damned poltroon, and scattered with a terrific eloquence of unprintable scorn." General Scott, who was known to be present was asked after the war if he had ever been witness to Washington swearing, where he answered immediately, "Yes, sir, I did once; it was at Monmouth and on a day that would have made any man swear. Yes, sir, he swore that day till the leaves shook on the trees. Charming! Delightful! Never have I enjoyed such swearing before or since. Sir, on that memorable day he swore like an angel from heaven!" Although the exact conversation may never be known, one fact remains. The retreat stopped right there in its tracks.

As well as being quick tempered and an eloquent swearer, Washington was well known to be an excellent equestrian, maybe the best in the Colonies at that time. He was always mounted on a great white horse, a gift from Governor William Livingston of New Jersey. An officer that was present had this to say of the moment, "As soon as his Excellency was finished dressing down General Lee, he took his reins hard in his gloved hands, gave his steed two quick jabs with his spurs, and was off like a hotshot." Washington, with Greene attempting to keep up, galloped along the road to Monmouth Court House, halting his troops along the way and screaming for them to go back and fight. As he crossed the bridge over the west ravine, he met Colonel Walter Stewart's 13th Pennsylvania Regiment, and Lieutenant Colonel Nathaniel Ramsay, with the 3rd Maryland. These were the last troops of the retreat, with the British coming after them with not more than 200 yards between them. Wayne was near by, and ordered to take command and form a new line with these two regiments on the north side of the road, while Washington and Greene went about organizing the rest of the men they could find for another new line.

Suddenly, a party of Light Dragoons attacked the two regiments under Wayne. Stewart was badly wounded and had to be carried from the field. The heavy pressure from the dragoons was held back, but the Maryland unit were slowly being driven back. Ramsay, the last to withdraw, was wounded during hand-to-hand fighting with one of the dragoons, eventually was overpowered by another and taken prisoner.

Washington sent Varnum's brigade and Lieutenant Colonel Eleazer Oswald, with six guns, to reinforce the two regiments in hard fighting. Four more guns were soon brought forward, and Knox took charge of the artillery. Colonel Henry Beekman Livingston's 4th New York Regiment was also added to the defenders. In all these movements while under sharp attack by the enemy, there was much confusion. There was also confusion on the road to the west, along which many of the men who had been retreating were amassed. Lee had been ordered to the rear by Washington, and no field general stepped up to calm the troops while heavy fighting had started between an attacking force of dragoons and grenadiers and the American soldiers standing by the side of the road.

Washington and Greene had been riding up and down the lines attempting to assemble fresh troops to a rise of ground just west of the western ravine. Washington told Greene to take command of these men, and assembled the remainder himself into a center force; meanwhile Stirling had come up from the left with his division. Lafayette had been given command of the second line, with artillery well posted on both wings, particularly well on the right by Greene's troops, and where it was placed on Comb's Hill as to enfilade an attacking force. Enfilade is gunfire that is directed along the length of a target, such as in this case, a column of troops. A British attack was aimed at Stirling's wing. The British light infantry, the 42nd of foot, and the famous Black Watch pressed forward and were met by a heavy fire from the guns of Lieutenant Colonel Edward Carrington's battery. British fieldpieces were brought up, and a smart artillery duel ensued. Within this artillery battery was a particular artilleryman by the name of John Hays. Within the line of troops, running from man to man with pitchers or buckets of water she had gathered at the nearby creek, was his wife Mary Ludwig Hays. The men just called her "Molly Pitcher," which was the name they gave most women who brought water to the troops during and after a battle. Mary had been at Valley Forge with her husband and was well tutored in the ways of a campfollower by this point. It was expected that campfollowers do any job or duty given to them. In return, they were given half amounts of their husband's rations and occasionally a few cents here and there.

Volley after volley of musketry and cannonade came from both sides. Stirling, with Washington and von Steuben, passed along the American line, encouraging the men, sometimes at the end of their hangers. For nearly an hour, the guns on both sides pounded their opponents, the muskets rained lead without cessation. The fighting and heat were terrific. In the midst of this volley, Mary Hays was ordered to bring water for her husbands gun battery, to cool the cannon, and keep it from overheating. At that moment, Mary's husband John succumbed to the heat and collapsed, leaving only two men to man the cannon. While Mary was attending to her husband, the gun commander ordered the piece to withdraw due to the lack of artillerymen to man it. Mary volunteered to work the worm and rammer, which her husband had shown her how to operate, and the gun was able to remain in service. At one point, Mary was standing off to the side as the cannon fired and a enemy ball bounced in front of her and was said to have passed directly between her legs, taking half her long, striped dress with it, and leaving a gaping hole in her shift. She merely tied what remained of her dress around her waist and continued to work the worm and rammer.

The fighting was still intense, two hours later. Under constant fire, Von Steuben was watching the American regiments in the Stirling line. They were brought up into position, wheeled his line "with as much precision as on an ordinary parade and with coolness and intrepidity of veteran troops." Alexander Hamilton said afterwards, and added, that until he saw those troops deploy and fight as they did, "I had not known or conceived the value of military discipline." Von Steuben was extremely proud to see the results of his tireless teaching and drilling, and in only the first opportunity for the troops to use what they had learned at Valley Forge. The pressure on Stirling's wing was relieved when the 1st and 3rd New Hampshire regiments and the 1st Virginia moved to the left through the thick woods and charged upon the extreme right of the British, who gave way and fell back out of the Americans fire and to re-form.

Clinton's attack on Stirling's left wing had been a complete failure. He decided to send another force against the right, and here was where Greene's troops stood. The British troops used to attack Greene's right was made up of "the very flower of the rear division and of the army," English and Hessian grenadiers, light infantry, the 37th and 44th regiments, the Coldstreamers, and another battalion of the Guards. Cornwallis in person directed the attack.

In the usual British fashion, they first came forward in line and under an enfilading fire from the six-gun battery on Comb's Hill, who was being commanded by the Chevalier de Mauduit du Plessis, one of the heroes of the battle for Fort Mercer, and Knox's brigade adjutant. The fire from this battery was directed right across the line of the attackers with such accuracy that one round shot struck the muskets from the hands of an entire platoon. The muskets of Greene's infantrymen were also ablaze, but the British pressed on. Although five of their officers, including the colonel of the Coldstream Guard and the lieutenant colonels of the 37th and 44th, and many of the men had been killed or wounded, they kept coming. But eventually, the American fire, especially the artillery crossfire, was too heavy to bear. The attack on the right wing also failed, the British attacking force fell back once again.

While the assault on the right was repulsed, a determined onslaught was made on Wayne's position, behind the hedge, by light infantry, grenadiers, and dragoons. They came on with such ferocity and speed that they were close to the American line before they met the first volley. But then a steady rain of lead balls hit them with terrific force, shattering their ranks and driving them back. They re-formed and charged again, but Wayne ordered his men to hold their fire until they were "within 50 rods of our position, and then we opened fire with a blast of grape and canister shot which stopped them once again." The British troops were forced to fall back, yet again.

It was nearly an hour before they made a third attempt. This time Lieutenant Colonel Henry Monckton of the 45th of Foot, the Sherwood Foresters, now commanded the 2nd Battalion of grenadiers. He formed his line to within five hundred feet from the hedge where Wayne's brigade was positioned behind, so close that Wayne remarked afterwards that he could hear Monckton talking to his men. Monckton gave the command "Forward to the charge my brave grenadiers!" and on they marched. Monckton was on the right of the line leading them on every step, and then had them dash forward at top speed. Wayne held his fire, telling his men, "Steady boys. Steady! Wait for the word, then pick out the king-birds!" At a distance of about forty yards, Wayne gave the word, and a volley crumpled the British ranks. Monckton himself fell onto the hedge and some of the American soldiers leaped out and seized his body and the battalion colors.

But the British would not quit. A fourth attack was planned and organized with a much larger body of troops on both sides of the hedge and was about to outflank Wayne. Resistance was futile, and so he gave orders for his troops to draw off in good order. They served their purpose well, to keep the main American line, from Stirling to Greene, intact and safe from any further attempt to take the position by assault. The line was too well posted and was no longer in danger of being moved from that position. Cannon fire on both sides continued for another hour or so, until the British withdrew in force around six o'clock to a strong position east of the middle ravine.

But Washington was less than pleased. Even though he had taken a retreat and turned it into a satisfying withdraw by the British, he wanted an all out victory. The Lee fiasco had heated his blood and he wanted a complete victory. He felt with fresh troops brought forward, he could rout the enemy and takes the field. However, before the troops could be organized and brought forward it was too late to risk an engagement in the dark.

The American army laid with their arms through the night, Washington himself within their midst, under the branches of a large oak tree with only his familiar cloak for covering, Lafayette nearby. Every man was ready to renew the fight in the morning, but when the first light of dawn shone, there was no enemy to fight. As silent as Washington had escaped Howe on Long Island, now Clinton employed the same tactics to get way from Washington. Clinton started to withdraw just after midnight, caught up with Knyphausen's division by daybreak and was in Middletown by ten o'clock in the morning. By the 30th his entire army was at Sandy Hook, and by the 5th of July they were in New York.

The usual criteria for winning a battle during the Revolutionary War were who had occupied the field. But in this case, both sides could claim that prize, but at completely different times. So, the Battle of Monmouth has always been considered a tie. In fact, Clinton had no desire for the field. What he wanted was New York, and he got it. All he was really doing was protecting his baggage train and his route to New York, playing a defensive game the entire battle. He accomplished that feat, so you could say he had scored a victory by his criteria. But Washington had been entirely in an offensive mode from the start that is until the Lee fiasco had retarded his ultimate goal, the complete victory of the British army on the field. The march pursuing the British had no strategic worth, but the pride of fighting a major engagement against the formidable professional soldiers of the British and Hessian army, and not coming out the loser was certainly an occasion for positive reflection. The epitaph of the battle was that both armies fought valiantly with notable courage displayed by the British, Hessians, and Americans, a first. It was also, by far, the longest battle of the war, and also the last that would be staged north of the Mason-Dixon line.

The woman that bravely stood by her husband's gun when he was unable to continue, Mary Ludwig Hays, better known to us in history as Molly Pitcher. Well, Greene had been informed of the woman's fortitude and had sent a note to Washington about her. Contrary to popular folklore, Washington never personally received her. But, he did give orders to have the rank of sergeant bestowed upon her, at half pay. Her husband John recovered from his heatstroke, and they both returned to Carlisle, Pennsylvania after the war where John was a barber where he died in 1789. Mary then married a family friend, George McCauly. The marriage was an unhappy one and she left George to take a job as a servant again, and was known thereafter as, Molly McCauly. In 1822, the state of Pennsylvania awarded Molly her full annual pension of 40 dollars in recognition of her wartime services. She died peacefully on January 22, 1832 an was laid to rest under a flagstaff and cannon in Carlisle, which commemorates her deeds during the Battle of Monmouth. She had been thought, until recently, to be of Irish descent, but was actually Dutch-German.

The most serious consequence that came out of the battle was what was to become of General Charles Lee. He had been publicly rebuked on the battlefield by his commander-in-chief, and all, if any, respect that was felt for him by the troops, was now wiped away. The talk within the camp was quite bitter towards him and there was even talk of having him ride the wooden horse. He squirmed under the pressure of being dressed up and down in front of the "lowly troops" and then the injustice of having his guarded pride injured to such a degree. On the 29th, he wrote Washington a letter, which began mildly, but grew bitter and hateful with each passing word, accusing Washington of "an act of cruel injustice" and to "demand some reparation." He added the threat of resigning "from service, at the head of which is placed a man capable of offering such injuries." He was quite confident; he would tell any and all that would listen, of justifying himself, "to the Army, to the Congress, to America and to the World in general."

Washington, furious over the letter, replied in kind to Lee, saying, "I am not conscious of having made use of any very singular expressions at the time of my meeting with you, as you intimate. What I recollect to have said, was dictated by duty, and warranted by the occasion. As soon as the circumstances will permit, you shall have an opportunity either of justifying yourself to the army, Congress, to America, and to the world in general; or convincing them that you were guilty of a breach of orders, and misbehavior before the enemy, on the 28th inst., in not attacking them as you had been directed, and in making an unnecessary, disorderly, and shameful retreat."

Lee, and his temperament, felt it necessary to reply to Washington. "You cannot afford me greater pleasure than in giving me the opportunity of showing to America, the sufficiency of her respective servants, I trust, that the temporary power of office, and the tinsel dignity attending it, will not be able, by all the mists they can raise, to obfuscate the bright rays of the truth."

Washington reflected on the situation and decided a Court of Inquiry would investigate the charges levied at General Lee. The charges Washington put before the court was for disobedience of orders and disrespect to the Commander-in-chief. But Lee struck again when he heard that the court was made up of more officers supportive of Washington than himself and wrote a third letter, "I have reflected on both your situation and mine; and beg leave to observe, that it will be for our mutual convenience, that a Court of Inquiry should be immediately ordered; but I could wish it might be a Court Martial: for, if the affair is drawn into length, it may be difficult to collect the necessary evidences, and perhaps bring on a paper war betwixt the adherents of both parties, which may occasion some disagreeable feuds on the Continent; for all are not my friends, nor all your admirers."

It has been suspected over two centuries that Washington was merely going to instill a bit of commander-in-chief wisdom on Lee, dismiss the checkered past of the two men, and nothing more. But when he received Lee's letter demanding an apology and the subsequent second and third bashing him, it forced the hot tempered Washington's hand and he could do nothing but bring charges against Lee. The request for a court-martial was granted, and the charge of, "Misbehavior before the enemy on the same day, by making unnecessary, disorderly and shameful retreat," was added to the court-martial. Lee was found guilty because of his actions during the battle and suspended from command for one full year. The verdict was sent to Congress for final approval, and was approved, but by a very close vote. Several months later Lee wrote an insulting letter to the Congress, and it finished the affair by resolving that it had "no further occasion for his services in the army of the United States." Washington was finally rid of the persistent thorn in his side, and need not suffer Lee's ego or bad advice ever again. When Congress was searching for the army's commander-in-chief, Lee had been a top contender for the position. Only by the strong disapproval and insistence against Lee by Benjamin Franklin was Lee kept from the position. Besides his enormous ego, Franklin had contended that Lee was "just too British."

Greene had not been involved in the battle when the incident with General Lee had occurred, so was not called upon as a witness. Although, for that exact reason Greene should have been chosen to sit in on the trial, because he was not directly involved with the incident and would have been able to listen to the testimony without knowing the full implications before hand. Of course, taking into account the close relationship Greene had with Washington, and his great affection for his commander-in-chief, it would be hard to imagine Greene not taking Washington's side in any such affair.

With the latest engagement with the enemy behind them, Greene did not have time to rest on laurels and threw himself back into his duties as Quartermaster-general. He was given the assignment of ordering new provisions for the portion of the army that would be on the march in a few days. Greene made a trip to Brunswick, trying to acquire the necessary supplies, but especially a new supply of horses to make up for the heavy losses the army sustained in the field at Monmouth and on the subsequent march afterwards. In both cases, a large amount were overcome by the heat and dropped dead on the field and along the road. When Greene had completed his task, the army moved on towards the Hudson, in hopes of securing the passes to the New York Highlands. From here, Greene writes to Washington on the 16th of July to report his findings; "Captain Drake's, seven miles from the ferry. General Varnum is also at this place, and has very lately returned from Rhode Island; he says that there are fifteen hundred State troops, including the artillery regiments. There is the Continental Battalion, commanded by Colonel Greene, about one hundred and thirty strong. Besides these, 4,500 militia are ordered from Massachusetts, Connecticut, and New Hampshire States, part of which are already arrived, and others daily coming in. General Varnum thinks there cannot be less than three thousand men already embodied under the command of General Sullivan, that can be depended upon. General Varnum thinks that there are not above three thousand of the enemy at Rhode Island and only six frigates. I find no place for encamping the troops short of nine miles from the ferry towards Crompond."

It would seem that Greene was doing his best to influence Washington into his next campaign, an expedition to Rhode Island with the American army. Unbeknownst to Greene, that is exactly where Washington was already making plans to go. Being always the cautious commander-in-chief, Washington was already calling councils daily to help reassure him of his decision. The next day

166

Greene was across the river into West Chester, but still had his mind on Rhode Island when he wrote to one of his deputies in Providence, Colonel Ephraim Bowen, and although he alludes to it, he makes no direct mention of an expedition to Rhode Island. "Your request by Mr. Martin for cash is gone to the Treasury. I hear this day he has been successful in his attempt; you may, therefore, expect the money very soon. I have written to my brother to furnish you with any articles you may want, that he has purchased, or may purchase for the public use. If you should want you will please to apply accordingly. Let us hear the news from your quarter every week, by the post. It is increasingly important."

On that same day, Greene writes to his wife: "I received your agreeable letter of the 8th this instant. I am very sorry to find you are unwell. Why did you ride in the night? What was your hurry? Why do you expose yourself unnecessarily and risk any disagreeable consequences that might follow? Sensible of your anxiety, and desirous of giving you the earliest information after the battle of Monmouth, I sent off an express, with a line to Colonel Hay, desiring him to forward your letter by the first opportunity; which I hope you have received long before this. You express a strong desire to see the army on the east side of the North River, and urge you have political as well as private reasons for it. Your private reasons I can interpret, but your political ones I cannot divine. You may rest assured that there must be something very uncommon to prevent my coming home; you cannot have a greater desire to see me than I have you and the children. I long to hear the little rogues' prattle. Besides which there are many other matters that I want to settle. You write you are politely treated in Boston. I am exceeding happy to hear it. You are envious then, I find; why so, Caty? (if) there are others more happy than you, are there not others less so? Look around you, my dear, and see where there are not many whose conditions and prospects are far less eligible than yours. I have been obliged in many instances to sacrifice the present pleasures to our future hopes. This, I am sensible, has done violence to your feelings at the time; but I trust the motives were so laudable and the consequences will be so salutary that I shall meet with no difficulty in obtaining your forgiveness hereafter. At the close of the war I flatter myself I shall be able to return to your arms with the unspotted love and affection as I took the field. I shall doubly relish domestic pleasures. To please my love and educate my children will be a most happy employment; my fortune will be small; but I trust by good economy we may live respectably."

As previously noted, it was generally known at the time that Washington had a very quick temper, and was often led to sudden and violent rages at what most of us would consider insignificant things. Few people close to him escaped witnessing at least one of these tirades, and if they were lucky, were not the direct recipient of it themselves. Each person was said to learn to deal with it according to their individual character. Alexander Hamilton, a person not exactly known for his benevolence, once said to Schuyler, "I always determined if there should ever happen a breach between us, never to consent to an accommodation." Nathanael Greene's personality, on the other hand, would have made it hard for him to absorb such a tongue-lashing. He absolutely loved and admired Washington, looking up to him as our savior. The only man who could guide us safely through the dangers and perplexities of the Revolutionary War, and grateful to him for the confidence he had shown Nathanael from the very beginning, and standing by him when others sought to keep him down. So, when the occasion finally arrived for Greene to be the subject of Washington' wrath, Greene was upset, but appealed to him as a friend, and not just as a subordinate.

"Your Excellency has made me very unhappy. I can submit very patiently to deserved censure, but it wounds my feelings exceedingly to meet with a rebuke for doing what I conceived to be a proper part of my duty, and in the order of things. When I left your Excellency at Haverstraw, you desired me to go forward and reconnoiter the country, and fix upon some proper position to draw the troops together at. I was a stranger to all this part of the country, and could form no judgment of a proper place until I had thoroughly examined the ground. Croton River was the only place I could find suitable to the purpose, all circumstances being taken into consideration. I wrote your Excellency what I had done and where I was, that if you had anything in charge might receive your orders. I wrote you the reasons for my not waiting upon you in person were I had my letters to answer and many matters to regulate in my departments, which prevented me from returning. Besides which it was almost half a day's ride, the weather exceeding hot, and myself not a little fatigued. And here I must observe that neither my constitution nor strength is equal to constant exercise. The security of the army, the ease and convenience of the troops, as well as to perform the duties of my office with a degree of reputation, all conspired to make me wish to fix upon the proper ground for the purpose. This it was impossible for me to do unless I came on before the troops. And I must confess I saw no objection, as your Excellency had wrote me nothing to the contrary, and what I wrote naturally led to such a measure. If I had neglected my duty in pursuit of pleasure, or if I had been wanting in respect to your Excellency, I would have put my hand upon my mouth and been silent upon the occasion; but I am not conscious of being chargeable with either the one or the other, and I cannot help thinking I have been treated with a degree of severity I am in no respect deserving of." The letter continues for more than three pages, explaining the same thing over and over again. Greene was injured to think Washington thought he was neglecting him and his job. Greene was in the process of doing his duty as Quartermaster-general, when Washington asked him to do another job. When Greene was finished with the job Washington had given him, he went back to his business as Quartermaster-general, a job he insisted that Greene take on. If Washington thought he was neglecting any of his duties, he could take the Quartermaster-general job and give it to someone else. Washington's reply is unavailable, but the strong bond the two men shared continued thereafter, so we can assume they reconciled their differences.

The French fleet under the command of Count d'Estaing had arrived and was anchored off the coast of New Jersey. Washington now turned his attention on plans as to how the fleet could be employed in the best possible circumstances. "I would propose writing to the French Admiral," Greene wrote to Washington, "that there are two objectives. One of the two may be improved as a blockade or an investiture, as circumstances and the practicability of entering the harbor of New York should be found. The French fleet to take station at Sandy Hook and block up the harbor. This army to take a position near the White Plains to cut off the land communication, and to all appearances seem to design some serious operations against New York and the troops there. General Sullivan to be wrote to desiring to know what force he has that may be confided in the character of regular troops. What force is from the neighboring States and expected in a few days and what militia can be brought together in eight days' time. In the mean while the admiral to make himself acquainted with the depth of water into New York and the ships and force there."

The channel, as had been feared, was not deep enough for the larger, heavier ships of the French squadron, and it was decided that they would turn their attentions to Rhode Island. The American army would meet their new allies in Newport and combined forces. "I am at once the most happy man in the world," Greene writes to Sullivan from Whit Plains on the 23rd of July. "What child of fortune. The expedition going on against Newport, cannot, I think, fail of success. You are the first General that has ever had an opportunity of cooperating with the French forces belonging to the United States. I wish you success of this expedition. I wish you success with all my soul, and intend, if possible, to come home to put things in a proper train in my department, and to take a command of part of the troops under you. I wish most ardently to be with you. I was an adviser of this expedition and therefore am deeply interested in the event. I wish a little more force had been sent. The Count d'Estaing will block up the harbor and you may wait until your plan is ripe for execution. I hope you won't precipitate matters until your force gets together. Everything depends almost upon the success of this expedition. Your friends are anxious; your enemies are watching. *I charge you to be victorious.* The Marquis de la fayette is coming to join you. Trust to your own judgement for forming the plan, as you have everything at stake; and pray give your orders positive for the execution. The late transactions at the battle of Monmouth make me drop these hints. You'll excuse the freedom, I take, and believe me, &c."

It is quite evident that Greene is bubbling at the anticipation of the expedition, and was even bursting to get into the fray. He probably thought, as did almost all of the people involved, that this would be an end-all to the conflict and the revolution. The now disciplined, well organized American army, fighting at the side of the well trained, experienced soldiers of France, would not only afford the opportunity to show the world what the Americans were now capable of, but they would finally prove to be a formidable force against the British troops. We could also notice the longing Greene was feeling inside. Up until now, he had only played small, and what he felt were insignificant roles, at Brandywine, Germantown, and Monmouth. This was his opportunity to shine in the spotlight, and he wanted the chance to earn a place in history with his comrades. It may have seemed egocentric or pompous, but Greene cared little what people thought then, only how he would be perceived in history.

He could finally respond to questions his deputies in Rhode Island had been asking for weeks. The plans were off the drawing board and about to be put into motion. Greene would write to Colonel Ephraim Bowen in Providence, "There is an expedition going on against Newport. The forces that will be collected for this purpose will be considerable. Great exertions, therefore, will be necessary in our department. You must get the most active men to assist you that you possibly can. A great number of teams and boats will be wanted upon the occasion. Pray do not let the expedition suffer for want of anything in our line. I am in hopes to come and assist you myself and join the expedition; but am afraid cannot obtain the General's assent. There is also a line of expresses established at the following places, to form an easy communication of intelligence from Providence to this camp. You must fix one at Mr. John Greene's in Coventry, to complete the communication. It must be done immediately."

By the 28th of July, Greene set out for Rhode Island. It took three days to travel the route that would take less than three hours today by automobile. "I arrived at this place last evening about nine o'clock," he writes to General Sullivan, "and being a little fatigued, I propose to refresh myself to-day and wait upon you to-morrow, unless there should be something special that renders my attendance necessary immediately; in which case I will set out without delay. You'll please to inform me by the return of the express. Inclosed is a letter from his Excellency, General Washington. I have forty ship-carpenters and boat-builders coming on to put things in readiness in the water department for the expedition, and there is a most excellent fellow at the head of them, Major Evans."

Nathanael Greene had not been home since he left for the army in 1775. Three years since he walked on his property, sat at his own dinner table, and played with his two children, the youngest, a daughter he had never laid eyes on. Friends and relatives would stop by and question him endlessly about the army and the officers and men with whom he served. Monmouth was the battle most discussed, because one of their own, a well known citizen from East Greenwich, a Captain Thomas Arnold, had left a leg behind on that battlefield. Forever more, the captain would be known in that area as "Monmouth Tom" to the children. Greene's brothers would also come up from Potowomut. They all noticed a distinct change in Nathanael, which they would comment on, again and again. No longer the same boy they knew, asking only to buy more books, and the leisure time to read them, but a man that would be in those books someday. Then everyone could read about their brother. They remembered the boy with the limp, who couldn't possibly be a soldier, let alone a major-general in the army at the side of General George Washington.

After a single day of rest and visiting, Greene was back on the road for his duties. It was decided that he would have "a command in the troops to be employed in the descent." Lafayette, whose command was divided by this new arrangement, accepted it with a cheerful frankness, which he would prove in a letter he wrote to Washington, "I have received your Excellency's favor by General Greene and have been muched pleased with the arrival of a gentleman who, not only on account of his merit and the justness of his views, but by his knowledge of the country and his popularity in this State, may be very serviceable to the expedition. I willingly part with half my detachment, since you find it for the good of the service, though I had great dependence on them. Anything, my dear General, which you shall order or can wish, will always be infinitely agreeable to me."

On the 2nd of August, Greene is at east Greenwich, in the old house where he grew-up. He was there to consult with the governor of Rhode Island, William Greene. This expedition would depend on the civil authority of the state. However, Nathanael Greene is dissatisfied with the act for calling out the militia, and after stating his objections to the Governor during their conversation, decides to emphasize his position in a letter a few days later. "Upon further inquiry I find there is an order from the council board for drafting one half of the whole militia in the State. I presume the intention of the board was to have one half of all those actually fit for duty drafted, and no others, for the intended expedition. If this indeed is the intention of the board, I am afraid both they and the General will be disappointed in their expectations; there being many drafted that are unfit for duty, and are now getting clearances. It will be necessary for the board to issue their orders for those one half-fit for actual service be drafted, and none others; or that those that are unfit for duty provide others to serve in their places. If something of this sort don't take place there will be a great diminution of the expected force. You will pardon the freedom I take at hinting these intentions to his Excellency."

On the 4th of August, Greene writes to Colonel Wadsworth. "I am here busy as a bee in a tar-barrel, to speak in a sailor's style. I am happy to inform you that everything in your department seems to equal our wishes; it was the first inquiry I made, and I received the most flattering answers. Will you want a quantity of rum? If you should, please to give the price to be delivered at Norfolk. My brothers have some; any service you can render them consistent with your trust will be duly acknowledged. Please to write me an immediate answer. We intend to give the enemy a cursed flogging. We are almost in readiness."

Up until now, everything seemed to be going as planned and the Americans had no reason to doubt otherwise. The soldiers were full of confidence, even the hopes of the timid and cautious civilians in the area were high. "We will show these French soldiers that we can fight as hard as they can," one foot soldier, still filled with old English and colonial prejudices left over from the French & Indian War, would write home. "We will show our allies that while we know what they are doing for us, we are prepared to do our parts like true men." Greene would establish his headquarters at Tiverton, doing double duty, Quartermaster-general and commander of a division. Amongst every order of the day contains a new charge for the Quartermaster-general. "The Quartermaster-general is directed to send over all the spare tents and distribute them among the troops that are destitute of covering, also all canteens." says an order written on the 10th of August. "The Quartermaster-general to see that the axes and entrenchment tools forwarded immediately after the army have marched. The Quartermaster-general will furnish proper tools for the pioneers," says an order on the 11th. Every third day finds Greene as Major general on duty. The increased workload soon makes it necessary for Greene to request an additional aide. By the 12th, a Major Jacob Morris is attached to "act as volunteer aid to Major-general Greene, and to be respected accordingly."

But soon, unforeseen difficulties arise. The French fleet came-to off Newport, by the 29th of July, and began the blockade. But the American levies were not yet on the ground, and Sullivan was reluctantly compelled to wait. At last they were all in, ten thousand men and more, and among the generals, John Hancock, fresh from serving his time as a representative of Congress. The plans call for a simultaneous advance by the French and Americans, and are agreed upon. The French will land near Dyer's Island, on the west side, the Americans at Howland's Ferry, on the east side. The British general, realizing their intentions, withdraws his forces from the strong works he had erected on the

170

north end of the island, and prepares to stand a siege in the lines near Newport. Sullivan, seeing the works empty, throws over a strong body to seize them, and crosses with his whole army as quickly as he can. This was a terrible breach of etiquette in 18th century warfare, a breach d'Estaing had some difficulty forgiving. The French allies were to land first, and Sullivan did not consult d'Estaing before the change in tactics. But the maneuver was fully justified by the circumstances that the British move caused. The French troops land on Conanicut, and hemmed in on all sides, British General Pigot, has no choice but to surrender.

At the same time, a British fleet of warships appears off Point Judith, thirty-six vessels in all, thirteen of them 64-gun ships of the line. The thin skinned d'Estaing, still bristled by his hurt pride, hurries his troops on board again, and sails out to meet the enemy, eager to show his strength and power. If he had not been upset at Sullivan, and had curbed his impatience, he could have contented himself with defending the mouth of the harbor, and victory would have been assured. Instead, the battle started off the coast, where the winds kept drawing the two fleets farther down the coast, and by the second day, just as they were about to engage in an enormous sea battle, a sudden gale blew up and scattered the ships to the four corners of the compass. Howe took his fleet and limped back to New York. D'Estaing was to take his crippled fleet to Boston. But Congress was in a political battle of their own with the great minds of Massachusetts who would not allow the French fleet into the harbor without assurances that they would be paid for the repairs needed on the ally ships. D'Estaing was forced to bring the crippled fleet, damaged by the violence of the storm, into Newport.

The storm did not only harass the two navies, but the soldiers on land as well. All of the provisions were completely destroyed by the torrential rain, their ammunition was wet, most of the tents had blown away, and the ground they were on was too muddy to walk on. Many of the soldiers ruined uniforms and blankets in the quagmire. Many of the men were forced to seek shelter by the stonewalls which are found everywhere in Rhode Island to take the place of fences, but many could find no shelter at all. It is reported that more men perished from exposure in the next few days than were killed and wounded in the skirmishes in and around Newport. An eyewitness writes, "I saw for the first time that these men were more hardy than horses," because many of the horses also perished, sinking down in the mud, unable to be removed, only to sink farther into the mud and slowly die. By the 14th, all repairs of the damage done was completed. On the morning of the 15th, the American army moved forward to within two miles of Newport, and began to prepare for regular approaches against the British lines. Now Greene's duties would be compounded, attempting to reconcile what was lost in the storm.

He was only a few miles from the crossroads to his house, and only two miles from the lines, where he took up headquarters. "I received your two letters to-day. I am sorry to find you are sick once again," he writes to his wife of the 16th of August. "I am afraid it is the effect of anxiety and fearful apprehension. Remember the same good Providence protects all places, and secures from harm in the most perilous situation. I feel your distress. My bosom beats with compassion and kind concern for your welfare, and the more so at this time as your situation is critical."

The Americans had expected to easily take Newport with the assistance of the French allies, but the disappointment at the lack of success to the enterprise soon came to a head. In general orders Sullivan indiscreetly censured the French, and in particular d'Estaing for not having remained to help their American allies. The French officers strongly resented this action, and d'Estaing quickly forwarded a letter he had written to Congress to explain "his chagrin and irritation" at the censure, which he felt "were but ill-conceived." Congress responded by resolving that "Count d'Estaing hath behaved as a brave and wise officer and that his Excellency and the officers and men under his command have rendered every benefit to these states, which the circumstances and nature of the service would admit of are fully entitled to the regards of the friends of America." D'Estaing was appeased, and harmony was restored. Contrary to the two-signed protests by Sullivan and Greene, the French fleet was refitted, and in due course, sailed away to Martinique, taking their 4,000 troops with them.

Greene was furious. Like Sullivan, he had hopes that a combined and sustained attack by the French and American forces would have convinced the British to give up Rhode Island all together and that they would have fallen back to New York. While all of this posturing was going on, Washington had moved his army from Haverstraw to King's Ferry, then across the Hudson and down to White Plains. He was fairly pleased by the fact that "after two years of Manoeuvring and undergoing the strangest vicissitudes" he was again at the place where it had all began after the retreat from Long Island, and now his enemy, then on the offensive, was now "reduced to the use of the spade and pick axe for defence." Washington was baffled by the inactivity of Clinton and his army, and wondered why they were happy to just sit quietly in New York. Washington was unaware that before Clinton had even taken command, the decision had already been made in England to desist from any further offensive operations in America.

"What shall we do next" was the question on everyone's mind. For the next few days, Greene was stationed on the west shore of Narraganset Bay, with his headquarters in Coventry, actually in his own house. But Greene was less than happy with the past month's occurrences. The expedition for which he had held great hope had failed miserably. That alone was of great disappointment to him. As he told his friend Reed, "I was dreaming of whole hosts of men and cargoes of generals to grace their triumph. But all at once the prospect fled like a shadow." Add to that, the mortification of public disappointment with the army, and even more discontent was to follow.

Two prominent merchants from Providence, whose interest were profoundly affected by the closing of the bay to their ships, personally blamed Greene. In their opinion the whole expedition had been badly planned and executed even worse, which proved Sullivan was a terrible general, and Greene was irresponsible with his command in Rhode Island. Greene was indignant at the unmerited accusations and wrote a letter of explanation. "Sirs, --This expedition was planned upon no other consideration than that of the French fleet cooperating with the American troops. The strength of the garrison was considered, and a force ordered to be levied accordingly, that might be sufficient to complete its reduction. The loss of the French fleet and troops was a sufficient reason for abandoning the expedition and of no fault of General Sullivan. You say you think the expedition was ill planned and worse conducted. I must beg leave to dissent from you in opinion. Was there any time lost by the Continental troops coming to Providence? There was not; for they all got together some days before the militia. I am not dependent upon the State of Rhode Island for either my character or consequence in life. Only to sacrifice my domestic pleasure to be given up to the service of my country. But I flatter myself I am not dependent upon the State of Rhode Island for either my character or consequence in life. However, I cannot help feeling mortified that those that have been at home, making their fortune, and living in the lap of luxury, and enjoying all the pleasures of domestic life, should be the first to sport with the feelings of officers who have stood as a barrier between them and ruin. I am, sir, your most Obedient and very Humble servant, N. Greene."

The way in which Greene signed the letter seems to be more than a little pointed towards sarcasm. Also, Greene would not know just how prophetic his one line would turn out to be, "I am not dependent upon the State of Rhode Island for either my character or consequence in life." The day after the letter was sent, brought more bad news, which made the strategic failure seem even more serious than first thought.

"By a letter this moment received from Major Courtland," writes Greene to Sullivan on the 7th of September, "I am sorry to hear of the destruction of Bedford. General Clinton deserves to be immortalized for this memorable action. It is highly worthy so great a commander. He has forgot how he run the other day in the Jerseys at the head of all his troops. If he had wanted to fight, he had then an opportunity. I am clear it is the intention of Clinton, if possible, to burn Providence, and he is making

172

these manoeuvers at New London and Bedford to divide and draw off our forces. Tyler's brigade is gone, and I suppose more force will be demanded at the eastward. In attempting to cover too much we shall expose everything; some principal objects should be attended to, and others must take their chance. Warwick is now left open. Will you have part of the troops at Pawtuxet ordered there or not? I wish to know your mind upon this matter. The artillery is wanted at Greenwich; please to order it forward, for fear Mr. Clinton should try his success this way."

Had there been nothing now but his military duties to occupy Greene's attention, he might have given himself up for a few days to be with his family and friends for a little rest and relaxation. But the demands of the Quartermaster's department were forever drawing the majority of his attention. By the middle of September 1778, he mounted his horse again and rode once more over the road to the Boston that he was beginning to learn and know so well. By the 16th, he writes to Washington to report on the progress of his duties: "Sir,--The growing extravagance of the people, and the increasing demands of the article of forage in this quarter, has become a very alarming affair. Hay is from sixty to eighty dollars per ton, and upon the rise; corn is ten dollars a bushel, oats four, and everything else that will answer for forage in that proportion. I am going to represent to the States of Rhode Island and Connecticut the absolute necessity of legislative interposition to settle the prices of things upon some reasonable footing. What effect it will have I cannot say; but if there is not something done to check the extravagance of the people, there are no funds in the universe that will equal the expense. I find by your Excellency's letter to General Sullivan that you expect the enemy are going to evacuate New York; and that it's probable they are coming eastward. I can hardly think they mean to make an attempt upon Boston, notwithstanding the object is important, there is no other object worthy their attention in New England."

The duties of his department were not the only circumstances that called Greene to Boston. The French fleet was still there, as his letters tell us, and there were still some ill-feelings between D'Estaing and Sullivan, which made it necessary for Greene to do a little backdoor diplomacy in that regard. Greene had won the Admiral's confidence, and he had always possessed Sullivan's. So when the correspondence between the two men seemed to be rapidly verging on bitterness, Greene naturally stepped in to play the friendly counsel to both. D'Estaing quickly showed his appreciation to Greene for playing the peacekeeper in a letter to him on the 1st of October 1778: "Sir,--It is from you and what you are, that it is doubtless suitable and flattering to judge of the respectable and amiable qualities of the American general officers whom I have not the honor of knowing by correspondence or personally. I hope that your Excellency and your respectable colleagues will not disapprove my conduct. To merit that it should please them will ever be one of my desires."

Another disaster adverted; Greene turned his attention to the business of clothing for the troops about to go into yet another winter of encampment. The memory of Valley Forge burnt into his mind, Greene held no regard for doing whatever was necessary to accomplish his goal of every soldier being completely outfitted with proper equipment before winter set in. "Colonel Bowen informs me there is some difficulty respecting the staff officers belonging to the quartermaster's department drawing clothing out of the public stores," he writes to Sullivan from Coventry, "All these who do business at the stated prices are, I conceive, as justly entitled to draw as the other officers; it being impossible for them to support themselves without this priviledge. Such of the staff as have been appointed in the grand army, have always and will always have free access to the store with other officers of the line. I believe I have made my position on this subject perfectly clear."

On the verge of another encampment, Greene made plans to be stationed wherever the army would be, rather than at home. "I was told yesterday that General Sullivan had wrote to your Excellency to have me stationed here (Coventry) this winter. However agreeable it is to be near my family and among my friends, I cannot wish it to take place, as it would be very unfriendly to the business of my department. I wrote yesterday to General Sullivan for leave to join the grand army, and expect his answer to-day." And with that, Greene departed his home on the hill which stands there to this day, never to return to it again. It is poetic justice that one of the bigger than life historic figures of the Revolutionary War would come from one of the smallest states in the Union. It is sad, however, that little is written today in the vacation pamphlets and catalogs that travelers to Rhode Island pickup while visiting the tiny state. They do not see much in the way of references, like the roadside signs that mark historic sites, to the General that was second in command of the Continental army behind only Washington. Could it be that the State of Rhode Island holds a grudge against Nathanael Greene for abandoning them in lieu of a state like Georgia that may have appreciated him just a little more? I leave that for you to decide.

Nathanael Green's home in Coventry, Rhode Island (front view).

Back view of Greene's house.

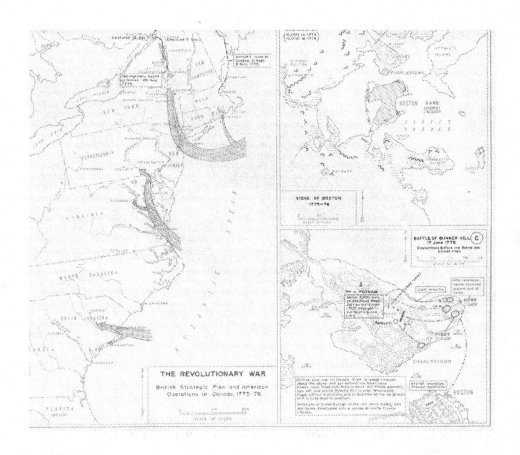

Illustration of British strategic plans and American operations in Canada, 1775-1776.
Notice the detail of the Battle of Breeds Hill and the Siege of Boston.

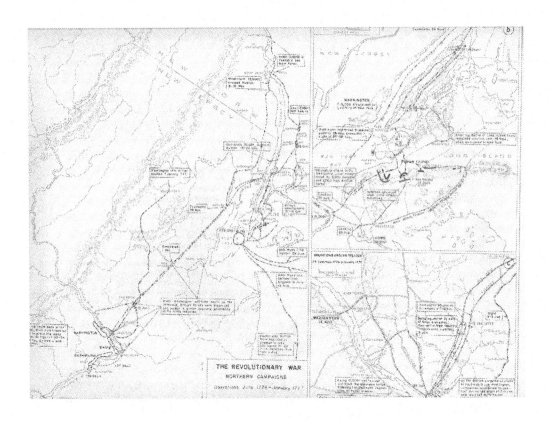

Detailed map of Fort Lee and Fort Washington with British troop movement during the battle in November 1776.

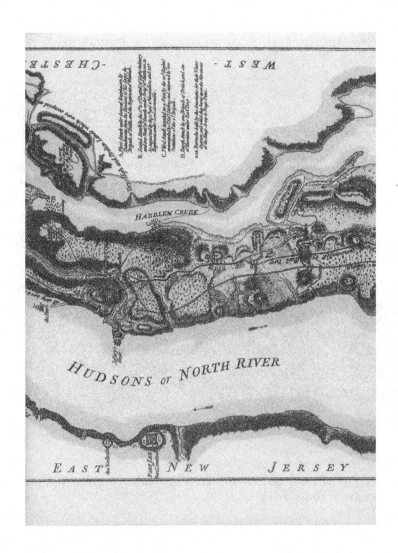

Illustration and map of troop deployment and movement from June 1776 to
January 1777 in particular, during the Battle of Long Island, 27 August 1776.

Present day photo looking across the Hudson River from Fort Lee National Park, NJ. On the New York side is the former location of Fort Washington.

Photo from Fort Lee National Park with the George Washington Bridge in the background.

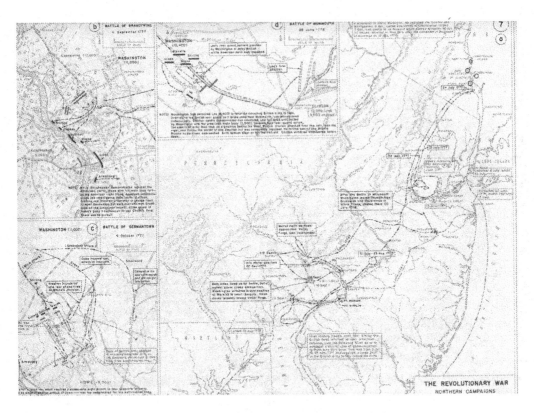

Illustration and map of Northern operations in Pennsylvania and New Jersey from May 1777 to July 1778, in particular, the Philadelphia Campaign.

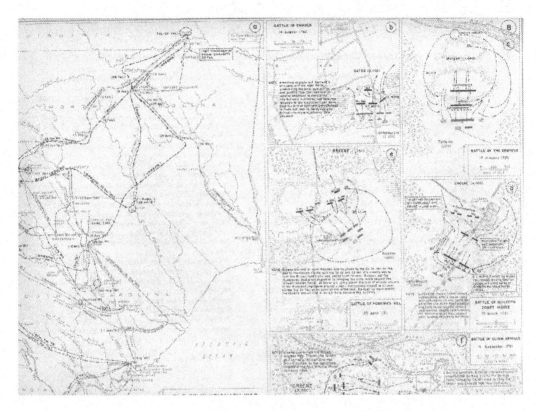

Map of operations in the Southern Campaign, 1778-1783. Note illustrations of British
and American troop movements of battles in the Carolinas

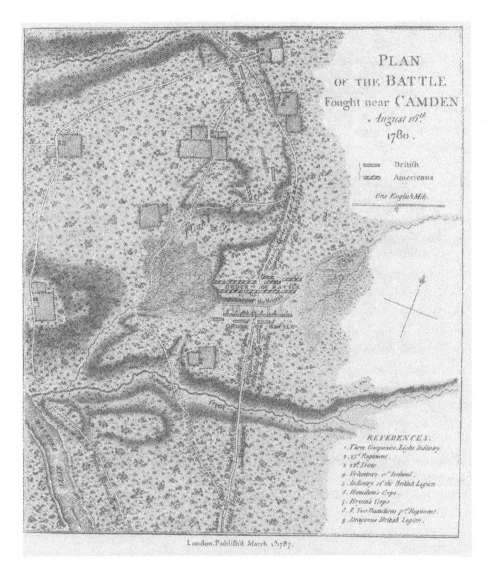

Plan of battle for British and American troops during the Battle of Camden,
16 August 1780.

Copy of the original painting entitled "Female Patriotism – Mrs. Steele & Maj-Gen Nathanael Greene." Painted by Alonzo Chapple in 1784. *Courtesy of Martin, Johnson & Co. Publishers.*

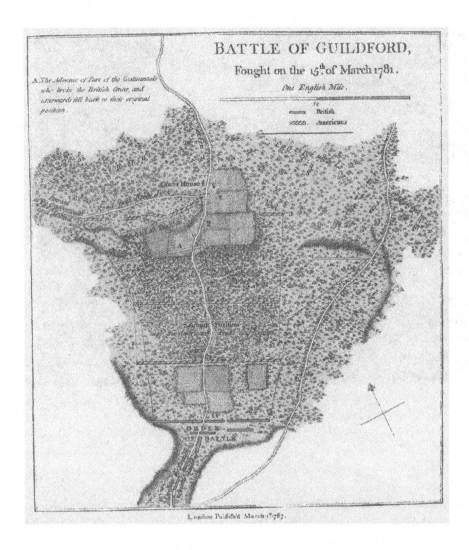

Map of troop deployment and movements during the Battle of Guildford Courthouse, 15 March 1781.

MULBERRY GROVE IN 1794

Copy of the only known illustration of what Greene's Mulberry Grove Plantation
may have looked like in 1794, when Whitney Was developing the cotton gin. *Artist
rendition courtesy of the Mulberry Grove Historical Society.*

Nathanael Greene State Historical Marker

Johnson Square, Bull St., Savannah

Photo of the monument marker near the spot of Nathanael Greene's final resting place. The fifty-foot obelisk at the Greene tomb is located at Johnson Square, Bull Street, Savannah, Georgia.

Chapter XIV

"The Armies Settle-in for the winter."

By late fall of 1778, Washington's army was the largest body of regular troops ever assembled under an American banner. There were 16,782 rank and file fit for duty; of these troops about 11,500 would winter over in White Plains, New York. Also, the army was rearranged to compensate the larger numbers of soldiers. Putnam, Gates, Stirling, Lincoln, De Kalb, and McDougall each commanded a division. Putnam was sent to West Point, De Kalb to Fredericksburg (now Patterson), New York, Gates and McDougall to Danbury, Connecticut, Stirling to a point between Fredericksburg and West Point. The active movement of the campaign now over, Greene was still relegated to the duties of Quartermaster-general. A job he had thrown himself into by now, mainly because he was not all that sure that the war would soon be over on the North American continent. He had theorized that the British would soon end their operations in America and concentrate their efforts in the direction of the West Indies. "A large part of the enemy at New York have embarked," he writes to General Varnum from the camp at Fredericksburg on the 24th of October. "Their destination is unknown. Many conjecture they are bound to Boston. I am rather of the opinion they are going to the West Indies. Another embarkation is said to be getting in readiness. Most people are of the opinion there will be a total evacuation; but I am not of that number. I think they will leave a garrison, if it is but a small one."

Rhode Island, however, he believed would soon be set free by the British. "We have been hourly expecting the arrival of the accounts of the evacuation of Newport," Greene writes to his cousin William Greene, now the Governor of the State. While military questions still received most of his attention and made up the primary subject of his letters, the majority of his physical time was devoted to the duties of the quartermaster department. Forever absorbed by the perplexing job at hand, yet no department in the army was more exposed to malignant criticism. This was mostly due to the direct relations he was forced to pursue with a public purse with private interest. "I thank you kindly," he writes to Henry Marchant from camp, "for your friendly hints upon the state of the Quartermaster's department. I am sensible of the difficulty of conducting such an extensive business without leaving some cause for complaints. Lord Chesterfield, speaking on the ministers of state said it best. They are not as good as they should be, and by no means as bad as they are thought to be. A charge against a quartermaster-general is most like the cry of a mad dog in England. Every one joins in the cry and lends their assistance to pelt him to death. I foresee the amazing expenditure in our department will give rise to many suspicious; and I make no doubt there will be some impositions and many neglects; but the great evil does not originate either in the want of honesty or economy in the management of the business, but in the depreciation of the money and the growing extravagance of the people."

Further accusations of Greene and Wadsworth's improprieties were always in the wind while Greene was involved in the duties of Quartermaster-general of the Army. Accusations that linger even today. But no one could fault the department for what they had accomplished in the past nine months. If improprieties existed, and this author can find nothing concrete, maybe they were done for the good of the men of the army and the cause for which they fought. In the end, the true test of the man is how the army was equipped under his tutelage and the amazing job the agents that worked under his command accomplished in their capacity. To form a correct estimate of the personal sacrifice that

Greene made to accept the office of quartermaster-general, we must remember that he was very ambitious for a place in history, along with the other founding fathers of the time. He constantly wrote to Washington about, "whoever read of a quartermaster in history as such, or in relating any brilliant exploit?" And again he writes to Marchant, "You mistake me if you think I complain of Congress or my friends in it, for not taking a particular notice of me. I freely confess I have never had an honest ambition of meriting my country's approbation; but I flatter myself to have not been more studious of deserving it. However, people are very apt to be partial to themselves; but I have sometimes thought my services have deserved more honorable notice than they have met with, not from Congress, but the army."

That aside, a welcome addition to his stores soon arrived from France. A very large shipment of always needed clothing and shoes arrived. The waistcoats and breeches were all the same color; off-white. But the coats were not all of the same color. The coats all had red facing, but some of them were blue, and the rest brown. Greene immediately assigned them to the different states by lottery: North Carolina, Maryland, New Jersey, and New York drew the blue; Virginia, Delaware, Pennsylvania, Massachusetts, New Hampshire, and Hazen's Canadians received the remaining brown. But it seems that there were more of the blues than the first states had needed, and a second lottery was held. This time, Massachusetts, Virginia, and Delaware were chosen to get the remaining blue coats. Pennsylvania, New Hampshire, and Hazen's Canadians remained with the brown. For the first time in American history the army had the closest attempt of a uniform army dress than had ever been accomplished.

Again the Continental troops huddled in huts for the winter. Unlike the winter at Valley Forge, the huts were better constructed, the men better equipped, and food was more plentiful. It did not hurt that the winter of 78-79 was "remarkably mild and temperate." The only shortage reported was "articles of Blankets and hats." As always, even with the supply the French had recently sent, shoes were always a scarcity. The problem was no longer a shortage of supplies, or even money. Congress had plenty of money for the asking, bushels of it. In fact, there was too much of it. The value of the Continental paper dollars had sunk steadily during the past two years in real value, in purchasing power; and it was still sinking by the spring of 1779. It was so depressed that, as Washington had written after being told by Greene, "a wagon load of money will scarcely purchase a waggon load of provision." Nobody in their right mind was going to exchange good beef or crops for vanishing paper money.

Neither army made any moves or performed any extraordinary feats during the winter of 1778. And with the dawn of another year upon them, the rebellion that many thought would be over within months was now into its fourth year as 1779 began. In early January, Greene joined Washington for a trip to Philadelphia. The object of the Commander-in-chief's visit was most likely to discuss the coming year's plan for its campaign, but also to come to an understanding with them on numerous questions of organization. One of the hot topics was the question of half-pay, in which Washington had supported his cause of the army against men like Samuel Adams and Henry Laurens. With Greene, Washington had a comrade who believed in the same causes as his commander-in-chief, and Washington needed all the support he could muster on such subjects as the ones they were about to debate. Greene writes of their meetings to Colonel Biddle: "The great scarcity of the article of forage produces too general a cry to leave the least doubt of the reality of the thing. I am happy to hear from camp, that the distress with cattle grows less and less. I find the Government and Council will do nothing more than recommend or enforce the old laws; although this is far short of our wishes, yet it is much better to have them with us than against us. The Governor and Council of this State complain that the State is overborne with cavalry and wagon horses. I have got an order for Pulaski's legion to go down into Kent and Sussex in the Delaware State. I don't think it advisable to order in horses out of Salem County in the Jerseys. I drank teas with your good lady and sisters this evening. The spirit of dueling, intrigue, and cabal goes on here as much as ever."

Seventeen hundred and seventy-nine was neither an active nor hopeful year for America and its army. By late December, Congress yielding to the urgent suggestions of Washington, finally gave up the absurd plan of another expedition to Canada. The New Year saw both sides listless in everything but personal schemes and party dissensions. In personal circles, Washington was now treated with confidence and respect. Greene was received with consideration and was always listened to with great attention. But neither man could overcome the inherent sluggishness of a legislative body called upon to perform the functions of an executive body. Members of Congress forever consumed precious time in endless debates when they should have thought only of immediate action. Sounds familiar, doesn't it? But still, after the experience of four years of war, repeating the errors and illusions of these first years should have been paramount in their minds. Recruits who, when the war began, might easily have been secured for the duration of the war, without any expense beyond their food, clothing, and pay, could hardly be obtained now at any price. The draft took the place of voluntary enlistments, but No State dared to enforce drafts for the war, or even for a minimum enlistment's, like three years. So they wound up making the enlistment's for a paltry nine months, and twelve months being the average. Eighteen was the utmost limit. In fact, very few were willing to engage for the war at any terms. To procure recruits Congress offered a bounty of $200. In today's monetary figures that would equate to about $2000. To fill quotas the State government outbid the Congress, so the army was forced to literally be created anew every year. Most of the officers remained year after year, but this meant the men of the rank and file were going off as their terms of enlistment's expired. Steuben's discipline was not thrown away on these men, because it soon became a part of the general military education of the entire country. But his labors still had to be renewed with new recruits at the beginning of every campaign. New recruits meant inexperienced men to replace veterans. This was not a good trade off considering that the British troops remained constant and even gained more experience with each battle fought on the North American continent.

Yet even with all these elements, delays, and distractions, a tolerable preparation might have been made, and the rudiments of discipline imparted to these new recruits before they would be called to the field, if they had been engaged in the campaign season. But, Congress would never do its share of the work at the right time, and so Washington could never have them trained in time. Unwilling to learn from past mistakes, Congress proceeded to make the same error in 1779. Therefore, the same old practices produced the same problems as they did the preceding years of the war. Finally, by the end of January, Washington was given the authority to reopen the enlistment rolls. But it was not until mid March that they called upon the States to fulfill their quotas. Thus, instead of an army that was drilled and ready by campaign time, they had an army that was yet to be raised.

Before long it was late March and everything remained as it had when the armies were well into their winter quarters. We hear little from Greene as well, except that he continued to labor under the guise of quartermaster-general and experience the trials and tribulations about which he often wrote to anyone that would listen. Although the list had grown shorter over his tenure, it was becoming harder and harder to find someone that would listen to his constant tirades. One individual that was saddled with the responsibility of listening whether he wanted to or not was the President of Congress. On the 25th of March 1779 Greene would write, "It has been impossible to obtain returns from the different branches of the Quartermaster's department for want of the necessary forms to direct the business at hand. This I am endeavoring to complete and flatter myself the agents in future will be able to make regular returns once a month. It was late in the season last year before I entered upon the business of this department, and finding it naked, distressed, and in a state of confusion; the wants of the army numerous and pressing; the business multiform and complex; myself and two gentlemen, my assistants, in a great degree strangers to the economy of it; that I have never had either leisure or opportunity to digest it into such form and order as I could wish, and as I conceive necessary for the just information of Congress, and for my own convenience ease, and security."

We can see that frustration must have been a contributing factor in Greene's personality at this time. All of the generals, including Washington, were waiting for something to happen, anything. On the other hand, Washington loved to play the game of contrition and waiting for the British to make a move before he had to. The chance that the enemy would make a wrong or false move was highly likely. After all, Clinton was required to pass most of his ideas and strategies past Parliament before making a move in the first place. Communication between England their troops was slower than people today can imagine. After all, it was made by ship, three thousand miles. The fastest trip may take 6 weeks, but on the average it was more like two months. Hard to fathom when you now can hit a key and send messages almost instantaneously across the globe from New York to Tokyo in this day in age.

Nathanael also missed home and hearth. His affections for his country could not hold a candle to his family. Although he knew the duty he was destined to perform was important. He also knew that family was the only true thing of which you could be sure. We know he kept to his reading, which he loved, but also to keep his mind off his loneliness. He spent a bit of his leisure time with on least a few pages of some favorite author before retreating to his bed, in hopes that the long winter would give way to the coming of spring. He anticipated the reunion and the time of enjoyment he would spend with his friends and family and the indulgence of parties they had missed while faced with the work at hand. That behind them, Nathanael writes to his wife. "The eastern jaunt I am afraid will prove very unfriendly to my wishes, as I am all impatient to see you. Never did I experience more anxious moments. Colonel Cox and Mr. Pettit are gone to Philadelphia. They wish you well and hope to see you this spring in Trenton."

His winter quarters were once more in the Jerseys at Middlebrook, with the division of the army which Washington kept nearest to him. Greene stayed in a house in Pluckemin, just down the road from Washington. Martha Washington was again at headquarters with her husband. By the 1st of April, almost all of the field general's wives were with them in camp. Caty Greene (again without the children), Mrs. Knox, Lady Stirling, and the ever present Lady Kitty. General Lott and his wife were in Morristown, just a carriage ride away and able to partake in any social gathering that may pop-up, which did quite often during the uneventful winter of '78 and spring of '79. "We had a little dance at my quarters a few evenings past," Greene writes to Colonel Wadsworth at the end of March. "His Excellency and Mrs. Greene danced upwards of three hours without once sitting down. Upon the whole we had a pretty little frisk. . . .Miss Cornelia Lott and Miss Betsy Livingston are with Mrs. Greene. This moment they have sent for me to drink tea. I must go."

In February the one-year anniversary of the French alliance was celebrated. But unlike the celebration at Valley Forge the year before, there was no review, but instead a artillery salute, and in addition to the dinner, fireworks and a ball. Washington even got into the spirit, although it was said he loved a good whirl. "There could not have been less than sixty ladies," wrote a correspondent of the "Philadelphia Packet" newspaper, who was present.

But soon, a new problem arose. Somewhat of a delusion was surfacing among the inhabitants of the Colonies and members of the army. "Now that France was with us, and Spain was soon to follow, so it would be impossible for England to continue the war at its long distance from the front." A positive factor that Washington and the army had used to their advantage up until now. Some people were beginning to theorize on a new found idea; and that was England would speedily withdraw her troops from all of the battlefields and transfer them from the continent to the islands surrounding it and its navy into the ocean. Many in Congress therefore reasoned, and not just a few in the army, Greene and Washington not being amongst them, that the enemy did not want to be led into a long, drawn-out war in America. It would be a vain attempt at securing colonies that no longer wanted securing, and a wanton waste of material and human life. The British, it was thought, would play out a sort of blockade, and wait out the rebels. The British would be forgetting that the rebels were almost self-reliant and now had the help of two of the three top navies in the world as allies.

The British had delusions of their own. Now with the French and Spanish cooperation a failure in their books, those involved reasoned that the Americans would see that their allies were unable to protect them. The old hatred of France and Spain, so deeply rooted to their Anglo-Saxon heritage, would be revived. The rebels would gladly accept the terms which they so rashly rejected in their hour of ill founded hope of independence, and returning to their allegiance, unite with their English brethren to crush the common enemy of their past peace and prosperity. To hasten this moment of fantasy, the British leaders resolved to complete the conquest of the Southern States. They would confine their operations in the northern and middle States to such a measure as would most effectively keep alive a constant feeling of insecurity all along the American seaboard from New Orleans to Boston. To begin this new project, England felt is was best to make the colonies feel powerless and that France could not protect them, and in turn make France feel like they would have nothing to hope for from the colonies if they lost confidence. The project was put into motion with Matthew's descent on Virginia in May, Tryon's expedition against Connecticut in July. In both cases, towns were burnt, shipping and stores destroyed and innocent lives lost. These were vain and wanton outrages indeed, but not against the Continental Army, but rather against civilians. By the British carrying out this death and desolation against American citizens, they actually did the opposite of what they were trying to accomplish. For what these atrocities did instead, was only awaken the thirst for vengence in the hearts and minds of Washington and the army and turn civilians that had previously stayed neutral into enemies. This was not the type of propaganda needed for winning back subjects to his majesty King George.

Meanwhile, the Americans held the line along the Hudson, keeping strong positions on both banks, and keeping at least part of their forces within striking distance of the enemy, wherever he might be at the time. But there were no military operations in the north during the winter of 1778, or in the spring of '79. Both armies lay in their winter quarters until the summer months were almost at hand. They seemed to be content playing a waiting game and expecting the other to blink first. Finally, in late May, Clinton made the first move. He assembled 6,000 of his best troops, British and Hessian grenadiers, light infantry, dragoons, Hessian jagers, and Provincial (Tory) regiments including the Simcoe's Queen rangers and Ferguson's corps. They embarked in a fleet of seventy sailing vessels and over one hundred and fifty flat-bottomed boats. On June 1st they landed on both sides of the Hudson by an area known as Stony Point and Verplanck's Point, just below Peekskill.

Washington had been concerned that the British would mount a movement up the Hudson and then try to capture West Point, and so he ordered St. Clair's division up to Springfield, and Stirling and De Kalb's divisions to Pompton. McDougall was already posted in the Highlands with five brigades of Continental troops and two North Carolina regiments. At Stony Point there was a small, unfinished fort with a handful of Americans. While across the river, on Verplanck's Point, lay Fort Lafayette, held by a captain and only seventy North Carolinians. Stony Point was taken quickly and without opposition. The garrison had burned down the blockhouse before fleeing at the approach of the enemy. Fort Lafayette was a small but complete works, with palisades and surrounded by a double ditch and an abatis. Because of the heavy cannon fire from the now captured Stony Point, British troops on the landside, and from the ships in the river, the fort was forced to surrender. The British immediately set about completing the works on Stony Point, a strong natural defensive position.

By July, the works at Stony Point were completed, and Washington knew he had to deal a sharp, quick blow at Stony Point if he was to dislodge the British stronghold there. Washington had been extremely disturbed by the taking of the two points by the British. He called for Anthony Wayne and asked him to employ a trustworthy and intelligent man to go into the British works, if possible, or otherwise find out the nature and strength of the garrison. The job was given to Henry Lee's "most active officer," Allen McLane, an astute and experienced scout. On July 2nd, in company with a Mrs. Smith who wished to see her two sons, presumably members of the garrison, he approached the fort with a flag of truce and was admitted. Wearing the clothes of a simple countryman, McLane was allowed to look about the fort at will and obtained all of the desired information he needed. One item of particular note was that the entrenchment's intended to connect several of the batteries in the inner fort walls were incomplete. On the basis of McLane report, Washington made a plan of attack and gave the command of it to Wayne.

At half past eleven on the 17th of July, the Americans advanced on the southerly side of the fort where the unfinished entrenchments were located. Meanwhile, another, smaller column attacked the front of the outside abatis, keeping up "a perpetual and gauling fire" to make it appear to the garrison inside the fort that this was the main attack, while the real attack was from the south. The garrison took the bait and concentrated their defense on the front. At the same time, the true main column quickly took the southern side, quickly advanced on the second line of abatis with only token resistance, and gained entry into the fort.

Inside the fort was a melee. Bayonet, sword, and spontoon thrust and parried, while the harried defenders began to fire into the mass of the attack. Turmoil reign supreme, with the men of the garrison seeing the battle lost and throwing down their muskets, crying for quarter. Within a half-hour the Americans won the fort. The estimates of losses were severe for the British: 63 killed, more than 70 wounded, and 543 captured. The Americans fared much better; with only 15 killed and 80 wounded. But more important, fifteen field artillery pieces were captured along with a tremendous amount of military equipment and stores.

Washington inspected the captured fort and commented that "it would require more men to maintain it then we can afford." It was therefore concluded that all of the arms and stores would be removed and the works should be destroyed. Soon after the Americans left, Clinton reoccupied the Points, rebuilt the works, and installed a stronger garrison. No military advantage was gained in the battle, beyond the capture of the military weapons and stores. But it was an inspiring display of how far the American army had come from the early days of defeat after defeat, and buoyed the spirit of the general public in the Colonies to their Army. Suddenly, there were whispers in the streets of towns and cities alike, that maybe, just maybe, we could actually win this fight.

The capture of Stony Point made its way to England where it was looked upon as another embarrassing defeat at the hands of the upstart rebels. Charles Stedman, a English historian saw it another way and wrote, "It was an enterprise of difficulty and danger, and the American general, Wayne, who conducted it, deserved great praise for his gallantry . . . as did the troops. . . for their bravery." Several British generals felt the same way and commented on their American foes in kind. General Pattison wrote, "as well as to all acting under orders, no instance of Inhumanity was shown to any of the unhappy Captives. No one was put to the sword or wontonly wounded." Commodore George Collier said, "The laws of war gave a right to the assailants of putting all to death who are found in arms. . .the rebels had made the attack with a bravery never before exhibited, and they showed at that moment a generosity and clemency, which during the course of the rebellion had no parallel." Respect from their enemies at last. The American army was now the British armies equal.

By August, Major Henry Lee, Jr., was the next American officer to "bask in the glory of such an achievement as Stony Point as it was for 'Mad' Anthony Wayne." Like Wayne, "Light-Horse Harry" as he was affectionately known, was never adverse to public recognition. "Stony Point had piqued my emulation." On August 19th, Major Lee attacked the British troops at Paulus Hook, a low-lying, blunt point of sandy land projecting into the Hudson directly opposite of New York City, now part of the State of New Jersey. The British, completely caught by surprise, were overwhelmed and the "men and equipment" soon fell into the Americans hands. Just like Stony Point, there was no significant military value of the attack, except the prisoners and stores that were taken was another inspiration of glory which had been sadly lacking in the prior years of the Revolution. Congress proclaimed, "the country resounded with his praise" for Lee's exploits and responded by presenting Wayne and Lee with a special gold medal for their achievements.

So ended the active military operations of the armies of Washington and Clinton for 1779. Washington would keep his men busy fortifying West Point and drilling them under von Steuben. Clinton, anticipating an intensification of the British effort in the south, abandoned Newport. Cornwallis arrived from England with reinforcements. These, added to the troops from Newport, brought the New York garrison up to 28,756 men, 13,848 of which were British regulars, 10, 836 were Hessian, and 4,072 Provincials. Washington's whole force, "including all troops combined of all sorts" amounted to 27,099 as reported in early November of '79. It was time for Washington to move his troops into quarters for yet another long winter.

Chapter XV

"The Quartermaster-General Retires"

With little going on militarily, Greene was forced to return to the only military duty he despised. It is also the position that Greene would forever be associated with throughout the pages of American History. But in truth, Major-general Nathanael Greene, in his time, was looked upon as the only man that would or could succeed Washington if ever necessary. If that had ever happened, he could have easily received the adoration that was reserved for the second most important man of the entire Revolutionary War. That subject was the office of Quartermaster-general. Now we shall look into the controversy and reasons Greene was labeled in an unjust light for almost two hundred and twenty years.

The difficulties and embarrassments of the department could be traced to four recurring causes. First: The condition of the finances. Second: Congressional delays. Third: The increased expenditure caused by the frequent calling out of the militia and the annual raising of a new army. And Fourth: The decreased interest in the war. The question of finances can be linked to the war of independence being directly connected in form with the question of taxation, that Congress did not and would not dare to begin its financial action by imposing taxes. Unconscious of its real power, which, founded on opinion, was absolute so long as that opinion retained its force, it hesitated where it should have acted, and waited for the public sentiment which it should have formed and led.

So when war came and money was required for the support of an army, instead of calling upon the people by direct taxation, the amount of which can always be estimated, it called upon them by indirect taxation, the amount of which has always outrun the estimate. Money was already scarce, credit abundant, and Congress, forgetting that between credit and money there is a certain proportion which cannot be passed, drew solely upon credit without making the corresponding provision of money. The enthusiasm, which raised the first army, sustained the first issues of Continental bills. But, obeying the natural law of human passion grew cool and languished as the progress of the war, imposing new sacrifices, brought into play its full proportions, the question of personal interest. Depreciation began almost immediately with the introduction of the paper dollar in place of the silver dollar. Men having once stopped to measure their loyalty to the cause by their faith in representation now only had the promise from Congress to pay what was owed, rather than having the hard money in hand. The moral and financial effects of this depreciation were put upon the common people as well as the army.

The first issue of Continental bills was decided in June of 1775, and limited to two million dollars. A third of a million was called for in July; three more in November of that year; five in February of 1776, five in May and five more in July. By the end of 1778 the issues were over a hundred million and by September of 1779, over a hundred and sixty million was called for. It was evident that this course could not be continued much longer, and Congress, in an eloquent and elaborate appeal to the people, pledged itself not to exceed the two hundred million which it had already reached. But when the summing up day came, it was found that, what with forgery by the Tories and with negligence, the limit had been exceeded by over one million dollars.

It was not until the issues had reached nine million that a sensible depreciation began, and even then, it has been questioned, whether the depreciation as manifested by the prices of goods was owing to a loss of credit or to an excess of the paper money. In January of 1777, inflation caused only one dollar and a quarter to a dollar, but by January of 1778, it was four dollars to one dollar. Throughout 1778 it went as high as six for one, but then back to four again, but then quickly rose in January of 1779 from seven to eight and by March to nine to a dollar. By April, it was already twelve, and then by May it was an astonishing twenty-two to a dollar. Throughout the summer and into fall it continued to drop until in November it hit forty-five. Then by December it dropped back to thirty-five and held there well into 1780, but after that it swiftly climbed to its precipice in the spring of 1781 to over one hundred dollars to a single dollar. When in May of 1781, Congress ceased to circulate paper money, although it was still bought up by speculators at four hundred and even one thousand for one.

Various attempts were made by Congress to arrest the progress of depreciation and give stability to the Continental paper currency, all to no avail. From very near the first issue of the bill, merchants refused to accept it as money. In it themselves, was becoming another unknowing enemy to the struggle for the United States to survive. Not as well known, but certainly as important as any attack the British could ever bring against our army at the time.

Equally unfair was the attempt to regulate prices on goods. Conventions met, examined the state of the market, and fixing prices by their own estimate of values, required everyone to accept the regulated price for all articles needed by the army and not actually required for domestic use. But the natural law of supply and demand refused the control of human enactments. Many injustices were perpetrated, many wrongs and losses were suffered, yet the attempt to regulate prices, like the attempt to create value to the goods, failed miserably.

At last an effort was made, in 1779, to form a sinking fund by calling upon the states for their quota of fifteen million dollars for that year and six million annually for the eighteen years that followed. The day of enthusiasm for the cause had passed, and the states did not answer with the willingness expected. There was one resource left to try. Over two hundred million in bills were in circulation. It was useless to think of redeeming them at their nominal value. But it was resolved to call them in by taxes at the ratio of forty for one, cancel them, and issue a new paper, one of the new for every twenty of the old, the whole redeemable species at the end of six years, bearing an interest of five percent. Of this new issue, six million were to be divided between the states, four million to be subject to the order of Congress, and the final payment to be made by the states in due proportion, under the guarantee of the United States. Some hopes were raised, and a good amount of curiosity to see if it would work. Men and women had come to look with great doubt upon the financial skill of Congress, and few were surprised when the trial showed, like every other attempt to pump life into a dead currency, but it came up short.

One bright spot was that some money had been raised by domestic loans, through loan offices, which were opened for that sole purpose in the different states. Some sale of the currency drawn on by Benjamin Franklin and other diplomatic agents in Europe, in anticipation or realization of foreign loans, some by lottery, some by taxes, and some by the sale of confiscated estates. But none of these resources was sufficient, either by itself or in conjunction with the others. The expenses of the government were constantly in advance of the spent receipts, and even the most zealous patriots felt that if they would make provision for their wives and children, they must not entrust their money to the keeping of Congress.

In turn, Congress did their best, in the conscious of real power, to try and throw the responsibility of action onto the states. The states brought in slowly and reluctantly their quota of taxes. To lighten their task while it made an attempt to make the tax payments, states in New England decided they would use corn and cattle to make payments of taxes and public contracts, the way states like Virginia, Maryland, and North Carolina had used tobacco in the past. An elaborate table of the wants of the army was prepared, and each state was called upon to fill its proportion of the army's necessary supplies.

The inherent defects of such a system quickly manifested itself. Disputes arose between State Officers and the officers of the United States. Questions concerning transportation gave rise to innumerable difficulties and delays, and when these had been overcome and the articles did finally reach camp, they were often found to be woefully deficient in quantity and especially low in quality. "Every day's experience," wrote Washington after a full and fair trial, "proves more and more, that the present mode of obtaining supplies is the most uncertain, expensive, and injurious that could be devised."

No one felt the burden of depreciation more than the people who were dependent on salaries and stipulated pay. The clergy suffered greatly, and in most cases their parishioners shared a large portion of the loss and were then effected themselves by trying to remedy the situation by supplementing the salary of the clergymen. In the case of the army, we find that in 1780, the pay of a Major-general would not hire an express rider, nor the salary of a captain allow him to buy himself a pair of shoes. Looking at the cost of items at that time, we find that a hat (typical tricorns used by soldiers) cost as much as four hundred dollars and a suit of clothes (pair of breeches, waistcoat, and coat) cost sixteen hundred.

People from all walks of life were becoming discontented with the inevitable consequences of the depreciation of the currency. Merchants and citizens would ask, "What compensation can we expect from our goods or labor? Soldiers would ask, "we have no clothing or food now, what is to keep us from not having either in the future? With all of these factors, the task of the Quartermaster-general must have bordered on the impossible and his relationship with the citizens and the men with whom he served must have been extremely difficult on a daily basis.

When Greene took the office, every part of it was in complete confusion. The public stores were wasted, articles essential to the comfort and protection of the troops were scattered along the road, discarded when the troops passed by, debts accumulated, and accounts neglected. The former quartermaster-general, Thomas Mifflin had seen the writing on the wall and had dealt with the problem as best he saw fit. He walked away and did nothing, said nothing. To meet demands of his situation, Greene took a more direct route to combat the shortfall of the department; he made constant calls to Congress and the Board of War for authority, for explanations, and for money. This route would bring him into conflict with the second cause for his embarrassment and expulsion from the ranks of the other historic heroes, Congressional delays.

It was one of the chief misfortunes of Congress of the Revolution that it was both a legislative and an executive body. Committees and boards administered laws that it made, on a whole. A habit of careful examination in making a law, usually turned into exhaustive discussions that became fatal in the end, and opposed the habits of prompt decision making and vigorous enforcement which were required for the execution of a law. Both Washington and Greene found it impossible to bring Congress to look at questions from the same point of view as themselves, the point of view that usually was associated with quick and responsive action. And so, month after month was lost in endless debate, and the debate had no power to enlighten, only the power to delay needlessly. Washington and Greene's letters are filled with humiliating and frustrating illustrations of this. We find it constantly forcing the two men to try any means at their disposal to try and rectify the stalemate. This only brought more frustration onto them from Congress.

Underlying all of those causes was the third act that diffused problems for all of them combined and that was the lack of enlistment's for the duration of the war. We have already peered into the necessity of preparing year by year the materials that were needed to wage war. All of them become a mute point if you do not have the necessary men to fight your battles in that war. Congress waited too long to come to grips with that fact. Not only with the enlisted men, but also among the officers who were needed to pass on the personal knowledge needed by their men. Continuity is a major factor in the training of troops even today. Numbers are not enough if they are not trained properly or experienced enough to have the knowledge of their appointed jobs when the time comes to use the knowledge they were either taught or gained in battle. Continuity was lost with the constant turnover of men, from the short enlistment terms and the annual bounty calls. Officers seemed to be constantly training men and marching them into battle month after month, only to watch helplessly as they walked out of camp at the end of their relatively short enlistment's, and then had to start all over again and train the new recruits that took their place. To further complicate the issue, there was reckless waste and consumption of necessary stores by militiamen and raw recruits that never saw a battle, causing rifts in camp between the new recruits and veterans and in turn undermining the entire moral sense of the camp community. This caused a drain on the officer's mental state and forced hundreds to walk out of camp in disgust, thus causing a hole in the chain of command infrastructure, resulting in raw officers teaching raw recruits. It was a deadly combination that bore witness in battle after battle between 1775 and 1778.

And last, but not least, we had the public at large who were quite tired of the war by 1777. The errors and dissension of Congress had destroyed any confidence which that body had inspired prior to and including 1776. Efforts, which had seemed a natural tribute for a good citizen in the first year of the struggle, seemed only to be questionable sacrifices by the fourth year. The raw enthusiasm, which had once made the members of Congress almost God-like, was completely gone. When the people were subjected to sudden invasions, like Knyphausen's into New Jersey, it showed that Congress and the army lacked the needed power and fortitude to protect the common peoples interest and well being. Their competency was now held in question and Congress and the army's credibility were weakened. The results were that supplies became hard to procure, taxes were almost impossible to collect, and the ranks of the army hard to fill. "We have now obtained military knowledge in an eminent degree," writes Duane to Washington in September 1780, "we have internal resources and reputation abroad; we have a great and respectable ally; of what then are we destitute but vigor and confidence in government, and public spirit in individuals?"

We remember how reluctantly Greene had accepted the office of quartermaster-general, and how burdensome he had found the duties through 1778 and 1779. There wasn't a day in either of those years at which point Greene would not have gladly transferred his commission to anyone whom Washington would have chosen in his stead. But the reasons that Greene accepted the position in the first place still existed in full force. It was necessary that the man, who shouldered the weight of "if and when" the army moved depended, had the full confidence of the Commander-in-chief at all times. Throughout the war, no one possessed Washington's confidence as much as Greene did. No one.

At the beginning of the winter of 1779 and 1780, it became evident that a change must be made in the powers of Quartermaster-general, and in the relationship of Congress. The true position of the department was never fully understood by either the people or Congress. Men were always ready to scream that the quartermaster department was conducted on a scale of dangerous extravagance. They were never prepared to show that with prices at their actual scale, and with a currency daily sinking in value, though still unchanged in name, its necessary work could have been done for much less. Few knew what the nature and extent of that work actually was, including all of "the details of the movement of the troops," or all the details of encampment and the quarters, or that it extended to a thorough exploration of the field of operations. This included the opening and repairing of all the roads on the line of advance and retreat, the building of bridges, the facilities for obtaining the means of transportation by water and land. If supplies were not to be had by the usual avenues, the responsibility of finding those supplies by forage or any means available fell to the quartermaster department. In fact, every provision possible for the army to march with ease, or encamp with convenience and safety was the responsibility of the quartermaster department. It should have been evident to every thinking man alive that such a job could not be performed without the help of several branches of government, local authorities, or the complete cooperation of the people of the United States. But it was not, and Greene bore the lion's share of blame every time some pint-sized merchant complained that he had not received proper compensation for the goods he had provided to that department.

Various attempts were made by Congress to correct the errors of their system. As early as November, 1778, Greene had written, "Whereas, It has become necessary not only that speedy and vigorous measures should be taken to regulate the Commissary's and Quartermaster's departments, but also that a constant attention should be paid to those departments: Resolved, that Mr. Scudder, Mr. G. Morris, and Mr. Whipple be a committee to superintend the same departments, and that they or any two of them, be empowered to take such steps relating to the same as they shall think most for the public service."

By May, 1779, the Board of the Treasury reported---"That in their opinion it will be impracticable to carry on the war by paper emissions at the present enormous expenses of the Commissary-general's, Quartermaster-general's, and medical departments; that it appears to them that a general opinion prevails that one cause of the alarming expense in these departments arises from allowing commissions to the numerous persons employed in purchasing for the army, and that a very general dissatisfaction has taken place on the account among the citizens of these United States; and that in their opinion it is necessary to put these departments on a different footing with regard to the expenditure of public money." The problem was they continued to buy on credit. Credit is fine, as long as you have currency to ultimately pay the bill. But, because of the constant change in the currency's value, many suppliers would demand payment when the currency was at its best value, and Congress just made more money to pay and only compounded the problem of inflation. The attempt to fix the problem failed and it was time to try again.

The next attempt was made in January, 1780, a new "commission of three" was formed to resolve the problem, one of whom was soon to become a member of Congress, and was given ample power to inquire into the condition and approbation of Washington, just what reform might be deemed necessary. Schuyler, Pickering, and Mifflin were the three men chosen for the committee. Mifflin as a committee member who was given the duty of fixing the quartermaster department was an odd choice at best. He was almost single handily responsible for the problems Greene now faced. It was if Congress were giving the reins of a runaway wagon to the man who had made the wagon a runaway in the first place. To complicate matters, Washington and Greene had been the individuals who quashed the infamous "cabal" to which Mifflin was a party. It was hard to believe that feelings had healed in that matter.

Before long, more committees were formed to assist the original committee. "It was then proposed that the committee should consist of one member from each State. The head of this committee was to be Matthews of South Carolina; known to have a deep and unfavorable dislike for Greene, the reason lost in time. They immediately set upon the task of "their attention to the business committed to them, in their plan for the arrangement of the staff department." This job concluded, the duty of "establishing a new system for the direction of the Quartermasters department and the Commissary-general issue in the discharge of their duties, and the third point at the regulation of the hospital department." The committee was directed to "pay particular attention. Public business is in a wretched train. All things at stand; and we don't believe the great departments of the army will be organized for a month to come." Those steps showed it could not be accomplished without the cooperation of Greene.

On the 12th of December Greene would write to the President of Congress, "It has been my wish for a long time to relinquish the office of Quartermaster-general. This is the close of the second campaign since I engaged in the duties of this office, and I feel a degree of hapiness in having it in my power to say with confidence that every military operation, whether in the main army or in any detachment, has been promoted and supported, as far as it depends upon this department. The Commander-in-chief has given me the most ample testimony of his approbation; and the success in every other quarter sufficiently evinces the ample provision that has been made."

Chapter XVI

"Another Hard Winter Encampment"

Another winter was upon the armies and Washington would have to find quarters yet again. Again, the question of enlistments would surface. A question that Washington was tired of trying to answer. Only 14,998 were enlisted for three years or the duration of the war; the remaining enlistments were expiring from month to month. Washington, writing to Congress proclaimed, "supposed Troops borne on Muster Rolls, were either in service, or really in existence, for it will ever be found for obvious reasons, that the amount of an army on Paper will greatly exceed its real strength."

Soon, Washington would face another problem of utmost importance. D'Estaing had taken his thirty-seven ships, his 2,000 guns, and his 4,000 men to besiege Savannah, Georgia. When his final attack there was beaten off, he raised the siege, sent some of his ships to the West Indies, and with the rest, sailed for France. Washington had been expecting d'Estaing for two weeks. He wrote to Lafayette, "we have been in hourly expectation of seeing Count d'Estaing off Sandy Hook." A month later he received the bad news. He immediately began to arrange for his troops to form winter quarters. Some would remain in Danbury, Connecticut, to have "an eye on the Sound towards Norwalk, Fairfield, &ca," the cavalry would be quartered near by. Four Massachusetts brigades would remain at West Point and a number of North Carolina and New York corps would be sent to New Jersey near Suffern, with Lee's Legion posted in Monmouth. But the main army would move to Morristown as they did the year before.

Meanwhile, Greene had remained inactive and participated in a few uneventful occurrences, but overall it had been a hard, annoying, thankless bit of labor for Nathanael. The Quartermaster's department was constantly besieged with relations that were more or less connected with personnel of questionable interest. The interest always seemed to be their interest, rather than the army's or the country's, and so was a constant source of restlessness to Greene. In spite of all the precautions he could muster, some of his agents became untrustworthy, and here again, the blame fell upon him. Greene always tried to make sure that the purchases and the contracts corresponded. But sometimes the samples that Greene had been shown by the contractor did not match up with the item that was promised and then delivered. With only the money of the fixed and recognized value, some purchases may have looked like they had been made for the advantage of the suppliers, but in other cases, the same could be said about Greene and his fellow quartermaster agents. Another problem Greene ran into was the cost of transportation at reasonable rates. Wagon companies knew they had the army at a disadvantage, because in most cases they were forced to use the local transportation because of the lack of their own. And so, transportation rates were astronomical. The money that Greene received was usually slated for only purchases of supplies and did not include transportation cost. Washington wrote to Greene in November, "But I am under no apprehension of a capital injury from any other source than the depreciation of our Continental money. This indeed is truly alarming, and of so serious a nature that every other effort is vain unless something can be done to restore its credit." To obtain an adequate supply of items needed for the department, Greene would have to use the depreciated currency. The same currency whose value would not allow forty-five dollars in Continental paper money to buy the same amount as one in silver. This caused the people to begin accusing the Quartermaster-general and his agents of "profuse and wanton expenditure."

The delays and hesitations of Congress hampered the system further. At a time and place where circumstances called for quick and timely decision making, the opposite was usually the case. Day after day and week after week would be wasted in profitless debates and discussion. Greene's, as well as Washington's letters of this time are peppered with evidence of these fundamental errors in these Congressional policies.

Heavy demands had been made on the country's natural resources since 1775, and the faith and resolve of the people were being severely tested. Foresight, the rarest and probably the most essential element of statesmanship, was woefully lacking in this time since the beginning of the war as well. It certainly was a noble sacrifice to break off ties with the mother country and renounce the luxuries of English manufactures. But after four years, the voluntary self-denial of the people was beginning to grow old. The lack of factory supplied goods was not only being felt by the civilians, but with the army as well. A few years of extensive and general imports would have secured enough supplies to carry an well-armed and clothed army through at least the first half of the war. In 1775, at the siege of Boston, the army nearly ran out of powder. Knox was forced to bring cannon down from Ticonderoga in the middle of December. It was no surprise when the Continental army celebrated endlessly when they captured a few military store transports early on in the war.

But as the war continued, occasional supplies came from France, and each new arrival was greeted with the same joy they had exulted when they captured supplies from the enemy. Industry was not a problem. There was the proper skilled labor and iron to manufacture arms. They had enough materials to produce powder. The farmers had two years of abundant yield to furnish enough grain and livestock for daily nourishment. And only a few years of hindsight could have produced the necessary supplies to enter into a war. But hindsight being 20/20, it is quite easy to judge over two hundred and twenty-two years later I suppose.

By mid January 1780, Greene had still not heard from Congress about his resignation. By the 22nd of January and with still no response from Congress, Greene decided to voice his displeasure with another letter to President Reed of Congress, "I did myself the honor to address Congress the 12th of last month on the subject of my reseigning the Quartermaster's department, as well as upon many other matters respecting the same. A whole month is now elapsed since I wrote, and I have not been favored with a reply. If I did not conceive that the public interest suffers from a delay, I should feel less anxiety upon the occasion; but when I view the alarming crisis to which things are drawing, and the necessity there is of applying a remedy before the evil becomes incurable, I cannot help pressing an answer."

One of the reasons Greene was not receiving the courtesy he was entitled was that Congress had passed Greene's correspondence to the new commissioner to such issues, Thomas Mifflin. Greene could not expect any return correspondence from the likes of Mifflin. So, still in the dark, but now embarrassed too, Greene decides to bypass channels and writes another letter on the 9th of February. This time addressed directly to President Reed. "Sir, You were kind enough, when you were at camp, to promise to give me full information what measures were adopting by Congress respecting the Quartermaster's department. I have been impatiently waiting the arrival of a letter from you; if there is no new objection to my receiving this necessary information through your means, you will do me the favor of preserving your first intention, as the intelligence you give can be more depended upon than from any other quarter."

Reed answered Greene on the 14th, "I had neither forgot or neglected my promise, when I had the pleasure of seeing you, but was prevented by two reasons; first, that I really could not find out what was doing at the civil head-quarters with sufficient certainty, and secondly, that I expected you daily here in town. I am almost afraid to commit to paper my real and undisguised sentiments on the present state of affairs with which you are so specially connected. I am fearful of trusting anything in so hazardous a channel. However, I will venture to tell you that you have nothing to expect from public gratitude or personal attention, and that you will do well to prepare yourself at all points for events. General Mifflin's appointment to his present office, without including the heads of the department, is a sufficient comment on my text, and by your letter I find you understand it as I do. In my opinion you ought not to delay an explanation on your affairs; if a tub is wanted to the whale you are as likely to be it as any. A torrent of abuse was poured on Wadsworth, but that has all died away, as ill grounded and unjust calumny ever will. I think he was a valuable officer, and wish they may not feel his loss. Your particular situation will enable you to leave the department not only without discredit, but your station in the line will preserve a certain respect which in other circumstances might be wanting. Whoever is quartermaster this year must work, if not mircles, at least something very near it, for I verily believe there will be not a shilling where pounds are wanted. Whatever you do or resolve must be done soon or you will be plunged in another campaign without any possiblity of retreat, and though the circumstances I have above alluded to is a favorable one, it is impossible to envy your situation; for whether you move or stand still, it may be improved to your disadvantage. If you quit, they will say that having made a large fortune you quit the department in distress when you could be of most service to your country. If you stand fast, you become responsible for measures and events morally impracticable. If an honorable retreat can be effected, it is beyond doubt your wisest and safest course; but I am not certain that this can be done even now, and every hour adds to the difficulty. When things go wrong, no matter where the wrong bias is given, every one concerned finds a pleasure in shifting the blame on his neighbor, or at least to divide it. Upon the whole I still retain my opinion of your being here as soon as possible, and in the meantime can only inform you of two things with certainty. 1st. That the plan of the department will be altered as to commissions. 2d. That nothing but necessity will induce them to continue the present department, for though it may have a great deal of the utile it has little of the dulce on the palate of Congress. But you will be drilled on till the campaign opens, and if they cannot do better, they may keep you."

A letter from Mr. Pettit the next day gives Greene some much-needed hope that the intentions of Congress may not be as unfavorable as President Reed had painted it.
"I have lately had conversation with some of the members of Congress whom I esteem free from intrigue, and who I believe, to be our friends respecting your resignation. They seem to think that if Congress accept your resignation it will be merely to gratify your desires, but that they really wish you to continue, and so of your assistants. The latest commission was not intended to offend you or the General, and they were told that the particular person in question would be acceptable and pleasing at head-quarters."

Greene was somewhat relieved by Pettit's letter of the situation, but things did anything but calm down. Greene was still Quartermaster-general and had work to do. Prices everywhere kept pace with the depreciation of the currency and the goods rose in the markets to the point that it took four hundred dollars to buy a hat, and sixteen hundred to buy a suit of clothes. Merchants organized conventions to discuss the problem and come up with solutions to get a fixed scale of prices. They tried, but failed miserably.
It was time for Congress to get involved, and laws were made to obey the natural laws of commerce versus the unnatural laws of restraint in profits. But Congress did not have the power to enforce the laws passed. States would pass laws for the sole purpose of protecting their own citizens, without any regard for the necessity of the military, thoughtlessly setting up individual interest in direct opposition to the general interest, and exposing the military service to a dangerous collision with the civil service. Because of this, the Quartermaster's department often demanded labor and materials when there was no money to pay them. State laws therefore required that payment be made before services could be rendered. Because of that stipulation, more than once it was impossible to feed the cattle and horses attached to the army, and essential for the transportation of its baggage and stores. In turn the thankless

job of labor and unfounded suspicion was chiefly the burden of the Quartermaster's department. "We indeed have a thankless task," wrote Greene that winter, "with difficulties and prejudices innumerable to contend with."

And as month after month passed, and the difficulties increased, Greene stopped hoping for relief by Congress. "Congress I am told," he writes, "have appointed another committee on finance. But in all matters of this sort the members themselves have such scattered and heterogenous ideas that none of them can form a tolerable judgement beforehand what will be the result of any motion or measure set on foot. . . . When necessity presses so hard that something or other must be done, they will then and not before, take some course by way of temporary expedient, trusting, as usual, to accident for the past."

Thus, another dreary winter was upon the American army. The severest and coldest of all eight winters of the war. Even worst than the one at Valley Forge. At the start of a new decade, on the 3rd of January 1780, there was a great snowstorm. Canvas tents and marquees were pushed over like twigs, and buried men and officers under the sheets like an avalanche. "My comrades and myself," says Thacher, "were roused from our sleep by the calls of some men for assistance; their marquee had been blown down, and they were almost smothered in the storm before they could reach our marquee, only a few yards away." No man could endure the violence of the storm for more than a few minutes without endangering his life. When the storm finally subsided, all of the roads were blocked and the fields covered by drifts reported to be "15 to 20 rods high." "We ride over the fences," writes Greene the next day, "but for a timely supply of straw, men and officers would have frozen to death; but by spreading their blankets on the straw, kindling large fires at their feet, and piling all the clothes they could collect over them, they succeeded in preserving warmth enough for life; comfort was beyond their reach. The poor soldiers with their single blanket, scanty clothing, and often naked feet, fared harder still."

Famine, too, reared its ugly head once again during a winter encampment. The snow, four, six, and by one account eight feet deep on the ground around them and constant snowdrifts at least twelve feet, had completely cut them off from their supplies. "The army at Morristown is upon the point of disbanding for the want of provisions," writes Greene to Colonel Hathaway, "the poor soldiers having been several days without, and there not being more than sufficiency to serve more than one regiment in this magazine. This is, therefore, to request you to call upon the militia officers and people of your battalion to turn out their teams and break the roads between this and Hackettstown, there being a small quanity of provisions there that cannot come on until this is done. Give no copy of this, for fear it should get to the enemy."

"What a winter is this!" writes Colonel Wadsworth from Hartford. "The Sound all frozen up; nothing can come into New London; the ice reaches out to the sea at Rhode Island." And Washington writing to Lafayette saying, "The severity of the frost exceeds anything of the kind that had ever been experienced in this country before. We have had the virtue of the army put to the severest test."

Badly fed and badly clothed, with starvation staring them in the face day after day, the soldiers did not feel they should be subjected to this two times in three years. Depreciation of the money had reached its lowest point. Even if the troops could spend their pay, the money was little more use than waste paper for the privies. If all of that wasn't enough, the Tories had successfully introduced a large amount of forged Continental currency. The end of enlistment's were steadily growing from week to week, forcing Congress to call upon each state to fill their own quotas. But some states could provide well for their troops, and others could not. And so when the men from all states were called on to enlist, the ill-provided soldiers envied the soldiers from the fortunate states and could not help feel as if the government had let them down as to be sent for equal service, only to be unequally rewarded in camp.

A great discontent was growing among the troops in Morristown. Those that had enlisted for the war, were now finding themselves deprived of the bounties that were being offered to the men who were engaged for limited terms of enlistment's, in order to get them to re-enlist again. At Washington's suggestion, a gratuity of $100 was given to all of the men who had "enlisted for the war previous to the 23rd of January, 1779. Still, many of the men evaded signing up in the hope of securing the state awarded bounties, and some went so far as to appeal to the civil authorities for protection. Washington, with his usual temperate firmness, explained the matter to Governor Livingston, and there the matter ended. "Certain I am," Washington explained, "unless Congress speak in a more decisive tone, unless they are vested with powers by the several States competent to the great purposes of war, or assume them as matter of right, and they and the States respectively act with more energy than they hitherto have done, than our cause is lost."

As bad as the suffering was in the horrible winter of 1780, it brought with it a single ray of good fortune. The rivers and bays were frozen, and the ice was so thick the heaviest cannon could be carried over it without as much as a groan from the ice. "A detachment of cavalry marched from New York to Staten Island on the ice." New York was no longer an island. "All is continent," wrote Knyphausen." The British ships which had been the protection at the double waterfront for years, were now frozen in at their moorings, and in anticipation of a sudden attack by the rebels, parts of the crews were drawn from the ships to serve on shore. "Nature," writes Greene, "has given us a fine bridge of communication with the enemy, but our men are too weak to take advantage of it."

One diversion, commanded by Stirling, was when a detachment of 2,500 men in over five hundred sleighs, crossed the snow into Staten Island for a surprise attack on the enemy's camp. But the enemy was less than surprised; they retreated to their strongholds, and nothing came out of the effort beyond the capture of a handful of prisoners, some tents, arms, and other assorted loot. Against that, Stirling reported, "6 men killed and 500 slightly frozen."

Winter wore slowly away amid anxious cares and hopes for the upcoming campaign. Martha Washington, Caty Greene, and the ever-present Mrs. Knox were again by the side of their husbands. This time, although Mrs. Greene again traveled without the children, they were not without a child to take care of. For while in Morristown, the Greene's celebrated the arrival of their second son, Nathanael Ray Greene. For the first time, Nathanael Greene was present at the birth of his third child, and was given the honor of holding his son at birth, rather than with the other children who did not see their father till they were each almost a year old.

However, Greene's happiness was short-lived. Problems within the quartermaster-general's department reared its ugly head yet again. By late February a Rhode Island delegate, John Collins, wrote to Greene, "I have not heard any mention of your resignation since my return to Congress. Neither have I heard of any new arrangements in your department; neither do I think there will be any soon." Congress remained oddly silent on the matter, and some of Greene's friends urged him to go to Philadelphia and try to see for himself what their intentions might be and to lobby for his own personal application. He hesitated, because he felt that such a step might only be construed as a wish for him to retain his office, which couldn't be farther from the truth. Colonel Pettit felt, "I do not think the objection is a whole conduct that may manifest a real desire for you to quit the department whenever you can do it without injury to the public; they cannot, therefore, find any ground to charge you with intriguing to keep it in opposition to your profession."

Greene's position on the matter became increasingly more embarrassing, as continued reports circulated about Greene's influence of personal enmity and in other cases a complete misrepresentation of his beliefs came forward. While Greene deliberated over what to do next, he received a letter from Schuyler. In it were all of the items that confirmed Greene's views on the intentions of Congress. It was becoming increasingly evident that Congress was not going to supply an immediate answer to his letter of resignation, although a draft of it was reported to be circulating within the halls of Congress. The latest draft had been referred to Mifflin's committee once again. When they would act upon it was anybody's guess. Greene resolved, with great reluctance, to try and gain an avenue to Congress by representing himself on a personal order rather than the professional one he had been using up until now. "I shall set out early in the morning for Philadelphia," he writes to Washington on the 22nd of March, "but can plainly see little is expected from it, unless it is dismissing myself from the department, which I devoutly wish, as well from what I discover from General Schuyler's letter to your Excellency and myself, and from what he relates to Dr. Cochran. I am confident there is a party business going on again, and as Mifflin is connected with it, doubt nothing of its being a renewal of the old scheme; and the measures now taking is to be prepared to take advantage of any opening the distresses of the army may introduce. I propose to take Colonel Biddle with me, that clear, full, and particular representation may be made of every branch of the Quartermaster's department, and the whole be brought to a speedy issue."

That letter was written on a Thursday evening. By Wednesday of the next week Greene wrote to Washington from Philadelphia. " Yesterday I finally had a conference with a committee of Congress. The public is insolvent to all intents and purposes. The treasury is without money, and the Congress are without credit. The best people who are in Congress think the new system for drawing supplies from the States, will be found totally incompetent to the business. There is a new arrangement of the Quartermaster's department made by Mifflin and others, and now under consideration before Congress for adoption. The scheme is so complex and tedious for such heavy and pressing demands as are frequently made on the department, that many think it will starve the army within ten days. I am told it is to be confirmed without alteration. It would add greatly to your Excellency's load of business and reduces the duties of the Quartermaster-general himself to almost nothing. It is thought by others, and General Schuyler is amongst them, that the plan of Mifflin's is to injure your Excellency's operations. I shall take no hasty steps in the business of the Department, as I think myself in a disagreeable situation."

The days in Philadelphia passed painfully slow for Greene, and his health began to suffer from the stress. By the 31st of March he wrote a heartfelt note to President Reed explaining the evils he feared were at work on the quartermaster's department issue. He thought that more damage lay ahead if it continued, and feared the new law of the State, which forbade the purchase of forage by the officers of the department, would be detrimental to the army. He also wrote a letter to Washington basically outlining the same issues, and how supporting the army by specific supplies, pointing out its evils and dangers, and how the total failure of the new arrangement could soon finish the army in no time. This deep perception and sound judgment of Greene's would soon show itself to all, and how it so often had in the past. He did not stop there. He wrote another letter, this time to Roger Sherman, outlining briefly the subject of his difficulties. In it he insisted that Congress send a committee to headquarters to study the effects of the quartermaster department on the men and to judge on the spot the question of revamping the department to the degree they were discussing.

He then wrote one more letter to Congress, but probably should have thought twice about this one. "Immediately on the close of the last campaign I communicated to Congress my inclination to decline the management of the Quartermaster's department, and at the same time made a pretty full representation of some new regulations necessary to take place for the well conducting of that department. Several other letters to the same purpose were written in the course of the winter, all which remained unanswered until I set out for this city. The business by this had got so deranged, and the opening of the campaign so near at hand, that his Excellency the Commander-in-chief urged the necessity of my repairing immediately to Congress, and to endeavour to bring the several subject-matters which had been laid before them respecting the department to a full explanation and conclusion. I have been waiting a full week for an answer, but as I find I am not likely to obtain one, and as I conceive my attendance is no longer necessary here, I propose to set out for camp the next day after to-morrow and there await the issue of the business."

Needless to say, when the letter was read, it was met with mixed emotions. "A resolution was proposed," Schuyler writes to Washington on the 5th of April, "that Congress has the full confidence in General Greene's integrity and ability, and requesting his future exertions. This brought on much debate; amendments were moved, and the House got into many heated debates; so strongly that an adjournment was deemed necessary to give the members time to cool. A member, more zealous for the General's reputation than prudent, observed that he was an officer in whom the Commander-in-chief had the highest confidence. He mentioned that he felt Greene was the first of all such subordinate generals in point of military knowledge and ability; that in case of an accident happening to General Washington, he would be the likely person to command the entire army; and that General Washington agreed. Another participant mentioned that he had a very high opinion of General Greene's military abilities, but that he believed no person on earth was authorized to say as much as the words scored implied. I will entreat General Greene to remain a day or two longer in town, that I may be able to advise with him on the measures necessary to prevent the ill consequences of his being driven to the necessity of resignation, which I conceive would be ruinous at this present conjuncture."

On the 5th Greene writes one last letter to Congress, proposing a method for settling the accounts of the department, in such a way as to meet all of the difficulties arising from the new method of supply they were proposing. And then, a very dissatisfied and frustrated Greene returned to Morristown. On his arrival, he finds that the army's chief supply of meat in Bucks County Pennsylvania has run dry. Without it, the army would go hungry in days. The major stumbling block at purchasing the beef again points to the farmer's dissatisfaction with Congress paying their bills. Credit had been cut off and the farmers demanded cash for the herds, and Greene did not blame them. He did, of course, blame someone else. "I have just received a note from Major Burnet (Greene's aide) requesting me to have a gallery built for the reception of the ambassador from France. I cannot comment on how many plains this request is improper, and it is not my power to do it for the want of boards. There is plenty in this county and not far from this, but they cannot be had without cash to purchase them."

The next day Greene writes a pointed letter to Reed. "My situation has become peculiarly disagreeable, and I have a most delicate and critical part to act. If I force myself out of the department, and any great misfortune happens, no matter from what cause, it will be chargeable to my account. If I stay in it, and things go wrong, or any failure happens, I stand responsible. What to do or how to act I am at a loss. I think upon the whole your advice is prudent, and on the safer side of the question. And therefore I determine to seek all opportunities to get out of the business."

As for the other business of the army, particularly on the war side, there were a few other unimportant forays on both sides during the remainder of that long winter, which accomplished nothing of any consequence. By the spring of 1780, the war in the north was all but over. The south would become and had continued to be the nation's principal battlefield. Nathanael would still have a few personal battles to wage before he could get back into the shooting war. A war of men, equipment, and weapons in which he would much rather fight, than the one he was embroiled in at the moment, which was a war of words and contrition that he loathed.

Chapter XVII

"Resignation as Quartermaster-general"

Greene could hardly be expected to hide his feelings toward the congressional committee members, but he did hide those feelings and continued to work with a body of men that had treated him with injustice and indignity. To do this, he would first need a deliberate expression of Congress' sentiments so as to know they were not the same as Mifflin's committee. The moment was critical. A delay had already been extended to a terrible extreme, and a prompt decision and action were demanded. After carefully considering Greene's letter, on May 3rd, after months and months of delay's, the committee finally replied. "It is the wish as well as the inclination of this committee to give you every satisfaction as far as their power extends. But to undertake an investigation into the state and conduct of your department at this moment, the business being of so diffuse and complex a nature, we conceive would be highly inconsistent with the public's welfare, as the consequent delay attending such an inquiry would evidently tend to defeat the great object we have primarily in view,---the immediate supply of the army."

But Greene's feelings had already been hurt too deeply. He would not accept their interpretation of the problem. It was true that his personal grievance should take a backseat to the welfare of the army, but in his judgment the problem included the welfare of the army. "I am very sorry to find the committee adverse to making an inquiry into the order and arrangement of the Quartermaster's department; nor can I conceive how they can execute their commission without it. On what ground can they make any alterations to confirm any part of the present plan without such an investigation? My own honor obliges me to insist upon this; If my further services are wanted by the public in the Quartermaster's department, I conceive it highly reasonable and absolutely necessary to remove every shadow of imputation which may affect my character or standing with Congress. But I will not agree to conduct the business where so much is left to be governed by discretion. Neither will I serve under the direction of any other superintending Board than that of the Board of War, unless they are directly belong to Congress. I shall be always happy to render the public every service in my power either with or without reward more than necessary for my family's support. Under such circumstances I hope it will not be expected that I either accept or continue in an employment. Neither do I see very little prospect of engaging others in so disagreeable an employment in which those who have gone before him have been treated more like galley-slaves and publik pickpockets than faithful agents."

Disagreeable as Greene supposed his situation to be, he continued to serve at it for the good of the army and because his duty toward Congress. When he was accused by implication of his agents he quickly asked for a full investigation which was refused, thereby allowing the same people to continue to rake his name through the muck. Most of Congress held him in great esteem and respected him as the second highest ranked in command under the Commander-in-chief of the army George Washington. But, a few were still whispering that his abilities lay in his association as Washington's friend and confidant, rather than in his military ability. The doomsayers asked, "What great feat of military do had Greene ever accomplished? His only record of command was the loss of Fort Washington."

If all of this were not enough for Greene to endure, yet another strike against him would be swung. He had finally made peace with the committee when word came down that the Treasury Board had some questions on certain moneys for which Mr. Pettit had signed. As always, Greene was being blamed for the acts of his agents when there was no evidence that he had any part in the case. "The letters in my possession from the Treasury Board seem to be hinting at so strange, new, and unexpected a doctrine, that I think it requires some immediate explanation; they imply a responsibility in me, for the expenditure of public money be persons of my appointing, that neither law nor reason will warrant; and such as neither the Committee of Congress, the Commander-in-chief, or myself ever had in contemplation at the time of my appointment. I have ever considered the office of Quartermaster-general as a place of great trust, with latitude to act at discretion for the interest of the public; and that he stands between the subordinate agents and the public; not accountable for their conduct but to judge of it as the only person having that intimate acquaintance with the nature and circumstances of the business which can make him capable of determining rightly between them and the public."

These new accusations did not fall on willing ears in Congress. Two members of the Board were also members of Congress, and it could hardly be expected that they would sit quietly as delegates while other members of Congress strongly condemned them on their acts as commissioners in Greene's case. The debates droned on for weeks, and Greene's letter of record was finally referred to a committee of three composed of Ellsworth, Duane, and Madison. By late July, they emerged with their decision, with a soft but unsatisfactory clause that when "abuses and frauds" occurred in spite of the "customary precautions" they would determine the "circumstances of the abuse and either make favorable or unfavorable allowances as the circumstances required." It is hard to believe that Greene would have consented to continue in an office with such a sword of Damocles suspended over his head. When the resolution of the 24th reached him, his formal letter of resignation was already written and ready for delivery.

The private feelings Nathanael felt at this time could best be expressed by a letter dated June 29th, 1780 to his cousin, Griffin Greene which said, "I beg you write to me by every opportunity, as nothing is more agreeable than domestic matters in this bustle of life. You are home among all your connections, and must think less of us who are absent day after day, than we of you. You are happy in your circle; we are not so, and equal to domestic happiness. This mode of life is living for ourselves, every other is living for other people. I wish the war was over, that I might return to my dear friends and fireside. The world is full of folly, superstition, and ignorance, and overrun with malice, prejudices, and distraction. Good intentions are no security aganist abuse, especially when ambition is to be gratified by prostituting honor and justice. What a novice did I find myself. The black passion of jealousy, and the cankering spirit of envy, had well-nigh worked my overthrow, before I had the least idea that I had an enemy in the world. I was an enemy to no man, and could not see why they should be to me. But so it was, and so it will be to the end of the world, in political life."

Meanwhile Congress was busy implementing their new Quartermaster department system. They had decided that they intended to run it as a temporary business for only the duration of each campaign in place, and therefore see a necessity of only a few assistants to run the entire system and work directly under the supervision of Congress. The system seemed easy, but reality was quite cumbersome and complicated. Most of the members of Congress that were going to be involved in it could not understand it themselves. Before the system could even be put into operation, Mifflin saw fit to go ahead and add several more pages to the already bulging system paperwork, complicating it even further. A few weeks later Shuyler wrote to Washington to discuss the systems progress and had this surprising revelation to report. "This plan of Congress appears to me much better than I had first expected. . . .The inferior objection to it are fewer than /I had supposed would arise in my mind, and such as might perhaps be removed without great difficulty if the department were well supported with money."

In April, Lafayette arrived from France with the promise of an army as well as a fleet. The news was not as welcome to some as others when the French actually arrived. "As an American citizen," wrote Major Shaw, an aide to general Knox, "I rejoice in the prospect of so speedy, and I hope, effectual an aid as our French allies; but as a soldier, I am dissatisfied. . . . 'Tis really abominable that we should send to France for soldiers, when there are so many sons of America idle." Beyond that, the question of what to do with the new arrivals in conjunction with the American troops was batted about for weeks. Finally, Washington decided he would do what he had planned to do when D'Estaing had first arrived two years before. "If we take New York, we shall put an end to the war."

After a careful examination, it had been decided to lay siege to New York. 5,000 French soldiers, thoroughly disciplined and perfectly equipped, were ready to arrange themselves under Washington's command. Where were the stores and supplies and means of the Americans though? Greene had first tendered his resignation in December of 1779. Congress had begun to take the condition of the department into consideration in late January. July 1780 was half gone, and no decision had been reached on Greene's request to be replaced as quartermaster-general. Greene put in his formal request on the 14th of July, with Washington putting in his two cents. "I have determined upon a plan of operations," he writes Greene that day. "You are hereby directed, therefore, to make every arrangement and provision in your department for carrying the plan of operations into execution. You will apply to the States for what they are bound to furnish, agreeably to the several requistions of Congress and their committee at camp. All such articles as the States are bound to furnish, which will be necessary for conducting the operations, you will provide; and for this purpose you will apply to the Treasury Board for the requiste supplies of cash. I have been in anxious expectation that some plan would be determined upon your department; but as it has not hitherto taken place, and as it is impossible to delay its operation a moment longer, I have to desire that you will yourself arrange it in some effectual manner, to dispatch and efficacy to your measures equal to the task."

Meanwhile, Knyphausen, the commander in New York, had plans of his own. Hearing news of the near riot in the American camp at Morristown caused by two Connecticut regiments that declared they would return home if they were not given adequate food and clothing, the Tories brought the news to the British commander. A little late, but better late than never they thought. Knyphausen was filled with the confidence that what he had always expected was about to come to pass. The American army would dissolve into general dissolution over their leaders. What Knyphausen did not know was that the uprising had been calmed almost as fast as it had started. The army was not disheartened at all and in fact was buoyed in their confidence to win the war soon by the arrival of the French.

So, when Knyphausen marched toward Springfield, Connecticut, he was more than a little surprised when he was set upon by musket fire from behind every fence and wayside along every turn in the road. The officers quickly saw that they had miscalculated their chances of counting on the "discontent" of the Americans. Disappointed but not disheartened, Knyphausen continued on to Springfield. Maxwell, a gallant cavalry officer, had thrown himself in front with a Jersey Brigade and a small party of militiamen. With a strong resolve he commented, "defile near the Farm Meeting House," and when told to retreat, continued to fight for every step of ground, "harassing the enemy right and left at will," and regaining ground at Springfield, by a desperate charge, the ground that had just before been lost.

Washington had taken a post at the Short Hills, just behind the village and was preparing to give battle. But night had fallen more quickly than expected due to an approaching storm. The Americans lay on their arms, expecting to fight the next morning. But the British were dissatisfied with the situation. The Americans had the high ground and Knyphausen did not realize the true strength of Washington's troops. So, at ten that evening Knyphausen gave the order to retreat. They passed along the order so quickly and quietly, that two company of Grenadier ran into each other in the darkness. Suddenly, the thunderstorm broke on them. The rain came down in buckets and the thunder was deafening. The lightning was so frequent that one soldier wrote, "it was lighted up as if day, and the flashes bewildered the men. Once or twice the whole army was compelled to halt."

Meanwhile, Washington was calling his generals together in his marquee for a council. "The enemy outnumbers us by half; what shall we do?" "When I compare their strength with ours," said Greene; "I am in favor of a retreat. If Knyphausen, as is probable, is making a feigned movement in this direction, and really aiming at the heights of the North River, our retreat will be merely a change of position." Von Steuben proposed a night attack. The council eagerly agreed on the suggestion and the time of the attack fixed for midnight. But, when the Americans reached the ground where the British had been, they saw that they had gone and quickly pursued them.

Knyphausen reached Elizabethtown Point unmolested "and somewhat in confusion," but happy that the invasion could have ended much worse than it had. The British were disappointed that the invasion of the Jersey's had ended in shame once again. Washington on the other hand, was compelled to bestow kudos all around for his troops. "Both regulars and militia had performed gallantly, and Colonel Dayton merits particular thanks for his participation."

Knyphausen lingered about Elizabethtown Point until late June, and Washington, knowing that Sir Henry Clinton was on his way north with troops fresh from the successful siege of Charleston, became to grow anxious of the development and disliked the odds and his unhealthy ground. What would the victorious Clinton do next? It was a question Washington found asking himself time and time again, whoever the commanding general of the British may be at the time. Would he seize West Point, the key to the Hudson Valley? Or would he march rapidly to Morristown with its strong mountain passes that had protected the American army for two winter encampments? Clinton decided that Morristown would be his destination. A sudden blow on the position would keep Washington in suspense and afford the British excellent defensive points until a decision for their final destination could be ascertained.

Washington was so certain of the enemy's intentions that he decided to move the main body of his army northward, leaving Greene to command Maxwell's and Stark's brigades, Lee's corps, and the militia, "to cover the country and the public stores. The disposition for this purpose," continues Greene's orders, "are left entirely at your discretion, with this recommendation only, that you use every precaution in your power to avoid a surprise and provide for the security of your corps." Washington was well aware of Greene's tendency to attack if the opportunity arranged itself. In this case, discretion would have to be the better part of valor. Particular attention was called also to the gathering and transmission of intelligence. This assignment was a welcome respite to Greene from the annoyances of the Quartermaster's department duties he had been saddled with for so long, and now very near their culmination, and to find himself at the head of even this little army was grand to him. He loved to command and would much rather lead men than organize requisitions, write letters to agents, and order supplies.

The next day at five in the afternoon he wrote, "At this moment our intelligence man has returned from Elizabethtown. He says that General Clinton with the whole British army will be in motion this evening." Their intention, according to the account, was to cut Washington off from the entrance of the Clove. "It is probable they are about to move," adds Greene, "but I think their route and object very uncertain. I shall watch their motions and give them all the trouble in my power, and will duly advertise you of everything necessary for your information. I have ordered the troops to be in readiness to move at a moment's warning. The enemy sent a small party out this afternoon about two miles. They were drove back with the loss of two or three killed and two prisoners."

But by ten o'clock that evening, the British still had not started to march. Greene waited impatiently for something to happen, but the British did not stir. Greene acknowledged, "The intelligence our man gave this afternoon has not bore fruit. No accounts received from the lines of the least appearance of a movement by the enemy. The intelligence received and the other information by Major Lee, induced me to believe that the enemy were about to make some movement. But I begin to have some apprehension whether this movement to the northward may not be given out with a view of forcing your Excellency as far towards the North River as possible in order to leave an open passage to Trenton."

Greene was beginning to have grave doubts about his intelligence reports. But the man responsible for the reports was willing to face death if the information he had provided was not the truth. Greene did not doubt his sincerity, only his ability to gather intelligence information. He decided to send one of his officers, Colonel Dayton, to gather new information from the front. Dayton later returned with basically the same information provided to Greene earlier and with two prisoners. But the prisoners were so drunk, that they were barely able to stand, let alone give them prudent troop movements. Greene waited through the night, and by six the next morning, he finally received the information on the British for which he had been waiting. "The enemy are out on their march towards this place in full force, having received a considerable reinforcement last night." By eleven, from "Near Bryant's Tavern: I informed your Excellency this morning that the enemy were on the advance in force. I now acquaint you that they proceeded with vigor until they gained Connecticut Farms. They have since advanced in two formidable columns on the Springfield and Vauxhall roads. After very obstinate resistance they are now in possession of Springfield with one column. With the other they are advanced near the bridge leading to Vauxhall where Angell's pickets lay. From present prospects they are directing their force against this post, which I am determined to dispute so far as I am capable. They are pushing a column to our left, perhaps to gain the pass in our rear towards Chatham. If they pursue this object we must abandon our present position.

Later that morning a report comes in, and when he resumes his letter, he adds: "The militia are collecting, and I hope to derive support from them." At five in the afternoon that day he writes to Lord Stirling from Connecticut Farms: "The enemy advanced this morning and forced their way into Springfield; there they were warmly opposed by several corps of the army, and after burning almost every house in town, they retreated. We are now pressing their rear, but the principal part of their army has already reached Elizabethtown."

The next day, Greene found more time to relay the prior day's engagement at length to Washington. "The enemy advanced from Elizabethtown about five o'clock in the morning, said to be about five thousand infantry, with a large body of cavalry and fifteen or twenty pieces of artillery. They moved in two columns, one on the main road leading to Springfield, the other on the Vauxhall road. Major Lee with the horse and pickets opposed the right column, and Colonel Dayton with his regiment the left and both gave as much opposition as could have been expected from such a small force. The enemy continued manoeuvering in our front for upwards of two hours, which induced me to believe they were attempting to gain our flanks. Colonel Angell, with his regiment and several small detachments, was posted to secure the bridge in the front of town. Colonel Shreve's regiment was drawn up at the second bridge to cover the retreat of those posted at the first bridge. Major Lee with his dragoons and the pickets commanded by Captain Walker was posted at Littell's Bridge on the Vauxhall road; Colonel Ogden was detached to support him. The remainder of General Maxwell's and General Starke's brigades was drawn up on the high grounds at the Mill. The militia were on the flanks.

While the enemy were making demonstrations to their left, their right column advanced on Major Lee. The bridge was disputed with great obstinacy and at great loss to the enemy; but by fording the river and gaining the point of the hill, they obliged the Major with his party to give up the pass. At this instant of time their left column began the attack on Colonel Angell. The action was severe and lasted about forty minutes, when superior numbers overcame obstinate bravery, and forced our troops to retire over the second bridge. Here Colonel Shreve's regiment warmly greeted the enemy; but as they advanced in great force with a large train of artillery, he had orders to join the brigade.

As the enemy continued to press our left on the Vauxhall road, which led directly into our rear, and would have given them the most important pass, and finding our front too extensive to be effectually secured by so small a body of troops, I thought it advisable to take post upon the first range of hills in the rear of Bryant's Tavern, where the roads are brought so near to a point that succor might readily be given from one to the other. This enabled me to detach Colonel Webb's regiment commanded by Lieutenant-colonel Huntington, and Colonel Jackson's regiment to entirely check the advance of the enemy on our left and secure that pass.

Being thus advantageously posted I was in hopes the enemy would attempt to gain the heights, but discovered no disposition in them for attacking us; and seeing them begin to fire the houses in town, detachments were ordered out on every quarter to prevent them burning any buildings not immediately under the command of their cannon and musketry. With almost every house in town ablaze, the enemy began their retreat. Captain Davis with a small detachment of one hundred and twenty men, fell upon their rear and flanks, and kept up a continual fire upon them all the way to Elizabethtown, which they reached about sunset.

The enemy continued at Elizabethtown Point until midnight, and then began to send troops across to Staten Island. By six this morning they had totally evacuated the point and removed their bridge. Major Lee fell in with their rear guard; but they were so covered by their works that little or no injury could be done to them. He did make some prisoners, and took a great deal of stores that they abandoned to expedite their retreat.

I have the pleasure to inform his Excellency that the troops who were engaged behaved with great coolness and intrepidity, and the whole of them discovered an impatience to be brought into action. The good order and discipline which they exhibited in all their movements do them the highest honor. The artillery under the command of Lieutenant-colonel Forest was well served. I have only to regret the loss of Captain-lieutenant Thompson, who fell at the side of his piece by a cannonball. It is impossible to fix with certainty the enemy's loss; but as there was much close firing, and our troops were advantageously posted, they must have suffered very considerably.

I am at a loss to determine what was the object of the enemy's expedition. If it was to injure the troops under my command, or to penetrate further into the country, they were frustrated. If it was the destruction of this place, it was a disgraceful one. I lament that our force was too small to save the town from ruin. I wish every American could have been a spectator; he would have felt for the sufferers and joined to revenge their injury. I cannot close without acknowledging the particular service of Lieutenant-colonel Barber, who acted as deputy adjutant-general, and distinquished himself by activity in assisting to make the necessary dispositions."

Greene and his officers were thanked in general orders, and Angell's brilliant stand at the first bridge was mentioned with a special commendation. The next few days passed with great uncertainty, although the thought of West Point being attacked was becoming less likely, the feeling throughout the general officers was that at this juncture, West Point could defend itself if it was attacked at all.

On the 10th of July news arrived that the first division of the French fleet, seven ships of the line and two frigates, bringing six thousand troops under Count Rochambeau, had arrived at Newport. Had Washington's plans been followed, the Americans would have been prepared to act with them and easily taken New York. But they had not been followed, and before any decisive step could be taken, the British were reinforced, and the French fleet was quickly blockaded in Newport harbor. Clinton resolved to take advantage of his superiority in numbers, and attack the French by land and sea. Eight thousand men were embarked. For a few days, Huntington Bay, the gathering place on Long Island, swarmed with ships and transports. If Clinton could capture or destroy the fleet and army of this division, it would be a deadly blow to the alliance that would not quickly be mended.

Washington had been expecting something like this to happen and was on the alert for it from the start. He called upon the militia to aid him in filling the thin ranks of troops. He crossed the Hudson and directed a march towards King's Bridge. This bold maneuver threatened the weakened garrison of New York and caught Clinton off guard. The British commander was forced to return to New York in haste and leave the British fleet in wait off of Block Island. Rochambeau was left at leisure to attend to his sick men, and strengthen his position by building new fortifications.

Greene, who was given the job of providing the means of transportation and securing supplies for the army, which had just been suddenly put into motion, felt that his position was difficult. He still had received no answer from his letter to Congress asking their view of the interpretation which the Treasury Board had put upon his responsibility by appointments, and now Washington wanted him to ask for a great deal of funds. He was obligated to obey the orders of his commander-in-chief for the good of the army. So, Greene set about accomplishing the duties he was still under an obligation to perform. But this time, he was probably doing them with the added fervor that he had lacked in he recent past because he was doing it directly for Washington and not the committee.

Without waiting for his long awaited answer, Greene instantly began his preparations for supplying the combined French and American army for what appeared to be the largest and most important campaign of the war. "Sir,--The Commander-in-chief has given me direction to make the necessary provision in the Quartermaster's department with the French forces which now lay in Newport Harbor. Mr. Bowen has instructions to collect all flat-bottomed boats in the State, which he could not affect without the want of money. In military operations one thing depends so much upon another, and the success of the whole upon the provision of each part, that nothing is more common than for great events to depend upon little things. Therefore what may appear a trifling consideration, often involves important consequences."

Greene also sent off a note explaining Washington's orders to the committee, who answered immediately. "We observe in your letter of the 19th ultimo to Congress, that you have stated the degree of responsiblity which you think ought to be required of you on the expenditure on moneys in the Quartermaster-general's department. As you have obtained the determination of Congress for conducting your department reported by this committee has not to our knowledge been decided upon. In justice to you, sir, we embrace this occasion to declare that after having examined your arrangement of the Quartermaster-general's department, we are convinced the measures you have adopted and the principles on which these measures were founded, were well calculated to promote the service, whilst they fully evinced your attention to the public interest."

Greene had finally been cleared to do the job he had originally set out to do almost three years before he was so rudely interrupted. He continued to work at supplying the army as best he could, and was encouraged by the swift and decisiveness of Congress when he requested their assistance or for funds. So while Washington, Greene and the committee were exerting themselves to make up for lost time, Congress brought its long labors upon the Quartermaster's department to a close. On the 15th of July the new system was approved. By the 26th, Greene received it from Washington at their camp in Preakness. Greene had thought and felt too much on this particular subject to hesitate one moment about his course of action. His views, Washington's views, had been freely communicated to Congress these past six months; and this was the reward of over two and a half years devotion to duty in a laborious and stress-filled office. He instantly wrote to the President of Congress. "His Excellency General Washington has just transmitted to me a plan for conducting the Quartermaster's department agreed to in Congress on the 15th of July, 1780, wherein I am to continue as Quartermaster-general, and directed to make the necessary appointments and arrangements in the department agreeably thereto as soon as possible. It was my intention from the peculiar circumstances of our affairs, and I have long since communicated it to the Commander-in-chief and the committee of Congress, to continue to exercise the office of Quartermaster-general during the active part of this campaign, provided matters were left upon such a footing as to enable me to conduct the business to satisfaction; and in order to remove every shadow of suspicion that might induce a belief that I was induced by interested motives to make more extensive arrangements than were necessary, I voluntarily relinquished every kind of emolument for conducting the business, save my family expenses. But however willing I might have been before to subject myself to the fatigue and difficulties attending the duties of this office, justice to myself as well as to the public constrains me positively to decline it under the present arrangement. It is unnecessary for me to go into the general objections I have to this plan. It is sufficient to say that my feelings are injured, and that the officers necessary to conduct the business are not allowed; nor is proper provision made for some of those that are. My rank is high in the line of the army, and the sacrifices I have made on this account, together with the fatigue and anxiety I have undergone, far overbalance all the emoluments I have derived from the appointment. Nor would double the consideration induce me to tread the same path over again, unless I saw it necessary to preserve my country from utter ruin and a disgraceful servitude."

The representatives of Congress were in camp at the time. The next day he wrote to them; "I do myself the honor to inclose you a copy of the letter of resignation I have sent to Congress. I think it my duty to give you the earliest information of everything that concerns the interest and well-being of the army, and therefore take the liberty to trouble you on this occasion." The same day, he also wrote to Washington. Not as his friend, Greene did not feel it was appropriate due the subject and circumstances. But as his Commander-in-chief and someone he respected above all other people he knew in the army or Congress. "I do myself the honor to inclose your Excellency a copy of a letter of resignation as Quartermaster-general to Congress, and another on the same subject to the committe which is in camp. I have only to regret that the measures of administration have laid me under the necessity at this critical moment. It is true it has been my wish for a long time to get out of the department; but as our political affairs were in so disagreeable a train I was willing to submit to many inconveniences in order to promote the public welfare, while I had a prospect of conducting the business to answer the expectations of the public and to the satisfaction of the army. But a new system of Congress has cut off all prospect, and left me without the shadow of hope. Since the commencement of this war I have ever made the good of the service the rule of my conduct, and in no instance have I deviated from this line; and where there has been a seeming variation, it has been only in such cases where I could not render my services without forfeiting my reputation."

To say that Congress reacted with extreme indigence would be an understatement. Several weeks passed with letters passing back and forth from member to member, from committee to Congress, both in support of General Greene and in blatant disrespect for the man who had performed admirably under trying conditions set upon him. The response from Congress was curt and to the point. "That General Greene's refusal be accepted. That general Washington be empowered and directed to appoint a Quartermaster-general. That General Greene be acquainted that Congress have no further service for him." And so, a chapter in Nathanael Greene's life that hurt him deeply till his last days on earth was over, but not forgotten.

Chapter XVIII

"The Armies Posture"

Greene could finally set his attention to his favorite part of military service; leading men. He decided that this would be a perfect occasion for a general such as himself, to add a bit of moral strength to the troops by explaining his conduct and motives to the army. On the 3rd of August1780, he wrote to Washington from Verplanck's Point: "Your Excellency will consider this a great movement, and has been very rapid. The march of the army has been very fatiguing. Without some explanation we shall not do justice to ourselves, nor will your Excellency to your own military character. The enterprise was great, the object noble, and the end for which it was undertaken appears to have been party answered if not fully so. To explain the reasons of the movement will give the army a high opinion of the confidence you have in their spirit and enterprise, and perfectly reconcile them all the past fatigues and to those, which may follow in regaining our former position. It will strike the enemy with the boldness of the design. It will reconcile the country to all the inconveniences they have felt, and prepare their minds for future exertions of a similar nature in full confidence that the object is worthy the preparations."

Washington was extremely disappointed when he saw the chances of an attack upon New York and a decisive campaign slip through his fingers. It was not his fault this time, that no adequate preparations had been made in time to turn the cooperation of our allies into their best use. Greene had felt that the turn of events was even more striking than most of those involved. He felt there was something idealistic, without regard to practicality in the idea of an enterprise that demanded men, money, and supplies. He had more reason for feeling so, since it was his department that carried the chief burden of its preparation. To know what they could, and could not do logistically, Washington and Rochambeau decided to meet in Hartford, and there they would discuss their plans and resources in a personal interview together.

Meanwhile on the 24th of August, Greene had been sent out on a foraging expedition to Bergen and in the neighborhood of the British encampment. "Such are the necessities," writes Washington in his instructions to Greene, "being all within the power of the enemy, that you will make the forage as extensive as possible in the articles of hay and grain, as well as in cattle, hogs, and sheep fit for slaughter, and horses fit for use of the army. All the articles are to be receipted for by the respective departments of which they will belong. . .Should the enemy attempt to interrupt you in the business, you must govern yourself according to circumstances. I leave you at liberty either to attack or retire, as you may think prudent, from the force in which they may appear."

The expedition was successful and was carried out without incident. Most of the necessary supplies were secured, but it brought into painful light the demoralization, which had crept into the army under the influence of hunger, lack of clothing, and a worthless currency. On the 26th of August Greene wrote to Washington from the Three Pigeons: "There has been committed some of the most horrid acts of plunder by some of the Pennsylvania line that has disgraced the American arms during the war. The instances of plunder and violence is equal to anything we have seen committed by the Hessians. Two soldiers were taken that were not upon the business, both of which fired upon the inhabitants to prevent their giving intelligence. I think it would have a good effect to hang one of these fellows in the face of the troops, without the form of a trial. It is absolutely necessary to give a check to the licentious spirit which increases amazingly. The impudence of the soldiers is intolerable. A party plundered a house yesterday in sight of a number of officers, and even threatened them if they offered to interfere. It is the opinion of most of the officers that it is absolutely necessary for the good of the service that one of these fellows should be made an example of, and if your Excellency will give permission, I will have one hung up this afternoon when the army are ready to march by. There is also a deserter taken three-quarters of a way over to New York, belonging to the 7th Pennsylvania regiment, which the officers of several other regiments, wish may be executed in the same way that I propose to execute the other in. I believe, it will also serve as a deterrent to the other fellows in league with this sort. I wish your Excellency's answer respecting the two culprits, as we shall march at five this evening."

Washington would write back with his answer; "I need scarcely inform you of the extreme pain and anxiety which the licentiousness of some of the soldiery has given me. Something must and shall be done, if possible, to put an effectual check to it. I entirely approve of the prompt punishment which you propose to have inflicted on the culprits in question. You will, therefore, please to order one of the soldiers detected in plundering, and also the deserter you mention, to be immediately executed." The orders were carried out without another word being spoken between Washington and Greene. The entire incident marked as just another misfortune of war.

Soon after Greene returned to camp, Washington, who had been preparing for his interview with Rochambeau, called a council of war, in order to collect the opinion of his officers upon a plan of operations. After laying out the subjects at hand for his officers, Washington requested that they give him their ideas in written form. The only general that was not in attendance was Benedict Arnold, who had recently requested, and was made, commandant of Washington's new shining crown of glory in the American army's ranks of fortifications, West Point. It would be the last time Washington and Arnold would correspond, and quite ironic that the last subject the two men would speak about would be on Washington wishing to know his views on the situation and prospects of the American army.

By the 11th of September, Greene would write of his views on the situation; "I have taken into consideration as far as my health would permit, the several matters submitted to the general officers in the council held on the 6th, and am of opinion that as the second division of the French fleet has not arrived, and there being little probability that it will be here in season to attempt anything to the northward, it would be a folly to persevere further upon our original plan of operations laid down for the campaign. The very great deficiency in our own preparation of men, provisions, and stores of every kind, for an attempt upon New York, furnish a stronger argument for changing our plan of operations. It is sufficient that we know that more powerful arguments cannot be offered to the people than has been, to draw forth either men or supplies of any kind. Nevertheless, should a large reinforcement arrive immediately from the West Indies, it would be our duty to attempt a cooperation, but I confess I doubt of its success while the business of finance and the supplies of provisions are upon so disagreeable a footing. Three objects claim out attention in the state of our affairs, which your Excellency has laid before me. This would be the force necessary to be kept in this quarter, the expedition into Canada, and for the situation of the southern States. The first is the great object, and the other two are to be considered only as appendages. It is a difficult point to determine how to employ our force, their time of service is so short and their future establishment so uncertain. Our prospects of provision and pay are still more distressing and disagreeable. Our present collective strength here, upon a Continental establishment, is equal to that of the enemy, but will be soon rendered greatly inferior by the expiration of the time of service for which the troops are engaged. Could there be a junction formed of a part or the whole of the French forces at Newport, and measures taken to recruit this army for the war, detachments might be made with a degree of safety and not without, unless the enemy detach before us. The French fleet might be safe in Boston harbor without their land force, and I believe they also might be safe up Providence River; but they are the best judges of what force and what place is necessary for their own security. Should the enemy detach largely from New York to the southward, it may lay us under the necessity of detaching also, or it may open new prospects with respect to prosecuting our original plan of operations, especially if a reinforcement should arrive from the West Indies to join the French army.

From all of the intelligence coming from Canada there appears a favorable disposition among the inhabitants for our undertaking an expedition into that country. But to undertake it with troops whose time of service will expire before the business is completed, would be a folly; and besides this objection, we have not the provisions or the stores necessary for such an attempt. However, if there should be no offensive operations to the southward, an expedition might be made into Canada in the winter, and for this purpose I would direct magazines of provisions and forage to be laid up at Albany and Cohoes.

What I would recommend with respect to our southern affairs would be to levy an army in that country, for the war if possible, of regular troops. My plan would be to act upon the defensive. If great bodies of militia are kept in the field, the country will soon become incapable of making any opposition. I would not employ a larger force than is necessary to secure great objects, and though this may not be so popular for the General, it will be more salutary for the people. When any offensive operations are undertaken for the reduction of Charleston, there must be a naval force to give it success. To attempt anything before, will only be agreeing that the country, from its own resources, is unequal to the support of an army sufficient for the reduction of Charleston and the expulsion of the enemy. Nor can I persuade myself that the same people who could not protect themselves, after having sufficient time to collect their force, can ever bring into the field an army sufficient to expel the enemy, unless the enemy should greatly diminish their strength, which is by no means the case in that quarter.

When our allies furnish a naval force, and we are in a position to furnish a land force to act in conjunction with those of our ally, which, joined by those in the southern States, will be sufficient to reduce the garrison of Charleston, then I would undertake offensive operations, and not before. Provisions and stores sufficient for the support of the army could go under convoy of the fleet. Until then I am persuaded all our efforts to regain possession of that country will be fruitless and ineffectual, and the more we attempt it the greater will be our distress in that quarter. Nothing but regular troops should be employed in a country where provisions and stores are so difficult to provide as they are to the southward, and as double their number of militia will not give equal security to the country." How prophetic much of what Greene would write in his opinions to Washington would bear fruit. But some of the future events would be dictated by a way that would have been scoffed by Greene just months before, as seen by the following events. Also, Greene would never have believed how closely he would be involved with its ultimate inception.

Chapter XIX

"The Loss and the Betrayal"

On the 17th of September Washington set out for Hartford and his meeting with Rochambeau. "In my absence," he writes to Greene, "the command of the army devolves upon you. I have such entire confidence in your prudence and abilities, that I leave the conduct of it to your discretion, with only one observation; that, with your present prospects, it is not our business to seek an action, nor to accept one, but upon advantageous terms." Washington wanted to make sure that Greene had his hands on the reins, but kept a low profile. This was something that was very hard for Nathanael to muster. Greene would add his own orders to those of Washington: "His Excellency the Commander-in-chief, going to be absent from the army for a few days, the knowledge of which may possibly reach the enemy and encourage them to make some movement in consequence thereof, the General desires officers of all ranks to be in perfect readiness to meet them on the shortest notice; and recommends to the outguards to be very vigilant and attentive, and the patrols to be watchful and active."

By the next day, Greene found himself in the Quartermaster-general mold, even as interim Commander-in-chief. An ample supply of food was again becoming a problem, and he was forced to enact stringent measures to supply the army. He would write to Colonel Butler, "You will take command of a party of horse and foot, detached this morning, and march them to the neighborhood of Newark Mountain meeting-house. The object of the detachment is to assist the civil magistrate in collecting a number of cattle in that country for the use of the army. I have entire confidence in your discretion and prudence that no insult or injury will be offered the people but what cannot be avoided from the nature of the service. I recommend secrecy and dispatch."

This expedition, like Greene's own foraging party, would have had appeared much like a failure in better times; but they were now becoming accustomed to having the army live hand to mouth. Greene had a feeling of real satisfaction that the expedition was successful, but also wrote "in the late scarcity the soldiers had threatened to disband," and he feared, "they will put it in execution in the next instance. In reporting to Washington on the 21st, Greene acknowledged "We are pretty well supplied with provisions for five or six days to come, with what is in camp and on the road from the eastward and the westward, we will make due for now."

Before Washington had left, he had given Greene orders to bring the army forward to Tappan, a spot that would soon become infamous in the war. On the 19th, Greene's aide issued the marching orders. "At seven o'clock to-morrow morning the general will beat the assembly at nine, and the army will march at ten. The General desires the march may be conducted agreeably to the regulations, and with the greatest regularity; for this purpose every officer is requested to attend to his particular command.

One of the main problems with marching the army wasn't the logistics or the timing. It was the serious consequences brought on by the demoralization of the desertions that occurred during the march to the next camp. In turn, the officers felt great apprehension during this time. "As the army is to march in the morning," Greene writes to Major Pace, "it is not improbable there will be a number of deserters attempt to get in to the enemy. You will, therefore, in order to intercept them, march your riflemen down the road towards Bergen, and take post a little this side of the road leading to Fort Lee, and there establish the proper patrols for your own security, and make the best disposition you can for intercepting the deserters. The army will take their old ground at Tappan."

Meanwhile, ten ships of the line had arrived at New York with ten more said to be on their way. "This confirms," writes Greene to Reed, "the report concerning the Count de Guichen's coming upon the coast, as it is not probable that the British would leave such a naval force behind as the combined fleets would form." Conjecture ran rampant at American headquarters. What were the British going to do? "Reports from New York say," Greene writes to Washington, "that Rodney is going to join Arburthnot, and that an attack is intended upon the fleet and army at Newport. I think this is possible but not probable. Preparations for a considerable embarkation has been making for some time in New York. The destination of the troops is unknown. But from a combination of circumstances I am led to believe they are going to Virginia; the refugees of that country being invited to engage in it." Writing to the President of Congress, Greene theorized, "the rescue of the convention troops is in contemplation . . . . These may be blinds, but I have thought it my duty to communicate matters as I receive them."

At this same time, the war was heating up in the South. It wasn't much more than a civil war. Furious and ferocious partisan warfare between the Tories and the southern militia and rebel fighters that continually became a thorn in the side of Clinton. Charleston captured and under the control of the British, Clinton's next move was to try and reduce the interior of the Carolinas to the subjection of the British crown. He continually sent out a series of detachments composed almost entirely of Tories, and for the next three months claimed victory after victory. The British regulars had little to do with any of the five engagements during this time. It was a true civil war. Brother against brother, but it would be seen again in a grander scale in less than one hundred years on the same ground as they were fighting in 1780.

To try and counteract this march by the British, Washington had sent De Kalb down to form some sort of troops into an army. De Kalb was a sight in the field. Six-foot tall, high forehead, keen hazel eyes, aquiline nose, strong chin, engaging to his men with an expression of good nature mixed with shrewdness on his face. His physical endurance was legendary; he often was said to make twenty to thirty miles in a day by foot, "preferring that exercise to riding." Though ambitious as the next officer, he was single-hearted and honest to a fault; energetic and enterprising, he would not expect his troops to do anything he was not willing to do himself. Although he tempered his actions with caution and common sense for the most part, he was also known to be brave to the point of recklessness, and so was an ideal leader for combat forces in this type of action.

The army had been living in the field, foraging as they went for months. Lincoln, formerly in command of the Southern Department, was in captivity. As senior officer in the department at the time, De Kalb was the obvious choice to assume command. But he was a foreigner, a son of a Barvarian peasant who had learned his trade as a young infantryman, and who ultimately gained a commission as a lieutenant and fought in the European wars from 1747 to 1767. When he came to America to fight in 1776, although he was widely known throughout the small military community of the time, he was little known in Philadelphia and had no influential friends or patrons to urge his merits to Congress. It was unlikely he would continue as commander very long, and would only command until Congress found a general they knew. De Kalb was never even considered for the job on a permanent basis.

The first pick to fill the position of Commander of the Southern department was obvious to Washington; Nathanael Greene, of course. But Congress did not share his enthusiasm of his choice and had its own man in mind for the job, none other than Horatio Gates; Hero of Saratoga. The man whose head hung an aureole of glory and victory laurels like Caesar. You could just ask him yourself, he would be more than willing to tell you how great a man he thought he was. Never mind that he had almost nothing to do with the entire engagement at Saratoga. That wasn't the point. What Gates did have, besides an inflated ego, was a great public relations team in Philadelphia during 1780. Congress loved him so "with almost unbecoming haste" and without even a word of advice from Washington, Commander-in-chief of the Continental Army, "though not ignorant of his opinion," Gates was the overwhelming choice by members of the United States Congress, and was so by ordered "to repair to and take command of the southern department."

Gates received word of his placement at his plantation in Virginia and gladly accepted it. He then received a cryptic warning from his friend and neighbor, Charles Lee: "Take care lest your Northern laurels turn to Southern willows." De Kalb got the news and was more than admirable saying, "I'm happy to hear of Gate's coming." He then proceeded to mention the present conditions of the troops and his ongoing difficulties with supplying them: "Altho I have put the troops on short allowance for bread, we cannot get even that. . . no assistance from the legislature or executive power… The design I had to move nearer the enemy to drive them from the Pedee River, a plentiful country, has been defeated by the impossibility of subsiding on the road."

De Kalb had marched the army to "Hollinsworth's Farm on Deep River" when Gates arrived on the 25th of July 1780. After assuming command from De Kalb, Gates immediately took stock of the "grand army" which consisted of "an army without strength, a military chest without money." All round him were depressed patriots, elated Tories that were swarming everywhere, and facing a victorious enemy of high morale, strongly posted, and planning to spread further conquest larger than the last.

Before Gates was named as the new commander, De Kalb had planned to move southwest toward Camden by way of Salisbury and Charlotte, no more than a village of thirty homes at that time. The route would be on good roads and fruitful for foraging, along with the fact that the people of that area were well affected by the British and would help the patriots in any way they could in the Rowan and Mecklenberg counties. Those lands were chiefly inhabited by the patriotic Scotch-Irish, and had magazines of supplies and hospitals throughout the area. But the forthright Gates took hold at once and would have none of that. His intention was to march at once, and by the most direct road to Camden. Although Gates proposed route was shorter by fifty miles, it also ran through thinly populated areas of infertile pine barrens and swamps, presenting another problem for the passage of artillery and the few baggage wagons that the army possessed. Further, the road would cross several waterways that would be swollen by the summer rains; scanty food supplies would be detrimental to the health and morale of the troops. But most important, the road proposed by Gates took them right through a region that was the most unfriendly of the South to the American cause.

Apart from all of those negative points Gates gave the order to march on the route while the "men and officers looked at each other with blank amazement" one of them would write later. Day by Day, the distress of the marching men grew more severe. Already on half rations, food was worse than scare. They ran out completely after a few days. Men lived on green corn from the outlying fields along the route, and some unripe peaches. The physical result was too obvious to mention. Of livestock on the few farms they passed, there were none. There weren't even any farmers; they had fled months before and had taken everything edible with them. The only thing remaining was the farmer's stray cows that had been left to run wild. Horribly lean creatures with barely any meat beneath their hanging skin, but they were devoured anyway. The officers took to making soup and thickening it with their hair powder. The men continued on their march, plodding through deep sand and wading through chest deep swamps.

The troops arrived at the crossing of the Pedee River on the 3rd of August. Half starved, the other half sick, all of them fatigued at the point of exhaustion, still the men had to continue on; and they did, for seventeen to eighteen miles a day. There were subtle murmurs among almost all of them, ominous glances at each other, and black looks that could burn holes for the commander. Sergeant Major William Seymour of the Delaware regiment put in his journal: "At this time we were so much distressed for want of provisions, that we were fourteen days and drew but one half pound of flour. Sometimes we drew half a pound of beef per man and that so miserably poor that scarce any mortal could make use of it--living chiefly on green apples and peaches, which rendered our situation truly miserable, being in a weak and sickly condition, and surrounded on all sides by our enemies the Tories."

Finally, the army arrived at Rugeley's where they joined up with General Edward Stevens and his 700 Virginia militia. There they were also met with some provisions of beef and corn which was ground up for meal, each man receiving half a pound. By now the army had a total of roughly 4,400 rank and file, with the enemy having about 6,240. On the 16th of August the Battle of Camden was fought. The British line was formed to the left of the Americans and advanced headlong into the troops that were mostly made up of unproved militia. The results were as they always were; they would shoot once, maybe twice and then drop their guns and run into the woods, leaving the Continentals to fend for themselves. And they did, bravely, but with disastrous effect. With both the center and left flanks quickly gone, the right wing was engulfed by murderous British attacks.

De Kalb had his horse shot out from under him. The gigantic form of De Kalb fighting on foot and trying to rally his brave Delaware and Maryland troops into movements must have been a sight to behold. De Kalb and his men, heavily outnumbered, were slowly being engulfed by the enemy. De Kalb, wounded and bloodied by a saber slash to the head, refused to give up and thought that victory could still be at hand. His adjutant of the Delaware regiment, Captain Peter Jaquett, hastily bandaged the general and begged him to retire. Still De Kalb refused, saying he neither had nor received orders from Gates to do so. That would be impossible for Gates to do, because during the early engagement, Gates had set-up his post about six hundred yards in the rear of the American lines. They had just received word that the American artillery was in full engagement with the British artillery which appeared to be about two hundred yards off. Otho Williams, Gates adjutant general, found the commander and reported; "The enemy are deploying on the right, sir. There's a good chance for Stevens to attack before they're formed." Gates turned, ever so slowly, looked at Williams and mumbled "Sir, that's right. Let it be done." It was the last order Gates gave in the battle or in any other until the end of the war.

Williams hurried to Stevens and gave him Gates' order to advance. The Virginians raggedly and reluctantly moved forward, but even if they had moved with speed and accuracy, it would have been too late to do anything. The British had already formed their line. As the British steadily advanced, a solid body of scarlet and glittering bayonets and with no regard for the American line, the Virginians suddenly stopped their movement, fired one volley, and then fell back in disorder. The moment Gates witnessed the British advance and the American troops complete collapse, an overpowering fear must have seized over Gates. Because just as he saw the eyes of the fear-stricken Virginians and North Carolinians burst through the 1st Maryland brigade reserve, in complete confusion and running for their lives, Gates must have suddenly thought it wasn't such a bad idea. He was seen to "rear his horse back, put his spurs into its hindquarters, and turned the beast at once, bringing the animal to a full gallop almost immediately." Gates didn't stop until he was in Charlotte.

"Never was victory more complete, or defeat more total." It has been described as the "most disastrous defeat ever inflicted on an American army." De Kalb, fighting to the end, had been hit with musketball after musketball. Blood was said to be pouring out of him, but the old lion had enough in him to cut down a British infantryman attempting to bayonet him. Unfortunately, that was his last stroke. Bleeding from eleven wounds in all, he fell and died on the spot. Colonel "No Quarter" Tarleton pursued the fleeing Americans and picked up several prisoners, including General Rutherford of the North Carolina militia. Rutherford was leading the way in their retreat, and Colonel Armand with several other officers who were apparently caught in camp, trying desperately to save the baggage train which was being looted by the retreating American militia.

Scattered in small groups or individually, looking vainly for their comrades and for any type of leadership. With Gates' flight, the men had no orders to assemble in case of defeat. The fugitives of the battle "came into Camden daily, but in a deplorable condition, hungry, fatigued and almost naked." until about 700 had assembled, the meager relics of Gates "grand army" of 4,000 men. By the 19th, Gates was in Salisbury. He had stayed overnight at Charlotte on the 16th, the night of the battle, then had pushed on and been in Hillsboro the next day and, as fast as fresh horses could carry him arrived in Salisbury. Two hundred miles in less than three days, a good record for even the fastest rider of the day. The only other officer of note to escape with his troops was Daniel Morgan. Gates's first job was to reorganize his shattered army. But the only troops to assemble were Continental soldiers. The militias had "fled different ways as their hopes led or their fears drove them." Lieutenant Caleb Bennett of the Delaware unit wrote long afterward, "We found ourselves in a most deplorable situation, without arms, ammunition, baggage and with very little sustenance and for sometime our situation was unenviable." What they needed was a savior. Thankfully, the Department of the Southern Army would soon get one.

The news of Gates' defeat at Camden made its way North in no time. Greene's earlier thoughts on the Southern theater was not as true as he thought, but still added "the more we waste our strength in such a fruitless attempt, the less we shall be able to give protection to the rest of the southern States not yet in the enemy's power." He could not be more wrong, and that was something out of the ordinary for Major General Nathanael Greene. The offensive or defensive fate of the entire United States rested in what happen to the South. Interesting that a man that thought so little of the aspects of that portion of the war would become such a large part of it.

It was no secret that Greene absolutely hated Gates. Their past occurrences had always been on thin ice and almost hostile toward each other. You can almost imagine the wry smile on Greene's face when he wrote the following; "General Gates late misfortune will sink his consequence and lessen his military character. He is bandied about and subject to many remarks, the common fate of the misfortune. Whether he has been to blame or not, I cannot pretend to judge, and shall leave those who were nearer at hand to fix the common opinion. The affairs to the southward are still more agreeable than the account I mentioned. Most of the prisoners taken in the action at Camden were rescued by Colonel Marion as they were on their march to Charleston. Upon the whole the British have got little to brag of. General Gates's first account was shocking and very premature." Again, Greene is either uninformed, misinformed, or kidding himself on the subject of the battle at Camden. The British may not have much to brag about, but it was a complete victory, and with the state of the army in the north, it should not have occurred in the circumstances in which it did. He was right about one thing, and that was Gates had underestimated his foes and overestimated his abilities as a field general.

The attention of Washington was now being drawn to reports that in New York the British were planning an expedition against Wilmington, North Carolina, and another against Portsmouth, Virginia. Greene would write, "But some people think the whole is intended against Newport." Now Greene was underestimating the campaign to the south, and again drawing to much attention to the north. There can be no doubt that the reason was because of his worry for his family and his state. But generals are not suppose to let sentimentality and homesickness cloud their objectivity and judgment. Greene would have to focus on the facts eventually and realize that the south was the primary concern for the Americans now.

Clinton had scattered his doubts broadcast, and spread his snares with the skill of a spy, but fate would be the major player in this game. "There has been some firing by the North River at the shipping which lay near Tellard's Point, but I have no account of what effect it had more than to make shipping move a little further upon the shore." No one knew exactly what the firing meant, but the firing would last for two days before its full meaning would be explained.

Greene, writing to the President of Congress passes what information he is privy to: "By intelligence from New York it appears that the enemy continue their preparations for a very extensive embarkation; they are collecting their force on Long Island for the purpose of embarking them at White Stone, and at the same time a number of transports have fallen down to the watering place to prepare for sea. They are repairing and taking in their stores with all possible expedition. The enemy have detached near five hundred of the best men from the new corps in garrison at New York, Paulus Hook, and Staten Island, with orders to join the main army near Whit Stone; they have laid a general embargo on all shipping, and continue to impress men for their fleet. All reports in the city of New York are alternately that they are intended for Rhode Island and Virginia. Further, I have enclosed a New York paper which shows that Sir Henry Clinton has removed General Robertson from the duties of commandant of the city, which is no doubt to answer some very particular purpose."

The 23rd of September 1780 started out as a typical day in camp. Von Steuben was doing an inspection and then drilling the troops under general exercises in the parade ground. Greene was witness to the event and wrote later, "The truly martial appearance of the troops yesterday, and the order and regularity with which they made the different marches, and the facility with which they performed the several manoeuvers, do them the greatest credit, and open the most flattering prospects of substantial service to the country and military glory to the army." Quite a profound and patriotic statement on the occasion of the country's most embarrassing events of American history and least patriotic acts.

The cares of the day over, Greene repaired to his headquarters; still in command of the army while Washington was away. The last correspondence from Washington to Greene told of his plans to visit one of his favorite generals at his proudest accomplishment. He was to have breakfast with Benedict Arnold on the morning of the 24th, and then make an inspection of the West Point fortifications, which had just been completed. However, when Washington and his aides arrived on the banks of the Hudson in the shadow of West Point, he was quite putout by the fact that no one met him at his arrival, especially Arnold. Arnold was far too busy to meet Washington. The night before Arnold had been informed by one of his officers that a spy by the name of Andre had been captured and had been carrying a pass from Arnold, along with plans to West Point. The officer was asking Arnold what to do with him? Arnold immediately made his plans to catch the ship Andre had come up north on, the Vulture, and run to the British side after his botched treason attempt. When Washington finally made his way to Arnold's house to find out what was happening, they were met by Arnold's servant and shown into his wife's bedchamber. Knowing before hand that Washington and his men were approaching, Mrs. Arnold changed into a loose fitting outfit. Making sure to have nothing underneath but her birthday suit and having only a single button attached at the collar, Mrs. Arnold made her entrance. Every move by Peggy Arnold was perfectly orchestrated, and when pressed by the hot-tempered Washington to the whereabouts of her husband, Peggy Arnold feigned an attack. It was reported by those in attendance that during the course of her convulsive episode, allowed her top button to come unhitched and her dress opened to fully expose her fine figure of womanhood. Washington and his aides, being the officers and gentlemen they were, attempted to assist the lovely Peggy and no longer pressed the issue, allowing Arnold to get a head start.

Meanwhile, the news of the treachery was beginning to filter through to the entire army and the country as well. It was nearly eleven in the evening on the 25th, and Greene had just laid down his pen from writing the next days orders, when an orderly entered with a letter. Greene recognized the writing and knew at once it was from Alexander Hamilton: "There has just unfolded at this place a scene of the blackest treason. Arnold has fled to the enemy. Andre, the British Adjutant general, is in our possession as a spy. His capture unraveled the mystery, which has just now been revealed. West

Point was to have been the sacrifice. All the dispositions have been made for the purpose, and 'tis possible, though not probable, to-night may see the execution. The wind is fair. I came here in pursuit of Arnold, but I was too late. I advise you putting the army under marching orders, and detaching a brigade immediately this way."

How Greene felt as he read the letter was shown in the letter he sat and composed almost the instant he finished reading Hamilton's. He took up his pen and wrote to the President of Congress: "Enclosed is a copy of the letter which this moment came to my hand from Colonel Hamilton, communicating the discovery of the blackest treason that ever disgraced human nature. I have thought it advisable to forward your Excellency this intelligence that you may take measures to search for his papers in Philadelphia, and those of the family with whom he is connected. Perhaps some discovery may be made which may lead to further scenes of villainy."

Greene allowed the troops to get some rest, but roused them at three in the morning, ordered two regiments of the Pennsylvania line to set out immediately for West Point, and the rest to hold themselves in readiness to start at a moment's notice. Just after four, a courier arrived with a letter from Washington. Its instructions were the ones Greene had already anticipated, and Greene responded: "Your Excellency, before the receipt of your letter I had already put the First Pennsylvania brigade in motion to your location. As the first brigade had marched I thought it most advisable to let the second follow them this morning. The rest of the army is in perfect rediness to move at the shortest notice. I beg leave to your Excellency on this unhappy discovery, but am struck with astonishment at the horrid treason."

The next morning, while assembled for parade before the days marching and at the reading of the orders of the day, you could have heard a pin drop when the Adjutant read the news to the troops. What would come next was impossible to tell, or in what direction the army for either side would move. But Greene was prepared for any sudden orders to march and decided to send the sick to a place with greater security and for their comfort. "The situation of Paramus," he writes to the head physician of the army, Dr. Tilton on the 27th, "and the uncertainty of our armies continuing at this place, induces me to think it will be for the interest of the service to send the sick to the huts at Morris. Please take measures for their immediate removal, having regard to the weather, so as not to expose the sick more than what is necessary, as we are not yet pressed for time."

From Washington's headquarters at Robinson's House across from West Point, Washington drew up new orders. "I have concluded to send to camp to-morrow Major Andre of the British army, and Mr. Joshua H. Smith, who also has had a great hand in carrying on the business between him and Arnold. They will be under an escort of horse, and I wish you to have separate houses in camp ready for their reception, in which they may be kept perfectly secure; and also strong, trusty guards, trebly officered, that a part may be constantly in the room with them. They have not been allowed to mingle together, and must be kept apart. I wish the room for Mr. Andre to be a decent one, and that he may be treated with civility; but that he may be so guarded as to preclude a possibility of his escaping, which he will certainly attempt to effect. Smith must also be carefully secured and not treated with asperity. I intend to return to-morrow morning, and hope to have the pleasure of seeing you in the course of the day."

On the 29th the Board of Inquiry into the matter of Andre's case was organized, and meeting in the Old Dutch church at Tappan, they read Washington's letter of instructions, and entered at once upon their duty. Greene was elected president of the Board; it was decided that no one present had higher qualifications in the discussion or question of military law. Greene had studied under Jacob's and Blackstone, experts of that time; he had also studied the law of nations in Vattel, the leading authority of the day. It was certain that all that knowledge would go to waste in the case of Andre. In initial interviews with his captures, he had admitted fully to his guilt, and there was no doubt as to the outcome and result of his trial. The young man was already well known, and quite liked by his peers in the American army officer corp. Many who were involved with the gracious and handsome young officer knew he was only doing his duty and the work his superiors had given to him. Most felt it was unfair for him to stand for the charge that should have been saved for Arnold, and only Arnold. Von Steuben had said to North, "It is not possible to save him, and yet if it was in my power I would gladly have saved him."

When the inquiry was assembled after the arrival of Andre, the graceful gentleman came forward and bowed to the court in silence. Every man assembled would have gladly given up his spot to another. "Read the names of the members," announced Greene, "and let the prisoner say if he has anything to object to any of them." "Nothing," was Andre's reply. "You will be asked various questions," Greene continued, "but we wish you to feel perfectly at liberty to answer them or not as you choose sir. Take your time for recollection and weigh well what you say." Andre told his story, and presented a written statement of it and gave it to the court of inquiry. "Did you consider yourself under the protection of a flag?" was one of the questions asked. "Certainly not; if I had I might have returned under it," was the quick answer. "You say that you preceded to Smith's house?" asked Greene. "I said 'a' house, but not whose house it was," he replied curtly with a grin. "True," said Greene, "Nor have we any right to ask this of you after the terms we have allowed. Have you any remarks to make upon the statements you have presented?" "None. I leave them to operate with the Board."

The guard escorted Andre back to his room and left the court to their devices. Eyewitnesses have stated that "the room remained silent for quite some time." Then Greene was the first to speak. "You have all heard the prisoner's statements and the documents that have been laid before you by the order of the Commander-in-chief. What is your opinion?" Each man was asked in turn and replied the exact same as the next. "That he is to be considered as a spy, and according to the laws and usages of nations ought to suffer death," was the answer. The opinion of the court was drawn up in full and handed to Greene for his signature. A few tears were said to have run off each mans face as Greene set his name to the death warrant, but his hand showed no sign of it when he finished his signature.

The report was laid before Washington. He too was deeply touched and had wished there were something they could have done. If they had captured Arnold, they would surely have let Andre go free in a prisoner exchange in was thought. Hamilton was asked to write his reply, which he refused. He had grown close to Andre over the course of the last few days and thought it was wrong that the young man suffers for Arnold's treachery. Washington did not disagree with Hamilton, but said nothing. He merely had another aide write up the deliberation and had it sent back to Greene: "The Commander-in-chief approves of the opinion of the board of general officers respecting the matter of Major Andre, and orders that the execution of Major Andre take place to-morrow, at five o'clock P.M."

Meanwhile Clinton had written a claim to the surrender of his adjutant, and in his answer back Washington to him, enclosed the opinion of the board. The British general, who was warmly attached to Andre, resolved to make one more effort to save him. Assuming the board could not have been rightly informed of all the circumstances essential to the formation of a correct opinion, he announced his intention of sending Lieutenant-general Robertson and two other gentlemen to give a true state of facts and to declare his sentiments and resolutions. On receiving this letter from Clinton, Washington postponed the execution, and ordered Greene to go to Dobb's Ferry and meet the English deputies party.

Greene was already on the spot when the *Greyhound*, arrived with its white flag at the masthead. A boat was quickly lowered, and within only a few minutes, an officer stood before Greene asking for permission to allow Lieutenant-general Robertson, the Honorable Andrew Elliot, Lieutenant-governor, and the Honorable William Smith, Chief Justice of the Province of New York, to land. The arrival of the chief justice was a blatant attempt to take the question of it being a military matter and transforming it into a civil law action. "No one but General Robertson will be permitted to land," was all that Greene replied. Robertson immediately landed, alone. Robertson was born in America, but had chosen to fall in for service to the king and the service of what he felt was his country. Robertson and Washington had been acquaintances, but Greene had never met Robertson before, but they both knew of each other. Robertson the American made English general, and Greene, the Quaker general, proposed by the British to be Washington's successor. Robertson was the first to speak with his compliments: "It is a great satisfaction to meet you upon an occasion so interesting to the army and to humanity." It was an obvious assumption that the question of Andre was still an open one. "You must understand from the outset," Greene replied, "the ground we stand upon. I do not meet you as an officer, but as a private gentleman. It is in this quality alone that General Washington allows me to meet you. The case of an acknowledged spy does not admit of discussion." Robertson spoke strongly. "I come to state facts and whatever character I may be supposed to speak in, I trust they will have their own weight." He then proceeded to attempt to prove that Andre was under the protection of a flag, and acted wholly by Arnold's directions. "The question of a flag truce has already been examined by the Board, General, and I find nothing in what you have said to change my opinion." Robertson tried to interject, "But Arnold also asserts that he was under a flag." Greene just smirked. "We would believe Andre rather than Arnold."

Failing to make any impression upon Greene, Robertson proposed that the question should be referred to Rochembeau and Knyphausen as two disinterested men, familiar with European usage. Greene was said to become angry and stated, "This sir, is not Europe. We are capable of performing at just such a usage in the United States. That also could not be done without impugning the deliberate decision of a competent tribunal, and that has already been done." The same objection was laid before Congress. Then as a last resort an open letter from Arnold to Washington was introduced. According to Marbois, Greene read it and threw it contemptuously at Robertson's feet. Greene was to look at Robertson and finally utter the obvious solution. "If you expect us to give up Andre we shall expect you to give up Arnold." Robertson was said to have said nothing, but "to look on Greene with indignant reproof." With every avenue exhausted, an appeal was made to humanity, and the consideration, which Clinton has shown to persons in whom Washington had taken an interest. It was Greene's turn to show contempt and merely looked at Robertson without uttering a word.

As they parted, Robertson called to Greene from the rowboat taking him back to the *Greyhound*, "I shall trust to your candor to represent my arguments to General Washington in the fairest light." He also announced his intention to wait until the next morning in the expectation of taking either Andre himself, or at least an assurance of his safety, back to New York with him. Greene did not answer, but retired to his desk and penned the following note to Robertson: "Agreeably to your request I communicated to General Washington the substance of your conversation in all the particulars, so far as my memory served me. It made no alteration in his opinion and determination. I need say no more after what you have already been informed."

The next question to decide was Andre's request in a letter dated the 1st of October, "not to die on a gibbet." Washington consulted his officers, and it has been asserted, though no contemporary evidence exist except a letter announcing the findings to Andre, that the vote amongst the officers was six for granting his request, and six against. As president of the Board, Greene had the deciding vote and cast it. Andre would be hung. Since Andre had been convicted as a spy, he held no military rank, and so if punished by the letter of the law, must be executed by the laws of war. Spies were hung. "Any other mode," Greene explained after his vote, "would in the actual state of our relations with England, throw a doubt upon our conviction of this crime."

On the day of the set execution was to be performed, it had been decided that the principal officers of the army should be present. Washington and his staff were absent, but Greene was there on horseback, and as onlookers watched, said that "Greene received and returned Andre salute as he passed to the gallows. And when the cruel act was done. There were tears, and all went their way."

Chapter XX

"A New Command"

In accepting the office of Quartermaster-general Greene had reserved and retained his rights as a Major general. His dislike of the duties of staff, and his intention to return to the line at the first moment that presented itself, made him extremely sensitive at any attempt to question his right to that rank. As soon as he had first tenured his resignation in the winter of '79, he wrote to several of his fellow officers whose claim to his former rank would have affected them. So, he asked them quite frankly for their opinion of the situation. The majority of them agreed with his assessment that he should be given his former rank immediately upon Congress's acceptance of his resignation. Washington was not among those that agreed, and also told him frankly, that it was up to the commander-in-chief whether he receive his former rank, and when or if, he should ever receive the rank of Major-general.

Finally relieved from the burden of staff duties, Greene was now free to direct his attention to the more congenial duties of the line. The optimistic plan for a northern campaign had failed. The French fleet was stuck in the harbor at Newport by a superior British force. The French army therefore was compelled to remain inactive until their fleet could be released. There was no prospect of any movements at the present, and the near future was just as gloomy and uncertain. Congress had taken on the job of a new system for the army in earnest, but they had gone ahead and formed it without consulting Washington, and it soon fell into total collapse which took precious time to correct. This was the perfect time for something like treason to occur, and Arnold soon made it so.

Soon after the treasonous episode on the heels of the southern campaign disaster at the battle of Camden, rumors that many of Washington's officers began urging him to assume a dictatorship, soon began circulating in Philadelphia. Soon after, another report throughout the colonies had the eastern states at the point of forming a new confederacy. Both reports appeared to be false, but innuendoes abound to this day that they were true facts when the nation was under a pall of dark thoughts and anxious minds of the public that saw the revolution crumbling right before their eyes.

Arnold's sudden "departure" as commander of West Point had left that position vacant, and the certainty that the condition of this key to the Hudson was well known to the English commander. This made it necessary to take immediate steps for assigning another person to secure the defenses of the Americans jewel of fortifications. St. Clair was ordered there to fill in as a provisional commander, but it was decided before hand that it was only temporary until permanent arrangements could be made. Greene was anxious to obtain the command. "I understand a new disposition of the army is going to be made," he writes to Washington on the 5th of October 1780, "and an officer appointed to the command at West Point and the district on the east side of the North River, I take the liberty just to indicate my inclinations for the appointment. Your Excellency will judge of the propriety, and determine as the honor of the army and the good of the service may require. I hope there is nothing indelicate or improper in the application. My first object is the freedom and happiness of my country. With these, your Excellency's reputation and glory are inseparably connected; and as it has been my constant wish, so it shall be my future endeavor, to promote the establishment of both."

Washington wasted no time in replying to Greene. "It is a matter of great question with me, whether West Point will not become head-quarters of the army, when we go into cantonments for the winter. I am very apprehensive that the diminution of our present force and the little prospect of recruiting the army in season, the importance of the West Point, and economical motives, will compel us to concentrate our forces on the North River, keeping light parties only on our flanks. If under this information you should incline to take the immediate command of the detachment which is about to march for the West Point, and the general direction of matters on the east side of Hudson's River, it will be quite agreeable to me that you should do so. But candor has led me to a declaration of the uncertainty of that post's being long removed from my immediate command. The army will march and separate to-morrow. Your immediate determination is therefore necessary, that the orders may be prepared accordingly."

Greene vigorously accepted, received his instructions the same day, and on the 7th of October, his two divisions, composed of the Jersey and York brigades, with the brigades of Starke and Poor, began their march up the west bank of the Hudson. The next day, while Greene and the troops were encamped at Verplanck's Point, an account from a British deserter came before him. Not taking any chances that he was a spy, due to the recent dealings in the area, Greene held him for the rest of the trip. He had told Greene that the British might be on their way in the next week. Greene took the information with a grain of salt, but took no chances for obvious reasons. The next day the troops marched for West Point as quickly as possible. They sent the baggage and covered wagons up the river ahead, and ordered Wayne to march with his troops from Haverstraw, and St. Clair to march with the other brigades the next day. By evening he reached West Point without incident and immediately penned his initial observations in his journal. "Four brigades to garrison this place. I got into garrison late last evening, and am sorry to find a place of such great importance is in such a miserable situation. The condition of the works, and the knowledge the enemy has of them from Arnold, makes it necessary that every exertion should be made to complete them; and I have it in charge from the Commander-in-chief to leave nothing unattempted to accomplish the feat. The force I command is but small, but if the garrison is but furnished with provisions, wood, and forage, I have nothing to fear from the enemy, being persuaded the discipline and bravery of the troops will make up for the smallness of numbers and the defect in the fortifications."

On the same day Greene detached 100 infantry and 40 cavalry to collect cattle under the governor's warrant; and writes to call Colonel Hughes to the Point to examine with him the question of supplies, "and many other matters too numerous to enter into the detail of." In order to lessen the consumption of provisions and forage, he directs "all officers horses to be sent out into the country to be kept," and adds, "It will be best to agree with the farmers to keep them by the week, if possible, and to take the entire charge of them."

By the 10th Greene writes to Colonel Hughes on another matter, "His Excellency, the Commander-in-chief is exceeding anxious to have the fortifications completed at this place, as well on account of Arnold's knowledge of them, and for the more certain security, should we at any time be obliged for want of provisions or other articles to reduce the garrison." The Artillery comes next for preparation, and so writes to his friend Knox. "I have been here so little time that I have not had opportunity to examine fully into the state of the artillery, but from the observations I have made, I see the gun-carriages are in bad order. I am told there is no artificers in your line, and by the return very few in the quartermaster's line, and a prodigious deal of work to do in every line, particularly in yours and the engineer's. I beg you, therefore, to order us a detachment of artificers from the main army. Everything here is in a bad state. But the worse of all is we have not a mouthful of flour in garrison except the little lodged in the forts."

The next day Greene goes to Poughkeepsie to consult with Governor Clinton about supplies for his ever growing of incoming troops. By the 13th, he begins to carry out his plan for the collection of supplies. "I have detached a party of two hundred men," he writes to the quartermaster of the post

Daniel Carthy, "for the purpose of assisting the Quartermaster's department in getting a supply of wood for the use of the garrison. You will also immediately provide a sufficient quantity of roots and vegetables of different kinds for the troops of the garrison." By now, the amount of the garrison had swelled to about 3,000 men. Clearly showing the seriousness, the Americans felt that the British would attempt to use the information Benedict Arnold had supplied for the capture of the fortification, and to what degree they were willing to go to prevent that very thing from happening. By the 1st of January 1781, the threat of an attack on West Point had decreased to the point that Washington believed it was safe to move some of the troops to other winter encampments, and so the garrison was reduced to little more than 2,000.

As yet another winter loomed, Greene was strenuously engaged in the duties of his new command. But, talk had been circulating for quite a few months that Major-general Nathanael Greene would soon be called to a broader and more important field of duty. As early as September, the rumors had already begun to circulate that even General Gates friends were prepared to admit it was time to recall the overwhelmed commander from the southern department of the war. One of those flies in the ointment was known other than Alexander Hamilton. By mid September, he wrote to Duane expressing his thoughts. "Was there ever an instance of a general running away, as Gates had done from his whole army? And was there ever so precipitous a flight? One hundred and eighty miles in three days and a half! It does admirable credit to the activity of a man at his time of life. But it disgraces the general and his brave soldiers. I've always believed him to be very short of a Hector or a Ulysses. All the world, I think, will begin to agree with me now. But what will be done by Congress? Will he be changed or not? If he is changed, for God's sake overcome prejudice, and send Greene. You know my opinion of him. I stake my reputation on the events, give him but fair play."

"Should a Major-general be detached to relieve General Gates, which is not improbable," Cornell wrote a few days later, "I believe you would be the man." Greene remembered what Washington had written to him before Gates was appointed. "I am sorry for the difficulties you have encountered in the department of Quartermaster, especially as I have been instrumental in some degree in bringing you into it. Your judgement must direct you; if it points to a resignation of your present office, and your inclination leads you to the southward, my wish shall accompany it; and if the appointment of a successor to General Lincoln is left to me, I shall not hesitate in preferring you in this command; but I have little expectation of being consulted on the occasion."

Washington was not consulted, and the favorite of Congress was met in a disastrous defeats and Gates showed his true coat of paint. But by now, Congress had learned to leave matters of military decisions to Washington, and at the least to ask for his opinion and consul on such matters in the future. The commander-in-chief should be listened to with deference of his character and the position he held. Plus, Washington was not one to allow you to make a mistake more than once on the same subject without demanding you leave his opinion to no doubt.

By October, Congress had sent Pettit to "bring intelligence from the southward of the past events of a certain general." Pettit was already a fan of Greene's from working with him in the quartermaster department. He needed no prodding to get to the truth of the events that up until now had been related by Gates. No one else was willing to speak, but Pettit pressed some with the use of spirits in several taverns, and soon "asked further explanations that had been wholly suppressed, though most people seemed desirous of keeping it secret, some from real regard to this general's fame, others from prudential motives, unwilling to be foremost in attacking so eminent a character (no matter how raised.)"

Soon, news came from Congress to "be obliged to break off all inquiries this morning. Congress is to form a Court of inquiry on the conduct of General Gates, which clearly suspends his command." Washington was asked to appoint a general to that command at once, but "that a southern gentlemen particularly seemed desirous, and that General Greene may be the appropriate choice of appointment." The member of Congress soon added that "they hoped he was not, because I know the fate of the officer who shall undertake it, especially if he be from the eastward; no eastern man can please those people, nor succeed in his command, unless he should be favored by circumstances which no man has a right to expect."

By the 10th of September, Congress ordered the court of inquiry, and almost at once suggested that Greene be the successor to the southern department. On that same day, Colonel Biddle wrote to Greene expressing his thoughts on the matter. "I shall hope that you may obtain this command, because I think you may serve your country and distinguish yourself. But, though you have warm and honest friends, you have your enemies also to oppose you, and to suggest you are the perfect candidate, only in wishing to see you fail or worse."

By the 5th of October, news of Gates' recall from command had become wide spread. The southern department had now become the talk on everyone's lips in the colonies from public figure to merchant. The people demanded quick and decisive action in the naming of the new commander. When Nathanael's old friend Henry Knox learned of the Gates' recall he wrote to him. "By this time, it is presumed, you are pretty well seated amidst the mountains of Hudson's River; but I pray you not to fix your affections too strongly on the craggy precipices that surround you; if you do, it is probable a seperation might cause you much pain. I am informed that General Gates is recalled to answer Congress on some matters respecting geography of the Southern States, and that his Excellency is directed to send some general in his stead. You will be that person? You may ask me that same question, but I protest I know not since I found of Gates recall. Poor fellow! The heat of the southern climate has blasted the laurels which were thought from their splendor to be ever Greene!"

On the 13th of October a resolution reached headquarters at the Falls of the Passaic, and with it a letter from Mr. Matthews. "I am authorized by the delegates of the three Southern States to communicate to your Excellency their wish, that Major-general Greene may be the officer appointed to the southern department, if it would not be compatible with the rules of the army." Without hesitation, Washington picked up his quill and sent his response by express rider to Congress and another letter to Greene. "By a resolution from Congress and a copy inclosed, I find it has been their pleasure to order me to direct a court of inquiry to be held on the conduct of Major-general Gates, as commander of the southern army; and also to direct me to appoint an officer to command it in his room, till the inquiry shall be made. As Congress have been pleased to leave the officer who shall command on this occasion to my choice, it is my wish to appoint you; and from the pressing situation of affairs in that quarter, that you should arrive there as soon as circumstances will possibly admit. Suppose that General Heath, if not already at West Point, is on his way from Rhode Island. I write him to take command of the post. If he is with you, be pleased to communicate to him your instructions with respect to it, and any other matters you may judge it to be material for him to know. If he has not arrived, General McDougall will command till he comes. I have only to add, that I wish for your earliest arrival, that there may be no circumstances to retard your proceeding to the southward, and that the command may be attended with the most interesting good consequences to the States and the highest honor to yourself."

This was a day Greene and Washington must have relished to some degree. They had both suffered from Gates' wrath and his weak ambition to discredit the two of them either seperate or jointly. Gates' hostility towards Greene had even extended to Caty Greene from his past rude and ungentlemanly comments on her less than motherly ways and flirtatious persona while in camp. Now, the mortification and disgrace was his, and no one was responsible for his folly except Horatio Gates. Both men's feelings toward each other had never had an occasion to manifest itself. In the past they had merely been comrades fighting a common enemy, whether it be political or military foe. Washington's appointment of Greene was an open approval of confidence at a moment when Greene could use it most. Greene's quick acceptance was a declaration that he felt himself worthy of the trust, even though he secretly dreaded the assignment.

However, Greene always responded to the call of duty with vigor and decisiveness and returned his answer to Washington's letter only hours after receiving it. "Your Excellency's letter of this morning, appointing me to the command of the southern army was just only delivered to me. I beg your Excellency to be persuaded that I am fully sensible of the honor you do me, and will endeavor to manifest my gratitude by a conduct that will not disgrace the appointment. I only lament that my abilities are not more competent to the duties that will require of me, and that it will not be in my power on that account, to be as extensively useful as my inclination leads me to wish. I will prepare myself for the command as soon as I can. But as I have five years and upwards in service, during which time I have paid no attention to the settlement of my domestic concerns, if it was possible, I should be glad to spend a few days at home before I set out to the southward, especially as it is altogether uncertain how long my command may continue, or what deaths or accidents may happen during my absence to defeat the business."

The army with universal satisfaction received Greene's appointment. "General Greene is to go," wrote Major Shaw to his brother William. "Let the people in that quarter furnish the men and the necessary supplies, and, if anything is to be expected from the abilities and exertion of a single person, I think no one will be more likely to answer every reasonable expectation than this amiable officer." Greene immediately began his preparations, but details from his past and his present command came down on him like a ton of bricks. Some of the problems were Greene's own making due to his habitual method of order and manners. Point in fact; Greene added to his already enormous preparation list by feeling it was necessary to write to the new Quartermaster's department to outline some unfinished appointments he felt responsible to straighten out before he left West Point. "Being appointed to the command of the southern army, I take the earliest opportunity to acquaint you therewith; that if there arise any difficulties in the Quartermaster-general's department, that they must be referred to Mr. Pettit, as it will be impossible for me to pay the least attention thereto."

As for Greene's request for a few days home to straighten out any personal affairs, Washington returned with a negative response. "I am aware that the command you are entering upon will be attended with peculiar difficulties and embarrassments," wrote Washington on the 18th of October, "but the confidence I have in your abilities, assures me you will do everything the means in your power will permit to surmount them. I wish that circumstances could be made to correspond with your wishes to spend a little time at home previously to your setting out; but your presence with your command as soon as possible is indispensable. The embarkation at New York sailed on the 16th, and is in all probability destined to cooperate with Earl Cornwallis, who by the last advices, was advanced as far as Charlotte. I hope to see you without delay, and that your health will be no obstacle to your commencing your journey." Greene had been suffering from "a fever" in the last two weeks prior to his being named the new commander of the southern department.

Nathanael was quite disappointed that he would not have the opportunity to see his children before he left. However, Caty immediately began arrangements to meet him in West Point before word came that the southern command was his. Nathanael sent out an express rider to meet her and tell her to arrange to meet him in Hackensack, New Jersey in the next two days. But Caty Greene, along with their oldest son George, and her traveling companion Mrs. Hubbard, had been delayed in New York due to the British troop movements there. She was forced to reroute her path which added several hours to her travel plans, and the express rider never found her. Greene would write to Washington, "Your Excellency's favor of the 18th came at hand this afternoon. I wrote to Mrs. Greene to come to camp, and expect her here every hour. Should I set out before her arrival, the disappointment of not seeing me, added to the shock of my going to the southward, I am very apprehensive will have some disagreeable effect upon her health, especially as her apprehensions have been all alive respecting my going to the southward, before there was the least probability of it. My stay shall not be more than a day longer, whether Mrs. Greene arrives or not."

As much as Greene loved to command troops and was fully aware that he was about to become the commander of the southern department, he and his wife dreaded the thought of it actually happening and prayed that it would not come to pass. He writes to Caty on the 6th of October, "General Gate's defeat to the southward, and the report prevailing of a French fleet's being upon the coast from the West Indies, prevents my being explicit upon the subject of your coming to camp. I am sorry to hear Nat is unwell, but am very glad he is getting better. I am happy to hear that the rest of the little flock are in good health. I also, have been unwell for some time, but in good spirits, and thoroughly recovering, except the old complaint of the asthma, which is troublesome o' nights. My stay here in West Point for the winter should correct things I hope."

With the word from the south growing darker from day to day, and then the message that he had dreaded arriving from his commander-in-chief, Nathanael quickly attempted to rearrange his meeting with his wife and went to Fishkill in hopes of meeting up with her. He went to the house of a friend, Mr. Mandervill, on the opposite bank of the Hudson. Throughout the night he waits, but with the dawn of the next day approaching, Nathanael realizes he is not going to have the opportunity to see his wife and son, and picks up his pen to say his farewells. "I am rendered unhappy beyond expression that fatal necessity obliges me to take my leave of you in this way. I have waited until the last moment, in hopes of your expected arrival, and have just returned from Fishkill, where I went this afternoon in hopes of meeting you and George. O Caty, how much I suffer, and how much more will you. Could I have seen you, it would have given my bosom great relief." Caty had been dissatisfied with Coventry for some time, and he wished to assure her that she must decide then on a new home. This move of his to the south would almost certainly make up her mind as to where she wanted to live. She would want to follow him, but with the current events in the southern states being what they were at present, Greene had grave doubts about bringing his children to live with him. He was virtually torn apart by the years he had been away from them and could stand it no longer. He secretly hoped that Caty would choose a new home in the south, but could not bring himself to make the decision for her, so he waited to hear her thoughts on the subject. But now, it would be quite a different story to arrange the move by way of letters, and would now delay such a move by weeks or even months and he was tired of waiting to see his family. But wait he must, once again. There is a saying to this day in the military, "Hurry up and wait." I suppose it was a true statement even in the eighteenth century.

Greene waited upon every last hope that his wife and son may still appear. But by morning all hopes had vanished with the night, and he wrote one last note and left it with Colonel Hughes who had traveled with him. "I am this moment setting off for the southward, having kept expresses flying all night to see if I could hear anything of you. But as there is not the least intelligence of your being upon the road, necessity obliges me to depart. Since I shall ride very fast on to the southward, and make a stop only of one or two days at camp to see his Excellency, and about the same time at Philadelphia, it will be impossible for you to get up with me. Therefore I recommend your immediate return home, whenever this reaches you. I have been distracted, I wanted to see you so much before I set out. Our fears of being ordered to the southward, though there was scarcely a possibility of the thing taking place, was what made me hurry away at such an early hour. God grant you patience and fortitude to bear the disappointment as I have done. My apprehensions for you and our children's safety distresses me exceedingly if a move is in order for all of us. If heaven preserves us until we meet, our felicity will repay all the painful moments of a long separation. I am forever and ever yours most sincerely and most affectionately."

Greene was concerned that his wife would still attempt to catch up with her husband and wrote another note to Colonel Hughes, "I beg you sir to forward the letter which accompanies this, to Mrs. Greene as soon as possible. It is to advertise her of my setting out, and to strongly advise her to return home, as there is but little chance of her overtaking me; and to attempt it, which I feel she shall, only to be disappointed, and then have that much longer to return at a much greater distance over this rough country, will only add to her affliction, already too great in her delicate constitution." But no sooner had Greene sent the note than a express rider arrived with one from Colonel Hughes saying, "Give me your leave at once sir, for on this same day, your lady, if possible without injury to herself, must see you. My God! She will ever suffer a thousand times as much by a disappointment, as she can by going ten times the distance. I shall personally accompany her out of danger, you may rely. I ordered the person that went to Danbury to caution her not by any means to go by the way of Peekskill."

Greene was only going to be in camp one more day before continuing on to Philadelphia. Although he was elated at the thought of seeing his wife, he knew Washington expected him to start his travels to the south in the next two days. Any delay would be completely against the wishes of his commander-in-chief and disobeying direct orders from Washington. He was extremely tempted, and wrote to Hughes. "The friendly manner in which you interest yourself in Mrs. Greene's happiness, and the feeling manner that you speak upon the subject, deserves my particular thanks. I must tell you I am greatly perplexed, and know not how to act. I wish to gratify Mrs. Greene; but I am afraid my stay will be so short at this place and at Philadelphia that it will not be possible for her to overtake me. However, as you have detained the letters, and as she must be far on her way by this time, I think it will be best for her to proceed on until she hears further from me. My motives for stopping her was to save her a long and disagreeable ride for uncertain advantages. If I shall find it impossible to wait for her to come up to me, she shall hear of it by a flying express. I shall be exceedingly obliged to you to see Mrs. Greene safe across the North River, and you will please to deliver her the letter that accompanies this."

But two days pass, and another letter comes from Hughes. "This moment, 8 o'clock on Tuesday, I have learned that your lady is at Litchfield, and does not expect to be in before Saturday. I shall send a messenger with your last letter to her in the morning. The others I shall have the pleasure to deliver to her myself when I have the honor of waiting for her. My reasons I presume are obvious, as I suspect the two first are discouraging. I confess, General, that I have taken unwarrantable liberty with you and your feelings on this occasion, and don't know but I may appear before a court-martial for my offense. But if I do, I will plead *Mrs. General Greene*. I wish she were with you. I am told she intends making a tour of the southward. I am certain this will detain you, General, or I am an utter stranger to your humanity. I sent a rider off by way of Danbury to prevent your lady taking the Peekskill route."

In the meantime, Greene was at the Preakness camp, meeting with Washington at the council board, sitting with his friends Hamilton and Knox for the last time before he was to depart. Washington, Hamilton and Knox wrote up his instructions as if giving last minute directions to a friend about to go on a trip of which they have never been. In them they outlined: "Congress having been pleased by their resolution, to authorize to appoint an officer to the command of the southern army, in the room of Major-general Gates, till an inquiry can be had into his conduct as therein directed, the proper choice for this purpose is Major-general Nathanael Greene. You will, therefore proceed without delay to the southern army now in North Carolina, and take command accordingly. No particular instructions can be given in that quarter, but must leave you to govern yourself entirely according to your own prudence and judgement, and the circumstances in which you find yourself. I am aware that the nature of the command will offer you embarrassments of a singular and complicated nature; but I rely upon your abilities and exertions for everything your means will enable you to effect. I have proposed to them to send Baron von Steuben to the southward with you. His talents, knowledge of service, zeal, and activity, will make him very useful to you in all respects, and particularly in the formation and regulation of the raw troops and militia who will principally compose the southern army.

You will give von Steuben a command suited to his rank, besides employing him as inspector general. I have put Major Lee's corps under marching orders, and so soon as he is ready, shall detach him to join you." With that, Nathanael Greene departed for the south.

Chapter XXI

"The Southern Campaign"

From here forward, the story becomes history as much as biography. Nathanael Greene was proposed to be the savior of the southern campaign and its lowly army. It was expected that the British would gain forces from those that had recently landed in the captured city of Charleston. They would slowly march their way north through North Carolina, then Virginia, then Maryland, and then onward to Pennsylvania. There they would meet up with their northern army and catch "the Old Fox Washington", as Cornwallis was prone to calling the American commander-in-chief, and crush the rebellion once and for all. Then, the British would begin to build the Crown's new utopia in the North American continent, which Cornwallis had already been told by England would be headed by him, along with a handsome amount of land on which to build his new kingdom. The land is encompassed millions of prime acres and was to the wilderness side of Fort Pittsburgh. The land he was to be given was from Lake Erie to the western boundary of the explored wilderness at that time, which was an area of land that is approximately the state of Ohio. All were to be Earl Cornwallis' when he dispatched the annoying rebels and their pitiful rebellion. All hopes had suddenly fallen on one man to single-handedly save the American southern campaign from ruin and stop the overwhelming superior British army from marching to their goal of complete victory and totally crushing the American rebellion. That would be Major-general Nathanael Greene.

Greene had one less thing to worry about before he started for the south. He had received word that his wife had indeed received all of his letters, including the strongly worded note to turn back and forget trying to catch up with him. She took his advice and had already turned around before reaching the border of Rhode Island and Connecticut. Greene received a kind note from Hughes, explaining his mortification with keeping his hopes up that his wife was still on her way and begged for his forgiveness. Greene was extremely disappointed he would not see his wife and older son George, but was also genuinely glad that she realized the danger of racing through hostile country and then make the trip back. He now had time to concentrate on the job at hand which was how he was going to accomplish this impossible duty that was laid before him.

The general description of the territory originally known as just Carolina was somewhat familiar to Greene. He had read a great deal about the south when he first entered the war. He was attempting to familiarize himself with an area that had not truly entered the war back in 1776, but would soon enough become a portion of the Colonies. He had always suspected the south would be a major player in the war of independence. That day had arrived with the capture of Charleston by the British, and their subsequent drubbing Gates and the Continental line had received since then. At that time, Carolina had been divided by later charters into what would become Georgia, North and South Carolina. Topography and the entire lay of the land, had always been a factor in Greene's determination of where to meet the enemy or at the least knowing what to expect at such a meeting. He had always put great importance to how and why an enemy might form a defensive position. What to do if the high ground or best field is already taken by the enemy and what to do in the circumstance of a worst case scenario especially concerning the path of retreat, water, hills, towns and escape route. Greene had used all of these factors to best use in places like Brandywine, Germantown, and Monmouth, but those were two defeats and one draw. Greene would have to greatly improve on that record in the instance of the southern department, and no one knew it better than he did.

The south as a whole was primarily comprised of all the same characteristics from southern Virginia to Georgia in the way of soil, climate, production, and population. At the time of the Revolution though, South Carolina had a seacoast of about two hundred miles inland and was the second largest seaport in the Colonies. North Carolina had a seacoast of more than two hundred and twenty miles, and Georgia, over one hundred. The greater part of the mainland was cut off from direct contact with the ocean by a string of barrier islands, many of them extremely long and narrow. They were covered for the most part with a natural growth of pine and palmetto trees, and formed a type of extensive and complex system of inland navigation.

The soil on the coast of South Carolina is a low and sandy wash, extending eighty miles inland without a hill, and almost without a stone of any significance, but gradually rising as you advance, to a hundred and ninety feet above sea level. Approximately sixty miles of sand hills follow, with some hollows between them, appearing like the sea on a choppy day. Farther beyond lie the fertile tract of highlands between the Savannah and Broad rivers, the Ridge, which was beyond that as far as North Carolina and extending with hills and dales, and both well wooded and well watered.

The soil of South Carolina was divided into the Pine Barrens, with its valuable timber, but desolate, sandy, unfruitful wilderness and interwoven with swamps. The Savannah's, vast natural lawns, like those found in Africa, without a single tree to protect a person from the brutal mid-day sun, but which every morning is thick and heavy with the dew from the night before, making the soil incredibly fertile. On these meadows the tall grass grew and farmers let their cattle to graze untouched. Next came the rivers, and around the mouths of those rivers, more low swampy ground of black earth and red clay. Last but not least was the low country, an area called the oak and hickory lands, with bright red earth growing chiefly corn. While in the back country they grew grains, tobacco, hemp, flax, cotton, and indigo.

In none of the parts of land mentioned, except Charleston, was the population dense. In the land farther to the northwest, lay the mountain chain that would eventually start the Appalachians and Alleghenies. In this area we find names like King's Mountain, on the northern boundary line of the two Carolinas, Cheraw Hill on the southern bank of the Pedee, Hobkirk's Hill, near Camden, and the High Hills along the Santee and the north bank of the Wateree. These were natural elevations that could easily be used for, or against troops in the coming battles. A waterway that would become even more important to Greene would be the Dan, a small stream formed by the confluence of several other streams so small as to not even be named on a map of the day. At first, the Dan runs eastward within the limits of North Carolina, but just midway, it crosses the boundary into Virginia, and by a slight northerly inflection, unites with the broader current of the Roanoke. Why are we spending so much time describing the geography of the land? Because it will play an enormous amount of importance in the next year, and be a direct partner in the success and heartache of the two armies that will fight and maneuver for every inch of ground described here. Each inch as important as the preceding inch.

The southern states had taken an early part in the contest with England, and the repulse of the British fleet at Fort Moultrie, just outside of Charleston had been one of the brilliant achievements early in the war, when victories were hard, if not impossible to achieve. However, it was not until after the defeat of Burgoyne, and the failure to make a permanent impression upon the north, that the British generals finally turned almost all of their attention to the south. In December 1778, a Lieutenant-colonel Campbell of the British army suddenly took Savannah, Georgia, and with it a strategic position was gained at the mouth of an important waterway, the Savannah River. A base of operation for the entire south campaign was secured for the British. Their fleet gave them a direct communication with New York, and from there they could easily draw supplies and reinforcements. The road to the interior was open by the river, and the road to Charleston was open by the mainland and the outer islands. How long the capital of South Carolina could hold out against such forces was elementary.

There had always been southern troops in numbers, and good southern officers to command them. But, none of these officers had ever experienced fighting the British on a large scale. Their fighting style was guerrilla tactics, the attacking from all sides of a British column or Loyalist unit and then scattering before they knew which way they went. It drove the enemy crazy, but did little to damage the British troops on a whole. Occasionally, the British commanders would get frustrated, and set up a trap that would silence the American units for awhile. Consequently, the southern delegates knew they needed experienced leaders and did not hesitate to request that Congress give them Lincoln, a Massachusetts man, who had distinguished himself in the great northern campaign of 1777. For fifteen months, with only 600 Continentals, and the constant fluctuating numbers of militia, Lincoln held his ground against superior forces in the open field, and for thirty days defended Charleston against the combined strength of Aburthnot and Clinton. Finally, on the 12th of May 1780, the English took possession of the first city in the south. The British possessed, New York and Newport, but the war was far from over for the Americans.

The progress of the war in the south had been anxiously watched by those in the north. Many letters and reports of the day were filled with rumors and conjecture and could not always be taken at face value. People longed for speedy news from the south, for those in the north, as well as the south, knew how much depended on Lincoln's little army keeping the English at bay. News traveled slowly in those days. It was May 30th, and through enemy publications out of New York, that the Americans encamped at Morristown heard the news about the fall of Charleston, and that Lincoln and over 5,000 troops had been taken prisoner. Congress was alarmed, but not disheartened. That was the second in command at Saratoga, but the first was still available. So, on the 13th of June, as fast as could be acted upon without consulting Washington, Congress "resolved unanimously that Major-general Horatio Gates immediately repair to and take command of the southern department."

Here finally, Gates must have thought, was his time to prove that he really should have possessed the title of commander-in-chief. He would show that he had the great qualities, which his friends so confidently claimed for him, time and time again. His army was small, but well disciplined, proven in battle, outstanding officers like DeKalb and Morgan commanding them, and now they would have the added genius and character of Gates as their commander. The small army had just been supported by Marion and Sumter, a large body of militia had been gathered and were battle tested and well disciplined for militia. In addition, two weary corps with DeKalb had just been increased by Armand's legion, composed of cavalry and infantry, and then three small companies of artillery. How could they possibly lose? For one thing, Gates did not believe in calvary in southern war, and took no pains to conceal his thoughts on the matter. Also, the troops had just been marched over rough terrain with little provisions and rest. For another, a general's first thought should be to provide magazines and supplies to his army. And lastly, Gates had been trained in the British army. He thought like a British officer and acted like a British officer. That type of tactics were not going to work against the British army. However, those were the exact tactics gates employed, but without the use of cavalry and the proper supplies for his artillery. After only about two hours, America had suffered the worse defeat it would see in the entire war, which would decimate the morale of the whole army. Greene would certainly have his work cut out for him at his new command.

By the 19th of August, more bad news arrived with the defeat of Sumter at Fishing Creek. The Americans were forced to fall back to Salisbury and regroup yet again. Unbelievably, most of the militia had stayed and not lost heart and ran away. These men were of stout blood and were not just fighting a cause for freedom, but for their homes, families, and neighbors. The units attached to Mecklenburg and Wazhaws reformed into small bands and renewed the fighting almost immediately. Then, a surprise to everyone occurred. Rather than follow-up on his overwhelming victories and carry the fight farther north, Cornwallis halted his troops and actually reversed his march and returned to South Carolina near Charleston. Luck was beginning to shine on the Continental army. If Cornwallis had advanced after his recent successes, he most certainly could have ended the war in the south and easily marched on to join his forces in the north and crushed Washington and the northern Continental army. The British would have won and the rebellion finally ended.

With the halt of the British advance, stragglers were given time to come in and meet up with other units. Officers were permitted to reestablish their authority and train troops, gather provisions, and recruit more soldiers. By early September a few hundred ragged, half-starved men were assembled around gates at Hillsborough. But they men were still considered leaderless. Gates had lost complete control of his command, his men had totally lost respect for his abilities, and word had it that Congress wanted some answers from Gates about the debacle at Camden. A small supply of clothing arrived and was distributed among the Continentals. The four companies of infantry were formed into a battalion and put under the command of lieutenant colonel Howard of Baltimore. The Continental brigade was given to Colonel Otho Williams, another Marylander, who was Gate's Adjutant general. Even Smallwood, who had alienated most of the officers in the south and north with his ambiguous conduct, was given command of the militia. The light troops were assigned to Daniel Morgan who would soon be made a Brigadier-general. By the end of November the little army of the southern department would advance to Charlotte, Smallwood to Providence, fourteen miles south of Charlotte, and a small contingent of militia stationed near Camden after the British withdrew. On the 2nd of December 1780, Greene would ride into camp at Charlotte and join his new army command. It was not an event to celebrate, because he and his officers had much to do as 1781 dawned and when the British would fall upon them.

Chapter XXII

"Greene Makes His Way South"

Greene was not new to Philadelphia, and knew every street as he did his own town of Coventry. But this time, the trip to the capital was different. Now he had a keener sense of responsibility than previously experienced. Before he was even to reach his new command, he would have to overcome two great calamities, which had fallen upon the southern department. Gates had dimmed his honorable reputation by the overwhelming defeat in Camden, and a great officer in DeKalb, had lost his life because of Gates cowardice. Greene had always liked DeKalb and had hoped to look to him for counsel and support. But he would now have to rely on his own intelligence, fortitude, and wits. Even with Greene's monstrous confidence, he still had the fear that he too could fail and had little reason to doubt it with what he was about to inherit. With the Carolinas and Georgia in the hands of the enemy, the preservation of Virginia would be difficult at best. A safe peace would have been difficult, but now it seemed impossible. The fate of the entire war and all of the questions surrounding it now depended on the preservation of the south, and Greene was beginning to feel the pressure. One thing Greene had decided upon arriving in Philadelphia was to ask Thomas Jefferson and the other Virginia delegates, what they could do to support the southern department. With Charleston captured, Virginia and its rich plantation owners had more to fear than ever. Surely, they could come up with more troops, funding, or supplies to help the cause in South Carolina so their need did not become Virginia's?

Greene's relations with Congress had never been what you would call friendly. Even though he now had a proclamation that was heartedly approved of by Congress to name him commander of the southern department, there were still men in Federal Hall who just three months before would have gladly voted him out of the service. Would these same men be able to put there prejudices aside and give him the help and support he so desperately required?

Armed with the letter Washington had written for him announcing to Congress his actions and instructions, Greene quietly strode into Congress and gingerly laid the document before them, along with a letter he had dictated himself. "Whether this appointment is considered a misfortune or otherwise, will depend upon future events. He is conscious of his deficiencies, but if he is clothed with proper powers and receives the necessary support, he is not altogether without hopes of prescribing some bounds to the ravages of the enemy. I am wholly unacquainted with the intentions of Congress with respect to the plan and extent of the war they mean to prosecute in the southern department, as well as the number and condition of the troops they mean to employ, or the States in which they are to be levied. I must request the orders and information of Congress upon all these points, and I will endeavor to make the most of the means put into my hands. Money is the sinews of war, and without a military chest, it is next to impossible to employ an army to effect. Although great articles and troops may be provided to equip them for the field, a thousand things essential to success will occur in the course of operations which cannot be foreseen or provided for. I have only to suggest to Congress my earnest wish of being with my command as soon as possible, and the necessity there is of making the proper arrangements before I go."

While Congress deliberated over the instructions, they formed a committee of five, including Sullivan and Cornell, who had recently passed through the army camp; Greene reacquainted himself with the particulars of his new department. He noticed that the majority of troops that made up the southern army were from Delaware and Maryland, but he had absolutely no authority to call upon those states for more recruits or supplies. He also noticed that a large portion of the supplies being collected were coming from the north, which meant an auditor-general of accounts would be required to do the business through dispatches, and that the "ordnance department was in a wretched, and deranged state," further delaying his departure. Concerning the medical department, Greene learned nothing. While Quartermaster-general at Valley Forge and Morristown, he had greatly concerned himself with his attention to that department. But for the south, they had no records, no leads, and no course of action. The military chest was the same problem. Two days later, after Congress was finished going over Washington's instructions and the committee over Greene's letter, they addressed the immediate problems that Greene brought to their attention.

This time there was no delay in the committee or Congress. "Giving the results of General Greene's inquiries into the state of the southern department, and inclosing estimates for a variety of articles in those areas, we find it absolutely necessary to enable his army to take the field, and must be had from the northern states as there was not the least probability of procuring an article of them to the southward." With that, there was no delay in committee or in Congress. Congress quickly agreed on the necessary articles and it was approved by the 30th of October. On that same day, Congress passed a series of resolutions. One approving Greene's appointment as commander of the southern department, another approving the assignment of von Steuben to that same command, assigning the army "all the troops raised and to be raised from Delaware to Georgia inclusive," giving Greene all the powers that had been given to Gates and extending to him all the instructions and resolutions that had been given to the southern department since Gates' appointment, and authorizing him to employ the army according to his own judgment, though subject to the control of the Commander-in-chief. Congress also "earnestly recommended the legislatures and executives of the states within his department to comply" with his requisitions for "men, money, clothing, arms, intrenching tools, provisions, and other aids and supplies" directing the heads of departments to furnish to his order such articles as the states could furnish, and authorizing him to negotiate a cartel for the exchange of prisoners.

So, the first step had been taken, and with a promptness and tenacious attitude not exhibited by Congress in some time, Greene was well on his way. But now, Greene would see just how far these good intentions could be carried out. Passing resolutions is one thing. Making it happen was a completely different story in most cases. His army, as far as he could make out, was "rather a shadow than a substance, having merely an imaginary existence." But this army was basically all he had with which to work. So, he had to make the best of it. The militia, never one of Greene's favorite branches of military units, would come and go at will most of the time and he could and would not rely on them. Although he knew he would be forced to take them into the field of battle, he knew that the only constant force he could rely on was Continentals. To try and procure as many regular soldiers as possible rather than militia, was his chief job during his eight days in Philadelphia.

While writing to Washington on the 31st of October, Greene would say, "My first objective will be to equip a flying camp to consist of 800 horse and one thousand infantry. This force, with the occasional aid of the militia, will serve to confine the enemy in their limits and render it difficult for them to subsist in the interior country. I see but little prospect of getting a force to contend with the enemy upon equal ground, and therefore must make the most of a kind of partisan war until we can levy and equip a large force."

Knox had promised him a company of artillery, and in a letter dated the 27th, Greene urges him to send it immediately forward without waiting for him to proceed with it. "Four field pieces and two light howitzers as complete as possible." Pickering had promised him two companies of artificers, and in a letter on the 1st of November Greene urges him to send them on also "as soon as possible, with orders to make as little stay in Philadelphia as might be."

For arms, which neither Congress or the southern States could supply, he had turned to Joseph Reed, a personal friend he knew he could rely on, and who as President of Pennsylvania had cooperated with him at every turn in the past. "I shall be exceedingly obliged to your Excellency," he writes to Reed on the 1st of November, "if you will be kind enough to lend us for the service of the southern army four or five thousand stand of arms. And I will engage they shall be replaced out of the Continental magazines. If you cannot furnish this number, let me have all that you can spare." Reed did all that patriotism and friendship could allow in meeting Nathanael's request, but the number of arms which he could supply fell woefully short of the demand by more than half. When all was said and done, between the Board of War and those Reed had supplied, it was found that the number of arms collected only numbered about fifteen hundred. Greene turned to the only man left that could help. That was Washington. "I must beg your Excellency, therefore," he writes on the 3rd of November, "to forward us three or four thousand arms from the eastern States, as it is impossible to get them here; we are not less deficient in cartouch boxes than arms."

Another problem that arose was the difficulty he was having procuring clothing. He felt that carrying unclothed men into the field in the midst of a winter campaign, even in the south, would only serve "to fill the hospitals and sacrifice valuable lives, and is doing violence to humanity and can be attended with nothing but disgrace, distress, and disappointment." Always the humanitarian, Greene also thought of another department he did not want to go into battle with in a less than fully supplied state. "Congress will be burdened with all the expense of a well-appointed army, without the least advantage from their services; for I am persuaded the expense of the hospital department will nearly equal that of the clothes and be twice as important."

But Congress had no clothes to give him, and it would be ludicrous to think that the southern States would supply them. He had an idea, and proposed the plan to merchants in a meeting "with some of the principal ones," that they agree to furnish "five thousand suits of small clothes and great coats, and take bills on France in payment." He wrote to Congress with his proposal and wrote of it, "I have taken the liberty to suggest this mode of providing clothing from an earnest desire that the troops which are to be under my command may be put in a condition to be as extensively useful as possible." Unfortunately, the proposal was declined. As he wrote to Washington, "The merchants excuse themselves as having engaged more already than they can perform. I intend to try to put subscriptions on foot in Maryland and Virginia for the purpose of supplying clothing. Whether it will produce any good or not time only can determine. At any rate, I shall have the satisfaction of having done all in my power; and if there is public spirit enough in the people to defend their liberty, they will well deserve to be slaves."

There was still one more obstacle that need to be hurdled, and this was an obstacle that was near and dear to Greene's heart from his days on the quartermaster's department. At the defeat at Camden nearly all of the public wagons had either fallen into enemy hands or been abandoned on the highway during the retreat. The means of transportation in the south, always incomplete, was almost utterly destroyed. In the north there were wagons and horses, but neither the money nor credit with which to procure them. The Quartermaster's department could do nothing to alleviate the problem for him. Greene was embarrassed, but had to turn to his friend Reed once again. Within days of a prompt resolution of the State Council, orders were issued for raising "a hundred road wagons for the purpose of forwarding the stores collected." Greene also applied to Pickering once again. "We are exceedingly in want of about forty covered wagons; if there was a possibility of detaching from the ordance or from any other branch of the army a small number to our assistance, it would afford us great relief."

Gates had always felt that using cavalry in the southern States would only be a waste of time. He did not feel the ground was correct for its use. Too soft and sandy with too many woods and patches of trees on most of the areas that he had decided would be used as battlefields. Gates had been

244

trained by the British army. Never mind that Cornwallis had been using cavalry for all of the battles in the recent southern campaign. Men like Colonel Banastre "No Quarter" Tarleton's 400-man Loyalist calvary, who quite effectively worked in close unit with infantry, was considered the "devil butcher of the south" with his run and hit tactics. They showed no mercy to the American regular and militia troops it had already encountered by December of 1780. Greene, was much to the contrary, and believed that "cavalry and partisan corps were best adapted to the make of the country and the state of the war in that quarter, both for leading and encouraging the militia, as well as protecting the persons and property of the inhabitants." The leader of the corps of which he spoke was Henry Lee, "Whose merit and services," he writes to Congress, "are so generally known and so universally confessed, that it is altogether superfluous for me to say anything in their commendation." But Lee was only a major, and his legion had "but one field-officer belonging to it. Two are absolutely necessary to perform the services that will be required of them; and therefore I beg leave to propose the promotion of Major Lee to Lieutenant-colonel, and captain Peyton to a Major." Congress acted on it immediately and Lee was made a Lieutenant-colonel, and the "further arrangements of the corps be referred to the Commander-in-chief to take orders."

There was one other promotion about which Greene felt very deeply. One of the select few amongst George Washington's military family was a Dr. James McHenry, of Maryland. McHenry was a very young man at the time from a wealthy family and was well liked by the officers and men of camp. He had studied medicine as a science rather than a profession, and had been in the army since the inception of the war. Greene and he were close friends. From the instant McHenry had learned Nathanael Greene was named as commander of the southern department McHenry was anxious to abandon the dull life of the northern camp and serve with Greene as his aide. Greene, in turn had an "earnest wish to have him along." But since McHenry had already served as aide to the Commander-in-chief, there was a rule that said he could not accept the same position with a lower ranked officer, without losing rank. "Nothing but a majority will engage him in this service," writes Greene to the President of Congress; and "if the indulgence can be consistently granted, it will lay me under particular obligations." The subject of promotions had always been a tender subject with Congress, and although it had been asked for by Greene and favored by Washington, and every consideration was being afforded the new commander, it would take months before the general subject of his promotion would considered. In the meantime, McHenry returned as one of the Commander-in-chief's aides.

Among the prisoners who had fallen into the hands of the British at the surrender of Charleston, was Lieutenant-colonel John Laurens, the son of Henry Laurens, former member and President of Congress, and recent minister to Holland. The senior Laurens had also been captured when a British man-of-war intercepted the ship in which he was traveling to Holland, and was now a prisoner in the Tower of London. Under the accusation of high treason for crimes against the Crown, the punishment of such a sentence was hanging. John Laurens was unaware of his father's fate when Greene began to negotiate his release. Laurens had also served as a Washington aide before his transfer to the southern department, and for the exception of perhaps Lafayette and Hamilton, no young officer was held in higher esteem or held such a high level of praise from the commander-in-chief. Greene was also a fan of the young Laurens and wrote to Washington to request permission to try and make his release and then offer him the aide position upon the exchange. "I have just had a letter from Lieutenant-colonel John Laurens. He is in good health, and is very anxious to be released and join my staff as soon as we can arrange his exchange. His valuable knowledge of the southern States and of the customs and manners of the people will render his services very necessary in that quarter."

Greene had now done all that he could hope to do in Philadelphia, and prepared to leave for his winter campaign camp. But Greene was hesitant to leave without first knowing that he may at least halfway count on Congress to live up to their promise to him. He knew it was asking a lot and expected to get only a part of the supplies he needed, but some was far better than none. So he was driven to write one last letter that he hoped would help in getting those much-needed provisions. "I beg your Excellency," he writes to Washington the day before he left Philadelphia, "to urge unceasingly the necessity of forwarding our supplies for the southern army, as it will be impossible to carry on a winter campaign without clothing. I have laid before Congress an estimate of our wants, but there is not a shadow of a prospect of their being furnished, unless constant attention is paid to the business. And I am apprehensive as soon as I am gone, and no one left to press the issue of our wants, they will soon forget us."

The duty of forwarding his supplies and reminding the different departments of their promises is entrusted to a Colonel Feibiger, with minute instructions for his guidance. Then one last provision had to be addresses before he left. The amount, which Congress had furnished for his traveling expenses, was insufficient. After paying for the transportation of his own baggage, and giving von Steuben the funds he would need in order to equip himself for the journey, there was not enough left "to defray the expense of the baron and myself, with our respective families, even as far as Virginia. I must therefore, request," he writes to the President of Congress, "a further immediate supply of sixty to eighty thousand dollars, at least."

His final words were reserved for his commander-in-chief. "I am at this moment setting out for the southern army." After a few lines of personal quotes and banter, he adds: "The British might receive a deadly blow in Virginia, if Count Rochambeau and Admiral Terny would suddenly embark their troops, and land in Virginia. The enemy's fleet there is much inferior to the one I saw with the French, and land force of the former greatly inferior to the latter when joined with the troops in Virginia and the militia of the country; but this will be thought too hazardous perhaps." Strange that Greene would make such a statement out of mere conjecture. Or perhaps it was his marvelous insight and a great vision. Maybe even more, it planted a thought in the mind of Washington for such a bold and skillful advance at a place like Yorktown. At last, Greene set out for the south and to meet what he called "my little army."

Chapter XXIII

"The Heavy Weight of Command "

   Greene was glad to finally be on the road. He was convinced that the enemy were hell bent on conquering North Carolina so that they could take possession of the lower part of Virginia and set up camp and supply lines for their move farther north. A winter campaign was inevitable, and he longed to be with his army. Von Steuben would accompany Greene for the first half of his journey, and with such a traveling companion there would be no lack of subjects of conversation. By the time they parted ways, Greene would comment later, "we did not lack for instructive conversation and delightful banter." Each of the generals; Greene, Colonel Morris and Major Burnet; von Steuben, Captain Benjamin Walker and Peter S. Duponceau had their aides with them. Major Clairborn, of whom Greene always wrote warmly about in his correspondence, traveled with the group in hopes of going to Virginia and reentering the Continental line there.

   For the first two days out of Philadelphia, Greene was on familiar ground. The road was the same one he had rode with Washington to check the advance of the British from their landing at Head of Elk, and returned in slow retreat after the defeat at Brandywine. The inn at Chester, in which they spent their first night, was the same inn Washington had used as his headquarters the day after the battle. Years later, Duponceau wrote in his memories about that evening's conversation. He was surprised when in the course of several subjects, Duponceau had brought up the subject of Latin classics, and how Greene seemed at home in even that regard, and then Latin poets, which Duponceau found to his surprise, Greene was also very knowledgeable and at home speaking about. The young genial Frenchman also made it an issue that Greene then produced a volume of Latin that he had been using as a traveling companion. Duponceau also noticed that the pages were worn and dog-eared. It was an obvious favorite read for the surprising American general.

   By the 5th of November the group was at Head of Elk, and Greene, whose thoughts were on his new army, drew up instructions to Donaldson. Gates, who was to supervise the forwarding of the stores as they came in from the north. "If they came in from the north. The whole southern operations will depend upon the stores coming from the northward." Greene wrote up in his instructions to Gates. The further south the group went, the more clearly Greene saw that his first impression was correct and that there was no prospect of drawing supplies for his army "from any other quarter than Philadelphia." On the 7th of November from Annapolis, he addressed an urgent letter to the Board of War. "General Gist is at this place, and says it is idle to expect service from the southern army unless they receive supplies from the northward, to put them into a condition to act, and that it is equally idle to expect anything south of this, especially clothing; nor will there be anything of consequence to be had in this State." Baltimore he found in so "defenseless a state, that a twenty-gun ship might lay the town under contribution. And in this defenseless town had been collected, as if to attract the enemy's attention, a large quanity of public shot and shell."

   On the 20th, Greene writes from Annapolis to Governor Caesar Rodney, of Delaware, informing him of his appointment to the command of the southern army, and telling him that he is authorized by Congress to "call for such supplies of men and other things as the southern service might require," enclosing a requisition, and urging the "earliest attention to the business, as the situation of the southern army presses hard for the most speedy reinforcements of men and supplies of every kind. . .

Every wise people, will keep the war as far from them as possible. The middle States have no way of effecting this but by giving timely support to the southern operations."

The Legislature of Maryland was in session, and he seized the opportunity to lay a statement of his wants before them. "They promise me," he writes to Washington, "all the assistance in their power; but candid enough to tell me that I must place but little dependence upon them, as they have neither money nor credit, and from the temper of the people are afraid to push matters to extremity." He also brought the subject before Governor Lee, urging "the necessity of giving prompt assistance to the southern States before their spirits were broken, and that they become convinced of their misfortunes." He reminded the governor that it "remained easier to keep hope alive than to revive the spirit of resistance." Maryland and Delaware came through as best they could with the much needed supplies, and pressed Gist to "continue with the applications in writing to all concerned, that it may appear that our justification be left to promote the public service. Let your applications be as pressing as our necessities are urgent; after which if the southern States are lost we shall stand justified. The greatest consequences depend upon their activity and zeal to the service that that does not occur."

One of the greatest problems Greene continued to encounter, was the difficulty in procuring correct intelligence of the conditions to the south. In Baltimore, he was told, "men were as much at a loss generally speaking, for authentic advices from the southward as if they were in the West Indies." A common misconception was that the people felt the army was on the threshold of capturing Cornwallis and his army. So, the Whigs were lulled in a false and dangerous sense of security, while the ignorant and uninformed continued on their merry way, persisting in their malignant efforts with unabated zeal. Gates's letters to the governor, promising him a speedy renewal of offensive operations, along with "recovering all our losses in the southern States," certainly did not hurt the situation and contributed "to fix the delusion we were winning."

This was a subject that was always close in the heart of Greene, having an unwavering state of the public's confidence in the army. Greene would comment that "By tossing the public's trust to and fro, from hope to extreme despair." Greene and others thought they would lose the public all together eventually and without the support of the public, the cause would surely be lost. An example of the false reports and subsequent crush of the truth was given in a letter to Greene from a Mr. Lux. "In three days came here the different accounts that the enemy had left our bay; Lord Cornwallis and his army had likely been taken; a French army and fleet off Charleston, the enemy still in the bay, and hemming in the Virginia militia, so as they could not escape; a complete victory by General Gates; that no battle had even been fought to southward; and lastly, that the British had gone up the James River, and expecting the last article, there is neither a confirmation nor a denial of these reports."

Greene had to put all of that out of his mind for the moment. He was rapidly approaching the scene of action, and looking forward to it, but also to his arrival at Richmond and a supply of "good information." On the 12th of November, at noon, he arrived at Mount Vernon, which Washington had not seen in over five years. Greene wrote to him and said, "nothing but the absolute necessity of being with my command as soon as possible could induce me to make my stay so short. Mount Vernon is one of the most pleasant places I have ever saw; and I don't wonder that you languish so often to return to the pleasures of domestic life here. Nothing but the glory of being Commander-in-chief, and the happiness of universally admired, could compensate for such a sacrifice as you make. Baron Steuben is delighted with the place, and charmed with the reception we met with. Mrs. Washington will set out for camp about the middle of next week."

The next leg of his journey takes him to Fredericksburg, where he had hoped to find his friend General Weedon, and hear information about the movements of the enemy. But Weedon was not with the militia which had been called out to meet the enemy in the neighborhood of Portsmouth. "I lodged at your house in Fredericksburg," he writes to Weedon, "and was treated with great politeness by Mrs.

Weedon, who I was very sorry to find exceeding unhappy at your going into service again. I left Mrs. Greene equally unhappy at my going to the southward."

On the evening of the 16th of November, Greene finally reached Richmond. At the moment he arrived, he received reports that confirmed his worse fears that he found everything in utter confusion; "the business of government almost at a standstill for want of money and public credit." A high state of alarm, too, had been started by the sudden appearance of a strong body of British troops in the area. The militia had been called out, and preparations for the defense of the town made, as time and circumstances permitted. But the British general in charge of the operation, "after making every preparation for establishing a permanent post at Portsmouth by fortifying the place strongly, had suddenly drawn in his advanced parties, evacuated the town, embarked his troops, and fallen back in mass to Hampton Roads," where he still lay when Greene arrived in Richmond. The few vessels the Americans had in the harbor were left untouched, "and shoals of negroes, were left on the shore." Greene was at a complete loss to account "for this sudden and strange change in measures." It certainly could not be for fear of Muhlenberg and Weedon, who were with their troops near "the great bridge on the west side of the James River," even though the American forces were respectable in numbers, they were "ill-provided and too imperfectly disciplined to attack a fortified post. There must be some foreign cause which must be left for time and further information to explain." Greene wrote to Washington on the 19th.

The Governor of Virginia at the time was Thomas Jefferson. At the time, Jefferson was indeed the original author of the Declaration of Independence, but was not yet a household name throughout the States. It was the first, and only time that Jefferson and Greene would meet. There is little written of the meeting, supposedly because Greene did not feel it was that important of a meeting. The little that I can ascertain from the meeting is my own interpretation. The subject of the militia was obviously discussed, a subject near and dear to Greene's heart, but one that brought only negative comments from him in most cases. It was when this subject was breached when the two gentlemen met that we learn of the guarded impression of Jefferson that Greene left the meeting. Either or, it was fairly obvious to me that Greene did not particularly take to Jefferson's strong accords on democratic tendencies when he said, "the illustrious Virginian did not share in my feelings concerning the militias. But to depend upon them as a principal, the very nature of the war would become so ruinous to the country, that through numbers for a time may give security, yet the difficulty of keeping this order of men long in the field, must soon put it out of our power to make further opposition. It tells me the man be of extreme folly to hazard our liberties upon such a precarious tenure when we have it so much in our power to fix them upon a more solid basis."

Greene's six days in Richmond were like his nine in Philadelphia, devoted to the interest of his command and nothing more. He writes yet another letter to the President of Congress, recalling their attention to the subject of clothing, provisions, and supplies of his "particular inquiries during my journey and could see no prospect of obtaining the necessary article but in the way that I had suggested to Congress before leaving Philadelphia." He also returns to the problem of transportation, which with clothing, might have been as important as feeding the troops. Jefferson had been trying for "three weeks and upwards to collect a hundred wagons," and although vested with the full power of the legislature, had only collected eighteen. If Greene had only thought he disliked Jefferson at their first meeting, he was sure of it now. "The want of money and the want of public credit are the bane of all business." Jefferson wrote. "I have no complaints to make of the Legislature of Virginia. They appear perfectly disposed to do everything in their power, but the enemy's late incursion and the heavy losses they have met with will render their exertions of less avail." Greene was thankful that provisions were abundant, and that foraging had produced a well-stocked pot for each man. But there were no magazines to store these items, and no means to keep them full. To make matters worse, 3,500 men had been drafted to serve eighteen months. But the number had fallen short by over 2,000, and a large number of those had been deserting in droves for lack of clothing, and of the rest, half of those would soon be hospitals due exposure from the same reason. If that was not enough, "my greater fears than our account of provisions, clothing, and soldiers, is the lack of arms and ammunition."

He would also write in his letter to Washington; "The governor of Virginia says their situation as to clothing is desperate. Nor is the business of transportation in a much more eligible condition. We cannot march the troops of this State, or transport the provisions necessary for their subsistence for want of wagons. . . . On my arrival at Hillsborough, I intend to have all the rivers examined thoroughly in order to see if I cannot ease this heavy business by water transportation. Unless I succeed in these two measures, I am afraid it will be impossible to subsist either in North or South Carolina a sufficient force this winter to prevent the enemy from holding their present possessions and extending their limits."

Meanwhile, Greene had received a letter from Colonel Feibiger, announcing that a brigade of ten wagons had set out from Philadelphia on the 8th, and that artificers with a traveling forge would set out on the 9th. However, he had "heard nothing from Colonel Pickering, and that the committee of Congress have determined nothing yet, and seem exceedingly averse to draw on France."

On the 20th, he writes to his old brigade commander, Muhlenberg, and directs him to report to von Steuben for orders. He then writes to von Steuben that he would be taking command of the forces in Virginia, and giving him instructions for the arrangement of the Virginia line, the inspection of all stores, the appointment of a deputy quartermaster-general, and to fix a plan for repairing all damaged arms.

Greene had spoken to every politician from Philadelphia to Richmond, he had written a baggage train of correspondence to every State legislature and body of government from Congress to the town of Hillsbourgh. He asked the help of every farmer, merchant, and wagonier he came across. Greene had done all that he could to procure provisions and supplies for his much needy southern army. All he could do now was wait. One evening, in a brief moment of weakness, Greene penned a private letter to Washington as a friend, and not a field general to his commander-in-chief. "Your Excellency, It has been my opinion for a long time that personal influence must supply the defects of civil constitution, but I have never been so fully convinced of it as on this journey. I believe that the view and the wishes of the great body of the people are entirely with us at this point. But remove the personal influence of a few and they are a lifeless, inanimate mass, without direction or spirit to employ the means they possess for their own security. I cannot contemplate my own situation without the greatest degree of anxiety. I am far removed from all my friends and connections, and have to prosecute a war in a country, in the best state attended with almost insurmountable difficulties. How I shall be able to support myself under all these embarrassments, God only knows. My only consolation is, that if I fail I hope it will not be at the expense of my men due to any peculiar marks of personal disgrace. It would mean the ruin of my family, and that hangs most heavy upon my mind. My fortune is small, and misfortune or disgrace to me would be the ruin to them. I beg you Excellency will do me the honor to forward the inclosed letter to Mrs. Greene by the safe conveyance. She is rendered exceedingly unhappy at my going to the southward and is ill with worry."

On the 21st, he resumed his journey south. At this time, he was traveling alone. Von Steuben was no longer with him, and the genial Duponceau, who Greene had had several enjoyable conversations with about his favorite subjects, was also with von Steuben. It only served to give Greene even more time to deliberate over his impending problems. More time to go over time and again what he was to do to make this army capable of fighting the superior British force he was to face. But, Greene's company of aides increased by two. A Major Pearce and Captain Pendleton had joined him in Richmond. They had come to him with outstanding references, and Greene could use all the help he could get.

250

By the 22nd, they were at Petersburg, Virginia, where he was met with reports that the enemy had turned around and retaken Portsmouth. Without checking the report, he ordered von Steuben to check the story himself, and if it proved to be true, to immediately move with the army, and take charge of the defense of Virginia. He also sent Lawson's brigade ahead to reinforce his army to the south. "Our weak side is not here, and therefore I wish to secure ourselves against the enemy's advancing into North Carolina, which will effectually frustrate the enemy's great design in taking possesion below."

On the same day he writes to General Sumner that he wishes "to see him as soon as possible, in order to call the officers of the North Carolina line upon the Continental establishment together, and fix with them those that are to continue in service, and those that are to retire. Please let me hear from you as soon as may be." He also writes to Colonel Lomagna, "You will please send to me a return of your legion as soon as possible, the number of men, horses, and accouterments of every kind. You will be particular in this return, that I may have a perfect knowledge of the state of the legion, and be able to give the necessary orders for putting it upon a proper footing for service."

By the 27th, he is finally at Hillsbourgh, and writes to von Steuben, "I arrived at this place last evening, and I shall leave it in about an hour. All the troops have marched from hence for Salisbury and some say for Charlotte. The Board of War also have removed to Halifax, with a view of being in the neighborhood of the enemy at Portsmouth. No information, therefore, of any kind can be obtained, which determines me to move on without loss of time. . . .I find confirmed in this State what I apprehended, that is, that the numerous militia which have been kept of foot have laid waste almost all the surrounding country, and the policy, if persisted in, would render it altogether impracticable to support a regular body of troops to give protection and security to the State. The expense attending this business in the waste of stores of all kinds exceeds belief. Twelve millions of money, I am told, has been expended since last spring. I hope Virginia will avoid this destructive policy, and I beg leave to recommend it to you, not to keep a man more in the field, especially militia, than is absolutely necessary for covering the country."

December 1st, Greene is at the end of his long journey and arrives in Salisbury. He immediately proceeds to take command and delegates duties that must be accomplished if the southern department has even a chance of defending the southern States from the British. His first order is always his most important thought; Transportation of supplies to the army. He orders Lieutenant-colonel Carrington to explore the Dan River; "it may be used for transportation up the Roanoke as high as the upper Sauratown." And, "I want General Stevens to appoint a good and intelligent officer with three able-bodied privates to go up the Yadkin as far as Hughes Creek to explore carefully the river, the depth, the current, the rocks, and every other obstruction that will impede the business of transportation. When the officer gets up to Hughes Creek, I wish him to take a horse and ride to the town of Bethania to the upper Saura town, and report the exact distance and condition of the roads there. At upper Saura, I expect the officer will meet the party exploring the Dan River. I wish him to get their report and forward it back to me whole." Next, "I also wish an officer to make inquiry respecting the transportation that may be had from the Yadkin to the Catawba River, and whether the transportation can be performed with batteaux down that river." Along with learning transportation routes, Greene could also use the information on the waterways in the area to his benefit if he ever found himself backed up to them by Cornwallis. The information gained would be more precious in the near future than even the forthright thinking Greene could imagine.

After Greene had felt his orders were understood to the fullest, he traveled to Charlotte. He reached the town on the afternoon of the 2nd of December 1780 and immediately proceeded to headquarters there. It was well known throughout the army from the newest recruit to the oldest veteran in Washington's staff that Greene's relation with Gates was not the friendliest on record, and so all eyes were fixed on the two major-generals when they exchanged greetings. Greene did his best not to show the pride that was bursting with personal triumph within him, and Gates tried not to feel terribly offended by this unfortunate changing of command, but he was crest fallen by all accounts of those in attendance. On the other hand, Greene, always showing himself to be simple and unaffected, could not help by fell sorry for his predecessor. Gates returned his greeting with dignified politeness, with the manners of a man of the world. It was said that both seemed to forget their past relations, and seemed to only be concerned with the job at hand. "It was a surprisingly elegant lesson of propriety," said an eyewitness to the meeting, "exhibited on a most delicate and interesting occasion. Fireworks were expected, but none were to be seen."

The next morning, Gates issued his final orders. For the day's parole or password he chose "Springfield," the scene of Greene's first battle, and for a countersign "Greene." On the orders of the day, the following was read to the troops: "The honorable Major-general Nathanael Greene, arriving yesterday, and being appointed by his Excellency General Washington, and the honorable Congress, takes command of the southern army, all orders will for the future issue from him, and all reports be made to him. General Gates returns his sincere and grateful thanks to the southern army for their perseverance, fortitude, and patient endurance of all the hardships and sufferings they have undergone while under his command. He anxiously hopes their misfortunes will cease therewith, and that victory and the glorious advantages attending it, may be the future portion of the southern army. Farewell."

"General Greene returns his thanks to the honorable Major-general Gates," say the orders of the following morning, "for the polite manner in which he was introduced and for his comments and good wishes for the success of the southern army. General Greene confirms and approves all of the standing orders." Greene would not allow the grass to grow under his feet and hit the ground running in headquarters. He was not alone in his lodgings. For his safety, John Rutledge, governor of South Carolina, had taken refuge in the camp after his home and property was confiscated after the fall of Charleston. Rutledge had heard of Greene's appointment and was there to help him form a larger army to take back South Carolina and personally retrieve what had been taken from him. Greene did not care that his motivation may have been purely personal, he saw it as an opportunity to use Rudledge's knowledge of the people and land to both their advantages.

Greene's first step now was to establish a direct relationship with his present staff and his new officers, and assign each one a specific duty as the position and nature of each man's command required. To do this, he first needed exact returns of force numbers from the various detachment commanders and as he adds, "their time of service, how posted, and where they are employed. Since militia totals fluctuate, a weekly report will be necessary, specifying numbers, condition, and time of service of troops under each commanders care."

The first returns did make Greene happy. His entire army consisted of 2,307 men; 1,482 of which were present and fit for duty, 547 had been given permission to go on leave, and 128 were detached on extra service, along with 90 cavalry and 60 artillery. This was the complete roll call of the entire southern army. The next fact made Greene absolutely cringe. His worse fears were realized. He had only 949 Continental regulars in camp. His whole "force fit for duty that were properly clothed and equipt(did) did not amount to 800 men." The majority of the force was made up of Greene's worse nightmare; Militia. It has never been a secret that Nathanael Greene deplored the militia. It may have been fostered by his friend and commander-in-chief's distaste for the "irregulars," as he was fond of calling them. The true fact of that matter can not be determined. The one we do know played a factor in Greene's mistrust for the militia, was their performance during battle. In almost every major engagement with which he had been associated, the militia involved had a tendency to drop their muskets at the very sight of the enemy advancing towards them, and unceremoniously running for their lives. Good sense maybe, but not sound military behavior.

As small as the southern army was, it was too large for his commissary and clothing officer.

"Many of the men were naked; others so nearly naked that it was impossible to put them on duty." (It is here that we should define naked in the late 18th century sense. In their description of naked, they mean that the men didn't have coats, shoes, no stockings, poor excuses for breeches or overalls, and a shirt that was in tatters or none at all. Literally naked meant tattered breeches and nothing more.) In one of his first official orders to von Steuben, Greene directs him to send no unarmed or unclothed men forward. "It is impossible that men can render any service, however well disposed." In a well directed letter to Jefferson, we see again that Greene does not appear to hold the Virginia governor to his proverbial bosom when he comments, "when your troops may literally be said to be naked, and I shall be obliged to send a considerable number of them away to some secure place to warm quarters, until they can be furnished with clothing, I will have you to suffer from it." Nathanael was never one to hold back from telling someone what he felt. But this was not the first time he had approached this subject to Jefferson, or any of the other politicians he had met along the way during his journey to his new command. He never seemed to grow weary of repeating his common mantra. Clothing and supplies for his men. Clothing and supplies for his men. Unfortunately the remedy sought was not altogether under the control of either Congress or the State legislatures. Along for the demand for the military, there was also an overwhelming demand for the supply of the public by the domestic manufactures. The uselessness of the currency and the risk of capture of imported goods, kept supplies from foreign market and allies at a minimum. To make matters worse, accidents and storms delayed France's help.

The commissary department was not much better off. When Greene entered camp, there were not three days of provisions available to the troops. He blamed it on "the wasteful habits of the militia, and the repeated incursions of the enemy." The fact remained; the army was living from hand to mouth by foraging and daily collections.

The Quartermaster's department was still in deplorable condition as well. Not only had the public wagons and horses been lost at the defeat at Camden, but all of those, which had been obtained from private individuals by hire, were also missing. Even with hard money it would have been difficult to build new wagons and buy new horses in a country in which armed parties of both sides had been living alternately for the past six months. Each had seized what came its way and used it at will, and if not consumed or carried off today, would surely fall into the hands of the enemy tomorrow. But it did not matter, because Greene's military chest was void of hard money.

Greene looked around and seemed to be accumulating difficulties day after day. Not one to sit and feel sorry for himself, Nathanael did what made him the measure of a great leader. He applied himself to bringing a remedy to his problems one by one.

In Virginia he had met Lieutenant-colonel Carrington, of the artillery, a well-respected man from a noted southern family, of good character, and "persevering energy" as Greene put it. Like many other good officers of the southern department under the command of gates, he had been thrown out of his command when Gates assigned one of his friends to that position prior to Camden. Carrington was now looking for a job, and Greene was anxious to give him one. Greene had always been a good judge of character, and having the experience of knowing what type of man you needed to run a quartermaster-general department, he saw Carrington possessed those tools. On the 4th of December he wrote to him and offered him the position. The times being what they were, Carrington accepted the appointment immediately. To make a long story short, Carrington did the job just as well as if Greene had held the position himself.

A day later he re-appointed Colonel Polk to the position of commissary-general. Polk had held the position under Gates, but Polk wrote back, "I am now too far advanced in years to undergo the task and fatigue of a commissary-general." Greene turned to Colonel William R. Davie. Davie, whose corps had been discharged about the last of November, was making arrangements to raise another body of troops at the insistence of General Daniel Morgan, who was charged with a separate command to operate on the left of the enemy. Davie was excited at the possibility of serving under the celebrated commander and was feverishly attempting to complete the task he had been assigned, when Greene approached him with the position of commissary-general. Davie informed Greene he would take a quick look of the situation he was asking him to tackle. When he was done, Davie said he had observed that if the troops were not properly supplied they would be forced to fall back to Virginia, thus allowing the enemy to take possession of two more southern States. Davie said that was not acceptable, but that he had no knowledge of money and accounts, and felt he could better serve the army and his country by therefore pursuing his present task. Greene told him, he would not be troubled with either of those, because there wasn't a single dollar in the military chest and any prospect of gaining any, and that he was required to accept the appointment for the same reason he wanted to decline it. The troops would not subsist for six more weeks without the proper man to supply them. With Colonel Carrington, no two men were better suited for the jobs. Only they could carry it out to its completion. Davie was convinced by the eloquence of the general and accepted the appointment with the clear understanding that it should only be for a short time, and then be allowed to serve under Morgan. Where had Greene heard that before? With the promise that the appointment would not last longer than six months, Davie became Greene's new commissary-general.

Among the powers which Congress had bestowed upon Greene was negotiating exchanges of prisoners, a thing usually, greatly desired by both sides, but after the fall of Charleston, the balance was largely on the British side now. Still, there were a sufficient number of enemy prisoners to justify the opening of negotiations. Greene wrote to Captain Maberly: "I find it necessary that a place should be immediately erected for the safe custody of the prisoners of war, and wish it to be placed in Salisbury. You will please take the necessary steps for having the charge of the business. I have written General Butler to furnish you with wagons and fatigue men, and give you every other assistance in his power to build the gaol."

Another subject that gave him anxiety was intelligence reports. Or, obtaining correct and constant information of enemy movements. Neither of which was furnished with regularity. Without it, he felt that every step he took was in the dark, and carrying out regular plans of operation would be impossible. But of all the services in the military, this was the most dangerous. An agent acted at the peril of an infamous death, as Colonel André learned, and his employer at the hazard of being detected and having the deception turned around on him. Great judgment, therefore, was required in the selection of the men to whom this perilous duty was entrusted. As this employment was always executed with the compensation to make exposure worthwhile, the first step for organizing this indispensable branch of the service was given to Francis Marion. Greene would write, "At present I am badly off for intelligence. It is of the highest importance that I get the earliest information of any reinforcements which may arrive at Charleston, or leave the town to join Lord Cornwallis. I wish you, therefore, to fix some plan for procuring such information, and for conveying it back to me with all possible dispatch. The spy should be taught to be particular in his inquiries, and to get the names, place from whence they came and where they are going. It will be best to fix upon somebody in town to do this, and have a runner between you and him to give you the intelligence, as a person cannot make these inquiries without being suspected, who lives outside of town. Whatever sums of money are advanced for these purposes shall be repaid."

General Gates was not expecting an early renewal of active operations, he was so sure of it he proposed to a council of war that they establish winter quarters at Charlotte. When Greene arrived, they had already begun to build huts for the army. Greene did not approve of Gates decision, because he thought this would retard the proper order and discipline of the troops. So long as they were depended on for the demoralizing effects of daily collections of food by foraging, the only process that they would be able to subsist in their present position. So, he decided to abandon those plans and make new ones. He wrote to Polish volunteer, General Tadeusz Kosciuszko on the 8th of December: You will go with Major Polk and examine the country from the mouth of Little River, twenty or thirty miles down the Pedee, and search for a good position for the army. You will report the make of the country, the nature of the soil, the quality of the water, quanity of produce, number of mills, and the water transportation that may be had up and down the river. You will also inquire respecting the creeks in the rear of the fords, and the difficulty, if any, of passing them; all which you will report as soon as possible directly to me."

By the 16th the army was put under marching orders, but owing to the recent heavy rains they had experienced, they did not actually march until the 20th of December. The spot that was chosen by Kosciuszko was on Hick's Creek, nearly opposite Cheraw Hill, on the east bank of the Pedee, and the site of the modern town of Chatham. Greene, who felt that the only way to "inspire his army with confidence and respect," was by independent action, changing the camp from Charlotte to the present position "by a single order" he would write his friend Alexander Hamilton a few days later, "I call no councils of war, and I communicate my intentions to only a trusted few." Unofficially, Greene's first attack was not against the British; it was against the demoralization of his troops. "This army," he writes to Washington, "is in such a wretched condition that I hardly know what to do with it. The officers have got such a habit of negligence, and the soldiers so loose and disorderly, that it is next to impossible to give it a military complexion." An example of one of these "disorderly complexions" was the dangerous and irregular custom the men had fallen into. It was, going home without permission or leaving no word that they had even left, staying as long as they wished and returning as if they had just gone down to use the privy. As was normal with Greene's command skills, he announced his intention to all of making an example of the first offender of this custom from this time forward. One simple-minded individual, not knowing Greene, tested his word a few weeks later. He was subsequently arrested at his home, put on military trial, convicted, and hanged in sight of the entire army, which was drawn up to witness the punishment. Needless to say, the impression was instantaneous. As one private in Greene's army acknowledged, "We must not do as we have done from here out, it is a new lord, new laws."

Now that the army was in its new position, Greene decided it was time to make preparations for living quarters. Orders were given to collect boards for barracks, to build boats for the transportation of stores, to collect provisions, and to do everything that could be done to render the new camp a camp that would be as comfortable and well managed as possible. They would need both rest and general organization to prepare the men for the active duties of the coming campaign. He was determined that if supplies failed, he was not going to be blamed. "An army cannot subsist itself; and if we are drove to the necessity, those in the neighborhood of camp will feel the disagreeable effects of the want of a regular supply. If the troops are not subsisted one way they must be by the other. . . I must have something to rest upon with certainty, and cannot be kept in the dark without hazarding the safety of the army and the loss of this country."

In the midst of all this a letter came from Cornwallis, complaining of the violation of a flag and the putting to death of some of the prisoners at Gilbert's Town. It was another difficult question, which required firmness, good judgment, and knowledge of the laws of nations to solve. Greene surely possessed all three. But first, this gave Greene the opportunity to raise the question of a prisoner exchange with the British commander. He asked for permission to open a line of correspondence with General Moultrie, commander of the garrison on Sullivan Island and the senior officer among the prisoners from Charleston. "I shall be happy," Greene writes to Moultrie, "to give them every relief in my power, until their exchange can be accomplished."

At last, the remaining troops arrived at camp on the day after Christmas. "It is no Egypt," Greene wrote to Morgan, "but food and forage are abundant and more easily obtained." Now if he could only clothed the men, he would most assuredly be able to bring the troops under better discipline. "No army," wrote von Steuben, "ever needed it more." And with 1780 drawing to close, details still crowded Greene's mind. "I have no secretary yet," he writes to his friend Bury Stoddard, "and no officer ever wanted one more, having all the business of the great departments of the army on my hands, besides a most extensive correspondence with governors, boards, committees, commissioners, and a great variety of other orders to numerous to enumerate."

Chapter XXIV

"Greene Prepares to Fight"

The first authentic returns of Greene's army gave him, 2,307 men, more than half of who were militia. Among them, were the two Continental regiments of Maryland and Delaware, these regiments were veterans of the northern campaign, proven soldiers that fought gallantly at Camden after the militia abandoned them, and trained in the rigid school of von Steuben. They formed the nucleus around which, if time and means were given, it would be possible to gather an efficient army. But time would not be an ally of the southern department.

To this small body was added 400 eighteen month men form Virginia, and Lee's legion of 300, partly cavalry and part infantry, were added in mid January. But if Greene wanted for arms, ammunition, and clothing to make his men effective in the field, he more than made up for it in officers under his command. They were all excellent, proven leaders, many of them with superior talents in tactics, staging, and knowledge of the country where the battles would be fought.

First in experience, and second in the ways of a soldier, was Daniel Morgan, best known, up until then, as a colonel of the rifle corps which had done outstanding service at Saratoga, and was now a brigadier-general. His immense strength and dauntless courage made him an idol to his men, and an inspiring spirit that made men fight for him. There is no better leadership ability than leading by example. Morgan never asked his men to do something he was not willing to do himself. Next was Otho Holland Williams, who had acted as Deputy Adjutant general under Gates. He had served from the beginning of the war, marching from Maryland to the camp set up outside of Boston in 1775, as lieutenant of a rifle corps. He had never served in a military profession before, and learned from the school of hard knocks how to find good officers under your charge and preserve discipline in an army that was ever changing. Williams was nothing like the rum swilling, exuberant spirit that was Daniel Morgan. If fact, Williams was a gentler, more confined soul. He led his men by appealing to their honor and acknowledging each and every one of their strengths and weaknesses. It was said that Williams knew every one of the men in his force on a first name basis. Respect and firm leadership goes a long way when asking men and boys to die for an ideal. Greene knew Williams since Brandywine, and his "conduct in the field, tempered judgement, and ardor of self-possession, brought bearing to his men in camp, insuring discipline and the fullfillment of every man under his command." Greene would write after the war. He brought Williams into his council in the southern department, and had confidence in him, which he seems to have felt with no other officer but Henry Lee.

"Light Horse Harry" as he was affectionately called throughout his military career, was born in Virginia into that noble family out of which so many famous men would come. A young, brash, horseman who was afraid of nothing. He had first served under Greene at Germantown, commanding his guard in that battle. The British, seeing a young officer and thinking him inexperienced, tried to surprise his right at Germantown, but his ever present vigilance foiled them. He even turned the tide of the attack and beat back 200 men who thought they had his forces surrounded. Washington loved what he called his "delightful and brilliant exploits." Greene had first met "Captain Henry Lee, of the Light Dragoons, by the tenor of his conduct at capturing twenty-four British prisoners at the battle of Brandywine." As Greene would write soon after that battle, "His exemplary zeal, prudence, and bravery, make him the material of a essential officer." Greene liked the way he treated his horses and

257

men with the same importance. "He never relaxed the reins of discipline, nor denied them any indulgence that was consistent with the good of the service." He also chose his horses the same way he chose his men, "with strict regard to speed and bottom, carefully trained and tended." On the 15th of January he joined Greene once again in the camp on the Pedee. Greene was amazed at how well the men and horses had held up on the long road down, and that "Lee was prepared to enter upon active service the very next morning."

John Eager Howard, who Greene had mentioned "deserved a statue of gold no less than the Roman and Grecian heroes," was also from Maryland. Born from a large land proprietor family, Howard was at the battle of White Plains and was a captain in Colonel Josias Hall's regiment. The regiment was disbanded in late 1776 and he became a Colonel in the 4th Maryland regiment. He fought at Germantown and Monmouth with them and marched south with DeKalb into South Carolina and was by his side when he was struck down at Camden. He immediately took command, and no one fought longer or more gallantly than he did that day. "He is a man of excellent parts, sound judgement, and a bearing which bordered close upon reserved, but a cool deliberate courage which makes him peculiarly useful in the decisive moment of battle," a superior would write to Greene of Howard.

Another Virginian was also brought in to lead with Greene. William Washington, a very distant relative of the Commander-in-chief, destined by his parents to be educated for the church. William Washington entered the service when war broke out under the command of the tutelage of Hugh Mercer, as a captain. He served the entire campaign through the Jerseys, fought gallantly at his regiment's head at Staten Island, and was wounded in the wrist at Trenton. He was made a major with Baylor's regiment, but soon was attached to serve under General Lincoln, in South Carolina. He was able to escape after the fall of Charleston and joined Gates in North Carolina where he applied to recruit a regiment. However, Gates was openly avowed at using cavalry, and refused his request. After the defeat at Camden, he was relieved when he learned that Greene would take command from Gates, and knew he would be permitted to raise the regiment again, which Greene directed him to do at once.

Part of the American army lay at Charlotte and part at New Providence, about twelve miles nearer to the enemy. Greene had received intelligence that the British foraging parties were becoming very active, and being well supported, often trusted themselves into hazardous positions. One party even ventured to forage between two divisions of the Americans. Morgan, who commanded the vanguard of the light troops, took exception to this, and in typical Morgan fashion, dashed forward to give them a blow. But the ever-watchful British eluded the attack, and retreated back to Camden. William Washington was at the head of the cavalry, and taking a larger circuit than the infantry, learned that a party of loyalist were within striking distance, at Rugeley's farm, about twelve miles from Camden. It consisted of 100 men, commanded by Rugeley himself, who selected his barn as the strongest point, had it secured by abatis against a cavalry charge. Nothing but artillery would reach him. Washington came up at full speed, but his hopes were dashed by the sight of the works that his horses could not mount, and behind him, he knew enemy marksmen would be checking his advance closely. Rugeley was known to be a weak, vain man, and knowing this, Washington instantly resolved to try and win by artifice what he could not seize by force. While surveying his next move, Washington had noticed the stump of a tree that looked remarkably like a cannon. He was able to produce an axle from a nearby wagon, and mounted the stump onto the wheels. He bodily brought the contraption forward, and to further the trick, sent a man ahead with a flag of truce to summon the loyalist surrender, or "be prepared to face the consequences of attempting to hold an untenable post." Without waiting for a second demand, the terrified loyalist surrendered without a shot being fired. It was this laughable, but distinctive feat that began Washington's brilliant career under Greene.

Francis Marion's story started on the sea. Without the money to pursue an education, the young Francis entered upon the crew of ship sailing out of Charleston, to the West Indies. But the ship

258

was destroyed in a storm and he was cast afloat for eight days with no water or food, watching as most of the crew died, he renounced the sea and tried being a farmer like his father. However, his attention to his work was soon drawn away by the Cherokee war and he was soon active as a soldier, which he liked very much. Although short, he was "a stout man and very healthy in appearance." He joined Moultrie in the defense of Sullivan Island, and soon was made a major. He was involved in the siege of Charleston, but he accidentally broke his leg and was sent to a hospital by the British which freed him after the city fell and allowed him to join Governor Rutledge whom immediately bestowed on him the rank of brigadier. When he entered Gates's camp he only had twenty men. Half of which were slaves that he had freed when Charleston fell. He soon would meet up with a figure he would attempt to pursue throughout the entire south, "No Quarter" Tarleton. His slender frame concealed "a lion heart, with his cold impassive face, there was a perpetual glow of tender sympathies." One of his men would write of their commander. "It is distressing," he would write, "to see women, and children sitting in the open air huddled round a fire, without blanket, or any warm clothing, but what they had when they fled the butcher. For he spares neither Whig or Tory." When his own commander joined in such deeds, he wrote, "Colonel Murphy's party have burnt a great number of houses on the Little Pedee, and intend to go on in that abominable work, which I am apprehensive may be laid to me; but I assure you, that there is not one house burnt by my orders or any of my people." He was the consummate partisan, "vigilance, promptitude, activity, energy, dauntless courage, and unshaken self-control." Morgan would write of him. He was prudent as well as bold. He had always said, "Never permit yourself to lull into ill-timed confidence, nor failure to depress your energy. Always remember, while watching your enemy, never forget that your enemy may be watching you." Two principals controlled his actions, and shaped all the means to an end. They were; pure, earnest, and profound love of country; and the sincere, undeviating, and incorruptible love of right. It would be a formidable force when met in battle, which the British would soon find out.

At the time Greene decided to take his post at Cheraw, he also made another decision that was a bold and daring step in the fundamental principals of warfare. He would divide his already insufficient forces in two. This was a direct violation of everything Greene had ever read or studied on the art of battlefield strategy. To divide an inferior force in the face of superior numbers invited the enemy to destroy one half and then the other. Strategically, Greene felt that the advantages far outweighed the negative aspects of this judgment call, and was willing to take the risk. Greene did not feel he had any choice seeing the provisions with which he had to deal. By dividing the army into two parts, he felt they had a much better chance to subsist on the country. The objective of Cornwallis had always been to conquer North Carolina and Virginia and bring the northern American army and Washington to their knees. But the recent disaster of King's Mountain in September had Cornwallis rethinking the strategy of an invasion to North Carolina and even force him back to central South Carolina. Instead of returning to his original position at Camden, the British general decided to move his camp to Winnsboro, a small village of between thirty to sixty homes, and a little further north, and on the west versus the east bank of the Catawba. To the rear lay Ninety-six, and on his extreme left covering the country, were the head waters of the Salunda, a natural defensive boundary. Directly below his was Fort Granby at the confluence of the Salunda and Congaree, and on his right Camden, the most important post of all. So the main army occupied a central position to the smaller posts, he has secured communications with Charleston, and rich fertile country for foraging to his rear. According to the latest returns, Cornwallis' troops consisted of 3,224 men, nearly 1,000 more soldiers than Greene's whole force. Knowing this, it astonished Cornwallis when he received the intelligence reports that Greene had divided his army. Add to it the fact that the British force was thoroughly disciplined, well clothed, armed, equipped, and fed, and it might as well have been 6,000 men to Greene's 2,200. What more could Lord Cornwallis possibly ask for?

It was evident to Greene that his adversary was still fixated on the conquest of North Carolina, and waiting only for the appropriate moment to enter upon a winter campaign. To meet the British in a frontal assault with an army so inferior in numbers, equipment, and discipline, would have been madness. But by dividing his forces, he might not only secure an abundant supply of good food for his men, but also at the same time confine the enemy within narrower bounds. This would cut them off from their supplies of the upper country, but revive the sagging morale of the local inhabitants, which was essential for the Americans livelihood. It could also establish rallying points for the militia on the east and the west, threaten posts and communications of the enemy, give his friends an opportunity to form small magazines in the rear of the troops and compel Cornwallis to suspend his threatened invasion.

Tarleton could not believe Greene would have divided his troops if he had known of Leslie's addition to the British army. It offered such a good opportunity for an advance from Winnsboro, "which, if executed with tolerable rapidity, might separate the two divisions of the American army and endanger their being totally dispersed or destroyed." But Cornwallis was not as hot headed as his young officer and saw the situation more clearly. He saw what Greene had seen: that if he attacked Huger's force Morgan might strike at Ninety-six and Augusta; if he went for Morgan the way to Charleston would be open to Greene. He therefore saw he could only follow the unorthodox example of his opponent and divide his own army-not into two parts, but into three.

Greene expected Cornwallis to counteract in that exact way. In fact, he banked on it. Therefore, before he set out on his march for the Pedee, he detached Morgan with 300 of his best troops, and Washington's regiment of light dragoons. They were given orders to take a position on the south of the Catawaba, where he was to be joined by 300 volunteers under General Davidson, and 450 Georgia and South Carolina militia under Colonel Clark and Colonel Few. This would open a brilliant field of action between Broad River and the Pacolet, and alarm Cornwallis for the safety of the important post of Ninety-six, and the equally important post of Augusta.

With the remainder of his forces, reduced by this detachment to 1,100, of which only 650 were Continentals, Greene took post at Hick's Creek on the Pedee. It was one of the immediate advantages of this position that it prevented the enemy from "attempting to possess themselves of Cross Creek, which would have given them command of the greatest part of the provisions in the lower country." The more Greene thought about this change in camps the better he liked it. "I am here in my camp of repose," he writes in a journal, "improving the discipline and spirits of my men, and the opportunity for looking about me. I am well satisfied with the movement, for it has answered thus far all the purposes for which I intended it. It makes the most of my inferior force, for it compels my adversary to divide his, and holds him in doubt as to his own line of conduct."

In the meantime, Cornwallis sent Leslie to hold Camden against an attack by Huger's division. He directed Tarleton to find and crush Morgan, while he himself, with his main army, moved cautiously and slowly up into North Carolina to intercept and destroy the remains of Morgan's force after the expected defeat by Tarleton's force. His orders to Tarleton, then posted at Ninety-six, were set forth, on January 2, in these terms: "If Morgan is still at Williams or anywhere within your reach, I should wish you to push him to the utmost. . . .No time is to be lost." To which Tarleton was reported to have replied: "I must either destroy Morgan's corps or push it before me over Broad River towards King's Mountain." Cornwallis answered that Tarleton had understood his intentions "perfectly. Now go do it."

While Cornwallis' put his plans into motion, Greene had something up his sleeve as well. Unbeknownst to his British antagonist, Greene was eagerly watching for an opportunity to open the campaign by attacking some post or party of his enemy. Marion was already actively engaged in the neighborhood of the Santee, between the High Hills and Neilson's Ferry, alarming the enemy by the boldness of his movements, and baffling all their attempts to intercept him, or take him by surprise. On the 12th of January 1781, Lee arrived with his Legion, in perfect order for immediate service. The next day he was sent to join Marion, with orders to strike Georgetown by surprise, and try to scare the enemy into the safety of the rear. His attempt on Georgetown was only partially successful. The Americans entered the town, made prisoners of the commander and several officers, and because of a mistake by their guides, would have captured the entire garrison. But the guides became "bewildered, a part of the enemy had time to take refuge in the fort. To carry the fight would have required artillery; which we had none, and we were compelled to withdraw." After a short halt to refresh his troops, Marion directed the march towards Neilson's Ferry, with the hope of surprising a body of English and loyalists under the command of a Colonel Watson. But Watson, getting timely notice of the danger from his pickets, threw a party of more than 80 men into the fort that bore his name, and with the rest of the force retreated to Camden. An attempt was then made to seize the enemy's stores by the Congaree, but before the plan could be carried out, an express rider came from headquarters. He carried with him orders from Greene to make a quick turn towards Salisbury, and join Morgan, who was retreating before a large British force being commanded by Cornwallis himself.

Morgan, with his 580 men, had crossed the Catawba on the evening of the 20th of December, and holding his way towards the Broad River, had passed it on the 25th, and encamped at Grindall's Ford, on the north bank of the Pacolet. Here, he was joined, in the course of the next few days, by Colonel Pickens and Major McCall, with 260 mounted Carolinians. On the 28th and 29th General Davidson arrived with a 120 men, instead of the 600 Morgan had been expecting. The British general had followed his old policy of advancing with the regular army, and instigating the Indians to break in on the surrounding frontier, and alarm the militia, who the Americans depended on for the safety of their families. Still there were 500 men already at Salisbury, and over 500 more were expected. Davidson, considered to be an enterprising and zealous officer, quickly returned to Salisbury to organize the force.

Meanwhile Morgan was concentrating on collecting supplies, and more especially the collection of frequent and reliable intelligence on the movements of the enemy, and by no means allowing an opportunity to strike a blow against them. That first opportunity presented itself in the form of a party of 250 Tories, under the command of Captain Waters, who were laying waste to the settlements around Fairfort Creek, and murdering the men, women, and children of that area. Washington, with his cavalry and a body of 200 mounted militia under Major McCall, were just biting at the bit to exact some revenge for what they had done to their friends and family, were sent forward to attack the Tory force. An extremely quick march of fifty miles brought them upon the Tories before they could even react. Over 150 were killed and wounded, 40 taken prisoners, and 60 escaped to tell the bloody tale and add to the terror that was beginning to run throughout the country of this new American force unleashed. Washington was now deep within the enemy's lines, but although aware of this danger, was unwilling to turn back without one more attack. About fifteen miles north of the settlement named Ninety-six (named because it was thought to be ninety-six miles between it and the Cherokee nation of tribes) and directly on the line of communications between there and Winnsboro, there was a stockade of log houses, garrisoned by 150 men. It was known as Fort William. To spring a surprise attack on the garrison of Fort William would make it a double blow after the blow inflicted on Captain Waters and his Tory force, and Washington was of a mind to attempt it. Colonel Hays was pushed forward with all speed at the head of 40 mounted militia. But the British commander of the fort had been given sufficient warning of the Americans advance, and when they came into sight, had already evacuated the fort and begun his retreat. The garrison managed to escape, but the fort was not so lucky. It was put to the torch and completely destroyed.

Two weeks passed without any further movements by either side, although Morgan with his wild spirit was chafing at the bit to attack someone or something. By the 8th of January 1781, there came a warning letter from Greene, who had quickly noticed some early inclinations at movement by the enemy. Morgan wanted to push forward into Georgia without wasting time, but Greene felt that the moment just wasn't right. "The Pedee rose over twenty-five feet the last week in thirty hours," he wrote to Morgan on the 19th. "Put nothing to hazard. A retreat may be disagreeable, but is not a disgrace. Regard not the opinions of the day. It is not our business to risk too much."

At the same time, the British were watching the Americans with equal interest. The arrival of General Leslie, with a reinforcement of 1,500 men, was a welcome addition to their strength, and made the chance of a design against North Carolina, and then Virginia all the more realistic with the added force. But the decision by Greene to divide his force made Cornwallis hesitate. He could not advance and leave Ninety-six and Augusta exposed to Morgan. He could not call Leslie over the Catawba, without leaving the region on its Right Bank open to Greene. In either case, immediate success and the presence of a protecting force would be necessary. After the destruction of Waters force, the subsequent evacuation and destruction of Fort William, and the presence of Morgan at the districts west of the Catawba, had made Parliament more than a little uneasy. The British political body was screaming for results in the wake of these slaps in the Kings face. Cornwallis had no choice, but to begin his advance into North Carolina without further delay, hoping to get between the two divided forces of Greene's American army, and crush them in one fell swoop. Leslie was immediately ordered to join the main army. Tarleton, who had already been sent forward to hold Morgan in check, was instructed to push his adversary to the utmost, and either crush him, or drive him across the Broad River. From there, Cornwallis himself, moving up its left bank, would be in a position to intercept his retreat, and compel Greene to either disband his forces, or take the chances of a all-out battle.

Tarleton was to Cornwallis, what Lee was to Greene. A bold, active, and enterprising officer, who had distinguished himself by his adventurous spirit, and was in complete harmony with what their commanders wanted and expected of them. That he was colored a cruel conqueror to the enemy, and merciless in laying waste to the districts occupied by the Whigs, does not seem to have tainted his reputation as a capable and trustworthy officer to the Crown. It has been noted by historians that, unlike Lee, Tarleton had a tendency to be quick in his judgment at times. Often rash, but only occasionally cautious when his adversary was at bay, and boldest when he was in pursuit of his fleeing enemy. The order to push Morgan was a welcome one to Tarleton, because he felt he was of far superior intellect than the American general, and especially stronger by discipline, equipment, and numbers. His entire force exceeded 1,100 men, including a detachment of Royal Artillery, with two field pieces. Cornwallis had no doubt that he would triumph, and moving slowly northwards, over roads heavy and broken by the recent rains, had to pass swollen water courses, and reached Turkey Creek, forty miles from Winnsboro, on the eighth day after breaking camp. Here, expecting Tarleton to be successful in his quest, decided to stay and wait for Leslie, whom he thought was not entirely safe from attack by Greene. The division of the American forces had forced Cornwallis to do the same, and so the advantage of superior numbers over the Americans had been seriously diminished.

Morgan was on constant alert as to the movements of his enemy. His frequent intelligence information had been both timely and accurate up until this point, and he saw no reason to keep from trusting the reports. With the information he had, Morgan at first had proposed to defend the passage to the Pacolet. But with further thought on the matter, it finally convinced him that Cornwallis and Tarleton were not working separately, but in concert with one another. So, he decided to alter his plans and fall back further towards the upper fords of the Broad River, where he would still be within reach of the reinforcements that had been promised him, and at the same time keep up communications with Greene. However hard Cornwallis might press him, he was still confident of a sure retreat by the fords of the Catawba.

It soon became evident that Tarleton was not going to cross the Broad River, and that Cornwallis was waiting to form a junction of some kind with Leslie before he moved up from the Turkey Creek. If these things continued to unfold, Morgan felt he had a chance to fight Tarleton on some sort of equal terms. Morgan broke camp at Grindall's Ford on the 15th, and detached several small parties to watch the fords of the Pacolet and bring him word when the enemy had crossed, while with his main body of troops, fell back to Burr's Mills on Thicketty Creek. The next day Morgan continued to march, and about sundown halted the men at the Cowpens. During the night he was joined by Colonel Pickens, with a fresh body of militia, about 150 in all, and more than 50 more showed up before morning. Morgan carefully examined the surrounding terrain, and decided it was a perfect battleground. Never in the mold of a "brass hat" the name enlisted men gave to some officers, Morgan visited the men around the campfires that evening, talking, joking and abiding in a couple of gills of rum with his men. He spoke to them in their own language in a cheerful voice, his manner always confident and reassuring. He told them that "the Old Wagoner would crack the whip over Ban Tarleton in the morning as sure as he lived. Just hold up your heads, boys," he said to the militia, "give them three fires and you're free." If the militia held their ground for just three volleys and then retreat, it would be just enough time to give the regulars the needed cushion between them and the British.

Morgan's position was anything but ideal. A true fighter in every sense of the word, he had been irked at having to retreat from Tarleton, and seemed to turn on his foe simply because he wanted to show him who was the better man. Something you may see on a schoolyard, but not in a military operation. Henry Lee commented that he thought the choice of field grew out of "irritation of temper which overruked his usually sound and discriminating judgement," and that "confiding in his long tried fortune, conscious of his personal superiority in soldiership and relying entirely on the skill and courage of his troops," he just decided to stop his organized retreat and fight it out with Tarleton where he just happened to be.

Chapter XXV

"The Battle of Cowpens"

Tarleton's forces would be comprised of his own Legion, 550 horse and infantry; a battalion of the 7th Royal Fusiliers Regiment numbering about 200; a battalion of the 71st Highlanders Regiment with about 200 men; 50 of the 17th Light Dragoons; a small detachment of the Royal Artillery, and a party of Tory militia of unknown numbers. In total, about 1,100 rank and file, with two light fieldpieces, 3-pounders called "grasshoppers." Morgan's entire corps, consisted of 320 Continentals, 200 Virginia militia riflemen, about 80 of Washington's dragoons, and Davidson's 140 and McDowell's 200 North Carolina and Georgia militia riflemen. During his march to Cowpens, McCall had joined Morgan with his 30 South Carolina and Georgia militia, making his total force about 1,100 as well. The numbers may have been equal to Tarleton's corps, but his trained regulars outnumbered Morgan's by more than three to one.

On the morning of January 17th, 1781, just after breakfast, Morgan formed his battle line. To the rear and the north of the ground where his men had camped was a slight elevation, rising gradually for about three hundred and fifty yards and then sloping northward into a swale. Behind that the ground ran to a lower elevation, which in turn sloped northerly into a plain, and beyond which ran the Broad River. Open woods covered the entire terrain.

The distribution of his men was as unorthodox as Greene's division of the army. On the southern and higher elevation, he formed his main line. Howard's Maryland light infantry and the Delaware Continentals held the center. On their right were Tate's Virginia Militia and a small company of Georgians, and on their left Triplett's Virginians. These militiaman were mostly old Continentals soldiers who had served their terms of enlistment and rejoined as volunteers. So unlike the usual raw recruits that made up most militia regiments, these men were seasoned veterans of the early campaigns and were better trained than most militiamen. On a whole, this line contained about 450 men, with Howard as its commander.

About one hundred and fifty yards in front of the main line, 300 North and South Carolina militia under Pickens were posted in open order in a thin line three hundred yards long. In front of them, at a similar interval, 150 hand picked riflemen; Georgians and North Carolinians under Major John Cunningham of Georgia and Major Charles McDowell of North Carolina were literally thrown out in a line as sharpshooters. Behind all of them, and back on the lower elevation, Morgan posted as a reserve 80 of William Washington's dragoons and 45 of Lieutenant Colonel James McCall's Georgia mounted infantry armed with sabers to operate as cavalry.

Morgan's field orders were simple, but the entire formation was very unusual for basic 18th century warfare, because it put the weakest contingents so far in front of the battle line to receive the first wave of the attack without immediate support from the regulars. Morgan's plan was well conceived by using the strength and weaknesses of each contingent in his troops and his enemy. The sharpshooters in the front line were to take irregular formation behind the cover of trees. They were to hold their fire until the advance of the enemy was within fifty yards, and then take careful aim at "the men with the epaulets." The officers. After three volleys they were to retire, slowly, firing at will as they retreated, and fall into spaces in the second line of militia.

The second line, thus reinforced, was to fire "low and deliberately," and not to break at any account, but, if pressed too hard, they were to retire to the left. From there they would maneuver around to the rear of the main formation to be used as reinforcements, if necessary, but Morgan told them, "be perfectly safe." Those orders were not given to just the officers, but to every man before the battle began, because Morgan wanted the second line to understand what was being done. He did not want them to be alarmed when the first line fell back in apparent defeat, and then turn a run themselves. It was all carefully planned and each unit had to perform so the next part of that plan could be accomplished. It was asking a lot of these soldiers, especially the militia, who were not known to follow orders to the letter, no matter who was leading them. But to reassure the troops, Morgan had arranged for the baggage to be sent and held under suitable escort a few miles in the rear, and the horses of the militiamen in the first two lines (they were all mounted) were tied to trees behind the cavalry reserve. Making such arrangements gave comfort to their owners and Morgan, because it meant they could hold a little longer, knowing they had a swift retreat awaiting them in case of disaster.

The men all in position and the orders understood by all involved, the men were told to "ease their joints" an old 18th century saying for sitting down, and told to rest until the enemy were sighted, but not to break formation for any reason. Morgan, always the cheerleader, rode amongst the men, encouraging the men with his backwoods wit and enthusiasm, exhorting things like, "Give them at least two fires at killing distance my boys, and I will make the victory sure." It helped to boast morale and instill confidence in the band of men. As a result, the men were in excellent spirits and ready for a fight.

Tarleton, eager to please Cornwallis' confidence in him and to fulfill his promise to destroy Morgan's corps or push it back towards King's Mountain, where Cornwallis would finish them off, had allowed his men only a short rest the night before. By three in the morning they were up and marching. For five hours, mostly in pitch-black darkness, and marching on muddy roads, through swamps and creeks and over broken ground, they covered eight long miles, before they came in sight of the American forces.

When he came into sight of his enemy, Tarleton, with a small party, rode forward to reconnoiter their position. A sight of the first riflemen kept him in check before he could get a clear view of the entire main battleline, and that played right into part of Morgan's plans. Tarleton immediately ordered his Legion cavalry forward to dislodge the sharpshooters. As the horsemen came on, they received a volley that emptied fifteen saddles. They recoiled in horror, and so convinced of the marksmanship of the always-dreaded American riflemen, Tarleton could not induce them to charge upon the American first line again. The first front-line men, still firing at will, began to slowly retire and take their places in the second line.

The English artillery now opened up, and the whole line advanced upon the second line of the Americans, who were waiting calmly until the enemy was within one hundred yards, when they poured a deadly fire onto them. The British wavered and slowed their pace for a moment. The worse casualties were felt in the officer ranks. Groups of them seemed to fall at every musket discharge, and a visible confusion began to take hold throughout the ranks. However, it was only momentary. The British army was driven by their severe discipline, and unlike the American soldiers, they were all too familiar to the sights and sounds of a battlefield, and virtually willed themselves straight into the deadly encounter, moving steadily forward with every deliberate step. Picken's men, according to orders, turned about and ran across to the American left to seek refuge behind the Continentals. Those on the right had to make a long traverse, and the British dragoons, seeing an easy target, swept down on them with shouts and huzzahs.

All of a sudden, to the total amazement of the enemy, Washington and McCall's horsemen appeared from behind the rise, which had concealed them so well. Short swords in hand, they had been ordered not to fire their pistols, they charged the pursuing British dragoons and routed them completely.

Pickens troops were able to gain the desired shelter behind the rise and rest before moving to their second position.

The flight of the first lines of the Americans was seen by the British as the beginning of the retreat of Morgan's entire army. The over-confident British therefore came rushing up to meet the main American line, expecting to overwhelm them with numbers. But Howard's Continentals and Tate's Triplett's Virginians surprised the Brits when they stood fast. Ordered to knell for better accuracy and to aim low, they fired volley after volley. Checked, but advancing once again, the equally brave British line came on relentlessly. This was "hot and furious close-in fighting at about 40 to 50 rods" as described later by a British officer, and the battle continued like this for the better part of half an hour.

Tarleton, not liking the way the battle was progressing, called on his reserve of Highlanders, extended them to his left, and sent them forward. Seeing this, Howard saw that the British line now outstretched his front and put his right flank into jeopardy. To meet the danger, he ordered his right company to change fronts, but mistaking the order, the men began to slowly back-up, and thus communicating the movement to the rest of the line and following suit. Even with the miscommunication, a common occurrence in the heat of battle, Howard saw that his men could still be counted on to perform the needed task ahead of them. Seeing that the men were performing the movement with military accuracy as if the were on the parade ground, instead of trying to counterman the order and risk complete confusion, he instead accepted it. He then calmly led them to the second hill on which the cavalry had been stationed, when Morgan came up to inquire about the change in plans. "What is this retreat, sir? cried the "old wagoner", in his harshest voice. "A change of position to save my right flank, nothing more," answered Howard. "Are you beaten?" asked Morgan. "Do men march such as this, look as though they are beaten?" countered Howard. "Right then; I will ride forward and chose you a new position, and when you reach it, face about and give the enemy another fire."

But before they could reach the new position, a messenger from Washington rode up, who had charged through the British cavalry. "They are coming on like a mob," the messenger said. "Give them another fire, and I will charge them." Seeing Howard's troops withdrawal, Tarleton was sure of victory. He ordered up his Legion cavalry and threw everything he had against the Americans. His men, each eager to out do the other, broke ranks and ran forward in disorder. Washington, pursuing the British dragoons, was in advance of the American line and saw the confusion of the British ranks, that was not visible to the others now behind the second hill. This is when he had sent the rider to warn Morgan that they were charging through.

Just then, as Picken's riflemen were completing their circuit of the field, Morgan ordered them to his right. He gave them similar orders that he had given to Howard's corps. He told the Continentals; "Face about, give them one or two good volleys and the day is ours." At that moment, the entire American turned about to face the British charge that was less than fifty yards away. The entire American line lowered their muskets as one, and the British were torn apart by the blaze of gunfire. Large groups of British soldiers fell tot the ground dead and dying, within moments the entire British advance halted, stunned by the devastation and bewildered turn of events that had suddenly unfolded upon them. Howard gave another order, "Load again, and prepare to fire another volley." The soldiers quickly cast about and held their muskets at the ready. "Fix bayonets." was the next order given. "Prepare to charge bayonets" was given soon after, and the entire American line lowered their flintlocks to the hip with a great "Huzzah!" With the British still in total confusion, some trying to reform, others bolting to the rear, Howard ordered a full volley of the line. "Fire!" he shouted. And the British regulars were torn to pieces. "Give them the bayonet. Charge!" Was the last order Howard proclaimed, as he seized the moment and charged with his sword headlong into the tangled ranks of Tarleton's infantry and the Royal Fusiliers. The Maryland and Delaware Continentals drove through them with devastating effect. At the same time, Washington and McCall struck them on the flank and in the rear simultaneously. Between the bayonets and the flashing sabers of the cavalry, the throng of redcoats were quickly torn to ribbons.

The shock to the British was irresistible. Some threw away their arms, and sought safety in flight, much like they had seen the American soldiers do in the past and scorned them for it. But a far greater number merely threw down their arms and screamed and begged for mercy. "Throw down your arms and we will give you good quarter! shouted Howard. Muskets clattered and banged to the ground, others cried like babies for their mothers. Many of the Americans were present at Camden and had to be held back from their foe as they cried, "Tarleton's quarter! Tarleton's quarter! Which meant to bayonet even disarmed men. With great difficulty, the officers were able in intercede and calm the men.

In the center, the battle was over, but on the American right the Highlanders held out gallantly, and the British dragoons from their left wing were still active. Picken's riflemen, reformed and ready, decided to open up on these poor souls as they had the first wave of cavalry. They hit them with such a destructive fire that the dragoons fled in disarray, but the Highlanders fought on. Not until the whole weight of the Americans fell upon them did the Highlanders yield. Only then, did their commander, Major McArthur, give up his sword to Colonel Pickens.

Meanwhile Tarleton has been urging his reserve of 200 dragoons to move forward from their post in the rear, but was met with little success. The men refused to move. He then tried to protect the artillery and remove it from the field. Washington quickly attacked his position and drove his men off the field, but the British artillerists stood by their guns. They died there, never surrendering. They were struck down at their posts attempting to save the cannons from the enemy.

Washington attempted to follow Tarleton, who, with a few officers and about 140 horsemen, was in full retreat. A circumstance that Lieutenant-colonel Banastre Tarleton was unfamiliar with in the past. In all of the excitement of the chase, the superior rider Washington, got well ahead of his troops and found himself upon the British, and alone. Seeing this, Tarleton and two of his officers turned and attacked him. One of them was about to stroke him with a well aimed saber, but an American sergeant who was close at hand quickly moved up and deflected the blow onto his saber and wounded the assailant in the arm. Another British officer was about to cut Washington down when a fourteen year old bugler shot him with his pistol, striking him in the head and killing him instantly. Tarleton was next to thrust at the American colonel, when the blow was parried, he fired his pistol, wounding Washington's horse and throwing Washington to the ground. Now, Tarleton quickly was outnumbered and galloped away. Washington jumped onto a British horse and tried in vain to purse Tarleton, but he was too far ahead. He instead decided to intercept the fugitive infantry and took many prisoners. The British baggage guard cut the horses loose, mounted them, abandoned the wagons, and got away.

The victory was complete in every way. The British lost over 100 killed, among them more than 30 officers. Prisoners totaled 830, with 600 of them unhurt, and 230 wounded. In all, nearly nine-tenths of the entire British force that attacked at the Cowpens were either killed or captured. Of the Americans only 12 were killed and 60 wounded. The two British guns, 800 muskets, 35 baggage wagons, 100 dragoon horses, 60 Negro slaves, and a quantity of ammunition to numerous to account, fell into the American hands.

The news of the victory spread across the country like wildfire and was received with delight by Greene in camp. At Cheraw, it was celebrated by a *feu de joie*, (a bonfire and the firing of muskets as a show of joy.) With Governor John Rutledge of South Carolina in camp, he instantly made Pickens a brigadier. A reward Greene would have enjoyed bestowing on the triumphant officer, but was under orders by Congress to refrain from doing. Greene quickly sent off letters to Virginia, North Carolina and Maryland with praise for his officers that were involved in the victory. He praised them to their

States leader with enthusiastic resolution for obtaining, "a complete and important victory over the select and well appointed detachment." In return for Greene's praise of the men, Virginia gave Morgan a prize thoroughbred horse and a sword. Congress awarded him a gold medal. To William Washington and Howard, silver medals and silver hilted swords were awarded and to Pickens a sword. The battle proved to Greene the value of militia, if properly handled. Also, it was the deathblow to Tarleton and badly damaged his reputation as military leader, all but ending his storied military career. On the other side, it vaulted Greene's reputation to new heights. It showed Greene was the strategic genius that Washington and only a select few had known up until then. It also allowed him to continue to conduct the southern campaign with "dazzling shiftiness" that would lead his opponent to a string of "unbroken chain of consequences that followed Cornwallis to the end of the war."

All of the back slapping and congratulating would have to be put aside for now. Cornwallis may have been thirty miles from Morgan, but that did not diminish the danger to him and his troops, and before nightfall Cornwallis would learn of the utter defeat of Tarleton at Cowpens. It was not expected that Cornwallis would lay down and lick his wounded pride, quite from it. He was closer to the fords of the Catawba than Morgan, which afforded a direct road to a junction with Greene. There was little doubt throughout Greene's camp that the British general would delay in striking a blow against his enemy who had just cast a bloody stain to this egotistical British commander. Instant retreat was Morgan's first duty, and making all his preparations without the loss of a single moment, he put his army in motion without resting from the ferocious battle they had just fought, and by evening was already on the north bank of the Broad River.

Giving his troops only a minimum amount of rest, Morgan had his men in motion at the crack of dawn and marched towards Ramsour's Mills, on the Little Catawba. Staying with the main body, Morgan sent Washington ahead to the higher ford with the prisoners so they would not slow their progress. The roads were mired and deep by recent winter rains, and had made the watercourses swollen to overflowing. He also thought it prudent to collect food day by day as he went along, and his men were beginning to feel the effects of the constant movement. Ten miles a day was all that he could muster from them, and all the while looking over his shoulder for the approach of Cornwallis.

Cornwallis fully intended to cut off Morgan's retreat, but the sudden blow by the Cowpens defeat seemed to momentarily bewilder the British commander. Instead of pressing his forces, upon the first intelligence reports of Tarleton's drubbing by the Americans, he paused to join Leslie. Then, figuring that Morgan would be drunk with success, would attempt to hold the precarious ground in the neighborhood of broad River, or even hazard an attempt to attack Ninety-six. So, Cornwallis directed his troops to move towards the little Broad River to the northwest, while Morgan, was busy suffering from a severe attack of rheumatism in his lower back. The pain was so crippling, that he could not ride his horse at more than a slow walk, thus delaying his flight and allowing Cornwallis to move closer to them. It did allow his weary troops to get some needed rest due to the slow pace, but it gave Morgan a few sleepless nights as he watched his adversary move within sight. Cornwallis had shifted his march yet again and marched north, and his mistake could not be reversed when the British general reached Ramsour's Mills on a fork of the Catawba. There he found that his adversary had already crossed at the same place two days before, and was already at Shrerrill's Ford, on the east bank of the main river.

Again Cornwallis had been disappointed. If he could have intercepted or overtaken Morgan, or at least rescued the prisoners of the Cowpens, he may have at least rescued something from the recent defeat. But instead, he had been foiled twice, and it was too much for the egotistical commander to take, being guilty himself of a slew of mistakes, making him feel humiliated to the fullest degree. In the heat of anger the British commander made a fateful decision. He collected all of the army's unnecessary baggage and had it burnt, and to encourage his men to do the same with their needless personal items, he showed the men the level of his own sacrifice by burning all of his own personal possessions. All he kept was four wagons for the sick and wounded, and those necessary for the conveyance of hospital stores, salt, and ammunition. Then, lightly equipped, just like his enemy, he prepared for a long and rapid march, and resumed his pursuit of Morgan and his men.

Meanwhile, Morgan was on the East Side of the Catawba, resting and refreshing his troops while he awaited the return of the detachment he had sent off with the prisoners. Pickens delivered them to a commissary for captives at Island Fort and were then to be sent onto Virginia. From there he crossed the stream and rejoined Morgan on the 28th. By the 1st of February the entire corps was together again when they triumphantly marched into camp, just as Greene was returning from a reconnoiter with an aide and a sergeant's guard of dragoons.

At first Greene was overjoyed at the victory, but as usual for Nathanael it was short lived. His next thought was for the half-clothed men he saw before him. As happy as he was of their good fortune, he first had to do something about the clothing and provision crisis. It would need immediate action, but he could only think of the difficulty of it when he wrote to his wife, "I am of a Spanish disposition, always the most serious when there is the greatest run of good fortune, for fear of some ill-fated stroke." Perhaps an eighteenth century version of Murphy's Law.

But whatever the chances, he did not hesitate at all. First he put the army under marching orders. Next, he ordered all his detachments to be called in, and all the stores that were lying in his marching line, were to be brought into camp. The commissary of supplies he had purchased by the seaboard, was now directed to be promptly brought inland. With the increase in prisoners with the Cowpens victory, his bargaining chips were now increased two-fold. He ordered the prisoner commissaries at Salisbury and Hillsboro to be at the ready to move the prisoners and all of the stores to the upper counties of Virginia on a moment's notice. He thought that he might have to cross the Dan, so he possibly would need boats. He charged the quartermaster-general with the task so they would be at the ready whether he needed them or not. Lastly, he appealed once again to the governors of North Carolina and Virginia, to at least fill the quotas of Continentals, and to call out the militia, and repeated his orders to von Steuben to hurry on his recruits. He had always wanted to use Marion as an agent on the rear of the enemy. Marion was a tremendous guerrilla fighter, and his partisans were well adapted to that sort of fighting. So, he wrote to him to ask his opinion about sending 300 or 400 horse across the Santee. In a conference, Morgan was for a quick retreat into the western mountains beyond probable, or even possible pursuit. A safe move if nothing more, so they may regroup and have longer to plan their next attack objective. But Greene had bigger plans. When Morgan told him of Cornwallis destroying his baggage, Greene could see that this was a moment to seize upon if they marched to the north. "Then, he is ours!" He then wrote to Huger that he hoped to ruin Cornwallis, if he persisted in this "mad scheme of pushing through the country," and urged him to meet with Marion at Georgetown and also to recall Lee's Legion if possible. Greene would exclaim, "If this is done, here is a fine field and great glory ahead."

Greene planned on retreating north, but not into the mountains, as difficult as that would make it for Cornwallis to pursue them. Greene wanted to do the complete opposite, and go through the country where the British commander could, and would follow him. Each day, he would stay just ahead of his pursuer and avoid being caught, but near enough to keep Cornwallis thinking he may catch them in battle. He would literally tease his opponent further and further from his supply magazines, while Greene would be getting closer to his own in Virginia and farther north. It was an insane and hazardous plan, and subject to the least problems which occur when marching an army over terrain that has been made more difficult with the weather conditions. Rain for days at a time, then temperatures near freezing at night, making roads impassable or at best, difficult on which to travel. Morgan saw it as an undue risk and flirting with disaster. He was completely opposed to it, screaming that he would not be accountable for the consequences to his men and the army if Greene tried this. "Neither will you, for I shall take the measure upon myself," Greene replied, "It is for the commander to take on such a burden." He issued orders that would set the plan in motion.

With Cornwallis dividing his army, he had sent part of them under the command of Lieutenant-colonel Webster. They comprised of the 33rd of Foot Regiment, the 2nd battalion of the 71st, and the Royal North Carolina Regiment of Tories, the Hessian jagers, the artillery, and all of the wagons, and ordered to approach Beattie's Ford as if he were going to cross it. While the main body of troops under Cornwallis and General O'Hara , with a brigade of Guards, the Hessian Regiment von Bose, the Royal Welch Fusiliers, 200 cavalry, and two light filedpieces, started for McGowan's around midnight, six miles below Beattie's. The British commander could see the left bank ablaze with the American watch fires, and felt this movement would take them by complete surprise and outflank the foe without a means of escape.

Although McGowans Ford was only four or five feet deep, it was over five hundred yards wide, with a rocky bottom and a swift and turbulent current. To make matters worse it was beginning to rain, thus making the ford impassable in a matter of hours. After all that he had risked so far, Cornwallis felt that it was better to take a chance of forcing the passage now, rather than waiting and allow Greene to muster more militia and having his army stronger than it was right now. The Guards were ordered to advance across first, led by a Tory guide, the soldiers were told to carry their cartridge boxes high on their shoulders to avoid getting the gunpowder wet, and to be unloaded, but have bayonets fixed. By just after 1 Am, the waters were already beginning to swell and become even more turbulent. But the roaring also helped to drown out the sound of the approaching British, and with the rain and dark, the American sentinels were unable to see the opposite bank to see the enemy advancing until they were within 100 yards from the side of the bank. Then the alarm was sounded by a diligent guard who had continued to scan the ford, even in the downpour. He noticed the first line of British troops in the light of the watch fires and within seconds, the small body of militiamen opened fire into the advance column. Their aim was deadly, as the well-directed rifle fire suddenly, visibly thinned the first three ranks. The entire column halted, then continued again, with men and horse beginning to stumble among each other in the turbulent waters and against the current and ever rising waters. This caused many to lose their footing, and eventually they were swept downstream, being dragged under from the weight of their equipment, but many remained upright and nevertheless continued to advance.

Cornwallis had his horse shot out from under him, but the animal was said to be conscious enough, "to struggle to shore, carrying his rider as far, and then dropping dead the moment he reached shore." The terrified Tory guide turned and ran for his life, and as is many such moments in war, actually saved the British army from complete destruction. For when he ran he broke off to the right in the same direction the horse landing was to be. Fortunately, the officers did not see him and continued to advance straight-ahead. If they had gone to the right, they would have come directly into Davidson's camp of 350 North Carolina militia, which had heard the firing and were already preparing to meet the British at the bank of the ford. Before they could get there, the British had managed to reach the bank. They were able to chase off the small band of militiamen that had spotted them, but not before losing Colonel Hall, who had so courageously led his men across. He was shot dead the second his foot hit the bank. Davidson finally managed to hurry his men to the site of the fighting, but the British were beginning to organize now, and seeing their disadvantage of numbers, decided to retreat. Unfortunately, just as he was mounting his horse, a bullet struck him in the chest killing him immediately. When he fell dead his men broke and scattered, with many of them losing heart altogether and dispersing, and returning to their homes and families. Of the 800 who had rallied around Davidson just the day before, the next morning there were only 300 still under arms.

All of these brave maneuvers served to accomplish nothing after all was said and done. Morgan was not outflanked. He and his troops had left camp under the direction of Greene the evening before. General Webster with the other division of the British crossed the Beattie's Ford later in the day without opposition. By the time Cornwallis was able to cross with his force, Morgan's troops had been given time to get thirty miles away, after marching all night and part of the next day on the road to Trading Ford on the Yadkin, the next river over. "The march," wrote Seymour, "was very unpleasant. . . it having rained incessantly all night, which rendered the roads almost inaccessible."

Morgan had already departed, but Greene, with two or three of his aides had stayed behind to arrange Davidson's militia to rendezvous at a certain point and join up with Morgan's force. Greene was anxious. He saw that this was a decisive moment, and felt confident that if they brought in the militia, they may be able to meet Cornwallis in open field battle. "It is necessary we should take every possible precaution," he wrote to Huger. "But I am not without hopes of ruining Cornwallis, and it is my earnest desire to form a junction as soon as possible for this purpose. Desire Colonel Lee to force a march to join us." While Morgan was hurrying as best he could to Yadkin, Greene had taken up a station at the selected rallying point for the militia beyond Tarrant's Tavern, on the road to Salisbury. Hours passed waiting, but without success of meeting the militia that was suppose to arrive. Greene had been waiting alone when a few of the militia started to assemble, when suddenly Tarleton's cavalry came galloping up in pursuit of them. The militiamen turned and delivered a hasty fire, ran to their horses, and escorted Greene down the road to Steele's Tavern. Tarleton gave up the pursuit, never knowing how close he had come to capturing the southern departments commanding general.

Greene waited throughout the night along the road for the militia until almost midnight. Finally, a messenger rode up and told him that Davidson was dead, the militia dispersed, and Cornwallis had crossed the river and was on this side now. He rode on alone, dejected, until he came to Salisbury and Steele's Tavern. There he dismounted, his arthritic right knee stiff and sore, and was greeted by his friend Dr. Read who had been awaiting his arrival. "What? Alone Nathanael?" "Yes," he answered "tired, hungry, alone, and penniless." Mrs. Steele, the proprietor of the tavern, heard Greene. She fixed him an enormous breakfast and then showed him to his room. There, Greene thanked her for her warm generosity and held out his hand towards her in friendship. She held out hers and handed him two small bags of hard money. Amazed. Greene looked up in disbelief to ask why? As the patriotic landlady exclaimed, "Take them, for you need them, and I can do without them." The two small bags of money Greene held in his hands was the entire military war chest of the Grand Army of the Southern Department. As Greene turned around he noticed a portrait of King George over the fireplace mantel. It showed the respect the American people had shown to their monarch before the hostilities broke out in the colonies. Greene walked over to the painting and turned the face to the wall, and wrote on the back of the picture. "Hide thy face, George, and blush." Here we have met yet another unknown hero who has passed without a word from history books or any novel, until now. Mrs. Elizabeth Steele.

Chapter XXVI

"Greene Retreats"

Cornwallis paused, and deliberated whether he should endeavor to try and get between the two divisions of the American army by crossing the Yadkin further down the river, or to cut them off from the fords of the Dan, and force them to fight at a disadvantage? Thus began one of the most famous annals of the Revolutionary War. The race or retreat to the Dan. It would be, the single most important consequence for the rest of the entire war.

There was a momentary pause, during which Greene was watching the movements of his adversary from a sure position in the forks of Abbott's Creek, not far from Salem. Cornwallis was effectively doing the same thing to his counterpart. He knew the Dan was the ultimate goal of the Americans. Once across it and in Virginia, Greene could call on reinforcements and supplies, and there was safety in the terrain. Greene was using the waterways to their optimum potential, and showed to Cornwallis the genius and foresight of Greene and the skill and energy of Carrington. Greene, on the other hand, had studied his opponent for years and knew his tactics and character well. Greene never left anything to pure chance, and was not without hope "that from Cornwallis' pressing disposition, and contempt he has for our army, we may precipitate him into some capital misfortune. If he knows his true interest he will pursue our army. If he can disperse it, he completes the destruction of the State; and without it he will do nothing to effect." Greene had hoped to deceive his enemy by attempting to strike the British commander from the upper fords of the Dan. However, when he reached the Sherrill's, hoping to form a junction with his main army in a few days, he wrote to Washington about his problem; "heavy rains, deep creeks, bad roads, poor horses, and broken harness, as well as delays from want of provisions, has prevented it." As a result, he was forced to change the place of junction from Salisbury to Guilford Courthouse. By the 8th of February he directed his movement of Morgan's detachment. On the 9th, Huger came up with the main army, which Lee had already joined. Expresses were sent out in all directions, with urgent appeals to the officers of the militia. While waiting for their return, Greene proceeded to make a careful study of the ground on which he hoped to meet the enemy.

But, Greene was disappointed yet again. The militia could not be convinced to join the army's ranks. It was about this time that an old friend, turned hated advisory came back on the scene. Benedict Arnold, fresh from his failed attempt to give up West Point for 20,000 L sterling and the rank of general, had only received 6,000 L sterling of the money he was promised, due to the failure of his little coup. However, he was given the rank of British brigadier-general and command of a band of regular and loyalist soldiers in Virginia. He and Greene would eventually be reestablishing the old acquaintance in a far darker light. But, the problem at hand far outshines the issue of Arnold. Von Steuben, still did not have the necessary trained recruits that Greene required. All of his men at this point only added up to 2,040 men under arms, with only 1,230 of them regulars. On the other hand, he was facing at least 2,500 British troops by his latest intelligence gathering, and as many as 3,100 strong. To attempt to fight against such a disadvantage in manpower would be suicide. Greene had to come to the realization that he must, once again, retreat. He assembled a council of war, something he had been reluctant to do up until this point, but sudden matters required one, and the council confirmed what he already had deduced.

As much as it pained Nathanael to fall back after the recent good fortune and victory, he was also encouraged at the fact that his army was getting closer and closer to their base of operation and a full contingent of desperately needed supplies. As badly as Jefferson had failed to raise recruits for Greene's army, he had done a masterful job of procuring provisions and equipment from the State of Virginia. The only other problem Greene saw with his retreat to Virginia was a political backlash he feared. How were the Whigs going to react at seeing the new southern department commander turning his heels and returning to Virginia after only a short time, and the apparent abandoning of North Carolina? Would the general do the same to them if the circumstances became the same in Virginia? Even the Tories took notice and had to feel they were witnessing a change in events that would only be in their favor.

Although it appeared so, Greene had not abandoned North Carolina. He did not trust the Tories as far as he could throw one, but he would need them as bait for deflection against the Whigs. Sumter had now recovered from his wounds and returned to take his command in the field to Greene's delight. He was immediately directed to the upper districts of South Carolina to organize the militia in that area as best he could. Marion was ordered to cross the Santee, and Pickens, who had now succeeded the late Davidson with the remnants of his militia, was to take his new command of the men he had under arms and march to the rear of the enemy. All of the stores and provisions were removed from Prince Edward's Courthouse, and Greene wrote to Governor Nash of North Carolina of his needs and prospects for receiving them. He even wrote to his old friend Patrick Henry, who was back in Virginia, appealing for Henry to use his persuasive ways in drumming up 1,400 to 1,500 volunteers that would be needed. The small military chest that had given to him by Elizabeth Steele was already long gone. The men were still "imperfectly clothed" as Greene put it, but their health and spirit had begun to climb. They were eating better and more regularly now, and they were beginning to catch the confidence their new commander was projecting. Their discipline and resolve were growing stronger, and they felt confident that the judgment and energy Greene was displaying had taught them "that he was an independent spirit and confided in his own resources." Which could only bode well for them in battle against the British.

Up until now, the distance to the Dan was seventy miles. This had not been a factor to Greene up until this moment. But the weather was becoming an issue. It was now mid February, the worst month of the year. The roads were through the red clay region, difficult to travel over in the summer months for civilians, let alone an army in the dead of winter. The roads had developed the deep, rough and broken marks of wagons that were slimy by day, and frozen by night. With every step, the soft clay would become mire in the daylight as horses and men's feet splattered the holes to make them bigger, while wagons broke the surface and drilled deep, cutting scars with every roll of the wooden wheels. It would not only weaken the road, but tired men and animal to exhaustion, as well as damage wagons beyond repair. The only comfort Greene could possibly find in this, was that the enemy had to travel over the same roads and endure the same pains. The difference was, the British were much better dressed for the occasion, with better shoes for marching on such roads, better clothing for warmth, good blankets for sleeping, and an abundance of good food everyday. The other side of the coin was the American army in their rag clad garments, wholly unsuited for the season, with maybe one blanket shared between three men, who foraged for their daily provisions of food.

Greene would comment time and again in his journal, "from neither officer or man would be heard a discouraging comment. For the fate of the entire south hung in the fate of every one of us." However, even the confident Greene was beginning to question his own wisdom. How could he hope to succeed against the best soldiers the world had to offer, led by the best generals? How could he keep the Tories from joining the British in force, now that the Crown troops were able to protect and incite them? As mentioned, Arnold was now directing an ever growing, well supplied detachment in Virginia. What was to stop him from working in orchestration with Cornwallis, and slowly squeeze

Greene and his troops until they were crushed somewhere in the middle? Nathanael Greene had never had a time to be in a deeper anxiety than at this moment. For the first time, the realization of the complete separation of the north and south seemed so imminent. "My hopes," writes Washington to Greene, "rest on my knowledge of your talents." How could he fail with the confidence of the commander-in-chief and the country looking upon him? It was his worse fear when he had first accepted the command of the southern department. For the first time, it was beginning to look like the worse could only be expected. "We wait the receipt of further accounts with the utmost anxiety," writes Major Shaw to his brother, when the news of Greene's re-crossing of the Dan reached the north. "The present is a time of great expectations."

Now, like two champion prize fighters eager to enter the ring to decide who was best, the two leaders prepared themselves for a struggle of their own. Cornwallis had refreshed his tired men, and had lightened their burden by the destruction of the baggage, divided his troops, had figured out his adversaries intentions, or so he thought at the time, and stood there prepared to rush forward in full pursuit of Greene. The American general had also put his heavy baggage into safekeeping. He had also tried to do all he could to raise the militia in the country behind the enemy and provide for a passage across the rivers whenever and wherever needed. Greene had then divided his army once again, pushing the main body forward on a direct road to Boyd's Ferry. He ordered the rest, 700 hand picked men, armed as light infantry troops, to be prepared to throw themselves in front of Cornwallis, giving their companions time to cross the Dan. The 700 men consisted of "the cavalry of the first and third regiments, and the Legion, two hundred and forty in all; a detachment of two hundred and eighty infantry, under Lieutenant-colonel Howard; the infantry of Lee's Legion, and sixty Virginia rifle-men." The first choice as commander of this elite band was offered to Morgan. But Morgan was almost incapacitated with the rheumatism in his lower back and was bed-ridden. Still he considered accepting, but was persuaded by an aide to decline for the good of the mission. So Greene's second choice was Colonel Otho Holland Williams.

No sooner were the final arrangements completed, than Greene put his troops in motion. It was the 10th of February 1781. His main body set forward on the direct road to Boyd's Ferry. The light troops under Williams threw themselves boldly in front of the enemy. Cornwallis, seeing a body of horse and foot before him, slackened his speed in order to bring his long line into closer order, and then moved swiftly but cautiously onward. Williams, inclining left, came out onto an intermediate road with the main army on his right, and Cornwallis, who still supposed that Greene could only cross at the upper fords, was confident of reaching them before him, on the left. But Greene's plan had succeeded fully once again. The movements of the main body were effectually masked by the movements of the light troops.

From behind this mask, Greene pressed forward on the direct road to the ferry, his weary men bravely advancing through the pain of privation and fatigue. They were still marching by day's end, resting only a few moments through the night, and like Valley Forge and Morristown before, leaving their bloody footprints on the broken frozen ground. They marched through rain and sometimes snow, bivouacked in crouched piles around the fires with only a single blanket among three men, trying to warm themselves from the frequent crossings in the waist deep waterways from the day before. The North Carolina militia lost hope, and by the third day all but 80 of them had deserted, captains and majors amongst them. "You have the flower of the army," wrote Greene to Williams, "do not expose the men too much lest our situation should grow more critical." The next morning he writes to Williams again with new orders, "Follow our route, as a division of our forces might encourage the enemy to push us further than they will dare to do if we are together. I have not slept four hours since you left me, so great has been my solicitude to prepare for the worst. I have great reason to believe that one of Tarleton's officers was in our camp the night before last." Maybe Greene was becoming a little paranoid. It could not be helped in the situation he faced.

Meanwhile, Williams was using every trick in the book to mislead his adversary and try to retard his march as best he could. "It is Greene's rear," thought Cornwallis aloud to one of his officers, "and I have him in my grasp." The British advance was led by O'Hara, the American rear guard by Lee. Both knew the nature of the stakes, and both were equally determined to win it. Williams weighed his chances carefully, and looked at the danger in all of its aspects. While day lasted, it was a question of vigilance and speed. But when night came, strategy and surprise would be the rule. If they could get the British general to commit to advance between the two American divisions, they would have his at their mercy. Half of the light troops were therefore put on guard at night, while the other half slept. Six hours out of forty-eight was the allotted time permitted and no more. So strong was the need for that precious few minutes, that it was said when the order was given for guard duty, that the remaining men who were allowed to sleep would hear the call, they would literally drop to the ground wherever they stood and fall fast asleep. But by three in the morning, the entire body was again under arms, pressing forward to secure a quiet breakfast, usually their only meal of the day.

This continued for three days, Cornwallis believing, all the while, that every step was bringing him nearer to the only point which his adversary could cross. He had no idea that Greene had collected every boat in the area, and they were sitting and ready on the south bank of the Dan, prepared for use by Greene and that Kosciusko was already busy on the north bank quickly throwing up a breastwork to cover the crossing.

By the third day, Cornwallis changed his course, crossing with the main body into the high road to Dix's Ferry, the road held by the American light troops, part of Tarleton's Legion pressing forward till it came into contact with Lee. It was the first time that the two legions had met face to face. In the sudden, sharp encounter, 18 of the British were killed but only 2 Americans. By afternoon on that same day, Lee himself barely escaped a surprise. Cornwallis discovered his mistake, and saw that his nimble adversary was again about to elude his grasp. He crossed into the right road to Irvin's Ferry, and continued the pursuit.

It was a question of speed now. Lee and O'Hara never lost sight of each other, and more than once they were within musket shot of each other. But neither seemed to be willing to take the chance of losing their stride in such an attempt. With every water crossing, the Americans steps were slowed to almost a halt, and their pursuers would rush forward and try to throw themselves on the rear of the band. But on more than one occasion they pursued only to pause, prepare for an encounter, and then remain stopped. It had soon become evident that the British were waiting for the Americans to make the first offensive move and the Americans were doing the same thing. So both parties decided not to waste any further energy on the sojourn and stayed at even paces apart as if they were part of the same army column.

The two armies met each other's maneuvers throughout that evening. The Americans, hoping for rest were sadly disappointed to find Cornwallis continuing his push on them. Finally, a little after midnight on the 1st of March, Cornwallis ordered the British column to halt. The exhausted Americans nearly fell where they stopped their march and gratefully captured some much-needed rest. Both armies built fires, and slept on their arms for only four or five hours. The next morning, struggling through the heavy morning mist, and still tired and weary from the long, forced march of the past few days, both armies seemed to be in a type of parley. They were allowing each other to enjoy a hot breakfast for the first time in quite awhile. In actuality, Cornwallis was so confident that he had his quarry nearly in his grasp, he probably felt as if he were a fox, playing with a captured meal. However, something was to happen that would frustrate the British commander yet again. At just that moment, a breathless horseman, splattered with mire, was galloping up to hand Williams a communiqué from Greene. "The greater part of our wagons are over," it said, "and the troops are crossing." They had done it. They had out foxed the old English gentleman once again, and they could not restrain their emotion, as a hail of Huzzah! was heard throughout the troops. Unwilling to admit defeat, Cornwallis must have merely brushed it aside and ordered his men to march onward against their fleeing quarry yet again. Later that evening, Greene sent another message to Williams, "Irvin's Ferry, 5 1/2 o'clock. All our troops are over, and the stage is clear. The infantry will cross here, the horse below. Major Hardman has posted his party in readiness on this side, and the infantry and artillery are posted on the other, and I am ready to receive and give you a hearty welcome."

That night, the entire American army slept on the north bank of the Dan. It had been a long and perilous journey since they had slept so soundly, and morale was sky high. They stood and watched the enemy's watchfires on the opposite side with just a bit of bravado. They now felt as if they were not merely holding on to the last hope any longer, but that they could finally feel the satisfaction of safety from the enemy and see that their cause could now be one of triumph and not just survival. Around the fires that night were many stories and tales spun of daring-do against their formidable adversary. Loud praises were heard of Williams and his brave light troops, as well as back slapping commendations for Carrington, who had done a masterful duty in the field and staff. But loudest of all was the admiration they felt for their general, Major-general Nathanael Greene, who had foreseen every danger, provided for each contingency, and inflicted the most severest wound on the British imaginable, a blow to their pride. A blow that would be strongly felt for the remaining course of the southern campaign.

When Greene did not find time for sleep, he could always find time for writing. Even during the retreat he could always find a few minutes to pen a note, a letter or message. Now he had time to do both and took up the duty with enthusiasm. "On the Dan River," he writes to Jefferson, "almost fatigued to death, having had a retreat to conduct for upwards of two hundred miles, maneuvering constantly in the face of the enemy, to give time for the militia to turn out and get off our stores." To Washington he wrote, "The miserable situation of the troops for want of clothing has rendered the march the most painful imaginable, many hundreds of the soldiers marking the ground with their bloody feet. The British army are so much stronger than I had calculated upon in my last. I have not a shilling of money to obtain intelligence with, notwithstanding my application to Maryland for that particular purpose. Our army is in good spirits none the less, notwithstanding their sufferings and excessive fatigue." Finally, to von Steuben, "We have been astonishingly successful in our late great and fatiguing retreat, and have never lost one instance anything of the least value." Washington wrote back on the 3rd of March: "You may be assured that your retreat before Cornwallis is highly applauded by all ranks, and reflects much honor on your military abilities."

Chapter XXVII

"The Battle of Guilford Court House"

Both armies were completely exhausted from their recent romp across the countryside. The British rested at Bell's Mills on Deep River, and Greene had made camp at the ironworks on Troublesome. Greene's first concern was the strengthening of his corps. Von Steuben had raised over 2,600 militia in Virginia and 400 new Continentals. He began to march them south. But soon after he started out, word came that Cornwallis was retreating to Wilmington and Greene was pursuing him with an overwhelming force. Therefore, von Steuben halted the militia and sent only the Continentals forward under the command of Colonel Richard Campbell. Out of North Carolina came two brigades of militia, over 1,060 under Brigadier-general John Butler and Colonel Pinketham Eaton. The Virginia militia, finally did arrive later with 1,693 men. They were separated into two brigades under the control of Brigadiers Robert Lawson and Edward Stevens.

By the 10th of March, Williams had rejoined Greene with his light troops, and the corps was dissolved "with the highest and best merited encomiums on the spirit and ability with which it had discharged its laborious and important duties." The men were all returned to their respective regiments, except Captain Kirkwood's Delaware company and Colonel Charles Lynch's Virginia riflemen, who were ordered to join William Washington's cavalry and form a new legion.

Now, Greene was prepared for battle. He was as well manned as possible. He could not delay, with the usual loss of men from sickness, desertion, terms of service expiring and the use of the militia for only six weeks, the time for action was now. He also was low on provisions and had exhausted his supplies in the outlying area. Now with the amount of troops in camp, that problem would only grow worse and the men would then begin to lose strength and morale if forced to ration again. The time was right for a fight and Greene knew it. He knew Cornwallis would be ready also, and the field of battle was all that was left to choose. But Greene had that decided by this time as well. The area surrounding the meeting house or better known as Guilford Court House was his choice.

Cornwallis was anxious to finally take on Greene and his force head-on. He had been frustrated and disappointed at the fool Greene had him made out to look like. A battle would also send a sharp blow to the inhabitants of the area, especially those who remained on the fence as to who to back, the "Congressional army" as Cornwallis called them, or the protection of the Crown. Cornwallis knew that, even if he won the battle, he would need the locals to hold it. He knew most of the inhabitants in the area were Whigs. To make matters worse, Cornwallis knew that he not only had to win the battle, but make it a decisive affair. Without it, he could not possibly win back North Carolina or even hold it.

The battle was just as necessary to Greene, but it did not necessarily have to be a victory. Another sharp blow, skillfully struck, could cripple the British army in its present condition by slowing it down further with wounded, and throw Cornwallis back into Wilmington.

The American army consisted of 4,243 foot, and 161 cavalry. Only 1,490 of them were Continental regulars. Even with their success at Cowpens, Greene still did not enjoy putting most of his trust on the militia. For instance, while there had been as many as 5,000 of them in the course of the last few weeks, over half had picked up after only six weeks of service and gone home without a word. Greene felt it would be impossible to carry out a regular plan of attack, or accomplish a remote object

277

with such materials and men. With the knowledge of how militia reacted when confronted by British regulars in battle, Greene knew that the majority of them would fire once, maybe twice from an unreasonable distance, throw down their arms, turn their backs and run. Most of these American militia were well-trained marksmen, who had built their own muskets for optimum effectiveness. Their arms were a little more reliable, and musketballs flew a little further and were a bit more accurate than the common flintlock being used by both sides. These men could be a terrific tool if used in the proper way. If they could be persuaded, even if it was only a majority of them, to hold and fire at least two good volleys into the British front line, the British would lose quite a few men and cause a panic amongst the survivors, at least for a moment. Cornwallis had everything to lose with defeat, total ruin of the campaign for one. At the worse, Greene would loss the field and the dispersion of the militia. This was certainly a risk worth taking.

Greene had remembered Guilford Court House from when he had used it as the junction point to detach Morgan, on the retreat to the Dan. The advantages which it offered as a battlefield for irregular troops such as his, so impressed Greene that he made this special trip to come back to this location in order to make his stand with Cornwallis. It lay in the midst of a large wilderness. Within it, there were small clearings, some which had been used as crop fields and so were well manicured. In the middle of one of those clearings, just on the outskirts of a large hill surrounded by other smaller hills, stood the building that gave the area its name. Running by it was the high road to Salisbury. The largest hill was formed by a gradual rise that was nearly a half-mile in length. Directly around the courthouse, the ground had been planted with shrubs and saplings in a type of garden. Just a few hundred feet away, down the slope a long, narrow field that had recently been planted with corn formed another opening. It extended on both sides of the road to Salisbury, out to the outskirts of a swamp. The swamp was fed by a small creek. From this direction, Greene expected Cornwallis and his force to arrive. The space between the two clearings mentioned was covered in an oak tree forest, and the clearings nearest to the courthouse were screened by a high growth of saplings. The whole tract was undulating into a slope, broken by several ravines, and abounding in strong positions for defensive and offensive purposes during battle.

From High Rock Ford to Guilford was a short march. When the army reached it, on the afternoon of the 14th of March, there was still light enough for Greene to survey the ground one last time before the battle orders were given out. When Greene completed his reconnoitering and returned to camp, his aides then issued their own orders. "Do not expose your person needlessly. Put our lives at every hazard if you must, but please be careful of your own sir. If we fall, our loss will not be felt; but your death would not only be fatal to the army, but in all probability greatly retarded, if not destroy, every hope of securing the independence of the south." The "declaration" was signed by all of his aides and several field officers. They knew Greene's penchant for battle, and knew he would especially want a good seat with this long awaited fury against Cornwallis himself. He promised nothing, but agreed the terms were just. That night the American army slept on their chosen field of battle. The same ground that many of them would be lying on the next morning in endless sleep.

There had been a light frost through the night, and the morning was cold. But the sky was clear, the sun rose bright, and there was exhilarating braceness in the air. This was going to be a decisive day. They all knew it, and felt that they were prepared for it. With breakfast finished, it was time to arrange the men into lines and range themselves for battle.

Meanwhile, Lee had been sent forward to watch for the enemy. Three or four miles from Guilford, Lee met Tarleton leading the British cavalry, the Hessian jagers, and the light infantry of the Guards. He fell back for a moment, with Tarleton pressing in on him, just until he embanked on the narrow lane. Then his cavalry wheeled about and charged, completely overthrowing Tarleton's first wave and driving the remainder back as well. Lee and his legion quickly pursued the British horsemen, but soon came upon the head of the main enemy army. There was a heated skirmish for a short while before Lee "retired precipitately" back to his own lines and to notify Greene that the British were on their way.

It was almost noon and Greene could hear the sounds of small arms fire, not far distant. Greene instantly proceeded to draw up his troops, and in so doing, remained loyal to his original plan of perhaps not winning the battle, but making sure that if there was to be a British victory, it would come at a heavy cost on their side, and their side only. He would separate them into three barriers, each of which would have to be overcome before the other could be reached. The first line was drawn up on the outskirts of the woods, with open ground in front of its center, and with its flanks extending into the wood.

The open ground was an old cornfield, about two hundred yards in length, and whose side opposite of the Americans was bordered by a small creek. The split-rail fences bordering the fields, were for the most part still standing, and formed a kind of light breastwork, behind which the militia could seek shelter if need be, and make good on their promise to deliver two to three well directed volleys before giving way. Morgan had written to Greene soon after Cowpens and warned about the next battle he knew was on the horizon and about "the great number of militia" on the American side: "If they fight, you will beat Cornwallis, if not, he will surely beat you." He advised flanking the lines of militia with riflemen under an enterprising officer he could trust. "Put the bloody militia in the centre with some hand picked troops in their rear to shoot down the first of those men to break and run."

Greene followed the advice and set up Butler's and Eaton's North Carolina militia across the road at the fence, so that the enemy emerging from the wood would have to cross five hundred yards of open ground in order to reach the fence and the skittish militia. The line of militia was supported on its right flank by the infantry of Washington's Legion, which at the time was made up of Kirkwood's light infantry and Lynch's Virginia riflemen. They were formed at an angle so that their fire could be raked down the length of the attacking column with devastating effects on the British troops when they came near the fence. Washington's cavalry was to their rear on the far right. Lee's Legion of infantry, Campbell's riflemen, and Lee's cavalry supported the left wing. Most of these troops were also raw militia, but Greene had specifically requested Jefferson to send out an urgent call for officers in the militia that had recently been released from service, and this request had been extremely effective.

The third, and by far, the most principal line was drawn up in a semi-circle along the open ground around the courthouse hill, about four hundred yards from the rear of the second line, and on the right of the high road from Salisbury. If you drew a line along the formation of the courthouse hill, they would have been drawn up with a double front. The two regiments of Virginia regulars under Greene and Hawes on the right, and the first and second Maryland under Gundy and Ford on the left, with Captain Jaquett's Delaware company in the center. Gundy commanded the only veteran regiment. It was hoped that the new regiments would be inspired by its example, and thus at the critical moment, put forth their combined strength, and complete the work of the first and second lines. Also in the center of the third line was the only artillery the Americans possessed. Two guns under Singleton in the center of the first line, and two under Finley in the center of the third. It was approximately half a mile from the third line to the first, and because of the woods, the second line was completely out of Greene's line of sight. There was no reserve at all. The entire army was on the ground and would have to live or die on their own.

Just after noon, the Americans could see the British front line advancing up the narrow avenue from the battlefield. With all the maneuvering that Greene could muster, he rode forward to the first line and passed along the entire length of it. In a clear, firm voice he called the men's attention to the strength of their position, and like Morgan at Cowpens exclaimed the same three words he extolled to the militia; "Just three rounds. Three rounds, my boys, and then you may fall back." The day was cool and cloudless, but several witnesses said later that Greene still had to remove his hat and wipe the perspiration off of his "ample forhead." And then taking his position again with the Continentals in the third line, he held his breath and waited for whatever duty the day may call for from him.

A little after one o'clock in the afternoon, the battle began in earnest with the British center advancing into the clearing in front of the North Carolina militia. Singleton immediately opened up with his two field-pieces. The British artillery was also brought up. Within minutes a sharp cannonade began and lasted almost half an hour. All the while, Cornwallis was arranging his men and drawing his lines for the advance. He formed them into one continuous line. With no reserve, he resolved to come at the raw militia with the tip of the bayonet and chase them from the field. It was unusual, but no music was playing in the British ranks, and the first wave crossed the first fence line, coming across more than half of the open ground. Then the entire first line of American muskets seemed to fire as one. Men in red coats fell all along the line, leaving huge gaps in it, but they steadily marched forward.

On Cornwallis' right he had placed Leslie, with the 71st Regiment, the Hessian regiment von Bose, and the First battalion of the Guards under Colonel Morton. On the left was Lieutenant-colonel Webster, with the 23rd and 33rd of Foot regiments, and Brigadier-general O'Hara with the grenadiers and the 2nd battalion of the Guards. In the woods, on the left of the artillery was jagers and light infantry of the Guards. The cavalry under Tarleton was ranged in columns on the road, with instructions to keep compact, and not to charge without getting orders directly from Cornwallis himself, except "in the case of the most evident necessity."

Cornwallis saw the first line decimate his advance corps and pushed the column across the creek, under the cover of his own artillery. He deployed the right and left in quick step, and brought them quickly into the line of battle as well.

Greene's first concern was that they not be permitted to cross the open field unbroken, and he strained his ears to listen for the North Carolina's second volley. But it did not come. When Cornwallis had brought up his right and left to merge with the first line, the militia quickly became unnerved when they saw the British advance in this tremendous column. They saw the gleam of their bayonets, witnessed their unbroken stride and determination and slowly began to shrink back without firing their second volley. As the British came even closer, the militia began to quicken their backward pace, and just as they heard the command to charge bayonets at quick step and then full charge, the militia dropped their muskets and broke into a full run to the rear. It looked like complete madness, wildly running and throwing first musket, then cartridge box, and anything else that would impede their flight. It was a waste of time, but the officers attempted to stem the torrent of the escapees, Eaton, Butler, and Davie threw themselves in front of them, flailing their arms, beseeching them to halt, but all in vain. Lee even ran through them in full gallop and threaten to attack them with their own cavalry, but it was useless. Complete terror had taken hold, and within seconds, the entire first line was beyond the sound of the officer's threats.

The British were now advancing with no one to oppose them for a hundred yards. But Washington and Lee quickly took command of their corps, seeing that their flanks were now exposed. Cornwallis countered and promptly wheeled the Regiment von Bose in front of Lee. The 33rd, with the light infantry and jagers were pushed against Washington, and he ordered the grenadiers with the 1st and 2nd battalions of the Guards to advance and fill up the breaks in the line. The Americans retired slowly, firing volleys as they went, and fell back. Within moments they found themselves in position with the second line.

With the clearing behind them, the British were now fighting in the woods. The Americans on both wings were retiring, taking cover behind each tree they came upon, then fired and retired again. Lynch and Kirkwood were now covered by Washington's corps and were able to make a right wheel into the American second line, the Virginia militia, which was commanded by veteran officers, held fast. Meanwhile, on the American left, Campbell and Lee had been joined by the remnants of the North Carolina troops under Captain Forbes, who had not fled the field. Campbell had intended to fall back at a position to the left of the Virginia line, but he had been delayed in an engagement with the 1st battalion Guard, while the Regiment von Bose had struck across his front and cut him off from his intended path. He and Lee were now being forced away from the rest of the Americans and had to take a position up on the height to the south of the main battlefield.

Here the Americans made a stand. Gunby's 1st Maryland, including Jaquett's Delaware company, Colonel Hawes' Virginia Continental regiment, and Kirkwood's light infantry, faced Webster's troops at a distance of two hundred yards. Webster sent in his jagers, and light infantry, along with the 33rd in a bayonet charge thinking he was up against raw militia. The Americans held until the enemy was within less than 30 yards and unloaded a withering volley of fire that halted the British in their steps. Before the British could reorganize, Gunby sent in his men with the bayonet. His 1st Maryland and Kirkwood's company lunged forward and drove the British back, down into the ravine and up the other side in complete disorder.

The tide was suddenly turning on Cornwallis. The Hessians had been engaged with Campbell's riflemen and Lee's Legion on the wooded height to the south of the main battlefield for some time. Stevens' Virginians were finally being forced back, and Webster's troops were beaten and demoralized. If Washington and Lee's cavalry could be thrown into the fray of the disordered enemy, the entire Continental line could charge down on Leslie and O'Hara as they had at Cowpens. The battle would be the Americans' and Cornwallis would be completely destroyed. However, that was not Greene's original plan. Unlike Morgan, Greene could not risk his entire detachment in an all-out attack. If he was defeated for some reason he would lose the entire army and thus lose the entire south. That was not an option Greene could live with. So, Greene halted Gunby and Kirkwood, thus allowing Webster to recover and return to his original position safely.

Cornwallis had another horse shot from under him, and was forced to mount a common dragoon horse, and in his haste, had left his saddlebags with all of his maps and documents under the belly of the dead animal. Cornwallis was a bit disoriented and had to be assisted by a sergeant of the Royal Welsh fusiliers, who saw his danger, seized the general's bridle and led him to safety on the outskirts of the woods. Cornwallis had witnessed a very confusing day. Although he had seen the first line of the Americans in full flight, he then saw his best troops routed and sent into disorder. The day would be lost if he did not attempt a counter attack of some kind.

O'Hara had been wounded in the previous melee with Washington, but was still attempting to command the grenadiers and the 2nd battalion of the Guards with Lieutenant-colonel Stuart. As the Virginians in the second line began to weaken, Leslie drew off the Welsh fusiliers and the Highlanders, and left the 1st battalion to deal with the Virginians on their own. The Hessians were still struggling with Campbell and Lee in the woods, but with those two armies engaged, the whole British army was now free to attack the Continentals of the third line.

Meanwhile Howard of the 1st Maryland and Kirkwood were wheeling their troops to the right to protect the third line. Washington had just finished sweeping through the Guards and killing Stuart, when Howard charged them full in their left flank. The British troops held their ground, as did the Americans. O'Hara, despite his wounds, took command and rallied the Fusiliers and Highlanders on their flanks and engaged the Americans in close hand to hand fighting which was said to be quite bloody and savage.

Cornwallis could see that his troops were getting the worse of it, even with the pockets of determined fighting some of his troops were putting up. When he was led out of the woods, he came upon his artillery unit on the ground above the clearing. He decided to take desperate measures and ordered his artillery commander MacLeod to open fire with grapeshot over the heads of the British engaged with the Americans. Grapeshot is like a giant shotgun shell and can not be fired with any accuracy. It would kill indiscriminately American as well as British soldiers. "Open on them at once!" Ordered Cornwallis. Just then O'Hara came up from the battle, still bleeding profusely from his wound and heard the order. "You can't be serious sir? It will destroy our own men as well as the enemy." Cornwallis glared at the British officer for daring to question his order and exclaimed, "I see it sir, and am well aware of it. But it is a necessary evil which we must endure to advert impending destruction." O'Hara was said to turn away in disgust and groaned as the cannons fired their deadly cargo upon the troops below with devastating effect to both armies. The effect worked though, and the Americans were forced to withdraw to their former line, which allowed the British to re-form.

Webster was the first to reorganize his men. Amongst what was said to be mounds of dead British and Americans, a third of the British troops, Webster re-crossed the ravine he had been pushed back on, and charged upon the American left of the third line. But here stood the 1st Maryland, Huger's two Virginia Continental regiments, Kirkwood's light infantry, and Lynch's riflemen. To the total surprise of the British, the Americans did not give an inch, and stood fast, and with a withering fire, drove Webster back once again.

There was a pause in the initial engagement while both sides collected their loses and totaled their wins. The American militia was gone, the 5th Maryland had disintegrated, Stevens' Virginia militia in the second line, saw their colonel wounded and had fled into the woods. But Campbell and Lee were still engaged with von Bose, while Webster was again in retreat from the third line. If Greene had known just how badly he had damaged Cornwallis and his army, he may have sent in his entire force and finished the British. But always true to his word, he decided to stick to the original script and not risk the destruction of the whole army for the chance of one moment of victory. He decided to withdraw at half-past three in the afternoon, and a "general retreat took place; but it was conducted with order and regularity," wrote Stedman, the English historian, who was witness to the battle.

Cornwallis may have called it a victory, but it was at an extremely heavy cost. Of over 1,900 men who had gone into battle for the British, more than a fourth were casualties: 93 dead and 439 wounded, many of them dying of their wounds later. General O'Hara and General Howard had suffered injuries that kept them out of the war for months, Webster died of his wounds some days later, and several junior field officers were killed. Greene's chief objective had been conquered, he had crippled Cornwallis and his army. Of course he would have rather had a victory in the battle, but faithful to his plan he did not expose his small band of regulars to needless danger. Cornwallis attempted to pursue Greene's army, but was soon driven back. At the Reedy Fork, three miles from the field of battle, he halted, drew up his men, and waited for the stragglers to come in. Then setting forward, Greene returned to his old encampment at the iron works of Troublesome Creek.

Chapter XXVIII

"Cornwallis Licks His Wounds"

The battle had hardly ended when the weather broke and a torrential downpour commenced. It grew cold and windy. The battlefield was over such a large area, it had been impossible to collect the dead and wounded in the few hours of daylight that remained. The night had grown unusually dark, which made it nearly impossible for the British soldiers given the task of searching for wounded through the wide area, made even harder by their hunger and exhaustion. All through that sad night their shrieks and groans were mingled among the British and the Americans. Men wrote that it was "fearful to hear them, as the big rain fell upon their unprotected bodies and the cold wind swept in gusts through the forest, bearing on its wild wailings the cry of human anguish." Sometimes a sharp shriek would be followed by a feeble groan, and the groan grew fainter until death had come and all was quiet. Before morning when the searchers were able to go out again, nearly fifty who had been only been lightly wounded, had died from exposure to the elements.

Cornwallis was doing all that he could to give comfort to the wounded. However, he had no tents, and there were no houses within reach to hold the poor souls. Reports were still reaching him of his "victory." Stuart, of the Guards had been killed, the younger O'Hara of the Royal Artillery had died, Talbot of the 33rd, and Grant of the 71st were also killed. The elder O'Hara was gravely wounded, Webster, one of Cornwallis' most trusted officers was wounded and lay dying of his injuries. Maynard, a close friend of Cornwallis who was in his first battle of the war and had seen his impending demise in a dream the night before the battle lay dead on the field, a victim of his own prophecy. Even Tarleton had been wounded, although only slightly. When the tally of the casualties was complete, Cornwallis had learned that the Royal arms had been weakened by over 600 men. If they had barely held their ground in the past, what could they possibly hope to accomplish now?

Greene on the other hand, was full of confidence before he had even left the field. He knew he had inflicted a severe blow to his enemy, but for the first few hours, due to the weather and improper intelligence reports, he was not sure just how much Cornwallis was suffering. The British had broken off their pursuit too quickly, and this was interpreted as a sign of just how dearly Cornwallis had paid for his dear victory. The final tally of which would not be shown for some time. Greene meanwhile, drew up his men on the northern bank of the Reedy Fork and waited until at least the greater part of the stragglers had come in. He then resumed his retreat, and moved his men even further back to the Speedwill iron works, on Troublesome Creek, about ten miles from the battlefield. It was a long, weary night's march over muddy roads, and under a pelting rain. At daybreak he reached his old encampment. Here his first thought was to send a flag of truce to Cornwallis, with a surgeon to attend to the American wounded.

Soon, the reports started to finally arrive. Of his Continentals over 300 had been killed or wounded, and over 290 of his militia were missing, mostly from the Virginia regiments, "gone home," Greene writes, "to kiss their wives and sweethearts." The North Carolina militia was missing over 550 men. The chief loss was that of Major Anderson, of the Maryland line. "A brave and gallant loss severely felt and deeply lamented," wrote Greene. Stevens and Huger were wounded, and would pull through, but their spots in the command structure at such a moment could not be spared. Even with the strategic loss, the men were in high spirits and morale was good. They were eager to fight the British again, and soon. "You will see next time," said a North Carolina militiaman who had held his ground with others from his State. "We will wipe out the disgrace of North Carolina."

A flag soon appeared from Cornwallis, and at first the troops had thought it was the British commander asking for the surrender of Greene and his army. One had written what they could do with their request, "We are ready to sell you another field at the same price." The troops morale, although dampened by the lack of food, good clothing, and the fatigue of the battle and subsequent march, was still high. Greene's letters a few days after the battle reflected that. "Our army are in the highest spirits," he writes on the 16th of March to Sumter, "and wishing for another opportunity of engaging the enemy. I myself, hope in a few days to fight again with more decided an advantage. The purchase was made at so great an expense that I hope it may yet effect their ruin." On the 17th, he directs General Eaton to re-collect the North Carolina militia, and urges him to persuade the North Carolina Legislature to fill their quota of Continental troops. On the 18th, he instructs Colonel Malmedy to attempt to cut off the enemy's supplies, and "inform the inhabitants of the result of the battle of the 15th," the importance of which was becoming evident to the Tories almost daily. He had no idea that Guilford Courthouse was to be the most decisive battle of the southern war. But, he certainly knew he and his army had performed well and had made the best of their chances considering what they had endured. In a letter to Reed he shows this:

"Here has been the field for the exercise of genius, and an opportunity to practice all the great and little arts of war; fortunately we have blundered through without meeting any capital misfortune. . . . . The battle was fought on the very place from whence we began our retreat after the light infantry joined the army from the Pedee. . . . . It was long, obstinate, and bloody. We were obliged to give up the ground, and left our artillery; but the enemy have been so soundly beaten, that they dare not move towards us since the action, notwithstanding we lay ten miles from them for ten days. . . . . I am happy in the confidence of this army, and though unfortunate, lose none of their esteem. . . . . We have little to eat, and less to drink, and lodge in the woods in the midst of smoke. Indeed our fatigue is great. I have never felt an easy moment since the enemy crossed the Catawba, until the defeat of the 15th. But now I am perfectly easy, persuaded it is out of the enemy's power to do us any great injury. Indeed I think they will retire as soon as they can get off their wounded."

That same day he writes to his wife, "We have had a very severe general action with Lord Cornwallis. Our army though obliged to give up the ground, retired in good order, and the enemy suffered so severely in the action that they dare not move towards us since. This day we retired toward the Yadkin. He has great pride and great obstinacy, and nothing but sound beating will induce him to quit this State, which I am in hopes of effecting before long. The evening after the action I received your letter, which was some consolation after the misfortune of the day. Thus the incidents of human life mix and mingle together; sometimes good, and sometimes bad. I see by your letter you are determined to come to the southward. I fear you will be disappointed in your expectations. Nothing but blood and slaughter prevail here, and the operations are in a country little short of a wilderness, where a delicate woman is scarcely known or seen. And while the war rages in the manner it does, you will have little opportunity of seeing me. Our fatigue has been excessive. I have not had my clothes off for upwards of six weeks; but am generally in pretty good health. God grant the day may not be far distant when peace with all her train of blessings, shall diffuse universal joy throughout America."

While Greene was looking forward to another fight, Cornwallis was preparing to flee. Everyday more difficulties emerged that brought his weakened position into light. He could not venture out to meet Greene again on the field without exposing his army's weaknesses and thus to complete destruction. He could not retreat without abandoning his wounded. The Tories were still supporting him, but they grew more in fear each day from the Whigs who seemed to be growing bolder with each passing day. They were more than willing to cheerfully give up their food and bed to the Royal troops, but were less than willing to press their bodies into action until they were sure they would be victorious.

On the 18th of March, Cornwallis stopped wallowing in his self-pity and decided to extend the power of the victor. He issued a proclamation screaming of their recent "victory" against the rebels, and called upon all loyal subjects to come to the assistance of the English Crown to restore authority in the region. The next day he promptly broke camp at location near Guilford, and began his retreat towards Cross Creek, leaving over seventy of his own wounded and all of the American wounded under cover of a flag. At first it was reported that he was, "retiring towards the Yadkin." But a few hours later, intelligence reports determined that "they are moving towards Bell's Mills," Greene writes to Morgan on the 20th. "We shall follow them immediately, with determination for another brush." On the 22nd, he was at South Buffalo, eighteen miles from Bell's Mills, and wrote to Colonel Polk. "I beg you will spread the news throughout the country, that the inhabitants may well be informed respecting the enemy's situation. Come prepared for another battle." He had all intentions of attacking the British while they marched. "Cornwallis must be soundly beaten before he will relinquish his hold," he wrote to Lee, and pressed forward quickly with a call to the militia to come out and support them. On the 23rd, he wrote to Jefferson from Buffalo Creek. "Their route is conjectured by some to be towards Corss Creek, but by others to the Pedee. If measures are not taken to furnish us with provisions immediately, we shall be compelled to fall back." The militia, as they were prone to do, had wasted ammunition, which took a day to have sent up from the rear. Another day was lost and Greene feared Cornwallis would escape. The roads were terrible, marching was a struggle, and the rains continued and made matters worse as each day passed. By the 26th, Greene finally received accurate intelligence on Cornwallis' route. He pressed on towards Cane Creek on the Rigdon's Ford on Deep Creek, and from there he wrote to General Lillington in the vicinity of Wilmington. He wanted him to "watch the English encamped in that region, and prevent them from advancing and supporting Cornwallis."

By the 23rd, Greene had written to Jefferson about the necessity of calling out fresh troops of militia to take the place of those whose terms of service were about to expire. On the 27th of March he wrote to Jefferson explaining the men were "counting their days from the day they left their different counties, and not from that of their entrance into active service. They insist they be permitted to set out for home in season to reach it by the expiration of their terms, and not wait until that date." But arguing with the men was useless. They had already made up their minds and were making plans to set out in mass in the next few weeks. Greene tried in vain to explain what the battle at Guilford had meant, and that the fatal blow to Cornwallis meant the end was near. That by staying the course now, they would have all of the time in the world in the very near future, if they just held on. There was only one hope left. There may still be a chance to fight the enemy before the bewitching hour and the enlistment's expired.

On the 27th, Greene and his army were at Rigdon's Ford, where he had hoped to cross the Deep River in time to attack the enemy on their march. But word came that they were still at Ramsay's Mill, twelve miles below their present position. Without worrying about all the problems he was facing, Greene advanced and "put his army in motion without loss of time, firmly believing that Cornwallis would fight again." However, Cornwallis had secured his passage over the river by throwing a bridge across it, and on the 28th, as Greene came up, was already on the Right Bank. Lee was in position to press his rear guard and prevent him from destroying the bridge. All the surrounding indications showed how determined Cornwallis was to continue his retreat and not press into battle. Dozens of the British wounded who had died laid unburied along the road. Beef was still hanging in quarters where they had been slaughtered, and the hungry American ate it eagerly, and still ravenous for food, seized upon the British garbage that had been thrown aside for the turkey buzzards and ate that as well.

The next day Greene wrote to Governor Nash from Ramsay's Mill. "The enemy are on the way to Cross Creek, and probably to Wilmington. I wish it was in my power to pursue them further; but want of provisions, and a considerable part of the Virginia militia's time of service being expired, will prevent our further pursuit. The greatest advantages are often lost by short terms of service."

On the 31st of March, the better part of the militia would leave. What was he to do? He wrote to Washington: "The regular troops will be late in the field in the southern States, if they are raised at all. Virginia, from the unequal operation of the law for drafting, is not likely to get many soldiers. Maryland, as late as the 13th of this month, had not a man, nor is there a man raised in North Carolina, or the least prospect of it. In this situation, far remote from reinforcements, inferior to the enemy in number, and no prospect of support, I am at a loss what is best to be done. If the enemy fall down towards Wilmington, they will be in a position where it would be impossible for us to injure them if we had force. In this critical and distressing situation, I am determined to carry the war immediately into South Carolina. The enemy will be obliged to follow us, or give up their posts in that State. If the former takes place it will draw the war out of this State, and give it an opportunity to raise its proportion of men. If they leave their posts to fall, they must lose more than they can gain here. If we continue in this State, the enemy will hold their possessions in both. All things considered, I think the movement is warranted by the soundest reasons, both political and military."

No sooner had Greene decide his course than he began to prepare for its immediate execution. He first wrote to Governor Nash of North Carolina, "I beg you Excellency to order to Hillsborough as soon as possible twenty hogsheads of rum for the use of the army. Without spirits the men cannot support the fatigues of the campaign." To Major Long he wrote for ammunition, and urges the prompt repair of all the arms he can muster. To General Lillington; "You shall be further supported as far as I have it in my power, consistent with the great plan of operations. In the meantime keep up the spirits of the people. If the State avail themselves in time of their resources you have nothing to fear." To Lee, who always seemed to be at the rear guard of Cornwallis and maneuvering back and forth to find the best position for a possible attack, he communicated his latest wishes on the 2nd of April. "I take the liberty to communicate to you my sentiments respecting your plan of operations. This conduct may eventually undo the successes gained by the enemy of the last campaign, and most probably render every effort of his lordship to establish himself in this State. Thousands of difficulties oppose your success, and yet as I said before, no other system can promise you aught but loss to the United States, and disgrace to your arms. I think the following matters claim your immediate attention: The passage of the Pedee; supply of ammunition; transported in such a manner that it cannot be damaged; an extra pair of shoes for each man; the 1st regiment of cavalry to be collected, and to join the troops left in this State; the most cautious instructions to the commanding officer of the Pennsylvania division, lest his ignorance of the mode of warfare in this country may expose his troops to ruin; and a proclamation pardoning deserters, pointing out the delusion of the Tories, and breaking up the paroles given to inhabitants taken from their houses by the enemy. I am certain that good consequences must result from a proclamation at this period; perhaps it may be proper for governments to do something of this same sort."

On Monday, the 2nd of April, the militia was dismissed, and the resolution of Congress to honor Morgan and the army of the Cowpens, was received in time to be communicated to the troops in the orders of the day. On the 3rd, the men were further ordered "to wash and clean themselves, to get their arms in good order, and be prepared to march at a short warning." By the 6th of April, 1781, the long, adventurous march began. So ended the events that had seen Greene arrive in December of 1780. The enemy having complete possession of South Carolina and Georgia, and held a line of posts extending from the seaboard to Augusta and Ninety-six. The British army numbered between 3,500 - 4,000 men in the field, with several hundred more garrisoned at Charleston and large bodies of loyalist, scattered throughout the area that could be called out at a moments notice. North Carolina was there for the taking from the south, while Arnold approached from the north. But even in the midst of overwhelming odds, Greene saw fit to divide his army, and engage in a series of hazardous movements. One which gave the Americans a brilliant victory, lured Cornwallis from his base, subsequently forcing him to fight a battle hundreds of miles outside his communication and supply lines, and on ground picked to the advantage of his adversary. This produced a hollow victory, leaving him burdened with sick and wounded and in the midst of "timid friends" and bitter enemies surrounding him. Cornwallis was forced to march his decimated battalions into Virginia, and was unable to continue his pursuit of the Americans. Soon after, the Battle of Guilford Courthouse was recognized as the high watermark for the British and the turning point of the southern war.

Virginia formed a part of Greene's command, and was the main source that he looked to for reinforcements, and for most of his supplies. Fully aware of this, Sir Henry Clinton was preparing to send a strong detachment against it by water, and open the way for a strong cooperation with Cornwallis. Arnold had already been sent south in December, and was ordered to move down along the James River to Richmond and destroy all of the valuable American stores he could find. He went further and destroyed any manufacturing plants or shops he came in contact with, burning them and plundering the immediate area, until he reached Portsmouth where he was forced to lay low while a strong detachment of Virginia militia searched for him. At Portsmouth, he began to fortify the area, with the apparent idea of making it the base of future operations. The Americans caught up with Arnold, but kept a safe distance while watching his movements with a keen and anxious eye. They did not only want to thwart his plans, but also crush him at the earliest opportunity and hopefully capture him for a quick and legal trial and hanging. Washington himself was excited at the prospect of seeing his former general at Arnold's expense, and even formed a plan for his capture. Unfortunately, it involved the, still absent French fleet, and could have easily succeeded, but did not come off.

Cornwallis was happy to see Major-general William Philips enter Chesapeake Bay with 2,000 choice troops from New York. Philips immediately took command of all British troops in Virginia, much to the chagrin of Arnold who had aspirations of being named to that post. From there Cornwallis turned his attentions back to the south and to his weary and destitute army. He needed reinforcements, more supplies, and a firm ground from which to conduct the plans for his next campaign in order to retake South Carolina and Georgia and to crush and demoralize Greene and his pitiful army. Cornwallis would soon find it difficult to demoralize anyone except his own troops.

On the 6th of April, Greene ordered Captain Oldham's company of Maryland Continentals with two pieces of artillery to join Lee's Legion and for them to converge on the Pedee in hopes of joining up with Marion. He wanted them to proceed down the Cape Fear River to mislead Cornwallis into thinking that their destination was Wilmington. From there, the three would combine their forces and move Fort Watson on the Santee below Camden.

Greene wrote to Brigadier-general Andrew Pickens, suggesting that he move on Ninety-six "if he felt able, at all events, to prevent a reinforcement of Camden from that post." On April 7th, Greene broke camp at Ramsey's Mill and proceeded down the Cape Fear as if he were moving on Wilmington also. But the next day he moved west, across the Little River, the Yadkin, and then the Rocky River. With an abundance of food and rum, their march was at a good rate of eighteen miles a day, and was not filled with hardships like they had experienced in mid-winter.

By the 17th, the Americans were at Lynch's Creek. The sick and excess baggage were moved to Salisbury under a small detachment and orders were given that "women who have children and all those unable to march on foot must also be sent off, as none will be permitted to ride on wagons or horses, on any pretext whatever." While Greene continued his march he wrote to Reed of what he found along his route. "All the way through the country as I passed, I find the people engaged in matters of interest, and in pursuit of pleasure, almost regardless of their danger. Public credit totally lost, and every man excusing himself from giving the least aid to Government, from the apprehension that they would get no return for any advances." At the same time, a young man in the militia had been summoned to attend the session of the Legislature, to which he had been elected while in the field. But he refused to go, and Greene had been notified of this. "What! Refuses to exchange the perilous retreat before a superior force in exchange for a safe seat in the General Assembly?" Greene was noted as saying. "Bring the man to me at once, so as I may judge him for myself." The young man went before Greene and was asked; "Why do you refuse to obey the governor of North Carolina's summons?" Unafraid the young man spoke up and said, "I have seen the faces of the British many times and never seen their back, and I mean to stay with the army til I do." Greene was both awed and inspired. This was exactly the type of assemblyman that he needed in the Legislature. Greene sat the young man down and convinced him that if he stayed in the army, it would only be adding one man to it. But as a member of the Assembly, he may assist in procuring many men, and the army would have a voice in their care that was much needed. The young man relented and agreed to leave. The young man's name was Nathaniel Macon, and he would go on to be one of the States' premier statesman for decades, and be remembered in history to this day.

Meanwhile, Lee and Pickens found Marion, and proceeded to Fort Watson and reached it on the 14th of April. A small fort, but well fortified by three rows of abatis and sitting on a rise about thirty feet in height, with a barren plain all around for two hundred yards. It was garrisoned by only 80 British regulars and two Tory militiamen commanded by a Lieutenant McKay. Lee and Marion decided to attack the fort, but had no artillery with them and no entrenching tools. The actual commander of the fort was Colonel Watson, a British regular officer that was out at the time searching for Lee and Marion and had 100 British regulars with him. Knowing that this detachment could return at any time, the Americans knew a siege was out of the question. By the 22nd, they had formulated a plan. Several trees were felled and made into a barricade that could be carried within rifle shot of the fort. From there, they erected a small structure that could look into the fort from a platform at the top. The next morning, a company of riflemen opened fire on the fort where no man was safe from the balls whizzing within the small confines of the fort. At the same time, under cover from this withering fire, two detachments attacked the abatis and were able to get through all three rows without a single shot at them. The fort promptly surrendered. The Americans lost only two men with six wounded. They took the entire garrison prisoner, thus making the first break in Rawdon's communication line with Charleston.

Greene's next move was to attempt to surprise Rawdon. However, reports of the American advance reached Rawdon in Camden on the 19th of April, the same day Greene arrived in that area. Stopping his march for the night a few miles outside of town, Greene decided to send Kirkwood's light infantry into a small village called Logtown, nothing more than seven or eight cabins in the middle of a large clearing on a slight elevation, but less than a mile from Camden. Kirkwood and his men marched and arrived at Logtown at ten o'clock in the evening. By midnight, he drove out the Tories holding the village, and throughout the night skirmishes broke out off and on. When morning came, the Americans had successfully repelled the last of the attackers and captured the village for good. Greene was ready to make his next move.

The town of Camden was a large military strong point. To the south and southwest was the Wateree River, which curved around the town about a half mile away, while on the east was the Pine Tree Creek, which was a fairly wide and deep waterway. To the north and west, a series of redoubts had been constructed surrounding a central fort of considerable fortification. Garrisoned here were about 900 troops in all, consisting of the 63rd Regiment of Foot and four detachments of Tory soldiers, the New York Volunteers, the King's American Regiment, and Fanning's Regiment, organized in 1776 in New York City, and the Volunteers of Ireland, Rawdon's own regiment. Along with 60 Provincial dragoons and a small party of militia, it made up a considerable force of veteran soldiers. The second in command, a Colonel Watson had taken 500 Tory troops out to look for Marion.

Greene soon realized that his small force was not sufficient enough to attack such a well-garrisoned fortress. He had hoped Sumter would soon be arriving with his substantial addition of men, along with Lee and Marion, fresh from capturing Fort Watson. In the meantime, he decided to withdraw to Hobkirk's Hill about a mile to his rear.

The next day, he sent Colonel Washington's horse and Kirkwood's light troops on a foraging party expedition to the west of Camden. They came back with provisions from "burn't a House in one of the British Redoubts. . . .took 40 horses and 50 Head of cattle before returned to camp." By the 21st, Greene learned that Watson and his party of 500 men were preparing to enter Camden to reinforce Rawdon. He knew he had to intercept them, and thought their best position would be from the East Side of town, the expected route that Watson would take. After receiving updated information on Watson's whereabouts, Greene moved back to Hobkirk's Hill and ordered the artillery and baggage moved back to Lynch's Creek, twenty miles away. He then sat and waited for Sumter, Lee, and Marion.

But Sumter in his usual independent fashion, had no intention of coming to Greene's aid, and Lee and Marion were too busy chasing Watson in the Santee country to give any thought to aiding Greene. A drummer from the Maryland line had deserted Greene's troops and was brought to Rawdon with news of Greene's predicament. Rawdon was told of the condition of Greene's troops, and that the artillery had been sent back with the baggage, and gave him a detailed description of the troops make-up, their distribution, and location on the hill. Rawdon decided to make up Greene's mind on when he was to fight.

Chapter XXIX

"The Battle of Hobkirk's Hill or The Second Battle of Camden"

Hobkirks' Hill was nothing more than a narrow, sandy ridge of no more height than 40 or 50 feet. It was a mile and a half from Camden, and so this is why some historians misname it the second battle of Camden. The area was covered by dense forest extending from the east and west. At the farthest edge of its eastern slope, the grade gradually descended to a wide swamp adjacent to the Pine Tree Creek and extending past to the southern defensive works outside of Camden. South of Logtown a large clearing reached all the way down to Camden as well. The main road from town to the Waxhaws ran north of Logtown and right down the middle of Hobkirk's Hill. There was no clear view of the approaches from the top of the hill due to the shape of the hill and the denseness of the forest. The first settlers of Camden called it Pine Tree due to that same forest. But the name was changed during the French and Indian War to show respect for the great English statesman of that period.

Greene would never allow himself the weakness of despising his enemy. He did not feel he could afford that luxury. By respecting your enemy, you never took them for granted and "respect breeds honor" he would always say. So when Greene had encamped only a mile and a half from his foe, it was not for lack of respect, but rather honor for battle. He decided to form his first line contrary to that at Guilford. This battle was not going to be an attempt to merely cripple his enemy. This battles sole purpose was to fight until complete victory was attained. So, the first line would not have militia, but instead would be composed of two regular brigades. The Virginia brigade under Major-general Huger, consisting of Campbell's and Hawes' regiments was on the right of the road. The Maryland brigade, commanded by Colonel Williams, and consisting of the Gunby and Ford regiments on the left a second line consisted of North Carolina militia under the command of Colonel Read. He placed Washington and his cavalry on their right, and Kirkwood with his light infantry in front to support the pickets, and to retard any enemy advance. The artillery had been brought back from Lynch's Creek and placed under Harrison, who placed a battery directly on the road behind the second line.

The Americans were prepared and held under arms from the 23rd until the morning of the 25th awaiting the baggage and stores to arrive. At the orders of the day the troops learned that they would be "furnished with two days provisions, and a gill (4 ounces) of spirits per man, as soon as the stores arrive." The men stacked their arms and proceeded to the distribution area, but were soon disappointed. The food had arrived, but the rum had been delayed and expected on the hour. They enjoyed a hearty breakfast and seemed to be eager to engage the British. Some rested at their assigned positions, while others ran off to wash their clothes in the creek. By ten o'clock in the morning the rum arrived and every man received his allotted amount. Greene even found time to partake in what he called "one of my few vices," a strong cup of coffee while he sat in his tent. But the drum began to beat, calling the men to formation, and in the distance small arms fire could be heard throughout the woods. The men were all in formation when the order came to "sit down in place." Soldiers slowly obeyed, but eyewitnesses said later, "An animated though solemn joy appeared to pervade the whole army." The soldiers had never been told to sit under arms before. Greene was attempting to keep the British from seeing where his troops had been aligned until the last possible moment.

Meanwhile Kirkwood had hurried with his light infantry to the support of the pickets under fire. Although he was putting up a terrific stand against the British regulars, he was slowly forced back, disputing every foot of ground, until he reached the hill where the entire American line was waiting. With the men sitting on the ground, the British could not see them. The Americans could only see the blue smoke of gunfire rising up from the trees. It was hard to tell how the battle was progressing and which direction the British were advancing. As Kirkwood moved his light infantry out of the woods and up the hill, the British emerged from the forest just in time for Greene to give the order to stand. Now Rawdon saw his foe and within minutes would be face to face with him.

The British general had arranged his men in a single line, with a corps of observation in the rear, the right wing supported by the Volunteers of Ireland, and to the left by Captain Roberston's detachment of troops. As Greene watched them form, he saw a quick chance at victory in the narrowness of their front, and resolved to strike simultaneously at front, flanks, and rear. Campbell was ordered to wheel onto their right flank, Ford on their left, Hawes and Gunby to charge bayonets to the front, and Washington to pass around them under cover of the forest and take on the rear with his cavalry.

But, like most grand plans before they are enacted, the success of the maneuvers rested on Campbell and Ford's regiments that were primarily made up of new recruits, and had not been under sustained fire before. To make matters worse, while Ford was attempting to press his men forward on horseback, he was struck by a musketball in the chest and thrown from his mount mortally wounded. Instead of moving forward to avenge their leader, they did what most raw troops did under the same circumstance; they shrank back in dismay. Campbell's men, seeing Ford's troops stop, did likewise at the critical moment, and with neither flank attacked, Rawdon had time to notice the danger and brought up the Volunteers of Ireland to extend his line and make the maneuver impossible.

Meanwhile Harrison's artillery had opened up a brisk cannonade, and the regiments of Gunby and Hawes were advancing steadily. Soon the enemy's small arms fire also began to grow heavy. Some companies on Gunby's right, forgetting the order to use only bayonets, returned musket fire and continued to advance on the British. But a moment later, Captain Beatty, a favorite officer of the rank and file, was shot through the heart and killed immediately at the head of the company. The company stopped dead in their tracks and became confused and disoriented, falling out of line and almost walking in circles. An officer from a nearby company said later, "that it seemed as if they were deranged." The other companies were still advancing, and if the rear companies had been pressed forward at quick time, the advance may have been preserved, but it was not to be. Instead of pushing all of them forward, Gunby ordered them to fall back to the foot of the hill to reform. The order turned out to be fatal. "We are commanded to retreat," said each soldier to the next, and with the British advancing closer, the entire regiment gave way. Williams, Gunby, Howard, all competent, veteran officers, could do nothing to qualm the disorder, and the same men that distinguished themselves at Cowpens, were now yielding to sudden panic, breaking, and running like green militiamen. Before they could be rallied again, the day was already lost.

Only one regiment remained unbroken, the regiment of Hawes. Greene had been with them during most of the fight. He noticed that they were suffering more than the other troops. Just as he was about to give them the command to retire, they were at it again and advancing with a bayonet charge. They were no more than forty yards from the British front line. Rawdon noticed the advance immediately and pressed his men up the hill to take the Americans flank and attempt to silence the artillery. Greene noticed the danger to his men, and quickly formulated a plan. He was as exposed to the fire as his men and "led his men like a captain of grenadiers" an aide had commented afterwards. When he saw his line broken by the misconduct of his favorite unit, and the enemy about to double on his flank in a moment against the only regiment holding their ground, he saw that he had no choice but to order retreat.

Gunby had finally succeeded in reforming his regiment, which now was at the foot of the hill, which would be a good rallying point for Campbell's and Ford's regiments. Hawes therefore covered them with his troops, firing volley after volley as they withdrew slowly. Still the artillery was in danger. Harrison had used it with excellent effect until Hawes was outflanked, and by then the matrosses, the men responsible for pulling the cannons by ropes and assisting the artillerymen were beginning to see their predicament and dropped the ropes and were about to bolt. The rest of the artillerymen were also starting to swivel their heads around in anxious anticipation of what they felt was the inevitable outcome, and were also thinking of running. But Greene did not lose sight of them. Jumping from his horse, he limped over to one rope and picked it up in his hand while holding the bridle of his horse in the other. With a bellowing voice, he did his best to encourage the men to hold on just a bit longer, thereby saving the guns from capture. Then the camp guards, led by a man named Smith, came to the general's and artillerymen's rescue by assisting them in pulling the guns back in retreat. All of the camp guard men were Irish immigrants and not one was under the age of forty.

Coffin, with the British cavalry, came up at the same time, and within seconds, Smith and all of the camp guards were put to the sword. The artillery seemed lost. Miraculously, at that exact moment when Greene seemed in imminent danger himself, Washington's cavalry appeared. Each rider had a prisoner behind him, in a second the prisoners were thrown from the horses and the American cavalry charged against Coffin's men. The British cavalry wasted no time in running for their lives and Greene and the cannons were saved.

The Americans retired from the field skirmishing, and in good order with the British making a faint attempt at pursuit, but soon gave up the fight. About three miles from the battlefield, Greene halted to collect his stragglers and refresh his men. Toward evening he fell back two more miles further. The night's orders read, "The army having received a slight repulse from the enemy, the troops are to encamp this evening at the passes on Saunders Creek and Gum Swamp."

The next morning the officers and men waited anxiously for morning orders to be read, because they all knew Greene was sadly disappointed by the loss. This was mostly due to the failure in battle of his favorite and most trusted unit, the 1st Maryland. He was so disgusted by the conduct of the unit that he implied that censure should be applied at the least. The men replied, "We were ordered to fall back," and most of the men acknowledged that as fact. Gunby requested an immediate inquiry, and it was granted without delay. "General Huger, Colonel Harrison, and Lieutenant-colonel Washington," say the orders of the 28th of April 1781 "are to compose a court to inquire into the conduct of Colonel Gunby, in the action of the 25th instant." By the 2nd of May, they made their report: "It appears to the court that Colonel Gunby received orders to advance with his regiment, and charge bayonets, without firing. This order he immediately communicated to his regiment, which advanced cheerfully for some distance, when a firing began on the right of the regiment, and in a short time became general through it. That soon after, two companies on the right of the regiment, gave way. That Colonel Gunby then gave Lieutenant-colonel Howard orders to bring off the other four companies, which at that time appeared disposed to advance, except a few. That Lieutenant-colonel Howard brought off the four companies from the left, and joined Colonel Gunby at the foot of the hill, about sixty yards in the rear. That Lieutenant-colonel Howard there found Colonel Gunby actively exerting himself in rallying the two companies that broke from the right, which he effected, and the regiment was again formed and gave fire at the enemy which appeared on the hill in front. It also appeared from other testimony that Colonel Gunby at several other times was active in rallying and forming his troops. In closing, it appears from the above report that Colonel Gunby's spirit and activity were unexceptionable. But his order for the regiment to retire, which broke the line, was extremely improper and un-military, and in all probability the only cause why he did not obtain a complete victory."

Greene confirmed the opinion and wrote some time later to President Reed: "The troops were not to blame in the Camden affair; Gunby was the sole cause of the defeat; and I found him much more blameable afterwards, than I represented him in public letters."

However, as disappointed as Greene's "chagrin and vexation" was with the loss in battle, it made no alterations to his general plan of operations to push the British from Camden. "We are now within five miles of Camden," he wrote to Marion the day after the battle, "and shall closely invest it in a day or two again." To von Steuben he wrote, "This repulse, if repulse it may be called, will make no alterations in our general plan to defeat the British at Camden again." And to the French minister, the Chevalier de La Luzerne he would write, "We fight, get beat, rise and fight again."

Chapter XXX

"The Partisan War"

The darkest feature of the southern war had always been the savage fury whenever Whig and Tory collided. Which of the two were more barbaric it will never clearly be revealed. Each group seemed to be drunk with revenge after each one attacked one or the others village, camp, town, or farm. Women or children were not spared, animals were wantonly slaughtered in the name of loyalty to the Crown or patriotism to America. Houses, churches, schools, shops, mills, and crops were burned, whole plantations laid to waste, families killed or survivors scattered, only to be hunted like beasts of prey through swamps and thickets and then butchered. These were common occurrences on both sides. Any triumph by the British was a signal for the Tories to rise up and burn or kill. The victories of the Americans were a warning to the Tories to seek shelter in the deepest and most inaccessible recesses of the swamps, forest or within the distant lines of Charleston where the British set up their stronghold only to be overrun by the loyalists and Tories. To whichever side was inclined to call for revenge on any given day, new fires of hate and destruction could be seen in the skies that night. Some of the most bitter Whigs were in the ranks of the American militia. Of the most virulent Tories, they followed the tracks of the British army.

The men that can not be blamed are the officers of the British and American armies. Cornwallis and Greene were both known to detest the partisan brutality and many of their letters express the shock and indignation held for them, which they both felt was detrimental to the people of the country. Both men predicted that the ill feelings would run deep for years to come after the war was over. Both commanders believed that even peace would not heal the ill feelings that had been burnt so deep into the inhabitant's minds. To this day, if you travel in the south the words Whig or Tory conjure up a stern look and expletive word from even the most passive southern gentlemen's lips.

It was in the midst of these scenes that Greene also issued a commission for the negotiation of a treaty of peace with the Native Americans in the western frontiers of the southern states. He then began the discussion of a cartel for the exchange of prisoners. Both equally important, because the Native Americans had proved useful allies to the British, and the wretched conditions of the Native Americans tribes who had declined to help the British and the American prisoners in custody called for immediate relief.

Greene had decided it was time to carry the war back into South Carolina, and was counting on the reinforcement of 1,500 to 2,000 men from Virginia, and the approximately 1,000 men from Carolina that had been promised him. This would have increased his force to over 5,000 soldiers. With that many men he could have easily blockaded Lord Rawdon in Camden, and made himself master of the posts on the Santee and Congaree, opening the way to Ninety-six and Augusta. As he advanced toward Camden, he kept Sumter advised of his progress, and the cooperation of which he expected from him. On the 15th of April, he wrote to Sumter, "Lieutenant-colonel Lee is on the march from the Pedee to the Santee, and will cross that river somewhere near Nelson's Ferry, and then come up on the other side. Perhaps you may make your movements cooperate with his and also those of General Pickens. You will keep in mind that our force thus far collected is very small; and therefore you should not lose sight of a junction should Lord Cornwallis move this way. You will also not fail to give me constant intelligence of your force and situation, as matters may grow very critical by and by. The Pennsylvania line and reinforcements from Maryland and Virginia are coming to join the army, but it will be some time before their arrival. North Carolina are collecting their troops also, by drafts, agreeable to the late law, and from present appearances, promise a reinforcement of twelve to fifteen hundred men. Much blood has been spilt, and more must be before this country can regain its liberty."

When his letter received no response, Greene wrote again on the 19th, and again on the 23rd: "I must depend entirely on you to secure us on the quarter from Ninety-six to Charleston on the West Side of the Wateree." But, Sumter merely sent a few supplies of corn and meal and refused to send a reply to Greene's early letters. Sumter was too proud to bring himself to be a subordinate to Greene, and continued to make excuses to his officers for holding back his troops from the main army. He had been accustomed to acting on his own without orders from a superior, and had been extremely effective in his raids on British posts and supply trains and keeping the partisan spirit throughout the countryside alive. In that respect, Sumter was a proven leader and commander. But what he failed to realize was that he could have done so much more if he had taken his band of volunteers and systematically incorporated them in with the regular army, controlled by Greene, and helped direct major accomplishments into a definite purpose, rather than a few tiny ones.

Greene was now seething with anger. He could not understand how a man who had performed as a patriot up until this juncture could suddenly be more concerned with his own feelings. But because of the timing, Greene was reluctant to pursue this blatant disobedience further, and deducted that Sumter would just resign in the wake of a complaint and so he let it drop instead. But that does not mean he kept quiet about the issue. To Lee he confided, "General Sumter has got but a few men; he has taken the field, and is pushing after little parties of Tories toward Ninety-six. Major Hyrne is gone to him, if possible to get him to join us; but this I know he will avoid, if he can with decency." Greene formulated a plan where he could use Sumter to his advantage and yet Sumter would not know he was serving the Major general. Sumter's erratic movements would certainly begin to get the attention of the enemy, if not already. The British may look upon them as a part of a general plan of Greene's, and give them more attention than was really deserved. So, when Major Hyrne returned with a negative response from Sumter to join his troops with his, he was annoyed, but began to use the situation to his best advantage.

Marion on the other hand, had conducted himself in the complete opposite way. When he had received orders from Greene, he promptly united his forces with Lee's, and acted with him in cooperation rather than considering him a superior, as in the siege of Fort Watson. Not only had he assisted in reducing that post, but he also quickly followed that up with throwing himself and his men in front of Watson in battle and retarding his movements from then on. Lee was so impressed by Marion that he wrote to Greene, "I wish you would write a long letter to General Marion. His services demand great acknowledgments, and I fear he thinks himself neglected." And Greene proceeded to write to Marion immediately. "When I consider how much you have done and suffered, and under what disadvantages you have maintained your ground, I am at a loss which to admire most, your courage and fortitude, or your address and management. Certain it is no man has a better claim to the public thanks, or is more generally admired than you are. Nothing will give me greater pleasure than to do justice to your merit, and I shall miss no opportunity of declaring to Congress, the Commander-in-chief, and to the world in general, the great sense I have of your merit and services."

Lee even carried his admiration so far as to ask permission to put "in some degree under Marion's command. It will please him, and I admire him." But no one excelled in zeal, intelligence, and bravery than Lee in those critical days. Lee had always agreed with Greene's assessment to carry the war back into South Carolina, and constantly wrote to him with eager allusions and sometimes explained his views, without giving them the full weight of the implications, as if he could triumph over the entire British army, almost single handily. He had written to Greene, "I beg you will send down a field-piece," he wrote from Fort Watson, "it can get to me in one day and a half. I will have horses to meet it, which will go off from me on hearing from you. Five minutes will finish the business, and it can immediately return." Later, after the fort surrendered, he requested, "a hundred picked riflemen, and fifty infantry." Such energy and enthusiasm delighted Greene, but also upset him that Lee did not think of overall operations and just for the moment. However, no one could deny he was a hard worker and zealous officer.

After the battle of Hobkirk's Hill, very little had changed strategically. Lord Rawdon found himself weaker by nearly 300 men, and only had Watson to look to for support and reinforcements. Greene had lost about as many men, but had the promise of reinforcements of both militia and regular soldiers. Provisions were beginning to grow scarce in the British garrison, and its communications with Charleston were already difficult. The British knew they were in no condition to hazard a second battle. If the Americans were able to conduct a blockade, they would be finished.

To draw a blockade and intercept Watson at the same time was the exact plan Greene had in mind. "We are now within five miles of Camden," he wrote to Marion a few days after the battle, "and shall closely invest it in a day or again. That we may be able to operate with more certainty against this post, I should be glad you would move up immediately to our assistance, and take post on the north side of the town."

By late April, word of the fall of Fort Watson had arrived. Greene gave orders for the army to "march immediately to join the baggage at Rugeley's Mill, where there was a better chance of recruiting the cattle."

Today, it is extremely hard to imagine what it must have been like to travel through such landscape in the late eighteenth century. Even though the country the soldiers traversed in the south is now much as it appeared in 1781, it has still been modernized to a great extent and fairly easy to travel through today. These were anxious days for Greene. "The country was extremely difficult to operate in, being much cut to pieces by deep creeks and impassable morasses. And many parts are covered with such heavy timber and thick underbrush, as exposes an army, and particularly detachments, to frequent surprises." Added to that, was the problem of establishing magazines in the rear. The main problem was, they never knew where their rear might be, due to the routes the army was forced to travel. Perhaps they would come upon a swamp or deep creek, and amend their course that brought them 10 miles south of their intended destination. This was a trying time for the army's Quarter-master general, and must have reminded Greene of his own experience in that role when he was in the north.

It was during one of these anxious days that Greene sent for Colonel Davie. Greene knew that he would have to step up the partisan war. Rawdon now had a superior force, and the Americans had moved to a far enough distance that allowed him to operate on any object he wished. Greene knew Rawdon would attempt to strike Lee and Marion at his earliest convenience, and then reinforce himself with all of the troops at his disposal and push to the mountains. The regular army troops were reduced to a handful, and the militia was staying put in their prospective neighborhoods, unwilling to come to the regular army's aid. Many had also joined with Sumter, who continued to disobey Greene's orders to join with his troops, and was now merely rambling through North Carolina, only attacking unconnected posts that were completely useless in a military standpoint. If the British were allowed to continue with this calculated measure of pushing the Americans back to the mountains, Rawdon would have a firm grip on the countryside. Cornwallis would then be permitted to establish a chain of posts along the James River, and the southern States would effectively "be cut off like the tail of a snake."

To add to Greene's increasing melancholy disposition was the ongoing wave of desertion that was putting the army in the icy grips of demoralization. Greene was again forced to deal with the problem in a harsh way that distressed him, but as the orders of the day reflect; "The General would be extremely happy if the offense of these unfortunate men deserved a punishment less severe. But desertion is a crime so dangerous to an army policy that it dictates this mode of correction." Subsequently, five deserters were "caught, arraigned, and after due consideration of the charges, evidence, and defense for and against, found guilty, and condemned to death by firing squad. In the case of these five men, it had been discovered that they "were marauding, and had burnt one or two houses that were used by women or soldiers of the American army." On the 26th of April, when the army was encamped at Twenty-five Mile Creek, the orders of the day announced that, "The rolls are to be called every hour, to confine the soldiers to camp and prevent such marauding."

Even with these diversions, Greene never lost sight of the enemy's movements in North Carolina. Dozens of rumors were found flying around headquarters, making it hard for Greene to determine what was false and what was factual intelligence. One involved a report that British detachment out of Camden was marching on Newbern. Greene immediately sent orders to General Sumner and General Butler on the 28th and wrote to Marion. "I have this moment got intelligence that Lord Cornwallis crossed the Cape Fear River last week, in order to begin his march towards this State. I beg you to take every measure to discover his route and approach." This was good news to Greene, because this was exactly what he had hoped Cornwallis would do. He had plans to counter such a move and welcomed further intelligence that would support the new emergency. However, as the day wore on, no such report emerged, and by the 29th, it was becoming increasingly evident that the movements that had been detected were only a rumor. Someone who did arrive on the scene was Tarleton, and Greene writes to Marion. "Keep a good lookout for Tarleton. I think he may be announcing Cornwallis' approach. It may be probable he is on the Georgetown route; but it is possible he may be on the upper route, as I hear of a guard being lately surprised near the Cheraws.

Further intelligence, though still confusing, came in on the 3rd of May. Greene contacted Marion; "I wrote to you that Lord Cornwallis was in motion, and that it was uncertain which way he meant to operate; it is necessary to collect our forces, for which purpose I have given orders to Lieutenant-colonel Lee to join the main army with the different detachments and the field-piece. I expect more intelligence to-night, which will enable me to decide our next move. Don't forget to give me an account of your numbers; and it would promote the service greatly if you could furnish sixty or eighty good dragoon horses." Sumter adds, "We shall halt upon the Twenty-five Miles Creek, till I hear further from you, Colonel Lee, and Lord Cornwallis."

A few hours later important intelligence reached Greene. But it was not what he had been looking for. Watson had eluded the vigilant Marion and Lee, and was on his way to Camden. "This is an unfortunate circumstance," Greene writes to Marion on the 7th of May, "as the enemy will now become impudent, and show themselves outside their works, which they have not ventured upon in some time. Our force divided, and the enemy collected, put matters upon an unmilitary footing. There is no further intelligence on Lord Cornwallis, which induces me to believe he is marching northwardly."

Meanwhile every preparation was made to expect the worse scenario. Orders were given to secure the public stores, carriers were kept in constant motion with details to the commanders, and Greene pondered every aspect of his current ground and all of the approaches to it. No detail was too small, every detail appeared to be large. Greene, usually the sedate and cautious commander, seemed almost cheerful on the eve of this latest battle with the British when he wrote to General Pickens on the 9th of May. "It gives me pleasure to find the people are still desirous of affording their assistance to expel the enemy, not withstanding all their suffering. Encourage all that you can; and as there is a scarcity of arms, I would take them from the old and infirm, and put them in the hands of the young and healthy, who are willing to aid the operations. Collect all the force you can, and hold them in perfect readiness for the close investiture of Ninety-six, which will soon be undertaken. Nothing new from the northward, only troops are coming to the southward very fast."

That Cornwallis was in motion was obvious. But, in what direction was the question. His last position, if it could be believed, had him moving either towards South Carolina or Virginia. "I am rather inclined to think," Greene wrote to Sumter on the 6th of May, "that he will leave everything here, and move northward. I am led to entertain this opinion from its being the original plan, and from the earl's being too proud to relinquish his object."

In either case, whether the British commander moved toward South Carolina as Greene had hoped, or towards Virginia as he feared, what should the American general do? He reasoned that the taking of Fort Watson had been a break in the enemy's chain of defenses. Camden, the strongest of all, was well supplied with provisions, and though capable of withstanding a hurricane, wholly unprepared to withstand a blockade. The additional fall of the posts on the Congaree was suspect from day to day. He needed more substantial fodder for his decision. He knew that the fall of Ninety-six and quickly followed by Augusta, either by surrender or evacuation, would be a great blow in the liberation of South Carolina. It was evident that Cornwallis was fully aware of the importance of the conquest of Virginia, and the basis for the conquest being the United States. He had Philips already there, and by joining with his forces with those of Philips, found himself at the head of a formidable army. Greene soon decided where his position must be. No other place, than in the front of his old antagonist.

Unwilling to commit his plan to writing, Greene sent one of his aides, Major Hyrne, to communicate the plan to Marion, Sumter, and Lee orally. Lee then sat down and wrote all of the parts involving the commander's, but did not approve of Greene's role. He felt it was too bold, decisive and dangerous a position for Greene to place himself. Responding to the letter Lee had written to Greene about the commander's role on the 9th of May, Greene wrote his reply to Lee. So concerned with secrecy, numbers were replaced for names. 306 representing Cornwallis and 310 being Greene. "It will give me leave to tell you that 306 is gone to the northward. The plan be laid, and a position taken, the rest will be a war of posts; and the most that will be left to be performed by the commanding officer, until we come to Camden, is to make proper detachments. Which would be more honorable, to be active there, or lying, as it were, idle here? I am confident nothing would come to this army, and all things be in confusion, if 310 was not to go northward. Therefore, whether taken up in military, personal, or public point of view, I am decided it is in his interest and duty to go. More advantage will result from 310's going than staying; for he can serve them more effectually yonder than there."

On the 14th, Greene communicated his intentions to Lafayette and von Steuben. In the meanwhile, he pushed on with his plans of operations against the British posts on the Congaree, and the sieges of Ninety-six and Augusta.

Watson had arrived in Camden on the 7th of May after eluding Marion and Lee, but that would be one of only a few fortunes in which the British would succeed. On the very night of Watson's arrival, Rawdon "crossed the Wateree at Camden ferry, proposing to turn the flank, and attack the rear of Greene's army." But because of Watson's success, the Americans decided to take up a new position at Sandy's Creek, "five miles higher up the river." Dissatisfied with this position to "risk an action in," Lee moved four more miles further up, to Colonel's Creek, "leaving on the ground the horse pickets and light infantry." The enemy followed, and mistaking the Americans corps of observers for the main army, drew up in battle formation, and drove in on the pickets. "I examined every point of the situation," wrote Rawdon later, "and I found it everywhere so strong that I could not hope to force it without suffering such loss as must have crippled my force for any future enterprise. I therefore returned to Camden the same afternoon, and after having in vain attempted to decoy the enemy into action, by affecting to conceal our retreat."

On the 9th, Lord Rawdon began his preparations for the evacuation of Camden. The British left the young town in "little better than a heap of rubbish." Although the inhabitants fared badly, losing the jail, mill, and several homes from fire, even the troops suffered from the evacuation, setting fire to "the greater part of their baggage" and leaving fifty-three of their fellow soldiers behind, three of them officers, "all too badly wounded to be moved." Rawdon first marched towards Neilson's Ferry, in the hope of rescuing the garrison of Fort Motte, but it was too late, the fort had already surrendered to Marion. He therefore moved in the direction of Monk's Corner, within thirty miles of Charleston. Greene "immediately took possession" of the deserted town, and began to level the works. Soon after, Fort Granby, Georgetown, several smaller stockades, and the larger, more formidable, Fort Cornwallis was already in preparation to be put under siege by Browne from Marion's corps, with Lee moving with his ever present speed toward Augusta. Greene was thrilled with the string of successes and wrote to Congress, "On the 11th of May, the post of Orangeburg, commanded by a colonel, and consisting of eighty men and several offices, some British, surrendered to General Sumter. It produced the surrender of a very strong post without loss of time or men. Great quantities of provision and some other stores."

Greene was still watching the movements of Rawdon, and was quickly planning the preparations for crossing the Congaree with the army. On the 24th, Greene wrote to General Butler; "Since we came into this State we have taken near eight hundred prisoners and fifty officers." In less than a month, Greene had taken four of the enemy's large posts, compelled the evacuation of two others, and now from the heart of South Carolina, was about to advance against the only two points beyond the seaboard where the British still had some authority, Ninety-six and Augusta. Greene was happy and proud to write to Governor Rutledge from his camp at McCord's Ferry on the 14th of May to report their progress. "Camden is evacuated, Fort Motte and Orangeburg taken, Ninety-six and Friday's Ferry besieged, and the probability of Neilson's Ferry being evacuated, which will lay open the whole country. I could wish that civil government might be set up immediately, as it is important to have the minds of the people formed to the habits of civil rather than military authority."

Greene then set his priority on an effort that had not been touched in some time. A cartel for the exchange of prisoners. Many of whom still languished in the stockades at Charleston. In the midst of all this activity following the evacuation of Camden, Greene was able to write to Washington. "I do myself the honor to inclose to your excellency a copy of conditions of a cartel agreed to for the exchange of prisoners in the southern department, which I hope will meet the approbation of Congress. The business has been a long while in hand, and many interruptions happened from the operations of the two armies, and the enemy insisting upon conditions contrary to the principles laid down as a rule of conduct for the government. Many hundreds of our people taken by the British enlist into their service. Indeed one third the force employed in the southern States, if we are to form a judgment from the prisoners we take, are deserters from our own army. A resolution of Congress declaring that all prisoners of war that engage in the enemy's service, shall be treated as deserters, if taken in arms against us, would have a good effect." Greene was now free to turn his arms against the only two remaining strong posts that remained, Ninety-six and Augusta.

Chapter XXXI

"The Battle for Ninety-six"

The strange name of the town, or stockade, of Ninety-six was so called because it was believed to be that number of miles from the old frontier fort of Prince George on the Keowee River. It had been an important link in the chain of posts maintained by the British in the Carolinas, mostly because it protected the interest of the Tory element that was so important to the success of the British cause. That was to keep the Tories happy by protecting their families and their homes from their patriot neighbors in the settlements to the west. It was also to maintain communication with the Native American tribes that seemed to favor the British, who they felt kept the onslaught of pioneers encroaching on their lands to a minimum.

Lee had already been ordered to march for Augusta, and had reached the town, over seventy-five miles away, in less than three days. Pickens and Clark were there to meet him with the militia, each occupying a position, which enabled them to prevent the enemy from receiving supplies or reinforcements. The preparations for a siege were well underway. The first thing that had to be done, was to reduce the garrison at Fort Galpin, also known as Dreadnought. This was a small stockade twelve miles below Augusta, and garrisoned by two companies of infantry. It was really only important in one respect. It was used as a deposit of the royal annual gifts to the Indians in the area. Examples were small arms, powder, balls, blankets, liquor, and other articles that could be used in the Americans' camp. Lee's strategy, and brilliantly executed by Captain Rudolph of his Legion, quickly put the possessions of the fort in the hands of the Americans. This was a great start for their current campaign. Not only did it weaken the British of two companies, but also it strengthened the Americans with much needed supplies, a few that would work well for the decreased morale. Greene wrote, "Your exertions, merit my warmest approbation; and Captain Rudolph and the officers and men under his command, my particular thanks." Everything was now set to begin the siege of Augusta.

Augusta stands in an oblong plain on the south bank of the Savannah River. In that day, thick forest covered its West End, while the river was on its East Side. Its defenses consisted of two forts, Fort Cornwallis, a strong and well planned work in the middle of town, and Fort Grierson, much weaker in fortification, and about half a mile up, on the border of a lagoon. The commander of the fort was a Lieutenant-colonel Brown, a brave and skillful soldier, but widely known and bitterly despised by the locals for his cruelty towards the patriots during the partisan wars. The besiegers first directed their attention towards the weaker, Fort Grierson, of which they quickly took possession. The greater part of the garrison were Tories and as was common place in the partisan wars, most were put under the bayonet and killed, with only a few escaping to Fort Cornwallis, and the rest taken prisoner.

Fort Cornwallis was going to be another subject all together. The garrison there was made up of mostly royalists, but had several British regulars in their ranks. Brown was a strong and gallant officer, and was not going to give up the fort easily. Regular attacks were made on one side, and frequent volleys at another, but the fort held solid. Not until the infamous Mahem tower, which was becoming a regular fixture in these sieges arrived, and after fifteen days of open trench attacks, did the fort surrender.

An example of how severe and cruel partisan bloodshed was came when the Americans were guarding the two commanders of the fallen forts and awaiting transportation for prisoner exchange.

Grierson and Brown were quietly sitting in their rooms in a house outside of the fort, when a man on horseback rode up to Grierson's bedroom window, pull out a flintlock pistol, and shot him in the head. He was killed immediately by the shot. The horseman promptly fled after the deed, and was quickly pursued by Grierson's American jailers, but his steed was too fast and he rode swiftly away. No one, not even the Americans, knew who the man was, and even after a large reward was offered for his discovery, he was never found. Brown's life was also in danger, but only the quick thinking of a junior American officer saved him, and only a strong escort by Continental regulars kept him safe. It was quickly learned that the Whig militia could not be trusted with the life of a Tory.

Now, only one British post in the interior, remained in their hands. Ninety-six stood alone. The village was situated a few miles to the south of the Saluda River, and about thirty-five miles from the Savannah, on the western boundary of South Carolina. With the fall of Camden, and the siege of Augusta, the line of defense for the western frontier had been broken, and rendered Ninety-six a useless commodity. Orders were sent to its commander, Major Cruger to withdraw his troops immediately, and retire to Augusta where he could better serve the British defense of the area. But the order never reached Cruger, because light parties of Americans had been hovering around the posts for weeks, cutting all lines of communication between the forts and Augusta.

Cruger's garrison consisted of 550 men, 350 of whom were British regulars, who had been in the Colonies since the beginning of the war and had seen action in several battles of the last six years. The remainder were South Carolina royalists, but expert marksmen, who staked their lives on their prowess with the long rifle. They had all witnessed the vicious brutality that had been inflicted on the soldier and civilian alike during the partisan wars, and many amongst them had been stained with the blood of their fellow countrymen. With such men fighting each other in a deadly grip of survival, it was not hard to see that a long and bloody siege was about to commence.

Indians had always surrounded the village with some light defenses as a protection against a sudden invasion. However, it did not amount to much more than a firm stockade, which may have been sufficient protection against ill equipped Indian tribes, but would be useless against artillery and siege equipment. Still, they had been well maintained by the British soldiers of the garrison, and a skillful engineer in Cornwallis' own staff had supervised a recent upgrading of the defenses only weeks before. Under that direction, an important improvement had been added; a strong redoubt, about eighty yards to the right of the village, roughly circular, but composed of sixteen salient and reentering angles, which gave it the name, the Star. From those angles, a destructive crossfire could be kept up, and to make matters worse, it was surrounded by a dry ditch, filled with frisework and an abatis, making it a formidable obstacle to an approaching enemy. On the opposite side, at a distance of one hundred and eighty yards, on a natural rise, was a stockade fort that had been built out of the jail, and been strengthened with two substantial blockhouses, forming a large, palisade fort. This was called Holme's Fort, and had a covered way that led from the main stockade to the only stream that supplied water to the village and the garrison. The covered way protected the water supply, and allowed the garrisoned soldiers to freely pass from each structure.

It was the 22nd of May when Greene arrived and surveyed this fortress with an army whose effective force was no more than 1,000. They were mostly regulars of the two Maryland and Delaware Continental regiments, and two battalions from Virginia and North Carolina, Kirkwood's light infantry, and only a few raw militia. His first job was to examine the enemy's works beginning at daylight, with Kosciusko and Pendleton, and not concluding until a heavy rain fell towards evening. One of Greene's aides made the entire circuit around the fortifications, with the enemy hearing him and fearing it as an all out attack, fired on this single man with everything they had, but he was able to ride to safety unscathed.

Greene determined quickly that the fortifications were too strong, and he was too under

301

manned for a direct attack on more than one side saying, "a very respectable work. . .so well furnished that our success is very doubtful." After stationing his army at four camps in the woods, making a rectangle around the fortress, and all within cannon shot of the stockade, he decided to operate in the classic manner of siege warfare, by applying parallel attacks. This would best be served by attacking the Star redoubt, the chief point of the defenses, which could be held independently of the others.

Ground was broken during the night, within seventy yards of the works. Construction of the trenches pushed on with the greatest intensity. But the next day, the garrison discovered the workmen. Under a well directed volley of Cruger's three guns and small arms fire, the British were able to sally out to the workers, attack them and put them under the bayonet. They then carried off their entrenching tools before an American rescue party could be formed to save the poor trenchmen. The approach was begun again, but this time several hundred yards out from where it had been begun before. Day and night the work went on. While one party worked in the trenches, and other stood by under arms to protect them. Every morning the besieged would attack the new work, obstinately disputing every inch of ground. However, despite all of their efforts, the second parallel was completed on the 3rd of June 1781. A mine from the first had already been begun, under the cover of a battery on the American right. But Cruger was again prepared for this new onslaught, and the work was again halted by the death of the workmen.

A third parallel was now begun, and although the men were worn down from the constant fatigue duty of their previous labor, they pressed on with renewed vigor. Here the Mahem tower came into play again, and rising above the works, gave the American marksmen a sure stand for their deadly trade. The enemy's fire was finally silenced during the day, because no man was fool enough to show his head above the ramparts and suffer greatly for it. An attempt was made to set fire to the Mahem tower by firing red-hot shot at it, but Kosciusko had foreseen that, and had purposely had the men construct the tower out of the greenest wood they could use.

On the morning of June 8th, Lee arrived with his Legion, fresh from the successful siege of Augusta, and was ordered to take post on the left, and direct his efforts against the stockade fort. He immediately broke ground, and pushed on his works with his characteristic authority. In four days he had made such progress that, in spite of the sallies and fire the garrison directed at him, he had almost cut the enemy off from the water supply. Every pail of water was now won at the risk of life and limb, and finally became too great a risk to be attempted at daylight. Cruger had enlisted dozens of black slaves to be used as forced labor to free up the soldiers from fatigue duty within the fort. They would now be used as water runners at night, as it was supposed their skin color would hide them from detection the American marksmen.

An attempt was made to set fire to the fort. A sergeant by the name of Whaling, cautiously approached the wall with nine other men, under the cover of darkness and a violent wind storm, and was about to light the abatis, when he was suddenly discovered and the group was fired upon. Only four of the ten men escaped, sergeant Whaling, who had served in the army since the siege of Boston would not be one of them.

The siege finally seemed to be drawing to a close with the approaches from every side advancing steadily now. It left little hope to the garrison that they would survive the siege much longer. Their cannon had already been silenced during the day by the riflemen in the four towers, and a battery within a hundred and forty yards of the works had been raised enough to give it an unobstructed view and firing line to the redoubt. Unless the danger could be promptly met, the men would be swept from their outworks, and compelled to surrender unconditionally. The parapet was already twelve feet high, and it was raised another three with sand filled bags so it could form gunports, through which the riflemen could keep up a constant fire on the Americans.

It was now the 12th of June, and the siege had continued for eighteen days. Many brave men had fallen on both sides, and many gallant feats of bravery had been performed as well. But the end was now quickly approaching, and it was evident that the British commander, could not hold out much longer. That evening, a local was seen riding along the lines south of the town, and conversing with a few of the officers and men on duty. Since this had been a constant event throughout the siege, not much was made of it. But on reaching the high ground that was the road to Augusta, he suddenly put his spurs to his steed, and began to dash towards town. No less than fifty musketballs instantly came flying towards him, but he had timed his dash so perfectly that not a single shot found him. The moment the rider found himself out of musket range, he raised his hand to the sky and revealed a letter. It was a dispatch from Rawdon, containing the news that he was making a speedy approach to the fortress with a strong force, to the relief of the besieged.

Greene had already been in possession of this intelligence report, and foreseeing that Rawdon would not delay a moment longer than absolutely necessary, Greene had taken every step to guard against this danger. Sumter and Marion, strengthened by Washington and Lee's cavalry, were ordered to form a junction, and leave no effort untried for harassing and retarding the progress of the enemy. At the same time great care was taken to cut off all communication between the town and the country to prevent more riders from reaching the garrison with news. Without the last rider's news, a triumph by the Americans was assured in a few more days.

Everything now depended on the movements of Lord Rawdon, who had set out from Charleston on the 11th, and was pressing forward on a forced march to the relief of Ninety-six. It was hoped that Sumter could, at least, retard Rawdon's approach with as much partisan inventiveness that he could muster. As far as Orangeburg, there could be no doubt about the British general's course, but from that point he might, thought Sumter, make a sudden dash to Granby to pickup supplies and more men. Sumter therefore brought up his reinforcements, in the reasoning of a partisan, and not a general. Rawdon would not have made any such side trip with the garrison of Ninety-six in the balance. He pressed on without turning to the right or to the left, and passed his adversary below the junction of the Broad River and the Saluda. Having once gotten between Sumter and the main army, he was too active and too skilled a general to neglect his advantage, and continuing his march with fortitude, was soon far on his way to Ninety-six. Due to Sumter's mistake, he could not check the progress of Rawdon or join Greene to enable him to meet the enemy in the field.

Greene wanted to fight Rawdon long before he came within supporting distance of Ninety-six, and made every effort to rouse the militia and collect as many reinforcements as he could muster. He called, in pressing terms, to the great militia leaders. "Let us have a field-day," he wrote to Clark, "and I doubt not it will be a glorious one." But Rawdon was close by, and with 2,000 men, a strong cavalry, and several field pieces. With his present troops Greene was hopelessly outmanned, and most of the men were worn down and weary from the constant labor of the siege. It was now the 17th of June, and not a minute to spare. Should they hazard an assault? His troops begged for it. After all of the work and the waiting, they did not want to let this ground go uncontested. "Give us one more chance general," wrote one officer. "We have a stain to wipe away," said another who had fought at Guilford and Hibkirk's Hill. Greene had to weigh his options carefully. He was not one to go running into a situation without all of the facts before him. Could the stockade fort be taken, and the lodgment made in one of the angles of the star, the garrison would be forced to yield to it. This could be accomplished by a few picked regiments, but a general storm might cripple the whole army. Orders were issued to prepare for an assault at noon the next day.

Lieutenant-colonel Lee was charged with the attack on the right, with the infantry, strengthened by a detachment of some of the best men from Kirkwood's Delaware's. Major Rudolph had the toughest assignment of all, leading his Legion against the fort itself. On the left Lieutenant-colonel Campbell, with his own regiment, the first Virginia, and a detachment of Marylanders, commanded the assault of the redoubt. Fascines (bundles of stick approx. 4 feet long and three feet in diameter) were constructed to fill the ditches, and behind them, men with hooks fastened onto long poles to pull down the sandbags on the parapets. At the exact instant they were to advance, volleys from the rifle towers, and the works were to clear a path to the fort and keep the enemy from the parapet, so as to cover their advance.

Lee was ordered to force his way into the fort, and then governs his movements by the result of the attack on the redoubt. Campbell's job was even more difficult and dangerous. He was to advance on the ditch that was in a direct crossfire from the angles of the redoubt. The parapet was so high by now, that it was difficult to reach the sandbags on top, even with the long poles. In the face of these obstacles Duval and Seldon were ordered to remove the abatis, and clear the angle if possible, while the hookmen advanced to pull down the sandbags. They were then to pile the bags on the fascines in the ditch. Campbell should then be able to force his way to the parapet under cover from the works.

The next morning every man was ready to do his part. At eleven in the morning the third parallel was manned, and the riflemen were seen taking their stations in the towers. Next followed the first gun from the center battery, and the men entering the trenches. They then waited for the signal to be given by Greene. It was given and the batteries and rifle towers opened fire, amid the thunder and smoke of the artillery, each party then rushed forward to their appointed position.

The work on the right was quickly done. Rudolph at the head, forced his way in to the ditch, and after a short struggle drove the enemy from the fort. Lee instantly prepared to follow up his success, and supported the attack on the left.

Here the battle raged long and fierce, and the result was deadly to the defender and the assailant. Duval and Seldon, with their brave group, leaped into the ditch, and began to throw down the abatis. But the enemy's fire met them full force at their approach, and thinned their ranks with every step with nowhere to hide between two walls of pouring fire from the reentering angles and the crevices of the fort. Above the parapet, the air bristled with a deadly array of pikes and bayonets. As the abatis finally yielded to their efforts, they became at every instant more and more exposed. Officers and men fell around on top of them from every side. Armstrong fell dead at the head of his company. Duval and Seldon were badly wounded, but still their men pressed on, and suddenly the curtain was won. Now the hook men struggled forward over the dead and dying to pull down the sandbags. If they could accomplish this, victory would be assured. Unfortunately, the depth of the ditch and the height of the parapet, rendered all their efforts useless. The poles were not long enough.

The desperate conflict had already lasted an hour, and the ditch was crowded with the dead and wounded. There was still a reasonable hope of success, for the fort had fallen, and not one man had as much as flinched from his duty. But Rawdon was sighted only a mile and a half away with his over powering army, and Greene, never forgetful of his responsibility as commander-in-chief, was unwilling to cripple his men for the field. Lee was then ordered to stop any further advance, and Campbell was ordered to retire. The greater part of the wounded was brought safely back to camp in face of a withering fire. The enemy gallantly restored the dead the following day for burial. The stockade was abandoned in the night.

The assault had failed, but Greene was very proud of his army. "I take great pleasure in acknowledging my high opinion of the gallantry of the troops engaged in the attack of the enemy's redoubts. The conduct of the army merits the highest encomiums, and must insure them perpetual honor. The consummate bravery of all the troops engaged, and the animated dispositions of those who were ready to engage, gains them the applause of their friends, and the respect of their enemies. I hope both officer and soldiers are given the earliest opportunity of reaping the fruits of their superior spirit by an attack in the open field upon the troops now led by Lord Rawdon."

It was now known by every man that Rawdon had been at hand, and that the reinforcements, which Greene had called for, had not materialized. At the orders read on the 19th of June, "The army will march at five o'clock, by the left, to-morrow morning." The news was received without much surprise, but with a bit of mumbling. Greene felt that the men's morale could use some uplifting, and at the first halt, "about five miles east of Suluda River," Greene wrote to the troops. "The zeal and attention of all the officers of the line and of the different departments, claim the General's particular acknowledgments; and the patience and fortitude of the troops, so uniformly manifested upon every occasion where duty was performed with fatigue and danger, entitle them to this particular regard."

Thus ended the siege and battle for Ninety-six. It had lasted twenty-eight days, and cost the American army 185 men. "The troops," Greene wrote in his report to the president of Congress, "Have undergone incredible hardships in the siege; and though the affair was not successful, I hope their exertions will merit the approbation of Congress. Their behavior on this occasion deserves the highest commendations bestowed; both the officers that entered that ditch who were wounded, and the greater part of their men who were either killed or wounded. I have only to lament that such brave men fell in an unsuccessful attempt."

Greene could not have been more disappointed by the results of the Ninety-six attack. "Our movement to the southward has been attended with very great advantages, and had not the Virginia militia failed us, the measure would have been crowned with complete success. It is mortifying to leave a garrison so nearly reduced." Some of his officers, it is said, lost heart, and would have persuaded him to fall back to Virginia. "I will recover South Carolina, or die in the attempt."

"I wish, therefore, you would join us with all the force you can," Greene writes to Sumter on the day after his retreat from Ninety-six, "for I am determined to maintain my ground in these States at all events." Greene was also giving way to personal irritation at the constant annoyances he received from "jealous authority watching to take advantage of me. But the objection is not sufficient to excuse you from rendering your further services to your country in this time of universal distress."

It was difficult to ascertain the enemy's intentions, and the equal uncertainty of the reinforcements he desperately needed to receive "to form a satisfactory plan for my next plan of action." One thing he was certain of was "to oblige, if possible, the British army to retire from the district of Ninety-six." Or as Lafayette had put it when he wrote to Greene a few days later, "I am endeavoring to oblige the British army into evacuating Ninety-six, and manoeuvre them down to the lower country where we can better deal with them."

Even if Greene could form a plan of operation, how far could it go without the cooperation of the surroundings States and their militia? To make matters worse, communication lines were breaking down. Greene was moving his camp so much in those days, that when a message was sent to another unit for a combined movement, it took as many as three days for the rider to search for the Greene to give him the response. By that time the plans had to be modified and it turned into a vicious circle where nothing was accomplished. "It was my wish," he wrote to Marion, "to have fought Lord Rawdon before he got to Ninety-six, and I could have collected your force and that of General Sumter and Pickens, I would have done it, and am persuaded we should have defeated him; but left alone I was obliged to retire. I am surprised the people should be averse to joining in some general plan of operation. It will be impossible to carry on the war to advantage, or even attempt to hold the country, unless your force can be directed to a point that meets with mine."

It also seems that the grand plan of meeting Cornwallis in Virginia had been laid by the wayside. "We want reinforcements in this quarter," he writes to Lafayette on the 23rd of June, "but I am afraid to call upon you, as I fear you are no less embarrassed and oppressed than we are. What a Herculean task we face!" Not the least of their problems during this period was the interference by Thomas Jefferson with the militia which had been called out to serve in the Carolinas. "I received word from the Marquis," he writes to general Lawson on the 27th of June, "that the militia ordered southward was countermanded by the governor of Virginia. Nothing could have been more unfortunate than the tardiness of the militia in the field at this time. Nor can I conceive the propriety of Mr. Jefferson or any governor of any State giving such an order that affects the general interest of the country. Before the force is granted for the service at large, the executive has it in his power to determine whether they will furnish the force or not, but after the order is given out they should have no power over those troops. How was he to know that such an order was not at the sacrifice of an army in the field, having taken the measures in expectations of support and then to be disappointed in a most critical and deadly situation. After this particular attention paid to the interest and protection of the southern States? After this particular attention was paid to the interest and protection of his State, it was mortifying as well as injurious to the common interest, to find myself deprived of a force on which I calculated on for giving success to our operation against Lord Cornwallis in this quarter."

As this attention is drawn toward Virginia, an early reference is mentioned by Greene about Yorktown. The French minister had written to him that the second division of the French fleet was approaching. On the 2nd of July he replies, "I have communicated to Governor Nash that I had hoped some preparations will be made for a plan of cooperation. Virginia, I think, affords the greatest object for this first operation. Lord Cornwallis' army and fleet and garrison at Portsmouth would be much in our power if the French fleet with a large land force should be allowed to enter the Chesapeake Bay." To Washington he writes on the same day, "We are anxiously awaiting the arrival of the second division of the French fleet. Virginia affords the most inviting object. The whole of the British army could be taken in three weeks or less; while New York or Charleston will produce a long, tedious, and uncertain siege."

But for now, Greene would have to think about retreat. A retreat that would not carry him too far to prevent him from turning on the enemy at a moments notice. "The fate of this country must be decided by an action," he wrote to von Steuben on the 23rd of July, "if his Lordship thinks proper to contend for that object." The army was on the move again, and the baggage and wounded had already been sent forward two days before. The southern summer heat was at its worse, and they marched very slowly, only going eleven miles the first day, and halting five miles east of the Saluda. "I am anxious," he writes to Sumter, "to collect our forces, to enable us to give the enemy the most effectual opposition. I beg you will march your troops and form a junction with us at the cross roads, near the fort at Williams plantation." But Sumter reports that the militia cannot be collected and he will not be able to join Greene's forces.

Meanwhile, Rawdon and his army had left Ninety-six and had been in pursuit of the Americans since the 23rd of June. Greene had marched fifteen miles and was encamped by the Enoree. They resumed their march the next day and reached the banks of the Broad River by seven o'clock that evening. Greene was still attempting to collect a large force and wrote to Lee, "It is next to impossible to draw the militia of this country from the different parts of the State to which they belong. Marion is below me, Pickens I can not account of, and Sumter wants to make a tour of Monks' Corner, and all I can say to either, is insufficient to induce them to join us."

It was becoming evident to Rawdon that he would not be able to continue his pursuit much farther. On the 23rd, Lee, who had been shadowing Rawdon reported, "His Lordship has no provisions, nor has he taken any measures to get any, except by hand-mills." Greene surmounted that they would not follow them any further, but continued his retreat for another eleven miles, until he halted at Timm's Ordinary, between Broad River and the Catawba, and waited for the development of the enemy's plans. Rawdon returned to Ninety-six, but knew he couldn't hold it with the loss of Augusta and the posts on the Santee and Congaree. With a heavy heart, the British commander assembled the loyalists and their families and announced that the British army was abandoning Ninety-six.

By this time, Greene had decided to collect a force as best he could, and began to move toward the Conagree to reestablish a force and meet up with Lee and Marion. Greene attempted to intercept a relief train of provisions for Rawdon in Charleston, but was only able to capture a few wagons. Pickens was now on the move and they arranged a meeting of all the American forces at Beaver Creek. Sumter also arrived with about 550 militiamen, mostly composed of men from Georgia, and the total force began their march on the 12th of July to attack the enemy at Orangeburg. But when they arrived, the British had fortified themselves so well they were unable to attempt an attack and safely retreated to the Edisto River. A day later, the troops from Ninety-six formed a junction with another British garrison at Monk's Corner and were moving towards Charleston. The British force amounted to about 800 men. Greene's force now numbered about 1,100, and was hoping to oppose this force as soon as possible and began to make plans for such an attack.

But during the attack, Sumter "detached his force too much, and had he not mistaken a covering party for an advance of an attack, he would have taken the garrison at Monk's Corner, amounting to six hundred men," Greene wrote in his journal the next day. They did manage to collect "between one hundred and forty or fifty prisoners, great quantities of stores were destroyed upon their retreat, upwards of two hundred horses, and a number of wagons captured, the entire baggage of the Nineteenth Regiment, and a considerable quantity of hard money."

Greene was extremely disappointed with what the outcome could have been, and evidently felt that Sumter had again made a major mistake in the engagement. Controlling his true feelings, he actually thanked Sumter, along with Marion and warmly commended their troops saying they, "behaved with great gallantry, and deserve the highest praise."

Now Greene was determined to start the new expedition he had been planning. On the 26th of July, he directed Sumter to take a post at Friday's Ferry, Marion at Nelson's Ferry, and Lee to join the main army on the High Hills of the Santee and to rest awhile before receiving their marching orders.

The High Hills of the Santee are a long, irregular chain of sandy hills, on the left bank of the Wateree, almost twenty miles north of its junction with the Congaree, and some ninety miles northwesterly from Charleston. The area was abundant with fruit trees and grain fields and the men had more than enough pure water for drinking and cooking. The men and officers had not enjoyed such an encampment in some time. The stress of the past year seemed to leave them and the vigor to continue their fight returned with full spirit.

With this time to rest, Greene also used it to reorganize his forces. North Carolina had deeply felt a disgrace due to its militias conduct. Governor Nash drafted appropriate measures to recall any man that had not fulfilled the required six month enlistment, as well as collecting men that had, up until now, refused to obey their draft orders. He now made the enlistment period twelve months and made good on his promise to Greene to "have fifteen hundred men deemed for Continental army service by the first of August." Although Burke soon succeeded Nash as governor, he made good on the promise and had the men in Greene's camp by early August.

Up until now, Virginia had borne a large part in causing the recent failures of the army at Camden and Ninety-six due to its absurd claim of controlling the militia after they had been given marching orders into Continental service, began to do its part. Nelson, her new governor, began to recruit soldiers and hoped to acquire 2,000 militiamen, as well as 300 horses for the cavalry. Greene was excited to have the horses, but cautiously urged Nelson to concentrate on the militia which were needed more gravely.

Greene then set his sights on South Carolina and Georgia for soldier quotas. He soon decided that South Carolina, which had no Continentals in the field since the fall of Charleston, had suffered more than its share from the enemy. The Tories in this war, and decided they could not bear the suffering any longer and put all of his efforts towards Georgia. Several districts of the State had already begun to answer the call and sent Greene several hundred militiamen with the promise of more very soon. Greene could not be more pleased and began to plan the next attack on the British.

While on the High Hills encampment, Greene was inundated with conflicting intelligence reports that usually turned out to be nothing but rumors. The British were seen moving towards Greene's position one day and to suddenly disappear when he sent out a party to search for them. Thousands of British had already moved to the north and Cornwallis himself was poised to attack Virginia. All were either found to be unsubstantiated, or just plain falsehoods that had been made up and passed along by the Tories, who were beginning to notice a definite turn in strength for the Americans. It was making them extremely nervous, as well as the British forces.

On the 5th of August, with new troops arriving everyday, Greene faced a grave problem in the midst of his increasing joy at finally getting his long awaited troops. It was brought to his attention that a Sergeant Radly of the Maryland line, had been saying dangerous statements about his country and its people, but especially the army. The lists of offenses were given to Greene. "First; He has spoken himself in a disaffected manner in the presence of his soldiers." Second; He has spoken disrespectfully of Colonel Howard his commanding officer. Third; He has frequently said in the presence of the soldiers he would never endeavor to injure the enemy."

Charges, which would be harmless in peace, are extremely grave in camp and during wartime. Before his court-martial, Radley pleaded "not guilty" when the charges were read and the punishment for a guilty verdict was acknowledged. Death. Over two dozen men are heard to bear witness against him without a single variation in their stories. The verdict to the serious charges is guilty, and two thirds of the court agree. Greene approved the sentence without the hesitation he had shown in the past for such verdicts. He considered this one of the most disgusting charges a soldier can perpetrate and saw to it that the execution was carried out the next day at six o'clock in the morning. "I do not wish to have this man in my company for one additional day." Greene would write in his journal. He dies as a soldier, by musketball, and not by cord. A sharp rattling volley of six flintlocks and Radly's days are at an end."

Greene moved on to more pressing matters by the 10th of August. The fall of Charleston threw over 5,000 prisoners into the hands of the British, nearly 2,000 of them Continental soldiers, 250 of them officers. By the terms implemented by the British, a distinction would be made between the militia and the Continentals. The former being held as prisoners of war until a regular exchange could be made. The latter being "permitted to return to their respective homes as prisoners on parole; and while on parole shall be secure from being molested in their property by the British troops."

Just ten days after the surrender of the city, Sir Henry Clinton called for a proclamation, and ordered that all paroles be annulled unless those held were willing to give their allegiance and be regarded as royal subjects of the English Crown. Within a few days he ordered another proclamation that all of the inhabitants, civilian or military, were now conquered subjects, and owed their allegiance to the conquerors, the British army. Clinton followed the proclamations with a system of enticement and menace, of corruption and terror, which ever was bested suited to the occasion. Prison ships, with their torture by starvation, small pox and the putrid smell of the unsanitary conditions caused many deaths. The others that were shipped off to St. Augustine, Florida. In utter violation of the articles of capitulation, these men suffered the same horrors as the prison ship captives. Added to the torture was listening to the daily propaganda of American defeats and the disasters befalling their families in the cities throughout the country that were fed to them by their British host.

Submitted to the proclamation, many lost heart and could no longer stand the suffering and the degrading atrocities of the British. But most did not and held true to the cause they had joined in support of their country, which was to fight against such persecution under which they had suffered for so many years. It had made the British torture these men even more. They were frustrated that the rebels would not break and could not understand how they rejected parole, only to continue to support a land that seemed to have forgotten them. Lord Cornwallis, who had once resolved to "extinguish the rebellion" in South Carolina, gave orders soon after Ninety-six, that "all the inhabitants" who had taken part in that or the revolt in Camden, should "be punished with the greatest rigor," and that "every militia man who had borne arms with the Crown and afterwards joined the Americans, should be immediately hanged."

The Americans followed the hanging of nineteen South Carolina militiamen after the victory at Camden with twelve loyalists hangings at King's Mountain. The British hung twenty-four more patriot militiamen after the battle for Ninety-six, and the Americans responded by burning every Tory village from Ninety-six to Charleston, killing hundreds of innocent victims who's men were off fighting for the British. Many did not discover the fate of their families, neighbors, or loved ones until after the war was over. Several bands of Tory and Whig units continued to attack and counter-attack each other years after the peace accord ended it in 1783. This is why feelings run deep even to this day over those lines. Few are probably aware that it is the remnants of those vicious battles known as the partisan wars, and described by many as the first Civil War.

By this time, Congress was realigning itself to become more effective as a functional governmental body. Governor Rutledge had just arrived into Greene's camp from Philadelphia with news of a military chest that was being collected from the sale of shares of the new bank that had just been formed by Robert Morris's direction. As an auxiliary source, Greene was authorized to draw on the superintendent for a specified amount. Greene was excited by the possibilities a regenerated war chest would have on his southern army. Unfortunately, it was not long before disappointment would take the place of optimism.

The government immediately put a limit on Greene of five hundred guineas a draft, which were to be strictly applied to the actual campaign at hand. Not on past campaigns or future campaigns, and solely dependent on whether the appropriate shares of stock had been sold. In the meantime, Rutledge, frustrated by the ineptitude the Congress continued to show on the subject of the army, came up with a plan of his own. He intended to fund Greene with the sale of a considerable quantity of indigo that had been seized from the Tories or hidden by the patriot planters over the last three years, in hope of a future market. The subject of hard money had been addressed, but the problem of troops continued. Greene had been promised reinforcements. They proved to only be available on paper. He did get 700 militia and levies from North Carolina, and they were not fully armed. 150 had been raised in Georgia by Colonel Jackson, but before he could march them they came down with small pox and all but 25 died. He had been promised 3,000 from Mecklenberg and Rowan counties, but only 500 arrived. The British proclamations and threats by them and their loyalist units had frightened the men and they decided to remain with their families. Greene was deeply annoyed. "I mean not to censure," he writes to Colonel Locke, who was to lead the Mecklenberg militia, "but to represent matters as they appear to me. It is true that the people are tardy in taking the field for the support of the liberties, and protection of their distressed brethren. But where the people manifest such a lukewarm disposition, and decay of patriotism, the laws should be brought in, to oblige them to do what their duty and interest require. You will pardon me if I speak feelingly on the subject; but my mean suffering and distressed situation will not allow me to be silent. I am not in pursuit of military glory; my object is the safety of the people and the establishment of our liberties. A becoming zeal to promote those ends, I hope, will not be displeasing to the honest citizens of America."

By early August it, was apparent that Greene was not going to get the reinforcements that he had been promised. So, again it was up to him to manufacture the troops from whatever he could scrape together and to make a plan of attack whether he had the added troops or not. He immediately wrote to Sumter with a request: "As soon as you arrive, and the troops have had a little relaxation, we will draw our forces to point, and attack the enemy wherever he may be found. Take care to refresh your cavalry as fast as possible, as we shall no doubt have severe duty in a few days. The militia should be warned to be in readiness at a moment's warning."

It was evident that Greene's original intention to cut the enemy off from the districts surrounding the Congaree, would have to be carried out without loss of time. However, Sumter suddenly came up with a mysterious aliment, and turned his command over to Colonel Henderson, giving him orders in a memorandum that were completely different from those he had received from Greene. "Move the troops immediately from the river swamps and encamp from three to five miles from the river on a bluff where there is good water; the horses sent into the river swamps with a guard, which the General wishes should be composed of the militia, and which shall serve them as a tour of duty. The General wishes the troops to have a respite from the service until the first of October, and as many as them furloughed home from time to time as the service of time will permit."

Henderson, a "gallant officer of great zeal," which had been stimulated by his recent imprisonment by the British, read the memorandum and took exception with it. He immediately wrote to Greene: "I received the enclosed memorandum from General Sumter; and many of it really surprised me, that I should come here for no other purpose than to furlough a parcel of troops, and that when the enemy is at our very doors, and their horses to be guarded by militia. No readier way to dismount the men could be devised. Should be much obliged to your opinion on every subject." Later that day, Henderson wrote to Greene again. "I came to take command of this brigade of State troops with the exception of finding four or five hundred men fit for the field, but I find General Sumter has played the old soldier with me, for I have not been able to collect quite two hundred fit for action, and they in a most shattered condition. If I could be assisted by a majority of the officers the men might yet be serviceable."

Greene had permitted Sumter's early services as a partisan to outweigh his glaring defects as a subordinate officer. But his constant unwillingness to change his tactics, his disregard for Greene's reports, letters and memos and the blatant disobedience he had shown his commanding officer was too much for even the patient Greene to bear. At the opening of the recent campaign, Sumter had come between Morgan and Greene, claiming he had a right to interfere with orders that came directly from the commander-in-chief. On the invasion of South Carolina, instead of coming directly into the field and following the line of attack marked for his troops, he held himself back at the most critical moments, until the attack was fully underway. Then, and only then skirting the outreaches of the battle and engaging the least amount of men as possible. Sumter had always used the excuse that he "was without a critical makeup of his brigade" as to why he would never fully engage himself in any full-scale attack. Even after his brigade was fully complemented with troops, he would always seem to be called away by the weakest pretext and following some useless line, would merely use his force to "push after small parties of Tories away from the fight." His continued orders from Greene to join the main army, were dispatched over and over, all without making a move to obey the request. Finally, Sumter decided to make a vain attempt at Fort Granby, but Lee lost no time in out maneuvering the second string commander, and took Granby without him. Sumter was so upset by the slight that he offered to resign his commission. Greene was too busy with other matters to be engaged with trivial, ego soothing.

Sumter only continued to build a case against himself. He was a total failure as a military officer in wartime. After finally joining the main army, Sumter continued to ignore Greene's orders and operated solely on his own. When Greene needed him at Friday's Ferry, he was high up the Catawba, out of the line of action. At Biggin's Church, he allowed his detachments to wander at their leisure and left his artillery in the rear, allowing an entire British regiment to slip through his hands. He did manage to take their baggage, and their regimental military chest containing seven hundred guineas

310

in gold. Instead of offering it to Greene, whose military chest was as empty as Sumter's patriotism, Sumter chose to divide the prize among his men.

Greene was fit to be tied, but in the absence of civil government, he allowed the blatant insubordination to go unpunished. He felt that if he brought Sumter to trial, it would only widen the division among an already divided people of the area. Greene was too wise a man to add fuel to the fire that was already burning out of control. He may have allowed Sumter to go unpunished due to logistic reasons, but carried a personal goal of seeing Sumter go before a judge at the conclusion of the war. In the meantime, he would continue to use Sumter as a stimulant for the exertion of the partisan corps.

By mid August, Greene had learned that the British had burned Georgetown on the 1st of August, killing and injuring dozens of civilians. The only excuse they produced for it was, that the stores there were filled with goods greatly needed by the American army. If the destruction of a flourishing town was sufficient, then they were right in doing it. Greene had already dispatched two units to seize the goods before they were destroyed. The little town basically paid the price for being commercially prosperous.

The communication between the North and South was slow and insecure. Even the horse express had become even more dangerous than usual, attacked by the enemy at every turn. The letters being sent were constantly being intercepted, and the information used to know the whereabouts and movements of the Americans. Greene was forced to withhold much of what he intended to write to Washington, and Washington did not dare write freely to Greene. All that Greene and the men at High Hills camp knew, was that the northern army was actively engaged in the siege of New York, and news of its success or failure was not getting through. "It is time to use the cooperation of our allies," Greene would write in his journal. "I am much at a loss what are Lord Cornwallis' intentions in Virginia. I am totally ignorant what is going on at New York, have heard nothing from his Excellency since June, which induces me to believe his dispatches are being intercepted or he fears sending any at all."

Greene was hoping the siege of New York was succeeding. His intelligence network was busy trying to uncover any news of the British intentions. He believed he could slow down the southern campaign if the British were busy in the North trying to unseat the siege. It was not until the day before the battle of Eutaws that he learned that the siege of Yorktown had been substituted for the siege of New York, and that Washington was "on his way to take command in Virginia." Greene excited at the prospects, felt obliged to write to Washington. "And if Cornwallis has been subdued, why not liberate Charleston? Charleston itself may be easily reduced, if you will bend your forces this way. And it will afford me great pleasure to join your Excellency in that attempt; for I shall be equally happy whether as principal or subordinate, so long as the public good is promoted."

Chapter XXXII

"The Battle of Eutaw Springs"

The summer of 1781 was quickly fading at the camp on the High Hills of the Santee. As the 22nd of August dawned, the morning orders announced that "The army will march tomorrow morning by the right, in the following order: The North Carolina Brigade, two pieces of artillery. Virginia Brigade, two pieces of artillery. Maryland Brigade. The baggage in the usual order, according to the line of march. The General will beat at four 0'clock, when all the small guards will join their corps; the Assembly in forty minutes after, and the March at five o'clock." Greene and army set forth to meet the enemy once again. "We are endeavoring," he wrote to Washington, "to draw a body of militia together at Friday's Ferry, and are on our march to that place to combine our forces, and make an attack on the enemy at McCord's Ferry, if our force will authorize the attempt when we are collected." Counting every single man at Greene's disposal, they amounted to 2,600 men. But in effective strength, it was only about 1,600.

As the crow flies, the two armies were only about sixteen miles apart. For Stuart, the British commander, he was encamped near the junction of the Wateree and Congaree. In-between Greene and Stuart were two large rivers, whose banks were overflowing with the advent of the recent heavy rains. The area was so waterlogged with rivers, streams, creeks, and swamps running together, that the surrounding country appeared as a single vast lake. Out of its waters rose tall trees, bearded with pendent moss, and vast tracts of cane that swayed with the winds and current. Due to this overwhelming obstacle, Greene was forced to make a seventy-mile circuit around the waters so he could reach his adversary. It was seventy miles of difficult marching country, over rough roads and through an area infected with malaria, typhoid, and yellow fever epidemics.

The late August sun was still burning hot at noon. Greene spared his men and only marched them during the cooler, afternoon and evening hours. At Camden, he crossed the Wateree, where Rawdon had crossed just a few weeks before. Still advancing at a safe pace as to care for the health of his men, they reached Howell's Ferry by the Congree on the 28th. Here he assembled the detachments he had sent out to reconnoiter the countryside, and learned that Stuart had fallen back a few days before at Friday's Ferry. They crossed the river and encamped at Mott's plantation. While there, he received updated intelligence that the enemy had been reinforced and were making preparations to establish a permanent post at Eutaw Springs, forty miles lower down the river. Greene decided that he could not allow the British to proceed with their plans. Greene ordered Marion to guard the heavy baggage and remove it to Howell's Ferry, on the line of retreat, and took only four field pieces comprising of two 4-pounders and two 6's, and two wagons with him. The wagons were laden with ammunition, hospital stores and rum, and he moved them "by slow and easy marches, as well to disguise his real intention as to give Marion time to join the main force." Marion arrived, and with news. "General Greene has the pleasure to receive a report from Brigadier-general Marion of the success of an enterprise against a detachment of the British army commanded by Lieutenant-colonel D. Brown, near Parker's Ferry on the Pompton River. The general and his detachment of two hundred, attacked and beat upward of three hundred British and Hessians, eighty dragoons, and a considerable body of Tories."

Greene was encouraged by the news, and joyful at the capture of three pieces of field artillery, forty horses, and the loss of only a few men. He continued the advance toward the enemy, and by the

7th of September they were at Brudell's plantation, and by that evening Marion joined them.

Unlike the battles at Kings Mountain, Cowpens, and Ninety-six, which had been mostly composed of American Tories, Stuart's army totaled over 2,000 men, and was almost entirely made up of British regulars. Stuart felt secure at the Eutaws, and had no prior reports that the Americans were approaching. The reason was that Greene had made it quite sure that Stuart could gain no intelligence, because he had effectively cut them all off, "waylaying the by-paths and passes through the different swamps, and even detaining different flags of truce."

The area, which made up the two Eutaw springs were the first and second appearance of subterranean streams that had come to the surface. From the lower of the two basins the water flowed into a winding stream, Eutaw Creek, which was between steep, heavily thicketed banks to the Santee. Nearby at the head of the creek, between it and the main highway which ran east to west, with a branch that ran to Charleston, there was a brick mansion of considerable size that was two stories high with garret windows indicating a third. In front of the mansion was a bowling green, with additional cleared area that encompassed about eight acres. Surrounding it was a palisade that was divided in half by the main road. On the side towards the creek and right beside the house was a formal garden, with a barn and several outbuildings scattered among the palisades. Surrounding the remaining area was sparse woods. Stuart had encamped his army in the clearing in the shadow of the mansion, of which he had taken as his headquarters.

The British commander had not chosen this position merely by chance. Stuart knew that by drawing his army up, he could take full advantage of his location. He drew them up into a single line on the border of the woods, only a few paces from the camp. The 3rd Regiment, called the Buffs, formed the right flank, and rested on the branch road leading to Charleston. Cruger, with the remains of his broken corps from Ninety-six and two Loyalist units made up of several dozen American Continental soldiers, made up the center, and the 63rd and 64th, two veteran regiments, formed to the left. For protection to the right, Major Majoribanks was posted with a battalion of light infantry, his right resting on the Eutaw Creek and his left stretching in an oblique line towards the flank of the Buffs. Coffin, at the head of the cavalry, guarded the left as well, which received no protection from the ground or which they stood. Two remaining infantry units formed in the rear as reserves ready to act as circumstances might require. Stuart had three field pieces, two 6-pounders and a 4. These were pushed to the front about a mile, to skirmish with the enemy in an attempt to retard his advance.

By ten o'clock, the Americans had broken camp and were preparing to march. Greene had already been on horseback for hours, preparing for the conflict which would most likely decide the fate of the Carolinas. He had arranged his army in two columns, each of which contained the materials for a line of battle. The first was composed of militia in four small battalions; two North Carolina units under the command of Colonel Malmedy were formed in the center, and two South Carolina, one for the right to be led by Marion, and one under Pickens for the left. In the second column, came the Continentals, the strength of the American army by far, in three small brigades of North Carolina, Virginia, and Maryland regiments, many of which were made up of British deserters. To such an extent had the interchange of men taken place by wars end that Greene would comment later: "At the close of the war, we fought the enemy with British soldiers; and they fought us with those of America."

The North Carolina brigade formed three small battalions, under Lieutenant-colonel Ash, and Majors Armstrong and Blunt, and was led by General Sumner, who by virtue of his rank, commanded the right. Campbell was to hold the center with his Virginians, two battalions under Major Sneed and Captain Edmonds on the left were assigned to Williams, and with two battalions of Marylanders, probably the best corps in the army, were led by Howard and Hardman. Lee with his Legion, and Henderson with the State troops under Hampton, Middleton, and Polk, formed the van of the army, and were charged with the protection of the flank. Washington and Kirkwood closed up the rear, forming a reserve of cavalry, along with the gallant infantry of Delaware. The artillery moved with the columns to which it was attached; the three pounders under Captain-lieutenant Gaines with the first, and the sixes under Captain Browne with the second.

At four o'clock the columns were put in motion, and advanced at a slow step by the main road to the Eutaws. The day was clear and calm, and the rising sun was beginning to cast shadows on the men. But it would soon become a cursed sun, for it would soon beat down unmercifully. The road they marched on ran through a sparse wood, but with thickets growing here and there throughout the trees, causing a tangled underbrush. The Americans moved forward, still slowly, cautiously, in the hope of coming up on the British pickets or patrol by surprise. The men were in high hopes, morale was good, and they had expectations of a great victory over their enemy.

It was eight o'clock when Greene and his force were about four miles from Stuart's camp. At the same time, a British rooting party had been sent out to gather sweet potatoes for their camp. Tagging along with them was Major Coffin who had 140 infantry and 50 cavalry intended on gathering intelligence information. At the same moment, along came Major John Armstrong of the American army, who had been reconnoitering ahead with a party of North Carolinians. "With a degree recklessness which indicated either his ignorance of its strength and the presence of the main body of troops or completely contempt for its service," Coffin charged headlong into the American band that had by now been reinforced with Lee's Legion and Henderson's column. "Coffin's infantry was utterly destroyed, with several killed under a shower of musketballs, and about 40 taken prisoner, along with their captain," Lieutenant-colonel Henderson would write later. Coffin's cavalry escaped only by turning their heels and taking flight, but the rooting party, made up of about 30 or 40 infantrymen, had heard the sound of gun fire and came to the scene to investigate, where they were immediately captured.

Meanwhile the firing had alerted Greene who had been in the rear. "He was so near me," wrote an eyewitness, "that our boots were actually in contact, when an aide-de-camp, galloping up, exclaimed, 'General Greene, there is a large body of enemy in our rear.' The General without turning his head, promptly replied, 'Well ride up to them sir, and tell them that if they do not immediately surrender, I shall be under the necessity of cutting them to pieces with my horse.' The order was obeyed and the enemy actually surrendered. I had been long accustomed to see men cool and collected in battle," continues the writer, "but I shall never forget the calmness and appearance of unconcern with which the general behaved that day."

Mistaking Coffin's detachment to be the enemy's van, Greene displayed his first column and moved forward in the order of battle, as fast as the nature of the ground would allow. Lee was still in front, and marching with his usual speed, he came up in about an hour of the enemy's advance corps, a body of infantry and one artillery piece. It was evident that this was not the main body. He promptly dispatched a rider to Greene, to advise him that the enemy must be nearby and approaching, and asked for support, and then pressed on to attack. He did not know it at the time, but they were about a mile from the British camp.

When the British heard the skirmish, they were on the ground and moving within a few minutes. Williams and Gaines coming up at full speed with two filed-pieces, ready to open up on the enemy column. The first line of the Americans soon followed Lee and Henderson, who diverged to the right and left, and firing obliquely as they moved, took post on their flanks, exactly according to the order of battle. The British van in the meantime, was quickly driven in, and the entire first line of the Americans, pressing steadily forward and firing as they advanced, soon found itself facing the entire British army. Stuart quickly saw that he had nothing but militia in front of him, and gladly thought they were the same that had been at Guilford courthouse. "Hold firm, my men, and drive them back without leaving your ground," Stuart commanded.

However, the British commander had miscalculated. These militiamen were under Marion and

Pickens, and their men were seasoned veterans. To punctuate their might, the American artillery was on both sides in full play; sometimes smashing massive branches from the trees surrounding the British, and sometimes cutting small trees in half when a ball sliced through them. The balls also found human targets, and sometimes-dashed full into the ranks, opening fatal gaps where men had just stood. Now, the only thing that remained in those gaps were the mangled bodies of what once were men and deep pools of blood wherever the living had to pass. Gaines plied his wares with such precision and effect, that the British artillery could not fire upon them due to the speed the Americans were firing on their position. The only thing that could stop the American artillery was that they had become unserviceable due to the amount of use in a short period of time. At about the same time, one of the British cannons suffered a direct hit from Gaines' last shot.

Meanwhile, the American first line was bearing up against the weight of the entire British army. Their adrenaline must have been sparked by the earlier skirmish, because their volleys ran from flank to flank with such precision, that the British line could not advance a single inch. The British answered with their open deep, regular volleys as well. But they could not gain the ground no matter how much they pushed the fight. "The fearful sound spread far and wide throughout the gloomy woods," an eyewitness related later.

Still the militia held their ground without wavering, and still the unshaken British line kept up its deadly fire. On the right, the Legion infantry was engaged with the 63rd of Foot, and on the left, Henderson was exposed to a galling fire from Majoribanks, secure behind the cover of the thickets. It was a mighty task for new troops, and the gallant Henderson would have gladly changed the circumstances by charging the British wing. Knowing his presence on the flank could not be jeopardized, and his men held firm and stood by him with unflinching loyalty.

But the conflict in the center was another story entirely. It was there that the untrained militia were formed and exposed to the constant fire of the 64th and part of the British center. The atmosphere was becoming unequal to last much longer, and the enemy, making a forward movement, forced the Americans to give ground and began to retire, though not until every man had emptied an entire cartridge box first. Sumner was ordered up to fill the chasm, but his corps, also were composed of new recruits. Greene had held back the strength of his line, the battalions of Williams and Howard, for the final blow. Sumner and his men came into action smartly, ranging with the corps of Lee and Henderson, still hotly engaged, and thus reformed the line of battle. The conflict was now fiercely renewed, and the British, thinking they had gained an upper hand, soon found themselves under heavy attack again and were forced back to their original position.

This was a critical moment for the British, because they knew that the greater part of the second line of the Americans had not been used yet, along with the entire cavalry and reserve which were still fresh as well. While the whole British army, except for the reserve, had already been engaged for some time now. Without missing a beat, Stuart brought up his reserve, and ordered Coffin to take a post to the left, where the open ground exposed him to a charge from the American horse. But his line was then condensed, and feeling the support, stood strong against the withering fire of the Americans. Suddenly on the left, Henderson was wounded, and reluctantly was carried off the field. For a moment, his men hesitated. But quickly Hampton moved to their head and took command, and seconded by Polk and Middleton, soon succeeded in restoring order. With the help of Sumner's brigade, who fought bravely, with coolness and the resolution of veterans, the entire line began to gain ground on the enemy. But the British line, sensing the turn of the battle, and strengthen by its reserve, became the stronger of the two, and although after a fierce and obstinate resistance, the American center was again forced to retire. The British shouted "Huzzah" and pressed forward, but in the excitement of their advance, the British line became disoriented and wavered. This was the moment that Greene had been waiting for; and this was the time for a decisive charge.

Williams and Campbell were ordered to advance their troops trailing arms, and reserve their fire. They were going to first sweep the field at the tip of the bayonet. A shout of "Huzzah" arose from the two brigades as the order was given to advance, and the men moved forward for the charge. At the same moment Lee, observing that the American right extended beyond the British left ordered Rudolph to turn his flank and pour in a raking fire. Now the air rang out with what seemed like a single crash, as the two armies fired volley upon volley at each other, causing thousands of explosions to sound as one. The British fire was quick and heavy, and "their bullets fell like hail" onto the advancing Americans. The Marylanders, obedient to their orders, pressed on without pulling a trigger. Williams and Howard were commanding them, and they knew that the bayonet alone could bring victory to them. But the Virginians, less trained, and unaccustomed to such a desperate struggle, stopped and returned the enemy's fire, endangering the Legion infantry by its delicate move on the flank they had made. Lee galloped down with his usual battlefield charm, and screamed at Campbell to take control of his men and follow the orders Greene had given him. As Campbell was about to explain to Lee, a musketball tore through his chest, and he dropped onto the pommel of his saddle without uttering a word. Lee directed his orderly to bear him back to the rear, and returned to his post, where his infantry, having succeeded in turning the enemy's flank, were bearing down on the British line.

The crisis to the British left soon spread to the center, and one by one their regiments began to give way and shrunk at the sight and shock of the bayonet. That is, all but the brave Buffs, who received the charge with a firm front line, returning the assault thrust for thrust till many on both sides began to fall. But the resolute of the Americans could not be withstood. They continued to press forward in a dense line, and pouring in a close fire onto the British ranks that was already beginning to shrink from the bayonet, was suddenly swept from the field, like the raking of leaves on a crisp, fall day. The enemy began to flee in every direction, some through the woods, some along the Charleston road, who did not stop until they were banging on the gates of the old city, crying of the terror of the battle and the defeat they had suffered so greatly. The staff officers began to break up their stores, and stove their rum puncheons. Everything was in complete disorder and wild dismay.

Although the battle was his, it would go into the record books as all of Greene's would; as a tie or loss. In those days, wins and losses were measured by the ground you won and occupied. Greene was never permitted the luxury of remaining on the hard fought battlefields he and his men had won. He was always onto his next objective, some other course of action, or tripped up by the weaknesses of these very human men that fought for him. On every occasion he either choose to withdraw for strategic sense, or was forced to allow the enemy to keep its ground. As the others, this one was no exception. The last, and by far the bloodiest of them all, half of his victory was wrung from him when all seemed within his grasp.

The British were in full flight. The Americans were in pursuit, though mostly just to preserve their comrades still engaged in the field, rather than tempered death lust against their enemy. The next thing they knew, they were among the British tents. Food and drink was everywhere they turned; hunger pulled at them, but thirst was screaming in their ears. It had been a hot, dirty, bloody, exhausting, and dry affair, and drink tempted the men beyond pain. For some it was too much to bear, and they broke ranks to find refreshment. The battle was won, and the day theirs, they thought. Should its hungry and thirsty winners be denied the poor pittance of a meal? They became like mice scurrying about, scattered among the British encampment in eager search for food and drink.

Some, however, among them Lee's gallant infantry of the Legion, passed on without as much as a passing glance at their comrades abiding, and followed after the fleeing British, and made prisoners at every step of the way.

The brick house that was at the edge of the encampment, was refuge for Sheridan and his New York volunteers. But the Continentals were close at hand, and quickly fell upon them. For a few tense

316

moments there was a life and death struggle at the front door as the loyalist attempted to close it behind them. Some of Lee's men had nearly foiled their attempt. One, a private struggled through the half open door with assistance from his so called friends, only to be thrown out again by the loyalist, who prevailed at shutting the door, but in their haste, leaving several of their own men and officers outside to fend for themselves. Several of the enemies ran to the third floor garret windows and began to pour down a close fire on the men surrounding the house. Placing the prisoners they had just been handed in front of them as a shield, the Americans fell back out of range of the house.

The conflict was far from over yet. On the British left, where Majoribanks fought behind the shelter of the impenetrable thicket, the battle was still raging with un-relented fury. When the British line broke, under the charge of Williams and Campbell, Washington had been ordered up with the reserve to dislodge Majoribanks from the thicket and Hampton was directed to support him. They were to move at the same moment, but Washington, spurring forward, was first on the scene, and attempted in vain to pierce the thicket with his horse. There was an open space to the rear, between the spring and the position held by the last remaining British. If this could be reached there would be clear ground for a charge. So, wheeling by sections, Washington attempted the extreme delicate maneuver directly under the guns of the enemy, who, pouring in a well directed fire, brought down every American officer but two, and thus spread death and confusion throughout the ranks. Washington had his horse shot out from under him, and while attempting to disentangle himself from his dead steed, was wounded and taken prisoner.

Kirkwood and Hampton were now at hand, and the men of the Delaware regiment pressed forward with their bayonets, while Hampton, collecting the shattered remains of Washington's cavalry, still bleeding but not beaten, made another attempt against the enemy. But the British position was too strong to be forced, and though Kirkwood held his ground, Hampton was compelled to retire rather than force the issue.

Still the defeat of the British line left Majoribanks exposed on his left; and to reopen his communications he began to retreat slowly towards the house, clinging to the cover of the woods and ravine all the way. Here he took a new position, with his rear to the creek, and his left resting on the picketed garden, while Coffin drew up his cavalry in an open field to the west of the Charleston road. Supported on his flanks, and protected by the fire from the house, Stuart attempted to form once more his line of battle.

Greene too had pressed forward expecting a victory, and brought up his artillery to batter the house. However, the field pieces were too light to make any impression on its solid brick walls, and the fire from the windows struck down everything in its range of fire. A few of the Americans were still scattered among the tents, enjoying their respite and rum. Coffin, seizing the opportunity, spurred forward to charge on them, while Majoribanks made a corresponding movement on the left. Greene ordered up the Legion cavalry to meet the attack; Pendleton, the aid who bore the order, could not find Lee with his cavalry, and gave the order to Major Joseph Egleston, second in command. The charge, though made bravely, was unsuccessful, and Coffin, pressing on, forced his way through the scattered Americans.

At this moment, Hampton came up. After a violent contest of hand to hand combat, he forced the British cavalry back under the cover of the house. The pursuit brought him within range of Majoribanks infantry, and this often challenged body of men poured one more well directed fire into the American onslaught, and the cavalry was repulsed and forced to withdraw. Hampton, collecting his scattered troops, retired under the cover of the woods, and Majoribanks, issuing from his thicket, seized the American artillery, the artillerymen having all been killed, wounded, or retreated, dragged it off in triumph. Then returning to the charge, Majoribanks drove before him and shattered remnants of the Americans, who still greedy for drink, were found lingering among the tents.

317

The British line was now reformed, and prepared to renew the battle. Greene, too, had rallied his forces in the border of the wood. Most of his corps was still fully intact and not demoralized, even the cavalry, though it had suffered severely The militia were proud of their resolute stand and should have been. The Continentals were satisfied with the charge they had made. Greene, tradition says, had been so delighted with it that he had ridden up and down the line in the heat of the action and had almost thanked them one by one. He may have renewed the battle with a good chance of driving the enemy off the field once and for all. As he had witnessed at Guilford Courthouse, he had accomplished his purpose for which he had fought, and crippled his adversary. Why risk the lives of these fine men, who had already done their duty with nothing of which to be ashamed? An unforeseen incident had deprived him of full victory again, but the banks of the Congaree and Santee would no longer be shaded by the profiles of the British army marching along them. Within forty-eight hours, Stuart would gather up the remnants of his broken force and be falling back to Charleston. At no point believing he had won the day, but winning by a technicality. When all was said and done, he had held the ground. As the echo of the guns still hung over the treetops, the cries and screams of the wounded were taking the places of the sounds of battle. Greene, dispatching Lee to propose to Stuart to have a joint funeral for their fallen comrades, which he agreed to. Leaving a strong picket with Hampton still on the ground, Greene fell back with the main body to Burdell's plantation where he had spent the days before the battle.

As always, casualty estimates were always either inflated or reduced by the respective army. The same could be said in this case, but estimates seem to be consistent on both sides. The American casualties as published by the Congress were 522 of all ranks: 139 killed, including 17 officers (the most of any battle in the war), 375 wounded, including 43 officers, and 8 missing. The British losses were even more severe, 866 in all, more than two-fifths of the British force in the struggle: 85 killed, 351 wounded, and 430 missing. The 430 had been taken prisoner by Greene and his men. Englishmen, Irish, and Germans who had fought their last battle, and would soon see the end of the war and could sense it after the "very bloody and desperate action of Eutaw Springs," Greene would write to his brother later. "Such was the heat of the action that the officers on each side fought hand to hand and sword to sword. It was by far the most obstinate fight I had ever saw."

After writing the necessary orders, reports and sending his letters to Washington and his wife, Greene performed the duty he most hated, but felt was extremely necessary, the visit to the wounded. They raised their weary heads as he passed slowly among them, with a kind word or encouragement for those that were suffering to the end. Three hundred human beings, most young, full of promise, husbands some, sons and brothers. All with nothing to be given by him but thoughtfulness and praise. "Hollow testament to the bravery these men showed today," he would write to his wife later. "When I entered the miserable hut where the wounded officers of Washington's cavalry lay, my feelings overcame me my dear. It was a trying duty I imposed upon them, but it was unavoidable. I could not help it, and I cried after leaving that sacred place. Four hundred and fifty four will be missing at tomorrow's roll call; and of these a hundred and thirty nine will never answer to their names again. It is almost too much for me to bear."

What would Stuart do? was the most asked question in the American camp. If he attempted to hold his ground, Greene was resolved to fight him again if he must. Marion and Lee were ordered to watch him. By the next evening, the question was quickly answered. Stuart broke camp, took up his stores, and leaving behind 70 of his wounded men behind, fell rapidly back by the road to Charleston. For a time, there would be no British posts within forty miles of the Congaree. In fact, except in around the town of Charleston and Savannah, the British now held no territory in the South. The State government in Georgia and the Carolinas were reestablished and were able to function without molestation till the end of the war. There would be no serious fighting in the three States after Eutaw

Springs, except the bloody partisan raids on both sides that would rage till well after the war.

Even though Stuart was retreating to Charleston, he would not escape altogether unharmed. Marion and Lee still hung around the rear of his corps, and cut off small parties by sudden charges. It was not until the reinforcements that he had ordered up, met him, that he could pursue his retreat undisturbed. Greene also hurried forward when he heard that the enemy was in motion, but the weather was still too hot for a long pursuit. So, he halted at Eutaw Springs for a few days, and made the necessary preparations for sending his wounded forward by water, an easier course for them. The army, crossing Nelson's Ferry on the 12th, returned by slow and easy march to the Hills by the Santee once more.

Chapter XXXIII

"The Politics of Peace"

Greene was encumbered by not only his 350 sick and wounded, but by that same number of the enemies as well. Sickness by "the fever" quite common for the south in that season were adding up day after day, with over 100 in Mayhem's corps alone. His hospitals formed a line extending as far up as Charlotte, and to make sure they were receiving the best care possible, he visited them all. "Our sick and wounded," Greene wrote to the President of Congress, "have suffered greatly. The extent of our hospitals, the malignity of disorders, and increasing sick since the battle of Eutaws, together with the numerous wounded on hand, and the great number of physicians that have fallen to sickness, have left our sick and wounded in a most deplorable situation. Several members of brave fellows have either bled in the cause of their country, have been eaten by maggots, and perished in other miserable conditions. Hospital stores and medicine have been exceeding scarce; not an ounce of bark have we in the department at this time."

Cinchona bark, which quinine was extracted from, was used effectively to treat "the fever" which we know as malaria. The men also could have been treated more effectively with trained hospital aides. The men they were using were merely soldiers that could not be used as useful soldiers on the battlefield or were injured or sick themselves. Many of them infected men that were already weak from injury or illness and in most cases hasten or caused their eventual deaths.

Much of the suffering the army was feeling might have been averted, if Greene could have obtained hard money for the purchase of supplies. Continental currency had completely disappeared. Even State issued money was now worthless out of the State in which in was issued. For example, Virginia had issued Greene over five hundred thousand dollars in Virginia currency and was on its way by early October. But the money was now virtually useless in North Carolina, and Major Clairborne wrote from Virginia on his way to Philadelphia, "It is almost unnecessary to send it now, as it cannot be useful where you are. Will you be kind enough, sir, to let me have it, and take the inclosed receipt." Greene was glad to be rid of the burden of it, and cheerfully consented to allow Clairborne to have it and use it for his own department in the north.

One of the more active and efficient men under Greene's command in the southern department, was one of his aides, Major John Burnet. The young officer had been a terrific officer under Greene's tutelage, but his health had failed recently, "falling under the weight of fatigue and exposure of this trying command." So, Greene decided to send him north to recuperate, but to also take advantage of this opportunity to have someone near Congress that he could entrust with several important commissions. One of them was a personal appeal to the Board of War, in favor of his half-clothed officers. When Burnet delivered the appeal, it was quickly accepted, the supplies voted on, and the Superintendent of Finance then approved the request. Greene was ecstatic at how well it had all worked out and how quickly, but soon found out it would come with a price tag. The procured funds would be forwarded, but under conditions. That they be purchased in Boston, so as to increase the labor and expense of transportation, and therefore prolong the suffering of the men it was procured for. Greene reluctantly agreed to the terms, feeling he had no choice, but he also had a trick up his sleeve. Burnet had several bills that Greene had incurred while buying supplies for the southern campaign. Greene felt that this was an opportunity to sneak this new bill into the others without the Board of

Finance realizing it until it was too late. Greene had Burnet order only the supplies that were the most pressing, and have the bill for twenty thousand dollars put in with the old southern campaign bills. Unfortunately, the Superintendent of Finance learned of the bill ahead of time and put a stop to the sale. Greene would have to submit to their terms and live with them, reluctantly.

About this time, gold and silver were now coming into general circulation, due in part to our allies the French and Spanish infusion of funds from trade in the West Indies, which was rapidly increasing due to their superiority on the high seas. Greene believed he would soon advantage from this significant revival of funding. However, such was not the case. Although Morris, a close friend of Greene's, was in charge of the money, he felt a deep responsibility to pay off old bills that had burdened the country since the beginning of the war. Greene and the southern department were considered new bills, and would have to wait their turn. Although Greene was disappointed with the philosophy, he knew he probably would have done the same thing. The best for the country is what needed to be observed, and not what was of the good of the most needy or in the cause of friendship. Morris did have a secret that he withheld from his friend Greene for the rest of their lives. He had indeed financed Greene on several occasions without anyone's knowledge. Morris hired an agent out of South Carolina to follow the southern campaign as closely as possible. When the request for funding for his department was received in Philadelphia, Morris already knew if the cause was justified or not from the information received from his agent. In most cases, he would send a portion of funds to his friend Greene and declare that it was from one of the southern States or an anonymous benefactor. These details were revealed only a few years ago from a researcher documenting Morris's correspondence.

Even with Morris's anonymous help, it was amazing what Greene and his army had accomplished considering the hardships they had to endure. The army had made long, dangerous marches throughout the southern States, it had driven the British army by hard fighting, and had wrestled the better part of the South from that enemy. But if the British had been privy to certain information, they would have known that Greene could have easily been crushed by them ten days after the battle at the Eutaws. The condition of his troops were kept secret, and for good reason. His encampment held, at most, 1,000 men fit for duty. He was seriously ill himself with a problem he had constantly battled while in the south; his asthma. Greene had always suffered worse from the condition during the summer, but in the humid, stifling conditions in the South, the illness constantly kept him short of breath. This made sleeping at night almost impossible and caused him to be forever tired and weak and thus susceptible to other maladies. But this was no time for complaining. Greene was up early every morning, and on his horse patrolling or working late into the night on correspondence and strategy.

Greene had received a letter from Governor Burke, which he had written before the battle of Eutaw Springs, "I do not delay a moment to send you this important intelligence contained in the inclosed extract: ---I left Halifax yesterday, and on the road heard a most furious cannonade which lasted several hours, and ended at the close of the day. It was heard by the people of Roanoke, and I wait with anxious impatience to know the event, which, as soon as I learn, shall be transmitted to you."

The extract Burke spoke of was a letter from Governor Nelson of Virginia. "But what raises our hopes and joys to the most exalted pitch, and which I have reserved to the last to crown the political feast which this letter will afford you, is a movement of our great General, who on the 27th of last month was at Chatham, with all the French troops of the northern army, and a body of Continentals, on his march to Virginia."

Other correspondence with similar news soon followed, along with information that Cornwallis, roused by the arrival of the French fleet and worried about the danger of his situation, was quickly preparing for a swift retreat through North Carolina to Charleston. Further news told of Stuart's army in the field again with 200 cavalry and a strong contingent of infantry reinforcements. It was an anxious moment for Greene. His bloodied and bone weary troops could not face a foe, especially an overwhelming one right now. Hampton and Marion, who had been shadowing Stuart's troops, were forced to fall back. British soldiers were again allowed to come within sight of the Congaree. Was their true intention to take the grain rich district all over again? Or was it to prevent Greene's army from disputing the advance of Cornwallis? Additional information would bring things to light.

However, the news did anything but clarify things. It was alarming. Hector McNiel, a daring loyalist, had surprised Hillsbourgh and captured Governor Burke, some of his members of council, and several military officers, and carried his prisoners off to Wilmington. After hearing the news, the loyalist, who had been rendered relatively quiet by the recent debilitating "victories" by their British brothers, began to give the partisan renewed hope and they began to ravage the surrounding lands of the Pedee once again. It put the heated partisan wars into motion once again, and new fighting along the Cross Creek region. A Major Butler met the Tories with an equal number of a Whig detachment and defeated them, dispersing them to the four corners of the wind. But General Rutherford did not allow the Tories to merely crawl away and hide. He set to tracking down as many of them as he could and showing no mercy, tortured and slaughtered all of them. To further his cause, the ones he could not find, he took to destroying their homes, property, and crops and killing the families or selling them into servitude. Reports of these injustices reached Greene who was livid at the barbarism amidst his command. He immediately wrote a stern letter of inquiry to his senior officers, outlining policy, justice, and the humanity required in the treatment of Tories and especially their innocent families, and sent a heavy detachment to capture Rutherford to answer to the accusations. Rutherford denied the accusations of course, and although Greene questioned his truthfulness, could not convict Rutherford due to lack of evidence. Greene used the occasion to expand and enforce his views on the subject though.

The capture of Governor Burke, a strong advocate of Greene's, was a serious blow both politically as well as morally. Greene was in desperate need of an advocate right now, and the capture of Burke could not have come at a worse time. Alexander Martin, the North Carolina speaker of the senate, became acting governor. He immediately opened an active correspondence with Greene. Greene felt that an active military officer would quell the concerns of the State government, as well as have a moral effect. He directed General Sumner to "set out immediately and make a tour through the State as far as Halifax and into such other parts as may find necessary to promote the public service." He was further instructed to prepare to oppose Cornwallis. "The particular situation of Lord Cornwallis in Virginia may induce him to attempt an escape through North Carolina; you will take every measure in your power to oppose his passage be securing advantageous passes; and by all means keep me constantly advised of his route and movements."

It was soon discovered that Cornwallis was at bay, and that the French fleet had hemmed him in on the waterside, with the allied army under Washington himself, on the landside. And so, on the 28th of September began the momentous siege of Yorktown, Virginia. Washington corresponded with Greene almost daily on the situation on the Virginia peninsula, telling Greene every detail from the progress on the works to the distribution of the French infantry units, soon to be under the command of their young charge, the Marquis de Lafayette. He spoke of the daily attempts at the outer redoubts, the visible effects of the incessant cannonade, until the 18th of October and the final capitulation.

In the meantime, these days brought trial and tribulations to Greene. Seven hundred recruits, men from Maryland and Delaware, were on the march for his army. Greene was becoming quite anxious in their arrival, due to the fact that the term of service of the Virginians was almost up. But the day the new men were to arrive, he instead receive a message from Washington's aide informing him that they had been stopped on their way and rerouted to Yorktown. He immediately wrote back to Washington: "Your Excellency. From a message on the 17th, I am informed that the Maryland troops, who were expected to reinforce this army, have been ordered to join the army in Yorktown. Our situation is truly distressing, and the want of a reinforcement very pressing; but if it will interfere with more important concerns, I am willing to struggle with every difficulty and inconvenience. However, I am told your force in Virginia amounts to no less than fifteen thousand men. If so, the Maryland troops will be of little or no consequence."

Maybe just a touch of sarcasm can be seen in that note to Washington. Probably one of the only times Greene ever questioned Washington's decisions. Many times prior, Greene had certainly put in more than his share of opinions. But when Washington made his final decision, Greene never wavered in his support for his commander-in-chief. Greene's officers were not so tolerant. "No troops coming on to you," wrote Lee to Greene on the 28th of September, "but a perfect monopoly has taken place of men and supplies, to fight a deranged, small army."

But as soon as Yorktown fell, what plans were to follow? With a superior French fleet to bottle up the communication by sea, Charleston could be taken in less than thirty days, Greene had reasoned. So more than ever, he prayed for the end at Yorktown. He wrote to Washington and begged him to follow up the siege of Yorktown with the siege of Charleston, and sent Lee as his envoy to press the point, worrying little of what the commander-in-chief would think of such a bold position by his second-in-command. But the French admiral had already pledged his word to the West Indies that he would return by a particular time, and that time was fast approaching. After the fall of Yorktown, Washington went back north to shadow New York, and left the conquest of Charleston to Greene.

The only post in North Carolina now held by the enemy was Wilmington, and against this Greene had planned his attack, even before the capture of Governor Burke. The plan was resumed when Greene realized he was not going to receive the reinforcements he desperately required. But when Yorktown fell, the British commander knew that the cause would quickly fail. Without the support of Cornwallis, he knew his own post was doomed in the long run and immediately evacuated Wilmington.

North Carolina was finally free. Virginia too, swept the occupied British from its land, and it was now occupied by French troops. Greene thought that surely Virginia would gladly send the troops he so desperately needed and thus end the southern war. But such was not to be. Even Lee's personal efforts to raise a Legion failed. Virginia had little thought for the war now. Effectively, it thought the war over, and did not give a single thought to the rest of the south and its continued plight.

But some good news was received. The Marylanders were finally on their way, along with the long expected Pennsylvanians under St. Clair and Wayne. Colonel John Sevier of North Carolina and Colonel Issac Shelby of Virginia joined Greene with a body of hand picked mountaineer riflemen, and were put under the command of Marion, with a slight suggestion that if he was to keep them he must keep them busy. Greene was extremely eager to finish the work he had been given. By the 18th of November he struck his tents on the High Hill of the Santee for the last time, and the army descended down into the low country to begin its march by Simon's and McCord's ferries to the Round O. But while Greene was marching, he received word from Marion that Sevier's and Shelby's men had deserted them. They had decided that with the defeat of the British at Yorktown, this expedition was useless and felt the loss of their lives at this juncture was pointless. This dangerously weakened Greene's forces, which were already weak to begin with. Even more, he had counted on the riflemen to be an intricate part in the execution of his plan. Stuart had advanced, but had led to no major confrontation. "They made their movements only in bravado," wrote Marion, "with a view to regain the hold on public retreat." Greene advanced on Stuart, and Stuart fell back to Goose Creek Bridge. The American general, optimistic by Staurt's unwillingness to fight, gave him courage to push the British commander even further back.

About eight miles west of Goose Creek Bridge, and fifteen miles northwest of Charleston, lay the village of Dorchester. It was a fortified post that possessed communication with Charleston by water via the Ashley River, and a secure retreat path by either of its banks. A garrison of 850 men held, 500 of who were regular infantry, and 150 cavalry. Greene resolved that he would outmaneuver them, counting upon the moral strength he had gained at the Eutaws. This would make up for the inferiority in physical strength of his troops. He assigned command of the main army to Otho Williams, with orders to continue the march southward. Then he took 100 cavalry from Lee's and Washington's commands, and 100 from Sumter's. He took the fine infantry of the Legion, and detachments from the Maryland and Virginia lines. Total, they formed a small army of 400 men. Greene put himself in the head of these troops, which seemed to make the men that more willing to perform in excellent form.

It was important to take the enemy by surprise. To accomplish this, the cavalry was extended over a broad front so as to cut off the enemy's communications. The most indirect path was chosen so they could keep out of sight for as long as possible. But the area was swarming with loyalists, and Greene's approach had already been discovered by the 30th of November. The garrison at the post was already on full alert that night, listening anxiously for every snap of a twig. By late morning on the 1st of December, the garrison grew restless and anxious and decided to send 50 loyalist out to reconnoiter the area. They soon came upon Greene's advanced guard and almost the entire 50 were put to the sword. But the pursuit of the survivors nearly brought the guard to the walls of the garrison. The British cavalry came out to meet them, and recoiling, shrank from the charge of Wade Hampton's swords. Not long after, Greene himself moved forward to reconnoiter, and was quickly recognized. The whole army was thought to be at hand, thought the British commander, and throwing his cannon into the river and destroying his stores, he retreated in great haste toward Charleston. At the quarter House, five miles from the city, where the isthmus was narrowest, he halted and reinforced. At the same time Stuart fell back from Goose Creek Bridge and joined them. Wild alarms by the loyalist in the area that Greene had upwards of 10,000 men and was about to attack, led to another large party of loyalist troops being added to the already strong garrison, numbering almost 3,300 troops. If that was not enough, all the slaves in the area that could be coaxed to fight for the British, were enlisted and armed. It was the first time that such a sight had been seen throughout the entire southern war.

But Greene was no fool, and had accomplished his goal, and knew his weakness too well to try and accomplish more. Kosciusko had been sent forward to select a place for encampment, and chose Colonel Saunder's place on the Round O. There, on the 7th of December the army halted. By the 9th, Greene joined them, and proceeded immediately to rearrange his troops. Marion held the enemy's right in check. Sumter occupied Orangeborough and the Four Hole Bridge. Wade Hampton, with 50 men of the State cavalry, was charged with the communications with Marion. Colonel Harden and Lieutenant-Colonel James Wilkinson kept watch over the movements of the enemy between Charleston and Savannah. Lee, with the light detachment, guarded the front, carefully concealing the fact, that Greene was headquartered with barely 800 men.

"Your success at Dorchester," wrote Williams to Greene, "would make your enemies hate themselves, if all circumstances were generally known; and the same knowledge would make your friends admire the adventure even more than they do now. I am very happy that you have obtained your wish with risking a general action, and I hope you will be able to keep what you have gotten, till the reinforcement under General St. Clair will enable you to take more."

"I had the pleasure," write Washington to Colonel John Laurens, "to receive your favor of the tenth of December, and also the report of the judicious and successful movement of General Greene, by which he compelled the enemy to abandon their outposts and hold them at bay, though hopelessly unnumbered. This brilliant manoeuvre is another proof of the singular abilities which General Greene possesses."

There were numerous advantages for being encamped on the Round O. It was in the midst of a rich rice region. Game was abundant in the woods, and wildfowl on the water, as well as good fishing beneath it. Officer and soldier, the well and the sick, for awhile ate delicacies and in abundance. It was the first time that both were available to Greene for his army since he had entered the war.

Yet from everywhere complaints and disheartening reports could still be heard. The governors of North Carolina and Virginia, still had no intention of sending additional troops. Quartermasters complained that they could neither get horses or wagons, commissaries complained that they were embarrassed on all sides in obtaining supplies. Arms and ammunition were wanting, and even with the excellent encampment being enjoyed by the troops, morale was at an all time low.

In the midst of all these problems, a new alarm was sounded and reached his ears. Through his spies in Charleston he learned of a large reinforcement from Ireland and New York which were on their way to South Carolina. If this report should prove true, how could Greene possibly hold his ground against such odds with nothing more than the shadow of an army? While attempting to find if the report was in fact true, he busied himself with urgent letters for support to Rochambeau in Virginia, the governors of North Carolina, Virginia, and Maryland, and wrote to Smallwood; "I fear the misfortunes of this country are never to be at an end. After driving the enemy into Charleston with the remains of our little army, I was in hopes to have a little respite; especially after General St. Clair should join us, which I expect will take place in three or four days. But alas! I got intelligence yesterday, that four regiments of infantry and two of dismounted dragoons were hourly expected from County Cork, and three regiments from New York. This force, with what the enemy had before, will make them upwards of eight thousand strong at Charleston, besides what they have at Savannah. Our force when collected together, even after St. Clair shall have joined us, will not amount to more than one third of the enemy's force. Unless I am speedily supported, I shall be obliged to abandon the country or expose the army to ruin."

His letters served only to bring out the source of his plight. Rochambeau could not move until Greene had pushed over the Dan. North Carolina was unable to get her legislature together since the capture of Burke. Virginia was embroiled in an internal quarrel between the governor and the State Superintendent of Finance. "I am sorry to say," wrote Governor Davie, "that I fear the whole power of the government would not be sufficient to reinforce you with two thousand men at this time."

Fortunately, the report of the British reinforcements, though true, was greatly exaggerated. Two regiments of infantry, with a hundred and fifty dismounted dragoons, were on their way from New York, and sixty artillerists had come from Ireland. Greene sighed with relief that he had escaped a catastrophe. "I have not been frightened," he wrote in his journal, "but as Doctor Skinner says, I have been confoundedly scared."

The constant embarrassments the army had suffered at trying to raise an army throughout the war, was still a thorn in the side of Greene as 1781 drew to a close. It had been brought to Greene's attention that out of the 248,139 inhabitants of the area, 120,000 were black. The enemy had made terrific work at trying to recruit these men, and had some luck with it by offering them their freedom, if they were not already, and a bounty. Greene had first approached Washington back in 1776 with the plan of using blacks as efficient recruits. The men that had volunteered without the promise of a bounty had proven their bravery and fortitude time and again at places like; Breeds Hill, Long Island, Trenton, Valley Forge, and Monmouth. Why not look to these men as soldiers now, when their support was needed most?

But Washington clearly showed his disfavor in 1775, just a few days after arriving in Massachusetts as the Commander-in-chief of the Army. From his headquarters in Cambridge, Washington issued the following order to recruiting officers: "You are not to enlist any deserter from the Ministerial army, nor any stroller, negro, or vagabond, or person suspected of being an enemy to the liberty of America. . . ." The order did not affect black soldiers who were already in service with the army. However, there was increasing pressure from the plantation owners and politicians from the southern States to make the Continental Army all white, but Greene was a northerner, and like many of the people of that region, Greene did not approve of such efforts.

Most southerners, including Washington, felt as the early English settlers in the south had put it a hundred years before, that "there must be great caution used in the military employment of Negroes, lest our slaves when armed might become our masters."

Many of our forefathers, gentlemen who would be instrumental in the writing of the Declaration of Independence, knew that there could not be a successful revolution unless the north and south were unified in the struggle. John Adams had expressed his concerns about using black soldiers to Brigadier-general John Thomas, a New England militia commander. Thomas would reply with, "We have some negroes in our company, and in action many of them have proved themselves brave."

Washington's feelings against arming black men must have still been powerful seven years later, since he was willing to ban them at a time when Greene and the Continental Army was so desperate for men.

When the British army landed in the south, Cornwallis had offered to provide the slaves with arms and clothes enough, and proclaim freedom to all the Negroes who would join his camp. Within a few weeks of British occupation of Charleston, twenty thousand Negroes would join it from the two provinces of South Carolina.

In the meantime, Greene had been constantly operating under what Lafayette had described as "the Herculean task of contending with the formidable enemy with only a handful of men." The logical answer to his army's manpower shortage was clear to Greene. It was the same one John Laurens, a native of South Carolina, had come up years before, to enlist slaves and give them their freedom. "That they would make good soldiers, I have not the lest doubt," he wrote Governor Rutledge of South Carolina. Greene went about attempting to enlist slaves under the condition that they be freed at the end of the war, along with the same bounty afforded white soldiers.

Instead of following Greene's suggestion, however, his constant source of aggravation, General Thomas Sumter, had been offering slave bonuses to any white man who would join his forces. Sumter based his bonuses on the enlistee's rank, starting with one adult slave for a private and going all the way up to three adults and one child for a colonel.

In the meantime, the Virginia Legislature, with Thomas Jefferson presiding, voted to give every new recruit his choice of a slave between the ages of ten and thirty, or L60 in gold or silver. But, by liberating the slaves and arming them, said James Madison when he heard of Jefferson's plans, "would certainly be more consonant to the principles of liberty, which ought never to be lost sight of in a contest for liberty."

Contrary to how Greene felt, and the agreement he had made with Madison that the slaves should be freed and armed, Greene, desperate for any men he could get, permitted Sumter to use slaves from a loyalist plantation as "down payments" for new recruits." With so many slaves running away, however, there must have been few to spare for such an endeavor. Soon the men in one regiment were owed 74 out of a promised 120 slaves. The men in the regiment of South Carolina's General Wade Hampton, said to be the wealthiest planter/slave owner in America, were somehow owed "ninety-three and three quarters adults and Three Quarters of a small Negro."

Despite the wretched treatment and terrible conditions the black men had been suffered, many still enlisted into Greene's army and served with distinction throughout the southern theater and were among the troops that stayed with Greene until the last days of the war. John Laurens, who had been a strong advocate for the release and rights of all slaves in the United States, was killed in October of 1782 in a meaningless skirmish near the Combahee River, between 30 Americans and a British foraging party. He is considered one of the last casualties of the war. Count Kosciuszko, another man who was sympathetic to the slave cause, asked Greene for permission to give Lauren's clothes to two black soldiers who were nearly naked, Greene quickly agreed. And so ended a sad chapter in the Greene saga, and a chapter he would probably want to reconsider if given the chance.

Contrary to all these problems Greene had to face, his main objective was still to turn to the troops that he now had against his enemy in Georgia. Greene felt it was a long overdue process that had to be accomplished if the Americans were going to bring total peace to the country. Along with the Pennsylvania troops came Wayne, Greene's comrade from his early military years, and someone he considered a close friend. Nathanael was looking forward to a general that he could rely on and give orders to and know they would not only be obeyed no matter how difficult the enterprise, but with intelligence and bravado. "Try," he would put in his instructions to Wayne, "by every means in your power, to soften the malignity and dreadful resentments subsisting between the Whig and Tory; and put a stop, as much as possible, to the cruel custom of putting men to death, after they surrender themselves prisoners."

Another subject that Greene felt was in need of his attention was the first meeting of the South Carolina Legislature in over two years. Where they should meet was the question on everyone's lips. Camden was the logical choice, but on further consideration everyone realized that having the meeting in a high profile location was the most important factor. By having the meeting in a location where more people would see it and learn about it, it would bring a deeper understanding of how much the end of the war had progressed. If not on just a military factor, but also on a morale factor, the location suddenly became more important than the actual meeting itself. Greene decided to take a squadron of cavalry on a reconnoiter mission to scout out an appropriate location near Jacksonboro, a small village on the Edisto, and thirty-five miles west of Charleston that he felt would be an ideal spot for the meeting. "Will General Leslie," he wrote in his journal, "resent the insult of convening the Legislature to sit and deliberate within hearing of his reveille?"

The enemy still held James and John Islands, two of that chain which stretches along the coast from Charleston to Florida. While John's Island remained in British control, Jacksonboro was exposed to a night attack. Greene resolved to seize Jacksonboro. The ground surrounding the area was carefully examined and the enterprise was given to Lee and Laurens. They decided on the night of January 13th, with the main army coming forward with the detachments, to lend support if needed.

The troops moved across the stream in water up to their waist, even though the tide was out. This should have been an indication to the two commanders that the water level would probably be higher on their trip back, but no one thought of this. Near by was a line of British galleys that lay at anchor no more than four hundred yards from their location and with guards posted on the ford nearby. If the British sentinels heard any sounds, they did not let on and probably mistook the ripples in the water to the ebbing tide as they called out, "All's Well" on the hour. Once on shore the first column halted. But where was the second? The reason they chose the 13th was that it was a new moon and the night was pitch black. The column stood for a few minutes and peered into the darkness, expecting the second column to emerge from its depths at any moment. But not a sole was seen. Laurens went as far as to lay his ear to the ground in hopes of detecting something, but not a sign of the second column was found. Dawn was about to break, and the one column had no chance of success alone. They decided to recross immediately, before the sun came up. The tide was already coming in and would be chest high by this time. Half freezing from standing in the chill breeze all night in soaking clothes, disappointed by the delay, they trudged off to cross the stream. Just as the last of Laurens column was reaching the bank, the sun shined and up marched the second column. Their guide had deserted them and they had wasted the whole night searching for this turn in the river that was the rendezvous point. They also met Greene along their travels. He had ridden forward after not hearing the sounds of a battle and had wondered what had happened. Although disappointed, Greene knew that it was better that Laurens had not attempted the attack on his own. "We will try it again," Greene said. But before they could, the enemy had discovered the danger they were in and withdrew. Had the Americans succeeded, the evacuation of Savannah would have been accomplished much sooner than it was.

On the 16th of January, Greene moved his troops to Skirring's Plantation, six miles from Jacksonboro, on the road to Charleston. Never had his war worn army found such accommodating quarters before. They were in the midst of the region occupied by the first settlers to Carolina. War had passed very lightly over it. The rice plantations still yielded an abundant harvest. Spacious houses were seen on every side of them, along with overflowing gardens of roses and other blooms. Delicate fruit trees that flourished in this warm climate filled the orchards. Limes were sheltered in shady walks and bowes. Delicate food, choice fruits, rich local wines covered the tables, beautiful women waited on each soldier as if he were in paradise, and the hopes and dreams of every man was awakened with the presence of these women. The rest can be left to your imagination.

By the 18th of January the Assembly met with John Rutledge in attendance, along with Christopher Gadsden and the unmistakable Francis Marion. When all of the participants were assembled, Governor Rutledge arose and addressed them in solemn words, recalling the dark days that had passed among them, and setting the duties before them that needed to be accomplished at the present hour. The House and Senate responded with the same feelings and thoughts when one of them arose and announced "the wisdom, prudence, address and bravery of the great and gallant General Greene, and the intrepidity of the officers and men under his command, --a general who is justly entitled, from his many signal services, to honorable and singular marks of his approbation and gratitude." Not stopping there, the Senate speaker, John Lewis Gervais, presented a special address to Greene, with the House passing a bill, "vesting in General Nathanael Greene, in consideration of his important services, the sum of ten thousand guineas." This would amount to the sum of about $75,000 today.

By the constitution of South Carolina, one of the first duties of the new Assembly was to choose a governor. Governor Rutledge, who was not eligible, stood by as John Mathews, a close advocate of Greene as a member of the 1780 congressional committee, was chosen as the new governor of South Carolina. It was a wise choice, because South Carolina was a member of the confederation, jealous of congressional influence, and always ready to assert its own dignity at the expense of the national government. With Mathews in the chair, it would be easier for Greene to do the work of both. With a friendly governor, it would always be less difficult to accomplish his goals, and sometimes, as the experience of the following year would show, impossible sometimes to avoid a collision of the two bodies.

With the close of 1782 Greene looked back on the military history of the campaign, he wrote to his northern friends that it had been "as dull and insipid as that of the preceding year had been critical and interesting." He general object by this point was to cover the country, confine the enemy within the narrowest limits, recapture Georgia, and if possible without the aid of a fleet, compel the evacuation of Charleston. The maneuvering and fighting were chiefly confined to Georgia, where Wayne found a fine field for the display of his military talents. The narrative of the Georgia conquest belongs to the history of that great soldier and not Greene. What must be related briefly, is that Wayne's campaign in Georgia was mostly leveled at the Native Americans in the area that were allied to the British. The Choctaws and Creek were awarded annual gifts near Augusta by the British for American scalps. But with Augusta now in the hands of the Americans, the Native Americans were directed to meet in Savannah with the Tory leader there, Colonel Brown. While there, the two tribes and the Tories got into an argument over a game of lacrosse and the tribes left to return home. Wayne thought this a perfect time to attack with the forces divided and descended on the groups. It was a complete and utter victory for Wayne who quickly moved on to Savannah as his next mission. By mid July 1782,

Savannah was evacuated, the regulars going to strengthen the garrison at Charleston, and the loyalist taking refuge in Florida. Wayne had ended the war in Georgia. "Georgia is ours," wrote Greene to Williams, in September, "and Wayne has acquitted himself with great honor."

In all respects, there are no other battles, strategy, or troop movement to relate. The war continued to paralyze industry, to fetter commerce, or bring sudden desolation to local families. The flame of war was gradually beginning to fade and brought the increased prospect that an official suspension of hostilities could be reached, but the history books fail to mention any. Due to the lack of troop movement, Marion's brigade was temporarily dispersed. The reason was because Georgia was utterly destitute and unable to support the troops. Even Wayne's army had drawn its supplies from South Carolina, but the burden was becoming to great for that State to continue. So it was thought by disbanding several units, the majority of the main army could continue to subsist on the supplies it could draw without putting an unwarranted burden on South Carolina any longer.

The men were still suffering from lack of clothing. All of their clothes were nearly worn out, many in tatters, some were said to be wearing only a remnant of some garment that was now unrecognizable and pinned around their waist with the thorn of a locust tree. Private citizens came to the rescue with contraband which had been secretly carried out of Charleston with the help of Lee and Laurens, some clothing, hospital articles, and some goods that were of no use to the army, but were used to obtain a good supply of rice. When the army advanced to Bacon's Bridge at the head of the Ashley, a communication was opened by water, and a brisker trade was carried on, with the authorities on the American and British sides looking the other way in consideration for goods for themselves. A larger, more productive commerce was opened through Georgetown and other posts along the coast. Rum, blankets, hospital stores, articles of clothing and the indispensable article of salt.

The monotonous months were wearing away slowly, bringing little alleviation to the long-suffering army. Murmurs began to be heard, low at first and then more distinctive and which were gradually swelling into mutiny. The Pennsylvanians "who had been well paid and well clothed" for their mutiny in the north years before, had brought with them that same bad spirit that some of the trouble makers that were present at the Morristown event south exhibited. The enemy spies quickly picked up on the discontentment of the American troops and quickly had several agents in contact with several of the angry men. A sergeant Gornell, who had led a regiment in the first mutiny was quickly won over by the British spies. Peters, Greene's batman (a type of butler in the field), became one of the conspirators. The two men sought to win over the equally discontented Maryland regiment, but failed in this attempt. American spies fed the symptoms of the mutiny by reporting suspicious movements within the British garrison, which put Greene on his guard. Greene ordered Colonel Harmar of the Pennsylvania line to keep a watchful eye on his men. In the midst of all of this a campfollower came out with a story that she said she had accidentally overheard. A party of horses were to approach the American camp in the night, and the mutineers were to seize Greene and his leading officers and deliver them to the British. Upon hearing this bit of news, Greene proceeded with his usual characteristic energy for such matters. The evidence against Gornell was complete. He was arrested, tried, and condemned to death within a day. The next night, twelve of the conspirators, fearing for their own lives, went over to the enemy. The next morning Gornell was shot, and five other sergeants were sent into the interior under guard. "This decisive step," wrote Greene to Williams, "put a stop to it, and you cannot conceive what change it has made in the temper of the army."

More trouble would soon follow. A great change had taken place among Greene's officers. Williams, who had been sick for some time, was in Maryland, waiting for the brigadiership for which Greene had urgently recommended him. Howard, too, was there, not yet recovered from his wounds, and Davie was in North Carolina. Of all these close knit family of officers, only one remained. Lee was beginning to complain that his services had not been properly recognized. Greene replied in as friendly a voice that he could muster. "No man in the progress of the campaign had equal merit with yourself, nor is there one so represented. . . .I think whoever reads my letters and knows the facts, will agree that I have done ample justice both to the friend and the officer." Lee was not heard to grouse again after that, and instead chose to retire from military service.

Two other officers, Horry and Mayhem, were divided by a question of rank. With a strong regard for Mayhem, Greene felt obliged to decide in favor of Horry. "I will also write to Lieutenant-colonel Mayhem, decidedly," he wrote to Marion, "upon the dispute of rank. I am sorry the colonel carries that matter to so disagreeable a length. Rank is not what constitutes the good officer, but his conduct. Substantial services give reputation, not captious disputes. A captain may be more respectable than a general. Rank is nothing unless accompanied with worthy actions."

But Greene's most serious trial came from the Legion, a body of men, which he likened to "the Praetorian guards." The ancient Praetorian Guards were the elite guard of the ancient Roman emperors. Augustus, the first Roman emperor, instituted the first Praetorian Guards in 27 BC as a separate force under his direct command. The Praetorian Guard was the only permanent body of troops allowed inside the city of Rome. On Lee's retirement, the Legion came under the command of Laurens, but they were greatly dissatisfied, going as far as to calling him "a bad cavalry officer, and not the type of officer to lead our storied corp." Sometime later, in forming a brigade for Brigadier-general Mordecai Gist, re-formation of several corps made it necessary to separate the infantry and cavalry, including the Legion.

By the end of the summer of 1782, the army had moved to Ashley Hill, where they found good water and good soil, but no relief from the dreaded fever (malaria). Men and officers suffered alike, but Greene was forced to watch helplessly without the power to alleviate the suffering. To make matters worse, hard feelings were beginning to surface between the civilians and the soldiers. The soldiers were constantly taking crops, animals, fruits, and just about anything that wasn't nailed down in the area. The civilians quite frankly were getting tired of the behavior and felt that the army's work was done. Why were they still hanging about and making the civilians life rough? This made Greene very anxious. "It is time the enemy were out of this country;" he wrote to General Barnwell. "The people appear to have far greater attachment to their interest than zeal for the service. They begin to think the army can live on air. Our troops are more than one third of the time without provisions."

The northern army had suffered greatly from the greed that ran rampant in the markets of New York and Philadelphia, where the British paid in gold and silver and were of want for nothing. At the same time the American camp was starving because they were forced to pay with Continental bills or commissary certificates, which the merchants would not take. Greene's army was suffering the same cause. "I beg leave, without reserve," wrote Governor Matthews, "to mention that one essential cause of the distress of the army, is the prodigious quantity of provisions that are daily carried into Charleston. This infamous traffic is carried on by the persons who will contribute nothing for the army, because they can get enormous prices and the cash for what they send into town. This gives great discontent to the good people of the country; and has in length produced even a backwardness to them."

In addition to all of these trials and tribulation, dysentery, the scourge of armies well into the twentieth century, had set in; seizing upon those whom malaria had spared. Summer dragged on and finally it was fall. By late October, Greene was at his wits end. On the 29th he writes orders for the day that read: "the General sincerely sympathizes with the army in their sufferings for want of provisions, and cannot but express the high sense he has of the dignity and patience with which they bear it; but as their sufferings are of a much longer continuance than he had the fullest assurance should happen, he is obliged, in order to relieve the present distresses of the army, to send out military parties to collect beef and hogs. As this mode is always disagreeable to the inhabitants, and creates animosities between them and the army, nothing but the last necessity can render it eligible, and when adopted, it should be conducted with the greatest prudence, delicacy, and equality among the people."

By early November 1782, Greene's grant for clothing and provisions from South Carolina had still not passed. Some of his friends thought that he was risking too much. But winter was at hand and supplies had to be procured. The military chest was completely empty. The Quartermaster-general's resources were almost gone. Day by day the powerlessness of the confederation "for the want of obligatory and coercive clauses on the States" was becoming more apparent. Congress had hoped for a windfall from their imposed duty of five percent. All of the States, except Rhode Island and Georgia had accepted it, but not willingly. When the refusal of those two States was reported, Virginia withdrew its acceptance of the duty. The prospect of feeding, clothing, and paying the army was quickly growing dim. Changes were beginning to be made in the army. Two complete regiments were formed out of the Pennsylvania and Maryland lines, and the rest were all sent home. But before they were set on their way for their long journey home, the clothing that had been procured at Yorktown was distributed amongst them. Now the two new regiments would have to be outfitted. But with what?

It was quickly becoming evident that Charleston was the only place in which clothing could be procured. Lincoln, the Secretary of War, gave Greene full authority to go and procure it, and Greene wasted no time in casting his plans in that direction. At this time, Greene met a man named John Banks. Mr. Banks had a proposition for Greene; "I will supply you and take bills from Mr. Morris in payment, if you will advance me seven hundred guineas." A receiver for the United States, Mr. George Abott Hall, who was an agent for Morris, happened to be in camp. Greene was well aware that Hall had public money in his possession, but for what purpose Greene did not know. Very reluctantly though, Hall advanced the sum required. Banks, whose Charleston friends had procured him the privilege of free communication with the city, promptly fulfilled his part of the bargain, and the army was soon clothed,--"better clothed," said Wayne, "than I have ever saw an American army before."

The transaction had gone much smoother than Greene anticipated. Banks had fulfilled all of his engagements, and with a hefty profit, but no more than was fair for the work he did. Greene soon came up with a logical summation. "If Mr. Banks could cloth the army, why not feed it as well?"

Proposals for supplying the army with provisions had been sent out into the country for several weeks now, but not a single reply had been received by Greene. Greene had already complained, "The price is too high, and the risk, was too great." Negotiations were opened up, and the price was gradually reduced from thirteen and one fourth pence sterling to the ration, to something less than eleven. But when the proposal was brought before the Legislature, the speaker, Hugh Rutledge said; "The terms are thought too high still, but as no others have been offered, and the pressing necessities of the army call for immediate relief, it is thought that it will be needless to keep open the contract any longer, under the idea that a more advantageous proposition will be received in the future."

It was now Christmas. The season we generally associate with rejoicing and pleasant gatherings around the table with one's family. "Poor Christmas!" wrote Colonel Harmar in his journal; "no beef nor rum for the men." Banks offer was accepted, and the army was well fed just in time for the holiday.

Soon after, questions began to arise about Banks' credibility. The bills on the Superintendent of Finance's desk began to build up and they began to be examined more closely. Banks was surely embezzling funds. Merchants began to refuse to take the orders except at a discount that would have quickly led to bankruptcy for them. The approach of peace slowed the sale of goods. The merchants knew that peace would bring a fuller market and lower prices. Banks creditors grew impatient and demanded payment immediately. Soon, Greene was involved because he was the first to introduce Banks as an agent. Greene was caught between a rock and a hard place. If he stopped payment on the bills the army would stop eating. If the army stopped eating, they would surely find a way to get food. Since they were armed, it was hard not to imagine what circumstances would follow next.

Under the circumstances the creditors offered to give up the assignment which they had held for Banks, if Greene would step in and take his place. Banks, in payment for the debts he had already assumed, agreed to assign to Greene for protection from the bills on Morris' desk, including the ones drawn under the contract for clothing, which were in the hands of an agent in Philadelphia. "All future bills for subsistence were to be made payable to the creditors." It was an anxious and trying moment for Greene. The grants of the Carolinas had finally been passed. Should he expose it to the chances of an agent's fulfillment, or lack of fulfillment of a contract? The army applied a great deal of pressure on him. Could he stand by while the army starved? It was learned that an old acquaintance was the holder of Banks' bills in Philadelphia, Mr. Pettit. Greene knew he could rely on Pettit to protect his interest. Greene also learned that Banks had hired Forsyth and Burnet, who Greene both knew. Forsyth was a former captain in Lee's Legion and Burnet was a Major and a aide in Greene's staff. Both were now retired from the military, and were to be Banks agents. With these three, trustful men involved, Greene felt it was safe enough to proceed. The danger was contingent, and the necessity of the army was urgent. The agreement was signed, and it soon became apparent to Greene that it was not a good idea to confide in the honor of a desperate speculator.

Greene was once again looked at with a weary eye. How much had he been involved with Banks' dealings? Correspondence and papers explain the connection between Banks and Greene and how it could appear to be a partnership from the beginning. The officers, like the soldiers, had not been paid in months. Their wardrobes were becoming shabby and were greatly reduced. So that they could procure the means of new wardrobes, Greene had requested that Morris allow them to accumulate bills for the clothing, which roughly amounted to two months pay. But the only house that would accept credit for the bills without charging an enormous fee, was the house of Forsyth & Co., which had been recommended by Banks, and had supposedly negotiated with the proprietor to take the payments made at their store. Greene felt that the house had rendered a great service to his officers, and was thankful to Banks for finding them and negotiating the deal. Later it was discovered that Banks had been a hidden partner with the owner of the house.

The house of Hunter & Co. was a Virginia firm of which Banks was a partner as well. When Banks had received his first bills, he forwarded them through the agency of Forsyth, who no one knew was connected with Banks in business, to Hunter & Co., his other partner in Fredericksburg, Virginia. Mail then was slow, irregular, and unsafe. As an officer of staff, Forsyth had a right to send dispatches through official military channels. As Forsyth was making up the parcel to send to Banks, Hunter & Co., a Captain Shelton of the wagonmaster's department was looking over Forsyth's shoulder. Something seemed amiss. Shelton hinted to Brigadier-general Charles Scott, to whom he was directed to deliver the parcel, via Governor Harrison, that something just did not seem right with the parcel. Scott opened the outer envelope, which contained only a short billet to Governor Harrison, requesting him to forward the package to its address, which was then to be delivered to Hunter & Co. But in the inner envelope, Scott found letters from Banks and Forsyth, with a full account of the transaction and a request that Burnet's connection with the dealings be kept secret. The next day brought another letter from Banks, showing that he had been dealing largely in false papers for importing salt and shipping tobacco. One passage referred directly to Greene:-- "I find General Greene an exceedingly agreeable man; and from hints dropt already, expect his proposals for an interest in a house we may establish in Charleston."

Another passage, seemed to refer to Greene as well. By the superior interests of my friends in Charleston, I have a passport, not only to return to camp, where General Greene advised my passing some time previous to evacuation; but have also leave to return to town, an indulgence not obtainable by any person in either party." Scott said, "In order to do justice to the public, and detect any species of speculation that might be at foot at the public expense, must forward copies of these letters to the governor."

Governor Harrison took a very different view of the matter all together. He had formed a very high opinion of Greene over the years, and to allow the mere suggestions of such a man as Banks that Greene may be involved was ludicrous. To Harrison, there was no doubt in his mind of Greene's upright standing as a man to whom the nation should owe a great debt. His council took the same view. The original letters of the 7th of November, covering bills, were forwarded to the address they were intended as if they had not been read. Scott was quite indignant at the thought that he was only trying to bring ruin to Greene, and in his own defense, sent copies of the suspected letters to Congress. It soon became evident that Burnet and Forsyth had formed a close relationship while officers in the army and had dealt in such matters while still engaged with the service. But how much was Greene involved?

On Christmas Eve, the Governor Harrison wrote to Greene calling his attention to a "dangerous partnership" into which some of the officers of his army had entered, and assured him that "Banks insinuations had made no impression upon him or his council. "Greene was still very upset and irritated. Here was the calamity of the Quartermaster-general's department all over again. He immediately sent for Wayne and Carrington. "What shall I do?" he asked the two men for council. They suggested summoning Banks and confronting his with the letters. Banks arrived and admitted to his misdeeds, but claimed no ill will meant toward Greene. The allusion to Greene in the letters could easily be explained. In the first interview between the two men, Greene had said that the war was nearly over, and Major Burnet, who was his aide at the time, but was a merchant before the war, proposed when he left the army, to go into business with his friends, if they approved. "Should he do so," Greene had said to Banks in the meeting, "I shall be obliged to you for any services that you can render him." Far less evidence than this has made great men fall. This evidence, however slender the foundation, was another mark on Greene's legacy.

When Banks came in front of Judge Pendleton to state his case on the speculation matters, his first words were "General Greene was not a willing participant in this calamity." Meanwhile, Wayne and Carrington had been in possession of the letters and were examining them very carefully. After an exhausting study of them they published a handbill exonerating Greene from all participation in the commercial part of the affair. However, Greene, who held that "no man was without his enemies but a fool," had bitter enemies of his own. To this day he is looked upon as someone who was involved with numerous under handed and shady dealings from the incident while Quartermaster-general of the army to the incident with Banks. Although this author believes he was innocent of any wrongdoing, it is hard for anyone with even a small amount of common sense to look at the two events and not wonder how a high profile officer could be involved, not once, but twice in inappropriate behavior. It is therefore hard to argue if people take the negative against Greene, but this author will continue to try.

This was a perfect time for Greene to think about the tranquil life of retirement from military service, and to take the friendly suggestion of Gouverneur Morris and allow his name to be entered as a candidate for head of the new department for the ministry of war. Congress had transferred the executive government to separate departments with a responsible head. Morris had been Superintendent of Finance since February of 1781. There were delays in filling all of the other departments. For the department of war, Lincoln, Schuyler, and Sullivan were candidates. Morris and many of Greene's other friends were anxious to add his name as well to the list of prospective candidates. But Greene, though anxious to escape public life, preferred to look to the labors of an office with which he was more familiar, or to the untried responsibilities of a new department. Morris wrote him a long, heartfelt letter, pleading for him to accept the offer. Greene replied: "I am too much a stranger to the nature and duties of the office, to wish the appointment, if there were no other objections. But when I consider the feeble powers of Congress, the difficulty of combining our force, the local policy of the States, the want of vigor, prudence, and zeal among our military men for the public good, in preference to their own pleasures and promotions, I can see many other objections. You think I am fond of an army and a busy scene; you mistake my feelings; I am truly domestic. The more I am in the army, and the more I am acquainted with human nature, the less fond I am of political life. To tell you the truth, my dear sir, I am poor, and I wish not to climb to a station from which I may be cast headlong in a moment, and lost without the means to support. Eminence always begets envy; and it is more difficult to support ourselves in high places than to arrive at them."

South Carolina still assumed its rights above those of the United States, and was less prepared to work harmoniously with a now efficient Congress. The present Legislature was largely composed of men who had been faithfully watching the movements of Greene's army, and was well aware that he was the single reason that they were able to re-establish themselves in Jacksonboro. But changes that were on the horizon would bring upheaval for Greene and the government of South Carolina. It started with horses. Kosciusko was ordered to capture a number of valuable horses while he was on his last expedition. The law of Congress said in general orders that the horses could be sold at auction and the proceeds of the sale, after a reasonable deduction had been made to the captors, be paid into a general treasury. But what about the rights of the original owners?

The citizens of South Carolina soon brought that question up after the evacuation of Charleston. Several citizens in the area came forward, claiming the horses were theirs. The governor wrote to Greene, who soon found himself in a question of postliminy; The right by virtue of which persons and things taken by an enemy in war are restored to their former state when coming again under the power of the nation to which they first belonged. It was hotly debated in the governor's council, and even discussed in a council of war. Greene suggested that the claimants be allowed to hold their horses until the question was decided by Congress.

A more serious question arose from the evacuation of Charleston. By the law of rotation, another new governor had taken office, Benjamin Guerard. Also, a new Legislature, glowing with different factions that had grown out of the confiscation laws, had taken the place of the Legislature in Jacksonboro. Greene had always been against the confiscation laws, and although no one was more aware that holding the Tories in check while they had arms, Greene was also ready to receive the former citizens with open arms, as long as they laid their arms down. "Where is there justice or wisdom," Greene said, "in punishing these people, who can no longer injure us, for having always continued to think as we all thought ten years ago?" This was enough to irritate the party of confiscationist, but he would soon take it one step further.

While he was lying with a small army in the neighborhood of Charleston, and everything depended on accurate intelligence to the movements of the enemy, Greene assigned Colonel Laurens to the task of opening a successful communication with Charleston. Laurens was quickly able to accomplish this feat by means of the loyalist anxious to help to buy forgiveness from their countrymen. The price for their service was a pardon and the restoration of their property. Had Laurens, a native son of South Carolina, lived, his personal popularity would have enabled him to fulfill that promise. After his death, Greene felt obligated to fulfill that solemn legacy. This stance on the subject was not looked at with anything but dissatisfaction.

Added to this problem, taxes and loans had failed to meet the demands of the Treasury and an impost of five percent had been levied on importation's. Rhode Island and Georgia had refused to enact the measure, Virginia had voted for the measure, but had pulled its support, and it was feared that South Carolina was about to follow suit.

This was a grave issue to Morris. Without the impost, the country would certainly go bankrupt, and he had counted on the funds for a means to pay the troops as well. Greene, with a half-starved, unpaid, and discontented army, saw mutiny and bloodshed in the very near future. Greene was always known for his continued communication with the governors of the country and especially the

States in which his army was moving through, even if the governors were no longer in civil authority. Jefferson, Burke, Harrison, Mathews, and Rutledge had even been present in his camp and seen him in action. Now that civil government was growing stronger everyday, wouldn't it be prudent to seek the counsel of supporters?

Greene did not hesitate, and wrote to the governor on the 8th of March 1783, calling his attention to the threatening aspect of the army in its current condition, both in the north and the south. The practice could only be a weakness of the Congress and the necessity of supplying the army with the means of fulfilling contracts, he said: "If we have anything to apprehend, it is that the members of Congress will sacrifice the general interest to particular interests in the States to which they belong. . . .More to be dreaded from their exercising too little than too much power. The eyes of the army are turned upon the States in full expectation of it. It is well known that Congress have no revenue, and the measures of the States will determine the conduct."

The governor, in turn, sent Greene's letter to the Legislature, along with a letter written of his own, enforcing the opposite views of Greene. The members could hardly contain their anger at Greene, while the letter was read, cries of "A Cromwell," by some, "A Dictator," by others. "Can we not manage our own concerns?" Are we to be terrified by threats of mutiny and violence? Let us first be paid our advances and then let Congress, or its swordsmen, require this duty!"

Greene was not only deeply wounded, but also greatly surprised. "I find my letter to your Excellency has been greatly misapprehended by some of the members of that great Assembly. I did not conceive it inparliamentary to receive information from military men, and that stating probable consequences, was invading parliamentary freedom of debate and decision. . . .I thought I was in the way of my duty in making the representation. I think so still; and if my expressions were less guarded than they might have been, it was from a persuasion I both had and merited the confidence of the people."

But the governor and Legislature were not convinced, and South Carolina withdrew her acceptance of the impost, leaving Congress with no visible source of income, and scrambling to find another means of fulfilling its agreement with the army. "The people of this State," Greene wrote to Washington on the 16th of March 1783, "are much prejudiced against Congress and the financier. Those who came from the northward think they have been amazingly neglected by both in their distresses. This State has contributed more than any other State, it is true, towards Continental expenses; but necessity obliged them. I wish all the States could see how much the tranquillity of each depended upon giving effectual support to Congress."

Another incident occurred in April that brought Greene and the South Carolina government to blows. A British officer, a Captain Kerr, had married a Charleston woman, but had left without her when the British army evacuated the city. He returned to collect his wife and their belongings so they could sail to England, and rode into town under the protection of a flag of parlay, and reported directly to the commandant at the military post. When Governor Guerard learned of the incident, he received the news as an infringement on his authority, feeling the flag should have been addressed to him and not the military attaché. Governor Guerard sent the sheriff to arrest Captain Kerr and the crew of the vessel that had brought him. The astonished officer appealed to Greene, who promptly assured him of his protection. The governor persisted, leaving Greene no choice but to take immediate action. But before he proceeded to act, he called a council of war and laid the papers before them. "Has Captain Kerr violated any of the usages of a flag?" "No!" was the unanimous answer. Then taking possession of the passes to the city, he ordered that no flag should be admitted without permission from headquarters. Kerr was released, but, as if adding insult to injury, ordered to leave the city at once and the State within ten days; without his wife and possessions. He again appealed to Greene. "The order sent to you by the Governor," wrote Greene, "you will pay no regard to. When I am ready to discharge your flag I will inform you. The time and manner of your leaving the State shall be made as agreeable as possible. . . .I am exceeding unhappy at this last instance of indelicate treatment you have met with." To General Lincoln he wrote, asking that the subject be referred to Congress, and assuring him "that precedents for such encroachments on the United States authority should not be founded on his failure to resist them. Never was there such an idle dispute; none but a lunatic would have engaged in such an action."

The months continued to wear away slowly. When Cornwallis was defeated at Yorktown, it was assumed it would mean a speedy evacuation of Charleston, and then an early peace. But by the summer of 1782, Laurens doubted an early evacuation would take place.

Then came word of De Grasse being defeated. Greene thought he could expect another invasion of Carolina at any time. "Fortune seems to smile upon the perseverance of Great Britain," he wrote to Washington, "Count de Grasse's defeat appears to be much more important than I expected." But as June ended, overtures were made about the possibility of an armistice. It was partly for the State government to decide and partly a measure for Congress. Anxious as Greene was for peace, he feared that by granting the freedom of purchase, which the armistice proposed, it would prolong the stay of the enemy in South Carolina. It was also suspected, that advantage might be taken of it and prepare for an attack on the French in the West Indies. The proposal was refused.

July came and went and Greene continued to doubt that there would ever be an end to the war. "The people of this country have their expectations raised," he wrote to Washington. "and are sanquine in their hopes that Charleston will be speedily abandoned. There are some preparations on which their opinions are founded, but I must confess they seem to be rather contracting their works than abandoning the place."

Appearances were a more decided aspect of the goings on towards the end of August. "It is said," Greene writes to Washington, "that Captain Pigot is on this coast with near thirty sail of the line to take off the garrison of New York. A part of the fleet is to take post at Beaufort, to take off the garrison of Charleston. But it is also said the enemy within a few days past have been meditating an attack upon us." No attack came, and no sails were seen off the coast.

In October the evacuation is reduced to a certainty, and Greene consults Washington about the fortifications. "On our possessing Charleston, the fortifications will come under consideration. To leave the town without any fortifications, will render trade so unsafe as to be highly injurious to the public finances; besides, the perpetual alarm to which the inhabitants will be constantly exposed, will render their situation exceedingly disagreeable."

Doubts about peace seem to linger in Greene's mind. "Although our prospects are flattering, and peace appears to be approaching," he wrote to General Weedon, "yet we ought to move with circumspection, as the British will practice every art to deceive us. And could they humble the pride of France, they would soon return to the charge here. But this, I hope, they will not be able to effect, and from necessity be obliged to submit to peace on terms of independence to the United States."

The British lingered. There were many preparations to make and many interests to consult upon. For instance, there were a large number of slaves who had been drawn into service by the British and Americans. Eight hundred were employed in the American engineer department alone. Almost every officer over the rank of subaltern had a slave employed as his batman or servant. What was to happen to them? Greene was against sending them back to their owners, but was under heavy pressure from Washington and Congress to merchants in Charleston to return the slaves to their original owners. There were also large British interests at stake also; goods sold on credit and property held by marriage settlements and as dower. Leslie, "a humane and equitable man to deal with" Greene wrote, wanted to arrange these interests to both sides general satisfaction. At the suggestion of Governor Mathews, commissioners were appointed and an arrangement nominally reached, by which all slaves within the power of General Leslie were to be restored, except those that had "rendered themselves obnoxious by

336

services rendered the enemy, and such as had been expressly promised their freedom." When the day for enforcing the treaty came, it was found that, under one pretext or another, the British carried the greater part of the slaves away. This would have been fine if they had been carried to freedom, but it was asserted then, and never disproved to this day, that they had actually been sent to a worse bondage than befell them in South Carolina, but to a worse one in the West Indies.

Then on the 14th of December, 1782, the day many dreaded, and others yearned for had finally arrived. The morning guns exploded and awakened the city as it had since the occupation began. But this day was different, because British forces would never fire again. The troops were mustered into their lines, with the American lines waiting outside the city gates. At a particular signal the march began, the British first; Wayne with his 300 infantry, 80 of the Legion cavalry, and a detachment of 20 artillerists, with two 6-pounders, following at the distance of two hundred yards. They slowly moved down King Street road, straight through the city gates with the British calling out every now and then to the Americans, "You come to fast for us." Once within the gates they filed off to Gadsen's wharf, where their boats were waiting. By 11 0'clock that morning they were all on-board, and the American troops, entering, took their post at the State House.

At three that afternoon, Greene strode through town on horseback, escorting the governor and his council. An officer and 30 of Lee's dragoons led the van, as they had often led it into battle. Greene and Mathews rode next to each other. General Moultrie and Gist followed, then came the governors council, and last but not least the remaining citizens in joyful procession. As they passed along the streets, old men and women, young children, and young maidens with flowers, cried to the two officials, "Welcome," and "God Bless You, General." Handkerchiefs were waved and wreaths cast down from balconies and crowded windows. Several faces had tears rolling down their cheeks. Some were of joy, others disgrace and fear. At Broad Street the cavalcade dismounted to take each other by the hand, and then every man and women went his own way, only to start again.

The next morning the sunrise brought an awesome and wondrous sight. In the harbor were over three hundred ships lined at anchor, and swaying with the tide. The British ships were waiting to take the army away. A few hours later, thousands stood and watched as the forest of white sails spread in the breeze and turned seaward for the last time. By that afternoon, it seemed as if life was back to normal in the old city. But really, it never would be the same again.

So, the war had finally passed from the south. Now all Greene had to do was wait for the peace accord to be signed. But when? Negotiations had been going on in Paris for several months without an end in sight. Greene wrote in his journal on the 21st of December 1782; "I can not persuade myself to believe that after reestablishing her supremacy on the seas, England will lightly forego so good an opportunity to strike another blow. If we would strengthen the hands of our commissioners in Paris, we must prove that we are ready for war again if need be." Washington entertained the same doubts. They both remembered that when the alliance with the French came, they were received by the whole country as the assurance of peace, and the hope of an early end to the war. Men in Congress thought it foolish to plan for another campaign, even high ranking officers in the American army like Charles Lee and Gates. Only Washington and Greene continued to think of plans for another campaign. Here it was, almost eight years later, and the British leaving the south, and still both men's thoughts were on future campaigns against the British. Their prophecy would be known thirty years later in 1812.

The prospects still were not encouraging when Greene wrote to Washington in January of 1783, "all of the southern States are in deplorable condition, and will require a great deal of nursing and care to establish good government and give proper spur to agriculture and commerce. At present there are no courts of justice in any States, and it is dangerous traveling in almost every part of the country, from the great number of robbers and private plunderers that infest the roads. From these circumstances your Excellency can judge how feeble must be the efforts of a people in this situation, reduced to poverty by continual depredations."

A month passes and the South's prospects do not brighten. "By all intelligence accounts," he writes to Washington, "the British have sailed to the West Indies. The Hessians and such Provincial corps as remain, are in New York, which is not to be evacuated until spring; nor do I believe it will then, if the peace accord has not been signed. I am afraid the southern States can produce but few men in the field, by any possible exertion in their power. South Carolina and Georgia, I am sure, cannot. The enemy's force at St. Augustine is not contemptible, which, aided by the savages and the militia, now numerous from its being a place of resort for the Tories, may make a serious impression upon Georgia. That State, without considerable force to protect it for some time, cannot recover from the ravages it has felt, or even prosecute any trade or agriculture. Charleston will be stripped and left defenseless until new fortifications can be raised and cannon provided. In this situation, and being altogether uncertain of the enemy's future plan of operations, I hope it will not be thought that I have detained too many troops for the present."

Soon, Greene learned that he had offended Congress. He had gotten himself in trouble once again with a political body, because of his penchant for speaking his mind without reservation. "I am told a letter of mine, some time past," he wrote to Colonel Biddle, "gave offense to Congress, wherein I portrayed the real situation of the army and the States generally. When a man is largely in debt and his affairs in confusion, he is loath to look into them; but it is impossible to apply a remedy without a knowledge of them, and he that will not submit to the inquiry must soon be ruined. I am sure Congress has not a faster friend than I am, nor has few done more to promote their interest; but they had rather be flattered than informed, and I am too honest to do this, and therefore I shall never be one of their favorites. They may employ me because they find their account in it, but they don't love me, and therefore lay hold of every little circumstance to pick a quarrel with me. But I will not quarrel with them, nor will I give them any just ground to complain, either in matters of duty or respect. In time they will be convinced of the truth of my observations, and perhaps discover their prejudices."

Caty Greene was on her way to see her husband, who she had not seen in over a year and a half. Again, it would be without their children. But this time, there was a very good reason. Their oldest son, George, had been deathly ill throughout the long New England winter. Fortunately, with the help of Mrs. Greene and their friend the Pettit family, the young man had been nursed back to health, but was unable to travel yet. Greene desperately wanted to see his family, but knew the long trip south would be too much for the entire family and asked that Caty Greene come alone. When she was sure of young George Greene's well being, she quickly agreed and made off for Greene's camp in Charleston. By March of 1783, Caty Greene had finally reached camp, restoring a cheerfulness that had been sorely lacking in Nathanael's life. Greene was almost giddy by the arrival of his loving wife, and many of his correspondence of the time reflect it. "I have just returned from a ride with Mrs. Greene, who rides on horseback," he wrote to Williams, "Mrs. Greene is not in good health, mostly due to the long journey I think, but is gay. They call her the French lady in Charleston."

There is little else to relate of any historical interest at this point in the inactive war in the months that remained. A brief danger of the Tories moving up from St. Augustine and Greene went to Georgia to make preparations for meeting the enemy there. Another incident of mutiny also surfaced. A detachment of cavalry that was stationed at Eutaw Springs under the command of a Major Swan, became restless one day, due to the lack of food, proper clothing, and no rum. Swan went to Charleston to ask for Greene's instructions on what he may do, but on his way back, met the entire corps on the march under the lead of their sergeants; their officers were following them, but at a safe distance. When Swan came upon them, the officers joined him and they made a valiant attempt at turning them back to camp. They appealed to their sense of duty, a promise that they would go unpunished, and explained that the major had just met with General Greene and that he would do all that he could to alleviate the problems they were facing. The men agreed to return, under the condition that they would only stay for three more months. If the conditions did not improve by then, they would certainly march home without delay. It was agreed upon and the conditions were somewhat alleviated for the men.

At last, on the 16th of April, 1783, peace was officially declared. On the 22nd of that month, there was a general illumination in Charleston, and on the 23rd, fireworks and a *feu de joie* (Fire of Joy) with the firing of guns and cannon's and a gigantic bonfire was built on James' Island. The army was called upon to join in the celebration, but they had little food on which to feast.

The fears and discontent of the northern army had reached Greene from information known as the "Newburg letters," written by John Armstrong about the grievances of the soldiers toward Congress and calling for a general take over of the country by the military. They were later discovered and addressed by Washington. Greene found them deeply alarming. He knew that some of the men with which he had served, believed that the only way of obtaining justice for the army from Congress and the States, was by a union of the army with all the public creditors." Greene actually sympathized with most of their beliefs, but felt there must certainly be a better way to accomplish their demands than declaring marshal law. "That Congress have not powers," wrote Gouverneur Morris, "I see, I feel, and I lament. If the foreign war, that great friend of sovereign authority, ceases, I have no hope, no expectation that the government will acquire force. I will go further, I have no hope that our union can subsist, except in the form of an absolute monarchy."

Greene shuddered at the idea of bringing in the army as a means of influencing the civil authority. Even Washington had written, "The patience and long sufferance of this army are almost exhausted, and there never was so great a spirit of discontent as at this instant." The main reason for the discontent was that an act of Congress had passed in October of 1780 that would give half-pay for life to those officers that had served in the army. But subsequent rumblings and events had made it evident that the funds for such a payment would never be voted on, let alone approved by all of the States. A committee was established with General Alexander McDougal named as chairman. The committee was sent to the various States to ask; if the payment was commuted from the half-pay for life to a single definite payment, would they then approve the measure? It would have been far more effective for Congress, if they had commuted the half-pay for life to five years of half-pay, which would have easily been agreed on. But instead they waited until the Newburg letters were released before addressing the issue.

Now the troops were beginning to ask when they would be discharged. "The war is over," they cried, "and we enlisted only for the duration of the war. When can we go home?" The problem escalated so badly in Greene's camp, that he went so far as to call out a detachment of Continental infantrymen to roll out a 8-pound cannon in plain sight of the mutinous rabble. They loaded it with canister shot, and had a man stand-by with a lit linstock pole, and prepared to fire at Greene's command. The troops, knowing Greene was not one to trifle with, especially when it came to duty and honor, backed down. All, except a hundred of the Virginia cavalry, who threw caution to the wind and began to march homeward, with a Sergeant Dangerfield at their lead, taking with them all of the choice horses that were in camp. They counted on a full pardon when the reached their home State, and found it when they arrived, much to the chagrin of Greene. By this example, he knew that the cases of troops marching home would increase, knowing there would be no retribution.

Soon after the incident, orders finally arrived from Washington to dismiss all of the troops on furlough. A small fraction of the pay they were promised was advanced. The North Carolina regiments and Virginians marched home to be furloughed. The Pennsylvanians and Marylanders were sent by ship, but they had so much difficulty obtaining transports for all of the men that it was early July, 1783 before they all embarked. A third of the troops who were already on the sick list, deserted, rather than

339

take the chance of suffering the deadly fever again, but desertion carried with it complete forfeiture of pay. One of Greene's last official acts as Commander of the Southern army was to write farewell letters to the governors of the States comprised in his command. As so often happened with Greene, he could not keep himself from imparting one last jab on those public figures. For while he congratulated them on this great time in the country's history and the return of peace, he also called their attention to the debt he felt they owed to the army. "Often," he wrote to them, "in the worse of times, have I assured you that the country would not be unmindful of the army's suffering and services; and humbly, yet confidently, do I hope that their just claims will not be forgotten."

And so, gradually the actors in this monumental play pass on into history. Officers like; Huger, who returned to his plantation. Sumter, who had resigned months before, would hold bitterness in his heart for Greene until making several vindictive comments over Greene's grave. Marion moved on to years of honors and domestic bliss. William Washington found a home in South Carolina and contentment. Burnet and Pearce went into business together, but both died soon after. Morris, lived up to Greene's prognostication that he would succeed in a "left-handed courtship and become a planter." Pendleton became an attorney. Williams married, went into business with his Father-in-law, but never fully recovered from his illness while in the service of the southern campaign and died some months later. Howard returned to Maryland and had a long and storied career in politics. Henry Lee went back to his family home in Virginia, married, and lived with adversity the remainder of his days. But one of Light-horse Harry's descendants would once again be involved with war in the Southern States almost a century later. The noble Kosciusko passes on to a broader field. He becomes the leader of his oppressed nation, triumphs marvelously, only to be crushed by overwhelming numbers, dies in exile, and is buried in a sepulcher in Warsaw, along with the rest of the kings of Poland.

Chapter XXXIV

"After the Peace, the
Road Back to Rhode Island"

For eight years now, Greene had never laid his head down on his pillow without thinking about what lay ahead when he awoke the next morning. He had not risen from his bed without feeling the burden of responsibility with each passing day. Now, his days were his again. Free to come and go as he pleased, without the duties of a major general to be fulfilled. He could finally play the role he had first set out to do; a husband and father. Too long had he been the absentee father and relished the thought of playing and teaching his children everyday. Yet, those first few weeks must have been a very tough adjustment period for Nathanael. To wake up now and ask himself; "What is my first care of the day?" he wrote in his journal. He had made up his mind years before that he would now remain, forever more, a private citizen. Never to claim the role as wartime hero or seek public office. Instead, he would become a planter, as well as bring his estate matters, that were long overdue, back into focus. He and his wife decided to divide the year between Rhode Island and Georgia. He would see friends in his home, but rarely travel to visit. He wanted to direct the affairs of a plantation, to watch over the education of his children, to indulge in his passion of books, and from his hard fought, quiet retreat, look out on a busy world and observe the progress of public events and not be involved with them. When Greene was on the last of the transports ferrying men home he took it as the signal for the beginning of his personal freedom from that time forward.

Many of his officers were in dire need, and they turned to him for help. As was his nature in war, so it would be in private life. Only when he was finished providing for his men was he at liberty to provide for himself. When he had completed the arrangement in South Carolina that provided for the men in need, he made a short visit to Georgia to inquire into the condition of his estate there. With his personal secretary, Major Hyrne, and one of his aides, Edwards, as companions, he finally set out northward and eventually, home. He continued to outline his daily routine in his journal. What better way to relate that trip then by allowing Greene to tell you in his own words.

"August 15, 1783.--We lodged this night at Colonel Horry's plantation on the Santee. His farmhouse is one of the most spacious as well as convenient I have met with in my travels. The plantation is upon the Santee, and finely cultivated.

August 19.--We left Georgetown today, which stands on a tongue of land, formed by three great rivers, the Pedee, Black River, and the Waccamaw on one side, and a small river called the Sampet Creek on the other. It was burnt by the enemy in 1781. It is well situated for trade, and in time will be considerable again. Ours horses had been sent up to Mr. Joseph Allston's, and Colonel Hamit was kind enough to furnish us with a fast sailing canoe to convey us up there by water. But Hamit would not let us pass his plantation without taking a look at his indigo works in all the pride of his wealth, melting under the scorching sun, and almost suffocating with the disagreeable smell of the place. Edwards got out of all patience, and I was afraid would not preserve his good breeding. However we left the Colonel in the most perfect good-humor. Our passage up to Mr. Allston's was pleasant and our arrival critical; for the moment we got into the house there came on a heavy shower. Mr. Allston gave us a cordial reception and regaled us with fine old wine.

August 22.--We set out for Wilmington, having poverty before us and leaving plenty behind us; and rode sixteen miles to Learward's Ferry. Edwards was taken with a fever, and Hyrne and he,

between them, led us in the party out of the way five or six miles. Edwards was very sick and with difficulty got to Wilmington, where we found good quarters and better cheer than we had met in our journey since leaving
Mr. Allston's.

August 27 & 28.-- We remained at Colonel Blount's for the recovery of my horse. His house is agreeable situated near the river Contentment, which runs a great distance into the country. His farm is large and fortune considerable.

August 29.--We set out for Halifax and lodged at Colonel Hardy's, and old gentleman who had lived with one wife upwards of fifty years, and was near eighty years of age. From this to Tarborough the country is hilly; generally pretty good land and very healthy. The people here would take no money from us.

August 31.--We arrived in Halifax after meeting a number of officers and citizens on the road who conducted us how to find Colonel Ashe's lodgings. Halifax is a little village, containing fifty to sixty houses, on the banks of the Roanoke, one hundred miles from the sea, and promises at some future day to be a considerable place.

September 3.--We left Halifax accompanied by a number of both officers and citizens. During our stay in Halifax there had fallen a considerable body of rain and there was a remarkable change in the air. The thermometer fell from 90 degrees to 58. This made the riding cool and the roads delightful. Our passage through North Carolina had been rendered as agreeable as possible by the polite attention of the inhabitants. It will be a long time before this State will begin to feel its importance.

September 4.--Arrived in Petersburg and breakfasted at Mr. Clevey's. This is a religious family and the happy fruits are visible in everything about them. This man affects a general acquaintance with the British nobility, and says he knew the king when he was a boy, and that his appearance was always more like a showblack than a royal prince. We stayed the day and talked with this man who wrote letters, was a good man and a natural genius. We had a genteel supper and spent the evening sociably.

September 5.--We left Petersburg for Richmond. Trade flourishes here, but the place is very sickly. Many families of distinction live in the neighborhood of this place, but few or none in it. Tobacco and flour are the great staples of trade at this place. The roads from Petersburg to this place are very uneven, not less so than the Northern States.

September 6.--We went this evening to Richmond, the capital of Virginia. The governor was out of town, but the corporation met and presented me with a polite address, and an invitation to a public dinner. I had the pleasure of seeing Clairborne, formerly one of my family in the staff. He was not altered, being as formal as ever.

September 8.--We set out for Frericksburg and lodged at Mr. John Baylor's, a man of considerable property, naturally very covetous and yet ostensibly generous. A great macaroni in dress, and was once the head of the Macaroni Club in London. He possesses middling abilities and a rather morose temper. But what makes me have a rather disagreeable opinion of the man is having witnessed how he treated his wife very ill, and who is a very agreeable woman. Edwards was so taken about by him that he mortified him by exaggerating his South Carolina fortunes.

September 9--We got to Fredericksburg, but dined by the way at General Spotwood's whose lady appeared to be an excellent breeder. General Weedon received us with open arms, and would not let us leave on the next day or the day after.

September 12.-- Set out for Mount Vernon, General Washington's seat. Within a few miles of Dumfires I overset my carriage, broke the top and harness and bruised myself not a little, but if I had not lifted up the carriage and let it pass over me, it is probable I might have killed or badly wounded myself, for the horse started upon a run and drawed the carriage after him until the harness gave way. I did fell the hurt at first, but even more afterwards.

September 13.--We dined at Mount Vernon, one of the most beautiful situations in the world. The house has more dignity than convenience in it. Nature never formed a finer landscape than may be seen at this seat. The Potomac River in full view, with several little bays and creeks. The plain and the hills, joined to the features of the waters, forms a most beautiful scene. Mr. Lund Washington, his lady, and Doctor Stewart and Miss Basset, were at the seat. We stayed and dined and then set out for Alexandria. hat evening I was taken very ill with a fever, after my arrival, which lasted me, with very little remission and no intermission, eight days.

September 21.--Finally I am well enough to travel. But before I take my leave of Virginia I cannot help remarking that the ladies appear to be brought up and educated with habits of industry and attention to domestic affairs, while the gentlemen attend to little but leasure and dissipation. This State is powerful in numbers, rich in revenue, and yet weak and poor. Its extent is the great difficulty of governing it properly. A want of a spirit of union perplexes their politics and weakens their counsels.

September 24.--We set out for Annapolis; dined and lodged at Mr. Deggs'. Governor Lee married his daughter, an only child. She is one of the most agreeable women in the world. She has the most interesting countenance I ever saw. Nature seems to have formed her to animate and please. Governor Lee is little less engaging than she is.

September 25.--We got to Annapolis and dined at the tavern. Major Jennifer invited me to take lodgings with him. Here I had the pleasure of seeing the celebrated Mrs. Loyd. She is a most elegant woman, but not so perfect a beauty as from some of my imagination had formed of her. The propriety of her conduct is not less remarkable than her beauty."

Much of the road that now lay before Greene was much more familiar, having reconnoitered it during the eventful campaign of 1777. He crossed the Brandywine, the site of his first test as a commander, and then on to Wilmington, where he stopped to rest. Greene had passed over the Brandywine three times before; once in advance, once in retreat, and the other on his journey to take command of the southern army. It must have felt considerably more pleasant to feel a lack of doubt and danger on this passage. After Wilmington, he took the road to Philadelphia, past Chester, and within cannon shot of Fort Mifflin. Here, soldiers and citizens learned of his arrival and came out in throngs to meet him. The streets into the city were crowded, the windowsills bursting. Children climbed walls and trees to get a glimpse of the general. But not a sound was heard. No cheers, no screams of joy. Only a vast crowd, solemnly silent, and merely gazing at him as if looking at a statue. The people must have only been recalling what he had done for them in the turning point of the war. When he reached the door of the hotel at which he had planned to stay, a sudden, long, loud shout arose at once. "Long life to Greene! Honor to the Victor of the South!" "It was then," wrote one of his aides who heard it, "I thought his triumph complete."

Congress was at Princeton, where it had been sent due to the disgraceful mutiny of the Pennsylvania line. Greene was anxious to close the business of his department and go home, and so he followed them there. He could not pass through Trenton without greeting his old friend Colonel Cox. Washington had just arrived a few seconds before and was still on the stairs to his room when Greene arrived. Washington grasped Greene's hand and held it, not saying a word. Then Greene embraced his commander-in-chief and wept openly. After a time, Washington stood back and wiped the tears from his face and said to Greene, "The trip northward must have been agreeable. You appear to be filled out."

The next day the two old friends set out together for Princeton. There is no record of the trip, for what material for conversation there must have been on every step of the way. Little did they know that it would be the last time they would ever journey together. A rider met them on the road to offer an invitation from the President of Congress to an informal dinner.

With a different feeling from any that Greene had ever experienced before in writing to him, Greene wrote to the President of Congress for the last time, October 7th, 1783:--"I beg leave to inform Congress that I have just arrived from my southern command, the business of which, I hope, has been closed agreeable to their intention, in furloughing all the soldiers and putting a stop to every Continental expense. It is now going on nine years since I have had an opportunity to visit my family or friends, or pay the least attention to my private fortune. I wish, therefore, for the permission of Congress to go to Rhode Island, having already obtained the consent of the Commander-in-chief."

In reply Congress resolved, "that a committee inquire and report a suitable expression of the approbation of Congress, of the general's conduct in his late command." The committee was composed of Mr. Madison, Ellery, and Duane, and reported their findings on the 18th of October. That two pieces of the field ordnance taken from the British army at the Cowpens, Augusta, or Eutaw, be presented by the Commander-in-chief of the armies of the United States, to Major-general Greene, as a public testimonial of the wisdom, fortitude, and military skill which distinguished his command in the southern department, and of the eminent services which amidst complicated difficulties and dangers, and against an enemy greatly superior in numbers, he has successfully performed for his country; and that a memorandum be engraved on said pieces of ordnance, expressive of the substance of this resolution."

"Resolved, That the Commander-in-chief be informed that Major-general Greene has the permission of Congress to visit his family at Rhode Island."

Greene then wrote to the President of Congress that "The letters and miscellaneous papers containing a history of the southern operations, which are now in my hands, may contain something which Congress or their officers may have some occasion to have recourse to. Loose files are easily disordered, and where they are frequently inspected the papers sometimes get lost. If the Congress should think it an object worthy the expense, and would indulge my wishes, I should be glad to get the whole papers properly arranged and transcribed into bound books.

Congress offered to "furnish General Greene with a clerk to copy into a book or books, the papers or letters in his possession relative to the southern operations; and that the record thereof be lodged in the Secretary's office."

The original plan was not fully carried out. But a selection from Greene's dispatches were copied and fitted into two folio type volumes which are preserved in the archives of the United States Department of State.

At last, Greene was able to make the final leg of his journey home. One of the first letters he wrote, once he was home, was a letter to Governor Samuel Greene: "I arrived at this place night before last, and am happy to set foot once more on the land of my nativity." Here for the first time he saw all his children together and received more honors and thanks from his Home State. Newport and Providence, along with other towns throughout the State presented him with addresses of thanks and congratulations for a job well done. But none, perhaps, touched him more than the addresses from East Greenwich and Coventry, and the welcome of his old comrades from the Kentish Guards, where he had started out in 1775 as an infantry private. The long journey from those days of marching to Massachusetts after the battle of Lexington and Concord, must have seemed like another world away. Varnum, their first colonel, had done great service to their name as a brigadier-general. Christopher Greene, their first major, had distinguished himself at Quebec, had won the honorable title of hero at the battle of Fort Mercer, and now lay in a shallow grave on the banks of the Hudson. Now the ranks were filled with new faces, mixed with some old, and ready to continue the work they had begun. As he looked out on the well-known streets filled with people that he had known all his life, he knew, he had finally come home.

But Nathanael knew his work had not been completed and was a long way from resting. While he was in Philadelphia on his trip north, he had devoted a portion of the time there to the examination and settlement of his public accounts; which had been meticulously kept by his secretaries. With the exception of two or three points, which required special legislation, the remainder was easily arranged. But his private accounts were another matter completely. The forges that the family had run in Potowomut and Conventry had been run by his brothers while he was away. All of Greene's property at the beginning of the war had been invested in the family firm when he entered the army, and he had used this as the chief means of supporting his family in that time. Jacob, the oldest brother, had gone to Conventry to live. However, when he did that, he left many of the duties to his younger siblings who had not pursued business with the same fervor Jacob had. Also, many businesses had made large fortunes in the form of speculating and privateering, trades that are looked on in disgust today, but considered good business in the late eighteenth century. The Greene brothers were anything but trained in such tactics, and were ill prepared for such business dealings. Instead, they continued to run the business as they always had, investing large amounts of money in share holds in different vessels until the end of the war. In 1778 the property of the firm was divided with Greene's brother Jacob, and his cousin Griffin managing Nathanael's portion of the investment. As the years passed, the expenses of a major general in the army and the irregularity of his pay from the family business, caused a serious drain on the small fortune he had accumulated before the war.

While Greene was quartermaster-general, he had no stocks to invest in at that time. The governments credit was running low, and many times he was forced to use his own private funds to supplement orders for the army that merchants would not offer with promises of Continental money, which was nearly useless by that time. He thought of going into private business for himself, but found no time to run it. Under those circumstances he was approached by Colonel Wadsworth, commissary-general, and Barnabas Deane of Connecticut, to form a firm under the name of Barnabas Deane & Co. Greene and Wadsworth supplied the greater amount of capital for Deane to undertake the management of the business. Greene also put other sums of money the hands of his friends Colonel Cox and Colonel Pettit, both of whom had been businessmen before the war to invest for him. But none of these investments did al that well and returned little in the way of fortunes.

In all respects, when Nathanael Greene crossed from major general to private citizen, he was broke. He knew he could not go back to Warwick to live. But he had to do something to provide for his family and their future. At one time, he entertained the idea of forming a partnership with Colonel Wadsworth, and living in New York. But soon after this, an acknowledgment of his service to the southern States was about to be bestowed upon him from South Carolina and Georgia. From South Carolina, the sum of 50,000 L sterling, and from Georgia, a plantation located on the banks of the Savannah River that had originally been the home of the last Royal Lieutenant Governor of Georgia, John Graham. In 1776, the area was controlled by militia and independent patriots called "The Liberty Boys," and Graham decided it was time to go back to England where it would be safer. In 1783, the Georgia government seized the property, declaring it Loyalist land and presented it to Greene for his military services.

Greene was overwhelmed by the generous present. Mulberry Grove had a substantial house that Graham had built in 1778 and the land that surrounded it was far greater than the property he had purchased in South Carolina; 2,141 acres as opposed to just over 700. But with the expanse of land that Greene was deeded came a perplexing question that would have to be addressed. Plantations in the south were so huge that they had to have an enormous labor force to run it or the land would wither and die, leaving the property not only profitless, but also worthless. A labor force that large could only be collected inexpensively in one way. The labor force Greene needed, would have to be made up of slave labor. Greene was perplexed and was said to have come down with an anxiety attack over the question.

"Could I become a slaveholder?" he wrote in his journal. "As for slavery, nothing can be said in its defense," he later wrote to a Quaker friend, who had been upset when Nathanael had forsaken his Quaker training by taking part in a war, but now he was contemplating accepting people as property. "But you are much mistaken respecting my influence in this business. With all the address I was master of, I could not obtain the liberty of a small number, even for the defense of the country; and though the necessity stood confessed, yet the motion was rejected. The generosity of the Southern States has placed an interest of this sort in my hands, and I trust their condition will not be worse or better."

In another letter, written to Greene by a Dr. Gordon, a historian of the time, "I shall rejoice to hear that you have tried and succeeded in the plan of admitting the Negroes to the rights of copy-holders, which, if it could be once effected, might possibly tend to their increasing so as to render further importation's of those people needless. Could you by your example, prove instrumental in demolishing slavery and the importation of negroes, I should think you rendered the human species nearly as much service as when you were fighting successfully against the British attempts to reduce the white inhabitants of America to the hard condition of slaves."

That plan, of which Dr. Gordon speaks, is nowhere to be found in any archives. The details may have been still in the planning stage when the tragedy that was soon to befall Greene prevented it from being implemented. The fact of the matter is, Greene received and purchased slaves to work on his Mulberry Grove plantation, and for this behavior there are no excuses. Like so many plantation owners before, during, and until the Civil War, Greene acknowledged the power of profit, over the rights of human beings.

The disgraceful business of slave labor aside, Greene hired a caretaker and foreman to look after his Georgia plantation while he turned his attention to conducting business in the north. He believed that his life would take on an air of domestic calm, now that the anxiety of how to provide for his family had been taken care of finally. He remained in the house at Warwick for now, content on the pleasures of his books and seeing friends and the mere sight of his children growing up around him. He had planned to rent a small house in Newport, until all of his business dealings could be straighten out before making the trip south.

But the momentary calm was short lived, when one day the name John Banks was heard once again. While Greene had become security for the house of Hunter & Banks, in order to enable those two men to fulfill their contract for feeding the army, it seems the bills had been deposited with Mr. Pettit for Greene's protection. But Greene was astonished when he learned that those same bills had been withdrawn by Banks and applied for other purposes, most likely for some illegal gain. Whatever transpired, the result was that the money was gone and the bills unpaid. Word had come that John Banks had died, and he was bankrupt. Burnet, who had also become connected with Banks and Greene in business, died. The responsibility of all those unpaid bills fell on Greene. An effort was launched by some members of the firm to do something for the relief of some of the responsibility to Greene, but it was unsuccessful. Creditors, knowing Greene did not have an original interest in the contract beyond the shear desire to feed his starving army and protect the citizens of Charleston from the violence that starving soldiers could have caused, still came to him for full payment of the debt. He was forced to sell, at a great loss of profit, his estate in South Carolina, and would have to confine his operations as a planter to the property in Mulberry Grove, Georgia. He was then forced to make long journeys back and forth to Philadelphia to untangle himself from the meshes of the law, and struggle with the embarrassment of all that the business entailed.

Had American credit in Europe been better, he may have been successful finding a loan which would have enabled him to carry out his plans for the improvement of the Mulberry Grove plantation, and within a few years have enabled him in meeting his debt obligations. But European capitalist looked with distrust on the weak handed confederation, and American capitalists had other use for their

346

money. After a long struggle of daily embarrassment, he addressed a statement of the whole transaction, expressing the hope that if all of the other modes of relief should fail; Congress would back him for losses incurred during a public cause.

Greene sold the house in Warwick to his brother, attempting to gather the necessary funds for his debts. He decided it was time to move to Newport, a stately house by an old stone mill which gave the street it name, Mill Street. This would be Greene's home for the better part of his stay in Rhode Island. He had many visitors to the house when he wasn't down south. Men like Kosciusko, von Steuben, and Lafayette visited. Greene and his family also made frequent trips back to Potowomut, Warwick, and Coventry to visit Caty's Aunt and Nathanael's family and his friends, like Samuel Ward. During these days, Greene fought with the decision of staying in his ancestral home or pick up and move down to Mulberry Grove permanently.

People were still clamoring for him to seek public office. In March of 1784, he was appointed one of five commissioners to negotiate a peace with the Native Americans. But he had resolved never to serve in public office. So he declined the nomination and asked to have his name withdrawn from any other consideration in the future. He lived the next two years in-between Mulberry Grove and Rhode Island. Then in 1786, he was appointed assistant judge of his county in Georgia. Again, he respectfully refused the appointment. That was not to say that Greene was no longer interested in public events. The five- percent impost, which had given him so much trouble in South Carolina, was now rearing its ugly head in Rhode Island. "I shall try by all possible measures," he wrote Robert Morris, "to bring this State into the general plan of finance, but it will take time, and in order to bring the thing about, I believe it will be necessary to get it to pass the Assembly under a qualified sense, which will be the groundwork of its finally passing agreeably to the plan of Congress. Nothing more can be done than this, and to urge it will defeat the whole."

While on one of his many trips south, Greene writes to Washington while traveling through South Carolina. "In this country many discontents prevail. Committees are formed and correspondences going on, if not of a treasonable nature, highly injurious to the tranquillity and well being of the people. The obstinacy of Rhode Island and the tardiness of some other States seem to be a message for more mischief. However, I can but hope that good sense of the people will correct our policy in time to avoid new convulsions. But I have spoken to many people who secretly wish that every State should be completely independent, and that as soon as our public debts are liquidated, that Congress should be no more;--a plan that would be fatal to our happiness at home as it would be ruinous to our interest abroad."

Although made president of the State Society for Rhode Island, Greene never took an active part in their meetings or any other actions involved with the group. It was thought that they merely used his name as a banner to recruit other high ranking officials to the group and provided Greene was a small stipend for the right to carry his name with their insignia.

Another duty that Greene was often asked to perform was mediator. Many of the officers who had served under him found themselves unable to discharge the debts they had incurred from the lack of pay while in the army, and the men appealed to him for some aid. Greene loaned or gave away a large amount of his cash in dozens of small sums, adding to his own personal financial difficulties. But Greene felt an obligation to the men. He had seen to their health and well being for so long, it was impossible to stop now.

On the other side of the coin, Greene also had to endure the penalties of those officers who had thought themselves wronged by their commanding officer. Back in 1782, a Captain Gunn had been involved with exchanging public horses with cavalry mounts. In one instance he traded a public horse with Captain Armstrong of Lee's legion, for two private horses and a slave. Greene had ordered a court of inquiry into the matter. To his surprise, the court justified the exchange, and called upon Greene to approve the court's decision. Greene saw it differently and disapproved of the court's findings, ordered the horses and slave be returned, and referred the whole question to Congress with the recommendation that Captain Gunn be censured. Congress agreed with Greene and Gunn had considered Greene his sworn enemy ever since. Gunn had settled in Georgia, married a lady of considerable wealth, and had entered public life. When Greene was on one of his numerous trips to Mulberry Grove, Gunn sent him a challenge to a duel through Colonel Jackson, Gunn's friend. Greene still harbored the personal responsibility of a commanding officers duty in relation to subordinates. The idea of Greene accepting the challenge of Gunn, his subordinate, would be a breach in military etiquette. He immediately refused the challenge and sent Jackson back to deliver the message to Gunn. When Gunn learned of the refusal he sent Jackson back with another challenge, but when Jackson found out what the feud was all about, he declined to be Gunn's messenger any longer. A Major Fishburne was found as the new messenger and delivered the challenge to Greene once again. Again Greene refused and persisted in his refusal over several weeks. Finally, Gunn sent word to Greene that "he would attack him whenever he met him." Greene smirked and said, "Tell him that I shall always carry both of my pistols; and that I'm quite handy with them." In fact, Greene was one of only a few officers in the Revolutionary War to carry pistols as well as his hanger and was known to be a terrific marksman. Gunn was known to steer clear of Greene from that time forward and they never met. Greene was afraid that people would look at him as a coward and wrote to Washington for advice. "As I may have mistaken the line of responsibility of a commanding officer, I wish for your sentiments on the subject."

Washington responded; "Under the state of the case between you and Captain Gunn, I give it as my decided opinion, that your honor and reputation will stand not only perfectly acquitted for the non-acceptance of his challenge, but that your prudence and judgment would have been condemned for accepting it; because if a commanding officer is amenable to private calls for the discharge of his public duty; he has a dagger always at his breast; and can turn neither to the right or to the left without meeting its point."

In late autumn of 1785, Greene had finally made the arrangements that would establish his family and himself at Mulberry Grove. In the winter months, the family would live at Mulberry Grove and the summer months would be spent in Rhode Island. The entire family packed up and sailed to Georgia. His children wrote years later about how their father called them up on deck one day and took them to the quarter-deck to watch a pod of whales that was passing close to the vessel. But, the trip was also a long a perilous journey of sixteen days, instead of the usual nine days. The ship ran into a late season hurricane and was tossed and turned about for days, in which one crewman was lost at sea when he fell overboard. Greene was said to have tried to save the man by throwing him a line, but the waves overtook the man and swallowed him whole. The rest of the trip was uneventful and the vessel eventually arrived in Savannah safely.

The family settled into their new dwelling and began to make it comfortable. Greene describes his new domestic life in Georgia in a letter to his friend Ethan Clarke of Newport, husband of Anna Ward. The first woman he had fallen in love with but could not win her heart. "We found the house, situation, and out buildings, more convenient and pleasing than we expected. The prospect is delightful, and the house magnificent. We have a coach-house and stables, a large out kitchen, and a poultry-house nearly fifty feet long, and twenty feet wide, parted for different kinds of poultry, also a pigeon-house on the top, which will contain not less than a thousand pigeons. Besides these, are several other buildings convenient for the family, and among the rest, a fine smokehouse. The garden is in ruins, but there are still a great variety of shrubs and flowers in it."

In addition to the supervising of his plantation, Greene was also busy preparing to employee the cutting of timber on nearby Cumberland Island, which he had purchased a large interest. On one of his visits to the island he was led to St. Augustine, where he was received with full military honors and was attended to by a guard of honor. Nearby, was the plantation of his friend Anthony Wayne, who had also received his property from the State of Georgia as a gift for his military services. In Savannah, just a day's ride from Mulberry Grove, his former aid, James Pendleton was in business for himself. The library in the plantation house was filled with his books, and between the letters he wrote and received, he was always busy with his pen. Then there was the shear delight he had at watching his children working and playing. He cherished the evenings when he could hold them on his knee and read to them. All the carefree thoughts and humor of his youth in Rhode Island came back to him through their eyes. A friend who visited the family wrote later that "General Greene was partial to the game Puss in the Corner; which he played with his wife and young daughter Patty (Martha)." Greene's youngest son Nat (Nathanael) later described him "as a tall man, who used to take me on his knee and teach me funny songs."

Greene writes another letter to Clarke describing the inroads with the plantation. "This is a busy time with us, and I can afford but a small portion of time to write you. We are planting. We have got upwards of sixty acres of corn planted, and expect to plant one hundred and thirty acres of rice soon. The garden is now delightful. The fruit-trees and flowering shrubs form a pleasing variety. We have green peas almost fit to eat, and as fine lettuce as ever you saw. The mockingbirds surround us evening and morning. The weather is mild, and the vegetable kingdom progressing to perfection. But it is a great deduction from the pleasure we should feel from the beauties and conveniences of the place, that we are obligated to leave it before we shall have tasted of several kinds of fruit. We have in the same orchard apples, pears, peaches, apricots, nectarines, plums of different kinds, figs, pomegranates, and oranges. And we have strawberries which measure three inches round. All these are clever, but the want of our friends to enjoy them with us renders them less interesting."

On the 12th of June 1786, he was called to Savannah to meet a Mr. Collet, one of the creditors associated with John Banks. His wife Caty was with him, and they had planned to pass the evening at Captain Pendleton's house. The next morning they started out early, intending to take breakfast and spend the day with a Mr. William Gibbons, who lived on the plantation just below Mulberry Grove. As a prospective rice planter, Greene was curious to see Gibbons fields of rice, and on Tuesday afternoon, the 13th of June, disregarding the intense heat of the day, Greene and Gibbons walked out to inspect the fields. His host had a servant follow him with an umbrella, but Greene being the old soldier, refused such treatment, and wore only a tricorn of straw, little defense from the brutal, afternoon Georgia sun. On his way home from his neighbors he complained to his wife that he had a terrible headache. On Wednesday, the next morning when he awoke, he was still suffering from it, and suggested it was from his asthma, which had been giving him fitful sleep the last few nights. He was still in extreme pain on Wednesday night, with no one even suggesting that it may be heatstroke, which was known and common in that day. On Thursday the 15th, the pain was so intense over his eyes he could not get out of bed, and there was the evident swelling of his forehead. That night Major Pendleton arrived, and was struck by Greene's terrible depression, and "unlike the General, did not want to engage in conversation." He communicated his concerns to Caty Greene, and a physician was immediately sent for. The physician, also saw nothing of the effects of sunstroke, and with the usual treatment for everything in the late eighteenth century, bled him a little with some leaches, and administered a few other common remedies, and then left.

The next morning the heatstroke had done its worst and Greene's head was greatly swollen, and the inflammation had spread to his shoulders, arms, and torso. Greene was drifting in and out of consciousness and complaining that he was on fire. Caty Greene brought in a second physician who immediately recognized the illness and began to apply a blister agent. Blood was drawn in pints, and all that could be done now was wait. To keep the house perfectly still, the children were sent to a neighbor's plantation, and no servants were permitted to the second floor unless called by the doctor.

Wayne soon arrived, but was seen to speak not a word and only weep silently. That night the doctor related in his journal that "the sick man sank into a stupor," probably a coma, "a state that no science could return him from." The family was permitted in to see him and the room was filled with friends and family who openly wept together, waiting out the inevitable result. Saturday and Sunday came and went with no change in Nathanel's condition. All through Sunday and into the night Wayne stood by his bedside. Towards dawn on Monday morning the dying man's heavy breathing grew fainter. By six o'clock on the 19th of June, 1786, the breathing stopped.

"I have often wrote you," wrote Wayne to Colonel James Jackson that morning, "but never on so distressing an occasion. My dear friend General Greene is no more. He departed this morning at six o'clock A.M. He was as great a soldier, greater as a citizen, immaculate as a friend. His corpse will be at Major Pendleton's home this night, the funeral from thence in the evening. The honors, the greatest honors of the war are due his remains. You, as a soldier, will take the proper order on this melancholy affair. Pardon this scrawl; my feelings are but too much affected because I have seen a great and good man die."

A messenger was dispatched to Savannah with the news. Men stood and stared when they heard it, because just a few days before, many of them had seen him walking those same streets in perfect health. He was only forty-four, young even by eighteenth century standards. His wife was inconsolable, wracked with grief, she had to be administered to by a physician. "There was still so much to do," Caty Greene kept crying, "we are in the perilous days. Who could supply his place?"

Hasty preparations were made for military honors for Greene's body. Tuesday morning the coffin was brought down the river, and landed in front of the house of Major Pendleton, the very house from which he had started six days before, on his fatal ride home. The militia of Chatham County, and a large concourse of citizens were gathered there to receive them. Minute guns were firing from Fort Wayne as they were put on shore. In the town there was silence and deep sorrow. The streets were deserted and all of the shops were closed. All the shipping in the harbor set their colors at half-mast. All of the inhabitants "suspended their ordinary occupations," who gathered in mournful procession. The light-infantry with reversed arms conducted the corpse to the left of the regiment, then filed off, right and left, to the front of the battalion. The dragoons took their place on the flanks of the coffin. And then the march began; the artillery in the fort firing minute guns as the long line advanced, and the band played a solemn dirge. The drums were muffled and gave a woeful sound. When they reached the burial ground at Christ Episcopal Church, the Graham vault that belonged to the former owner of Mulberry Grove, John Graham, was used. The regiment filed off to the right and left, resting on their arms, and facing the vault, until the coffin and pallbearers and long train of mourners had passed through. The Honorable William Stevens, in the absence of a clergyman, took his stand by the head of the coffin, and with a trembling voice read the funeral service of the Church of England. When the body was placed in the vault, it was discovered that a body was already inside. It was the remains of a British officer, a Lieutenant Colonel John Maitland from Scotland, who had died during the siege of Savannah. Thinking it wrong to have a dead British soldier lying in the grave with one of Americas greatest military hero's of the time, it was decided that they would remove the British officer after the mourners left, and would re-bury Maitland somewhere else in the burial grounds. The file of the vault was closed, and marching up to the right of the vault, gave three general discharges. The artillery then fired thirteen rounds, and with trailed arms, the soldiers all slowly and silently withdrew.

Then the members of the Society of the Cincinatti, who Greene had been a member, retired to their meeting house and made a motion that was carried: "That as a token of the high respect and veneration in which this society hold the memory of their late illustrious brother, Major-general Nathanael Greene, deceased, George Washington Greene, his eldest son, be admitted a member of this society, to take his seat on arriving at the age of eighteen years." But the irony of life, George

Washington Greene never became a member of the Masons, because in 1793, just after his eighteenth birthday, he was found drowned in the Savannah River and buried next to his father for eternity in the Graham vault.

The news of Greene's death spread fast and far through the land. It reached Mount Vernon through Lee, then a member of Congress at Philadelphia. "Your friend and second, the patriot and noble Greene, is no more. Universal grief reigns here. How hard is the fate of the United States, to lose such a man in the middle of life. Irreparable loss! But he is gone and I am incapable to say more."

Washington took the news very hard and it was said that it sadden him every day of his life. "General Greene's death," he wrote to Lafayette, over a year later, "is an event which has given me such general concern, and is so much regretted by his numerous friends, of which I count myself amongst, that I can scarce persuade myself to touch upon it, even so far as to say that in him you have lost a man who affectionately regarded and was a sincere admirer of you." And when the political horizon began to grow dark and the future was filled with foreboding, Washington wrote to Knox "In regretting, which I have often done with the keenest sorrow, the death of our much lamented friend General Greene, I have accompanied it of late with a query whether he would not have preferred such an exit to the scenes which, it is more than probable, many of his compatriots may live to bemoan?" And then wrote to Rochambeau; "General Greene lately died at Savannah, in Georgia, and the public as well as his family and friends has met with a severe loss. He was a great and good man indeed, and I miss him greatly."

Congress appointed a committee, of which Carrington, Lee, and Pettit were members, to report on a proper monument for the deceased hero. "Resolved, That a monument be erected to the memory of Nathanael Greene, Esquire, a native of Rhode Island, who died on the 19th of June, 1786, late major-general in the service of the United States, and commander of their army in the southern department. The United States in Congress assembled, in honor of his patriotism, valor, and ability, have erected this monument."

In 1820, the Council of Savannah appointed a committee to search for the burial place of Greene. But the stone was unmarked and they failed in their attempt. Peace for Nathanael Greene, and his son George, did not last long. During the Civil War and Sherman's infamous "March to the Sea," Union soldiers occupied the grounds surrounding Christ Episcopal Church, and while there, broke open several vaults in the old burial ground, searching for valuables to steal. They also amused themselves by altering epitaphs on some of the graves with limericks and jokes. One of those was the grave of Nathanael and his son, George Greene. Many years after the war, another search was begun for the remains of the father and son by the Rhode Island Society of the Cincinatti. The remains were finally found and transferred to zinc-lined boxes for preservation, and then taken to the Southern Bank of the State of Georgia for safe keeping. On 14 November 1902, an elaborate ceremony was held when the remains were transferred from the bank vault to the Johnson Square memorial at the end of Bull Street in Savannah, Georgia.

And so ends the life and times of Nathanael Greene. Quaker, blacksmith, merchant, businessman, politician, husband, father, planter, slave owner, and militaryman who started as a common foot soldier and reached the rank of major-general and second only to George Washington in command of the Continental army. Nathanael Greene had made mistakes in his life, took the blame when deserved, and lived with the ones he could do nothing about. With his military genius, he and his army changed the complete character of the Revolutionary War and caused the British to give up their claim to America. If nothing else, Nathanael Greene should, and must be remembered for that single fact. Without him, the war very easily may have droned on for many, many years. When the roll call of Heroes in the history of the United States is called, the name Major-general Nathanael Greene should be at the very top of the list.

Glossary of Military Terms

Abatis – A defense formed by placing trees that have been cut down and lengthwise, stacked one over another, with the branches sharpen and turned toward the enemy line.

Amuse – To occupy or divert the attention of the enemy from the actual point of attack.

Banquette – A raised step along the inside of a parapet or bottom of a trench, upon which soldiers stand to fire at the enemy.

Bastion – A pointed projection of a fortification thrusting out from the face of the main wall or at an angle at its corners.

Battalion – A body of soldiers, consisting of several companies and being part of a regiment. During the Revolutionary War a regiment was often called a battalion.

Battalion Companies – The companies left in a regiment after the grenadier and light infantry companies had been withdrawn from it.

Berm – The narrow space between the ditch and the base of the parapet of a fortification.

Brigade – A subdivision of an army composed of two or more regiments.

Canister – Small round shot packed in a case fitting the bore of a cannon, which scatter on discharge.

Carcass – An iron shell packed with ignited combustibles and pierced with holes through which the flame blazes, for setting fire to buildings or ships.

Chandelier – A wooden frame filled with fascines.

Chevaux-de-frise – A framework of heavy timbers fitted with iron spikes on the top and pointed at the enemy to check their advance, and also sunk in river channels to prevent the passage of ships.

Cohorn – A small mortar for throwing grenades.

Column – A formation of troops narrow laterally and deep from front to rear.

Counterscarp – The outer wall or slope of the ditch surrounding a fortification.

Covered way – A space about thirty feet across extending around the counterscarp of the ditch, being covered by the parapet.

Curtain – The part of the wall of a fortification connecting to bastions.

Demilune – An outerwork, like a curved bastion, to protect a bastion or curtain.

Deploy – To spread troops out from a main column into a line of battle.

Dragoon – A mounted infantryman; but often used primarily as a cavalryman.

Embrasure – An opening in a parapet to permit the firing of a gun.

Epaulement – The shoulder of a bastion where it meets the curtain, or simple outwork added to a fortification.

Fascine – A long, cylindrical bundle of brushwood or sticks, firmly bound together, used to fill ditches or to construct temporary batteries.

Fieldpiece – A light, portable cannon for use on a field of battle.

Flank – The side of a marching column or the end of a line of battle.

Flank Companies – The companies of grenadiers and light infantry drawn from a regiment.

Fleche – A small earthwork, **V**-shaped and open at the rear.

Forlorn Hope – A picked body of soldiers, detached to the front to begin the attack; a storming party.

Fraise – A palisade of pointed timbers planted in an upward slanting poistion.

Gabion – A cylindrical wicker basket open at both ends, to be filled with earth or rocks and used in fortifying a position or erecting a battery.

Glacis – The sloping approach to the parapet of a covered way.

Grapeshot – Small iron balls enclosed in an open frame fitting the bore of a gun, which scatter when the gun is discharged.

Grasshopper – A 3-pound cannon, so called because it was mounted on legs instead of a wheeled carriage.

Gun – Any firearm except a pistol, but usually a cannon of whatever caliber and not a musket or rifle.

Howitzer – A short, light gun to fire a heavy projectile at a high angle of elevation and low velocity.

Invalids – soldiers disabled from active service.

Linstock – Instrument holding slow burn matches with which cannon were fired.

Mask – To hinder or hold from activity an enemy fortification or body of troops.

Matross –A soldier next in rank below an infantryman, assisting with the guns.

Merlon – The part of ordnance with a large bore having trunnions on its breech to throw shells at high angles.

Ordnance – Heavy guns.

Parallels – Trenches approaching a fortification by a series of zigzags.

Parapet – The wall of a fortification.

Picket – A small, detached body of troops set out in front of a camp to discover the approach of the enemy.

Platoon – A small body or squad of infantry acting as a unit, as when firing.

Pound – The rating of a gun by the weight of its projectile.

Provincials – Troops raised in the colonies on the side of Great Britian; Tory troops.

Quarter – Exemption from being put to death after vanquished troops surrender.

Rank and file – The common soldier, privates.

Ravelin – An outerwork of two faces forming a salient angle constructed outside the main ditch and in front of the curtain of a fortification.

Redan – A simple form or earthwork, not completely enclosed, with two faces forming a salient angle, like a fleche.

Redoubt – A small independent earthwork, usually square or polygonal, completely enclosed.

Regiment – A body of troops made up of companies and commanded by a colonel.

Royal – A small mortar.

Sally port – An opening in a fortification for the passage of troops.

Sap – A covered trench or tunnel for approaching or undermining a fortification.

Saucisson – A sausage-shaped fascine.

Spontoon – A pike or halberd carried by infantry officers.

Stand of colors – A complete set of colors; flags.

Traverse – A barrier thrown across the approach to a fortification or across its interior to cut off a part.

Bibliography

Reference Works, Atlases, Maps, Illustrations, Photos, Bibliographies:

Alden, John Richard, "General Gage in America." Baton Rouge, La., 1948

Anderson, Troyer S., "The Command of the Howe Brothers During the American Revolution." New York: 1936

Arnold, James Truslow, ed "Atlas of American History." New York: Scribner, 1943

Arnold, James, "The Vital Record of Rhode Island, 1636 –1850. 21 vols. Providence: R.I.: Narragansett Historical Publishing Co., 1891-1912.

Ashburn, Percy M., "A History of the Medical Department of the United States Army." Boston, 1929

Atlas, Lawrence Martin, editor, "The George Washington atlas." United States George Washington Bicentennial Commission. Washington, D.C., 1932

Barber, John W., "History and Antiquities of New England." New Haven: Conn, 1870

Belcher, Henry, "The First American Civil War." 2 vols. London: 1911

Bennett, Caleb P., "Narritve of the Delaware Regiment." pps. 451-462 PA. Magazine of History and Biographies, IX, 1st edition, 1885

Boatner, Mark Mayo, "Encyclopedia of the American Revolution." New York: D. McKay, 1974

Burnett, Edmund C., editor, "Letters of Members of the Continental Congress, 1775 1783." 8 vols., Washington, D.C.: 1921

Calloway, Colin G., "The American Revolution in Indian Country." New York: Cambridge University Press, 1995

Capen, Lester, ed. "Atlas of Early American History." Princeton: Princeton University Press, 1976

Clarke, Clorinda, "The American Revolution 1775-83; A British View." New York: McGraw-Hill, 1967

Cook, Frederic, ed. "Journals of the Military Expedition of Maj.-general John Sullivan Against The Six Nations of Indians in 1779." Ann Arbor: University Microfilms, 1967

Cox, Clinton, "Come All You Brave Soldiers." New York: Scholastic Press, 1999

Cowell, Benjamin, "Spirit of 76 in Rhode Island." Boston: A.J. Wright, 1850

Darby, William, and Dwight, Theodore, Jr., "Dictionary of American Biography." 21 vols. New York: Scribner, 1943

"Documents: Letters of George Washington Bearing on the Negro." Journal of Negro History, vol. 2, 1917

Draper, Lyman C., "Kings Mountain and Its Heroes." Cincinnati: 1881

Dupuy, R. Ernest, and Trevor, N., "Encyclopedia of Military History." New York: Harper & Row,

1970

"An Outline History of the American Revolution." New York: Harper & Row, 1975

Eelking, Max von, "The German Allied Troops." Albany: New York, 1893

Fitzpatrick, John C., ed., "The Writings of George Washington from the Original Manuscript Sources, 1745-1799. 39 vols. Washington, D.C.: Library of Congress, 1931-1944

Flexner, James Thomas, "The Traitor and the Spy: Benedict Arnold and John Andre." Boston: Little, Brown and Co., 1975

Forbes, Harriette Merrifield, "New England Diaries, Orderly Books and Sea Journals." Topsfield, MA: Privately Printed, 1923

Foner, Eric, "Thomas Paine and Revolutionary America." New York: Oxford University Press, 1976

Forbes, Peter, ed., "American Archives." 4th Series, 6 vols. Washington, D.C., 1837-46

"American Archives." 5th Series, 3 vols. Washington, D.C., 1848-53

Franklin, Benjamin, "Autobiography." New York: Modern Library, 1932

Frothingham, Richard, "History of the Sege of Boston." Boston: 1851

Fuller, J.F.C., "Decisive Battles of the United States of America." New York: 1942

Gottschalk, Louis R., "Lafayette Comes to America." Chicago: 1976

Greene, George Washington, "The Life of Nathanel Greene." 3 vols., Boston: Houghton, Mifflin And Co., 1851

Greenman, Jeremiah, "Diary of a Common Soldier in the American Revolution – 1775 to 1783." Republished by Northern Illinois University Press, 1978

Harris, Caleb, "A Map of the State of Rhode Island – 1795. Reprint. Providence, R.I.: Rhode Island Historical Society, 1969

Hartley, Cecil B., "Life of Major General Henry Lee." Philadelphia: 1889

Heitman, Francis Bernard, "Historical Register of Officers of the Continental Army During the War of the Revolution, April 1775 to December 1783. New, revised, ed., Washington, D.C.: Rare Book Shop Publishing Co., 1914

Hibbert, Christopher, "Redcoats and Rebels: The American Revolution Through British Eyes." New York: Avon Books, 1990

Hosmer, James K., "Samuel Adams." New York: Chelsea House, 1980 "Index of Revolutionary War Pension Applications." Washington, D.C.: National Genealogical Society, 1966

Jackson, John W., "The Delaware Bay and River Defenses of Philadelphia 1775-1777." Philadelphia Maritime Museum, 1977

Jones, Charles C., "The History of Georgia." 2 vols., Boston: 1883

Journals of the Continental Congress, 1774-1789." Edited by Gaillard Hunt, 34 vols. Washington, D.C.: Government Printing Office, 1904-37

Klein, Milton M., "New York in the American Revolution, A Bibliography." Albany: New York State Bicentennial Commission, 1974

Leckie, Robert, "George Washington"s War: The Saga of the American Revolution." New York: HarperCollins, 1993

Lee, Henry, "Memoirs of the War in the Southern Department." New York: 1862

Manders, Eric I., "Notes on Troop Units in the Flying Camp, 1776." Military Collector & Historian, pps. 257-90, XXVI, no. 1, Spring 1974,

Martin, Joseph Plumb, "Private Yankee Doodle." Boston: Little, Brown, 1962

Maryland Archives, "Journal and Correspondenceof the Council of Maryland. 1777"

Maslowski, Pete, "National Policy Toward the Use of Black Troops in the Revolution." South Carolina Historical Magazine, pp. 1-17, Jan. 1972,

McCrady, Edward, "The History of South Carolina in the Revolution, 1775-1780." R, I, New York: 1901

        "The History of South Carolina in the Revolution, 1780-1783." R, II, New York: 1902

Meltzer, Milton, "The American Revolutionaries: A History in Their Own Words, 1750-1800." New York: Thomas Y. Crowell, 1987

Mitchell, Robert G., "After Yorktown: the Wayne-Greene Correspondence, 1780-1786." Chicago: 1978

Montresor, John, "Journals." Edited by G.D. Scull. New York: New York State Historical Society, 1882

Moore, Frank, comp. "The Diary of the American Revolution, 1775-1781." New York: Washington Square Press, 1967

Muhlenberg, Henry M., "The Journals of Henry Melchior Muhlenberg." 3 vols. Philadelphia: Muhlenberg Press, 1958

Papers of Nathanel Greene (UNC-Chapel Hill, NC) 7 vols. , 1995

Rice, Howard Crosby, Jr., and Brown, Anne S.K., eds. "The American Campaigns of Rochambeau's Army, 1780, 1781, 1782 & 1783." 2 vols. Princeton: Princeton University Press, 1972

Ryan, Dennis P. ed., "A Salute to Courage: The American Revolution as Seen Through Wartime Writings of Officers of the Continental Army and Navy." New York: Columbia University Press, 1979

Sabine, Lorenzo, "The American Loyalists." Boston: 1847

Scott, John Anthony, "Trumpet of a Prophecy: Revolutionary America, 1763-1783." Alfred A Knopf, Inc., 1969

Seymour, William, "A Journal of the Southern Expedition, 1780-1783; Historical & Biographical Papers of the Historical Society of Delaware, Vol. II." Wilmington: Delaware, 1896

Ships Registers and Enrollments of Providence, Rhode Island, 1773-1939." Providence: R.I. Works Projects Administration, 1941

Thacher, James, "Military Journal of the American Revolution." Hartford: Conn, Hurlbut, Williams And Co., 1862

Trussell, John B.B., "Birthplace of an Army: A Study of the Valley Forge Encampment." Harrisburg: Pennsylvania Historical and Museum Commission, 1976

U.S. Congress, "Debates and Proceedings." 2nd Congress, 1st & 2nd Session, Philadelphia, PA, 1775-1776

U.S. War Department, "Pension Rolls." Washington, D.C., 1835

Van Doren, Carl, "Mutiny in January." New York: 1943

Ward, Christopher, "The War of the Revolution." 2 vols. New York: The MacMillian Co., 1952

Ward, Samuel, "Correspondence of Governor Samuel Ward, May 1775-March 1776." Compiled by Clifford P. Monahan, Providence: Rhode island Historical Society

Zinn, Howard, "A People's History of the United States: 1492-Present." New York: HarperCollins, 1977

Lee Patrick Anderson is a Philadelphia-area native who first realized his passion for seeking the truth in American history at a very young age. At the age of eight, during a visit to Valley Forge, he learned that no battles had actually been fought at that historic site. This was confusing to an eight-year-old, considering the cannons that lined the borders of the park. From that point forward, he endeavored to learn the truth about American history and the lives and times of her people. He resides in Mullica Hill, New Jersey with his wife and daughters.

CPSIA information can be obtained
at www.ICGtesting.com
Printed in the USA
FSOW03n1443151216
28620FS

9 781581 126358